MAGILL'S ENCYCLOPEDIA OF SOCIAL SCIENCE

PSYCHOLOGY

MAGILL'S ENCYCLOPEDIA OF SOCIAL SCIENCE

PSYCHOLOGY

Volume 4
Separation and divorce: Children's issues–Work motivation
Appendices
Index

Editor
Nancy A. Piotrowski, Ph.D.
University of California, Berkeley

Project Editor
Tracy Irons-Georges

SALEM PRESS, INC.
Pasadena, California
Hackensack, New Jersey

Editorial Director: Christina J. Moose
Project Editor: Tracy Irons-Georges
Copy Editor: Leslie Ellen Jones
Assistant Editor: Andrea E. Miller
Acquisitions Editor: Mark Rehn
Photograph Editor: Philip Bader
Research Supervisor: Jeffry Jensen
Production Editor: Cynthia Beres
Page Design/Graphics: James Hutson
Layout: Eddie Murillo

Some of the updated and revised essays in this work originally appeared in *Magill's Survey of Social Science: Psychology*, edited by Frank N. Magill (Pasadena, Calif.: Salem Press, Inc., 1993).

Library of Congress Cataloging-in-Publication Data

Magill's encyclopedia of social science: psychology/ editor, Nancy A. Piotrowski.
   p. cm.
Includes bibliographical references and index.
ISBN 1-58765-130-0 (set : alk. paper) — ISBN 1-58765-131-9 (v. 1 : alk. paper) —
ISBN 1-58765-132-7 (v. 2 : alk. paper)— ISBN 1-58765-133-5 (v. 3 : alk. paper) —
ISBN 1-58765-134-3 (v. 4 : alk. paper)
1. Psychology—Encyclopedias. I. Piotrowski, Nancy A.

BF31 .M33 2003
150'.3—dc21

                                      2002151146

Fourth Printing

Table of Contents

MAGILL'S ENCYCLOPEDIA OF SOCIAL SCIENCE

PSYCHOLOGY

Separation and divorce

Children's issues

TYPE OF PSYCHOLOGY: Developmental psychology; social psychology

FIELDS OF STUDY: Adolescence; childhood and adolescent disorders; coping; infancy and childhood; interpersonal relations; stress and illness

Marital separation and divorce are stressful life transitions to which children must adapt in many ways. Several perspectives to explain the impact of divorce on children have been developed. Research identifies common issues for children of divorce, but individual adjustment may vary significantly as a result of a variety of factors.

KEY CONCEPTS
- divorce-stress-adjustment model
- family composition perspective
- family process viewpoint
- individual risk and vulnerability perspective
- parental distress perspective
- stress and socioeconomic disadvantage viewpoint
- stressful family transition

INTRODUCTION

At the beginning of the twenty-first century, more than one million children in the United States experienced the divorce of their parents every year, according the U.S. Bureau of the Census. It was estimated that about 40 percent of all children would experience divorce before they reached eighteen years of age.

Most studies regarding children's issues in divorce conceptualize the separation and divorce process as a stressful family transition to which children must adapt. These studies focus on the specific factors that children face in divorce, the protective factors that may assist them, and the range of outcomes experienced by all children of divorce. Divorce is not a discrete event but a process that begins with the specific factors in place in a particular family prior to the marital separation and continues through the divorce to the adjustment period afterward. Children are involved throughout the process and may experience a range of psychological, social, academic, and health issues as a result of the divorce. Children from different ethnic and cultural groups may experience different rates of parental divorce and remarriage and variations in specific effects.

The study of children's issues before, during, and after separation and divorce is controversial because of the different social and political viewpoints held by family life scholars. Some scholars believe that children need two-parent homes to achieve optimum development and that divorce and single-parent families have a negative impact on the institution of the family, resulting in many social problems. Other scholars believe that it is possible for children to develop well in different family structures, including single-parent families and stepfamilies. These scholars suggest that divorce may resolve home problems and ultimately benefit the development of children by creating more healthy and positive home environments. The differences among scholars can lead to alternative interpretations of research results and very different reports of the implications of research findings for families and society.

PERSPECTIVES ON CHILDREN'S ADJUSTMENT

American psychologist E. Mavis Hetherington identified five perspectives that help to explain the relationship between divorce and children's adjustment to it. The individual risk and vulnerability perspective proposes that some parents may have characteristics or psychological problems that make it more likely that they will experience divorce. These individual factors will also have an impact on the way the parents handle the divorce and the consequences of divorce for their children. On the other hand, children have individual characteristics that may safeguard them from the negative consequences of divorce or increase their vulnerability to negative outcomes.

The family composition perspective predicts that any family structure other than the two-biological-parent family may be related to increased problems for children. Research concerning the father's absence after divorce is related to this perspective.

The stress and socioeconomic disadvantage viewpoint notes that divorce may lead to an increased number of stressful life events, including new roles, change of residence, loss of social networks, child-care problems, conflict with the ex-spouse, and decreases in family finances. Children and parents may be affected negatively by these events. Research on the frequent financial problems of former spouses, especially custodial mothers, originates from this viewpoint.

The parental distress perspective indicates that tremendous variability exists in how individual parents handle all the issues and difficulties involved in divorce. Some parents are able to manage the events well and continue to provide consistent parenting to their children; other parents experience a noted deterioration in their parenting skills following divorce.

Finally, the family process viewpoint recognizes that divorced families may demonstrate disruptions in family relationships and interactions, having an impact on such processes as child discipline or child rearing. Hetherington suggests that the five perspectives complement each other and form a transactional model for understanding the impact of divorce on children.

Sociologist Paul R. Amato of Pennsylvania State University proposed a divorce-stress-adjustment model that incorporates the multiple perspectives noted by Hetherington into three factors: mediators, moderators, and adjustment. Amato noted that the divorce process may begin months or years prior to separation with a cycle involving overt conflict between the parents, attempts to renegotiate the relationship, and/or avoidance and denial of the problems. It is not unusual to note increased behavior problems in children at this early stage that reflect the marital discord.

Individual differences, however, may be noted between children. Some children may experience significant distress as a result of parental conflict prior to separation, so that the level of distress diminishes after marital separation. Other children may be unaware of the marital difficulties until the separation occurs, precipitating significant distress at that point. Children experience mediators or stressors that continue throughout the divorce process. They may include a decline in parental support and effective control, loss of contact with one parent, continuing conflict between parents, and economic decline.

In Amato's model, moderators or protective factors interact with the stressors throughout the process to determine the ultimate adjustment of the child. Moderators include individual resources (such as coping skills), interpersonal resources (such as extended family support), structural resources (such as school programs and services), and demographic characteristics (age, gender, race, eth-

nicity, and culture) that combine to determine how a particular child will respond to the stressors of divorce. Adjustment refers to the time and intensity of psychological, behavioral, and health problems for children before they adapt to the new roles required of them by the divorce.

MOST COMMON ISSUES FOR CHILDREN

Research on the effects of divorce on children between 1960 and 2000 consistently showed that children whose parents had divorced scored lower than children whose parents remained married on several outcome measures. Amato analyzed the research several times and noted small, but statistically significant, differences on measures such as conduct, academic achievement, psychological adjustment, self-concept, social competence, and long-term health. These effects continue even though more children are experiencing family divorce, the social stigma of divorce appears to have diminished, and support services for children of divorce have increased. A few studies indicate that divorce has positive results for some children, especially when divorce ends chronic high-conflict marriages that had created negative home environments, but the number of children in this type of situation is relatively low.

Research conducted by sociologist Yongmin Sun at Ohio State University confirmed that divorce is a multistage process, beginning prior to separation. Sun studied 10,088 students and compared the results of 798 students (8 percent) whose parents divorced over a two-year period to students whose parents did not divorce. He found that families in the predisruption phase, the period when the family is still intact prior to disruption of the marriage, show evidence of different family processes than do families that remain intact. The families that eventually divorced experienced deterioration in relationships between the parents and the children at least one year prior to the divorce. These parents did fewer things with their children, had lower expectations for the children, and were not as involved in school issues and events. The children had lower school math and reading scores and exhibited more behavior problems than did children in families that did not experience divorce.

After divorce, children may experience a variety of effects. One major problem for children of divorce is the continuation of preseparation conflict between the parents into the postdivorce period. By the second year after separation, one-third of parent relationships are still conflicted, one-fourth have achieved a cooperative coparenting relationship, and one-third are disconnected and do not interact about parenting. Continuing conflict is a problem because exposure to angry exchanges and fighting is itself a stressor for children. Conflict may also result in decreases in the quality of the parent-child relationship, including less consistent discipline, less demonstration of affection toward the child, emotional dependence upon the child, less ability to control parental anger, and using the child as a co-combatant in disputes with the former spouse. Conflict that involves the child directly (such as fights in the child's presence, or arguments that focus on the child or child rearing or include the child in the dispute) is most harmful to the child. In general, the greater the degree of conflict between the parents, the more likely it is that the child will experience psychological distress. Interventions that diminish conflict are likely to have beneficial results for children of divorce.

Many children have diminished contact with their fathers following the divorce. Studies indicate that when the mother has primary physical custody, more than one-fourth of all children report that they did not see their father in the last year and only about one-fourth saw their father at least weekly. More than half of fathers are not involved at all in making decisions about their children, and half did not pay any child support during the previous year. Fathers who have joint custody, live near their children, or had stronger emotional relations with their children prior to the divorce are more likely to have regular contact after the divorce.

The effects of divorce on children often continue over time, although the immediate emotional disruption and behavioral problems may be resolved within the first two years. Interview research by Judith Wallerstein with children of divorce over a twenty-five-year period suggested that even as children grow into adulthood, there is a continuing impact of divorce on their attitudes and behaviors toward relationships and marriage. Other researchers note a variety of effects later in life, including an increased probability of divorce for the children of divorce.

Sources for Further Study

Amato, Paul R. "The Consequences of Divorce for Adults and Children." *Journal of Marriage and the Family* 62 (2000): 1269-1287. This article summarizes research in the 1990's concerning the consequences of divorce, using a divorce-stress-adjustment perspective and explanatory diagram. The author uses some technical statistical language, but the primary findings can be understood by readers without statistical knowledge.

Emery, Robert E. *Marriage, Divorce, and Children's Adjustment.* 2d ed. Thousand Oaks, Calif.: Sage Publications, 1999. The author presents a multi-disciplinary perspective that includes psychology, social science, law, and policy dimensions. Summaries at the end of each chapter encapsulate the main ideas; the reader may then look back to the chapter to expand on areas of interest. Charts and graphs throughout the book provide helpful information.

Hetherington, E. Mavis, ed. *Coping with Divorce, Single Parenting, and Remarriage: A Risk and Resiliency Perspective.* Mahwah, N.J.: Lawrence Erlbaum, 1999. Outlines Hetherington's five perspectives that explain the relationship between divorce and children's adjustment.

Teyber, Edward. *Helping Children Cope with Divorce.* Rev. ed. San Francisco: Jossey-Bass, 2001. This is a practical book for parents who want to help their children as they go through the divorce process, written by an experienced clinical psychologist.

Thompson, Ross A., and Paul R. Amato, eds. *The Postdivorce Family: Children, Parenting, and Society.* Thousand Oaks, Calif.: Sage Publications, 1999. This book incorporates perspectives from scholars in psychology, sociology, law, and family studies regarding continuing family life after divorce.

Wallerstein, Judith S., and Joan B. Kelly. *Surviving the Breakup.* 1980. Reprint. New York: Basic Books, 1996. This book is based on the early findings of the Children of Divorce Project, a study of sixty families during the first five years of divorce. In-depth interviews were conducted with family members to determine their experience of divorce.

Wallerstein, Judith S., Julia Lewis, and Sandra Blakeslee. *The Unexpected Legacy of Divorce: A Twenty-five Year Landmark Study.* New York: Hyperion, 2001. Readable book that reviews the long-term results of divorce on the children of divorce, using an in-depth interview research methodology.

Mark Stanton

SEE ALSO: Family life: Children's issues; Father-child relationship; Mother-child relationship; Parental alienation syndrome; Separation and divorce: Adult issues; Stepfamilies.

Separation anxiety

TYPE OF PSYCHOLOGY: Developmental psychology
FIELDS OF STUDY: Anxiety disorders; childhood and adolescent disorders

Separation anxiety is characterized by fear upon separation from home or parents/caretakers. Separation anxiety, while a normal part of the developmental process, can become a behavior of concern when it is persistent, intense, and impairing.

KEY CONCEPTS
- behavioral inhibition
- cognitive-behavioral therapy
- school refusal
- separation anxiety disorder

INTRODUCTION

Anxiety is often defined as apprehension related to the expectation of real or imagined danger. Many of the anxieties seen in childhood are expected in the course of normal development, cause mild discomfort, and have a quick resolution. Separation anxiety may be defined as fear upon separation from home or parents/caretakers and has been identified and described both as a part of the normal developmental process and as a sign of disorder since the early 1900's. Sigmund Freud (1856-1939), John Bowlby (1907-1990), and other personality theorists have described the phenomenology and significance of this common fear. Separation anxiety usually begins between six and nine months of age, reaches a peak between ten and eighteen months, and often resolves by the end of the second year. Parents may first notice separation anxiety in their young child as clingy, crying, tearful, or protesting behaviors that begin upon separation and typically disappear upon reunion. Once children begin daycare or school (ages two through six), it is not uncommon to see a resurgence of separation anxiety during morning drop-offs or at bedtime. Typically, this separation anxiety is mild, and chil-

dren calm down shortly after their parents' departure. While the separation anxious behaviors (such as crying) are a cause of discomfort and strain for the parents, generally, separation anxiety is not a cause for concern. Separation anxiety is considered a normal part of the developmental process.

There are times, however, when separation anxiety does become a cause for concern. Separation anxiety becomes a clinical concern when the anxiety is excessive, of relatively long duration, and a significant source of interference for the parents and/or the child. If the separation anxiety is disproportionate to the situation, persists beyond age-appropriate reactions, and keeps the child and/or family from doing the things they want or need to do, then the behavioral patterns are likely outside the range of what is considered normal. When separation anxious behaviors become atypical given the child's age and developmental course, the behaviors may be characterized as symptoms of a clinical disorder.

SEPARATION ANXIETY DISORDER

Separation anxiety first made its appearance as a childhood anxiety disorder in 1980 with the American Psychiatric Association's publication of the third edition of the *Diagnostic and Statistical Manual of Mental Disorders* (DSM-III). Although the fourth edition text revision of the *Diagnostic and Statistical Manual of Mental Disorders* (DSM-IV-TR, 2000) recognizes the possibility of separation anxiety in adults, this presentation is regarded as rare. Separation anxiety disorder is characterized by developmentally inappropriate and excessive anxiety upon separation from home or from attachment figures. Prevalence rates range between 2 and 5 percent of children.

Separation anxiety disorder is manifested as the refusal to be left alone. The child will actively, even vehemently, avoid separations with parents by refusing to stay home alone, go to school, go to sleepovers, or sleep by themselves. Children may demand that parents do not vacation, leave home, or even be in another area or room of the house without them. They anxiously anticipate separations (for instance, worrying weeks before the parents' vacation) and experience extreme distress during the separations. School refusal (frequent calls home during the school day or multiple trips to the school nurse) is not uncommon for children suffering from separation anxiety disorder. These children have difficulty not only separating for school in the morning but also separating at bedtime. Many children with this disorder sleep in their parents' beds or insist that a parent accompany them to bed.

Children with separation anxiety disorder frequently worry that during the separation, some danger or harm will befall their loved ones. They fear permanent separation, such as the parent being in an accident, the death of the parent, or their own abduction. The child often views the world as a dangerous place—a place where various and numerous untold, untoward events may occur. Children with this disorder often experience physical symptoms of anxiety. They complain of stomachaches, nausea, vomiting, headaches, hyperventilation, and rapid heartbeat.

POSSIBLE CAUSES

Little research has specifically targeted the origin or causes of separation anxiety disorder. However, a fair amount of research has been accumulated that has examined the origins of childhood anxiety more generally. Research has identified several risk factors for childhood anxiety disorder, including attachment style, parental anxiety, child temperament, negative life events, and parenting style. Attachment style (the style of relating to attachment figure) has been identified as a potential risk factor for childhood anxiety. Parental anxiety has been demonstrated to be predictive of anxiety disorders in children. Anxious children are more likely than nonanxious peers to have an anxious parent. Additionally, children who possess the temperamental characteristic of behavioral inhibition (a shy, fearful personality style) and who experience negative life events are at increased risk for the development of a childhood anxiety disorder. Last, several parenting characteristics or styles have been associated with child anxiety. Researchers found parents of anxious children to be more overcontrolling, more overprotective, and more likely to allow or encourage their children to avoid feared situations than other parents.

DEVELOPMENTAL OUTCOMES AND TREATMENTS

Several researchers have noted the link between anxiety in childhood and anxiety in adulthood. More specifically, researchers have suggested a link between separation anxiety disorder in childhood and panic and agoraphobia in adulthood.

A number of approaches have been used to treat childhood separation anxiety, most notably behavioral (such as exposure-based techniques

---

DSM-IV-TR Criteria for Separation Anxiety

SEPARATION ANXIETY DISORDER (DSM CODE 309.21)

Developmentally inappropriate and excessive anxiety concerning separation from home or from those to whom the individual is attached

Evidenced by three or more of the following:

- recurrent excessive distress when separation from home or major attachment figures occurs or is anticipated
- persistent and excessive worry about losing, or about possible harm befalling, major attachment figures
- persistent and excessive worry that an untoward event (such as getting lost or being kidnapped) will lead to separation from a major attachment figure
- persistent reluctance or refusal to go to school or elsewhere because of fear of separation
- persistent and excessive fear or reluctance to be alone or without major attachment figures at home or without significant adults in other settings
- persistent reluctance or refusal to go to sleep without being near a major attachment figure or to sleep away from home
- repeated nightmares involving the theme of separation
- repeated complaints of physical symptoms (such as headaches, stomachaches, nausea, or vomiting) when separation from major attachment figures occurs or is anticipated

Duration of at least four weeks

Onset before eighteen years of age; early onset occurs before six years of age

Disturbance causes clinically significant distress or impairment in social, academic, or other important areas of functioning

Disturbance does not occur exclusively during the course of a pervasive developmental disorder, schizophrenia, or other psychotic disorder

In adolescents and adults, not better accounted for by Panic Disorder with Agoraphobia and contingency management) and cognitive (such as problem-solving training). Most often, however, these approaches are used in combination as cognitive-behavioral therapy. Cognitive-behavioral approaches address both thoughts and behaviors while emphasizing their reciprocal relationship—thought affects behavior and behavior affects thought. In the 1990's, treatment research flourished, and cognitive-behavioral interventions have shown real promise in helping children with clinical levels of separation anxiety.

SOURCES FOR FURTHER STUDY

Bowlby, J. *A Secure Base: Parent-Child Attachment and Healthy Development.* New York: Basic Books, 1990. The author examines the nature and importance of parental bonding in early child development and presents a model for how such attachment promotes later psychological health and well-being.

_____. *Separation: Anxiety and Anger.* New York: Basic Books, 2000. The author examines the effect of separation on child development and discusses the psychopathology that may result from such separations.

March, J. S., ed. *Anxiety Disorders in Children and Adolescents.* New York: Guilford, 1995. Edited volume in which experts in child anxiety explore neurobiological foundations, risk factors, assessment strategies, current literature on specific disorders, and treatment approaches.

Silverman, W., and P. Treffers, eds. *Anxiety Disorders in Children and Adolescents: Research, Assessment, and Intervention.* New York: Cambridge University Press, 2001. Edited text exploring the theory, research, and treatment of anxiety disorders in children and adolescent. Chapters include discussions of historical, genetic/biological, temperamental, and psychosocial perspectives, as well as current information on treatment techniques and prevention strategies.

Vasey, M., and M. Dadds, eds. *The Developmental Psychopathology of Anxiety.* New York: Oxford University Press, 2001. Edited volume in which authoritative experts in the field of child anxiety present factors that contribute to the etiology and maintenance of anxiety disorders in childhood, adolescence, and adulthood. Book sections include preliminary issues; predisposing, protective, maintaining, and ameliorating influences; and integrative examples.

Ellen C. Flannery-Schroeder

SEE ALSO: Anxiety disorders; Attachment and bonding in infancy and childhood; Bed-wetting; Childhood disorders; Cognitive behavior therapy; Conduct disorders; Dyslexia; Family life: Children's issues; Father-child relationship; Learning disorders; Misbehavior; Mother-child relationship; Psychotherapy: Children; Separation and divorce: Children's issues; Stuttering.

Sex hormones and motivation

TYPE OF PSYCHOLOGY: Motivation

FIELDS OF STUDY: Endocrine system; physical motives; sexual disorders

Sex hormones control sexual maturation and exert an important influence on sexual motivation. The role of the sex hormones varies across species; they play only a limited role in humans.

KEY CONCEPTS

- androgens
- antiandrogen drugs
- estradiol
- hormones
- pheromone
- progesterone
- testosterone

INTRODUCTION

Sex hormones exert an important influence on behavior. These hormones control sexual maturation at puberty, and they have an impact on the sex drive and on sexual activity throughout the life span. In most animal species, sex hormones completely control sexual behavior. In humans, their role is more limited. Human sexual motivation is the result of the complex interplay of hormones, psychological factors, and social factors.

At puberty, the brain releases several hormones which travel through the bloodstream to target organs. In males, the targets are the testes; in females, the ovaries. In response to the hormones released from the brain, these targets begin to produce the sex hormones. The principal male sex hormone is testosterone (the name refers to the fact that it is produced by the testes). With the production of testosterone at puberty in human males, facial and body hair grows, bones and muscles develop more fully, the voice deepens, and the genitals enlarge. In females, two sex hormones are produced by the ovaries at puberty, estradiol (often called estrogen) and progesterone. Estradiol is responsible for breast development, changes in female appearance (for example, wider hips), and maturation of the genitals and uterus. Progesterone plays a major role in preparing the female body for menstruation and pregnancy. It should be noted that although testosterone is called the "male sex hormone," it is also found in females, though in much smaller quantities. The same applies to the female sex hormones, which are found in males.

After puberty is completed, the sex hormones continue to play a role in sexual motivation. In most mammal species, the female goes through a regular cycle, the estrous cycle, during which sex hormones are released, causing an increase in sex drive. During this phase of the cycle, a female will seek a male partner with the goal of reproduction; she is said to be "in heat." In the presence of a female in estrus, the male experiences an increase in the sex hormone testosterone, and he will be sexually attracted to the female. For example, male rats will ignore a female whose ovaries have been removed and who thus cannot produce estradiol; however, an injection of estradiol will make the female interested in sex, and males will approach her for sexual activity. In these animals, sexual behavior is largely determined by the females' sexual readiness, which depends on the phase of estrus.

In most animal species, the male learns of a female's sexual readiness by the presence of a chemical she emits called a pheromone. Pheromones are usually derived from vaginal secretions during estrus. If pheromones are collected from an animal in estrus and applied to another that is not in estrus, males will approach the nonreceptive female and attempt sexual intercourse. In humans, pheromones do not appear to play a significant role in sexual attraction.

THE HUMAN CONDITION

Humans are quite different from other animals in other respects. While the sex hormones do have an important influence, they do not control sexual motivation and behavior. Research has shown that males who have abnormally low levels of testosterone have problems achieving erection and often

have a very low sex drive. Injections of testosterone restore the ability to obtain normal erection in these cases. Abnormally high levels of testosterone, however, do not cause an unusually high sex drive. Apparently, there is a minimum level of testosterone necessary for normal sexual behavior, but higher levels do not seem to have any significant effect.

Like females of other animal species, the human female goes through a cycle during which levels of sex hormones are increased. This cycle in humans and primates is called the menstrual cycle. Although human females experience cyclic increases in the sex hormones estradiol and progesterone, there is no clear indication of change in sexual motivation during this phase. For most women, sex drive does not vary with sex hormone levels. For example, women who have had their ovaries removed continue to experience a normal sex drive. The same usually applies to women who have undergone menopause, the stage of the life in the late forties during which the ovaries cease producing sex hormones. Most postmenopausal women continue to enjoy a normal sex life in spite of their reduced sex hormone levels.

Though the role of the sex hormones in sexual motivation in human females is limited, it appears that testosterone plays a role. In women, small amounts of testosterone are produced by the adrenal glands, small glands which secrete several hormones and are located atop the kidneys. Removal of the adrenal glands often abolishes the sex drive in women. In adult female monkeys whose adrenal glands and ovaries have been removed, injections of testosterone restore sex drive and sexual activity. In human females, while testosterone appears to play a role, many psychological factors such as attitudes and religious beliefs seem to be more important in understanding sexual motivation.

HORMONES AND SEXUAL DYSFUNCTIONS

Knowledge about sex hormones and their role in sexual motivation has been used in several ways. With the discovery that castration, or removal of the testes, drastically lowers sex drive, it was concluded that some cases of impaired sex drive in males may be caused by low levels of testosterone. For example, a soldier was castrated by an explosive during World War I. As a result, he lost interest in sex, was unable to obtain an erection, and lost significant muscle mass; his hips also expanded. After receiving five injections of high doses of testosterone, he was experiencing normal erections, his sex drive returned, and he began to gain weight and muscle mass. For males whose sexual difficulties are caused by abnormally low levels of testosterone, regular injections tend to restore a normal sex drive and the ability to achieve erections. Studies reveal, however, that not all individuals who are castrated experience changes in sexual behavior. For reasons which are unclear, some males appear capable of sexual behavior in spite of the removal of the testes.

Giving doses of estradiol or progesterone to human males has several effects. First, excesses of these hormones cause a sharp decline in the production of testosterone, which may interfere with sex drive, erection, and ejaculation. Administering estradiol also causes breast enlargement in men. When given to men, progesterone causes a decrease in sex drive and erection ability. It does not tend to make males develop a female appearance, as estradiol does. This knowledge has been applied to treating sex offenders. Compulsive sex offenders,

especially child molesters, are sometimes given injections of progesterone to help them control their sexual urges. When combined with counseling, this treatment may be useful in helping these persons gain some control over their sexual activity. While receiving the injections, the sex offenders often lose their sex drive and have trouble achieving erections. These effects are only temporary and disappear when progesterone is no longer given.

Women with unusually low levels of estradiol do not appear to suffer from direct sexual problems. They do experience difficulties with vaginal lubrication. Vaginal dryness makes sexual intercourse difficult and painful as a result of friction. One remedy for this problem is the use of a lubricant.

One early theory of homosexuality proposed that an imbalance in the sex hormones was responsible for sexual attraction to members of the same sex. According to the theory, male homosexuality was caused by a deficiency in testosterone or an excess of estradiol. This would explain why some men display the behavior expected of women: attraction to men and, according to popular stereotypes, effemi-

Hormones play a major role in romantic attraction and the selection of mates. (CLEO Photography)

nate mannerisms. Female homosexuality was believed to be caused by excess testosterone and, possibly, insufficient estradiol. Scientific tests of the theory have consistently failed to support it. Homosexuals, both male and female, do not differ from heterosexuals in their circulating sex hormone levels. Therefore, the hormone imbalance theory of homosexuality is no longer accepted. In fact, abnormally low levels of testosterone in men do not make them sexually attracted to men; the typical result is a decrease in sexual interest for any type of sexual partner. In women, excessively elevated levels of testosterone do not cause lesbianism; if anything, they tend to increase women's sexual interest in men. Factors other than levels of sex hormones are important in understanding homosexuality.

Another application involves the treatment of transsexuals. Transsexualism is a rare but interesting condition in which the person feels that nature made a mistake and placed him or her in the body of the wrong sex. A transsexual man is an anatomical male who firmly believes that he is a woman in a man's body. A transsexual woman believes that she is a male in a female body. Transsexuals who strongly desire to change their sex will sometimes receive hormone treatments. For a transsexual male, this consists of taking regular doses of estrogens. As a result, the male will experience breast growth, smoother skin, loss of muscle mass, and decreases in erection and sperm production. The treatment does not change facial and body hair or raise the pitch of the voice, but physical appearance will become femalelike. For transsexual women, testosterone is administered, which leads to growth of facial and body hair, deepening of the voice, and the end of menstruation. After living with these changes for two years, those who are seeking a sex change operation may do so at one of several specialized centers. The sex change surgery for males involves the removal of male genitals and creation of an artificial vagina. For females, the breasts and reproductive organs are removed, and an artificial penis and testes may be created. The results of these procedures are still controversial, as there are many possible problems, and not all transsexuals are satisfied with the outcome.

INSTINCTS AND CULTURE

The term "hormone" is derived from the Greek *hormaein*, which means "to set in motion." It was first used in 1904 to refer to those bodily substances which can have a profound influence on human development and behavior. All knowledge about the sex hormones is relatively new. Undoubtedly, much more will be discovered as medical technology continues to develop rapidly.

Knowledge about the effects of castration dates back to ancient China and Arabic countries. In these countries castration was practiced to provide safe guardians of the royal harem. The castrated guardians, or eunuchs, were considered safe since their sexual motivation was impaired as a result of testosterone deficiency. In Europe, up to the beginning of the nineteenth century, boys in church choirs were sometimes castrated to ensure their continued ability to sing soprano.

Thus, a general understanding about the importance of the testes in affecting human development and behavior is not new. Information about the exact nature and role of sex hormones, however, is relatively new. For example, the eighteenth century physician Simon Tissot believed that the results of castration were caused by impairments in semen production. According to his view, the loss of semen caused a decrease in strength, passivity, and a variety of other complications. It was not until the twentieth century that the loss of testosterone was identified as the mechanism underlying the effects of castration.

Although sexual motivation in lower animals is readily understood in terms of sex hormones and instincts, human sexual behavior is much more complex. A number of cultural and psychological factors, in combination with sex hormones, interact to determine human sexual motivation and behavior. The range of sexual activities in lower animals is limited and rigidly controlled by the phase of the female's estrous cycle. In humans, there is tremendous variability in types of sexual behavior, timing and frequency of sex, choice of partners, number of partners, and context of sexual activity. These variables are influenced by cultural standards regarding sexual activity. In permissive cultures, such as in Polynesia, sexual experimentation is encouraged and expected. Other cultures are more restrictive and discourage sex before marriage.

Within each culture, other factors such as peer group influence, familial and religious beliefs and values toward sexuality, and individual fears (such as pregnancy and sexually transmitted diseases) can also have an impact on human sexual behavior. For example, the threat of acquired immunodeficiency syndrome (AIDS) has led some individuals to change their sexual behavior. Abstinence and monogamy are advocated by some, while others, including many adolescents, have adopted few changes. On the other hand, the development of drugs such as Viagra that overcome the effects of the normal decline of male sex hormones with age is part of a movement to increase conscious control of and prolongation of sexuality.

Thus, although sex hormones play an important role in human sexual behavior, especially with respect to sexual maturity and sex drive, several cultural and psychological influences are more important. In order to address the problems of teenage pregnancy and sexually transmitted disease, including AIDS, all factors which determine human sexual motivation and behavior must be explored in depth.

SOURCES FOR FURTHER STUDY

Carlson, Neil R. *Foundations of Physiological Psychology*. 5th ed. Boston: Allyn & Bacon, 2001. One of the standard texts on the physiological basis of human and animal behavior. The importance of sex hormones in development and motivation is emphasized throughout the chapter on reproductive behavior.

Katchadourian, Herant A. *Fundamentals of Human Sexuality*. 5th ed. Fort Worth, Tex.: Holt, Rinehart and Winston, 1989. One of the best and most readable books on human sexuality. The discussion of sex hormones in chapter 4 is through and clear; psychological and cultural influences on sexual motivation are covered in chapters 8, 9, 20, and 21. The presentation is accessible to high school and college students.

Masters, William H., Virginia E. Johnson, and Robert C. Kolodny. *Human Sexuality*. 3d ed. Glenview, Ill.: Scott, Foresman, 1988. An overview of human sexuality by some of the world's foremost sex researchers. Although the coverage of sex hormones is limited, the material on the other determinants of human sexual motivation is thorough, detailed, and understandable.

Pinel, John P. J. *Biopsychology*. 4th ed. Boston: Allyn & Bacon, 1999. Another good introductory text to the physiology of human and animal behavior. The chapter "Hormones and Sex" is detailed and

clearly presented; several good case studies are offered to illustrate how hormonal problems can affect human sexual development.

Richard D. McAnulty

SEE ALSO: Gonads; Homosexuality; Hormones and behavior; Psychosexual development; Sexual behavior patterns; Sexual dysfunction; Sexual variants and paraphilias.

Sexism

TYPE OF PSYCHOLOGY: Social psychology
FIELDS OF STUDY: Prejudice and discrimination

Sexism is prejudice against persons on the basis of their gender. Sexism may exist at the interpersonal level, where it is expressed in individual beliefs and behaviors; alternatively, it may become institutionalized when social institutions and practices encourage gender bias.

KEY CONCEPTS
- discrimination
- expressiveness
- instrumentality
- male-as-normative principle
- prejudice
- psychological trait
- role
- stereotype

INTRODUCTION

The psychological basis for sexism, as for other forms of prejudice, is the human tendency to form stereotypes about persons who are members of certain social groups. Stereotypes may be either positive or negative; they consist of sets of interrelated beliefs and expectations that a person holds about a particular social group. When these stereotypes affect people's interpersonal behavior, sexism can result, leading to prejudice—a negative attitude toward a social group—and discrimination.

Gender stereotypes are reflected in beliefs and attitudes about the general nature of men and women as members of distinct social groups. In addition, gender stereotypes are related to the development of expectations about men's and women's psychological characteristics, interests, aptitudes, and behaviors. For example, if a person believes that women are more nurturant than men, then he or she might expect that women are more likely than men to be employed as child-care workers. In turn, these expectations may affect how people behave in social situations. The presence of different expectations for male and female performance may lead to differential treatment on the basis of gender. For example, if the director of a child-care center expects women to be superior nursery school teachers, then he or she may be likely to discriminate against males who apply for an available teaching position.

AMERICAN GENDER STEREOTYPES

Psychological research has established that gender stereotypes are quite pervasive in American culture. Considerable attention has been directed toward identifying the content of gender stereotypes. Psychologists are interested in the particular nature of beliefs that individuals hold about men and women in American culture. In a classic study, Paul Rosenkrantz, Inge Broverman, and their colleagues asked Americans to describe characteristics of the typical American man and woman. Their findings, which were first reported in the late 1960's, have been supported by subsequent research. Thus, their research appears to provide an accurate portrayal of the gender stereotypes commonly held by American adults.

These researchers found that subjects tended to describe men and women in terms of two different clusters of psychological traits, or personality characteristics. Women were more likely to be characterized by a group of traits which could be summarized as representing an expressiveness cluster. That is, men and women agreed that, as a group, women were caring, warm, and emotionally expressive. In contrast, men were characterized by a group of traits that could be described as an instrumentality cluster. In this instance, the typical man was perceived to be assertive, dominant, and competent. Thus, perceptions of men and women, as members of social groups, were conceived in terms of opposing psychological characteristics.

In the early 1980's, Kay Deaux and Laurie Lewis conducted a series of studies that elaborated upon this pioneering research. They hypothesized that instrumentality and expressiveness are only two possible distinctions between men and women. Deaux and Lewis believed that additional factors were likely to play an important role in gender stereotyping. In their research program, male and female subjects were given a list of gender-relevant characteristics. Subjects then were asked to estimate the likelihood that a man or woman possessed each characteristic. The results of these studies indicated that gender stereotypes do in fact consist of a number of related components. Subjects reliably associated certain psychological traits, role behaviors, occupations, and physical characteristics with gender.

The male stereotype consisted of the instrumentality cluster coupled with masculine psychological and physical characteristics. Subjects perceived the typical male to be strong, masculine, likely to hide his feelings, sexy, and muscular. Men typically were described as breadwinners and as being likely to take the initiative in encounters with the opposite sex. The typical male roles included blue-collar worker, businessman, athlete, and "macho man." In contrast, the female stereotype consisted of the expressiveness personality cluster coupled with feminine psychological and physical characteristics. Subjects described the typical woman as being smart and attractive, but also feminine, sensitive, and emotional. Women often were stereotyped as housewives and were perceived to be likely to be engaged in domestic chores such as child rearing and cooking. On the other hand, female stereotypes were not simply relegated to the domestic role. Subjects also held stereotypes that were representative of female athletes, businesswomen, and "sexy women."

Although there appears to be some overlap between male and female categories, it is clear that gender stereotypes do parallel the common roles that men and women typically assume in society. In addition, males and females are perceived to be members of distinctly different social groups. For the most part, people expect men and women to display opposing psychological characteristics and role behaviors. Finally, it should be noted that psychologists have found remarkable cross-cultural similarity in the content of gender stereotypes.

THE CONSTRAINTS OF STEREOTYPES

A large body of psychological research has investigated the effects of sexism. Some psychologists have investigated how gender stereotypes may influence people's perceptions of women in certain social roles (for example, as leaders). Others have studied how the use of sexist language might be related to the formation and maintenance of gender stereotypes.

The effects of gender stereotypes are particularly pronounced when people must form first impressions and make social judgments about others on the basis of little information. Natalie Porter and her colleagues have studied the factors that persons consider when they are asked to identify the leader of a small group. They asked subjects to view a photograph of an all-male group, an all-female group, or a mixed-sex group. Subjects were then asked to guess which person in the photograph held the position of group leader.

First, Porter and her colleagues found that subjects were likely to rely upon spatial configuration as an important cue in determining which person was the leader of the group. In the cases of all-male and all-female groups, the majority of subjects identified the person at the head of the table as the group leader. When the group consisted of both male and female members and a male was seated at the head of the table, this person also was designated as leader by a majority of subjects. When a female occupied the head position in a mixed-sex group, however, her position at the table was disregarded. In this situation, any of the other males in the group was selected. It is clear from these results that women are less likely than men to be seen as leaders of mixed-sex groups. The results of this study are consistent with the content of gender stereotypes described by Deaux and Lewis.

SEXISM AND LANGUAGE

Gender stereotypes are also apparent in the everyday use of language. For example, many linguists have pointed out that the English language traditionally has regarded the male linguistic forms as normative. The male-as-normative principle refers to the tendency for "man" to be used to refer to all human beings. Thus, the male is considered to be the representative, or prototype, of the human species. An example of the male-as-normative principle is the use of the pronoun "he" as a generic pronoun that is intended to refer to both males and females. An example of the use of "he" as a generic pronoun is, "While stress is a normal concomitant of our daily lives, man's ever-increasing pace of life may in fact shorten his life span."

The use of the male-as-normative principle has been subjected to two primary criticisms. First, the use of a male-gendered pronoun is often ambiguous. When a writer asserts that "man's ever-increasing pace of life may in fact shorten his life span," the reader may assume that men are more susceptible to the negative effects of stress than women. An alternative interpretation is that humans, regardless of sex, are negatively affected by stress. The second criticism focuses on issues of gender equality. The use of the male-as-normative principle implies that women are exceptions to the general rule. Critics argue that the use of the male generic encourages people to think exclusively of males, rather than including females. Further, they claim that language and thought are closely related and that sexist language may foster gender stereotypes.

In the early 1980's, psychologist Janet Shibley Hyde investigated the effects of sexist language on children's thought processes. She was particularly interested in discovering whether children understood the male-as-normative principle. She asked elementary school children to complete a story about another child. Each of the children was given a sentence with which to begin his or her story (for example, "When a kid goes to school, _____ often feels excited on the first day"). One-third of the sentences provided "he" in place of the blank, one-third included "they," and one-third included "he or she." Hyde found that children's stories indeed were influenced by the use of gender pronouns. When "he" or "they" was provided to the child, fewer than 20 percent of the stories were about females. This effect was especially pronounced when boys were tested. Not one boy who was provided with the pronoun "he" wrote a story about a girl. In contrast, when the pronouns "he or she" were supplied, 42 percent of the stories were about females. Hyde concluded that when children hear the word "he," even when used as a generic pronoun, they tend to think of males.

A number of practical suggestions have been made to avoid the use of sexist language. One simple change is to use the pronoun "they" in place of "he." The results of Hyde's study, however, would suggest that the use of "he or she" would be a better alternative. Others have argued that the single pronouns "he" and "she" might be used with equal frequency throughout written text. Such suggestions are not trivial. Since the 1970's, many textbook publishers have issued guidelines that forbid the use of sexist language. The American Psychological Association (APA) has provided similar guidelines for manuscripts that are submitted for publication in journals published by the APA.

DIFFERENTIAL PSYCHOLOGY

Psychological research investigating the causes and effects of sexism is rooted in the specialized field of differential psychology, which investigated ethnic and gender differences in psychological variables such as intelligence and mental abilities. As early as 1879, Gustave Le Bon provided a description of gender differences in which he noted women's innate inferiority to men, an observation echoed by many other differential psychologists of that period. Hence, the tendency to observe differences between social groups was reflected in both the attitudes and research efforts of early psychological researchers and continues today.

Historically, social psychologists have studied people's beliefs about differences between social groups and their attitudes toward members of other social groups. The first study of stereotypes was conducted in 1922 by Walter Lippmann, a public opinion researcher. His identification of the stereotype concept provided a means for the scientific study of ethnocentrism. The rise of fascism and its thesis of group superiority and inferiority in pre-World War II Europe concerned many social scientists and provided an impetus for the development of systematic studies of intergroup relations. While perceptions of different ethnic groups was the focus of social psychological studies of stereotypes conducted before the 1940's, the study of gender stereotypes was initiated by the publication of a study conducted by Samuel Fernberger in 1948.

Social psychologists continued to study stereotypes and their relation to prejudice in the post-World War II era. Gordon Allport's *The Nature of Prejudice* (1954) provided a theoretical model that explained the process of stereotyping and the development and maintenance of prejudice. In Allport's view, stereotypes are negative attitudes toward the members of other groups that are accompanied by rigid, inflexible thought processes. His conceptualization of stereotypes and prejudice remained unchallenged until the late 1960's, when social psychological research demonstrated that categorization and stereotyping were normal consequences of human thought processes.

The political unrest that characterized American society during the Vietnam War era was reflected in an explosion of social psychological studies of racism and sexism. In addition, the prevailing societal concerns about political and social inequality coincided with demands among feminist scholars for the conduct of nonsexist psychological research. This resulted in the emergence of a new field in the early 1970's, the psychology of women. Nonsexist, gender-fair psychological research has been promoted as a legitimate field of study by the establishment of a specialized section within the APA (Division 35) that is dedicated to the psychology of women. Scholarship in this field is dedicated to the study of sexism, gender differences and similarities, and other aspects of gender-role socialization.

SOURCES FOR FURTHER STUDY

Bem, Sandra Lipsitz. *The Lenses of Gender: Transforming the Debate on Sexual Inequality.* New Haven, Conn.: Yale University Press, 1994. Discusses contemporary theories about the gender relations through the lenses of androcentrism (taking male experience for the norm), gender polarization (placing male and female experience at opposite ends of a cultural spectrum, with nothing in between), and biologic essentialism (using biological differences to account for cultural realities).

Swann, William B., Judith H. Langlois, and Lucie Albino Gilbert, eds. *Sexism and Stereotypes in Modern Society.* Washington, D.C.: American Psychological Association, 1998. A collection of essays addressing the history of gender research, the complexity of gender stereotypes, and modern forms of sexism and their consequences.

Tavris, Carol, and Carole Wade. *The Longest War: Sex Differences in Perspective.* 2d ed. New York: Harcourt Brace Jovanovich, 1984. An entertaining and easy-to-read introduction to the psychology of women. Gender differences and similarities are discussed, in addition to the biological and social factors relevant to gender-role socialization.

Thorne, Barrie, Cheris Kramarae, and Nancy Henley. *Language, Gender, and Society.* Rowley, Mass.: Newbury House, 1983. Contains an excellent collection of papers that address the nature of sexist language and research findings on gender differences in language use. Draws parallels among gender, power, and social class and their relationship to language and its use. An accessible and valuable source of information.

Walsh, Mary Roth, ed. *The Psychology of Women: Ongoing Debates.* New Haven, Conn.: Yale University Press, 1987. Using a debate format, noted authorities on the psychology of women present their arguments about controversial issues. Topical issues include mental health, psychological characteristics, differences, and social issues. A very accessible yet informative introduction for the general reader.

Williams, John E., and Deborah L. Best. *Sex and Psyche: Gender and Self Viewed Cross-Culturally.* Newbury Park, Calif.: Sage Publications, 1990. The authors have conducted one of the best global studies of stereotypes. Here they present the results of a cross-cultural study of sex-role stereotypes, ideologies, and values in thirty countries. A wealth of statistical data is summarized in a format suitable for the college-level reader.

Cheryl A. Rickabaugh

SEE ALSO: Ageism; Causal attribution; Cognitive ability: Gender differences; Feminist psychotherapy; Gender-identity formation; Prejudice; Racism; Social schemata; Women's psychology: Carol Gilligan; Women's psychology: Karen Horney; Women's psychology: Sigmund Freud.

Sexual behavior patterns

TYPE OF PSYCHOLOGY: Motivation
FIELDS OF STUDY: Endocrine system; nervous system; physical motives

Sexual behavior patterns help to ensure the survival of virtually all species. There is a rich diversity of patterns in the animal kingdom, each shaped by evolutionary, ecological, and environmental factors on one hand and hormonal and neural factors on the other.

KEY CONCEPTS
- monogamy
- pheromones
- polyandry
- polygyny
- proximate cause
- sex hormones
- sexual selection
- ultimate cause

INTRODUCTION

Sexual behavior patterns represent one of the most important aspects of an organism's life. These patterns not only provide for the successful perpetuation of the species but also allow the individual to contribute genetically to future generations. Sexual behavior is unlike other physical motives, such as feeding and drinking, which are required for the individual's survival and which are initiated to some extent by measurable changes in blood sugar and cellular hydration. Engaging in sexual behavior is neither necessary to live nor stimulated by the depletion of a bodily fluid or chemical substance.

Two types of questions, relating to ultimate and proximate causality, must be addressed when sexual behavior patterns are examined. The first question asks why the pattern developed; the second asks how it occurs. For example, many species breed only during particular seasons, and the onset of these periods is often associated with changes in plumage or coloration, or the growth of anatomical structures such as antlers. Why do these changes take place? This question of ultimate causality is really asking about purpose or function; in these examples, one answer could be that the alteration makes the animal more attractive to a potential mate.

The second question, concerning proximate causation, asks how these changes come about or what the more immediate cause is. In this case, the answer could be related to a change in the animal's hormonal secretions. Thus, the sexual behavior pattern of a given species is determined by many factors, each with ultimate and proximate causes.

SEXUAL SELECTION AND MATING SYSTEMS

One of these factors is sexual selection, a concept originated by Charles Darwin in *The Descent of Man and Selection in Relation to Sex* (1871) and related to the example mentioned above. There are two kinds of selection, intersexual and intrasexual. In the first, one sex's ability to secure a mate is related to its anatomical and behavioral traits. Examples that pertain to males include antlers, the peacock's feathers (and the way the male displays the fully fanned-out feathers for the female), and the songs of some bird species used to "advertise" the male's availability for mating as well as the fact that he has obtained a territory relatively free of intruders.

Intrasexual selection involves those anatomical and behavioral traits that are used to compete with members of the same sex for access to a member of the other sex. The battle between males to establish dominance that for the winner often leads to the opportunity to mate is a common example. A well-known phenomenon in mice, the Bruce effect, provides a different sort of intrasexual selection example. The presence of an unknown male during the early stages of pregnancy can cause a female to abort, which results in her becoming sexually receptive and hence a potential mate for the strange male. In this case, the ultimate cause is that this enables the male to sire more offspring, while the proximate cause is that his odor alters the female's hormone secretions in such a way as to terminate pregnancy.

Various mating systems have evolved that also determine the type of sexual behavior pattern. Monogamy represents a sexual relationship between one female and one male, sometimes for life. One advantage is that it precludes the effort necessary to search for a mate during each breeding cycle or season. It may, however, sometimes be more advantageous for a female to enter a good territory already inhabited by a male and one or more other females than to form a monogamous relationship with a male who lives in a dangerous territory or one with fewer resources. These systems are called polygynous, as opposed to those that are polyandrous, in which one female has a sexual relationship with more than one male. Although polyandrous systems are uncommon, polyandry does occur in situations in which the female can lay many eggs in various nests while the different males do most or all of the incubating.

Unlike some species, such as humans, who reproduce throughout the year, most species breed only during one or more restricted times of the year. The ultimate cause could be that hatching or birth occurs at a time when the environmental features are more optimal in terms of temperature, predators, or food availability. Proximate factors have been well studied, and it is known that changes in the amount of light per day or temperature can cause an animal's endocrine system to become reproduc-

tively active. In female mammals, these periods are called estrous cycles; it is only during these cycles that pregnancy can occur. Animals kept in laboratories and maintained with constant and optimal amounts of light and other environmental factors will breed all year long.

The changes in hormonal secretions that precede the onset of a breeding period are critical for several reasons. Physiological processes such as maturation of the egg or ovum, the formation of the hard shell of the egg in birds and reptiles, ovulation, preparation of the uterus for implantation of the ovum in mammals, and development of sperm depend upon particular hormones. Hormones are also important because they act directly on regions of the brain to increase an organism's motivation to reproduce. In addition, by affecting sensory processes, hormones directly or indirectly enable an animal to communicate its reproductive readiness over distances. Examples include pheromones, which are odors that are emitted by many species to attract a sexual partner, some types of singing in birds and croaking in frogs, and the increased swelling and reddening of the genital region in monkeys.

SEXUAL BEHAVIOR IN DOVES
Sexual behavior patterns are extremely varied; only by studying them in detail have scientists uncovered some general principles that apply to various groupings of species. Appreciating the differences between even closely related species prevents oversimplified generalizations from one species to another.

Many species of birds have relatively prolonged and intricate courtship and mating patterns. The ring dove was extensively studied in the laboratory by Daniel Lehrman and his colleagues in the 1950's and 1960's and by a number of other scientists since then. Although the dove has breeding cycles in nature, it reproduces almost the entire year if kept in the laboratory under constant conditions of fourteen hours of light and ten hours of dark per day and 22 degrees centigrade.

The male dove's courtship begins with cooing sounds while in a bowing posture. This continues for a period of time until he selects a nest site and then coos from that location. When sufficiently aroused, the female also "nest-coos," which tells the male that it is time to gather material for the nest. Eventually the female ovulates, and the birds mate. She lays two eggs; both parents incubate the eggs, and both participate in feeding the young squabs by regurgitation.

Experiments have shown that androgens, the male sex hormones secreted from the testes, stimulate the male dove's courtship behavior, which in turn stimulates the female's ovaries to release the female sex hormones estrogen and progesterone. Hearing her own nest coos affects the female's physiology by playing a major role in the development of the follicles, the ovarian structures that contain her gametes, or eggs, which will be fertilized by the sperm. These hormones are important for ovulation and for mating behavior. Behavioral participation in the building of the nest produces further hormonal changes, which increase each partner's motivation to sit on the eggs. Visual and tactile sensory input from the eggs stimulates prolactin from the pituitary gland in both sexes, which functions to keep the parents incubating until the eggs hatch; it also causes the production of crop milk, the partially digested food that is regurgitated for the hatchlings. These behavioral-hormonal interrelationships have been shown to exist in other species, and they point out the importance of particular sexual behavior patterns for successful reproduction.

SEXUAL BEHAVIOR IN RATS

Another example of the role of behavior patterns in the survival of the species comes from experiments on rats by Norman Adler. A female rat comes into "heat" or estrus on only one day during the latter portion of her four-day estrous cycle. Her period of heat begins several hours before ovulation and ends several hours afterward. It is only during this time that she will mate and can become pregnant. During the first few days of the estrous cycle, the female secretes hormones that cause growth of the follicles, ovulation, and sexual behavior. If her eggs or ova are fertilized, her estrous cycling stops until after delivery of the litter. As in the case of the dove, a female rat will continue to have estrous cycles all year long under constant environmental conditions in the laboratory, unless she becomes pregnant.

Under those constant conditions, the male continues to secrete androgens and is almost always ready to mate. Placing a sexually receptive female and sexually active male together in a cage results in a predictable sequence of behaviors. The male will investigate the female and, on the basis of certain odors attributable to her estrogen and progester-

one, will find her "attractive." In response to the male's interest in her and her attraction to him, she engages in proceptive behaviors—sexually stimulating activities that maintain the pair's interaction. In the rat, these behaviors include a "hopping and darting" form of locomotion and ear quivering. The male will mount the female, and if sufficiently motivated, she will show receptivity by adopting the lordosis posture (characterized by immobility, arched back, and raised genital region). On many of these mounts, the male will be able to intromit his penis into her vagina; after an average of ten to fifteen intromissions, he will ejaculate. A number of minutes will elapse and the sequence will begin again; it will be repeated several times in a single sexual session.

In one experiment, males were allowed to intromit a varying number of times with a first female; then, before ejaculating, they were each placed with a second female. In this way, various females received different numbers of intromissions prior to an ejaculation. The significant finding was that the female needs a number of intromissions plus an ejaculation to become pregnant. If she receives only one or two intromissions prior to an ejaculation, her likelihood of becoming pregnant is greatly reduced. The stimulation she receives from these intromissions is necessary to alter her hormonal secretions in preparation for pregnancy. Additionally, males who intromit fewer than six times prior to an ejaculation release fewer sperm, hence reducing the probability that their partners will become pregnant. This result is related to the fact that subdominant male rats have fewer intromissions and reduced fertility, but only when a more dominant male is nearby.

SEXUAL BEHAVIOR IN PRIMATES

Scientists study primate species both because they are interesting in their own right and because the researchers wish to gain some understanding of human behavior. The rhesus monkey, a commonly studied primate, is polygynous and native to India; it has a breeding season that begins in the fall and lasts about five months. Instead of an estrous cycle, it has a menstrual cycle that is almost identical to that of human females.

Mating behavior is not controlled as exclusively by hormones as it is in lower species, but the frequency of copulation is greatest around the time of ovulation. Attractivity of the female is enhanced by

estrogen, but (as is not the case in the rat) it is reduced by progesterone, the hormone that is at its
highest level after ovulation in the second half of
the menstrual cycle. Experiments have shown that
for optimal mating behavior to occur, androgen is
necessary for the male, and both estrogen and androgen are required in the female. Female monkeys, like female humans, normally secrete androgen, although at much lower levels than males do
(just as male monkeys and humans secrete female
sex hormones). Studies on human females have
shown that levels of androgen during the menstrual
cycle correlate with increased sexual motivation and
gratification.

FROM EVOLUTION TO ETHOLOGY

Charles Darwin was influential in convincing scientists and nonscientists alike that humans and other
animals are products of evolution and that they
share common ancestors. Further, Darwin and his
successors have argued that behavior, like anatomy,
has changed as a result of natural selection, the process whereby traits that allow an organism to produce more offspring will be inherited by subsequent
generations.

In part because of Darwin's emphasis on the similarity between animals and humans, William James
in the late nineteenth century and William Mc-
Dougall in the early twentieth century proposed
that much of human behavior is based on instincts.
Instincts are behaviors that are characterized by
their lack of dependence on learning, fairly rigid
performance, and presence in all members of at
least one sex of a species.

The question of instincts is a key issue in the
long-standing controversy in psychology between
"nature" and "nurture," or the relative role of inborn versus environmental or learned factors in behavior. Over the years, some behaviors that were
thought to be pure instincts have been shown to be
affected by learning or experience, and other behaviors have been shown to be more inborn than
originally thought. Furthermore, simply calling a
behavior an instinct does little to shed light on either its ultimate or its proximate causes.

Partly as a result of the debate over instincts, the
study of animal and human behavior has taken two
somewhat separate paths. On the one side are primarily psychologists, psychobiologists, and neuroscientists who investigate the more proximate causes

of sexual behavior patterns in the laboratory under
controlled conditions. Their progress has helped
to gather information on the nervous system, the
endocrine system, the interaction between the two,
and their relationship to environmental factors
such as light, temperature, and the presence of potential mates.

Evolutionary biologists, animal behaviorists,
sociobiologists, and ethologists tend to study sexual
and other behaviors under natural conditions.
Ethologists Konrad Lorenz and Nikolaas Tinbergen
focused on more instinctive, species-specific behaviors emphasizing ultimate causation.

It is often difficult for a laboratory scientist to devote much attention to evolutionary concerns, and
it is equally difficult for the animal behaviorist to focus on the nervous and endocrine systems. Information from one approach often complements the
other, however, and a complete understanding of
the effect of all relevant factors is necessary for the
study of sexual behavior patterns.

SOURCES FOR FURTHER STUDY

Crews, David, ed. *Psychobiology of Reproductive Behavior: An Evolutionary Perspective.* Englewood Cliffs,
N.J.: Prentice-Hall, 1987. Twelve articles cover a
wide range of species, including humans. The
emphasis in this book is on ultimate and proximate causation of reproductive behavior, and the
articles are written by experts in their fields.

Hutchison, John Bower, ed. *Biological Determinants of
Sexual Behaviour.* New York: John Wiley & Sons,
1978. A collection of twenty-four articles covering
the role of development and experience, physiological mechanisms, sensory stimulation, evolutionary concerns, and reproductive strategies in
the sexual behavior of animals. Included are several readings pertaining to humans and other
primates.

Komisaruk, Barry R., et al., eds. *Reproduction: A Behavioral and Neuroendocrine Perspective.* New York:
New York Academy of Sciences, 1986. More than
forty articles, all written by individuals who were
or are associated with the Institute of Animal Behavior at Rutgers University, a program that emphasizes evolutionary physiological issues in the
study of reproduction.

Lehrman, Daniel S. "The Reproductive Behavior of
Ring Doves." *Scientific American* 211 (November,
1964): 48-54. This article presents a classic exam-

ple of the relationships between and among the mating partners, internal physiological mechanisms, and the environment.

Harold I. Siegel

SEE ALSO: Animal experimentation; Endocrine system; Gonads; Hormones and behavior; Instinct theory; Psychosexual development; Sex hormones and motivation.

Sexual dysfunction

TYPE OF PSYCHOLOGY: Psychopathology
FIELDS OF STUDY: Sexual disorders

Sexual problems are influenced by both health-related and psychosocial factors. Stress-inducing situations, interpersonal communication problems, or chronic illness can affect sexual functioning in both men and women. Sex therapy is aimed at helping individuals and couples to understand the underlying causes of sexual distress and to adopt new behaviors conducive to a more satisfying sex life.

KEY CONCEPTS
- arousal disorders
- dyspareunia
- feminist perspectives
- hyperactive sexual desire
- hypoactive sexual desire
- orgasmic disorders
- sexual aversion
- sexual minorities
- vaginismus

INTRODUCTION

A satisfactory sexual life is an integral component of a person's physical and psychological health. It plays an important role in both an individual's self-esteem and an enriching and fulfilling couple relationship. A strong association exists between sexual dysfunction and an impaired quality of life.

Sexual problems can be caused by various medical conditions, such as cardiovascular problems, diabetes, and hormonal imbalances. A majority of sexual disorders, however, are associated with significant psychological difficulties in an individual's personal and interpersonal life. Those suffering from sexual problems are also likely to experience distress, reduced self-esteem, and symptoms of anxiety and depression. In some cases, psychological problems are a consequence of sexual problems. In other cases, sexual problems reflect coexisting psychopathology. In still other cases, sexual problems may even result in other unspecified physical, psychological, interpersonal, or social problems.

Treatment strategies include a comprehensive assessment of the physiological and psychological factors contributing to the dysfunction, appropriate psychotherapeutic interventions, interpersonal intimacy training, and, in certain cases, surgical procedures such as penile implants.

In the early twentieth century, Sigmund Freud conceptualized sexual problems as symptoms of deep-rooted disturbances of personality originating from early childhood experiences. Treatment usually consisted of lengthy psychoanalysis that did not always alleviate the problem. In the early 1960's, behavior therapies such as systematic desensitization were used to treat sexual problems, specifically erectile dysfunction in men and so-called frigidity (lack of sexual desire) in women. These therapies, however, were mostly aimed at relieving symptoms rather than examining the underlying causes.

THE SEXUAL RESPONSE

In 1966, William H. Masters and Virginia E. Johnson proposed a comprehensive model of sexual response cycle consisting of four stages: excitement, the initial stage of increasing arousal in which the skin becomes flushed, the penis or clitoris becomes engorged with blood, and vaginal lubrication increases; plateau, the stage of full arousal in which the penis becomes enlarged to maximum erection and the outer third of the vagina becomes engorged with blood; orgasm, the stage involving muscle contraction throughout the body in which men ejaculate sperm-filled semen and women's vaginal contractions facilitate conception by helping propel the semen into the vagina; and resolution, the stage during which the body gradually returns to an unaroused state in which muscles relax and engorged genital blood vessels release excess blood.

For the first time, Masters and Johnson documented the genital and extragenital physiological changes that typically occur during each of these stages. They argued not only that men's and women's physiological changes are remarkably similar as they approach and achieve orgasm but also that the physiological expression of an orgasm is similar regardless of how it is achieved. Based on their model, Masters and Johnson subsequently published the book *Human Sexual Inadequacy* (1970), which described a sex therapy combining behavioral and psychotherapeutic approaches. The focus of this therapy was mostly on the relationship between the couple. Their treatment of individuals using sexual surrogates raised certain ethical dilemmas.

During the late 1970's, Helen Singer Kaplan observed that many of her sexually troubled patients complained of a lack of interest in sex or even an aversion to sexual activity. She concluded from her observations that there is an important stage preliminary to the excitement phase, one that she labeled sexual desire. This stage involves an individual's cognitive and emotional readiness for and interest in participating in sexual activity. Masters and Johnson's original sexual response cycle has since been revised to include sexual desire as a primary component, and the cycle is now recognized of having five main stages: desire, excitement, plateau, orgasm, and resolution.

THE DEFINITION OF SEXUAL DYSFUNCTION

The revised fourth edition of the American Psychiatric Association's *Diagnostic and Statistical Manual of Mental Disorders* (2000), more commonly known as the DSM-IV-TR, defines sexual dysfunction as a disturbance in sexual desire and the psychophysiological changes that characterize the sexual response cycle that causes marked distress and interpersonal difficulties. While the DSM-IV-TR provides a clear framework for classifying sexual problems, decisions about the presence or absence of a dysfunction may often reflect the values and standards of both clinicians and patients, which in turn are affected by the constantly shifting cultural opinions regarding sexual mores and behavior. Thus, the definition and understanding of sexual dysfunctions can be rather complex and, at times, controversial, particularly when the sexual behavior implies a reference to a perceived normal level of activity or interest.

Sexual dysfunctions can be classified under for four major areas: sexual desire disorders, arousal disorders, orgasmic disorders, and physical pain experienced during intercourse. These dysfunctions are not always discrete, and specific problems may

overlap as to their origin, presentation, and intensity.

SEXUAL DESIRE DISORDERS

Sexual desire disorders include hypoactive sexual desire, hyperactive sexual desire, and sexual aversion. Properly speaking, these disorders affect the brain's arousal capabilities rather than physiological responses. Individuals with sexual desire disorders have the ability to respond physically but have little or no emotional investment in sexual activities. It is as if the brain's erotic centers have shut down.

Hypoactive sexual desire, also known as inhibited sexual desire, is a low or absent sexual desire. The person suffering from hypoactive sexual desire has little or no interest in sexual matters, will not actively pursue sexual gratification, and, if a sexual situation presents itself, is not readily moved to avail himself or herself of the opportunity to engage in sexual activity. Hypoactive sexual desire generally stems from deeper, more intense sexual anxieties such as sexual performance anxiety. By developing a low interest in sexual activity, the person avoids the unpleasant feelings of embarrassment, loss of self-esteem, and frustration as a result of perceived sexual failure.

Depression can be one of the major causes of hypoactive sexual desire. Hypoactive sexual desire may also have roots in various unresolved relationship problems. Suppressed and unacknowledged anger and resentment toward one's partner can often manifest in hypoactive sexual desire. Stress, a traumatic marital separation or divorce, or loss of employment can also result in hypoactive sexual desire. Drugs, hormonal imbalance, and chronic illness are major contributors to hypoactive sexual desire. Some individuals may use lack of desire as a defense against a generalized anxiety around situations involving intimacy, closeness, and even physical touch.

Individuals with excessive desire disorder often experience uncontrollable sexual urges. They are obsessed with sexual thoughts that permeate all their actions and feelings, and they demand immediate gratification. These individuals are unable to control their sexual appetite and view sex as a magical cure for depression. Sex becomes an addiction for such people. Hypersexuality can occur with or without frequent masturbation. A person with excessive sexual desire uses sex as a substitution for involvement in other activities. For such a person, sex

---

DSM-IV-TR Criteria for Sexual Dysfunctions

SEXUAL AVERSION DISORDER (DSM CODE 302.79)

Persistent or recurrent extreme aversion to, and avoidance of, all (or almost all) genital sexual contact with sexual partner

Disturbance causes marked distress or interpersonal difficulty

Sexual dysfunction not better accounted for by another Axis I disorder (except another sexual dysfunction)

HYPOACTIVE SEXUAL DESIRE DISORDER (DSM CODE 302.71)

Persistently or recurrently deficient (or absent) sexual fantasies and desire for sexual activity; judgment of deficiency or absence made by clinician, taking into account factors affecting sexual functioning, such as age and life context

Disturbance causes marked distress or interpersonal difficulty

Sexual dysfunction not better accounted for by another Axis I disorder (except another sexual dysfunction) and not due exclusively to direct physiological effects of a substance or general medical condition

FEMALE SEXUAL AROUSAL DISORDER (DSM CODE 302.72)

Persistent or recurrent inability to attain, or to maintain until completion of sexual activity, an adequate lubrication-swelling response of sexual excitement

Disturbance causes marked distress or interpersonal difficulty

Sexual dysfunction not better accounted for by another Axis I disorder (except another sexual dysfunction) and not due exclusively to direct physiological effects of a substance or general medical condition

MALE ERECTILE DISORDER (DSM CODE 302.72)

Persistent or recurrent inability to attain, or to maintain until completion of sexual activity, an adequate erection

Disturbance causes marked distress or interpersonal difficulty

Erectile dysfunction not better accounted for by another Axis I disorder (other than a sexual dysfunction) and not due exclusively to direct physiological effects of a substance or general medical condition

FEMALE ORGASMIC DISORDER (DSM CODE 302.73)

Persistent or recurrent delay in, or absence of, orgasm following normal sexual excitement phase; diagnosis based on clinician's judgment that woman's orgasmic capacity is less than reasonable for her age and sexual experience and the adequacy of sexual stimulation

Disturbance causes marked distress or interpersonal difficulty

Orgasmic dysfunction not better accounted for by another Axis I disorder (except another sexual dysfunction) and not due exclusively to direct physiological effects of a substance or general medical condition

(continued)

---

is impersonal, with little or no positive feelings or emotions associated with the sex act.

Sexual aversion is a consistently phobic response to sexual activities or even thoughts of such activities. A person suffering from sexual aversion experiences an overwhelming anxiety about any kind of sexual contact. A mere kiss, touch, or caress may create fear that the initial contact might lead to sexual arousal or activity. Anticipating the sex act may provoke greater anxiety than actual participation in the sexual activity. Sexual aversion may result from strict and authoritarian parental attitudes during childhood, from sexual trauma such as rape or sexual abuse, or from consistent and increasing sexual pressure from a long-term partner. Sexual aversion may also be a result of adolescent difficulties with self-esteem and perceived body image.

AROUSAL DISORDERS

Arousal disorders among males include disorders of the erectile process, such as dysfunctional arousal and plateau phases. Erectile difficulties may be defined as persisting or recurrent inability to attain and/or maintain a penile erection sufficient to permit vaginal penetration and satisfactory conclusion of sexual intercourse. Erectile difficulties in men are commonly known as impotence and are the most frequently occurring male sexual dysfunctions. Impotence can be of great concern to not only the patient but also his sexual partner.

Total erectile dysfunction is rare and is caused by serious disruption in the blood supply to penis or the leakage of blood from penile cavernous bodies. Cardiovascular problems and diabetes may sometimes cause nerve damage, leading to sexual arousal

MALE ORGASMIC DISORDER (DSM CODE 302.74)

Persistent or recurrent delay in, or absence of, orgasm following normal sexual excitement phase during sexual activity that clinician, taking into account person's age, judges to be adequate in focus, intensity, and duration

Disturbance causes marked distress or interpersonal difficulty

Orgasmic dysfunction not better accounted for by another Axis I disorder (except another sexual dysfunction) and not due exclusively to direct physiological effects of a substance or general medical condition

PREMATURE EJACULATION (DSM CODE 302.75)

Persistent or recurrent ejaculation with minimal sexual stimulation before, on, or shortly after penetration and before person wishes it; clinician takes into account factors affecting duration of excitement phase, such as age, novelty of sexual partner or situation, and recent frequency of sexual activity

Disturbance causes marked distress or interpersonal difficulty

Premature ejaculation not due exclusively to direct effects of a substance, such as withdrawal from opioids

DYSPAREUNIA (DSM CODE 302.76)

Recurrent or persistent genital pain associated with sexual intercourse in male or female

Disturbance causes marked distress or interpersonal difficulty

Disturbance not caused exclusively by Vaginismus or lack of lubrication, not better accounted for by another Axis I disorder (except another sexual dysfunction), and not due exclusively to direct physiological effects of a substance or general medical condition

VAGINISMUS (DSM CODE 306.51)

Recurrent or persistent involuntary spasm of musculature of outer third of vagina interfering with sexual intercourse

Disturbance causes marked distress or interpersonal difficulty

Disturbance not better accounted for by another Axis I disorder (such as Somatization Disorder) and not due exclusively to direct physiological effects of a general medical condition

SEXUAL DYSFUNCTION NOT OTHERWISE SPECIFIED (DSM CODE 302.70)

Specify for each disorder:
- Lifelong or Acquired
- Generalized or Situational
- Due to Psychological Factors or Due to Combined Factors

---

disorders. Situational erectile dysfunction, on the other hand, usually has a psychological basis. The man is able to obtain an erection but is unable to experience erection with his partner or cannot sustain his erection when sexual intercourse is attempted.

Among women, arousal disorders include failure of vaginal swelling, the lack of sufficient lubrication, and a lack of sensation that is usually associated with sexual excitement. For some women, the hormonal changes that occur after childbirth may impair the normal vaginal response to sexual stimulation.

ORGASMIC DISORDERS

Orgasm is defined as the building up and release of tension. During release of the tension, contractions are felt in the genital area and, after the peak of excitement, a period of relaxation follows. In women, rhythmic contractions occur in the uterus, the vaginal barrel, and the rectal sphincter, gradually diminishing in intensity, regularity, and duration.

Women who are diagnosed as having primary anorgasmia have never experienced an orgasm. Women suffering from secondary anorgasmia are those who have previously experienced orgasm in sexual intercourse but are either no longer able to do so or are only able to have an orgasm in certain situations such as masturbation. These women suffer from orgasmic infrequency and are not always aware of the conditions that restrict them from being orgasmic.

Orgasmic disorders among males include inability to achieve orgasm and disturbances of ejaculation. Premature ejaculation in men is a persistent or recurrent ejaculation with minimal sexual stimulation before, during, or shortly after penetration and before the man's desire for it to occur. Men suffering from premature ejaculation fail to fully experience the orgasmic release, usually the most pleasurable sensation of the sexual activity. Failure to emit or eject seminal fluid can also raise concerns, primarily in those situations in which fertility is desired. A less common male sexual disorder is retarded ejaculation, which is the persistent or recurrent delay in, or absence of, orgasm following a phase of normal sexual excitement.

PHYSICAL PAIN DURING INTERCOURSE

In women, painful intercourse, or dyspareunia, often occurs because the woman is not entirely aroused before her partner attempts intercourse. Sexual inhibitions, lack of appropriate foreplay, a poor relationship with the partner, and hormonal imbalances can contribute to a woman's dyspareunia. Postmenopausal women may suffer from decreased vaginal lubrication and, as a result, lose much of the vaginal elasticity. Related to painful intercourse is vaginismus, a condition in which the muscles around the vaginal entrance go into involuntary spasmodic contractions, preventing the entrance of the penis. Vaginismus is essentially a conditioned response that reflects fear, anxiety, or pain. It may be a result of negative attitudes about sexuality, harsh early sexual experiences, sexual abuse or rape, or painful pelvic examinations.

SEXUAL MINORITIES

Sexual problems experienced by gay men, lesbians, and bisexuals are not significantly different from those experienced by heterosexuals except that the traditional concepts of monogamous sexual relationship cannot always be taken for granted when working with members of such populations. As in the general population, gay men and lesbians also suffer from desire, arousal, and orgasmic disorders. They also have a set of problems that sets them apart from the general heterosexual populations. Gay men, for example, tend to experiment with various forms of sexuality that may include open and frequently changing relationships, which sometimes leads to insecurity and instability in their relationships. Some gay men entertain fantasies of domination and overpowering others in their sexual repertoire.

Many lesbian relationships are based on feminist principles that incorporate equality and nonexclusivity in their relationships. Some lesbians tend to prefer bisexual relationships. They appear to be looking for a sense of community and spirituality in their relationships. Frustration in attainment of those ideals can sometimes lead to a generalized lack of sexual desire.

A SYSTEMS APPROACH TO SEXUAL DYSFUNCTION

Psychologist David Schnarch advocates a combination of physical stimulus and internal focus that brings together the physiological experience of sex and the phenomenological meanings that people attach to it. He distinguishes between clinical and subjective arousal and creates a clinical framework that can accommodate such subjective constructs as sexual potential and intimacy. He attempts to explore the roots of human inability to tolerate high levels of eroticism and intimacy, and he presents a model that integrates behavioral, object relations, and systematic approaches to help patients achieve the developmental maturity to tolerate high level of emotional salience.

According to Schnarch, a couple's sexual problems are a window to latent unresolved issues in the individual, in the couple, or in the extended emotional system of the couple, including the family of origin as well as lovers and friends. These unresolved issues can inhibit satisfying sexual-marital functioning and the full exploration of sexual potential.

TREATMENT OF SEXUAL DYSFUNCTIONS

Sex therapists are nationally certified by the American Association of Sex Educators, Counselors, and Therapists upon completion of the required training and supervision. Sexual dysfunctions are also treated by licensed marriage and family therapists, physicians, psychologists, psychiatrists and social workers. Treatment usually begins with a comprehensive assessment of physiological and psychosocial factors that could be contributing to the presenting problem. In the absence of a significant medical finding, the therapist attempts to uncover the emotional and interpersonal issues underlying the sexual problem and helps the patients find ways to resolve them. In addition to office visits, some therapists may assign homework aimed at gaining greater awareness of one's own feelings and those of one's partner and enhancing interpersonal intimacy. Psychotherapeutic treatments may include cognitive behavior therapy, mental imagery, psychodynamic therapy, and systematic desensitization. For patients with physiological deficiencies, medical interventions may include the use of hormonal treatments, appropriate antidepressants, Viagra (sildenafil), and, where necessary, penile implants.

A FEMINIST PERSPECTIVE ON SEX THERAPY

Traditional sex therapists mostly use the diagnostic framework of sexual dysfunctions as articulated in the DSM-IV-TR, which many feminist therapists consider as very poorly suited to women's and sexual minorities' sexual reality. By ignoring the social context of sexuality, these minorities assert that the DSM-IV-TR nomenclature perpetuates a dangerously naïve and false vision of how sex really works.

Feminist sex therapy encompasses the two domains of insight and skill. The first includes corrective genital physiology education, assertiveness training, body image reclamation, and masturbation education. The second rejects sexual drive in favor of contact comfort, mutual masturbation, and new ways of sexual understanding and exploration.

Feminist sex therapy attempts to move beyond restrictions and inhibitions created by the prevalent body/mind conflict, depreciation of women's sexuality, and preoccupation with procreation. It also attempts to bypass the restrictions and inhibitions embedded in gender roles and stereotypes. The focus in feminist sex therapy is on the personal meaning and subjective nature of sexual activity, feelings, and relationships.

SOURCES FOR FURTHER STUDY

American Psychiatric Association. *Diagnostic and Statistical Manual of Mental Disorders: DSM-IV-TR*. Rev. 4th ed. Washington, D.C.: Author, 2000. A reference manual used as an aid in diagnosing mental disorders.

Heiman, J., L. LoPiccolo, and J. LoPiccolo. *Becoming Orgasmic: A Sexual Growth Program for Women*. 2d ed. Englewood Cliffs, N.J.: Prentice-Hall, 1988. The authors offer guidance for enhancing the emotional experience of sexual activity. Areas of discussion include sexual expectations, sexual awareness, communication with one's sexual partner, and the enhancement of intimacy.

Kaplan, Helen Singer. *Disorders of Sexual Desire and Other New Concepts and Techniques in Sex Therapy*. New York: Brunner/Mazel, 1979. Focuses on inhibited sexual desire, including its identification and treatment. Presents case histories and examines the effects of medical conditions and drug interactions on sexual function.

Masters, William H., and Virginia E. Johnson. *Human Sexual Inadequacy*. Boston: Little, Brown, 1970. Based on direct observations of sexual activity in a clinical setting, the authors present definitions of various sexual dysfunctions and offer treatment approaches.

_____. *Human Sexual Response*. Boston: Little, Brown, 1966. The authors propose a comprehensive model of the sexual response cycle based on their clinical research of the sexual activities of numerous volunteers.

Saral, Tulsi B. "Mental Imagery in Sex Therapy." In *Healing Images: The Role of Imagination in Health*, edited by A. A. Sheikh. Farmingdale, N.Y.: Baywood, 2002. This article explores the use of mental imagery in the diagnosis and treatment of sexual dysfunctions and presents a series of imagery exercises for use in treating specific sexual disorders.

Schnarch, David M. *Constructing the Sexual Crucible: An Integration of Sexual and Marital Therapy*. New York: W. W. Norton, 1991. Schnarch presents a framework for integrating biological functioning, emotional experience and spiritual awareness to achieve optimum sexual gratification. The book also brings together individual, couple, and marital psychotherapies to propose an effective sex therapy model.

Tiefer, Leonore. "Towards a Feminist Sex Therapy." In *Sexualities*, edited by Marney Hall. Binghamton, N.Y.: Harrington Park Press, 1996. This article argues that traditional approaches of therapeutic intervention for sexual dysfunctions are biased toward the medical/symptomological model. Tiefer advocates a more holistic approach integrating emotional factors, interpersonal skills, and social awareness.

Wincze, J. P., and M. P. Carey. *Sexual Dysfunction: A Guide for Assessment and Treatment*. New York: Guilford, 1991. The authors offer a biopsychosocial model of sexual behavior, discuss the main categories of sexual dysfunctions, and present guidelines for the assessment and treatment of sexual problems.

Tulsi B. Saral

SEE ALSO: Endocrine system; Gonads; Homosexuality; Hormones and behavior; Nervous system; Psychobiology; Psychosexual development; Sex hormones and motivation; Sexual behavior patterns; Sexual variants and paraphilias.

Sexual variants and paraphilias

TYPE OF PSYCHOLOGY: Psychopathology
FIELDS OF STUDY: Sexual disorders

Sexual variations, or paraphilias, are unusual sexual activities in that they deviate from what is considered normal at a particular time in a particular society; paraphilias include behaviors such as exhibitionism, voyeurism, and sadomasochism. It is when they become the prime means of gratification, displacing direct sexual contact with a consenting adult partner, that paraphilias are technically present.

KEY CONCEPTS
- exhibitionism
- fetishism
- frotteurism
- sexual masochism
- sexual sadism
- transvestic fetishism
- voyeurism
- zoophilia

INTRODUCTION

Paraphilias are sexual behaviors that are considered a problem for the person who performs them and/or a problem for society because they differ from the society's norms. Psychologist John Money, who has studied sexual attitudes and behaviors extensively, claims to have identified about forty such behaviors.

TYPES OF PARAPHILIAS

EXHIBITIONISM. Exhibitionism is commonly called indecent exposure. The term refers to behavior in which an individual, usually a male, experiences recurrent, intense sexually arousing fantasies or urges about exposing his genitals to an involuntary observer, who is usually a female. A disorder is present if the individual acts on these urges or the thoughts cause marked distress. The key point in exhibitionistic behavior is that it involves observers who are unwilling. After exposing himself, the exhibitionist often masturbates while fantasizing about the observer's reaction. Exhibitionists tend to be most aroused by shock and typically flee if the observer responds by laughing or attempts to approach the exhibitionist. Most people who exhibit themselves are males in their twenties or thirties. They tend to

be shy, unassertive people who feel inadequate and afraid of being rejected by another person. People who make obscene telephone calls have similar characteristics to the people who engage in exhibitionism. Typically, they are sexually aroused when their victims react in a shocked manner. Many masturbate during or immediately after placing an obscene call.

VOYEURISM. Voyeurism is the derivation of sexual pleasure through the repetitive seeking or intrusional fantasies of situations that involve looking, or "peeping," at unsuspecting people who are naked, undressing, or engaged in sexual intercourse. Most individuals who act on these urges masturbate during the voyeuristic activity or immediately afterward in response to what they have seen. Further sexual contact with the unsuspecting stranger is rarely sought. Like exhibitionists, voyeurs are usually not physically dangerous. Most voyeurs are not attracted to nude beaches or other places where it is acceptable to look because they are most aroused when the risk of being discovered is high. Voyeurs tend to be men in their twenties with strong feelings of inadequacy.

SADOMASOCHISM. Sadomasochistic behavior encompasses both sadism and masochism; it is often abbreviated "SM." The term "sadism" is derived from the Marquis de Sade (1740-1814), a French writer and army officer who was horribly cruel to people for his own erotic purposes. Sexual sadism involves acts in which the psychological or physical suffering of the victim, including his or her humiliation, is deemed sexually exciting. In masochism, sexual excitement is produced in a person by his or her own suffering; preferred means of achieving gratification include verbal humiliation and being bound or whipped. The dynamics of the two behaviors are similar. Sadomasochistic behaviors have the potential to be physically dangerous, but most people involved in these behaviors participate in mild or symbolic acts with a partner they can trust. Most people who engage in SM activities are motivated by a desire for dominance or submission rather than pain. Interestingly, many nonhuman animals participate in pain-inflicting behavior before coitus. Some researchers think that the activity heightens the biological components of sexual arousal, such as blood pressure and muscle tension. It has been suggested that any resistance between partners enhances sex, and SM is a more extreme version of this behavior. It is also thought that SM offers people the temporary opportunity to take on roles that are the opposite of the controlled, restrictive roles they play in everyday life. Both sadism and masochism are considered disorders when the fantasies, sexual urges, or behaviors cause significant distress or impairment in social, occupational, or other important areas.

FETISHISM. Fetishism is a type of sexual behavior in which a person becomes sexually aroused by fo-

---

DSM-IV-TR Criteria for Paraphilias

EXHIBITIONISM (DSM CODE 302.4)

Over period of at least six months, recurrent, intense sexually arousing fantasies, sexual urges, or behaviors involving exposure of one's genitals to an unsuspecting stranger

Person has acted on these urges, or sexual urges or fantasies cause marked distress or interpersonal difficulty

FETISHISM (DSM CODE 302.81)

Over period of at least six months, recurrent, intense sexually arousing fantasies, sexual urges, or behaviors involving use of nonliving objects

Fantasies, sexual urges, or behaviors cause clinically significant distress or impairment in social, occupational, or other important areas of functioning

Fetish objects not limited to articles of female clothing used in cross-dressing (as in Transvestic Fetishism) or devices designed for purpose of tactile genital stimulation

FROTTEURISM (DSM CODE 302.89)

Over period of at least six months, recurrent, intense sexually arousing fantasies, sexual urges, or behaviors involving touching and rubbing against a nonconsenting person

Person has acted on these urges, or urges or fantasies cause marked distress or interpersonal difficulty

PEDOPHILIA (DSM CODE 302.2)

Over period of at least six months, recurrent, intense sexually arousing fantasies, sexual urges, or behaviors involving sexual activity with a prepubescent child or children (generally thirteen or younger)

Person has acted on these urges, or sexual urges or fantasies cause marked distress or interpersonal difficulty

Person is at least sixteen and at least five years older than child or children; does not include individual in late adolescence involved in ongoing sexual relationship with twelve- or thirteen-year-old

Specify Sexually Attracted to Males; Sexually Attracted to Females; Sexually Attracted to Both

Specify if Limited to Incest

Types: Exclusive Type (attracted only to children) or Nonexclusive Type

SEXUAL MASOCHISM (DSM CODE 302.83)

Over period of at least six months, recurrent, intense sexually arousing fantasies, sexual urges, or behaviors involving act (real, not simulated) of being humiliated, beaten, bound, or otherwise made to suffer

Fantasies, sexual urges, or behaviors cause clinically significant distress or impairment in social, occupational, or other important areas of functioning

SEXUAL SADISM (DSM CODE 302.84)

Over period of at least six months, recurrent, intense sexually arousing fantasies, sexual urges, or behaviors involving acts (real, not simulated) in which the psychological or physical suffering (including humiliation) of the victim is sexually exciting to the person

Person has acted on these urges with a nonconsenting person, or sexual urges or fantasies cause marked distress or interpersonal difficulty

TRANSVESTIC FETISHISM (DSM CODE 302.3)

Over period of at least six months, in a heterosexual male, recurrent, intense sexually arousing fantasies, sexual urges, or behaviors involving cross-dressing

Fantasies, sexual urges, or behaviors cause clinically significant distress or impairment in social, occupational, or other important areas of functioning

Specify if with Gender Dysphoria (persistent discomfort with gender role or identity)

VOYEURISM (DSM CODE 302.82)

Over period of at least six months, recurrent, intense sexually arousing fantasies, sexual urges, or behaviors involving act of observing an unsuspecting person who is naked, in the process of disrobing, or engaging in sexual activity

Person has acted on these urges, or sexual urges or fantasies cause marked distress or interpersonal difficulty

PARAPHILIA NOT OTHERWISE SPECIFIED (DSM CODE 302.9)

cusing on an inanimate object or part of the human body. Many people are aroused by looking at undergarments, legs, or breasts, and it is often difficult to distinguish between normal activities and fetishistic ones. It is when a person becomes focused on the objects or body parts, called fetishes, to the point of causing significant distress or impairment that a disorder is present. Fetishists are usually males. Common fetish objects include women's lingerie, high-heeled shoes, boots, stockings, leather, silk, and rubber goods. Common body parts involved in fetishism are hair, buttocks, breasts, and feet.

PEDOPHILIA. The term "pedophilia" is from the Greek language and means "love of children." It is characterized by a preference for sexual activity with prepubescent children and is engaged in primarily by men. The activity varies in intensity and ranges from stroking the child's hair to holding the child while secretly masturbating, manipulating the child's genitals, encouraging the child to manipulate his or her own genitals, or, sometimes, engaging in sexual intercourse. Generally, the pedophile, or sexual abuser of children, is related to, or an acquaintance of, the child, rather than a stranger. Studies of imprisoned pedophiles have found that the men typically had poor relationships with their parents, drink heavily, show poor sexual adjustment, and were themselves sexually abused as children. Pedophiles tend to be older than people convicted of other sex offenses. The average age at first conviction is thirty-five. For a diagnosis of pedophilia, the abuser should be at least sixteen years old and at least five years older than the child or children who are abused.

TRANSVESTIC FETISHISM. Transvestic fetishism refers to dressing in clothing of the opposite sex to obtain sexual excitement. In the majority of cases, it is men who are attracted to transvestism. Several studies show that cross-dressing occurs primarily among married heterosexuals. The man usually achieves sexual satisfaction simply by putting on the clothing, but sometimes masturbation and intercourse are engaged in while the clothing is being worn. A disorder is diagnosed if the fantasies, sexual urges, or behaviors cause clinically significant distress or impairment. In some cases, gender dysphoria, persistent discomfort with gender role or identity, is also present.

FROTTEURISM. Frotteurism encompasses fairly common fantasies, sexual urges, or behaviors of a person, usually a male, obtaining sexual pleasure by pressing or rubbing against a fully clothed female in a crowded public place. Often it involves the clothed penis rubbing against the woman's buttocks or legs and appears accidental.

ZOOPHILIA AND NECROPHILIA. Zoophilia involves sexual contact between humans and animals as the repeatedly preferred method of achieving sexual excitement. In this disorder, the animal is preferred despite other available sexual outlets. Necrophilia is a rare dysfunction in which a person obtains sexual gratification by looking at or having intercourse with a corpse.

CULTURAL CONTEXTS AND DIAGNOSIS

A problem in the definition and diagnosis of sexual variations is that it is difficult to draw the line between normal and abnormal behavior. Patterns of sexual behavior differ widely across history and within different cultures and communities. It is impossible to lay down the rules of normality; however, attempts are made in order to understand behavior that differs from the majority and in order to help people who find their own atypical behavior to be problematic, or to be problematic in the eyes of the law.

Unlike most therapeutic techniques in use by psychologists, many of the treatments for paraphilias are painful, and the degree of their effectiveness is questionable. Supposedly, the methods are not aimed at punishing the individual, but perhaps society's lack of tolerance toward sexual deviations can be seen in the nature of the available treatments. In general, all attempts to treat the paraphilias have been hindered by the lack of information available about them and their causes.

Traditional counseling and psychotherapy alone have not been very effective in modifying the behavior of paraphiliacs, and it is unclear why the clients are resistant to treatment. Some researchers believe that the behavior might be important for the mental stability of paraphiliacs. If they did not have the paraphilia, they would experience mental deterioration. Another idea is that, although people are punished by society for being sexually deviant, they are also rewarded for it. For the paraphilias that put the person at risk for arrest, the danger of arrest often becomes as arousing and rewarding as the sexual activity itself. Difficulties in treating paraphiliacs may also be related to the emotionally impoverished environments that many of them experienced throughout childhood and adolescence. Convicted sex offenders report more physical and sexual abuse as children than do the people convicted of nonsexual crimes. It is difficult to undo the years of learning involved.

Surgical castration for therapeutic purposes involves removal of the testicles. Surgical castration for sexual offenders in North America is very uncommon, but the procedure is sometimes used in northern European countries. The reason castration is used as a treatment for sex offenders is the inaccurate belief that testosterone is necessary for sexual behavior. The hormone testosterone is produced by the testicles. Unfortunately, reducing the amount of testosterone in the blood system does not always change sexual behavior. Furthermore, contrary to the myth that a sex offender has an abnormally high sex drive, many sex offenders have a low sex drive or are sexually dysfunctional.

In the same vein as surgical castration, other treatments use the administration of chemicals to decrease desire in sex offenders without the removal of genitalia. Estrogens have been fairly effective in reducing the sex drive, but they sometimes make the male appear feminine by increasing breast size and stimulating other female characteristics. There are also drugs that block the action of testosterone and other androgens but do not feminize the body; these drugs are called antiandrogens. Used together with counseling, antiandrogens do benefit some sex offenders, especially those who are highly motivated to overcome the problem. More research on the effects of chemicals on sexual behavior is needed; the extent of the possible side effects, for example, needs further study.

Aversion therapy is another technique that has been used to eliminate inappropriate sexual arousal. In aversion therapy, the behavior that is to be decreased or eliminated is paired with an aversive, or unpleasant, experience. Most approaches use pictures of the object or situation that is problematic. The pictures are then paired with something extremely unpleasant, such as an electric shock or a putrid smell, thereby reducing arousal to the problematic object or situation in the future. Aversion therapy has been found to be fairly effective but is under ethical questioning because of its drastic nature. For example, chemical aversion therapy involves the administration of a nausea- or vomit-inducing drug. Electrical aversion therapy involves

the use of electric shock. An example of the use of electric shock would be to show a pedophile pictures of young children whom he finds sexually arousing and to give an electric shock immediately after showing the pictures, in an attempt to reverse the pedophile's tendency to be sexually aroused by children.

Other techniques have been developed to help clients learn more socially approved patterns of sexual interaction skills. In general, there has not been a rigorous testing of any of the techniques mentioned. Furthermore, most therapy is conducted while the offenders are imprisoned, providing a less than ideal setting.

DISTURBANCES OF COURTSHIP BEHAVIOR

Beliefs regularly change with respect to what sexual activities are considered normal, so most therapists prefer to avoid terms such as "perversion," instead using "paraphilia." Basically, "paraphilia" means "love of the unusual." Aspects of paraphilias are commonly found within the scope of normal behavior; it is when they become the prime means of gratification, replacing direct sexual contact with a consenting adult partner, that paraphilias are technically said to exist. People who show atypical sexual patterns might also have emotional problems, but it is thought that most people who participate in paraphilias also participate in normal sexual behavior with adult partners, without complete reliance on paraphilic behaviors to produce sexual excitement. Many people who are arrested for paraphilic behaviors do not resort to the paraphilia because they lack a socially acceptable sex partner. Instead, they have an unusual opportunity, a desire to experiment, or perhaps an underlying psychological problem.

According to the approach of Kurt Freund and his colleagues, some paraphilias are better understood as disturbances in the sequence of courtship behaviors. Freund has described courtship as a sequence of four steps: location and appraisal of a potential partner; interaction that does not involve touch; interaction that does involve touch; and genital contact. Most people engage in behavior that is appropriate for each of these steps, but some do not. The ones who do not can be seen as having exaggerations or distortions in one or more of the steps. For example, Freund says that voyeurism is a disorder in the first step of courtship. The voyeur does not use an acceptable means to locate a potential partner. An exhibitionist and an obscene phone caller would have a problem with the second step: They have interaction with people that occurs before the stage of touch, but the talking and showing of exhibitionistic behaviors are not the normal courtship procedures. Frotteurism would be a disruption at the third step, because there is physical touching that is inappropriate. Finally, rape would be a deviation from the appropriate fourth step.

As a result of social and legal restrictions, reliable data on the frequency of paraphilic behaviors are limited. Most information about paraphilias comes from people who have been arrested or are in therapy. Because the majority of people who participate in paraphilias do not fall into these two categories, it is not possible to talk about the majority of paraphiliacs in the real world. It is known, however, that males are much more likely to engage in paraphilias than are females.

SOURCES FOR FURTHER STUDY

Allgeier, E. R., and A. R. Allgeier. "Atypical Sexual Activity." In *Sexual Interactions*. Boston: Houghton Mifflin, 1998. A highly readable description of sexual variations. Contains photographs, charts, and tables which help make the material understandable. Provides a multitude of references. The book itself is an excellent, thorough textbook.

Laws, D. Richard, and William O'Donohue, eds. *Sexual Deviance*. New York: Guilford, 1997. Twenty-five essays providing a complete reference on paraphilias such as exhibitionism, fetishism, masochism, voyeurism, and transvestic fetishism.

Rosen, Michael A. *Sexual Magic: The S/M Photographs*. Reprint. San Francisco: Shaynew Press, 1992. Contains essays written by people who engage in sadomasochistic activities. Includes photographs of the people. In general, provides a personal, honest look into the lives of real people, using a case-study approach.

Stoller, Robert J. "Sexual Deviations." In *Human Sexuality in Four Perspectives*, edited by Frank A. Beach and Milton Diamond. Baltimore: The Johns Hopkins University Press, 1977. Provides a review of several common atypical sexual behaviors, along with several case studies. Concise and readable. Part of an interesting, well-rounded book on sexuality in general.

Weinberg, Thomas S., and G. W. Levi Kamel, eds. *S and M: Studies in Sadomasochism*. Rev. ed. Buffalo, N.Y.: Prometheus Books, 1995. Composed of eighteen articles that provide thought-provoking information on a variety of issues relating to sadism and masochism.

Deborah R. McDonald

SEE ALSO: Abnormality: Legal models; Abnormality: Psychological models; Adolescence: Sexuality; Homosexuality; Law and psychology; Rape and sexual assault; Sex hormones and motivation; Sexual behavior patterns; Sexual dysfunction.

Shock therapy

TYPE OF PSYCHOLOGY: Psychotherapy
FIELDS OF STUDY: Biological treatments

Electroconvulsive therapy (ECT), or shock therapy, is the controlled application of an electric current to the brain to induce a seizure. This treatment is used primarily for severe and debilitating mental disorders, such as major depression. It is a controversial treatment that has both proponents and opponents.

KEY CONCEPTS
- anterograde amnesia
- brain hemispheres
- depression
- grand mal seizure
- mania
- neurotransmitters
- psychotropic medication
- retrograde amnesia
- schizophrenia
- somatic therapy

INTRODUCTION

Electroconvulsive therapy (ECT), also known as shock therapy, is a somatic, or physical, form of therapy that is used for some individuals who suffer from severe mental disorders. It involves the direct application of an electric current to the brain. Typically, this current lasts for up to one second at a rate of 140 to 170 volts. The purpose of this electrical charge is to induce a grand mal seizure that will usually last for thirty to sixty seconds. The seizure that is induced is similar to those experienced in some types of epilepsy. It is through this grand mal seizure that ECT has its beneficial effect in reducing the symptoms of the patient.

The use of electrical charges as a medical treatment has been reported for centuries. As early as 47 C.E., Scribonius Largus used an electric eel to treat headaches. During the sixteenth century, Ethiopians were reported to have used electric catfish to expel evil spirits from the bodies of the mentally ill. Direct electric charges for the treatment of nervous complaints were also reported during the eighteenth century in Europe.

The modern application of electric current for the treatment of individuals with mental disorders began in 1938. It was at this time that two Italians, Ugo Cerletti, a psychiatrist, and Lucio Bini, a neuropathologist, invented the first ECT machine for use on humans. Cerletti and Bini first used their newly developed ECT machine to induce convulsions for the treatment of schizophrenic patients, and they reported that the treatment was a success.

ECT was introduced into the United States in 1940, at which time it quickly became the major somatic treatment for all severely disturbed individuals, regardless of mental disorder. By the mid-1950's, its use began to decline rapidly for several reasons, including the introduction of psychotropic medications, increasing demands for civil rights for the mentally ill, and concerns about potential adverse effects of ECT. Subsequently, however, a growing body of research has indicated that ECT is an effective treatment for some severe mental disorders. This research has led to a gradual increase in the acceptance of its use, particularly in the treatment of severely depressed individuals.

When ECT was first used for the treatment of mental disorders, the patient would be strapped to a table and, without any medications or other medical safeguards, would be administered the electrical current and sent into a convulsion. During this convulsion, the patient would thrash around on the table, often being left with broken limbs and other physical complications. In its current use, prior to administration of the ECT, the patient is given a muscle relaxant, which completely immobilizes the body, and anesthesia, which makes the patient completely unconscious. The result of these safeguards has been a much safer treatment of the patient.

THEORIES OF EFFICACY

Although ECT has been demonstrated to be an effective treatment, it is not known how and why ECT works. The theoretical basis of the original use of ECT had to do with the observation that schizophrenia and epilepsy rarely occur together, suggesting that the two are mutually exclusive. Based on this observation, it was hypothesized that, if a seizure could be induced in a schizophrenic, the schizophrenic symptoms could be eliminated. Physicians had tried previously to induce such seizures by means of injections of insulin, camphor, and other chemicals, but these approaches proved to have more disadvantages relative to ECT.

Although this early theory of the mechanics of ECT has been refuted, there still is little knowledge of how and why ECT actually works. The only fact that has been firmly established is that it is the seizure that ECT induces that creates any positive changes in the patient's symptoms. There is no clear-cut explanation, however, of how the seizure creates the changes. Several theories have been developed to explain the process, most of which center on ECT's effect on neurotransmitters.

Neurotransmitters are chemicals that are used in the brain to transmit messages from one cell to another. One well-accepted theory holds that abnormalities in the level and utilization of certain neurotransmitters lead to the development of mental disorders such as depression, schizophrenia, and mania. Consequently, it is thought that ECT, through the creation of a seizure, somehow affects the level and utilization of some of these neurotransmitters, and that it is this process that reduces the patient's symptoms of mental disorder. While research to investigate how ECT works continues, it is important to remember that, as with all somatic treatments, ECT does not cure the disorder; it provides only temporary relief from the symptoms.

Despite its reported effectiveness, ECT remains a controversial treatment for mental disorders. Opponents point to potential adverse effects that ECT can cause, particularly the possibility of permanent brain damage resulting from the induced seizure. These opponents, who highlight the negative effects that ECT can have on a patient's memory, prefer the use of alternative treatment methods. The public media have served to exacerbate negative perceptions of ECT by depicting it as an inhumane treatment that is used only to control and punish malcontents, not to help the severely disturbed. There is perhaps no better example of the media's distorted depiction of ECT than that found in the film *One Flew over the Cuckoo's Nest* (1975), in which ECT was used as a brutal method to control and manage the main character. As a result of these misunderstandings and distorted perceptions, ECT is often not used when it might be helpful.

Uses

It has been estimated that each year 60,000 to 100,000 people in the United States receive electroconvulsive therapy. This form of treatment has been used to treat a variety of mental disorders, including severe major depression, schizophrenia, and mania. Several surveys have indicated that more than three-fourths of individuals who receive ECT have been diagnosed as suffering from severe major depression. The second-largest group of individuals receiving ECT consists of those who have been diagnosed as schizophrenic. While there is substantial evidence that ECT is effective in the treatment of severe major depression, the evidence supporting the use of ECT to treat other disorders is not as strong.

Generally speaking, ECT is not seen as a treatment of choice. It will most likely not be the first treatment given to someone suffering from a severe mental disorder. Instead, it is typically viewed as the treatment of last resort and is used primarily to treat individuals who do not respond to any other treatments. For example, a typical course of treatment for an individual suffering from debilitating severe major depression would be talking therapy and one of the many antidepressant medications. For most people, it takes two to four weeks to respond to such medications. If the patient does not respond to the medication, another antidepressant medication may be tried. If, after several trials of medication, the patient still does not respond and continues to be severely depressed, ECT might be considered a viable option.

There are few individuals for whom ECT might be considered the treatment of choice. These individuals include those who are in life-threatening situations, such as those who show symptoms of severe anorexia or strong suicidal tendencies, or those for whom medications would be damaging. ECT might be used to treat pregnant women, for example, since it presents fewer risks for a fetus than medica-

tion does, or individuals with heart disease, for whom medications can cause severe complications.

Because of the stigma attached to ECT as a result of its historical misuse and its characterization in the popular media, many physicians believe that ECT is not used as widely as it could and should be. Often, ECT is suggested as the treatment of choice, but because of its stigma, other approaches are tried first. The effect of this decision is to deprive the patient of an effective treatment and delay or prevent remission.

Techniques and Effects

When ECT is indicated for the treatment of a mental disorder, it usually involves five to ten applications of ECT administered at a rate of two or three per week. The number of ECT treatments given, however, will vary depending on the individual's medical history and the severity of the presenting symptoms. ECT is always administered by a physician; it cannot be ordered by a psychologist. When ECT is applied, many medical safeguards are used to prevent or minimize adverse effects. They include the use of a muscle relaxant, anesthesia, and oxygen. These medical procedures have made the use of ECT much safer than it was during the days when the patient would thrash about the table, breaking bones.

Additional refinements in the use of ECT have made it even safer. One such refinement is the application of unilateral, rather than bilateral, ECT. In unilateral ECT, the electric shock is sent through only one of the brain's two hemispheres. Usually, the shock is sent through the right hemisphere, which controls abstract thinking and creativity, rather than the left hemisphere, which controls language and rational thinking. While usually as effective as bilateral ECT, in which the shock goes through the entire brain, unilateral ECT has been shown to cause fewer adverse side effects.

Despite the refinements in ECT and the caution exercised in its use, there are several documented potential adverse side effects. Although most research indicates that these effects are temporary, some researchers suggest that ECT can cause permanent brain damage. The major adverse effects of ECT relate to how well the patient's brain functions after the treatment. The most common effect is extreme confusion and disorientation in the patient upon awakening after an ECT treatment. Generally, this confusion will last for only a few minutes to a few hours.

Another serious concern about ECT's effects on the cognitive functioning of the patient has to do with the patient's memory. ECT can cause retrograde amnesia, the inability to remember things from the past, and anterograde amnesia, the inability to memorize new material. Both forms of amnesia are most noticeable in the first days and weeks after the ECT treatments have stopped. With the passage of time, the patient will slowly remember more from the past and will regain or strengthen the ability to remember new material. In most patients, this recovery of memory will take no more than two to six months. The patient may, however, permanently lose memories of events that occurred immediately prior to the ECT treatments or while the patient was hospitalized for the treatments. The degree of memory loss appears to be related to the number of ECT treatments the patient received.

Research investigating permanent brain damage from the use of ECT has been mixed. Some research has indicated that any application of ECT will cause brain damage and that more brain damage will occur as more treatments are applied. Long-term impairment in the patient's memory is one effect that has thus been identified as permanent. Other researchers, however, have reported that ECT does not cause permanent brain damage. In the meantime, ECT is used cautiously, and research continues into its potential adverse effects.

CHANGING ATTITUDES

Prior to the advent of psychotropic medications, there were few effective treatments for the severely mentally ill. Numerous treatment methods were attempted to help relieve the symptoms of mental illness. Among these methods were bloodletting, the use of leeches, and immersion in water. Perhaps the most common approach was the permanent institutionalization of severely mentally ill individuals. This was done not only to control patients but also to protect others, since patients were viewed as a threat to others and themselves.

As a result of the ineffectiveness of these treatments and the growing concern about the institutionalization of the mentally ill, a number of new treatment approaches were developed and applied. Among these new approaches was electroconvulsive

therapy. Electroconvulsive shock therapy was first used on schizophrenic patients, and the treatment met with some success. It was also tried on depressed and manic patients, with even greater success. As a result of these successes and the lack of other effective treatment approaches, ECT quickly came to be a commonly used treatment for individuals who suffered from a variety of mental disorders.

Many factors caused ECT to fall out of favor during the late 1950's. First, the earlier applications of ECT held significant dangers for the patient. The risk of death was approximately one in one thousand, and the risk of physical damage, such as broken bones, was even greater—in fact, such damage was noted in up to 40 percent of the patients. Concerns about complications continue today, and their focus is the impact of ECT on cognitive functioning.

Another factor that led to the decline in the use of ECT was the development and introduction of psychotropic medications. These medications revolutionized the treatment of the mentally ill and led to thousands of patients being deinstitutionalized. In terms of both effectiveness and safety, it soon became evident that the use of these medications was substantially preferable to the use of ECT.

A third major influence on the decline of ECT's use was the growing civil rights movement for the mentally ill. Many community and religious leaders began to advocate the fair and humane treatment of the seriously mentally ill. These individuals saw ECT as an undesirable treatment method, used as an instrument for controlling and punishing individuals who could not defend themselves. This view of ECT as inhumane soon came to be widely held. ECT was perceived as a method to control, rather than help, patients—as a punishment rather than a therapy.

These and other factors led to the substantially decreased use of ECT. Subsequently, however, well-designed research has begun to define ECT as a relatively safe treatment method that may be the best therapy in certain situations. Additionally, refinements in the application of ECT have increased its effectiveness and reduced its complications. As a result of not only the ambiguity about its potential adverse effects but also the emotional issues related to its use, the controversy about ECT and its relative risks and benefits is likely to continue for many years.

SOURCES FOR FURTHER STUDY

American Psychiatric Association. *Electroconvulsive Therapy: Report of the Task Force on Electroconvulsive Therapy of the American Psychiatric Association.* Washington, D.C.: Author, 1978. This report provides the results of a major task force charged with examining the clinical use of ECT. It thoroughly reviews the issues in a very readable format. Extensive recommendations for the use of ECT are provided.

Baldwin, Steve, and Melissa Oxlad. *Electroshock and Minors: A Fifty-Year Review.* Westport, Conn.: Greenwood Press, 2000. Reviews the history and development of guidelines and resolutions for the use of ECT on children from three years old through adolescence, and cite case histories by decade from the 1940's to the 1990's.

Breggin, Peter R. *Electroshock: Its Brain-Disabling Effects.* New York: Springer, 1979. This book describes many adverse effects of ECT, but severe mental dysfunction in particular. Citing research from both animal and human research, this author makes a strong argument against the use of ECT, stating that it is no more effective than a placebo, but considerably more dangerous.

Fink, Max. *Electroshock: Restoring the Mind.* New York: Oxford University Press, 1999. Provides a thorough review of numerous issues surrounding the use of ECT. Includes a study of its effectiveness, risks, and legal, economic, and ethical concerns, as well as a comparison of ECT with other treatment methods. Several chapters are committed to a technical review of the mechanisms of ETC. Written to be understandable by laypersons.

Friedberg, John. *Shock Treatment Is Not Good for Your Brain.* San Francisco: Glide, 1976. Provides a strong condemnation of ECT. The author believes that mental illness is a myth and that the use of ECT is unnecessary as well as inhumane. This book, which is written in a personal, nontechnical manner, includes interviews with seven individuals who have received ECT and are opposed to its further use.

Mark E. Johnson

SEE ALSO: Abnormality: Biomedical models; Clinical depression; Depression; Drug therapies; Madness: Historical concepts; Neuropsychology; Psychosurgery; Schizophrenia: Theoretical explanations; Synaptic transmission.

Short-term memory

TYPE OF PSYCHOLOGY: Memory
FIELDS OF STUDY: Cognitive processes

Short-term (or working) memory refers to the mental process of temporarily retaining and manipulating information for the production of a wide range of cognitive tasks, including comprehension, problem solving, and learning.

KEY CONCEPTS
- anterograde amnesia
- elaborative rehearsal
- maintenance rehearsal
- phonological loop
- trace life
- visuo-spatial sketchpad

INTRODUCTION

A woman needs to make a telephone call and a friend has just told her the number to call; she does not have pencil and paper to write down the number. Two options are immediately available to help her remember the number. She could repeat the number over and over until she makes the call (a technique known as maintenance rehearsal), or she could give the number some kind of meaning that would help her recall it (elaborative rehearsal). The mental process that allows a person to perform those operations is commonly called short-term, or working, memory.

William James, in 1890, used the term "primary memory" to describe the information under conscious awareness (immediate memory) and the term "secondary memory" to describe inactive information (indirect memory). This type of dualism evolved into the terms "short-term memory" and "long-term memory," a distinction that was based upon the idea that each memory type was independent and was the result of different underlying mental processes.

Richard Atkinson and Richard Shiffrin, in 1968, further developed this approach by proposing a stage model, or modal model, of memory that included the sensory register, the short-term store, and the long-term store. Subsequently, extensive research programs focused on the short-term store. These experimental findings resulted in the view, postulated by Alan Baddeley in 1986, that emphasizes the mental processes involved in the memory function rather than describing a static (inactive or passive) storage bin where information is saved. With this approach came the label "working memory" and the metaphor of a mental workbench performing a wide range of cognitive operations. As Henry Ellis and Reed Hunt explained in 1991, "Memory is determined by what is done to the information, not by where the information is stored." This is the view of an active, mental process characterized by specific functions and limitations.

CHARACTERISTICS

Three basic characteristics define short-term memory: trace life, storage capacity, and nature of the code. With respect to trace life (the amount of time information can be retained in working memory without further processing), Lloyd Peterson and Margaret Intons-Peterson demonstrated in 1959 that current, active information in the working memory bank is subject to rapid forgetting (in about twelve seconds) if the information does not receive further processing. They showed that if people are not allowed to rehearse or elaborate information they have just encountered, that information is lost. For example, they asked people to recall a series of letters, but immediately after they indicated the letters to be recalled, the people in the experiment were required to count backward by threes. The activity of counting backward interfered with remembering the letters. Similarly, if one is trying to recall a telephone number one has just heard but is interrupted on the way to the telephone to call it, the telephone number is usually lost.

In 1956, George Miller wrote a paper entitled "The Magic Number Seven, Plus or Minus Two" that made a strong and influential case regarding the storage capacity of short-term memory. His notion has been tested in a variety of settings, using a variety of information units. Whether people are asked to remember a list of letters, numbers, or words, or even a group of objects, most people remember about seven items. This finding has produced a wide range of applications. Telephone numbers, one may note, are composed of seven numbers.

Further study of the capacity of short-term memory revealed the ability to "chunk" information and, in so doing, remember more information than merely seven individual, independent bits of information. This process involves reorganizing single bits of information (with the assistance of information previously encoded in long-term storage) into larger units of information. For example, one could remember each individual letter of the word "chunk" and recall five letters, c-h-u-n-k (hence, five units). One might also form the letters into one unit and, instead, recall the word "chunk" (one unit). Chunking dramatically increases the amount of information that can be retained in short-term memory.

To account for the nature of the code (the form used to understand and store information), Baddeley designed a model of working memory that includes the phonological loop (a concept describing the coding of speech-based information in working memory) and the visuo-spatial sketchpad. A wide range of experimental evidence indicates that a phonetic (or acoustic or sound) code is used in short-term memory. For example, if a person is asked to retain a list of words or letters and the items sound alike, fewer items are recalled and more errors are found. On the other hand, if the items sound different, recall is better and fewer errors are found. Baddeley referred to this as the phonological similarity effect and explained that this effect occurs because the short-term memory store is based on a phonological code. Accordingly, items that sound similar will have similar codes.

Also related to the phonological code is the word-length effect. In essence, this refers to the finding that words with more syllables take more time to read and are less likely to be recalled from short-term memory than are monosyllabic words. On the other hand, if a word takes longer to read and to pronounce (either aloud or to oneself), the opportunity for a strong memory trace is greater.

The visuo-spatial sketchpad in Baddeley's model refers to the use of an imagery code in short-term memory. For example, one might imagine one's kitchen and focus on the location of the sink. To do this, one most likely generates a mental image of the kitchen. Another example of the visuo-spatial sketchpad involves recognizing words or patterns when a person is reading. Still another example of this function is the process in which people engage when comparing two shapes. In a test in which people are asked to indicate whether geometric clusters are similar or different when they are presented in different orientations, experimental evidence indicates that most people engage in mental rotation to make their decisions about the figures. In other words, they imagine the particular geometric cluster turned in different directions and compare it to each of the other figures.

IMPORTANCE TO DAILY LIFE

The essential role of short-term memory is usually taken for granted until some event disrupts the memory process. In a hypothetical example of the consequences of not having a properly functioning short-term memory system, a man named Bill wakes up one morning without one. First, he gets out of bed (he can still walk, because he has the benefit of long-term memory) and trips over his cat. He finds himself on the floor but cannot remember how he got there. He walks to the bathroom to brush his teeth, but when he gets there he does not remember why he is there. He wanders into the kitchen to make coffee; he puts water into the coffeemaker and bends down to pet the cat. Then he rises and fills the coffeemaker with water again, because he does not remember the event that happened only a few seconds before.

The telephone rings, and Bill answers it. His friend Jane asks him to meet her in fifteen minutes; he agrees and hangs up. In the meantime, the water from the coffeemaker is spilling over the kitchen counter, and Bill has no idea why that is happening. The doorbell rings, and his next-door neighbor asks to borrow some milk. Being a good neighbor, Bill agrees to get some milk and goes into the kitchen. Once there, Bill realizes that he must turn off the coffeemaker. He steps in the spilled coffee, then goes into the bedroom to change his socks. Meanwhile, the neighbor whom Bill has forgotten leaves. Eventually Jane calls to ask why Bill did not meet her.

One's very existence and quality of life depend on the functioning of short-term memory. The preceding example may seem preposterous, yet there are a large number of cases of people who have impaired short-term memory. Several types of events can result in memory deficits and disorders, including head injuries, strokes, and disease-related dementia.

AMNESIA

The term "amnesia" refers to a class of disorders that involve various types of memory dysfunction. Some types of amnesia are associated with loss of long-term memory functioning. In these cases, a person may be able to learn new information but has difficulty recalling previous information. Other types of amnesia are associated with impaired short-term memory. These people have difficulty learning new information but can recall previously learned information. There are amnesiacs who have memory deficits relating to both short-term and long-term memory.

In general, when short-term memory is impaired, people are unable to process and retain new information effectively. The case of William Scoville's patient H. M., described in the 1950's, provides an interesting example of short-term memory impairment. H. M. suffered from a severe form of epilepsy that could not be controlled by medication. Scoville surgically removed portions of H. M.'s brain (the temporal lobes) in an attempt to remedy the epilepsy problem.

After the surgery, H. M. experienced striking short-term memory impairment, called anterograde amnesia. H. M.'s memory disorder was studied in depth, and many of the characteristics that define short-term memory functions were illuminated. H. M. was able to remember information from his past, but he was unable to remember new information. For example, H. M.'s mother reported that he could still mow the lawn, because he remembered how to do so, but he was unable to find the lawn mower when he left it parked somewhere.

H. M. was unable to remember or recognize anyone he met or any place he visited after the surgical procedure. He engaged in intense conversations with people but subsequently could recall neither the conversation nor the person with whom he had the conversation. Moreover, H. M. was taught procedures for accomplishing tasks, and his performance of a task revealed that he had learned the task; however, H. M. consistently claimed that he had never before performed the task. In other words, he did not remember the event of learning the task, but his performance revealed that he had retained some of the skills associated with the learning event.

Clearly, the short-term memory process, though often taken for granted, is an essential and integral part of mental functioning. This process also plays a major role in the study of psychology.

EARLY INTEREST IN MEMORY

With the first humans came the first speculations about mental processes. Inherent in studies of mental activities are studies of memory, since memory is necessary for learning. The role of memory was a central element of philosophies of the mind. This point is exhibited in historical accounts of the mind that referenced memory processes. These accounts reveal the underlying theories of mental processes postulated at the time of the philosophies.

For example, both Aristotle and Plato used the analogy of a wax tablet to describe the memory process. According to this perspective, experience was merely stamped into the brain. These views are consistent with the idea of memory being a static store or receptacle rather than a dynamic process. These static views assume a passive organism rather than an active, dynamic information processor.

This concept of memory continued through the ages, changing very little until the science of psychology arose in the late nineteenth century. As psychology evolved, so did the field of memory. This evolution is reflected in a change from the static, storage view of memory to the idea of memory as an active process. This change parallels the evolution of the image of humans as passive experience-storage units to seeing humans as active information processors; this evolution is often called the cognitive revolution. Whether the change is called evolution or revolution, it happened largely as a result of the foundation provided by innovative research such as that conducted by Hermann Ebbinghaus.

EBBINGHAUS'S CONTRIBUTIONS

In the early 1880's, Ebbinghaus moved the study of memory from the domain of philosophy to the domain of science when he embarked on an intensive investigation of the memory process. Ebbinghaus used himself as an experimental subject and spent two years memorizing nonsense syllables to see whether simple repetition would facilitate the recall process. Keeping copious notes in a strict scientific environment, he found that rote rehearsal improved the memory retrieval process.

Ebbinghaus's work was particularly important because it showed that mental processes could be simplified and studied using a rigorous, scientific method. In addition, he provided data that are fundamental for understanding memory processes and that paved the way for the vast program of memory research that is flourishing today.

Studies associated with short-term or working memory focus on dynamic, immediate, cognitive activities. In general, these mental processes are involved in understanding the world; specifically, these investigations advance knowledge about learning, comprehension, problem solving, thought construction, and expression. Trends include mapping regions of the brain and discovering neurotransmitters (brain chemicals) that are affiliated with working memory activities. The working memory process provides a rich domain for investigations of mental activities. Many researchers believe that future investigations of the process will reveal the keys to discovering the essence of mental activity.

SOURCES FOR FURTHER STUDY

Baddeley, Alan D. *Human Memory: Theory and Practice.* Rev. ed. Boston: Allyn & Bacon, 1997. Provides a comprehensive review of the memory process, by drawing from a wide range of literature domains, including cognitive psychology, psychobiology, neurology, cognitive science, and early historical accounts. In addition, Baddeley offers a thorough account of the working memory hypothesis.

_____. *Working Memory.* Oxford, England: Oxford University Press, 1986. Provides a scholarly report of working memory that has been very influential in the memory field. The writing may be too technical for readers who desire only an overview of general concepts, but it is essential for those interested in a deeper understanding of working memory.

Deutsch, Diana, and J. Anthony Deutsch, eds. *Short-Term Memory.* New York: Academic Press, 1975. This text consists of fifteen papers written by short-term memory researchers. Both the topics and the writing style are rather technical; however, this edition is very useful for anyone needing classical, comprehensive, detailed information about the intricacies of the short-term memory process.

Ellis, Henry C., and R. Reed Hunt. *Fundamentals of Human Memory and Cognition.* 5th ed. Dubuque, Iowa: Wm. C. Brown, 1991. A very readable text composed of numerous examples and illustrations of empirical evidence and practical applications that bring the information to life. Ellis and Hunt employ their expertise in effective, efficient encoding strategies to produce a text that describes complex cognitive processes in a manner that facilitates understanding and recall. They include both historical and current theoretical accounts of short-term memory.

Miyake, Akira, and Priti Shah, eds. *Models of Working Memory: Mechanisms of Active Maintenance and Executive Control.* New York: Cambridge University Press, 1999. Presents current models of working memory by asking a series of experts with differing approaches to answer the same set of questions about their theories.

Neath, Ian. *Human Memory: An Introduction to Research, Data, and Theory.* Belmont, Calif.: Wadsworth, 1997. An up-to-date textbook on memory. A particularly interesting feature is the book's carefully and simply planned experiments that can be conducted by the reader to illustrate the core issues.

Solso, Robert L. *Cognitive Psychology.* 6th ed. Boston: Allyn & Bacon, 2000. An undergraduate text for courses in cognitive psychology. Solso provides an account of memory that is written on a level appropriate for most high school and college students. Can be used not only to learn more about short-term memory but also to learn about memory processes in general.

Wyer, Robert S., and Thomas K. Srull. *Memory and Cognition in Its Social Context.* Hillsdale, N.J.: Lawrence Erlbaum, 1989. Wyer and Srull take a social cognition approach to the discussion of short-term memory, using the label "work space" to describe this process. They argue that the social context in which mental processes occur must be considered to provide an accurate and useful model of cognitive processes.

Pennie S. Seibert

SEE ALSO: Cognitive maps; Encoding; Forgetting and forgetfulness; Kinesthetic memory; Long-term memory; Memory; Memory: Animal research; Memory: Empirical studies; Memory: Physiology; Memory: Sensory; Memory storage.

Shyness

TYPE OF PSYCHOLOGY: Personality; psychopathology; social psychology
FIELDS OF STUDY: Anxiety disorders

Shyness is characterized by social interaction that is inhibited by anxiety and negative self-preoccupation and is often considered a form of social anxiety disorder. Its prevalence increased by 10 percent in the 1990's. Cognitive-behavioral and/or pharmacological treatment strategies have proven to be effective.

KEY CONCEPTS
- genetic environmental interaction
- inhibition
- isolation
- loneliness
- personality trait
- physiological arousal
- social functioning
- social phobia

INTRODUCTION

Shyness is characterized by inhibited behavior and feelings of awkwardness and anxiety in social situations. It can include symptoms that are behavioral, physiological, cognitive, and emotional. It can adversely affect social or professional functioning. Among those who are predisposed toward the personality trait of shyness, it can become a part of their self-concept; it can also be induced by experiences of failure or rejection in social situations that lead to poor self-esteem among some previously without the trait.

Research supports a genetic/environmental interaction explanation for shyness. The expression of shyness in children can be modified by parents and other environmental factors, although slight tendencies to act shyly in novel situations will remain. Cognitive-behavioral strategies and/or pharmacological interventions that focus on decreasing social withdrawal and increasing social participation have proven effective.

POSSIBLE CAUSES

Jerome Kagan and colleagues' work supports shyness as being a function of both nature and nurture. Longitudinal studies that followed three- to four-year-olds into adulthood reported shyness to be one of the most persistently stable traits; studies that followed children into the eighth year reported that 75 percent of children maintained their earlier shy or sociable styles. Also, parents and grandparents of inhibited compared with uninhibited children are more likely to report also being shy. The genetic predisposition involves easily aroused sympathetic nervous systems in fetuses and infants; later in life, social and performance situations stimulate these easily aroused nervous systems, resulting in social fear and anxiety and inhibited behavior.

In 25 percent of cases, those who are predisposed do not become shy, usually through environmental factors. Parents, for instance, may moderate the expression of shyness by helping predisposed children learn to not act shyly through balancing the levels of comfort versus harshness which they extend to upset infants and by promoting social interaction. However, underlying tendencies to behave shyly in new circumstances among those who are so predisposed remain.

Shyness can be situationally induced and develop in adulthood among some who were not shy at younger ages as a result of social performance and achievement failures, feelings of unattractiveness, or other reasons that can lower self-esteem and create future evaluation apprehension and social fear.

DIAGNOSIS

Lynne Henderson and Philip Zimbardo report that the prevalence of shyness increased in the United States from about 40 percent to 50 percent during the 1990's. Shyness has been considered a variant of social phobia (the third most widespread mental health problem in the country), which has a prevalence of only 13 percent, suggesting that those who are shy are not seeking treatment. The manifestations for both shyness and social phobia are similar: discomfort concerning interpersonal interaction (including conversing with and meeting others), the establishment of intimacy, participation in small groups, situations of authority, and assertiveness.

In social situations, shy individuals report experiencing behavioral symptoms, such as inhibition, nervousness, and avoidance of feared situations and eye contact; physiological symptoms, such as an increase in heartbeat, muscle tension, perspiration, and feelings of faintness, dizziness, nausea, and stomach unsettledness; cognitive symptoms, such as negative thoughts and beliefs about the self, the situation, and others; and emotional symptoms, such as low self-esteem, excessive self-consciousness, sadness, dejection, loneliness, depression, and anxiety.

TREATMENT

Treatments for shyness are successful and similar to those for social phobia, according to Henderson

and Zimbardo. They may include pharmacological treatments and/or cognitive-behavioral therapy, which focuses on moving individuals from being socially withdrawn, anxious, and self-preoccupied with negative thoughts to being comfortable with social participation and interpersonal relationships. The strategies can include exposure to the feared situation simulated in treatment, in vivo, or using visualization in imaginal desensitization; flooding, or exposure to the feared situation in vivo or imaginally until anxiety is lowered (extinction); anxiety management; progressive muscle group relaxation and/or controlled breathing; social treatment; communication, coping, and assertiveness skills training; and the replacement of negative thinking and emotions with more positive ones. Paradoxical intention, where clients learn to control their fear responses, and writing up positive self statements called affirmations have also been found to be effective. Individual, group, and home therapy are used.

IMPACT

Shyness appears to be a universal phenomenon, varying from a prevalence as low as 31 percent in Israel to a high of 57 percent in Japan. Shyness can result in a pattern of avoidance of people to the extent that self-imposed isolation and painful, heartwrenching loneliness can result. Fewer opportunities for social skills development due to technology and other social and economic factors, such as the replacement of interactional board and other games with solitary television and computer entertainment and social interaction with computer and telephone recording devices, may play a role in exacerbating the problem of shyness, according to Zimbardo and colleagues.

SOURCES FOR FURTHER STUDY

Henderson, L., and Philip Zimbardo. "Shyness." In *Encyclopedia of Mental Health*, edited by Howard S. Friedman. San Diego, Calif.: Academic Press, 1998. Summarizes shyness and the authors' own work in the area of research and treatment.

Jones, W. H., and B. N. Carpenter. "Shyness, Social Behavior, and Relationships." In *Perspectives on Research and Treatment*, edited by W. H. Jones, J. M. Cheek, and S. R. Briggs. New York: Plenum, 1986. Overview of the impact of shyness on social and interpersonal interactions.

Kagan, J. "Temperament and the Reactions to Unfamiliarity." *Child Development*, 68 (1997): 139-143.

Reports on studies about physiological reactivity to novel stimuli of those predisposed to shyness.

Kagan, J., D. Arcus, and N. Snidman. "The Idea of Temperament: Where Do We Go from Here?" In *Nature, Nurture, and Psychology*, edited by R. Plomin and G. E. McClearn. Washington, D.C.: American Psychological Association, 1993. Summarizes the authors' and other research on genetic and environmental origins of shyness.

Schmidt, L. A., and J. Schulkin, eds. *Extreme Fear, Shyness, and Social Phobia*. New York: Oxford University Press, 1999. Presents up-to-date research on psychological and biological determinants of shyness.

Debra L. Murphy

SEE ALSO: Anxiety disorders; Aversion, implosion, and systematic desensitization; Introverts and extroverts; Phobias.

Sibling relationships

TYPE OF PSYCHOLOGY: Developmental psychology
FIELDS OF STUDY: Adolescence; adulthood; infancy and childhood; interpersonal relations

Sibling relationships have been the object of increasingly detailed theoretical analysis and scientific investigation since the 1970's. Such relationships show both change and stability over the life span. They are characterized by both rivalries and helpfulness, with helpfulness predominating.

KEY CONCEPTS
- attachment theory
- bidirectional influences
- blended family
- family systems theory
- secure attachment
- social cognition

INTRODUCTION

Sibling relationships grow out of interactions among children within a family. Such interactions occur on many levels and involve behaviors as well as the emotions and cognitions that accompany them. Sibling relationships begin at the time the first child becomes aware that a brother or sister has

been added to the family and often continue into old age, ceasing only upon the death of a sibling. Because they often last from early childhood to old age, sibling relationships are frequently the longest-lasting relationships in an individual's life. Siblings' relationships differ from those among friends in that they are not voluntary, cannot be terminated at will, and—during childhood—are daily and intimate in nature.

Prior to the 1970's, research concerning children's development within families tended to stress parental influences on children's behavior. By the 1970's, however, developmental psychologists had discovered that they needed more elaborate theoretical explanations to account for the variety of child behavior seen in their studies. In 1968, Richard Bell reviewed the existing literature and concluded that parents influence children and children also influence parents. This has been called a pattern of bidirectional influences.

As developmental researchers came to accept the bidirectional influences view, other theorists soon broadened perspectives on family dynamics still further. Family systems theory was articulated by writers such as psychiatrist and family therapist Salvador Minuchin in his 1974 book *Families and Family Therapy*. In this view, the behaviors and roles of all members of a family are interdependent, each influencing the others. Relationships frequently became researchers' fundamental units of analysis, with all relationships seen as having the potential to influence one another and the entire family system. An ongoing rivalry between two brothers, for example, has the potential to erode the quality of their parents' relationship. In the 1980's and 1990's, systems-oriented researchers incorporated into their understanding of sibling relationships additional variables, including social class, culture, genetic factors, child temperament, and individuals' levels of social cognition (the ability to think and reason about interactions among people). Researchers also began to consider the relevance of ideas proposed by British psychiatrist John Bowlby in his three-volume work *Attachment and Loss* (1969-1980). Bowlby's attachment theory, which suggested that humans are biologically predisposed to form early social relationships, reinforced the notion that relationships develop early and are important in the subsequent development of the individual. At an early age, infants can become emotionally attached to familiar persons, including siblings.

The history of scientific attempts to understand sibling relationships, then, has been characterized by increasing appreciation for the complexity of such relationships and the diversity of contexts in which siblings learn to relate to one another. This complexity has created numerous methodological challenges for researchers.

METHODOLOGICAL ISSUES

Disparities among families with regard to number of children and spacing between children complicate investigators' attempts to discover general principles that describe all sibling relationships. In addition, children's gender is a variable that could influence relationships between siblings, and gender mix, too, varies across families. Birth order—being an oldest or youngest child in the family, for example—also may influence children's interactions with brothers and sisters.

With so many variables operating and so much diversity possible across families, researchers have tended either to do relatively straightforward descriptive studies or to restrict their investigations to a subset of all possible family types. Early research attempted to assess the impact of global factors such as birth order, family size, or gender on variables such as personality or intelligence. As family systems theory began to influence research, however, investigators began studying relationships among siblings and the various forces to which these relationships respond. Studies carried out in the systems theory framework have generally limited their scope to a particular family type, such as two-child families with children under the age of five.

Even with such necessary limitations, however, investigators still have to consider several other methodological issues. They must decide whether they will get information through interviews, questionnaires, or direct observation of sibling interactions. If using an interview or questionnaire, they must decide whether to question parents, children, or both. If observations are to be done, should they be done in a laboratory or in participants' homes? Another consideration is the type of siblings that will be studied. It has been common practice to study full siblings who share the same mother and father. However, half siblings, stepsiblings, and adoptive siblings may also be of interest, and researchers must decide whether to include them in their studies as well.

Psychologist and researcher Victor Cicirelli, in his 1995 book *Sibling Relationships Across the Life Span*, argued that sibling relationships must be studied longitudinally. Because sibling relationships can last a lifetime, it is valuable to know how they both change and remain the same over the entire life span. Only by studying such relationships over the long term can researchers develop an integrated, coherent body of knowledge about siblings' lifelong relationships.

CHILDHOOD

As infants and children grow, they change. The same can be said of childhood sibling relationships, for both members of any particular sibling pair are changing as individuals as their relationship grows. Research on the development of sibling interactions during childhood has been limited, but based on available information, some general observations can be reported.

Infants often do become emotionally attached to a sibling, just as they do to their mothers, fathers, and other caregivers. When the sibling relationship is positive and supportive, a secure attachment is likely to develop. Secure attachments during infancy predict healthy patterns of exploration as children get older, as well as successful adjustment to school and social situations.

Older children, being cognitively and physically more advanced than their younger bothers or sisters, tend to be leaders in sibling interactions. Younger siblings often imitate older brothers or sisters. Older children frequently act as linguistic interpreters as younger siblings learn to talk. As both siblings grow, the younger child becomes increasingly capable of actively participating in mutual activities; simultaneously, the older child may show increasing interest in the relationship.

An older sibling attends school and begins relating to peers earlier than a younger brother or sister, who may seek the advice of the older child when starting school. From the preschool period to school age, sibling pairs tend to remain fairly stable with regard to the proportions of positive and negative behaviors they exhibit. As children get older, they typically experience less adult supervision, which may pose a risk for sibling pairs with a predominantly negative relationship.

An observational study of the development of early sibling relationships published in 1982 illustrates the influence of family systems thinking on research. Judy Dunn and Carol Kendrick observed the development of sibling relationships for the first fourteen months after families had a second child. Older siblings were one and a half to three and a half years old when the new baby arrived. Dunn and Kendrick visited families in their homes several times and found that a majority of firstborns became more demanding and more likely to engage in naughty behavior in the weeks immediately following the younger child's birth. Crying, clinging, and jealousy increased. Despite the negative reactions, however, most older siblings also reacted positively to the new child, cuddling the baby, helping take care of it, and showing concern when it cried. They also showed gains in taking care of their own needs independently. Siblings were especially likely to develop a close relationship with one another if, when speaking to the older child, mothers referred to the baby as an individual with interests, needs, and preferences. This finding is in keeping with family systems theorists' belief that relationships within a family are interdependent.

ADOLESCENCE

The course of sibling relationship development during adolescence is less well understood than is the case for younger children. There is some evidence that the intensity of sibling relationships—for both positive and negative elements—may peak during early adolescence. Thereafter, power tends to become increasingly equivalent, and there is less tendency and less need for the older sibling to nurture the younger one. Conflict tends to be greater for siblings who are closer in age. Generally, same-sex siblings remain closer during this stage of life than do brother-sister pairs. Middle-aged siblings report recalling a drop in sharing and understanding during adolescence, followed by a resurgence of those characteristics during adulthood.

ADULTHOOD

Little research on adult sibling relationships was done before the 1980's. That done thereafter tended to be largely descriptive or normative in nature. Cicirelli contends that this has occurred in part because researchers studying adulthood have worked in isolation from those studying childhood and adolescence.

Existing investigations suggest that affection characterizes most adult sibling relationships and

that feelings of closeness may increase as siblings age. This may be particularly true for sisters. Relationships among adult siblings tend to be similar to friendships and often involve family celebrations or recreational activities. Elderly siblings often discuss family issues and reminisce.

Negative feelings between adult siblings are also reported, but overt hostility is rare. Affectionate feelings among siblings appear to be somewhat lessened in adults who spent part of their childhoods in a blended family (that is, a new family created by the remarriage of a parent). The few adult siblings—probably less than 11 percent—who have relatively little contact with one another have not been systematically studied.

RIVALRY AND HELPFULNESS

Both rivalry and helpfulness characterize sibling relationships across the entire life span. Joan Newman reviewed the literature on these features of siblings' interactions in 1994 and suggested that conflict between siblings may be inevitable, owing to maturational discrepancies in social cognition between children of differing ages who are involved in an intense, complex, daily relationship. In part, the complexity of such relationships derives from their having both egalitarian qualities and inherent inequities (such as when one sibling is old enough to drive and the other is not). Newman points out that cognitively immature youngsters could hardly be expected to negotiate such relationships without feelings of competition, jealousy, or frustration.

Questionnaire and interview studies of older children and adults reveal widespread memories of competition, arguing, and verbal aggression in childhood sibling relationships. Memories of physical aggression are rare. Observational studies suggest that although children show negativity in interactions with siblings more often than with peers or parents, negativity is not the predominant mode of relating.

Observational studies by Gene Brody and colleagues in 1982 and 1984 showed that eight- to ten-year-olds who were playing with a younger sibling tended to adopt cooperative but unequal roles (such as teacher and pupil). As children got older, there was some tendency for girls to play with a younger sibling more so than boys, perhaps because girls engage in more nurturant play activities and boys engage in more competitive physical activities.

Different studies have reported different proportions of positivity and negativity in sibling relationships. In part, the inconsistencies may be due to the methods used. Newman points out that parents' reports may overemphasize rivalries while direct observations of children reveal relatively placid interactions. Children often report a mixture of feelings and attitudes. Further, because sibling relationships themselves often embody considerable variability, researchers can expect fluctuations in their findings.

SOURCES FOR FURTHER STUDY

Brody, Gene H. "Sibling Relationship Quality: Its Causes and Consequences." *Annual Review of Psychology* 49 (1998): 1-24. The author reviews scientific literature on children's characteristics, family processes, and sibling relationships and offers a model for understanding their interactions. He explores the role of sibling relationships in cognitive and psychosocial development.

_____, ed. *Sibling Relationships: Their Causes and Consequences.* Norwood, N.J.: Ablex, 1996. This collection of chapters by leading investigators provides coverage of many important research topics related to sibling relationships.

Cicirelli, Victor G. *Sibling Relationships Across the Life Span.* New York: Plenum, 1995. An accessible and interesting academic review of literature on sibling relationships, with theoretical suggestions for advancing research.

Dunn, Judy. *From One Child to Two.* New York: Fawcett Columbine, 1995. A leading researcher of sibling relationships offers this book for a popular audience, basing her advice on scientific findings.

Dunn, Judy, and Carol Kendrick. *Siblings: Love, Envy, and Understanding.* Cambridge, Mass.: Harvard University Press, 1982. This classic work presents the observational research of the authors, who studied developing sibling relationships between preschoolers and new siblings. Emerging sibling relationships are understood in light of parent-child relationships.

Newman, Joan. "Conflict and Friendship in Sibling Relationships: A Review." *Child Study Journal* 24, no. 2 (1994): 119-152. This readable review focuses on rivalry and helpfulness among siblings. It highlights the role of social cognition in siblings.

Faye B. Steuer

SEE ALSO: Affiliation and friendship; Attachment and bonding in infancy and childhood; Birth order and personality; Family life: Children's issues; Stepfamilies.

Signal detection theory

TYPE OF PSYCHOLOGY: Sensation and perception
FIELDS OF STUDY: Cognitive processes; methodological issues

Signal detection theory is a mathematical model for understanding how sounds or other stimuli are detected in the presence of background noise. It replaces classical threshold theory in psychophysics and provides a method for separating a person's sensitivity to a stimulus from any bias or response criterion.

KEY CONCEPTS
- bias
- catch trial
- correct rejection
- false alarm
- hit
- miss
- noise
- psychophysics
- sensitivity
- threshold

INTRODUCTION

Signal detection theory is not a "theory" in the traditional sense as much as a term used to describe certain types of measurement procedures. Developed by mathematicians and engineers at the University of Michigan, Harvard University, and the Massachusetts Institute of Technology in the 1950's, signal detection theory is based on a method of statistical hypothesis testing and on findings in electronic communication. It provides a method to measure two factors independently: a person's sensitivity to sound or other stimulation, and any bias (a consistent tendency to respond positively or negatively in a situation) or decision criterion the person might adopt that affects the person's performance during a sensitivity test.

A typical measurement procedure might involve detection of sound in a quiet room. Invited into the acoustically insulated chamber, an individual puts on earphones and is told to pay attention to a small warning light that comes on periodically. The instructions are to report, for each occurrence of the warning light, whether a sound is heard through the earphones at that time. The sounds coming through the earphones vary in intensity, though not in frequency; they may initially be of very low amplitude, or they may be readily audible. Indeed, the warning light may come on with no sound at all; this is a "catch" trial—a situation designed to catch someone who simply pretends to hear a sound every time the light comes on. No matter what the sound, the individual being tested must respond with "Yes, I heard a sound" or "No, I heard nothing."

Much of the time the response is "yes" when a sound is present; this is called a hit, because it is a correct recognition of the stimulus. Often, when no sound is presented, the individual says "no," giving a correct rejection. Sometimes, however, the response is "yes" when no sound is present, a false alarm, and sometimes the individual says "no" when the sound is in fact present, a miss. Thus the experimenter collects data showing the number of hits, false alarms, misses, and correct rejections for each individual participant.

Individuals are told exactly what proportion of the trials will be catch trials (in a study measuring sensitivity to certain stimuli, a trial in which no stimulus is presented). This gives them some idea of what to expect. If the experiment were set up with 90 percent catch trials and participants in the study were given no knowledge of this, they might think, hearing so little, that something was wrong with the earphones. These same people would expect a session with 20 percent catch trials, for example, to sound very different. When there is a lower proportion of catch trials, individuals tend to respond "yes" more than when the proportion is higher; thus, they maximize hits and (since there are few catch trials) cannot make many false alarms. If there is a high proportion of catch trials, individuals tend to say "no" more, thus making fewer false alarms, but also making fewer hits. Thus, both hits and false alarms vary depending on the number of catch trials even though the sound intensities are exactly the same in each of these conditions.

ROLE OF EDUCATED GUESSING

If one took part in this without putting on the earphones, one could only guess whether a sound is present. In guessing, however, one might guess "yes" more frequently if told there would be few, rather than many, catch trials. This educated guessing is what a normal participant does. When unsure as to the presence of a sound, people guess; the probability of guessing "yes" is given by the proportion of catch trials. The psychologist collecting these data determines the number of hits and false alarms for each individual and compares them with a "guessing line," the percentage of hits and false alarms for one who merely guesses. The degree of difference between these two modes of response is a pure measure of sensitivity; bias has been eliminated with the guessing baseline. Sensitivity is high when the individual hears most of the sounds presented and has to guess on few of them, and it is low when many of the responses are guesses.

DETERMINING BIAS AND EFFECT OF PERSONALITY

There is another measurement: The experimenter also determines each person's bias, or decision criterion in responding. The decision criterion, which changes whenever the number of catch trials changes, may also be influenced by other factors. For example, there is always some noise going on when a stimulus is received. Even in an acoustically quiet chamber, there are sounds from one's own heart, blood rushing through vessels, and breathing. These vary from moment to moment, and they do influence perception of sound, particularly those that may seem very weak. Outside a quiet chamber there are other noisy backgrounds, hums of air conditioners, computers, street traffic, and so on.

In addition, people who participate in these measurement studies bring different decision criteria that are characteristic of their own personalities. For example, a participant may not respond with a "yes" unless absolutely certain that a sound is present, saying "no" otherwise and thus failing to make all the hits—but also making few false alarms. Another might respond with a "yes" whenever it seems as though a sound could conceivably be present and say "no" only when absolutely certain there is no sound. These two people might have the same sensitivity; that is, they could perceive the sounds equally well, but the number of sounds presented that they identify correctly would be different. They would therefore achieve equal measures of sensitivity but very different measures of bias. Signal detection theory, then, provides an ingenious method for the measurement of an individual's sensitivity to sounds or other stimuli independent of factors that impinge on that individual's decision.

PERCEPTUAL VIGILANCE

Signal detection methods are applied in studies in which a stimulus or event is to be detected. Used to separate sensation from motivational bias, these methods are most successful with simple stimuli.

One of the earliest and simplest of these studies involves perceptual vigilance. The basic task is to detect a few signals against a background pattern of noise similar to the signal. The best known of these displays is the Mackworth clock, which presents clockwise jumps of a black pointer across a white field. The signal jumps are twice as large as the repetitive background jumps, and they occur at irregular time intervals ranging, for example, from forty-five seconds to ten minutes. The noise occurs at a high rate and is constant, regular, and monotonous.

An observer sits in a small cubicle for half-hour periods watching this moving pointer, monitoring it and responding only when the pointer makes a long jump. At the beginning, attention is high and the observer makes few errors. After all, it is an easy task. As time goes on, however, the observer tires, loses concentration, and begins missing signals. The jumps all begin to look alike; after an hour or so, one in every four or five long jumps may be missed. There are few, if any, false alarms.

This vigilance decrement occurs with listening tasks as well. In fact, it is a common observance in nearly all tests of attention and is applicable to many everyday situations: factory workers monitoring displays on shift, inspectors in industry examining merchandise for flaws, even students sitting in classrooms listening for important points in lectures. Although psychologists were aware of these declines before the theory of signal detection was formulated, their study of this changed with the method. They began to address new questions. What difference does the nature of the noise make? How might the observer shift the bias, or criterion of response, over time or over situations?

It is perhaps not surprising to find that sensitivity is higher when the signal is most different from the background noise. More interesting is the finding that if there are very few signals, there often is no measurable decline in sensitivity even if the observers miss more signals over time. This occurs because

they also make fewer false alarms over the same time; that is, they become more cautious in their response—a shift in bias. One sees shifts of bias of this sort in many situations. For example, a physician may diagnose a disease on the basis of insufficient data in cases where failure to detect it would be disastrous and making a false alarm would be relatively insignificant. On the other hand, military personnel would not want to begin sending out retaliatory nuclear weapons against an enemy unless absolutely certain the attack to which they are responding is actually occurring. A false alarm here is unthinkable, so they exhibit extreme caution—a very high bias against a response.

USE IN HUMAN RESEARCH AND PSYCHOLOGY

Signal detection theory has been helpful in applied human research, in perceptual studies, and in studies of memory. Measures of sensitivity in memory parallel those in perception. Effects of variables such as aging, epilepsy and other brain dysfunction, brain insults such as concussions, or periods of oxygen deprivation have been examined more recently for their effects on sensitivity. In a 1977 signal detection study of head-injured patients, Diane McCarthy found that patients recovering from concussions show, during the acute stages of head injury, sensitivity scores similar to an elderly population and considerably lower than normal control subjects. They also show some residual deficit six weeks later, even when the head injury is not severe. Interestingly, this shows a period of reduced sensitivity to stimulation, not merely confusion.

Signal detection theory has provided a routine method in experimental psychology. It is applied in situations where a pure measure of sensitivity, unaffected by changing criteria, is desired. Additionally, it may be used when the target of interest is the criterion or bias itself—for example, in studies of personality factors in response decisions.

STUDY OF THRESHOLD

In the late nineteenth century, experimenters in psychophysics (the study of the relationship between the physical properties of a stimulus and the way in which they are perceived) questioned how accurately people's perceptions correspond to the physical stimulation they receive. They asked to what extent a person's reported perception actually reflects the physical changes going on in the real world.

One way of answering this was to try to discover how strong a stimulus needed to be before people noticed or detected that stimulus. There are sounds, for example, so soft that they cannot be heard, or can be heard only by a few individuals, and there are sounds so intense that all hearing individuals detect them. At what point in increasingly intense levels is a sound just barely detectable? Psychophysicists called this level the threshold. They assumed that this level of intensity, this limen, was like the threshold of a door in which one was either inside or outside, never in between. They assumed that all sounds less intense than the threshold, all stimulation that is subliminal or below the limen, would never be detected and that all sounds more intense than the threshold would always be detected.

With this theory in hand, experimental psychologists began measuring thresholds. They determined empirically, for example, how much sugar must go into a certain amount of distilled water at a given temperature before it can be tasted, how intensely a 440 hertz sound has to be played under certain acoustical conditions before it is heard, and how intense a spot of white light has to be in a darkened room for a dark-adapted subject to detect it in peripheral vision. They made measurements and ran into difficulties.

Measured thresholds were always imprecise, as the only measurement taken was the occurrence of hits. They were unlike the threshold of a door, a line with no breadth. Sometimes an individual would report hearing a sound that was very weak, then report not hearing a sound that was quite a bit more intense. Most of the time, however, intense sounds were heard and weak ones were not, so that researchers calculated an average, an intensity of sound that a subject reported hearing 50 percent of the time. This they defined empirically as the threshold, assuming that their inability to measure a point perfectly was attributable simply to procedural error or imprecise measurement.

Increasingly, however, researchers began to recognize that threshold measures were contaminated, or confounded, by other factors, such as how important it seemed to a person not to let a sound go unnoticed or not to appear foolish saying a sound was heard when it might not have been there at all. Signal detection theory provided an alternative, a method for determining a person's sensitivity to a stimulus independent of any bias in response. These methods are now a standard part of experimental psychology, providing another way to determine how perceptions correspond to physical changes in the real world.

SOURCES FOR FURTHER STUDY

Commons, Michael L., John A. Nevin, and Michael C. Davison, eds. *Signal Detection: Mechanisms, Models, and Applications.* Hillsdale, N.J.: Lawrence Erlbaum, 1991. A collection of scholarly papers based on the tenth annual Harvard Symposium for the Quantitative Analysis of Behavior. The chapters, quantitative and theoretical in approach, illustrate sensitivity and bias as independent parameters in signal detection theory. The final three chapters give clear articulation to major applications and are of interest in themselves.

Gescheider, George. *Psychophysics: The Fundamentals.* 3d ed. Hillsdale, N.J.: Lawrence Erlbaum, 1997. A thorough introduction to psychophysics, focusing on measurement techniques and signal detection theory.

Levine, Michael W. *Fundamentals of Sensation and Perception.* 3d ed. New York: Oxford University Press, 2000. A college textbook for students of sensation and perception, this proceeds from an introductory chapter to a clear and well-illustrated discussion of psychophysics. The pages on signal detection theory are replete with figures and diagrams, and the theory is described in historical and theoretical context. A short, enjoyable, and highly readable introduction.

Ludel, Jacqueline. *Introduction to Sensory Processes.* San Francisco: W. H. Freeman, 1978. Requires no prior study of sensory processes, anatomy, physiology, or perception. More than an introduction, Ludel gradually and clearly explores topics in depth. Her description of signal detection theory unfolds in the chapter on auditory perception. Conversational in tone, the book also contains mnemonics and pronunciation guides.

Wickens, Thomas D. *Elementary Signal Detection Theory.* New York: Oxford University Press, 2001. Explains the theoretical and mathematical underpinnings of signal detection theory. Intended as an undergraduate textbook.

Bonnie S. Sherman

SEE ALSO: Attention; Decision making; Hearing; Pattern recognition; Sensation and perception.

Skinner, B. F.

BORN: March 20, 1904, in Susquehanna, Pennsylvania

DIED: August 18, 1990, in Cambridge, Massachusetts

IDENTITY: American behaviorist psychologist

TYPE OF PSYCHOLOGY: Learning

FIELDS OF STUDY: Behavioral and cognitive models

Skinner was the founder of radical behaviorism and one of the most influential psychologists of the twentieth century.

Burrhus Frederic Skinner spent his boyhood in a middle-class family in a small town in Pennsylvania. He studied literature and received a B.A. from Hamilton College in New York. After an unsuccessful year as a writer, Skinner was inspired to enter graduate school in psychology by the works of Ivan Petrovich Pavlov and John Broadus Watson. At Harvard University, where he was influenced by William J. Crozier and Walter S. Hunter, Skinner proved to be a clever inventor of apparatus used to study the behavior of white rats. He earned his Ph.D. in 1931 and remained at Harvard until his first faculty appointment, in 1936, at the University of Minnesota. In 1945, Skinner became professor and chair of the department of psychology at Indiana University. He returned to Harvard in 1948 for the duration of his career. He retired as professor emeritus in 1974, remaining professionally active until his death in 1990.

Skinner's science of behavior was controversial and often misunderstood. He maintained that the behavior of organisms, including people, was a function of three factors: genetic heritage, past experiences, and current circumstances. He advocated an understanding of behavior based on directly observable aspects of the environment, not because unobservable factors such as thinking and feeling did not exist, but because they were not readily accessible for study and control. His techniques of behavior management through changing aspects of the environment, usually the consequences of behavior, have proven powerful and useful for many species and situations.

Between 1930 and 1990, Skinner published numerous articles and books. *The Behavior of Organisms* (1938) laid out the beginnings of his science of behavior. He wrote two books explaining his views to a

B. F. Skinner. (Alfred A. Knopf)

broad audience: *About Behaviorism* (1974) and *Science and Human Behavior* (1953). A utopian novel, *Walden Two* (1945), was about a fictional community guided by his principles of behavior. His most controversial book, *Beyond Freedom and Dignity* (1971), argued that a technology of behavior could help solve societal problems.

Skinner founded two areas of psychology: the experimental analysis of behavior, which investigates basic behavioral principles; and applied behavior analysis, which seeks solutions to specific problems. His work spawned dozens of scientific journals devoted to these issues. Skinner was widely recognized as the most influential psychologist in the twentieth century. He received numerous awards, including in 1990 the first-ever Citation for Outstanding Lifetime Contribution to Psychology from the American Psychological Association.

SOURCES FOR FURTHER STUDY

Bjork, Daniel W. *B. F. Skinner: A Life*. New York: Basic Books, 1993. Comprehensive biography of Skinner's life and work by an eminent historian of psychology.

_____. "Burrhus Frederic Skinner: The Contingencies of a Life." In *Portraits of Pioneers in Psychology*. Vol. 3, edited by Gregory A. Kimble and

Michael Wertheimer. Hillsdale, N.J.: Lawrence Erlbaum, 1998. Chapter-length summary of Skinner's life and work.

Wiener, Daniel N. *B. F. Skinner: Benign Anarchist.* Needham Heights, Mass.: Allyn & Bacon, 1996. Biography of Skinner by a student and colleague. Contains a complete bibliography of his work.

Amy L. Odum

SEE ALSO: Behaviorism; Conditioning; Radical behaviorism: B. F. Skinner.

Sleep

TYPE OF PSYCHOLOGY: Consciousness
FIELDS OF STUDY: Sleep

The study of sleep stages and functions involves descriptions of the electrophysiological, cognitive, motor, and behavioral components of various sleep stages as well as the potential functions served by each. The sleep-wake cycle is one of several human circadian rhythms that regulate human attention, alertness, and performance.

KEY CONCEPTS
- circadian rhythms
- desynchronized electroencephalogram (EEG)
- hypnagogic imagery
- myoclonia
- nonrapid eye movement (NREM) sleep
- paradoxical sleep
- rapid eye movement (REM) sleep
- synchronized electroencephalogram (EEG)

INTRODUCTION

Sleep, one of the most mysterious of human circadian rhythms (human biological cycles that fluctuate on a daily basis), can be characterized as a naturally induced alteration in consciousness. Although the sleeper may appear to be unconscious, many complex cognitive, physiological, and behavioral processes occur during sleep. For example, parents may sleep through a nearby police siren yet easily awaken to their crying infant.

Efforts to understand sleep have focused on behavioral and electrical changes that occur each night. During every moment of a person's life, the brain, eyes, and muscles are generating electrical potentials that can be recorded by a polygraph. Minute electrical signals are conveyed through tiny disk electrodes attached to the scalp and face, which are recorded by the polygraph as wave patterns that can be described in terms of frequency, amplitude, and synchronization. Frequency is measured by the number of cycles that occur per second (cps), amplitude by the distance between the peaks and troughs of waves, and synchronization by the regular, repetitive nature of the waves.

MEASURING STAGES OF SLEEP

Use of the polygraph has resulted in the identification of four stages of nonrapid eye movement (NREM) sleep, as well as a special stage referred to as rapid eye movement (REM) sleep. Each stage is described in terms of electrical changes in brainwave patterns, speed and pattern of eye movements, and muscular activity in the body. Brain-wave activity is measured by the electroencephalogram (EEG), eye movement patterns by the electrooculogram (EOG), and muscle activity by the electromyogram (EMG).

Three EEG patterns can be described for NREM sleep. First, as a sleeper progresses from stages one through four, the waves increase in amplitude or voltage from approximately 50 to 100 microvolts in stage one to about 100 to 200 microvolts in stage four. Second, the frequency of the waves decreases gradually from 4 to 8 cps in stages one and two to 1 to 4 cps in stages three and four. Last, the waves become progressively more synchronized from stages one to four, so that by stage four, the waves assume a slow, regular pattern sometimes called S sleep, for slow-wave sleep or synchronized sleep. Each of these patterns is reflected in the type of brain-wave activity present, with stages one and two consisting predominantly of theta waves and stages three and four of delta waves.

In addition to the changes in brain electrical activity, the EMG records a gradual diminution of muscular activity as the sleeper progresses through each stage of NREM sleep. By the onset of stage four, the EMG is relatively flat, revealing a deep state of muscular relaxation. In fact, virtually all physiological activity is at its lowest during stage four, including respiration, heart rate, blood pressure, digestion, and so on. In this sense, stage four is considered to be the deepest stage of sleep.

DSM-IV-TR Criteria for Dyssomnias

BREATHING-RELATED SLEEP DISORDER (DSM CODE 780.59)

Sleep disruption, leading to excessive sleepiness or insomnia, judged to be due to sleep-related breathing condition

Disturbance not better accounted for by another mental disorder and not due to direct physiological effects of a substance or another general medical condition (other than a breathing-related disorder)

CIRCADIAN RHYTHM SLEEP DISORDER (DSM CODE 307.45)

Persistent or recurrent pattern of sleep disruption leading to excessive sleepiness or insomnia due to mismatch between sleep-wake schedule required by person's environment and circadian sleep-wake pattern

Sleep disturbance causes clinically significant distress or impairment in social, occupational, or other important areas of functioning

Disturbance does not occur exclusively during course of another sleep disorder or other mental disorder

Disturbance not due to direct physiological effects of a substance or general medical condition

Types:
- Delayed Sleep Phase Type: Persistent pattern of late sleep onset and late awakening times, with inability to fall asleep and awaken at desired earlier time
- Jet Lag Type: Sleepiness and alertness at inappropriate time of day relative to local time, occurring after repeated travel across more than one time zone
- Shift Work Type: Insomnia during major sleep period or excessive sleepiness during major awake period, associated with night shift work or frequently changing shift work
- Unspecified Type

PRIMARY HYPERSOMNIA (DSM CODE 307.44)

Predominant complaint is excessive sleepiness for at least one month (less if recurrent) as evidenced by either prolonged sleep episodes or daytime sleep episodes occurring almost daily

Excessive sleepiness causes clinically significant distress or impairment in social, occupational, or other important areas of functioning

Excessive sleepiness not better accounted for by Insomnia, not occurring exclusively during course of another sleep disorder, and not accounted for by inadequate amount of sleep

Disturbance does not occur exclusively during course of another mental disorder

Disturbance not due to direct physiological effects of a substance or general medical condition

Specify if Recurrent (periods of excessive sleepiness lasting at least three days occurring several times a year for at least two years)

PRIMARY INSOMNIA (DSM CODE 307.42)

Predominant complaint is difficulty initiating or maintaining sleep, or nonrestorative sleep, for at least one month

Sleep disturbance (or associated daytime fatigue) causes clinically significant distress or impairment in social, occupational, or other important areas of functioning

Sleep disturbance does not occur exclusively during the course of Narcolepsy, Breathing-Related Sleep Disorder, Circadian Rhythm Sleep Disorder, or a parasomnia

Disturbance does not occur exclusively during the course of another mental disorder (such as Major Depressive Disorder, Generalized Anxiety Disorder, a delirium)

Disturbance not due to direct physiological effects of a substance or general medical condition

NARCOLEPSY (DSM CODE 347)

Irresistible attacks of refreshing sleep occurring daily over at least three months

Presence of one or both of the following:
- cataplexy (brief episodes of sudden bilateral loss of muscle tone, most often in association with intense emotion)
- recurrent intrusions of elements of rapid eye movement (REM) sleep into the transition between sleep and wakefulness, as manifested by either hypnopompic or hypnagogic hallucinations or sleep paralysis at beginning or end of sleep episodes

Disturbance not due to direct physiological effects of a substance or another general medical condition

DYSSOMNIA NOT OTHERWISE SPECIFIED (DSM CODE 307.47)

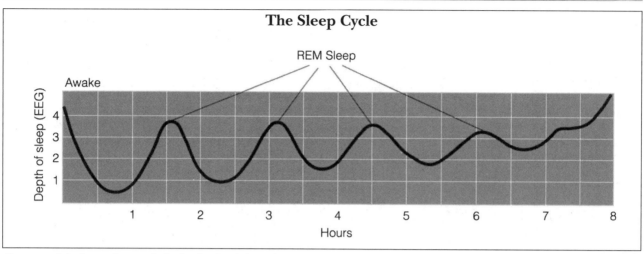

Over an eight-hour sleep period, the depth of sleep fluctuates and is punctuated by periods of rapid eye movement (REM). (Hans & Cassidy, Inc.)

COGNITIVE ACTIVITY CYCLES DURING SLEEP

As stated previously, the sleeper is not in an unconscious state but is in a different level of consciousness. Cognitive activity is present in all stages of NREM sleep. Hypnagogic imagery, consisting of dreamlike images sometimes indistinguishable from REM dreams, is present in stage one. Subjects are easily awakened during this sleep stage, and regressions to a waking state are quite common. Often, these regressions occur because of myoclonias, which are brief jerking movements of the muscles. Since stage one is sometimes viewed as a transitional state between sleeping and waking, it should not be too surprising that sleep talking occurs primarily in this stage. Stage one sleep lasts for approximately fifteen minutes.

The sleeper is somewhat more difficult to arouse during stage two, and the cognitive activity present is more thoughtlike and fragmentary than in stage one. If the subject recalls any mental activity, it is rather sparse. Stage two also lasts for approximately fifteen minutes.

It was once assumed that dreams only occur in REM sleep, but it is now common knowledge that dreams of a different variety occur in stages three and four. These dreams are not of the narrative or storylike variety found in REM sleep; rather, they resemble nonsequential thoughts, images, sensations, or emotions. As might be expected in the deepest sleep stage, it is quite difficult to awaken the sleeper who is in stage four. Paradoxically, a subject awakened in stage four will often claim not to be sleeping. Finally, sleepwalking, night terrors, and bedwetting, all of which are developmental disorders, occur predominantly in stage four. Stage three lasts approximately ten minutes, while the first episode of stage four usually lasts about fifty minutes.

Suddenly, about ninety minutes after falling asleep, the subject rapidly regresses back through the stages of NREM sleep to a special stage usually called stage one-REM sleep, or sometimes simply REM sleep. Three major changes occur in the electrical activity measured in this stage. First, the EEG pattern becomes highly desynchronized, resembling a combination of waking and stage one-NREM brain-wave activity. For this reason, REM sleep is sometimes called paradoxical sleep, because it is paradoxical that elements of a waking EEG should be present in a sleeping condition. Second, the EMG recordings become almost completely flat for most skeletal muscles, resembling paralysis. Finally, there is an onset of rapid eye movements, as measured by the EOG.

Cognitive activity, in the form of narrative or storylike dreams, is rich and varied in REM sleep—hence the term "D sleep," for dreaming or desynchronized sleep. It is interesting to note that the rapid eye movements correspond closely with dream content. For example, if a person dreams of something running from left to right, the direction of rapid eye movements will also be left to right.

Throughout the remainder of the evening, a cycle of approximately ninety minutes will be established from one REM episode to the next. All together, the sleeper will experience four to five REM episodes in a typical eight-hour sleep period, with each one lasting for a longer interval than the previous one. The first REM episode may last only five to ten minutes, while the final one may be thirty to forty minutes or longer in duration. In contrast, S sleep episodes decrease in length throughout the evening, and will disappear completely after two to three episodes.

STUDY OF SLEEP DEPRIVATION

Although a description of sleep stages can be provided with relative ease, identifying a clear function for sleep is a more difficult proposition. Yet applications of sleep research are inextricably linked with the functions of sleep. For the typical layperson, the seemingly obvious function of sleep is to repair and restore the body after daily mental and physical exertion. This commonsense approach has been formalized by science as the repair and restoration theory. One of the most frequently used methods to assess this theory is to examine the mental and physical effects of sleep deprivation. If the primary function of sleep is to repair the body, then loss of sleep should disrupt cognitive, motor, and behavioral processes. Early laboratory research with animals seemed to support this position. If sleep deprivation persisted for a sufficient time, usually between three and twenty days, death ensued in laboratory animals. Unfortunately, to maintain sleep deprivation in animals, it is necessary to keep them active. Perhaps the continuous activity, rather than the sleep deprivation, killed the animals.

If it were possible to allow animals to rest and relax, but not sleep, would the sleep deprivation still prove fatal? This question was addressed by anecdotal accounts of human sleep deprivation during the Korean War. As a means of extracting confessions from American soldiers, Korean military intelligence operatives commonly subjected prisoners of war to sustained bouts of sleep deprivation. In the face of overwhelming exhaustion and clear signs of personality disintegration, American soldiers were often induced to sign confessions of their alleged war crimes. Yet Randy Gardner, a seventeen-year-old high school student, experienced sleep deprivation for 264 hours to get his name in the *Guinness Book of World Records* with no apparent permanent effects and no profound temporary deficits. Why would people respond in such radically different ways to

sleep deprivation? One hypothesis proposes that severe adverse effects arise as a function of stress and inability to rest and relax, rather than from the loss of sleep. Furthermore, laboratory investigations with volunteer subjects suggest that those individuals who exhibit severe reactions to sleep deprivation almost always have some predisposition to abnormal behavior. Sleep researchers would not deny that sleep serves to restore the body; however, rest and relaxation may serve the same restorative functions in the absence of sleep, which would suggest that repair and restoration is not the sole or even primary function of sleep.

ADAPTIVE THEORY OF SLEEP

To redress the shortcomings of the repair and restoration theory, an alternative theory of a need to sleep has been proposed. The adaptive or evolutionary theory postulates that the need to sleep arose in the course of biological evolution as an adaptive mechanism to conserve energy during the evening hours, when it would be inefficient to search for food and other resources. Sleep, according to this view, serves a function similar to the hibernation observed in several species of mammals. These animals reduce their metabolic processes to barely detectable levels during winter to conserve energy when food resources are scarce. To do otherwise would threaten the survival of these animals. It is important to note that the adaptive theory still considers sleep to be a real need; in essence, sleep is a remnant of the human evolutionary past when human forebears did not have the convenience of twenty-four-hour supermarkets to acquire their sustenance. Humans deprived of sleep will become just as irritable and ill-tempered as a groundhog prevented from hibernating.

Several predictions have been generated from the adaptive theory, most of which have been supported by scientific observations. First, the theory predicts that predators such as large cats and bears, which obtain most of their nutrients in one large meal per day, would sleep much more than grazing animals such as cattle and horses, who must eat frequently to survive. A second prediction of the theory is that predators such as wolves and mountain lions, which have few natural enemies, would sleep more than prey such as rabbits and guinea pigs, which are at risk if they fail to maintain constant vigilance. Finally, animals such as bats, which are well protected by the environment in which they live, would sleep for relatively long periods of time. These predictions are documented by scientific observations, which provide support for the adaptive or evolutionary theory of sleep.

CLINICAL APPLICATIONS

The functions of sleep are extremely important in clinical applications. If the repair and restoration theory lacks strong scientific support, attempting to recover lost sleep time may serve no functional purpose. Indeed, most subjects expect to sleep for several hours longer than normal after staying awake for twenty-four hours, presumably because they believe sleep is required for repair and restoration of the body. In practice, however, most subjects report only four to six total hours of poor-quality sleep fol-

lowing such deprivation. Even after 264 hours of sleep deprivation, Randy Gardner slept for only fourteen hours and forty minutes the first evening, then resumed a normal nocturnal sleep pattern of eight hours per evening.

Knowledge of sleep stages may be especially valuable in diagnosing and treating sleep disorders, since the frequency, patterns, and symptoms of these disorders may be associated with specific stages of sleep. For example, knowledge of the muscular paralysis that accompanies REM sleep has been instrumental in diagnosing the cause of male impotence. Partial or total erections are present in about 95 percent of REM periods. Therefore, men who complain of impotence yet demonstrate normal REM erections can be diagnosed as suffering from psychologically based impotence. These pa-

---

DSM-IV-TR Criteria for Parasomnias

NIGHTMARE DISORDER (DSM CODE 307.47)

Repeated awakenings from major sleep period or naps with detailed recall of extended and extremely frightening dreams, usually involving threats to survival, security, or self-esteem; awakenings generally occur during second half of sleep period

On awakening from frightening dreams, person rapidly becomes oriented and alert (in contrast to confusion and disorientation seen in Sleep Terror Disorder and some forms of epilepsy)

Dream experience, or sleep disturbance resulting from awakening, causes clinically significant distress or impairment in social, occupational, or other important areas of functioning

Nightmares not occurring exclusively during course of another mental disorder (such as a delirium, Post-traumatic Stress Disorder) and not due to direct physiological effects of a substance or general medical condition

SLEEP TERROR DISORDER (DSM CODE 307.46)

Recurrent episodes of abrupt awakening from sleep, usually occurring during first third of major sleep episode and beginning with panicky scream

Intense fear and signs of autonomic arousal, such as tachycardia, rapid breathing, and sweating, during each episode

Relative unresponsiveness to efforts of others to comfort person during episode

No detailed dream recalled; amnesia exists for episode

Episodes cause clinically significant distress or impairment in social, occupational, or other important areas of functioning

Disturbance not due to direct physiological effects of a substance or general medical condition

SLEEPWALKING DISORDER (DSM CODE 307.46)

Repeated episodes of rising from bed during sleep and walking about, usually occurring during first third of major sleep episode

While sleepwalking, person has a blank, staring face, is relatively unresponsive to communication efforts by others, and can be awakened only with great difficulty

Amnesia for episode on awakening (either from sleepwalking episode or the next morning)

Within several minutes after awakening from sleepwalking episode, no impairment of mental activity or behavior seen (although short period of confusion or disorientation possible)

Sleepwalking causes clinically significant distress or impairment in social, occupational, or other important areas of functioning

Disturbance not due to direct physiological effects of a substance or general medical condition

PARASOMNIA NOT OTHERWISE SPECIFIED (DSM CODE 307.47)

tients may benefit from psychotherapy or sexual counseling. In contrast, men who do not achieve REM erections are diagnosed as suffering from organically based impotence and require hormone therapy or surgical implantations.

Nocturnal enuresis, or bed-wetting, is a stage four developmental disorder present in about four to five million children annually in the United States. The exact cause of this disorder is undetermined, although the extreme muscular relaxation during stage four sleep likely contributes to its occurrence. To prevent nocturnal enuresis, the patient must learn to associate a full bladder with waking up. Typically, a special apparatus is placed under the child, which sounds a loud buzzer when urine completes the circuit. Eventually, the child will learn to associate the feeling of a full bladder with waking up in the absence of the buzzer.

EMERGENCE OF RESEARCH

Since sleep is a universal human experience, it is probably safe to conclude that it has interested people since the dawn of humanity; however, scientific inquiry into sleep is a relatively recent phenomenon. Early interest in sleep arose during the late nineteenth century from a need to isolate the brain structure responsible for lethargy syndromes. Similarly, the electrophysiological study of sleep originated with a discovery in 1875 by the English physiologist Richard Caton that the brain continually produces low-voltage waves. This discovery was largely ignored until 1929, when a German psychiatrist, Hans Berger, found that he could record from large groups of neurons by attaching electrodes to the scalp and the forehead. Berger's discovery marked the beginning of modern electroencephalography. With the advent of EEG recordings, it was not long before A. L. Loomis, E. N. Harvey, and G. A. Hobart found, in 1937, that EEG recordings could be used to differentiate stages of sleep. In 1952, Nathaniel Kleitman at the University of Chicago gave Eugene Aserinsky, one of his new graduate students, the assignment of watching the eye movements of sleeping subjects. Aserinsky quickly noted the rapid, darting nature of eye movements during certain times of the night, which differed from the usual slow, rolling eye movements observed at other times. William Dement later coined the term "REM sleep"; sleep in which slow, rolling eye movements predominate later came to be known as NREM sleep (for nonrapid eye move-

ment sleep). Finally, in 1957, Dement and Kleitman presented the current system of four NREM sleep stages and stage one-REM sleep.

IMPORTANCE TO PSYCHOLOGY OF CONSCIOUSNESS

As a naturally induced alteration in consciousness that can be studied objectively with electrophysiological recording equipment, sleep has assumed a prominent role in the psychology of consciousness. Electrophysiological recording techniques that were originally developed in sleep research are now widely used to study other aspects of consciousness, such as hemispheric asymmetries, meditation, sensory isolation, biofeedback, dreams, and drug effects on the brain and behavior. In addition, sleep is one of the few alterations in consciousness that plays a central role in several areas of psychological inquiry. For example, physiological psychologists are concerned with the neurobiological mechanisms underlying sleep, as well as the functions of sleep. From their perspective, sleep is simply one of many human behaviors and cognitive processes whose biological basis must be ascertained. Developmental psychologists are interested in age-related changes that occur in sleep and attempt to develop applications of those findings for concerned parents of young children. Finally, physicians and clinical psychologists are often presented with patients who suffer from physical and/or psychological stress as a function of sleep disorders. These professionals are interested in developing effective drug and psychological therapies that can be used to treat sleep-disordered patients. Sleep is a concern in many areas of psychology.

Because sleep is universal in humans, it will continue to play a major role in consciousness studies and throughout the discipline of psychology. Future research will likely focus on applications of sleep research to industrial settings that employ shift workers. The emphasis will be on reducing fatigue and improving performance among employees by gradually adjusting them to shift work and by changing employee work schedules infrequently. In addition, research will seek ways to improve diagnostic procedures and treatments for a variety of sleep disorders, including insomnia, hypersomnia, sleep apnea, narcolepsy, and enuresis. The focus will be on developing effective drug and psychological therapies. Finally, pure research will continue to examine the functions of sleep, and to delineate more clearly the adverse effects of sleep, even those of a temporary nature.

SOURCES FOR FURTHER STUDY

Coren, Stanley. *Sleep Thieves*. New York: Free Press, 1997. A wide-ranging exploration of sleep research. Coren is one of the major researchers in the relationship between sleep deficit and major industrial accidents, such as the 1989 Exxon *Valdez* oil spill, the 1986 Chernobyl nuclear plant disaster, and the 1986 *Challenger* space shuttle explosion.

Dement, William C. *The Promise of Sleep*. New York: Dell, 2000. Dement, founder of the sleep disorders clinic at Stanford University, provides a nontechnical, personal report of current findings in sleep research, drawing a connection between sleep and general health. Offers a guide to remedying sleep deficits and alleviating insomnia.

Empson, Jacob, and Michael B. Wang. *Sleep and Dreaming*. 3d ed. New York: St. Martin's Press, 2002. An overview of scientific sleep research and popular beliefs about sleep.

Hobson, J. Allan. *Sleep*. Reprint. New York: W. H. Freeman, 1995. A broad and interdisciplinary view of sleep research, combining knowledge drawn from neurology, psychology, and animal behavior studies. The nontechnical language and lavish illustrations are two major advantages of this book. Highly recommended for high school and college students.

Jouvet, Michel. *The Paradox of Sleep*. Translated by Laurence Gary. Cambridge, Mass.: MIT Press, 1999. The scientist who discovered the relationship between REM sleep and dreaming discusses the stages of sleep, the meaning and evolutionary function of dreams, and many other topics.

Richard P. Atkinson

SEE ALSO: Brain structure; Circadian rhythms; Consciousness; Consciousness: Altered states; Dreams; Insomnia; Reticular formation; Sleep apnea syndromes and narcolepsy.

Sleep apnea syndromes and narcolepsy

TYPE OF PSYCHOLOGY: Consciousness
FIELDS OF STUDY: Sleep

Sleep apnea syndromes are a class of sleep disorders which result in repeated pauses in breathing during the night and cause repeated interruptions of the sleep cycle. Sleep apnea may be caused by physical obstruction of the upper airway or by neurological difficulties. Narcolepsy, another sleep disorder, is characterized by excessive daytime sleepiness, cataplexy, sleep paralysis, hypnagogic hallucinations, and irregular manifestations of REM sleep. The disorder is lifelong, and its origin is unknown.

KEY CONCEPTS

- apnea
- cataplexy
- electroencephalography
- hypnagogic hallucinations
- insomnia
- polysomnogram
- rapid eye movement (REM) sleep

INTRODUCTION

Sleep apnea syndromes include a variety of conditions, all of which result in the temporary cessation of breathing during sleep. Sleep apnea may affect people of all ages, but it is more common among elderly patients. Individuals with sleep apnea do not necessarily have breathing difficulty while awake, and while many people who do not have apnea experience pauses in breathing during sleep, sleep apnea patients experience much longer pauses (typically fifteen to sixty seconds), and these may occur one hundred to six hundred times per night. Three basic types of apnea exist: obstructive, central, and mixed.

SLEEP APNEAS

Obstructive sleep apnea (OSA) is caused by an obstruction of the upper airway during sleep and is the most common type of apnea. Breathing effort continues with OSA, but it is ineffective because of the patient's blocked airway. Individuals with OSA will commonly report that they experience excessive daytime sleepiness (EDS). Also, they snore loudly at night, which is a result of the vibration of tissues in the upper airway and the passage of air through a narrow airway. Another feature which is common in OSA patients is excessive body weight. OSA occurs more often in males than in females.

Children are also affected by this disorder; the most common cause is swelling of the tonsils. Therefore, all children are at risk of developing OSA, though some groups of children, such as those with Down syndrome, facial malformation, or muscular disorders, are more at risk than others. Children with OSA are typically underweight, because they usually have difficulty swallowing; they may even enjoy eating less because they are not able to smell or taste food as well as others.

Patients with obstructive sleep apnea frequently report falling asleep while driving, watching television, or reading, but some patients report little or no EDS. OSA patients may also experience intellectual or personality changes, which are usually related to EDS, but in severe cases may be attributable to lowered levels of oxygen reaching the brain. Another symptom associated with OSA is erectile impotence.

Central sleep apnea (CSA) is caused by a temporary absence of the effort to breathe while sleeping, and it is considered to be a rare disorder; fewer than 10 percent of all apnea patients experience CSA. CSA differs from OSA in that there is no obstruction of the upper airway and breathing effort does not continue as it does in OSA. Patients rarely have

CSA alone; the majority have both CSA and OSA episodes during the night. CSA is usually diagnosed when more than 55 percent of the episodes are central. Many authors point out that the mechanisms responsible for the two types of apnea may overlap; CSA may be attributable to a failure of the systems which monitor oxygen levels in the blood, resulting in the periodic loss of the breathing effort. CSA patients may experience between one hundred and three hundred episodes per night.

Central sleep apnea patients commonly complain of insomnia, which is poor, insufficient, or nonrefreshing sleep. Other symptoms associated with CSA are depression and decreased sexual drive. Patients with neurological disorders such as encephalitis, brain-stem tumor, and Shy-Drager syndrome may also have CSA. The range of disorders associated with CSA makes it difficult to make absolute statements about the cause of this form of apnea.

The third type of apnea is mixed sleep apnea (MSA). MSA is a pause in breathing which has both obstructive and central components. Most patients with MSA are generally considered to be similar to OSA patients in terms of symptoms, physical causes, and treatment options; however, there are also those MSA patients whose apneic episodes are characterized by long central components, and these individuals are more similar to CSA patients in terms of symptoms, cause, and treatment.

DSM-IV-TR Criteria for Sleep Apnea and Narcolepsy

BREATHING-RELATED SLEEP DISORDER (DSM CODE 780.59)

Sleep disruption, leading to excessive sleepiness or insomnia, judged to be due to sleep-related breathing condition (such as obstructive or central sleep apnea syndrome or central alveolar hypoventilation syndrome)

Disturbance not better accounted for by another mental disorder and not due to direct physiological effects of a substance or another general medical condition (other than a breathing-related disorder)

NARCOLEPSY (DSM CODE 347)

Irresistible attacks of refreshing sleep occurring daily over at least three months

Presence of one or both of the following:
- cataplexy (brief episodes of sudden bilateral loss of muscle tone, most often in association with intense emotion)
- recurrent intrusions of elements of rapid eye movement (REM) sleep into the transition between sleep and wakefulness, as manifested by either hypnopompic or hypnagogic hallucinations or sleep paralysis at beginning or end of sleep episodes

Disturbance not due to direct physiological effects of a substance or another general medical condition

NARCOLEPSY

Narcolepsy is a sleep disorder which includes symptoms such as EDS, overwhelming episodes of daytime sleep, disturbed nocturnal sleep, cataplexy (sudden, brief episodes of muscle weakness or paralysis which are emotionally triggered), hypnagogic hallucinations, sleep-onset rapid eye movement (REM) periods (or SOREMPs, the occurrence of REM sleep within fifteen minutes of sleep onset as indicated by electroencephalographic, or EEG, analysis), and sleep paralysis. Four symptoms—EDS, cataplexy, sleep paralysis, and hypnagogic hallucinations—are often referred to as the narcoleptic tetrad, although all four symptoms are rarely seen in the same patient. Narcoleptics rarely have problems falling asleep at night, but they do awaken more frequently and exhibit more body movements during sleep than normal subjects. Narcoleptics are also frequently disturbed by vivid dreams.

The EDS associated with narcolepsy is most often experienced during boring, sedentary situations, but it may also occur when the person is highly involved with a task. Though narcoleptics may awaken from a "sleep attack" feeling refreshed, narcoleptic sleepiness is persistent and cannot be alleviated by any amount of sleep. For years, many believed that the sleep attacks associated with narcolepsy could be attributable to a sudden urge to sleep, but more recent thought suggests that these sleep episodes may result from a sudden failure to resist the ever-present sleepiness that narcoleptics experience.

Not all patients with narcolepsy experience cataplexy. In a study to determine the differences between narcoleptics with cataplexy and those without cataplexy, it was determined that patients who experienced cataplexy had a higher prevalence of hallucinations, sleep paralysis, and nocturnal sleep disturbance. Thus, cataplectics generally seem to be more impaired both during sleep and while awake. For this reason, some have suggested that two groups of narcoleptic patients may exist: those with cataplexy and those without cataplexy. During a cataplectic episode, the narcoleptic patient maintains consciousness; however, if the episode is particularly long, the patient may enter REM sleep. Patients with severe cataplexy may experience complete paralysis in all but the respiratory muscles; these episodes can result in injury, although the most common episodes could be characterized by the patient dropping objects, losing posture, or halting motions.

Sleep paralysis in narcolepsy is experienced as the inability to move during the onset of sleep or upon awakening. These episodes may last from a few seconds to ten minutes and can be reversed by external stimuli such as another person touching the patient or calling his or her name. Sleep paralysis can be particularly frightening, although many patients learn that these episodes are usually brief and will end spontaneously. Adding to this fright, however, are the visual, auditory, or tactile hallucinations which may accompany sleep paralysis. Sleep

paralysis and hypnagogic hallucinations occur in about 60 percent of narcoleptic patients. Much like patients with sleep apnea, narcoleptics may exhibit psychopathology, but it is most likely related to effects of their disturbed sleep rather than to the sleep disorder itself.

EFFECTS

Individuals with apnea may repeatedly experience dangerously low levels of oxygen in their blood while sleeping. Oxygen is essential to the body's proper functioning, and if one does not receive the amount of oxygen the body needs, health may be affected in some way; heart disease and stroke are strongly associated with the occurrence of apnea. While it is not known if apnea actually causes these complications, the association is important nevertheless. Exposure to such low levels of oxygen in the blood over a prolonged period may result in increased blood pressure and poor circulation, as well as disturbance of heart rhythms.

Since both narcolepsy and apnea patients often experience nocturnal sleep difficulties, their quality and quantity of sleep are lowered. As a result, many patients with these disorders experience excessive daytime sleepiness. This may present itself as a problem during such activities as work or driving. Studies indicate that narcolepsy and apnea patients are more likely to have automobile accidents, poor job performance, and less job satisfaction than those without a sleep disorder, in part because these patients often fall asleep during such activities. Diagnosis of sleep apnea and narcolepsy in a sleep disorders clinic involves a number of measurements. The Multiple Sleep Latency Test measures the tendency of a patient to fall asleep during the day. This test, in addition to polysomnographic recording and the patient's medical history, aids in determining the proper treatment for these disorders.

TREATMENTS

Treatment of sleep apnea depends on a number of factors, which include frequency and type of apnea, quality of nighttime sleep, amount of oxygen in the blood during sleep, frequency and type of heart rhythm disturbance, and the tendency to sleep during waking hours. CSA patients may be treated using oxygen administration during sleep, which reduces the number of central apnea events, drug therapy, or mechanical ventilation, but all treatments for CSA have the potential to increase the occurrence of OSA in these patients. Various treatments available to patients with obstructive or mixed apnea include weight loss, drug therapy, surgery, and medical management.

Weight loss can be an important part of treatment for patients with OSA. In many cases, weight loss alone results in a reduction of the frequency and severity of apnea. Since adequate weight loss may take months, however, this option alone is not likely to be feasible for serious cases of apnea. Drug therapy has met with limited success in treating apnea patients, but many drugs are being studied that may prove effective in treating the disorder. Surgical treatment for severe cases of apnea was, in the past, limited to tracheostomy. More recently, however, removal of unnecessary tissue in the area of obstruction has been found to reduce apnea events significantly in certain patients. Facial reconstruction is also an option in more severe cases.

Treatments for apnea which involve medical management are constantly being developed. These include the insertion of a tube which bypasses the point of obstruction, allowing normal breathing to occur, and continuous positive airway pressure (CPAP). CPAP is a technique that uses air pressure to eliminate the closure of the airway in the nasal passages. In effect, CPAP provides a "splint" for the area that causes the obstruction; it also increases lung volume. This treatment is comfortable and easy to use for most patients and is thus very promising.

Treatments for narcolepsy all center on managing its symptoms, as there is no cure for narcolepsy itself. Fortunately, cataplexy, sleep paralysis, and hypnagogic hallucinations improve or disappear over time in approximately one-third of all narcoleptic patients. Medication may be prescribed to decrease the severity of daytime sleepiness, nocturnal sleep disturbance, and cataplexy. Regularly scheduled naps throughout the day may be used as an effective supplement to medication. Such naps may also reduce the need for medications by relieving the effects of insufficient sleep. Many doctors employ this method of treatment because it is important for patients to adjust their lifestyle in order to deal with the effects of narcolepsy.

SLEEP DISORDER STUDY

The scientific study of sleep began in the nineteenth century, although there was certainly interest in sleep prior to that time. Technological advances during the 1930's and 1940's allowed scientists to investigate the processes of sleep with more precision than before. In 1929, Hans Berger first recorded the EEG activity of humans. This development led to the discovery of patterns of brain-wave activity during sleep and the later description of REM sleep. This period of technological growth began the modern era of sleep studies; since that time, much has been learned about sleep and how it relates to other physiological processes.

Recognition of sleep apnea as a distinct sleep disorder began in 1966, and it is estimated today that as many as one in every thirty to fifty adults has sleep apnea to the extent that their quality of life is affected in some manner. Since its description, sleep apnea has received intensive investigation by a variety of medical specialists; in sleep apnea studies, it is not uncommon to see a heart surgeon working with a psychologist and a child specialist. This is attributable to the fact that sleep apnea can be the result of a number of physical or neurological problems, and it affects patients in a number of different ways.

Between one in one thousand and one in ten thousand women and men experience narcolepsy, and the usual age of onset is between fifteen and thirty-five. In half the cases, the onset of narcoleptic symptoms is preceded by severe psychological stress, an abrupt change in the sleep-wake schedule, or some other special circumstance. Scientists suspect a genetic factor in the occurrence of narcolepsy that may involve the immune system, but data also suggest that a strong environmental factor may play a role in the development of the disorder.

In an essay in *Principles and Practice of Sleep Medicine* (1989), Christian Guillemenault writes that the word "narcolepsy" was first used in 1880 to describe a pathological condition characterized by recurring, irresistible episodes of sleep which were of short duration. Interest in the disorder grew, and in 1960 it was discovered that a narcoleptic patient exhibited sleep-onset REM periods. This phenomenon became one of the cornerstone symptoms in the diagnosis of narcolepsy, and narcolepsy has since been described as primarily a disorder of REM sleep.

Investigation of sleep is showing how important sleep is to human physical and psychological health. Many theories exist which attempt to account for why people sleep; studies indicate that tissue restoration is enhanced during sleep, the ability to concentrate suffers if one is deprived of sleep for a significant period of time, and one may experience distinct mood changes without proper sleep. As stated earlier, cardiovascular complications are frequently associated with sleep apnea, as are work-related accidents and changes in intellectual ability. Sudden infant death syndrome (SIDS) is thought by some to be associated with sleep apnea. For these reasons, the study of sleep apnea, narcolepsy, and sleep in general is crucial to the health of many people. As psychologists and physicians further understand the processes involved in human and animal sleep, they will come closer to providing more effective treatment for patients with sleep apnea and narcolepsy.

SOURCES FOR FURTHER STUDY

American Psychiatric Association. *Diagnostic and Statistical Manual of Mental Disorders: DSM-IV-TR.* Rev. 4th ed. Washington, D.C.: Author, 2000. Overview of sleep disorders and narcolepsy emphasizing diagnostic categories and etiology.

Bradley, T. Douglas, and John S. Floras, eds. *Sleep Apnea: Implications in Cardiovascular and Cerebrovascular Disease.* New York: Marcel Dekker, 2000. Extensive monograph covers disruption of sleep, influence of normal sleep, effects of sleep apnea, and pathophysiological interactions of apnea and other systems.

Dement, William C. *Some Must Watch While Some Must Sleep.* San Francisco: W. H. Freeman, 1974. A book by a scientist who many consider to be the leading authority in the field of sleep studies. Easily read by high school or college students. Very informative; provides an excellent starting point for further study.

Fairbanks, David N. F., and Shiro Fujita, eds. *Snoring and Obstructive Sleep Apnea.* New York: Raven Press, 1994. Technical presentation for professionals. However, it can be used as reference for the public. Contains updates on surgical and nonsurgical interventions.

Guilleminault, Christian, and Markku Partinen, eds. *Obstructive Sleep Apnea Syndrome: Clinical Research and Treatment.* New York: Raven Press, 1990. Collection of research presentations and papers describing surgical and nonsurgical treatments for obstructive sleep apnea syndrome.

Loughlin, G. M., John L. Carroll, and Carole L. Marcus, eds. *Sleep and Breathing in Children: A Developmental Approach.* New York: Marcel Dekker, 2000. Highly technical collection of research on normal and abnormal children's breathing patterns and behaviors.

Alan K. Gibson and Shirley A. Albertson Ownes;
updated by Daniel L. Yazak

SEE ALSO: Attention; Brain injuries; Insomnia; Neurons; Sexual dysfunction; Sleep.

Smell and taste

TYPE OF PSYCHOLOGY: Sensation and perception
FIELDS OF STUDY: Auditory, chemical, cutaneous, and body senses

The senses of taste and smell, which are closely related, depend on sensory receptors known as chemoreceptors. These receptors detect molecules of various kinds and respond by generating nerve impulses. Chemoreception is believed to depend on proteins in receptor cell membranes that can recognize and combine with molecules from the environment.

KEY CONCEPTS
- adaptation
- chemoreceptors
- olfactory sensory neurons
- papillae
- taste buds

INTRODUCTION

The senses of taste and smell, which are closely related, depend on a type of sensory receptor cell known as a chemoreceptor. This receptor detects molecules of various kinds and responds on contact with them by generating nerve impulses. Although the basis for the detection is incompletely understood, chemoreceptor cells are believed to contain proteins in their surface membranes that are able to recognize and combine with various kinds of molecules. Combination with a recognized molecule causes the protein to open an ion channel in the surface membrane. The resulting ion flow creates an electrical change in the membrane that triggers generation of a nerve impulse by the chemoreceptor cell.

TASTE

Chemoreceptors for taste occur primarily on the upper surface of the tongue. A comparatively few taste receptors are also located on the roof of the mouth, particularly on the soft palate, and in the throat. The taste receptors in these locations are parts of taste buds, which are small, pear-shaped bundles of modified epithelial cells. Molecules from the exterior environment reach the taste receptor cells through a small pore at the top of a taste bud. All together, there are about ten thousand taste buds on the tongue and throat. The taste buds of the tongue, which are only 30 to 40 micrometers in diameter and thus microscopic, are embedded in the surfaces of small, moundlike outgrowths called papillae. The papillae give the surface of the tongue its rough or furry texture.

Taste receptor cells occur in taste buds along with other cells that play a purely supportive structural role. Individual taste receptor cells are elongated and bear thin, fingerlike extensions at their tips that protrude through the pore of a taste bud. Combination with chemicals from the environment, which must dissolve in the saliva of the mouth to reach the taste buds, probably occurs in the membranes of the fingerlike processes at the tips of the taste receptor cells. The opposite end of the taste receptor cells makes connections with sensory nerves serving the taste buds.

Each taste receptor cell probably has membrane proteins that can combine with a variety of molecules from the environment; however, individual taste cells, depending on their location on the tongue, typically combine more readily with some molecular types than with others. Taste cells with a preponderance of membrane proteins recognizing and combining with organic molecules, such as carbohydrates, alcohols, and amino acids, are crowded near the tip of the tongue. Combination of these taste receptors with organic molecules gives rise to nerve impulses that are interpreted in the brain as a sweet taste. Just behind the tip of the tongue is a region containing taste receptor cells that combine most readily with inorganic salts; combination with these substances gives rise to nerve impulses that are interpreted in the brain as a salty taste.

Farther to the rear of the tongue, particularly along the sides, are taste receptor cells that combine most readily with the hydrogen ions released by acids; this combination is perceived as a sour taste.

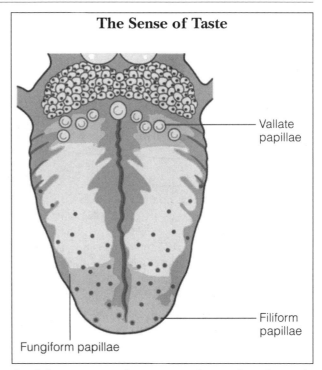

The Sense of Taste

Vallate papillae

Filiform papillae

Fungiform papillae

Specials receptors on the tongue send nerve impulses to the brain that are registered as the various tastes of bitter, sweet, salty, and sour. (Hans & Cassidy, Inc.)

The rear of the tongue contains taste receptor cells that combine most readily with a wide variety of organic and inorganic molecules, particularly long-chain organic molecules containing nitrogen and a group of organic substances called alkaloids. All the alkaloids, including molecules such as quinine, caffeine, morphine, and strychnine, give rise to a bitter taste. People tend to reject substances stimulating the bitter taste receptors at the rear of the tongue. This may have a survival value, because many bitter substances, including alkaloids produced by a variety of plants, are strongly poisonous. Many of the organic molecules with a bitter taste differ from those with a sweet taste by only minor chemical groups. A few substances, such as pepper, primarily stimulate pain rather than taste receptors when present in foods. Trigeminal nerves in the nose and mouth also contribute a generalized chemical sensitivity sometimes referred to as chemesthesis. Trigeminal response describes the fizzy tingle from carbonated beverages, the pungency of mustard or horseradish, and the irritant response to hot peppers or raw onions.

The distribution on the tongue of regions of strongest taste does not mean that the taste receptor cells in these areas are limited to detecting only sweet, salty, sour, or bitter substances; all regions of the tongue can detect molecules of each type to at least some extent. Four pairs of nerves innervate the tongue, making the sense of taste difficult to degrade substantially even during disease or the aging process.

Traditionally, the wide range of different flavors that humans can differentiate, which easily amounts to thousands, has been considered to be the result of subtle combinations of the four primary flavors: sweet, salty, sour, and bitter. There are indications, however, that the picture may be considerably more complex than this. Other taste categories which have been proposed include metallic, astringent, and umami. Persons can be "taste-blind" for certain very specific, single molecules, such as the chemical phenylthiocarbamide (PTC). The ability to taste this substance, which has a bitter flavor, is hereditary; some persons can taste PTC, and some cannot. The pattern of inheritance suggests that a membrane protein able to combine with PTC is present in some persons and not in others. Persons taste-blind for PTC do not have the specific membrane protein and cannot respond to the presence of the chemical even though other bitter flavors can be detected. It is possible that there are a wide variety of specific membrane proteins like the one responsible for detecting PTC distributed in the surface membranes of the taste receptor cells of the tongue. On the other hand, there are also "supertasters" of PTC who are hypersensitive to the taste.

SMELL

The chemoreceptors responsible for the other chemical sense, the sense of smell, are located within the head at the roof of the nasal cavity. The receptor cells detecting odors, called olfactory cells,

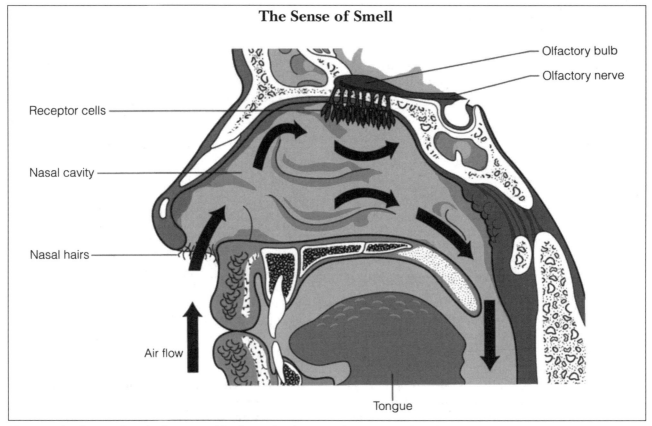

The Sense of Smell

Olfactory bulb

Olfactory nerve

Receptor cells

Nasal cavity

Nasal hairs

Air flow

Tongue

Receptors in the nasal cavity interact with odor molecules to send nerve impulses through the olfactory nerve that are registered as various smells. (Hans & Cassidy, Inc.)

are distributed among supportive cells in a double patch of tissue totaling about 5 square centimeters in area. Although limited to this area, the olfactory region contains between 10 and 100 million olfactory cells in the average person. Unlike taste receptor cells, olfactory receptor cells are nerve cells, often called olfactory sensory neurons.

Each olfactory cell bears between ten and twenty fine, fibrous extensions, or cilia, that protrude into a layer of mucus that covers the olfactory area. The membranes of the extensions contain the protein molecules that recognize and combine with chemicals to trigger a nerve impulse by an olfactory cell. In order to reach the fibrous extensions, molecules detected as odors must dissolve in the mucous solution covering the olfactory region.

The olfactory sensory neurons have a long arm, or dendrite, that extends to the surface of the nasal passage and ends in a knoblike swelling. From these knobs protrude ten to thirty fine hairs, or cilia. The cilia reach through a layer of mucus. The olfactory sensory neurons have another arm, or axon, which extends through the bony shelf of the cranium into the region of the brain called the olfactory bulb. Short axons terminate in globular structures called glomeruli. Additional neurons in the glomeruli send axons through the olfactory tract into the central nervous system.

Efforts to identify primary odors equivalent to the primary sweet, salty, sour, and bitter flavors have been largely unsuccessful. Studies of the genetic coding for the olfactory receptor proteins suggest that as many as one hundred to one thousand primary olfactory sensations exist. Similar to taste blindness for PTC, discrete odor blindness has been identified for more than fifty substances.

ADAPTATION

The chemoreceptors responsible for the senses of taste and smell typically adapt rapidly to continued stimulation by the same molecules. In adaptation, a receptor cell generates nerve impulses most rapidly when first stimulated; with continued stimulation at the same intensity, the frequency of nerve impulses drops steadily until a baseline of a relatively few impulses per second is reached. Adaptation for the senses of taste and smell also involves complex interactions in the brain, because discernment of tastes and smells continues to diminish even after chemoreceptors reach their baselines.

For the sense of taste, adaptation is reflected in the fact that the first bite of food, for example, has the most intensely perceived taste. As stimulation by the same food continues, the intensity of the taste and a person's perception of the flavor steadily decrease. If a second food is tasted, the initial intensity of its taste is high, but again intensity drops off with continued stimulation. If the first food is retasted, however, its flavor will again seem stronger. This effect occurs because adaptation of the receptors detecting the initial taste lessens during the period during which the second food is tasted. If sufficient time passes before the first food is retasted, the flavor will appear to be almost as strong as its first taste. For this reason, one gains greater appreciation of a meal if foods are alternated rather than eaten and finished separately.

Taste receptor cells have a life expectancy of about ten days. As they degenerate, they are constantly replaced by new taste cells that continually differentiate from tissue at the sides of taste buds. As humans reach middle age, the rate of replacement drops off, so that the total number of taste receptor cells declines steadily after the age of about forty-five. This may account for the fact that, as people get older, nothing ever seems to taste as good as it did in childhood. Smoking also decreases the sensitivity of taste receptor cells and thereby decreases a person's appreciation and appetite for foods.

Olfactory cells also adapt rapidly to the continued presence of the same molecules and slow or stop generating nerve impulses if the concentration of the odoriferous substances is maintained. This response is also reflected in common experience. When engaged in an odor-generating activity such as cooking or interior painting, a person is strongly aware of the odors generated by the activity only initially. After exposure for more than a few minutes, the person's perception of the odor lessens and eventually disappears almost completely. If the person leaves the odoriferous room for a few minutes, however, allowing the olfactory receptors and brain centers to lose their adaptation, the person is usually surprised at the strength of the odor if he or she returns to the room.

The region at the top of the nasal cavity containing the olfactory cells lies outside the main stream of air entering the lungs through the mouth and nose. As a result, the molecules dissolving in the mucous layer covering the olfactory cells are carried to this region only by side eddies of the airflow through the nose. Flow to the olfactory region is greatly improved by sniffing, a response used by all air-breathing vertebrates as a way to increase the turbulence in the nasal passages and thereby to intensify odors from the environment. Head colds interfere with people's sense of smell through congestion and blockage of the nasal cavity, which impedes airflow to the olfactory region.

Although humans are not nearly as sensitive to odors as are many other animals, their ability to detect some substances by smell is still remarkable, particularly in the case of smells generated by putrefaction. Some of the mercaptans, for example, which are generated in decaying flesh, can be detected in concentrations in air as small as 0.0000000002 milligram per milliliter. One of these substances, methyl mercaptan, is mixed in low concentration in natural gas. The presence of this mercaptan allows people to detect natural gas, which otherwise would be odorless, by smell.

HISTORY, GENETICS AND RESPONSES

The idea that taste and smell receptors operate by recognizing specific molecular types is an old one, dating back to the first century B.C.E., when Titus Lucretius Carus proposed that the sense of smell depends on recognition of atomic shapes. Definitive experimental demonstration of this mechanism for the sense of smell, however, was not obtained until 1991, when Linda Buck and Richard Axel finally isolated members of a large family of membrane proteins that can actually do what Lucretius proposed: They recognize and bind specific molecular types and trigger responses by olfactory cells. Axel and Buck have obtained indications that there are hundreds of different proteins in the family responsible for molecular recognition in the sense of smell.

One of the many interesting features of the family is that, as with the sense of taste, many people inherit a deficiency in one or more of the membrane proteins so that they are congenitally unable to detect a particular odor. There are in fact many thousands of different odors to which persons may be insensitive, which directly supports the idea that the family of membrane proteins responsible for detecting individual molecular types is very large indeed. Another interesting feature of the mechanism is that there are many odors for which people must be "educated." People cannot recognize them on first encounter but later learn to discern them. This indicates that membrane proteins recognizing previously unknown molecules may be induced; that is, they may be newly synthesized and placed in olfactory cell membranes in response to encountering a new chemical in the environment. People can also smell, and often taste, artificial substances never before encountered by humans or indeed any other animal. Thus, the chemoreceptors have membrane proteins capable of recognizing molecules not encountered in animal evolution.

Both taste and smell receptors are linked through nerve connections to regions of the brain stem that control visceral responses, as well as to the areas of the cerebral cortex registering conscious sensations. As a result, different odors and tastes may give rise to a host of involuntary responses, such as salivation, appetite, thirst, pleasure, excitement, sexual arousal, nausea, or even vomiting, as well as to consciously perceived sensations. The odor of a once-enjoyed food may make someone ill in the future if the person became sick after eating the food; previously unobjectionable or even pleasant odors and tastes may become unpleasant and nauseating to women during pregnancy. The odor of other foods, such as some of the ranker cheeses, may be repulsive at first experience but later become appetizing as a person learns to enjoy them. The degree to which many substances are perceived as pleasant or unpleasant is also related to their concentration. Many substances perceived as pleasantly sweet in low concentration, for example, taste bitter and unpleasant at higher concentrations.

SOURCES FOR FURTHER STUDY

Firestein, Stuart. "How the Olfactory System Makes Sense of Scents." *Nature* 413 (September, 2001): 211-218. The author provides a review of the anatomical organization of the sensory neurons and how signal transduction works. Although fairly sophisticated with biochemistry explanations, the summaries are easily understood by the high school reader.

Guyton, Arthur C. *Textbook of Medical Physiology.* 9th ed. Philadelphia: W. B. Saunders, 1996. Chapter 53, "The Chemical Senses: Taste and Smell," presents information on the sensation of taste and the sense of smell, as well as on receptors, nerve transmission, and responses. Intended for college and medical students, but easily understood by readers at the high school level.

Lawless, Harry T., and Hildegarde Heymann. *Sensory Valuation of Food: Principles and Practices.* Gaithersburg, Md.: Aspen, 1999. Chapter 2, "Physiological and Psychological Foundations of Sensory Function," presents the physiology of taste and sensory interactions, as well as information on sensory testing and psychological methods. Intended for college students, but easily understood by readers at the high school level.

Lindemann, Bernd. "Receptors and Transduction in Taste." *Nature* 413 (September, 2001). The author presents information on receptor functioning for taste, as well as additional information on umami and taste interactions. Although fairly explicit in its biochemistry, the summary and descriptions are clear enough to be understood by nonscientists.

Stephen L. Wolfe;
updated by Karen Chapman-Novakofski

SEE ALSO: Hearing; Sensation and perception; Signal detection theory; Taste aversion; Touch and pressure; Vision: Brightness and contrast; Vision: Color; Visual system.

Social identity theory

TYPE OF PSYCHOLOGY: Social psychology
FIELDS OF STUDY: Prejudice and discrimination

Social identity theory examines the relationship between group membership and self-esteem. It has provided insights into intergroup conflict, ethnocentrism, cultural affirmation, and self-hatred, predicting both individual and group responses to an unfavorable self-concept.

KEY CONCEPTS
- distinctiveness
- in-group bias
- minimal group situation
- personal identity
- self-image
- social categorization
- social change approach
- social comparison
- social mobility

INTRODUCTION

Social identity theory maintains that all individuals are motivated to achieve and maintain a positive self-concept. A person's self-concept derives from two principal sources: personal identity and social identity. Personal identity includes one's individual traits, achievements, and qualities. Social identity includes the group affiliations that are recognized as being part of the self, such as one's image of oneself as a Protestant, a blue-collar worker, or a conservative. Some individuals emphasize the personal aspects in their quest for a favorable self-image, while others emphasize their social identities. Social identity theory focuses on the latter. It attempts to explain when and how individuals transform their group affiliations to secure a favorable self-concept.

Psychologist Henri Tajfel introduced social identity theory in 1978. The theory maintains that a person's social identity emerges from the natural process of social categorization. People categorize, or classify, themselves and other people by many criteria, including occupation, religious affiliation, political orientation, ethnicity, economic class, and gender. An individual automatically identifies with some categories and rejects others. This creates a distinction between "in-groups," with which one identifies, and "out-groups," with which one does not identify. A person who identifies himself or herself as a Democrat, for example, would consider other Democrats members of the in-group and would view Republicans as members of the out-group. Individuals inevitably compare their groups with other groups; the goal of the comparisons is to establish the superiority of one's own group, or the group's "positive distinctiveness," on some level, such as affluence, cultural heritage, or spirituality. If the comparison shows that the individual's group memberships are positive and valuable, the social identities become an important part of the self. If, however, one's group appears inferior, one's self-image acquires "negative distinctiveness." The individual is then motivated to acquire a more satisfactory self-concept.

ENHANCING SELF-CONCEPT

Tajfel and John Turner proposed three strategies that can be used to enhance one's self-concept:

"exit," "pass," and "voice." The first two strategies represent attempts to validate the self. Both involve rejecting or distancing oneself from the devalued group to improve identity; both presume the existence of social mobility—an individual-based strategy for image enhancement whereby a person "exits" an inferior group or "passes" as a member of a more prestigious group. Exit involves simply leaving the group. This response is possible only within flexible social systems that permit individual mobility. Although individuals cannot usually shed affiliations such as race or gender, they can openly discard other affiliations, such as "Buick owner" or "public school advocate." If dissatisfied with an automobile, one trades it in for another; if unhappy with the public school system, one may exit and move one's children into a private school. Pass, a more private response, occurs when individuals with unfavorable group memberships are not recognized as belonging to that group. A Jew may pass as a Gentile, for example, or a fair-skinned black person may pass as a Caucasian. Typically in such cases, the objective features that link the individual to the devalued group are absent or unnoticeable.

Voice, the final strategy for identity improvement, is a collective response: Group members act together to alter the group's image and elevate its social value. Also called the "social change" approach, it is common in rigid social systems in which individual movement away from the disparaged group is impossible. It also occurs when psychological forces such as cultural and personal values bind the individual to the group. Members of such physically identifiable groups as women, blacks, or Asians might adopt the social change strategy, for example, as might such cultural or religious group members as Irish Catholics or Orthodox Jews.

Voice is a complex response. Simply recognizing that social mobility is blocked for members of one's own group is insufficient to prompt social change activity. Two additional perceptions of the overall social structure are important: its stability and its legitimacy. Stability is concerned with how fixed or secure the social hierarchy seems. Theoretically, no group is completely secure in its relative superiority; even groups that historically have been considered superior must work to maintain their favored position. If members of a denigrated group believe that alternatives to the current social hierarchy are possible, they are encouraged to reassess their own value.

Legitimacy, in contrast, involves the bases for a group's negative distinctiveness. If a group believes that its social inferiority is attributable to illegitimate causes, such as discrimination in hiring practices or educational opportunities, group members will be more likely to challenge their inferior position.

SOCIAL CREATIVITY AND DIRECT COMPETITION

Voice challenges to negative distinctiveness take two general forms: social creativity and direct competition. Social creativity involves altering or redefining the elements of comparison. The group's social positions and resources, however, need not be altered. In one approach, a group may simply limit the groups with which it compares itself, focusing on groups that are similar. A group of factory workers may choose to compare itself with warehouse workers or postal employees rather than with a group of advertising executives. This approach increases the chances that the outcome of the comparison will be favorable to one's own group. The group might also identify a new area of comparison, such as bilingual fluency, in its effort to enhance group distinctiveness.

Finally, the group might recast some of its denigrated attributes so that its value is reassessed. A new appreciation for group history and culture often emerges from this process. The Civil Rights movement, an important force for social change in the 1960's, caused this to occur. In the context of that movement, the label "Negro" was replaced by "black," which was recast by African Americans to symbolize group pride. Under the slogan "Black is beautiful," the natural look became more valued than the traditional European American model. African Americans were less likely to lighten or straighten their hair or use makeup to make their skin appear lighter.

Direct competition, in contrast, involves altering the group's social position. It is often an institutional response; consequently, it encourages competition among groups. Displaced groups target institutions and policies, demanding resources in an effort to empower the group politically and economically. In the 1960's, for example, black students demonstrated for curricular changes at colleges and universities. They demanded greater relevance in existing courses and the development of Black Studies programs to highlight the group's social and political contributions. In the 1970's, the women's movement demanded economic and political changes, including equal pay for equal work, and greater individual rights for women, such as abortion rights and institutionalized child care.

IN-GROUP BIAS

Social identity theory has been used to explain several intergroup processes. Among these are the phenomenon known as in-group bias (observed in laboratory experiments) and the actions of some subordinate groups to challenge their relative inferiority through collective (voice) approaches. The response of African Americans in the 1950's and 1960's to negative perceptions of their group illustrates the latter process.

In-group bias is the tendency to favor one's own group over other groups. In laboratory experiments, young subjects have been put in groups according to simple and fairly arbitrary criteria, such as the type of artwork they preferred. The goal was to establish a "minimal group situation": an artificial social order in which subjects could be easily differentiated but which was free of any already existing conflicts. Once categorized, subjects were asked to perform one of several tasks, such as distributing money, assigning points, evaluating the different groups, or interpreting group members' behavior. In all the tasks, subjects repeatedly showed a preference for their own groups. They gave to in-group members significantly more points and money than they gave to out-group members—despite a lack of previous interaction among the subjects. When describing in-group members, they attributed altruistic behavior to the person's innate virtuous and admirable qualities rather than to outside causes. When describing out-group members, however, they reversed the pattern, attributing altruistic behavior to situational factors and hostile behavior to personal character. Thus, even without any history of competition, ideological differences, or hostility over scarce resources, subjects consistently demonstrate a preference for their in-group.

Social identity theory predicts this pattern. The powerful need to achieve a positive self-image motivates a person to establish the value of his or her group memberships. Since groups strongly contribute to an individual's self-image, the individual works to enhance the group's image. Group successes are, by extension, the individual's successes. Daily life offers many examples of group allegiance, ranging from identification with one's country to support of one's hometown baseball team. Experiments in social identity suggest that ethnocentrism, or the belief in the superiority of one's own ethnic group, serves important psychological needs.

STUDY OF NEGATIVE GROUP SELF-IMAGE

Social identity theory also explains why some subordinate groups challenge their relative inferiority through rebellion or social change while others do not. The theory predicts that individuals who are objectively bound to negatively distinct groups—by gender or skin color, for example—will have fewer options for self-enhancement. Because they are driven by the powerful need to obtain a worthy self-image, however, they are unlikely to engage in self-hatred by accepting the denigrated image imposed on them by others. Instead, they will engage in some form of voice, the collective approach to image improvement.

Psychologists studying social identity do not directly explore the historical background of a group's negative self-image. Rather, they perform laboratory experiments and field studies designed to determine individuals' actual perceptions of groups—how individuals identify groups and whether they see them as having a positive or negative image. Social psychologists also attempt to measure the changes that occur in group self-image over time; they can then infer that social or political movements have affected that image. Studies involving African American children—for whom the essential identifying element is a physical one, race—provide an example.

In the landmark 1954 Supreme Court decision *Brown v. Board of Education*, which mandated school desegregation, social scientists presented evidence that educational segregation produced feelings of inferiority in black children. Support was drawn in part from a 1947 study by Kenneth and Mamie Clark, in which they compared the preferences of black and white children between the ages of three and seven for dolls with either dark or fair skin tones. Approximately 60 percent of the black children said that the fair-skinned doll was the "nicer" doll, the "nicer color" doll, or the doll they "preferred to play with." The dark-skinned doll, by contrast, "looked bad." Based on a combination of this negative self-image and the fact that African Americans are objectively bound to their group by their race, social identity theory would predict collective action for social change.

COLLECTIVE ACTIVITY AND POSITIVE SELF-IDENTITY

The Civil Rights movement embodied that collective, or voice, activity, and it offered blacks a new context within which to evaluate black identity. Results from studies performed in the 1970's suggest that, indeed, there was a significant rise in black self-esteem during that period. A replication of the Clarks' study by other researchers showed a clear preference for the dark-skinned doll among black children. Later analyses of comparable doll studies showed that such preferences for one's own group were most common among young subjects from areas with large black populations and active black pride movements.

A positive self-image may also emerge when social and cultural themes and historical events are reinterpreted within a group. A group's cultural image may be emphasized; its music, art, and language then become valued. To continue using the African American example, in the twentieth century, black music, which once had been the music of the oppressed—work songs and spirituals—evolved into a music that communicated ethnic identity in a new way. Blues and jazz became a focus of group pride; jazz, in particular, become renowned worldwide. The acceptance of jazz as a valuable art form by people of many races and nationalities illustrates another frequent outcome of activity for generating a positive self-concept: It often initiates a response from the larger society that improves the group's relative position in that society.

PERSONAL AND INTELLECTUAL ORIGINS

Social identity theory evolved from a series of experiments conducted in England at the University of Bristol in the 1970's. Originated by social psychologist Henri Tajfel, the theory represents the collaborative efforts of Michael Billig, John Turner, and several other European associates over a decade-long period.

Like many social science theories, social identity theory has both personal and intellectual origins. Tajfel's own identity as a European Jew who survived World War II contributed significantly to his desire to understand conflicts between groups. His early work in the psychology of prejudice and his personal distrust of reductionist or oversimplified mod-

els of psychological processes laid the foundation for the theory. Other concepts, including stereotypes, values, ethnocentrism, and the social psychology of minorities, became incorporated into the theory; these themes contributed to the attractiveness of the theory in Europe, a region recognized for its religious, linguistic, and social diversity and for the conflicts this diversity has caused.

RELATED GROUP RESEARCH

Group processes have long been emphasized in American social psychology, but the main thrusts have varied over the years. Kurt Lewin's work in the late 1940's, for example, focused on leadership in small groups; research in the mid-1950's examined the relationship of intergroup contact to prejudice and discrimination. In the late 1950's, Muzafer Sherif studied intergroup relations in socially created groups that he and his colleagues observed in real-life settings for extended periods of time. In the 1960's, however, internal conflicts in the field of social psychology led to the development of two distinct subdisciplines: sociological social psychology and psychological social psychology. Intergroup relations began to seem too sociological a topic for psychologists to study. This split, coupled with a renewed emphasis on studying individual cognitive processes, resulted in the displacement of intergroup studies in American social psychology in the 1970's.

Social identity theory revived American research on intergroup relations in the early to mid-1980's. Following more than a decade of political and social turmoil in the United States, social psychologists were looking for better ways to understand conflict between groups. They began to ask new questions and to adopt a wider variety of methodologies, including surveys and field studies. Race, class, and gender were recognized as critical psychological variables. The "group member," an individual with a sociocultural history that affected social behavior, became accepted as a respectable research subject. Social identity theory provided both theorists and researchers with a broad paradigm from which to investigate intergroup conflict, group identification, ethnocentrism, hostility, and social change strategies.

The three central psychological processes—motivation, emotion, and cognition—are incorporated into social identity theory in a logical and sophisticated manner. Earlier social psychological theories usually emphasized one or two of those processes.

Both comprehensive and complex, the theory offers a way of understanding a wide range of psychological topics.

SOURCES FOR FURTHER STUDY

Brown, R. "Intergroup Relations." In *Introduction to Social Psychology*, edited by Miles Hewstone, Wolfgang Stroebe, Jean-Paul Codol, and G. Stephenson. New York: Basil Blackwell, 1988. Brown summarizes intergroup relations literature in this accessible chapter in a social psychology textbook. Locates social identity theory in the broader context of intergroup relations and explains important terms clearly, providing excellent examples; can be understood by the college or high school student.

Ellmers, Naomi, Russell Spears, and Bertjan Doosje, eds. *Social Identity*. New York: Blackwell, 1999. A collection of essays on contemporary social identity research, covering theoretical issues and empirical research, including perceptions of self and others, communication between groups, and behavioral consequences of social identity issues.

Messick, David M., and Diane M. Mackie. "Intergroup Relations." In *Annual Review of Psychology*. Vol. 40. Stanford, Calif.: Annual Reviews, 1989. Reviews intergroup relations theory and research from a cognitive perspective. Categorization, ingroup and out-group effects, and intergroup bias are emphasized. Tajfel's social identity theory dominates the section on intergroup bias; his work is examined and critiqued. Variants of social identity theory are discussed.

Tajfel, Henri. *Human Groups and Social Categories*. Cambridge, England: Cambridge University Press, 1981. An easy-to-read account of Tajfel's conceptualization of intergroup conflict, accessible to college students. This book incorporates his early work on prejudice, essays on social perception and categorization, stereotypes, children's images of insiders and outsiders, and social identity theory. Includes both theory and research, emphasizing descriptions of the former. Tajfel provides an extensive bibliography.

_____, ed. *Differentiation Between Social Groups: Studies in the Social Psychology of Intergroup Relations*. London: Academic Press, 1978. Presents the work of the team of European social psychologists that conceptualized and formalized social identity theory. Thorough and detailed, it is important to those who wish to replicate key experiments or to understand the empirical and theoretical foundations of the theory.

Tajfel, Henri, and John Turner. "The Social Identity Theory of Intergroup Behavior." In *Social Psychology of Intergroup Relations*, edited by Stephen Worchel and William G. Austin. 2d ed. Chicago: Nelson-Hall, 1986. An excellent summary of social identity theory. This chapter focuses on the origin and importance of the theory, including intergroup competition and conflict. It offers examples of the concepts and attempts to answer practical questions.

Turner, John C. *Rediscovering the Social Group: A Self-Categorization Theory*. New York: Basil Blackwell, 1987. Turner's book argues for the group as an important social phenomenon and articulates assumptions made about the relationship between the individual and the group in social identity theory. Provides the reader with a valuable backdrop for understanding many of Tajfel's predictions in a readable blend of theoretical and empirical work.

Jaclyn Rodriguez

SEE ALSO: Aggression; Attributional biases; Causal attribution; Groups; Intergroup relations; Prejudice; Racism; Self-esteem; Social perception; Social schemata.

Social learning

Albert Bandura

TYPE OF PSYCHOLOGY: Personality
FIELDS OF STUDY: Behavioral and cognitive models; cognitive learning

Albert Bandura's social learning theory, later called social cognitive theory, provides a theoretical framework for understanding and explaining human behavior; the theory embraces an interactional model of causation and accords central roles to cognitive, vicarious, and self-regulatory processes.

KEY CONCEPTS
- determinism
- model

- observational learning
- outcome expectancies
- reciprocal determinism
- reinforcement
- self-efficacy

INTRODUCTION

Social learning theory, later amplified as social cognitive theory by its founder, social psychologist Albert Bandura, provides a unified theoretical framework for analyzing the psychological processes that govern human behavior. Its goal is to explain how behavior develops, how it is maintained, and through what processes it can be modified. It seeks to accomplish this task by identifying the determinants of human action and the mechanisms through which they operate.

Bandura lays out the conceptual framework of his approach in his book *Social Learning Theory* (1977). His theory is based on a model of reciprocal determinism. This means that Bandura rejects both the humanist and existentialist position viewing people as free agents and the behaviorist position viewing behavior as controlled by the environment. Rather, external determinants of behavior (such as rewards and punishments) and internal determinants (such as thoughts, expectations, and beliefs) are considered part of a system of interlocking determinants that influence not only behavior but also the various other parts of the system. In other words, each part of the system—behavior, cognition, and environmental influences—affects each of the other parts. People are neither free agents nor passive reactors to external pressures. Instead, through self-regulatory processes, they have the ability to exercise some measure of control over their own actions. They can affect their behavior by setting goals, arranging environmental inducements, generating cognitive strategies, evaluating goal attainment, and mediating consequences for their actions. Bandura accepts that these self-regulatory functions initially are learned as the result of external rewards and punishments. Their external origin, however, does not invalidate the fact that, once internalized, they in part determine behavior.

COGNITIVE MEDIATING FACTORS

As self-regulation results from symbolic processing of information, Bandura in his theorizing assigned an increasingly prominent role to cognition. This was reflected in his book *Social Foundations of Thought and Action: A Social Cognitive Theory* (1986), in which he no longer referred to his approach as social learning but as social cognitive theory. People, unlike lower animals, use verbal and nonverbal symbols (language and images) to process information and preserve experiences in the form of cognitive representations. This encoded information serves as a guide for future behavior. Without the ability to use symbols, people would have to solve problems by enacting various alternative solutions until, by trial and error, they learned which ones resulted in rewards or punishments. Through their cognitive abilities, however, people can think through different options, imagine possible outcomes, and guide their behavior by anticipated consequences. Symbolic capabilities provide people with a powerful tool to regulate their own behavior in the absence of external reinforcements and punishments.

According to Bandura, the most central of all mechanisms of self-regulation is self-efficacy, defined as the belief that one has the ability, with one's actions, to bring about a certain outcome. Self-efficacy beliefs function as determinants of behavior by influencing motivation, thought processes, and emotions in ways that may be self-aiding or self-hindering. Specifically, self-efficacy appraisals determine the goals people set for themselves, whether they anticipate and visualize scenarios of success or failure, whether they embark on a course of action, how much effort they expend, and how long they persist in the face of obstacles. Self-efficacy expectations are different from outcome expectations. While outcome expectancies are beliefs that a given behavior will result in a certain outcome, self-efficacy refers to the belief in one's ability to bring about this outcome. To put it simply, people may believe that something can happen, but whether they embark on a course of action depends on their perceived ability to make it happen.

RELEVANCE TO OBSERVATION AND MODELING

Perhaps the most important contribution of social learning theory to the understanding of human behavior is the concept of vicarious, or observational, learning, also termed learning through modeling. Before the advent of social learning theory, many psychologists assigned a crucial role to the process of reinforcement in learning. They postulated that without performing responses that are followed by reinforcement or punishment, a person cannot learn. In contrast, Bandura asserted that much of social behavior is not learned from the consequences of trial and error but is acquired through symbolic modeling. People watch what other people do and what happens to them as a result of their actions. From such observations, they form ideas of how to perform new behaviors, and later this information guides their actions.

Symbolic modeling is of great significance for human learning because of its enormous efficiency in transmitting information. Whereas trial-and-error learning requires the gradual shaping of the behavior of individuals through repetition and reinforcement, in observational learning, a single model can teach complex behaviors simultaneously to any number of people. According to Bandura, some elaborate and specifically human behavior patterns, such as language, might even be impossible to learn if it were not for symbolic modeling. For example, it seems unlikely that children learn to talk as a result of their parents' reinforcing each correct utterance they emit. Rather, children probably hear and watch other members of their verbal community talk and then imitate their behavior. In a similar vein, complex behaviors such as driving a car or flying a plane are not acquired by trial and error. Instead, prospective drivers or pilots follow the verbal rules of an instructor until they master the task.

In summary, Bandura's social learning theory explains human action in terms of the interplay among behavior, cognition, and environmental influences. The theory places particular emphasis on cognitive mediating factors such as self-efficacy beliefs and outcome expectancies. Its greatest contribution to a general theory of human learning has been its emphasis on learning by observation or modeling. Observational learning has achieved the status of a third learning principle, next to classical and operant conditioning.

STUDIES OF LEARNING AND PERFORMANCE

From its inception, social learning theory has served as a useful framework for the understanding of both normal and abnormal human behavior. A major contribution that has important implications for the modification of human behavior is the theory's distinction between learning and performance. In a now-classic series of experiments, Bandura and his associates teased apart the roles of observation

and reinforcement in learning and were able to demonstrate that people learn through mere observation.

In a study on aggression, an adult model hit and kicked a life-size inflated clown doll (a "Bobo" doll), with children watching the attack in person or on a television screen. Other children watched the model perform some innocuous behavior. Later, the children were allowed to play in the room with the Bobo doll. All children who had witnessed the aggression, either in person or on television, viciously attacked the doll, while those who had observed the model's innocuous behavior did not display aggression toward the doll. Moreover, it was clearly shown that the children modeled their aggressive behaviors after the adult. Those who had observed the adult sit on the doll and hit its face, or kick the doll, or use a hammer to pound it, imitated exactly these behaviors. Thus, the study accomplished its purpose by demonstrating that observational learning occurs in the absence of direct reinforcement.

In a related experiment, Bandura showed that expected consequences, while not relevant for learning, play a role in performance. A group of children watched a film of an adult model behaving aggressively toward a Bobo doll and being punished, while another group observed the same behavior with the person being rewarded. When the children subsequently were allowed to play with the Bobo doll, those who had watched the model being punished displayed fewer aggressive behaviors toward the doll than those who had seen the model being rewarded. When the experimenter then offered a reward to the children for imitating the model, however, all children, regardless of the consequences they had observed, attacked the Bobo doll. This showed that all children had learned the aggressive behavior from the model but that observing the model being punished served as an inhibiting factor until it was removed by the promise of a reward. Again, this study showed that children learn without reinforcement, simply by observing how others behave. Whether they then engage in the behavior, however, depends on the consequences they expect will result from their actions.

DISINHIBITORY EFFECTS

Models not only teach people novel ways of thinking and behaving but also can strengthen or weaken inhibitions. Seeing models punished may inhibit similar behavior in observers, while seeing models carry out feared or forbidden actions without negative consequences may reduce their inhibitions.

The most striking demonstrations of the disinhibitory effects of observational learning come from therapeutic interventions based on modeling principles. Baudura, in his book *Principles of Behavior Modification* (1969), shows how social learning theory can provide a conceptual framework for the modification of a wide range of maladaptive behaviors. For example, a large number of laboratory studies of subjects with a severe phobia of snakes showed that phobic individuals can overcome their fear of reptiles when fearless adult models demonstrate how to handle a snake and directly assist subjects in coping successfully with whatever they dread.

SELF-EFFICACY MECHANISM

In later elaborations, the scope of social learning theory was amplified to include self-efficacy theory. Self-efficacy is now considered the principal mechanism of behavior change, in that all successful interventions are assumed to operate by strengthening a person's self-perceived efficacy to cope with difficulties.

How can self-efficacy be strengthened? Research indicates that it is influenced by four sources of information. The most important influence comes from performance attainments, with successes heightening and failures lowering perceived self-efficacy. Thus, having people enact and master a difficult task most powerfully increases their efficacy percepts. A second influence comes from vicarious experiences. Exposing people to models works because seeing people similar to oneself successfully perform a difficult task raises one's own efficacy expectations. Verbal persuasion is a third way of influencing self-efficacy. Convincing people that they have the ability to perform a task can encourage them to try harder, which indeed may lead to successful performance. Finally, teaching people coping strategies to lower emotional arousal can also increase self-efficacy. If subsequently they approach a task more calmly, the likelihood of succeeding at it may increase.

Bandura and his associates conducted a series of studies to test the idea that vastly different modes of influence all improve coping behavior by strengthening self-perceived efficacy. Severe snake phobics received interventions based on enactive, vicarious, cognitive, or emotive treatment (a method of per-

sonality change that incorporates cognitive, emotional, and behavioral strategies, designed to help resist tendencies to be irrational, suggestible, and conforming) modalities. The results confirmed that the degree to which people changed their behavior toward the reptiles was closely associated with increases in self-judged efficacy, regardless of the method of intervention. It is now widely accepted among social learning theorists that all effective therapies ultimately work by strengthening people's self-perceptions of efficacy.

THEORETICAL INFLUENCES

Social learning theory was born into a climate in which two competing and diametrically opposed schools of thought dominated psychology. On one hand, psychologists who advocated psychodynamic theories postulated that human behavior is governed by motivational forces operating in the form of largely unconscious needs, drives, and impulses. These impulse theories tended to give circular explanations, attributing behavior to inner causes that were inferred from the very behavior they were supposed to cause. They also tended to provide explanations after the fact, rather than predicting events, and had very limited empirical support.

On the other hand, there were various types of behavior theory that shifted the focus of the causal analysis from hypothetical internal determinants of behavior to external, publicly observable causes. Behaviorists were able to show that actions commonly attributed to inner causes could be produced, eliminated, and reinstated by manipulating the antecedent (stimulus) and consequent (reinforcing) conditions of the person's external environment. This led to the proposition that people's behavior is caused by factors residing in the environment.

Social learning theory presents a theory of human behavior that to some extent incorporates both viewpoints. According to Bandura, people are neither driven by inner forces nor buffeted by environmental stimuli; instead, psychological functioning is best explained in terms of a continuous reciprocal interaction of internal and external causes. This assumption, termed reciprocal determinism, became one of the dominant viewpoints in psychology.

An initial exposition of social learning theory was presented in Bandura and Richard H. Walters's text *Social Learning and Personality Development* (1963). This formulation drew heavily on the procedures and principles of operant and classical conditioning. In his later book *Principles of Behavior Modification*, Bandura placed much greater emphasis on symbolic events and self-regulatory processes. He argued that complex human behavior could not be satisfactorily explained by the narrow set of learning principles behaviorists had derived from animal studies. He incorporated principles derived from developmental, social, and cognitive psychology into social learning theory.

EVOLUTION OF THEORETICAL DEVELOPMENT

During the 1970's, psychology had grown increasingly cognitive. This development was reflected in Bandura's 1977 book *Social Learning Theory*, which presented self-efficacy theory as the central mechanism through which people control their own behavior. Over the following decade, the influence of cognitive psychology on Bandura's work grew stronger. In *Social Foundations of Thought and Action*, he finally disavowed his roots in learning theory and renamed his approach "social cognitive theory." This theory accorded central roles to cognitive, vicarious, self-reflective, and self-regulatory processes.

Social learning/social cognitive theory became the dominant conceptual approach within the field of behavior therapy. It has provided the conceptual framework for numerous interventions for a wide variety of psychological disorders and probably will remain popular for a long time. Its founder, Albert Bandura, was honored with the Award for Distinguished Scientific Contributions to Psychology from the American Psychological Foundation in 1980 in recognition of his work.

SOURCES FOR FURTHER STUDY

Bandura, Albert. *Principles of Behavior Modification*. New York: Holt, Rinehart and Winston, 1969. Presents an overview of basic psychological principles governing human behavior within the conceptual framework of social learning. Reviews theoretical and empirical advances in the field of social learning, placing special emphasis on self-regulation and on symbolic and vicarious processes. Applies these principles to the conceptualization and modification of a number of common behavior disorders such as alcoholism, phobias, and sexual deviancy.

_____. *Social Foundations of Thought and Action: A Social Cognitive Theory*. Englewood Cliffs, N.J.: Prentice-Hall, 1986. Presents a comprehensive coverage of the tenets of current social cognitive theory. Besides addressing general issues of human nature and causality, provides an impressive in-depth analysis of all important aspects of human functioning, including motivational, cognitive, and self-regulatory processes.

_____. *Social Learning Theory*. Englewood Cliffs, N.J.: Prentice-Hall, 1977. Lays out Bandura's theory and presents a concise overview of its theoretical and experimental contributions to the field of social learning. Redefines many of the traditional concepts of learning theory and emphasizes the importance of cognitive processes in human learning.

Evans, Richard I. *Albert Bandura, the Man and His Ideas: A Dialogue*. New York: Praeger, 1989. An edited version of an interview with Bandura. Easy to read, presenting Bandura's thoughts on the major aspects of his work in a very accessible form. The spontaneity of the discussion between Evans and Bandura gives a glimpse of Bandura as a person.

Feist, Jess, and Gregory Feist. *Theories of Personality*. 5th ed. Belmont, Calif.: Wadsworth, 2001. Chapter 11 of this book contains an excellent summary of Bandura's work. Gives an easy-to-read overview of his philosophical position (reciprocal determinism), discusses his theory (including observational learning and self-regulatory processes), and presents a summary of relevant research conducted within the framework of social cognitive theory. An ideal starting point for anyone who would like to become familiar with Bandura's work.

Edelgard Wulfert

SEE ALSO: Aggression; Bandura, Albert; Cognitive behavior therapy; Cognitive social learning: Walter Mischel; Learning; Observational learning and modeling therapies; Phobias.

Social networks

TYPE OF PSYCHOLOGY: Psychological methodologies; social psychology; stress

FIELDS OF STUDY: Coping; depression; stress and illness

A social network is the total set of people with whom a person interacts, and from whom a person can potentially receive help in time of need. The positive consequences of having good social networks have been rigorously studied and have been shown to relate to a range of health outcomes and psychological well-being.

KEY CONCEPTS
- health outcomes
- perceived integration
- role-based measures
- social integration
- social participation

INTRODUCTION

In almost every culture in the world, men and women live embedded within a network of other people. Young infants are surrounded by caregivers; toddlers, growing children, and adolescents have their peers; and young, middle-aged, and older adults have varying numbers of friends and relatives with whom they interact. Trained research psychologists and laypeople alike have recognized that the presence of others—friends, family, and sometimes even strangers—can be very comforting. A large body of research has focused on how the number and quality of one's interactions with other people influence psychological and physiological health and well-being.

Within formal network theorizing, the term "network" refers to the ties that connect a specific set of entities, be they people, groups, or organizations. Social networks can be described as the sum total of an individual's connections with others. They encompass the different contacts a person may have in one or more distinct social groups (people who are seen on a regular basis for business or pleasure); the types of roles a person plays (mother, coach); the number of friends, family, and relatives a person has; and even the different types of activities in which a person participates (such as attending weekly softball games, where the team becomes part of the network). In psychological writing on the topic of social relationships, a clear distinction is made between social networks, also referred to as structural social support, and functional social support (processes by which people give resources, information, or help to promote emotional or physical well-being). Although social networks can and

do serve important functions, such as providing a person with emotional social support or tangible resources in times of need, research on social networks focuses more on the health benefits that are gained from the participation in one or more distinct social groups (the structure of, and stable pattern that exists between, one's ties). This approach and understanding of social networks makes possible the use of more direct measurements of connections, such as how many people an individual speaks to in a week. The underlying assumption in much of this work is that others can influence how people think, feel, and behave through interactions that may not be explicitly intended to exchange help or support.

HISTORICAL BEGINNINGS

Sociologists were the first to write on and study the psychological relevance of social ties or social integration. The French sociologist Émile Durkheim conducted the earliest study of the influence of social networks in 1897. He contended that the breakdown in family, community, and work ties that occurred when workers migrated to industrial areas would be bad for psychological well-being. Durkheim wanted to see if there was any relationship between the number of social ties that a person had and their likelihood of committing suicide. He identified persons who had taken their own lives and looked into their social relationships, collecting information from those who knew them and local public records. He found that suicide was most common among individuals who were not married and lacked ties with the community and the church. Some years later, the American sociologist Robert Faris tested if being culturally isolated had anything to do with the development of mental illness. His paper, published in the *American Journal of Sociology* in 1934, emphasized the importance of social contacts and showed that socially isolated individuals were more at risk for developing schizophrenia.

One of the most important studies on the role of social networks was conducted in the late 1970's by the American social epidemiologists Lisa Berkman and Leonard Syme. Whereas the work of Durkheim and Faris was correlational in nature, in that they looked at cases of suicide and schizophrenia and worked backward to assess the factors that were associated with the outcome, Berkman and Syme con-

An old man begs for change in the streets of New York City, c. 1900. Homelessness has always been a risk for those who lose their social networks. (Library of Congress)

HEALTH BENEFITS OF SOCIAL NETWORKS

There are many benefits to having good social connections. Together with being associated with longer life, having good social networks has been related to a large number of positive health outcomes. Socially integrated people have been found to be less likely to have heart attacks; tend to recover faster from colds and other illnesses; are more likely to survive breast cancer; cope better with stress; are more likely to eat better, exercise, and be physically active; and are less likely to start smoking, and have a slightly easier time quitting if they do. In perhaps one of the most impressive demonstrations of the health buffering ability of social networks, American psychologist Sheldon Cohen exposed a large group of consenting volunteers to a cold virus (delivered via a nasal spray). The participants who reported having more social support and higher quality social networks were less likely to develop upper respiratory illnesses. Cohen randomly sampled his participants such that anyone in the general population had an equal chance of being in his study, allowing generalization of his results and assurance that there was nothing else influencing his findings.

Good social networks are especially important for healthy aging. Many studies have shown that having a close confidant or intimate social partner is associated with increased longevity. Increased social network size is associated with a reduced risk of mortality. This is an important finding, as research shows that the networks of the elderly often shrink with age, as a result of both death and changes in activities that reduce social contact. As a result, a large number of studies have investigated whether support from one source, such as a friend, can substitute and compensate for support from another, such as a spouse. Results on this issue have been mixed. Some studies show that friends and relatives can make up for less support from spouses or children, while others suggest that this may not always be the case. One clear conclusion is that studies of

ducted a nine-year longitudinal study. They first measured the social ties of close to seven thousand residents of Alameda County in the western U.S. state of California. They asked the participants in the study what hobbies they had, what groups they attended on a regular basis, if they were members of clubs, if they went to church, and other questions that tapped into their connection with others. Nine years later, they assessed how many of the people were still alive. They found that the people who were more socially integrated at the beginning of the study (had more social connections) lived longer than their counterparts who had fewer social connections. Having social contacts enabled women to live an average of 2.8 years longer and men to live an average of 2.3 years longer. These effects were not caused by differences in education, income level, health status at the beginning of the study, or the practice of health habits. This result was not a fluke. Similar results were found in other large studies conducted since that time.

social support should assess support from many different sources.

One aspect of the health benefits of social networks needs special attention. Since Durkheim's early work showing that people who were married were better off psychologically, many psychologists and studies proclaimed that just being married is enough. This oversimplifies the issue and is inaccurate. The fact seems to be that the benefits of being married vary for each sex. Whereas being married is very important for the well-being of men, it is not always the case for women. For women, having a close female confidant seems to be the critical element for well-being. This sex difference extends over many forms of social support. In general, women have been found to be better at creating social networks and keeping them alive and functioning, to benefit the most from networks, and to give and receive more functional forms of social support from networks than do men.

MEASUREMENT

Social networks can be measured in many different ways. To make them easier to understand and study, psychologists separate social networks into different components. The first main distinction can be made between the behavioral component of networks and the mental component of interacting with networks. The behavioral component comprises measurements of active participation in a wide range of activities, often comprises a direct count of items such as the number of social groups to which people belong or how many people with whom they talk on the phone each week, and is perhaps the most common approach to studying social networks. Behavioral components are further subdivided into measurements of recognized social positions or social identities, termed role-based measures, and measures that assess the frequency and number of social activities, termed social participation measures. The mental component of social networks refers to how people think about their networks and what resources they believe they have. This category of measures, commonly called perceived integration measures, focuses purely on the perceptions of the individual, regardless of whether the perceptions are an accurate reflection of reality. Although this may seem like a problematic issue—how an individual's perceptions of something can be measured other than by using that individual's own report—psychologists

have found that even believing that one has many people to whom to turn in case of need has many benefits.

One of the first researchers actively to study how roles influence social networks was the American psychologist Margaret Thoits. Using data collected from a large study of the community in New Haven, Connecticut, she constructed a tool assessing participation in eight key social roles: parent, spouse, relative, worker, friend, neighbor, student, church member, volunteer, and group member. Consistent with earlier work on this topic, she found that people who possessed more roles experienced less stress and had fewer psychological problems. Extensions of her work have added additional roles such as lover, son or daughter, son-in-law or daughter-in-law, relative, hobbyist, athlete, and stepparent. Building on this work, Sheldon Cohen created the Social Network Index (SNI), a popularly used measure of social networks that assesses participation in twelve types of social relationships similar to those used by Thoits. Participation in a relationship is defined as talking to the person on the phone or in person at least once every two weeks. The total number of persons communicated with thus provides a measure of network size.

Social participation measures assess how often individuals interact with others regardless of the number of roles that they may have. This work focuses both on the type of activities (going to church versus going to a party) as well as the number of activities (how many times things are done in general). For example, Swedish researchers developed a questionnaire, the Welin Activity Scale, that assesses the degree to which people participated in three main categories of activities: social activities, home activities, and outside home activities. Respondents estimate how often they engage in thirty-four different activities over the course of a year, using three main response options (never, occasionally, and often). A twelve-year study conducted in Gothenburg, Sweden, with this scale showed that people with higher scores on this measure of social participation were less likely to die from heart problems. The American psychologist James House developed a similar measure of social participation in 1982. House and colleagues assessed participation in four main categories of social activity: intimate social relationships, formal organizational involvements outside of work, active and relatively social leisure, and passive and relatively social leisure. Together, these measures of social participation help assess the extent to which social participation contributes to well-being.

Perceived integration measures often provide the most direct ways to capture the psychological benefits of networks. Believing that others will help one in time of need can provide a sense of security and comfort. Very often, perceptions actually map onto reality when members of an individual's social networks help the individual cope with stressors and supply needed tangible resources such as money, materials, or information. Perceived integration has been measured in a variety of different ways, most commonly by asking individuals to think about whom they could turn to if they needed help.

It is important to note that researchers are not certain whether the effects of social support on health represents a slope (where a person is less likely to die the more social connections they have) or a ceiling (where social networks are very important for people with few or no connections, but not as important for people with many connections). Some answers to this problem can be found by looking at how social support does change over time.

THEORETICAL APPROACHES TO SOCIAL NETWORK CHANGE

Two main theoretical frameworks have been proposed to predict and account for age-related changes in social networks. The American psychologist Toni Antonucci proposed that people are motivated to maintain their social network sizes as they age. Calling her theory the social convoy model, Antonucci suggested that although there may be many changes in the composition of the networks, people are thought to sift through their relationships, retaining those they value most. According to American psychologist Laura Cartensen's socioemotional selectivity theory, people prune their social networks to maintain a desired emotional state depending on the extent to which time is perceived as limited. Correspondingly, whereas the sizes of older adults' social networks are smaller than those for younger adults, the numbers of close relationships are comparable. Both theories have been well supported and indicate that it is not the size of the network (structure) but the quality of transactions (perceived and received social support that may vary in function) that is critical. Even though networks may some-times decrease, the quality of support may in fact increase.

SOURCES FOR FURTHER STUDY

Cohen, Sheldon. *Social Network Index.* http://www.psy.cmu.edu/~scohen/. Cohen's index, available on the World Wide Web, helps gauge the nature and strength of a person's social network.

Cohen, Sheldon, Lynn G. Underwood, and Benjamin H. Gottlieb, eds. *Social Support Measurement and Intervention: A Guide for Health and Social Scientists.* New York: Oxford University Press, 2000. Provides a comprehensive review of the social support literature, highlighting many different theoretical approaches, surveying main research findings, and providing in depth coverage of the main ways of measuring and using social networks. The contributors in this book represent the major contemporary researchers of social networks.

James, S., Karl R. Landis, and Debra Umberson. "Social Relationships and Health." *Science* 241, no. 4865 (1988): 540-545. A rigorous scientific article showing that prospective studies, which control for baseline health status, consistently show increased risk of death among persons with a low quantity, and sometimes a low quality, of social relationships.

Sarason, Barbara R., G. Sarason Irwin, and Regan A. R. Gurung. "Close Personal Relationships and Health Outcomes: A Key to the Role of Social Support." In *Personal Relationships: Implications for Clinical and Community Psychology,* edited by B. R. Sarason and S. W. Duck. New York: John Wiley & Sons, 2001. An in-depth examination of how one particular aspect of social networks, close relationships, can influence a variety of outcomes. Illustrates how close relationships can vary, points out which aspects of relationships can be detrimental to happiness, and provides pointers for how to optimize one's close relationships.

Seeman, Teresa. "Social Ties and Health: The Benefits of Social Integration." *Annals of Epidemiology* 6 (1996): 442-451. A clear scientific article on the health benefits of being connected.

Uchino, Bert N., John T. Cacioppo, and Janice K. Kiecolt-Glaser. "The Relationship Between Social Support and Physiological Processes: A Review with Emphasis on Underlying Mechanisms and Implications for Health." *Psychological-Bulletin*

119, no. 3 (1996): 488-531. In this review, the authors examine more than eighty-one studies and describe the evidence linking social support to physiological processes. Social support and social networks were reliably related to beneficial effects on aspects of the cardiovascular, endocrine, and immune systems.

Wills, Thomas A. "Social Networks and Social Support." In *Handbook of Health Psychology*, edited by Andrew Baum, Tracey A. Revenson, and Jerome E. Singer. Mahwah, N.J.: Lawrence Erlbaum, 2001. A critical look at the specific ways social networks influence health outcomes such as pregnancy, coping and recovery from illnesses, arthritis, diabetes, and substance abuse.

Regan A. R. Gurung

SEE ALSO: Altruism, cooperation, and empathy; Affiliation and friendship; Affiliation motive; Coping: Social support; Health psychology; Helping; Support groups.

Social perception

TYPE OF PSYCHOLOGY: Social psychology
FIELDS OF STUDY: Interpersonal relations; social perception and cognition

Social perception deals with how people think about and make sense of other people—how they form impressions, draw conclusions, and try to explain other people's behavior. Sometimes called social cognition or the study of "naïve psychology," social perception focuses on factors that influence the way in which people understand other people and on how people process, organize, and recall information about others.

KEY CONCEPTS
- actor-observer bias
- causal attribution
- correspondence bias
- disposition
- fundamental attribution error
- primacy effect
- priming
- schema (*pl.* schemata)
- self-fulfilling prophecy

INTRODUCTION

Social perception deals with two general classes of cognitive-perceptual processes through which people process, organize, and recall information about others. Those that deal with how people form impressions of other people's personalities (called person perception) form the first class. The second class includes those processes that deal with how people use this information to draw conclusions about other people's motivations, intentions, and emotions in order to explain and predict their behavior (called attribution processes). This importance of social perception in social psychology is revealed in the fact that one's impressions and judgments about others, whether accurate or not, can have profound effects on one's own and others' behavior.

People are naturally motivated to understand and predict the behavior of those around them. Being able to predict and understand the social world gives people a sense of mastery and control over their environment. Psychologists who study social perception have shown that people try to make sense of their social worlds by determining whether other people's behavior is produced by a disposition—some internal quality or trait unique to a person—or by something in the situation or environment. The process of making such determinations, which is called causal attribution, was developed by social psychologists Fritz Heider, Edward Jones, Keith Davis, and Harold Kelley in the late 1950's and early 1960's.

According to these attribution theorists, when one decides that a person's behavior reflects a disposition (when, for example, one decides that a person is friendly because he acted friendly), one has made an internal or dispositional attribution. In contrast, when one decides that a person's behavior was caused by something in the situation—he acted in a friendly way to make someone like him—one has made an external or situational attribution. The attributions one makes for others' behaviors carry considerable influence in the impressions one forms of them and in how one will behave toward them in the future.

INACCURACIES AND BIASES

Unfortunately, people's impressions and attributions are not always accurate. For example, in many situations, people seem to be inclined to believe that other people's behavior is caused by dispositional factors. At the same time, they believe that their own behavior is the product of situational causes. This tendency has been called the actor-observer bias. Moreover, when people try to explain the causes of other people's behavior, especially behavior that is clearly and obviously caused by situational factors (factors such as a coin flip, a dice roll, or some other situational inducement), they tend to underestimate situational influences and overestimate the role of dispositional causes. This tendency is referred to as correspondence bias or the fundamental attribution error. In other words, people prefer to explain other people's behavior in terms of their traits or personalities rather than in terms of situational factors, even when situational factors actually caused the behavior.

In addition to these biases, social psychologists have examined other ways in which people's impressions of others and inferences about the causes of their behavior can be inaccurate or biased. In their work, for example, psychologists Daniel Kahneman and Amos Tversky have described a number of simple but efficient thinking strategies, or "rules of thumb," called heuristics. The availability heuristic is the tendency to explain behaviors on the basis of causes that are easily or quickly brought to mind. Similarly, the representativeness heuristic is the tendency to believe that a person who possesses characteristics that are associated with a social group probably belongs to that group. Although heuristics make social thinking more efficient and yield reasonable results most of the time, they can sometimes lead to significant judgment errors.

INFLUENCE OF SCHEMATA AND PRIMACY EFFECT
Bias can also arise in social perception in a number of other ways. Because of the enormous amount of social information that they must process at any given moment, people have developed various ways of organizing, categorizing, and simplifying this information and the expectations they have about various people, objects, and events. These organizational structures are called schemata. For example, schemata that organize information about people's membership in different categories or groups are called stereotypes or prototypes. Schemata that organize information about how traits go together in forming a person's personality are called implicit personality theories (IPTs). Although schemata, like

heuristics, help make social thinking more efficient and yield reasonable results most of the time, they can also sometimes lead to significant judgment errors, such as prejudice and discrimination.

Finally, social perception can be influenced by a variety of factors of which people are unaware but which can exert tremendous influence on their thinking. Social psychologist Solomon Asch was the first to describe the primacy effect in impression formation. The primacy effect is the tendency for things that are seen or received first to have a greater impact on one's thinking than things that come later. Many other things in the environment can prime one, or make one "ready," to see, interpret, or remember things that one might not otherwise have seen, thought about, or remembered. Priming occurs when something in the environment makes certain things easier to bring to mind.

During the 1970's and 1980's, social psychologists made numerous alterations and extensions of the existing theories of attribution and impression formation to keep pace with the field's growing emphasis on mental (cognitive) and emotional (affective) processes. These changes focused primarily on incorporating work from cognitive psychology on memory processes, the use of schemata, and the interplay of emotion, motivation, and cognition.

STEREOTYPE AND CONFLICT RESEARCH
Social psychologists have argued that many social problems have their roots in social perception processes. Because social perception biases can sometimes result in inaccurate perceptions, misunderstandings, conflict between people and groups, and other negative consequences, social psychologists have spent much time and effort trying to understand them. Their hope is that by understanding such biases they will be able to suggest solutions for them. In a number of experiments, social psychologists have attempted to understand the social perception processes that may lead to stereotyping, which can result in prejudice and discrimination.

For example, one explanation for why stereotypes are so hard to change once they have been formed is the self-fulfilling prophecy. Self-fulfilling prophecies occur when one has possibly inaccurate beliefs about others (such as stereotypes) and acts on those beliefs, bringing about the conditions necessary to make those beliefs come true. In other words, when one expects something to be true about another person (especially a negative thing), one frequently looks for and finds what one expects to see. At other times, one actually brings out the negative (or positive) qualities one expects to be present. In a classic 1968 study by social psychologists Robert Rosenthal and Lenore Jacobsen, for example, children whose teachers expected them to show a delayed but substantial increase in their intelligence (on the basis of a fictitious intelligence test) actually scored higher on a legitimate intelligence quotient (IQ) test administered at the end of the school year. Presumably, the teachers' expectations of those students caused them to treat those students in ways that actually helped them perform better. Similarly, social psychologists Rebecca Curtis and Kim Miller have shown that when people think someone they meet likes them, they act in ways that lead that person to like them. If, however, people think a person dislikes them, they act in ways that actually make that person dislike them.

The behaviors that produce self-fulfilling prophecies can be subtle. For example, in 1974, social psychologists Carl Word, Mark Zanna, and Joel Cooper demonstrated that the subtle behaviors of interviewers during job interviews can make applicants believe that they performed either poorly or very well. These feelings, in turn, can lead to actual good or poor performance on the part of the applicants. What was most striking about this study, however, was that the factor that led to the subtle negative or positive behaviors was the interviewers' stereotypes of the applicants' racial group membership. Black applicants received little eye contact from interviewers and were not engaged in conversation; the behaviors displayed by interviewers in the presence of white applicants were exactly the opposite. Not surprisingly, black applicants were seen as less qualified and were less likely to be hired. Clearly, subtle behaviors produced by racial stereotypes can have major consequences for the targets of those stereotypes.

PRIMACY EFFECT IN ACADEMIC SETTINGS

The relevance of social perception processes to everyday life is not restricted to stereotyping, although stereotyping is indeed an important concern. In academic settings, for example, situational factors can lead teachers to form impressions of students that have little bearing on their actual abilities. Social psychologist Edward Jones and his colleagues examined the way in which primacy effects operate in ac-

ademic settings. Two groups of subjects saw a student perform on a test. One group saw the student start out strong and then begin to do poorly. The other group saw the student start out poorly and then begin to improve. For both groups, the student's performance on the test was identical, and the student received the same score. The group that saw the student start out strong and then falter thought the student was brighter than the student who started out poorly and then improved. Clearly, first impressions matter.

CORRESPONDENCE BIAS

Finally, research on the correspondence bias makes it clear that one must be very careful when trying to understand what people are like. In many situations, the demands of people's occupations or their family roles force them to do things with which they may not actually agree. Substantial research has shown that observers will probably think these persons have personalities that are consistent with their behaviors. Lawyers, who must defend people who may have broken the law, debaters, who must argue convincingly for or against a particular point of view, and actors, who must play parts that they did not write, are all vulnerable to being judged on the basis of their behavior. Lawyers may not actually believe that their clients are innocent, but must defend them as though they do. Debaters often argue for positions with which they do not agree. Actors play roles that do not match their personalities. Unless one is particularly sensitive to the fact that, when they are doing their jobs, these persons' behaviors do not reveal anything about their true personalities, one may actually (and incorrectly) believe that they do.

INFLUENTIAL RESEARCH AND THEORIES

The study of social perception has multiple origins that can be traced back to a number of influential researchers and theorists. It was one of the first topics to be emphasized when the modern study of social psychology began during World War II. Current perspectives on social perception processes can be traced to the early work of Solomon Asch, a social psychologist who emigrated to the United States before the war. His work yielded important demonstrations of primacy effects in impression formation.

Also important to the development of an understanding of social perception was the work of Fritz

Heider, another German émigré, who came to the United States as World War II was ending in Europe. Heider's influential book *The Psychology of Interpersonal Relations* (1958) arguably started the cognitive approach to social perception processes. In many circles, it is still regarded as a watershed of ideas and insights on person perception and attribution.

Perhaps the most important historical development leading up to the modern study of social perception, however, was the work of Jerome Bruner and other "new look" cognitive psychologists. Following World War II, a number of psychologists broke with the then traditional behaviorist/learning theory perspective and applied a Gestalt perspective to human perception. They emphasized the subjective nature of perception and interpretation and argued that both cognition (thinking) and situational context are important in determining "what" it is that a person perceives. Using ambiguous figures, for example, they demonstrated that the same object can be described in many different ways depending on the context in which it is seen. One of Bruner's students, Edward Jones, made significant contributions to the understanding of attribution and interpersonal perception during his career.

THEORETICAL COMMONALITIES

The perspectives offered by all these theorists share some common themes. First, they all acknowledged that social perception is inherently subjective; the most important aspect of understanding people is not what is "true" in an objective sense, but rather what is believed to be true. Second, they acknowledged that people think about other people and want to understand why people do the things they do. Finally, they believed that some general principles govern the ways in which people approach social perception and judgment, and they set out to demonstrate these principles scientifically.

FUTURE RESEARCH DIRECTIONS

During the 1960's and 1970's, social perception research experienced unprecedented attention and enthusiasm. Attribution theories were developed and refined, and in the 1970's cognitive psychology's influence on the field began to grow. In the future, social perception research and theory will continue to focus on basic theoretical problems (such as cognitive processes and the role of emotion in perception and cognition) that have substantial so-

cial applications (such as finding solutions to the problems posed by prejudice and misperception). Understanding the broader scope of human social perception—the interplay of complex thinking "systems"—will no doubt become a priority as the field attempts to deal more comprehensively with the enduring mystery of how to understand what makes people tick.

SOURCES FOR FURTHER STUDY

Deaux, Kay, and Gina Philogene, eds. *Representations of the Social: Bridging Theoretical Traditions.* New York: Blackwell, 2001. A concise and up-to-date collection of papers by well-known experts on social perception, intended as a textbook for undergraduates.

Eiser, J. Richard. *Social Judgment.* Pacific Grove, Calif.: Brooks/Cole, 1991. Presents a detailed and broad overview of topics in social judgment, including categorization, the effects of emotion on judgment, causal attribution, and other issues. Describes major theories and research in detail, and provides useful context within which to understand social perception's importance in everyday life.

Heider, Fritz. *The Psychology of Interpersonal Relations.* New York: John Wiley & Sons, 1958. This classic text presents Heider's attribution and balance theories as well as a number of ideas that were to influence the field for more than twenty years; intended for advanced college students and graduate students.

Jones, Edward Ellsworth. *Interpersonal Perception.* New York: W. H. Freeman, 1990. Presents a detailed overview and review of topics including impression formation, emotion perception, causal attribution, and attributional biases. Describes major theories and research in detail, and provides useful context within which to understand social perception's importance in everyday life. Available in paperback; engagingly written.

Jones, Edward Ellsworth, et al. *Social Stigma: The Psychology of Marked Relationships.* New York: W. H. Freeman, 1984. A collection of notable social psychologists collaborated on this book while they were all Fellows at the Center for Advanced Study in the Behavioral Sciences at Stanford University. It presents a broad selection of work (both empirical and theoretical) on stigma and its effects on social perception and judgment.

Zebrowitz, L. A. *Social Perception.* Pacific Grove, Calif.: Brooks/Cole, 1990. Presents a detailed and broad overview of topics in social perception, including impression formation, emotion perception, causal attribution, and attributional biases. Describes major theories and research in detail, and provides useful context within which to understand social perception's importance in everyday life. Available in paperback, this book will appeal to college students and those who have a serious interest in the topic.

John H. Fleming

SEE ALSO: Attributional biases; Causal attribution; Emotions; Memory; Motivation; Prejudice; Racism; Self-presentation; Social schemata.

Social psychological models
Erich Fromm

TYPE OF PSYCHOLOGY: Personality
FIELDS OF STUDY: Humanistic-phenomenological models; psychodynamic and neoanalytic models

Erich Fromm studied the effects of political, economic, and religious institutions on human personality. Fromm's work provides powerful insight into the causes of human unhappiness and psychopathology as well as ideas about how individuals and social institutions could change to maximize mental health and happiness.

KEY CONCEPTS
- dynamic adaptation
- escape from freedom
- freedom from external constraints
- freedom to maximize potential
- mental health
- personality
- productive love
- productive work

INTRODUCTION
The approach of Erich Fromm (1900-1980) to the study of human personality starts from an evolutionary perspective. Specifically, Fromm maintained that humans, like all other living creatures, are mo-

tivated to survive and that survival requires adaptation to their physical surroundings. Humans are, however, unique in that they substantially alter their physical surroundings through the creation and maintenance of cultural institutions. Consequently, Fromm believed that human adaptation occurs primarily in response to the demands of political, economic, and religious institutions.

Fromm made a distinction between adaptations to physical and social surroundings that have no enduring impact on personality (static adaptation—for example, an American learning to drive on the left side of the road in England) and adaptation that does have an enduring impact on personality (dynamic adaptation—for example, a child who becomes humble and submissive in response to a brutally domineering, egomaniacal parent). Fromm consequently defined personality as the manner in which individuals dynamically adapt to their physical and social surroundings in order to survive and reduce anxiety.

Human adaptation includes the reduction of anxiety for two reasons. First, because humans are born in a profoundly immature and helplessly dependent state, they are especially prone to anxiety, which, although unpleasant, is useful to the extent that it results in signs of distress (such as crying) which alert others and elicit their assistance. Second, infants eventually mature into fully self-conscious human beings who, although no longer helpless and dependent, recognize their ultimate mortality and essential isolation from all other living creatures.

Fromm believed that humans have five basic inorganic needs (as opposed to organic needs associated with physical survival) resulting from the anxiety associated with human immaturity at birth and eventual self-consciousness. The need for relatedness refers to the innate desire to acquire and maintain social relationships. The need for transcendence suggests that human beings have an inherent drive to become creative individuals. The need for rootedness consists of a sense of belonging to a social group. The need for identity is the need to be a unique individual. The need for a frame of orientation refers to a stable and consistent way of perceiving the world.

FREEDOM AND INDIVIDUAL POTENTIAL
Mental health for Fromm consists of realizing one's own unique individual potential, and it requires two

kinds of freedom that are primarily dependent on the structure of a society's political, economic, and religious institutions. Freedom from external constraints refers to practical concerns such as freedom from imprisonment, hunger, and homelessness. This is how many people commonly conceive of the notion of freedom. For Fromm, freedom from external constraints is necessary, but not sufficient, for optimal mental health, which also requires the freedom to maximize one's individual potential.

Freedom to maximize individual potential entails productive love and productive work. Productive love consists of interpersonal relationships based on mutual trust, respect, and cooperation. Productive work refers to daily activities that allow for creative expression and provide self-esteem. Fromm hypothesized that people become anxious and insecure if their need for transcendence is thwarted by a lack of productive work and love. Many people, he believed, respond to anxiety and insecurity by an "escape from freedom": the unconscious adoption of personality traits that reduce anxiety and insecurity at the expense of individual identity.

PERSONALITY TYPES AND FREEDOM ESCAPE

Fromm described five personality types representing an escape from freedom. The authoritarian person reduces anxiety and insecurity by fusing himself or herself with another person or a religious, political, or economic institution. Fromm distinguished between sadistic and masochistic authoritarians: The sadistic type needs to dominate (and often hurt and humiliate) others, while the masochistic type needs to submit to the authority of others. The sadist and the masochist are similar in that they share a pathetic dependence on each other. Fromm used the people in Nazi Germany (masochists) under Adolf Hitler (a sadist) to illustrate the authoritarian personality type.

Destructive individuals reduce anxiety and insecurity by destroying other persons or things. Fromm suggested that ideally people derive satisfaction and security through constructive endeavors, but noted that some people lack the skill and motivation to create and therefore engage in destructive behavior as an impoverished substitute for constructive activities.

Withdrawn individuals reduce anxiety and insecurity by willingly or unwillingly refusing to participate in a socially prescribed conception of reality; instead, they withdraw into their own idiosyncratic versions of reality. In one social conception, for example, many devout Christians believe that God created the earth in six days, that Christ was born approximately two thousand years ago, and that He has not yet returned to Earth. The withdrawn individual might singularly believe that the earth was hatched from the egg of a giant bird a few years ago and that Christ had been seen eating a hamburger yesterday. Psychiatrists and clinicians today would generally characterize the withdrawn individual as psychotic or schizophrenic.

Self-inflated people reduce anxiety and insecurity by unconsciously adopting glorified images of themselves as superhuman individuals who are vastly superior to others. They are arrogant, strive to succeed at the expense of others, are unable to accept constructive criticism, and avoid experiences that might disconfirm their false conceptions of themselves.

Finally, Fromm characterized American society in the 1940's as peopled by automaton conformists, who reduce anxiety and insecurity by unconsciously adopting the thoughts and feelings demanded of them by their culture. They are then no longer anxious and insecure, because they are like everyone else around them. According to Fromm, automaton conformists are taught to distrust and repress their own thoughts and feelings during childhood through impoverished and demoralizing educational and socializing experiences. The result is the acquisition of pseudothoughts and pseudofeelings, which people believe to be their own but which are actually socially infused. For example, Fromm contended that most Americans vote the same way that their parents do, although very few would claim that parental preference was the cause of their political preferences. Rather, most American voters would claim that their decisions are the result of a thorough and rational consideration of genuine issues (a pseudothought) instead of a mindless conformity to parental influence (a genuine thought—or, in this case, a nonthought).

IMPACT OF HISTORICAL CONSTRAINTS

In *Escape from Freedom* (1941), Fromm applied his theory of personality to a historical account of personality types by a consideration of how political, economic, and religious changes in Western Europe from the Middle Ages to the twentieth century affected "freedom from" and "freedom to." Fromm argued that the feudal political system of the Middle Ages engendered very little freedom from external constraints. Specifically, there was limited physical mobility; the average person died in the same place that he or she was born, and many people were indentured servants who could not leave their feudal lord even if they had somewhere to go. Additionally, there was no choice of occupation: One's job was generally inherited from one's father.

Despite the lack of freedom from external constraints, however, economic and religious institutions provided circumstances that fostered freedom to maximize individual potential through productive work and productive love. Economically, individual craftsmanship was the primary means by which goods were produced. Although this was time-consuming and inefficient by modern standards, craftsmen were responsible for the design and production of entire products. A shoemaker would choose the design and materials, make the shoes, and sell the shoes. A finished pair of shoes thus represented a tangible manifestation of the creative energies of the producer, thus providing productive work.

Additionally, the crafts were regulated by the guild system, which controlled access to apprenticeships and materials and set wages and prices in order to guarantee maximum employment and a fair profit to the craftsmen. The guilds encouraged relatively cooperative behavior between craftsmen and consequently engendered productive love. Productive love was also sustained by the moral precepts of the then-dominant Catholic church, which stressed the essential goodness of humankind, the idea that human beings had free will to choose their behavior on Earth and hence influence their ultimate fate after death, the need to be responsible for the welfare of others, and the sinfulness of extracting excessive profits from commerce and accumulating money beyond that which is necessary to exist comfortably.

The dissolution of the feudal system and the consequent transition to parliamentary democracy and capitalism provided the average individual with a historically unprecedented amount of freedom from external constraints. Physical mobility increased dramatically as the descendants of serfs were able to migrate freely to cities to seek employment of their choosing; however, according to Fromm, increased freedom from external constraints was acquired at the expense of the circumstances necessary for free-

dom to maximize individual potential through productive work and productive love.

IMPACT OF CAPITALISM

Capitalism shifted the focus of commerce from small towns to large cities and stimulated the development of fast and efficient means of production, but assembly-line production methods divested the worker of opportunities for creative expression. The assembly-line worker has no control over the design of a product, does not engage in the entire production of the product, and has nothing to do with the sale and distribution of the product. Workers in a modern automobile factory might put on hub caps or install radios for eight hours each day as cars roll by on the assembly line. They have no control over the process of production and no opportunity for creative expression, given the monotonous and repetitive activities to which their job confines them.

In addition to the loss of opportunities to engage in productive work, the inherent competitiveness of capitalism undermined the relatively cooperative interpersonal relationships engendered by the guild system, transforming the stable small-town economic order into a frenzied free-for-all in which people compete with their neighbors for the resources necessary to survive, hence dramatically reducing opportunities for people to acquire and maintain productive love. Additionally, these economic changes were supported by the newly dominant Protestant churches (represented by the teachings of John Calvin and Martin Luther), which stressed the inherent evilness of humankind, the lack of free will, and the notion of predetermination—the idea that God has already decided prior to one's birth if one is to be consigned to heaven or hell after death. Despite the absence of free will and the idea that an individual's fate was predetermined, Protestant theologians claimed that people could get a sense of God's intentions by their material success on Earth, thus encouraging people to work very hard to accumulate as much as possible (the so-called Protestant work ethic) as an indication that God's countenance is shining upon them.

CALL TO EMBRACE POSITIVE FREEDOM

In summary, Fromm argued that the average person in Western industrial democracies has freedom from external constraints but lacks opportunities to maximize individual potential through productive love and productive work; the result is pervasive feelings of anxiety and insecurity. Most people respond to this anxiety and insecurity by unconsciously adopting personality traits that reduce anxiety and insecurity, but at the expense of their individuality, which Fromm referred to as an escape from freedom. For Fromm, psychopathology is the general result of the loss of individuality associated with an escape from freedom. The specific manifestation of psychopathology depends on the innate characteristics of the individual in conjunction with the demands of the person's social environment.

Fromm argued that while escaping from freedom is a typical response to anxiety and insecurity, it is not an inevitable one. Instead, he urged people to embrace positive freedom through the pursuit of productive love and work, which he claimed would require both individual and social change. Individually, Fromm advocated a life of spontaneous exuberance made possible by love and being loved. He described the play of children and the behavior of artists as illustrations of this kind of lifestyle. Socially, Fromm believed strongly that the fundamental tenets of democracy should be retained but that capitalism in its present form must be modified to ensure every person's right to live, to distribute resources more equitably, and to provide opportunities to engage in productive work.

THEORETICAL INFLUENCES

Fromm's ideas reflect the scientific traditions of his time as well as his extensive training in history and philosophy, in addition to his psychological background. Fromm is considered a neo-Freudian (along with Karen Horney, Harry Stack Sullivan, and others) because of his acceptance of some of Freud's basic ideas (specifically, the role of unconsciously motivated behaviors in human affairs and the notion that anxiety-producing inclinations are repressed or prevented from entering conscious awareness) while rejecting Freud's reliance on the role of biological instincts (sex and aggression) for understanding human behavior. Instead, the neo-Freudians were explicitly concerned with the influence of the social environment on personality development.

Additionally, Fromm was very much influenced by Charles Darwin's theory of evolution, by existential philosophy, and by the economic and social psychological ideas of Karl Marx. Fromm's use of adaptation in the service of survival to define personality is derived from basic evolutionary theory. His analysis of the sources of human anxiety, especially the awareness of death and perception of isolation and aloneness, is extracted from existential philosophy. The notion that human happiness requires productive love and work and that capitalism is antithetical to mental health was originally proposed by Marx. Fromm's work has never received the attention that it deserves in America because of his open affinity for some of Marx's ideas and his insistence that economic change is utterly necessary to ameliorate the unhappiness and mental illness that pervade American society. Nevertheless, his ideas are vitally important from both a theoretical and practical perspective.

SOURCES FOR FURTHER STUDY

Becker, Ernest. *The Birth and Death of Meaning*. 2d ed. Reprint. New York: Free Press, 1985. Becker presents a general description of Fromm's ideas embedded in a broad interdisciplinary consideration of human social psychological behavior.

Fromm, Erich. *Anatomy of Human Destructiveness*. 1973. Reprint. New York: Henry Holt, 1992. An in-depth examination of the destructive personality type.

_____. *The Art of Loving*. 1956. Reprint. New York: HarperCollins, 2000. A detailed analysis of how to love and be loved. Distinguishes between genuine love and morbid dependency.

_____. *Escape from Freedom*. 1941. Reprint. New York: Henry Holt, 1995. Fromm's early seminal work, in which his basic theory about the relationship between political, economic, and religious institutions and personality development was originally articulated. All of Fromm's later books are extensions of ideas expressed here.

_____. *Marx's Concept of Man*. 1962. Reprint. New York: Frederick Ungar, 1982. An introduction to Marx's ideas, including a translation of Marx's economic and philosophical manuscripts of 1844.

_____. *The Revolution of Hope: Toward a Humanized Technology*. New York: Harper & Row, 1968. A detailed discussion of how capital-based economies can be transformed to provide opportunities for productive work without sacrificing productive efficiency, technological advances, or democratic political ideals.

Sheldon Solomon

SEE ALSO: Fromm, Erich; Humanism; Psychoanalytic psychology and personality: Sigmund Freud; Self; Self-esteem; Social psychological models: Karen Horney.

Social psychological models

Karen Horney

TYPE OF PSYCHOLOGY: Personality
FIELDS OF STUDY: Personality theory; psychodynamic and neoanalytic models; psychodynamic therapies

Karen Horney's social psychoanalytic theory focuses on how human relationships and cultural conditions influence personality formation; the theory describes how basic anxiety, resulting from childhood experiences, contributes to the development of three neurotic, compulsive, rigid personality styles: moving toward others, moving away from others, and moving against others. Normal personality is characterized by flexibility and balance among interpersonal styles.

KEY CONCEPTS
- basic anxiety
- externalization
- idealized self
- neurosis
- neurotic trends
- search for glory
- self-realization
- tyranny of the should

INTRODUCTION
Karen Horney (1885-1952) spent the major part of her career explaining how personality patterns, especially neurotic patterns, are formed, how they operate, and how they can be changed in order to increase individual potential. In contrast to Sigmund Freud's view that people are guided by instincts and the pleasure principle, Horney proposed that people act out desires to achieve safety and satisfaction in social relationships. She was optimistic about the possibility for human growth and believed that, under conditions of acceptance and care, people move toward self-realization, or the development of their full potential. She wrote almost exclusively, however, about personality problems and methods for solving them.

ROLE OF CULTURE
Horney believed that it is impossible to understand individuals or the mechanisms of neurosis (inflexible behaviors and reactions, or discrepancies between one's potential and one's achievements) apart from the cultural context in which they exist. Neurosis varies across cultures, as well as within the same culture, and it is influenced by socioeconomic class, gender, and historical period. For example, in *The Neurotic Personality of Our Time* (1937), Horney noted that a person who refuses to accept a salary increase in a Western culture might be seen as neurotic, whereas in a Pueblo Indian culture, this person might be seen as entirely normal.

The neurotic person experiences culturally determined problems in an exaggerated form. In Western culture, competitiveness shapes many neurotic problems because it decreases opportunities for cooperation, fosters a climate of mistrust and hostility, undermines self-esteem, increases isolation, and encourages people to be more concerned with how they appear to others than with fulfilling personal possibilities. It fosters the overvaluing of external success, encourages people to develop grandiose images of superiority, and leads to intensified needs for approval and affection as well as to the distortion of love. Moreover, the ideal of external success is contradicted by the ideal of humility, which leads to further internal conflict and, in many cases, neurosis.

ROLE OF THE FAMILY
Cultural patterns are replicated and transmitted primarily in family environments. Ideally, a family provides the warmth and nurturance that prepares children to face the world with confidence. When parents have struggled unsuccessfully with the culture, however, they create the conditions that lead to inadequate parenting. In its most extreme form, the competitiveness of the larger culture leads to child abuse, but it can also lead to parents' preoccupation with their own needs, an inability to love and nurture effectively, or a tendency to treat children as extensions of themselves. Rivalry, overprotectiveness, irritability, partiality, and erratic behavior are other manifestations of parental problems.

Within this negative environment, children experience fear and anger, but they also feel weak and helpless beside more powerful adults. They recognize that expressing hostility directly might be dangerous and result in parental reprisals or loss of love. As a result, children repress legitimate anger, banishing it to the unconscious. By using the defense mechanism of reaction formation, they develop emotions toward parents that are the opposite of anger, and they experience feared parents as objects of admiration. Children unconsciously turn their inner fears and anger against themselves and lose touch with their real selves. As a result, they develop basic anxiety, or the feeling of being alone and defenseless in a world that seems hostile.

DEFENSE AND COPING STRATEGIES

In order to cope with basic anxiety, individuals use additional defensive strategies or neurotic trends to cope with the world. These involve three primary patterns of behavior: moving away from others, moving toward others, and moving against others. In addition, neurotic individuals develop an idealized self, an unrealistic, flattering distortion of the self-image that encourages people to set unattainable standards, shrink from reality, and compulsively search for glory (compulsive and insatiable efforts to fulfill the demands of the idealized self) rather than accept themselves as they are.

Horney wrote about these in rich detail in *Our Inner Conflicts: A Constructive Theory of Neurosis* (1945), a highly readable book. The person who moves toward others believes: "If I love you or give in, you will not hurt me." The person who moves against others believes: "If I have power, you will not hurt me." The person who moves away from others thinks: "If I am independent or withdraw from you, you will not hurt me."

The person who moves toward others has chosen a dependent or compliant pattern of coping. The person experiences strong needs for approval, belonging, and affection, and strives to live up to the expectations of others through behavior that is overconsiderate and submissive. This person sees love as the only worthwhile goal in life and represses all competitive, hostile, angry aspects of the self. The moving-against type, who has adopted an aggressive, tough, exploitive style, believes that others are hostile, that life is a struggle, and that the only way to survive is to win and to control others. This

person sees herself or himself as strong and determined, and represses all feelings of affection for fear of losing power over others. Finally, the moving-away type, who has adopted a style of detachment and isolation, sees himself or herself as self-sufficient, private, and superior to others. This person represses all emotion and avoids any desire or activity that would result in dependency on others.

The interpersonal patterns that Horney discussed are no longer known as neurotic styles, but as personality disorders. Many of the behaviors that she described can be seen in descriptions of diagnostic categories that appear in the American Psychiatric Association's *Diagnostic and Statistical Manual of Mental Disorders: DSM-IV-TR* (rev. 4th ed., 2000), such as dependent personality disorder, narcissistic personality disorder, and obsessive-compulsive personality disorder. Like Horney's original criteria, these categories describe inflexible and maladaptive patterns of behavior and thinking that are displayed in various environments and result in emotional distress and/or impaired functioning.

USE OF PSYCHOANALYSIS

In her practice of psychoanalysis, Karen Horney used free association and dream analysis to bring unconscious material to light. In contrast to Freud's more passive involvement with patients, she believed that the psychoanalyst should play an active role not only in interpreting behavior but also in inquiring about current behaviors that maintain unproductive patterns, suggesting alternatives, and helping persons mobilize energy to change.

Horney also made psychoanalysis more accessible to the general population. She suggested that, by examining oneself according to the principles outlined in her book *Self-Analysis* (1942), one could increase self-understanding and gain freedom from internal issues that limit one's potential. Her suggestions indicate that a person should choose a problem that one could clearly identify, engage in informal free association about the issue, reflect upon and tentatively interpret the experience, and make specific, simple choices about altering problematic behavior patterns. Complex, long-standing issues, however, should be dealt with in formal psychoanalysis.

INFLUENCES

Karen Horney was one of the first individuals to criticize Freud's psychology of women. In contrast to

Freudian instinct theory, she proposed a version of psychoanalysis that emphasized the role that social relationships and culture play in human development. She questioned the usefulness of Freud's division of the personality into the regions of the id, ego, and superego, and viewed the ego as a more constructive, forward-moving force within the person.

Horney's work was enriched by her contact with psychoanalysts Harry Stack Sullivan, Clara Thompson, and Erich Fromm, who also emphasized the role of interpersonal relationships and sociocultural factors and were members at Horney's American Institute of Psychoanalysis when it was first established. Horney's work also resembled Alfred Adler's personality theory. Her concepts of the search for glory and idealized self are similar to Adler's concepts of superiority striving and the superiority complex. Furthermore, Adler's ruling type resembles the moving-against personality, his getting type is similar to the moving-toward personality, and his avoiding type is closely related to the moving-away personality.

CONTRIBUTIONS TO THE FIELD

Horney anticipated many later developments within cognitive, humanistic, and feminist personality theory and psychotherapy. Abraham Maslow, who was inspired by Horney, built his concept of self-actualization on Horney's optimistic belief that individuals can move toward self-realization. Carl Rogers's assumptions that problems are based on distortions of real experience and discrepancies between the ideal and real selves are related to Horney's beliefs that unhealthy behavior results from denial of the real self as well as from conflict between the idealized and real selves. In the field of cognitive psychotherapy, Albert Ellis's descriptions of the mechanisms of neurosis resemble Horney's statements. He borrowed the phrase "tyranny of the should" from Horney and placed strong emphasis on how "shoulds" influence irrational, distorted thinking patterns. Finally, Horney's notion that problems are shaped by cultural patterns is echoed in the work of feminist psychotherapists, who believe that individual problems are often the consequence of external, social problems.

SOURCES FOR FURTHER STUDY

Horney, Karen. *Neurosis and Human Growth: The Struggle Toward Self-Realization.* 1950. Reprint. New York: W. W. Norton, 1991. Presents Horney's theory in its final form. Describes the ways in which various neurotic processes operate, including the tyranny of the should, neurotic claims, self-alienation, and self-contempt. Discusses faulty, neurotic solutions that are developed as a way to relieve internal tensions through domination, dependency, resignation, or self-effacement.

_____. *The Neurotic Personality of Our Time.* 1937. Reprint. New York: W. W. Norton, 1994. Outlines the manner in which culture influences personality difficulties and describes typical behavior problems that result from the exaggeration of cultural difficulties in one's life.

_____. *New Ways in Psychoanalysis.* 1939. Reprint. New York: W. W. Norton, 2000. Describes major areas of agreement and disagreement with Freud, as well as important elements of her own theory; highly controversial when first published.

_____. *Our Inner Conflicts: A Constructive Theory of Neurosis.* 1945. Reprint. New York: W. W. Norton, 1993. Identifies and describes, through rich detail and examples, the three neurotic trends of moving toward others, moving away from others, and moving against others; highly readable and a good introduction to Horney's main ideas.

_____. *Self-Analysis.* 1942. Reprint. New York: W. W. Norton, 1994. Provides guidance for readers who may wish to engage in informal free association, self-discovery, and personal problem solving.

Quinn, Susan. *A Mind of Her Own: The Life of Karen Horney.* New York: Summit Books, 1987. Readable, honest, fascinating biography of Horney's life; provides insights into personal factors that influenced Horney's theoretical and clinical work.

Westkott, Marcia. *The Feminist Legacy of Karen Horney.* New Haven, Conn.: Yale University Press, 1986. This book integrates Karen Horney's earlier papers on the psychology of women with the more complete personality theory that emerged over time.

Carolyn Zerbe Enns

SEE ALSO: Antisocial personality; Borderline personality; Ego defense mechanisms; Histrionic personality; Horney, Karen; Individual psychology: Alfred

Adler; Narcissistic personality; Psychoanalysis; Psychoanalytic psychology and personality: Sigmund Freud; Self-actualization; Social psychological models: Erich Fromm; Women's psychology: Karen Horney; Women's psychology: Sigmund Freud.

Social schemata

TYPE OF PSYCHOLOGY: Social psychology
FIELDS OF STUDY: Social perception and cognition

Social schemata are certain clusters of information that people have stored in their memories; each cluster concerns a person, group of persons, or social event. Having such clusters of information already stored in memory can help people understand their social world yet can also lead people to have a biased perception of their social world.

KEY CONCEPTS
- cognition
- cognitive processes
- relational scheme
- schema (*pl.* schemata)
- script
- self-fulfilling prophecy
- self-schemata
- social cognition
- stereotype

INTRODUCTION

Life would be very complicated if people did not have the ability to store things in memory or to organize the information that did get stored; people would have to relearn information over and over. Because of memories of past experiences, people do not have to relearn what an apple is, for example, or what to do with it each time they come in contact with one.

A well-organized memory system also helps people make educated guesses. One is able to conclude that, because of an apple's texture, it will not make a satisfactory baseball. One is able to make educated guesses because the human brain has the ability to categorize objects and to generalize from past experiences to new experiences. Indeed, social psychologists believe that the brain not only has the ability to categorize; it also has the tendency to do so. For example, a very young city child who is taken to the zoo may point to a goat and say, "Doggy!"

The brain's memory system categorizes objects, people, and events by connecting different pieces of related information together. Social psychologists call this collection of related information a schema. The young child knows that "doggies," for example, have fur, four legs, and wet noses. Somehow, the brain links these pieces of information together. In the child's mind, there is an idea of the typical characteristics an object must have in order for it to be a "doggy."

TYPES OF SOCIAL SCHEMATA

All people have many schemata, covering the entire range of topics about which a given person knows things. Some of these topics are social in nature; some are not. If the content of a schema concerns a person, group of people, or social event, the schema is called a social schema. One type of social schema is a script. A script is a schema about a social event, such as a "good party" or "going to class." Another type of social schema is a stereotype, which is a schema about a group of people. If one were to list, for example, everything one could think of regarding "criminals," including one's opinions or personal experiences, one would have listed the contents of one's "criminal" stereotype.

A third type of social schema is a self-schema. Each of a person's many self-schemata combine to make up the person's overall self-concept, and the self-schema most salient at any given moment is called the working self-concept. A person might, for example, have a self-schema regarding himself or herself as a student, another one as a male or female, and yet another regarding his or her athletic abilities. Each self-schema might have many, or few, pieces of information. One's self-schema as a student, for example, might include information about where one goes to school, which classes one is taking, whether one enjoys being a student, memories of oneself in one's first kindergarten class, or of books one read that made an impact. Some of these pieces of information might also be included in other schemata; the information stored in the "student" self-schema might also be stored in a script about school, for example.

Another type of social schema is the relational schema. Relational schemata are cognitive structures that exist within an interpersonal, interdependent context. Relational schemata are truly social psychological in nature, as they reflect one's views about self and others, not in an isolated context but in the context of others. Relational schemata are composed of three aspects. First is the self-schema in relation to another person, or how the self is experienced in interaction with another. A good example of this relational self-schema is the distinct self-schema one has when interacting with a parent or romantic partner. The second component of relational schemata is a partner or particular other schema within the context of an interaction or relationship. For instance, one holds a distinct schema of a parent, unique to one's particular parent/child relationship. Finally, relational schemata also include an interpersonal script composed of expectations about how the relationship will and should transpire based on past experiences within the relationship. These three components of relational schemata interact to influence expectations and behavior. As a result, a person having a relational schema with a parent would have a specific self-schema when interacting with the parent ("When I'm with Mom I feel incompetent"), a specific schema of the parent within the interaction ("When Mom is with me, she is very critical"), and finally, an interpersonal script specific to the parent/child relationship ("If I bring up school, Mom will start yelling at me").

SOCIAL SCHEMATA AS MENTAL SHORTCUTS

Schemata, whether they are self-schemata, scripts, stereotypes, relational schemata, or other types of schemata, help people organize and understand new events. They function as shortcuts to help one navigate through both one's physical and social worlds. Just as one's schema for an apple helps one recognize and know what to do with an apple, one's social schemata help one function in social situations. For example, most high school juniors know what to do in a new classroom without having to be told because their "classroom" schema, created during previous semesters, already holds information about how to behave in class. Schemata, then, help people simplify the world; they do not constantly have to relearn information about events, concepts, objects, or people.

To understand how social schemata help people simplify the world, social psychologists study the cognitive processes that schemata affect. This area of study is called social cognition. Cognitive pro-

cesses are thinking processes, such as paying attention, that enable the brain to perceive events. Research has shown that schemata affect what people pay attention to, what they store in permanent memory and then later recall, how they interpret events, and even how people behave (although "behaving" is not considered a cognitive process).

IMPACT ON MEMORY AND INTERPRETATION

Research in social cognition shows that having a schema makes it more likely that a person will pay attention to events that are relevant to the schema than to events that are irrelevant. Schemata also make it more likely that a person will store in permanent memory and later recall new information that confirms the beliefs that person already has in his or her schemata.

An interesting study illuminating this tendency had research participants view a videotape of a woman eating dinner with her husband. Half of the participants had previously learned that this woman was a librarian, while the other half had been told that the woman was a waitress. The researchers found that when they later asked participants to recall what they had seen on the videotape, those who had been told the woman was a librarian recalled more information consistent with the "librarian schema," such as the fact that the woman wore glasses or that she played the piano. Those participants who had been told the woman was a waitress recalled more information consistent with a "waitress schema," for instance, that the woman had a bowling ball in the room or that there were no bookshelves.

There are exceptions to this general rule. When a schema is either very new or very well established, inconsistent information becomes more important and is often more likely to be recalled than when a schema is only moderately established. For example, if one is just getting to know a new person or if the person is one's best friend, information inconsistent with one's schema is more likely to stand out.

Schemata also affect how people interpret events. When people have a schema for an event or person, they are likely to interpret that event or the person's behavior in a way that is consistent with the beliefs already held in the schema. For example, researchers found that when participants were exposed to either a list of words designed to bring to mind a schema of an adventurous person (brave, courageous, daring) or to invoke the schema of a reckless person (foolish, careless), their later judgments of a paragraph they read about a fictional person named Donald, who loved to go white-water rafting and skydiving, were influenced. Specifically, participants whose adventurous schema had been activated judged Donald positively, while those whose reckless schema had been activated judged Donald negatively.

Finally, people tend to act in ways that are consistent with the schemata they hold in memory, and their actions can affect the actions of others in such a way as to confirm the original beliefs. All these cognitive memory biases result in confirmation of the beliefs that are already held; thus, these biases often produce self-fulfilling prophecies.

THE NEGATIVE IMPACT OF SOCIAL SCHEMATA

Although social schemata can facilitate people's understanding of their social world, they also can bias people's perceptions. Often, people are not accurate recorders of the world around them; rather, their own beliefs and expectations, clustered and stored as schemata, distort their perceptions of social events. Such distortions help answer the social psychological question, Why are stereotypes so difficult to change?

If a person has a schema, a stereotype, about criminals and then meets a man who is introduced as a criminal, perceptions of this person can be biased by the schema. Since schemata affect what people notice, this person will be more likely to notice things about this man that are consistent with his or her schema than things that are irrelevant. Perhaps the person believes that criminals use foul language but has no expectations regarding the type of listening skills a criminal might have. In this case, the person might be more likely to notice when the criminal swears than to notice his empathic listening skills. Then, because schemata affect what is stored in and recalled from memory, the person might be more likely to put into memory, and later remember, the criminal's swearing. Even if the person did notice his good listening skills, he or she would be less likely to store that in memory, or to recall it later, than to store information about his swearing.

On the other hand, if a person believes that criminals are not very empathic, he or she might be especially likely to notice this new acquaintance's em-

pathic listening skills. It is unlikely, though, that a person would change his or her schema to fit this new information; what is more likely is that he or she would interpret this information in such a way as to make it fit the stereotype—for example, consider this one criminal to be the exception to the rule, or conclude he developed his listening skills as a con to get out of jail more quickly.

Finally, a person very well might treat a criminal in a way that fits his or her beliefs about him. For example, a person who believes criminals lie might express doubt over things he says. The criminal might then respond to these doubts by acting defensively, which might then confirm the other person's belief that criminals act aggressively or that they have reasons to feel guilty. The criminal also might respond to doubting comments by actually lying. He might have the attitude, "If you expect me to lie, I might as well." What has happened, in this case, is this: A person's beliefs have affected his or her behavior, which in turn has affected the criminal's behavior, and the criminal's behavior now confirms the person's stereotype. This chain of events is one of the problems created by schemata. Very often, negative beliefs make it more likely that a person will find or produce confirmation for these beliefs.

These biases in information processing also can apply to how people perceive themselves, and thus explain why it can be difficult to change a negative self-concept. If a woman sees herself as incompetent, for example, she is likely to notice when her own behavior or thoughts are less than adequate, she is likely to store those examples in memory, and she is likely later to recall such examples from memory. Furthermore, if she engages in an activity and her performance is up for interpretation, she will be more likely to evaluate that performance as incompetent than as competent. Finally, if she believes she is incompetent, this can lead her actually to act that way. For example, her belief may lead her to feel nervous when it is time to perform, and her nervousness might then lead her to perform less competently than she otherwise might have. This provides her with more proof of her own incompetence, another self-fulfilling prophecy.

HISTORY OF SOCIAL SCHEMATA RESEARCH

Research in social cognition, the area of social psychology that focuses on social schemata, evolved as a hybrid from two areas of psychology: social psychology and cognitive psychology. In 1924, Floyd Allport published a book titled *Social Psychology;* this early text was the first to assert that an individual's behavior is affected by the presence and actions of other individuals. In the 1950's, though, Kurt Lewin asserted, as social psychologists still assert, than an individual is more influenced by his or her perceptions of other individuals than by what the other individuals actually are doing. For many years after, a popular subfield in social psychology was person perception. Researchers studying person perception discovered many factors that influence people's judgments and impressions of others. For example, researchers showed that individuals are more influenced by unpleasant than by pleasant information when forming an impression of a stranger. Person perception research focused on how individuals perceive others, rather than on how individuals are influenced by others, and such research provided one of the main foundations for the field of social cognition.

The second main foundation was research on cognitive processes. In the 1980's, researchers studying person perception realized they could better understand why people perceive others as they do by learning more about cognitive psychology. Cognitive psychology was first developed to explain how individuals learn—for example, to explain the relationship between a child's ability to pay attention, put information into memory, and recall information and the child's ability to learn information from a textbook. As cognitive psychologists created techniques for studying these cognitive processes, researchers studying person perception realized that the same processes that affect a schoolchild's ability to learn textbook material also might affect how individuals learn about other individuals. As these new cognitive research techniques began answering many questions in the field of person perception, that field branched into a second field, the field called social cognition.

PRACTICAL APPLICATIONS OF RESEARCH

In the 1970's and 1980's, Aaron T. Beck demonstrated that individuals who are depressed have a self-schema for depression and also a hopeless schema about the world in general. Beck's work has been extremely influential in the understanding of depression. Because of his work, one of the major approaches to treating depression is to help the de-

pressed individual change his or her thoughts and cognitive processes.

Understanding that schemata can bias people's thinking can help people resist such biases. Resisting the biases can help people change parts of their self-concepts, their stereotypes of others, or even their schemata about their loved ones. If one sees one's roommate as messy, for example, one might be especially likely to notice and remember his messy behaviors, and it is possible that one might respond to his messiness by cleaning up after him, nagging, or becoming more messy oneself. The roommate might then rebel against all these responses by becoming even more messy himself, resulting in a downward spiral. If one's roommate also is one's spouse, this can lead to marital problems. Not all self-fulfilling prophecies have these types of unpleasant consequences, but to stop the cycle of those that do, people need to search actively for evidence that disconfirms their schemata.

One of the earliest contributions from the field of social cognition and social schemata research was a better understanding of interracial problems. Prior to their understanding of social schemata, social psychologists had been interested in discovering the factors that lead to unpleasant feelings toward other racial groups and the conditions that would eliminate such feelings. Research on social schemata helped explain unpleasant intergroup relations by showing that thoughts, that is, schemata, can be resistant to change for reasons that have nothing to do with unpleasant feelings toward a group; the biases in attention, storing information in memory, recalling information, and interpreting events can occur even when unpleasant feelings are not present. Just as a young child's brain perceives a goat to be a "doggy," an adult's brain also tends to perceive new events in ways that fit information already held in memory.

Social psychologists now understand that cognitive processes also affect many other psychological phenomena that formerly were explained by emotional processes alone. For example, social schemata contribute to psychologists' understanding of why crime victims do not always receive help, why bullies initiate fights, and why some teenagers are so angry with their parents.

Social schemata, studied by social psychologists, have such far-reaching effects that researchers in areas of psychology other than social psychology also study them. For example, personality psychologists study how social schemata affect self-concept, and clinical psychologists study how social schemata can inhibit or facilitate therapy sessions. Social schemata themselves may simplify people's understanding of social events, but the study of schemata has greatly enriched the understanding of the social perceiver.

SOURCES FOR FURTHER STUDY

Baldwin, Mark W. "Relational Schemas: Research into Social-Cognitive Aspect of Interpersonal Experience." In *The Coherence of Personality*. New York: Guilford Press, 1999. Scholarly overview of research into the relatively new theory of relational schemata. Places relational schemata within the broader context of social schema research.

Baumeister, Roy F., ed. *The Self in Social Psychology. Key Readings in Social Psychology*. Philadelphia: Psychology Press/Taylor & Francis, 1999. This collection of influential and academically significant social psychology articles introduces theories and concepts most investigated. Includes a seminal article on self-schemata. A thorough text with extensive bibliographies, geared toward a scholarly audience.

Beck, Aaron T. *Love Is Never Enough*. New York: Harper & Row, 1988. A famous therapist and researcher explains how negative thoughts can interfere in a marriage and teaches the reader how to change unrealistic scripts regarding relationships. Not a typical self-help book; the tone and writing style are serious, although not difficult.

Burns, David D. *Intimate Connections*. New York: Signet, 1985. This popular self-help book by a colleague of Aaron Beck shows how beliefs and expectations can influence people's feelings toward themselves and others. Includes a helpful chapter on how to change such thoughts, and another on how to overcome feelings of inferiority. Also addresses unrealistic relationship scripts.

Fiske, Susan T., and Shelley E. Taylor. *Social Cognition*. New York: McGraw-Hill, 1991. Explains how memory, attitudes, emotions, and motivation combine to affect people's perceptions of others and themselves. Although the writing includes the terminology used by social psychologists, the authors provide many definitions and examples. One of the most comprehensive books available on social cognition.

Lassen, Maureen Kirby. *Why Are We Still Fighting? How to End Your Schema Wars and Start Connecting with the People You Love*. Oakland, Calif.: New Harbinger, 2000. This book, written by a clinical psychologist in private practice, applies scientific research on social schemata to a relationship context. Geared toward a general audience and easy to read, it suggests various ways to identify and change unconscious self and other schemata to help resolve conflicts and improve relationships.

Taylor, Shelley E., Letitia Anne Peplau, and David O. Sears. *Social Psychology*. 9th ed. Upper Saddle River, N.J.: Prentice-Hall, 1997. This undergraduate textbook provides a well-written, broad introduction to social schemata including interesting examples from psychological research and everyday life. Good initiation into the topic of social schemata for the lay reader. Includes an extensive bibliography.

Julie A. Felender;
updated by Michelle Murphy

SEE ALSO: Attributional biases; Causal attribution; Cognitive psychology; Intergroup relations; Prejudice; Prejudice reduction; Racism; Social perception.

Speech disorders

TYPE OF PSYCHOLOGY: Language
FIELDS OF STUDY: Behavioral therapies; infancy and childhood; organic disorders

Speech disorders may have an organic or learned origin, and they often affect a person's ability to communicate efficiently. As a result of a speech disorder, a person may exhibit a number of effects on behavior, such as the avoidance of talking with others and low self-esteem.

KEY CONCEPTS
- communication
- self-esteem
- social interaction
- speech
- vocal folds

INTRODUCTION

The ability to communicate is one of the most basic human characteristics. Communication is essential to learning, working, and, perhaps most important, social interaction. Normal communication involves hearing sounds, interpreting and organizing sounds, and making meaningful sounds. The ear takes in sounds, changes them into electrical impulses, and relays these impulses to the brain. The brain interprets the impulses, assigns meaning, and prepares a response. This response is then coded into the precisely coordinated changes in muscles, breath, vocal folds, tongue, jaw, lips, and so on that produce understandable speech.

Between 5 and 10 percent of Americans experience speech and/or language difficulties, often referred to as speech disorders. For these individuals, a breakdown occurs in one of the processes of normal communication described above. People with speech disorders may exhibit one or more of the following problems: They may be difficult to understand, use and produce words incorrectly, consistently use incorrect grammar, be unable to hear appropriately or to understand others, consistently speak too loudly, demonstrate a hesitating speech pattern, or simply be unable to speak. Speech disorders can be categorized as one of three disorder types: disorders of articulation, of fluency, or of voice. Articulation disorders are difficulties in the formation and stringing together of sounds to produce words. Fluency disorders, commonly referred to as stuttering, are interruptions in the flow or rhythm of speech. Finally, voice disorders are characterized by deviations in a person's voice quality, pitch, or loudness.

TYPES OF SPEECH DISORDERS

Articulation disorders are the most common types of speech errors in children. Articulation errors may take the form of substitutions, omissions, or distortions of sounds. An example of a substitution would be the substitution of the *w* sound for the *r* sound,

---

DSM-IV-TR Criteria for Speech Disorders

PHONOLOGICAL DISORDER (DSM CODE 315.39)

Failure to use developmentally expected speech sounds appropriate for age and dialect

Examples include errors in sound production, use, representation, or organization (substitutions of one sound for another, omissions of sounds such as final consonants)

Speech sound production difficulties interfere with academic or occupational achievement or with social communication

If mental retardation, speech-motor or sensory deficit, or environmental deprivation is present, speech difficulties exceed those usually associated with these problems

STUTTERING (DSM CODE 307.0)

Disturbance in the normal fluency and time patterning of speech inappropriate for age

Characterized by frequent occurrences of one or more of the following:
- sound and syllable repetitions
- sound prolongations
- interjections
- broken words (such as pauses within a word)
- audible or silent blocking (filled or unfilled pauses in speech)
- circumlocutions (word substitutions to avoid problematic words)
- words produced with an excess of physical tension
- monosyllabic whole-word repetitions

Fluency disturbance interferes with academic or occupational achievement or with social communication

If speech-motor or sensory deficit is present, speech difficulties exceed those usually associated with these problems

---

as in "wabbit" for "rabbit." Substitutions are the most common form of articulation errors. An example of an omission would be if the *d* sound was left out of the word "bed," as in "be_." Finally, sounds can also be distorted, as in "shleep" for "sleep."

Stuttering is defined as an interruption in the flow or rhythm of speech. Stuttering can be characterized by hesitations, interjections, repetitions, or prolongations of a sound, syllable, word, or phrase. "I wa-wa-want that" is an example of a part-word repetition, while "I, I, I want that" is an example of a whole-word repetition. When a word or group of words such as "uh," "you know," "well," or "oh" is inserted into an utterance, it is termed an interjection. "I want uh, uh, you know, uh, that" is an example of a sentence containing interjections. There may also be secondary behaviors associated with stuttering. In order for an individual to extricate himself or herself from a stuttering incident, secondary behaviors may be used. A stutterer may blink the eyes, turn the head, tap his or her leg, look away, or perform some other interruptive behavior to stop the stuttering. In therapy, secondary behaviors are very difficult to extinguish.

While articulation disorders and stuttering are often seen in children, voice disorders are common among adults. Voice disorders are categorized into disorders of pitch, intensity, nasality, and quality. A person with a voice disorder of pitch may have a vocal pitch which is too high. A person may speak too softly and thus exhibit a voice disorder of intensity. Still others may sound as though they talk through their nose (hypernasality) or always have a cold (hyponasality). The most common voice disorder is a disorder of quality. Examples of disorders of vocal quality include a voice that sounds hoarse, breathy, harsh, or rough. This type of voice disorder may be caused by vocal abuse, or an overusage of the voice, and might be found among singers, actors, or other individuals who abuse or overuse their voices. If the vocal abuse continues, vocal nodules (like calluses) may appear on the vocal folds. Vocal nodules may be surgically removed, and a person may be put on an extended period of vocal rest.

Speech disorders may be caused by a variety of factors. They may result from physical problems, health problems, or other problems. Physical problems such as cleft lip and palate, misaligned teeth, difficulty in controlling movements of the tongue, injury to the head, neck, or spinal cord, poor hearing, mental retardation, and cerebral palsy can contribute to poor articulation. The exact causes of stuttering are not known; however, a variety of factors are thought to be involved, including learning problems, emotional difficulties, biological defects, and neurological problems. Problems with voice quality can be caused by too much strain on the vocal folds (for example, yelling too much or clearing the throat too often), hearing loss, inflammation or growths on the vocal folds (vocal nodules), or emotional problems.

SPEECH AND COMMUNICATION
Speaking, hearing, and understanding are essential to human communication. A disorder in one or more of these abilities can interfere with a person's capacity to communicate. Impaired communi-

cation can influence all aspects of a person's life, creating many problems for an individual. Behavioral effects resulting from the speech disorder can be found in both children and adults. Children with speech disorders can experience difficulties in learning and find it hard to establish relationships with others. Speech disorders in adults can adversely affect social interactions and often create emotional problems, which may interfere with a person's ability to earn a living. Disorders such as those described above can interfere with a person's relationships, independence, well-being, and ability to learn. People who have trouble communicating thoughts and ideas may have trouble relating to others, possibly resulting in depression and isolation. Furthermore, job opportunities are often limited for people who cannot communicate effectively. Thus, they may have trouble leading independent, satisfying lives. Emotional problems may develop in people who exhibit speech disorders as a result of embarrassment, rejection, or poor self-image. Finally, learning is difficult and frustrating for people with speech disorders. As a consequence, their performance and progress at school and on the job can suffer.

When trying to communicate with others, individuals with speech disorders may experience other negative behavioral effects as a result of the disorder. These effects include frustration, anxiety, guilt, and hostility. The emotional experience of speech-disordered persons is often a result of their experiences in trying to communicate with others. Both the listener and the speech-disordered person react to the disordered person's attempts to communicate. In addition, the listener's reactions may influence the disordered individual. These reactions may include embarrassment, guilt, frustration, and anger and may cause the disordered individual to experience a sense of helplessness that can subsequently lower the person's sense of self-worth. Many speech-disordered people respond to their problem by being overly aggressive, by denying its existence, by projecting reactions in listeners, and/or by feeling anxious or timid.

TREATMENT AND PREVENTION
Treatment of speech disorders attempts to eliminate or minimize the disorder and related problems. Many professionals may be involved in providing therapy, special equipment, or surgery. In

therapy, specialists teach clients more effective ways of communicating. They may also help families learn to communicate with the disordered individual. Therapy may also include dealing with the negative behavioral effects of having a speech disorder, such as frustration, anxiety, and a feeling of low self-worth. In some cases, surgery can correct structural problems that may be causing speech disorders, such as cleft palate or misaligned teeth. For children with articulation disorders, therapy begins with awareness training of the misarticulations and the correct sound productions. After awareness is established, the new sound's productions are taught. For individuals who exhibit voice disorders, therapy is designed to find the cause of the disorder, eliminate or correct the cause, and retrain the individuals to use their voices correctly. Therapy for stutterers, however, is an entirely different matter. There are many methods for treating stuttering. Some are self-proclaimed "cures," while others help individuals live with their stuttering. Still other types of stuttering therapy help the stutterer overcome his or her fear of communicating, or help him or her develop a more normal breathing pattern.

Though there are many ways to treat speech disorders, disorder prevention is even more important. Certain things can be done to help prevent many speech disorders. All the methods focus on preventing speech disorders in childhood. Children should be encouraged to talk, but they should not be pushed into speaking. Pushing a child may cause that child to associate anxiety or frustration with communicating. Infants do not simply start talking; they need to experiment with their voice, lips, and tongue. This experimentation is often called babbling, and it should not be discouraged. Later on, one can slowly introduce words and help with correct pronunciation. When talking with young children, one should talk slowly and naturally, avoiding "baby talk" and gibberish. Children will have difficulty distinguishing between the baby-talk word (for example, "baba") and the real word ("bottle"). Having children point to and name things in picture books and in real-world surroundings allows them to put labels (words) on the objects in their environment. Increases in the number of labels a child has learned can subsequently increase the number of topics about which the child can communicate. It is most important to listen to what the child is trying to say rather than to how the child is

saying it. Such prevention strategies will encourage positive behavioral effects regarding the act of communicating. These positive effects include feelings of self-efficiency, independence, and a positive self-image.

SPEECH-LANGUAGE PATHOLOGY

Early identification of a speech disorder improves the chances for successful treatment, and early treatment can help prevent a speech disorder from developing into a lifelong handicap. Professionals who identify, evaluate, and treat communication disorders in individuals have preparations in the field of speech-language pathology. A speech-language pathologist is a professional who has been educated in the study of human communication, its development, and its disorders. By evaluating the speech and language skills of children and adults, the speech-language pathologist determines if communication problems exist and decides on the most appropriate way of treating these problems.

Speech-language pathology services are provided in many public and private schools, community clinics, hospitals, rehabilitation centers, private practices, health departments, colleges and universities, and state and federal governmental agencies. There are more than fourteen hundred clinical facilities and hundreds of full-time private practitioners providing speech services to people throughout the United States. Service facilities exist in many cities in every state. A speech-language pathologist will have a master's or doctoral degree and should hold a Certificate of Clinical Competence (CCC) from the American Speech-Language-Hearing Association and/or a license from his or her state.

Responsibilities of a speech-language pathologist include evaluation and diagnosis, therapy, and referral to other specialists involved with speech disorders. By gathering background information and by direct observation and testing, the speech-language pathologist can determine the extent of the disorder as well as a probable cause. The speech-language pathologist chooses an appropriate treatment to correct or lessen the communication problem and attempts to help the patient and family understand the problem. When other treatment is needed to correct the problem, the patient is referred to another specialist. Audiologists, special educators, psychologists, social workers, neurologists, pediatricians, otolaryngologists (also known as ear, nose, and throat specialists), and other medical and dental specialists may be involved in the diagnosis and treatment of a speech disorder. For example, psychologists may be best suited to treat the emotional or behavioral aspects of having a speech disorder (that is, anxiety, frustration, anger, denial, and so on). Otolaryngologists are often involved in the diagnosis of voice disorders. Audiologists determine whether an individual's hearing is affecting or causing a speech disorder.

Speech disorders can affect anyone at any time. The chances are good that everyone at one time has either had, or known someone with, a speech disorder. Since communication is so overwhelmingly a part of life, disordered speech is not something to take lightly. With good prevention, early identification, and early treatment, lifelong difficulties with communication can be prevented.

SOURCES FOR FURTHER STUDY

Curlee, Richard F. "Counseling in Speech, Language, and Hearing." *Seminars in Speech and Language* 9, no. 3 (1988). In his introductory article to this issue, Curlee presents a clear and interesting overview of counseling strategies for the speech-language pathologist. Counseling of parents and spouses of persons with speech disorders is detailed.

Riekehof, Lottie L. *The Joy of Signing.* Springfield, Mo.: Gospel Publishing House, 1987. A comprehensive book of sign language. Includes origins of the signs, usage of the signs, and sign variations.

Shames, George H., and Norma B. Anderson, eds. *Human Communication Disorders.* Boston: Allyn & Bacon, 2001. This general text covers a wide range of communication disorders. Includes a section on speech-language pathology as a profession. Also includes sections on cleft palate, aphasia, and cerebral palsy.

The Speech Foundation of America. *Counseling Stutterers.* Memphis, Tenn.: Author, 1989. The Speech Foundation of America is a nonprofit, charitable organization dedicated to the prevention and treatment of stuttering. It provides a variety of low-cost publications about stuttering and stuttering therapy. This publication is written to give clinicians a better understanding of the counseling aspect of therapy and to suggest ways in which it can be used most effectively.

_____. *Therapy for Stutterers.* Memphis, Tenn.: Author, 1989. A general guide to help those who work or plan to work in therapy with adult and older-adolescent stutterers.

Jennifer A. Sanders Wann and Daniel L. Wann

SEE ALSO: Aphasias; Grammar and speech; Language; Stuttering.

Speech perception

TYPE OF PSYCHOLOGY: Sensation and perception
FIELDS OF STUDY: Auditory, chemical, cutaneous, and body senses

Speech perception involves a set of enigmatic phenomena, and no completely acceptable theory explaining all of its aspects has been developed. During speech perception, people rapidly extract meanings from a complex spoken signal in the face of many apparently insurmountable obstacles.

KEY CONCEPTS
- acoustic
- articulation
- formant
- motor neurons
- phonetic

INTRODUCTION

The perception of human speech signals involves a variety of phenomena which initially appear trivial; upon closer inspection, however, the phenomena are found to be exceedingly complex. The basic phenomena are the ability to perceive the same speech message correctly when it is presented by various speakers, or by the same speaker performing under different conditions (the phenomenon of perceptual constancy); differences in the perceptual processing of speech and nonspeech sounds; the ability to discriminate well among sounds from different speech sound categories, but only poorly among sounds from within the same speech sound category (categorical perception of speech); and the problems presented by the signal's immediate speech sound (phonetic) context for the correct identification of the signal (the phenomenon of context-sensitive cues).

Each of these phenomena is so complex primarily because of the nature of the speech signal. A spoken language is perceived by a native listener as a sequence of discrete units, commonly called words. The physical nature of the typical speech signal, however, is more accurately described as a continuous, complex acoustic wave. In this signal, not only do the sounds associated with consecutive syllables often overlap considerably, but also the sounds of consecutive words often overlap.

The ultimate goal of speech perception research is the development of a theory that explains the various phenomena associated with the perception of the human speech signal. To achieve this goal, two basic types of information are needed: a detailed description of the speech signal, to test whether any acoustic cues exist that could be used by listeners; and accurate measurements of the acts of speech perception, to test hypotheses related to the different theories of speech perception.

Consonant and Vowel Distinctions

When describing the speech signal for a given language, researchers have noted that the signal is composed of a set of basic units called phonemes, which are considered to be the smallest units of speech. The phonemes can be thought of (though this analogy is imprecise) as corresponding somewhat to the letters in a written word. For example, American English is said to comprise twenty-five consonant phonemes and seventeen vowel phonemes. The distinction between consonant and vowel speech sounds is based on the degree to which the vocal tract is closed. Consonants are generated with partial or complete closure of the vocal tract during some point of their production. Vowels are created with the vocal tract in a more open state.

Since consonants are produced by closing or nearly closing the vocal tract, they contain relatively little acoustic energy. Because of the dynamic changes occurring in the shape of the resonant cavities of the vocal tract during consonant production, the consonants are difficult to specify exactly in terms of acoustic patterns. Consonants commonly contain bursts of noise, rapid changes of frequencies, or even brief periods of silence, which all may take place within twenty-thousandths of a second.

Vowels have less complex acoustical characteristics, primarily because they are produced with the vocal tract open and do not change its shape so dra-

matically. They are of relatively long duration and tend to have more constant acoustical features than consonants. The most important features of vowel sounds are their formants, which are narrow ranges of sound frequencies that become enhanced during vowel production. The formants result from basic physical characteristics of the vocal tract, chief among these being its shape for a particular vowel, which cause most of the vocal frequencies to become suppressed, while only a few narrow bands of frequencies (the formants) are reinforced. Formants are numbered in increasing order from the lowest- to the highest-frequency band. The relative-frequency relationships among the formants of a vowel sound characterize that vowel.

Experiments show that the vowel sounds in English speech can be distinguished from one another by reference to the frequency values of formants one and two. For any given vowel sound, however, there is a range of frequencies that typically occurs for the formants, depending on the person speaking and the conditions under which he or she speaks. There is even some overlap between the ranges for some vowels.

Vowels and consonants can be further subdivided according to the articulatory features that characterize production of the sound. Articulatory features include the location of the greatest constriction in the vocal tract, the degree of rounding of the lips, the place of articulation (that is, where in the vocal tract the sound tends to be primarily produced, such as the lips or in the nasal cavity), and the manner of articulation (for example, "voiced" means the vocal folds vibrate, and "voiceless" means the vocal folds do not vibrate). These factors are important because of their possible use by a listener during the process of speech perception.

The nervous system can be viewed as consisting of two main subdivisions: transmission systems and integrative systems. For speech perception, the transmission systems both transmit and process the nervous signals that are produced by acoustic stimulation of the sensory structures for hearing. The integrative systems further process the incoming signals from the transmission systems by combining and comparing them with previously stored information. Both systems are actively involved in the processes of speech perception. Much research has been done concerning the exact mechanisms of signal processing in the nervous system and how they enable listeners to analyze complex acoustic speech signals to extract their meaning.

Theoretical Approaches

Theories of speech perception can be described in several ways. One way of categorizing the theories labels them as being either "top down" or "bottom up." Top-down theories state that a listener perceives a speech signal based upon a series of ongoing hypotheses. The hypotheses evolve at a rather high level of complexity (the "top") and are formed as a result of such things as the listener's knowledge of the situation or the predictability of the further occurrence of certain words in a partially completed sequence. Bottom-up theories take the position that perception is guided simply by reference to the incoming acoustic signal and its acoustic cues. The listener then combines phonemes to derive the words, and the words to produce sentences, thereby proceeding from the simplest elements (the "bottom") up toward progressively more complex levels.

A contrasting description is that of "active" versus "passive" theories. Active theories state that the listener actively generates hypotheses about the meaning of the incoming speech signal based upon various types of information available both in the signal and in its overall context (for example, what has already been said). The listener is said to be using more than simply acoustic cues to give meaning to what has been heard. Passive theories state that the listener automatically (passively) interprets the speech signal based upon the acoustic cues that are discerned.

Perceptual Constancy and Processing

Often, major differences in acoustic waves are produced by different speakers (or the same speaker performing under different conditions) even when speaking the same speech message. Nevertheless, native listeners typically have little trouble understanding the message. This phenomenon, known as perceptual constancy, is probably the most complex problem in the field of speech perception.

Variations in the rate of speaking, the pitch of the voice, the accent of the speaker, the loudness of signal, the absence of particular frequency components (for example, when the signal is heard over a telephone), and other factors are handled with amazing speed and ability by the typical listener. Many variations result in drastic changes or even to-

tal elimination of many acoustic cues normally present in the signal.

There is experimental evidence to support the hypothesis that when speech occurs at a higher-than-normal rate, the listener uses both syllable and vowel durations as triggers to adjust the usual stored acoustic cues toward shorter and faster values. This automatic adjustment permits accurate speech perception even when the speaking rate approaches four hundred words per minute.

Another difficult task is to explain the ease with which a listener can understand speech produced by different persons. The largest variations in vocal tract size (especially length) and shape occur between children and adults. Even among adults, significant differences are found, the average woman's vocal tract being nearly 15 percent shorter than that of the average male. These differences introduce quite drastic shifts in formant frequencies and other frequency-dependent acoustic cues. Nevertheless, experiments show that even very young children generally have no difficulty understanding the speech of complete strangers, which indicates that the nervous system is able to compensate automatically even before much speech perception experience has been garnered.

Studies of human perceptual processing using speech and nonspeech sounds as stimuli provide evidence for differences in the way people deal with these two categories of sounds. The implication is that specialized speech-processing mechanisms exist in the human nervous system. A major difference is a person's ability to process speech signals at a higher rate than nonspeech signals. Experiments show that phonetic segment information can be perceived as speech at rates as high as thirty segments per second (normal conversation rates transmit about ten segments per second). The rate of perception for comparable nonspeech signals, however, is only about four sounds per second.

Categorical Perception of Speech

The phenomenon of categorical perception of speech refers to the fact that people discriminate quite well among sounds from different speech sound categories (for example, a /b/ as opposed to a /p/ sound, as might occur in the two words "big" and "pig"); however, people's discrimination of different acoustic examples of sounds from within the same speech sound category (for example, variations of the /b/ sound) is not as good. One theory to explain categorical perception proposes that the auditory system is composed of nerve cells or groups of nerve cells which function as "feature detectors" that respond whenever a particular acoustic feature is present in a signal. In the example of the sounds /b/ and /p/ from the spoken words "big" and "pig," according to this theory, there are feature detectors which respond specifically to one or the other of these two consonants, but not to both of them, because of the different acoustic features that they each possess. One problem for proponents of the theory is to describe the particular features to which the detectors respond. Another problem is the number of different feature detectors a person might have or need. For example, is one detector for the consonant /b/ sufficient, or are there multiple /b/ detectors which permit a person to perceive /b/ correctly regardless of the speaker or the context in which the /b/ is spoken (and the consequent variations in the acoustic patterns for the /b/ that are produced)?

CONTEXT-SENSITIVE CUES

Although variations in the immediate speech sound (phonetic) context often result in major changes in the acoustic signature of a phoneme (the phenomenon of context-sensitive cues), a person's ability to identify the phoneme is remarkable. People can recognize phonemes even though the variations found in the acoustic signatures of a given phoneme when spoken by even a single speaker but in different contexts (for example, for /d/ in the syllables "di," "de," "da," "do," and "du") make it difficult to specify any characteristic acoustic features of the phoneme.

Research shows that many acoustic cues (such as short periods of silence, formant changes, or noise bursts) interact with one another in determining a person's perception of phonemes. Thus, there is no unique cue indicating the occurrence of a particular phoneme in a signal since the cues depend on the context of the phoneme. Even the same acoustic cue can indicate different phonemes, according to the context. A complete theory of speech perception would have to account for all these phenomena, as well as others not mentioned.

RESEARCH QUESTIONS

Speech sounds represent meanings in a language, and a listener extracts the meanings from a speech

signal. What has remained unclear is how the nervous system performs this decoding. One hypothesis is that there are sensory mechanisms which are specialized to decode speech signals. This idea is suggested by the experimental results which indicate differences in the processing of speech and nonspeech signals. An alternative hypothesis is that special speech-processing mechanisms exist at a "higher" level, operating on the outputs of generalized auditory sensory mechanisms.

In the 1960's, the study of speech perception developed rapidly; three major theories were presented. These motivated a wealth of research projects, assisted by advances in electronic instrumentation, and have formed a basis for the development of newer theories. All three theories specify an interaction between the sensory representation of the incoming speech signal and the neuromotor commands (that is, the pattern of signals that the nervous system would have to generate to activate the muscles for speaking) which would be involved in the production of that same signal. Two of the theories are briefly described below.

MOTOR THEORY

The first and probably most influential of the theories is Alvin M. Liberman's motor theory of speech perception. Briefly stated, the motor theory maintains that a listener decodes the incoming speech signal by reference to the neuromotor commands that would be required to produce it. The process of speech perception therefore involves a sort of reverse process to that of speech production, in which a speaker has a message to send and generates appropriate neuromotor commands to enable the articulatory muscles to produce the speech signal. According to the motor theory of speech perception, the listener has an internal neural pattern, generated by the incoming speech signal's effects on the sensory apparatus. This pattern can be "followed back" to the neuromotor commands that would be necessary to produce an acoustic signal like the one that has just produced the internal (sensory) neural pattern. At this point, the listener recognizes the speech signal, and perception occurs by the listener's associating the neuromotor commands with the meanings they would encode if the listener were to produce such commands when speaking.

Among the problems facing the motor theory, a major one has been to explain how infants are able to perceive surprisingly small differences in speech signals before they are able to produce these same signals, since it would seem that they do not possess the necessary neuromotor commands. Another problem has been the inability for the supporters of the theory to explain how the "following back" from the incoming signal's generated neural activity patterns to the appropriate neuromotor commands occurs.

AUDITORY MODEL

At the other end of the theoretical spectrum from the motor theory, Gunnar Fant's auditory model of speech perception places greater emphasis on an auditory analysis of the speech signal. This theory proposes that the speech signal is first analyzed by the nervous system so that distinctive acoustic features get extracted or represented in the activity patterns of the nervous system. Then these features are combined into the phonemes and syllables which the listener can recognize. Much as in the motor theory, this recognition depends on the listener possessing basic knowledge about the articulatory processes involved in speech production—in particular, the distinctive phonetic features possible in the language being heard.

In contrast to the motor theory, Fant's model supposes an ability of the listener's auditory system to pick out distinctive acoustic features from the phonetic segments being heard. The auditory model, therefore, separates the auditory and articulatory functions more distinctly than the motor theory does.

One of the problems of the auditory model is that distinctive acoustic features of phonetic segments are difficult to specify unambiguously. Supporters of the model argue that the important features are more complex than the relatively simple ones normally proposed and represent characteristic relationships between various parts of the signal.

SOURCES FOR FURTHER STUDY

Eimas, Peter D. "The Perception of Speech in Early Infancy." *Scientific American* 252 (January, 1985): 46-52. Discusses the human infant's ability to detect phonemic categories long before the age at which speech production has begun. This clearly presented article explains some of the speech perception research techniques that can be used with infants. The results suggest that at least some speech perception mechanisms are innate.

Fodor, Jerry A. *The Modularity of Mind.* Cambridge, Mass.: MIT Press, 1983. Although this is a philosophical presentation of Fodor's theory of mind, much of the text is concerned with speech and language. The discussions may be difficult for high school students, but they are valuable lessons in an alternate approach to what may seem to be a topic restricted to scientists.

Liberman, Alvin M. "On Finding That Speech Is Special." *American Psychologist* 37, no. 2 (1982): 148-167. The author is the chief developer of the motor theory of speech perception. This explanation of the theory and critical experimental results that support it includes many good figures, but most references are to articles in specialist journals. Good for advanced high school and college-level readers.

Matthei, Edward, and Thomas Roeper. *Understanding and Producing Speech.* New York: Universe Books, 1985. Recommended for high school and college readers, this text about psycholinguistics contains clearly written chapters about both human speech production and perception. Includes a good index and suggestions for further reading.

Morgan, Nelson, and Ben Gold. *Speech and Audio Signal Processing: Processing and Perception of Speech and Music.* New York: John Wiley & Sons, 1991. An up-to-date review of speech and audio signal processing, including the physiology and psychoacoustics of hearing, pitch and speech perception, vocoding methods, and automatic speech recognition (ASR) systems.

Perkins, William H., and Raymond D. Kent. *Functional Anatomy of Speech, Language, and Hearing.* Reprint. Boston: Allyn & Bacon, 1991. An excellent text for the serious high school or college student. One chapter is dedicated to speech acoustics, while three chapters treat the neurology of speech (input processing, central processing, and output processing). Good appendixes are included for anatomical terminology and selected readings.

John V. Urbas

SEE ALSO: Aphasias; Bilingualism; Brain structure; Hearing; Language; Linguistics; Split-brain studies.

Split-brain studies

TYPE OF PSYCHOLOGY: Biological bases of behavior
FIELDS OF STUDY: Cognitive processes; nervous
system

*Split-brain studies provide insight into cognitive
asymmetries in hemispheric functioning following
surgery to sever the major interconnecting fiber tracts
that allow communication between the cerebral hemispheres. Knowledge of hemispheric asymmetries is
useful for understanding the organization and information-processing abilities of the human brain.*

KEY CONCEPTS
- cerebral commissures
- cerebral hemispheres
- commissurotomy
- dichotic listening
- dyslexia
- expressive aphasia
- hemispheric asymmetries
- lateralities
- receptive aphasia
- tachistoscope

INTRODUCTION

The study of laterality, or the specialized asymmet-
ric functions throughout the body, is not a new and
novel field, as might be suggested by the populariza-
tion of "left brain-right brain" dichotomies. Lateralization of functions in the brain, sometimes referred
to as hemispheric asymmetries, was demonstrated
in 1861 by Paul Broca, a well-known physician at the
time. He found that patients suffering from damage
to certain regions of the left cerebral hemisphere
exhibited more frequent speech and language disorders than did those with right cerebral hemisphere
damage. Based on these findings, Broca correctly
reasoned that the left hemisphere is specialized for
speech and language in the vast majority of people. Unfortunately, these results were quickly transformed into an overly simplistic dichotomization of
cerebral functioning in which the left hemisphere
was conceptualized as the dominant hemisphere and
the right hemisphere as a rather minor, perhaps
even unimportant, hemisphere. From split-brain
studies performed since 1940, it has become obvious that the right hemisphere is essential for normal visuospatial functioning.

COMMISSUROTOMY EFFECTS

Split-brain surgery, sometimes referred to as commissurotomy, was first performed on a human patient by the neurosurgeon William Van Wagenen in
1940 to reduce the severity of life-threatening epileptic seizures. Other early commissurotomies were
performed by two neurosurgeons, P. J. Vogel and
Joseph Bogen. The rationale for commissurotomies
is rather simple: By severing the cerebral commissures, the major interconnecting fiber bundles that
allow communication between the cerebral hemispheres, surgeons can prevent epileptic seizures from
spreading beyond their focal hemisphere. Commissurotomies are performed only as a last resort, after
traditional drug therapy fails to control seizure activity.

Surprising as it may seem, commissurotomy patients show few long-term alterations in behavior.
All subjects suffer from acute disconnection syndrome, in which they are mute and partially para-
lyzed on the left side of the body for an interval
ranging from a few days to a few weeks. Otherwise,
commissurotomy patients exhibit relatively normal
behavior. Moreover, the severity and frequency of
seizure activity decline, sometimes quite dramatically, in response to this surgical procedure.

HEMISPHERIC ASYMMETRIES IN INFORMATION
PROCESSING

Upon closer examination with a tachistoscope (an
experimental apparatus for presenting visual information very briefly to the right or left visual field,
sometimes called a T-scope) of split-brain patients,
however, hemispheric asymmetries in information
processing are evident. These asymmetries are investigated in T-scope or divided visual field studies.
The split-brain patient is required to fixate on a central point, while visual stimulation is presented to
the right or left visual field. Assuming that the patient is fixated on the central point, stimulation in
the right visual field is projected to the left hemisphere, and left visual field stimulation to the right
hemisphere. Once the information is available to
the left or right hemisphere of a split-brain patient,
it is not able to cross the cerebral commissures,
principally the corpus callosum, since those fibers
have been partially or completely severed.

The pioneering studies of the divided visual field
in split-brain patients are described in *The Bisected
Brain* (1970) by Michael Gazzaniga, who was a

coprincipal investigator with Roger Sperry in those studies. In one of their investigations, pictures of common objects were presented to either the right visual field or the left visual field of split-brain patients. All patients were able to identify the information verbally when it was presented in the right visual field (left hemisphere), but not in the left visual field (right hemisphere). These results suggested specialization for verbal tasks in the left cerebral hemisphere but did not address functioning in the right cerebral hemisphere.

To assess the psychological functions of the right cerebral hemisphere, the researchers repeated the procedure described in the previous experiment, except that subjects were asked to reach under a curtain with their left or right hand to select the object from among several alternatives (rather than verbally identifying the picture of the object). Subjects were able to perform this task competently with their left hand, which is controlled primarily by the right cerebral hemisphere. Therefore, stimulation presented to the left visual field is projected to the right cerebral hemisphere, which controls the left hand. The opposite is true for stimulation presented to the right visual field. Correct identification of objects with the left hand indicated right cerebral hemisphere involvement in recognition of nonverbal stimuli.

Support for the superiority of the right hemisphere on visuospatial tasks came from a study in which split-brain patients were required to assemble patterned blocks into particular designs. Even though all patients were right-handed, they were much better at this task with the left hand, presumably because the right cerebral hemisphere controls that hand. Yet another test of the abilities of the left cerebral hemisphere was performed by requesting subjects to copy pictures of line drawings. Again, despite being right-handed, all subjects performed better with the left hand. Their left-handed efforts were rather clumsy, but the spatial dimensions of the line drawings were proportionally correct. Overall, split-brain studies seem to indicate left-hemisphere superiority on verbal tasks and right-hemisphere superiority on nonverbal, visuospatial tasks.

Further proposals for differences between the right and left hemispheres have been suggested from split-brain research. For example, it now appears that the left hemisphere is specialized for verbal tasks, but only as a consequence of its analytical,

logical, information-processing style—of which language is one manifestation. Similarly, the right hemisphere is specialized for visuospatial tasks because of its synthetic, holistic manner of processing information. Support for these hemispheric asymmetries was derived from a 1974 study conducted by Jere Levy in which split-brain patients were given ambiguous instructions; they were simply to match similar pictorial stimuli. These pictures could be matched either by their functions, such as a cake on a plate matched with either a spoon or a fork, or by their appearance, such as a cake on a plate matched with a hat with a brim. When the pictures were presented to the right visual field (left hemisphere), matching was accomplished by function, while pictures projected in the left visual field (right hemisphere) were matched according to appearance. Matching by function was construed to involve logical, analytical information processing; matching by appearance was interpreted as involving holistic, synthetic information processing.

Most of the basic findings on hemispheric asymmetries in split-brain patients have been extended to normal subjects whose cerebral commissures are intact, with the exception that right-hemisphere superiority for visuospatial tasks seems to be slightly weaker in normal subjects. Investigations with normal subjects require measurement of reaction time, because information projected to one visual field can quickly and easily transfer to the opposite hemisphere.

Real-World Phenomena

When generalizing basic laboratory research findings to real-world situations, it is important to note that information transfer across the cerebral commissures is nearly instantaneous in normal subjects. In addition, the real-world environment provides prolonged visual stimulation, which is typically scanned with continuous eye movements. In these situations, environmental stimulation is available to both cerebral hemispheres. Therefore, one must be cautious not to overstate the case for a relationship between hemispheric asymmetries and real-world phenomena. The two cerebral hemispheres do work in combination as a unified brain in normal subjects. Even in split-brain patients, the prolonged availability of environmental stimulation and continuous eye scanning movements result, for the most part, in unified overt behavior. Behavioral, perceptual, and motor differences in split-brain patients are only evident with highly specialized and artificial laboratory testing with such instruments as the tachistoscope. Generalizations, then, from divided visual field studies of asymmetry to everyday situations require actual research evidence rather than the speculation that is popular among some segments of both the scientific and lay community.

STUTTERING RESEARCH

Stuttering is one real-world phenomenon for which laterality research has practical implications. There is some evidence that stutterers are bilaterally represented for speech and language to a greater extent than are nonstutterers. In one investigation, R. K. Jones, a neurosurgeon, was presented with four stutterers who had blood clots or tumors located near the normal speech center in the left hemisphere. Because of concern that removal of the blood clots or tumors would produce muteness in his patients by damaging the speech center, Jones performed the Wada test to determine where the speech center was located in each patient. This test involves the injection of an anesthetic agent, sodium amobarbital, into the right or left carotid artery. The carotid arteries provide the frontal regions of the brain, where the speech center is located, with oxygenated blood. The sodium amobarbital anesthetizes the particular hemisphere into whose carotid artery the drug is injected. If speech is disrupted by this procedure, either the speech center is located in the opposite hemisphere or the patient is bilaterally represented for speech. Additional testing of the opposite hemisphere will reveal whether the patient is bilaterally represented.

Using this procedure, Jones found that all four stutterers possessed bilateral speech representation. After the surgery, all four patients stopped stuttering and began to speak normally. These findings raise the question as to why stuttering is related to bilateralization of speech functions. One explanation is that stuttering occurs in these patients because, unlike normal people, they have a speech center in one hemisphere that is competitive with the speech center in the opposite hemisphere. Neural impulses from the two speech centers arrive out of synchrony at the muscles that control speech, which produces stuttering. What are the practical implications of these findings? It is quite obvious that producing irreparable damage to the brain for

the sole purpose of eliminating a speech disorder, such as stuttering, would be highly unethical at current levels of medical technology and knowledge about the brain. Additional research on the hemispheric basis of stuttering will need to be conducted, and technological advances will be required before stuttering can be eliminated in bilaterally represented patients by means of neurosurgery; however, findings such as these may be increasingly useful in future applications of laterality research.

DYSLEXIA RESEARCH

Yet another phenomenon linked with laterality research is dyslexia, a disorder of reading that is not associated with sensory impairment, retardation, or emotional disturbances. In 1937, a physician by the name of Samuel T. Orton was the first to propose a link between hemispheric asymmetries and dyslexia. He observed mirror-image reversals of letters and words in reading and writing among children with reading problems. Orton also noted that many of these children exhibited unstable hand preferences, often accomplishing tasks normally reserved for a preferred hand with either hand on a given occasion. To account for these observations, Orton proposed that these children were insufficiently lateralized for speech and language functions. In other words, neither hemisphere was specialized for speech and language.

Evidence to support the hypothesis that dyslexia is attributable to incomplete lateralization was generated in 1970 by E. B. Zurif and G. Carson, who compared the performance of fourteen normal readers in the fourth grade with fourteen dyslexic fourth graders on a dichotic listening task. Dichotic listening involves presenting simultaneous, competing verbal stimuli of differing content to each ear through headphones. The subjects' task is to identify the words, letters, or digits presented to each ear. Since the right ear primarily transmits auditory input to the left hemisphere, and the left ear to the right hemisphere, detectable differences in the processing of verbal stimulation can be used to suggest hemispheric asymmetries. In the foregoing study, presentation of a dichotic digits task showed a significant right-ear (left-hemisphere) advantage for the normal children and a weak, insignificant left-ear (right-hemisphere) advantage for the dyslexic children. Failure to find a significant hemispheric advantage in processing dichotically presented verbal stimulation suggests that dyslexic children may, indeed, be incompletely lateralized for speech and language. Before practical applications of this finding are realized, further explorations on the development of hemispheric asymmetries will be necessary to determine whether lateralization of functions can be influenced by environmental manipulation. Only if such modifications are possible can the development of incomplete lateralization be altered in dyslexics.

EARLY ROOTS OF RESEARCH

Modern research on hemispheric asymmetries has its origins in a short paper read at an 1836 medical conference in Montpellier, France. Marc Dax, an obscure country physician, reported that aphasia (any loss of the ability to use or understand language) is related to left-hemisphere brain damage and concluded that each hemisphere is specialized for different function. Unfortunately, the paper received little attention and Dax died the following year, never knowing that he had anticipated one of the most exciting and productive research fields to emerge in the twentieth century. Because Dax's paper was not widely known, credit for the discovery of hemispheric asymmetries was incorrectly given to Paul Broca, who presented a similar paper in 1861 to a meeting of the Society of Anthropology in Paris. Broca does deserve some of the credit for the discovery of hemispheric asymmetries in that he suggested an exact area of the left frontal lobe that produces an expressive aphasia when damaged. Furthermore, Broca presented a much more impressive case for left-hemisphere lateralization of speech and language; his paper was received with enthusiasm and controversy.

In 1868, a British neurologist, John Hughlings Jackson, proposed the idea of a "leading" hemisphere, which preceded the modern concept of "cerebral dominance," the idea that one hemisphere is dominant for psychological functions over the other hemisphere. By 1870, Carl Wernicke, a German neurologist, had presented evidence that a specific region of the temporal lobe in the left cerebral hemisphere is essential for comprehending language and, when damaged, produces a receptive aphasia. In combination, these findings led to a widely held position that one hemisphere, usually the left, is dominant for verbal tasks and other higher functions, while the opposite hemisphere, usually the right,

possesses no special function or only minor, limited functions. Even though the term "cerebral dominance" is still used today, it is generally recognized that there are no "major" or "minor" hemispheres; they are simply specialized for different tasks and information-processing styles.

The strongest early evidence for a specific function mediated primarily by the right hemisphere came from widespread assessment of brain-damaged patients on spatial relationship tests. After testing more than two hundred brain-damaged patients, T. Weisenberg and K. E. McBride concluded in 1935 that the right hemisphere is specialized for spatial relationships. These results refuted the notion of a single dominant hemisphere for all psychological functions.

Modern contributions made by Roger Sperry, Michael Gazzaniga, and their colleagues have been, perhaps, most instrumental in establishing the functions of the cerebral hemispheres. Their results, as well as those of neuropsychologists, have been incorporated into such areas as biological psychology, cognition, and perception. Biological psychologists are concerned with establishing the functions of various brain structures in normal subjects, including the cerebral hemispheres. Neuropsychologists contribute to laterality research by specifying the cognitive, motor, and behavioral deficits that arise following brain damage to a specific region in the cerebral cortex. Laterality research also provides information about hemispheric specialization for cognitive and perceptual processes.

Future explorations on laterality will continue to examine performance for specific tasks and information-processing strategies in each hemisphere, but with greater emphasis on localizing functions to specific brain structures. In addition, more effort will be expended on developing practical applications of laterality research in clinical and educational settings.

SOURCES FOR FURTHER STUDY

Bryden, M. P. *Laterality: Functional Asymmetry in the Intact Brain.* New York: Academic Press, 1982. A comprehensive book on laterality research and methods for each sensory modality. In addition, such specialized topics as the genetics and development of laterality, sex differences in laterality, and individual differences in laterality are reviewed. Although very comprehensive, the book is highly technical and would be appropriate only for advanced students.

Davidson, Richard J., and Kenneth Hugdahl, eds. *Brain Asymmetry*. Cambridge, Mass.: MIT Press, 1996. Twenty-three essays on the phylogenetic antecedents and anatomical bases, perceptual, cognitive, and motor lateralization, attention and learning, central-autonomic integration, emotional lateralization, interhemispheric interaction, ontogeny and developmental disabilities, and psychopathology of brain asymmetry.

Hellige, Joseph B. *Hemispheric Asymmetry: What's Right and What's Left*. Cambridge, Mass.: Harvard University Press, 1993. Discusses the evolution and function of brain asymmetry in humans. Split-brain studies are referenced throughout.

Springer, Sally P., and Georg Deutsch. *Left Brain, Right Brain*. 5th ed. New York: W. H. Freeman, 1997. Springer and Deutsch have written a comprehensive introductory book on laterality. They address research with split-brain and normal subjects in considerable detail, and provide thorough coverage of potential practical applications of laterality research. The book is very readable and is highly recommended for high school students, college students, and adult readers.

Richard P. Atkinson

SEE ALSO: Aphasias; Brain injuries; Brain specialization; Brain structure; Speech disorders; Speech perception; Stuttering.

Sport psychology

TYPE OF PSYCHOLOGY: Cognition; emotion; learning; motivation; personality; social psychology; stress

FIELDS OF STUDY: Aggression; aging; attitudes and behavior; behavioral therapies; cognitive therapies; humanistic therapies; motivation theory; psychodynamic therapies; social motives

Involvement in sports as a participant or a spectator serves similar psychological functions for individuals: Both help people create and maintain a positive self-concept, allow them to feel a part of important social groups, and provide a pleasant source of stimulation.

KEY CONCEPTS
- anxiety
- arousal
- attribution
- imagery
- motivation
- participant
- self-esteem
- social identity
- spectator
- stress

INTRODUCTION

An individual's motivational level is a critical determinant of his or her involvement in sports, either as a participant or as a spectator. Involvement in sports by both participants and spectators is a result of similar motivational factors: the desire to maintain a positive self-concept, the need to affiliate with or belong to meaningful social groups, and the need for positive levels of stress.

POSITIVE SELF-CONCEPT

As illustrated by the work of social psychologists such as Henri Tajfel, John Turner, and Jennifer Crocker, who have all tested aspects of social identity theory, people attempt to maintain a positive view of themselves. Evaluations that people make of the groups to which they belong have consequences for their social identity. For many persons, the goal of feeling positive about themselves can be accomplished, at least in part, through involvement with athletics—either actively as participants or passively as spectators. For the athlete, self-esteem begins to play an important motivational role in early childhood. Children tend to choose activities in which they are successful, allowing them to feel proud of their accomplishments. Those children who find success in athletic games played at the gym or at recess begin to prefer them to other recreational or intellectual activities; however, physical ability also plays a role in children's decisions to participate in sports. Those with the most skill (presumably a genetic predisposition derived from athletic parents) tend to show the most enthusiasm for sports participation. Success and its subsequent self-esteem benefits fuel their desire to continue or increase their participation in athletics.

When studying the motivation of children, it is important to distinguish between intrinsic motivation and extrinsic motivation. When an individual is

Human-Animal Athletic Dynamics

Sport psychology does not apply only to humans. Some athletes who interact with animals for sport use psychological techniques to enhance performances. Sport psychologists help human-animal athletic teams. Horse and dog trainers learn about their emotions and animal behavior to communicate effectively with their four-legged partners. Humans mentally practice how to focus themselves and their animals on tasks to be performed such as penning calves, jumping obstacles, or completing an obedience trial.

The relationship between humans and animals is crucial for success. Competitions can cause both people and animals to feel anxious and vulnerable to distractions. While preparing for competition, people can consult with sport psychologists in an effort to control the person's and animal's emotions, including fear and nervousness. Sport psychologists aid human athletes to utilize their emotional energy by comprehending negative thoughts and feelings instead of ignoring them.

People are encouraged to condition themselves mentally to have positive emotions which calm them and their animals. Sport psychologists design training exercises to develop people's strategy skills and guide them to be aware of how arousal affects their animal partners.

Animals can detect and react to humans' physiological changes, such as tense muscles and increased heart rate caused by emotional stress. As a result, the team performs poorly. Mental preparation and practice to think positively and be relaxed and confident enable more consistent performances by both human and animal. A combination of physical and mental practice helps human-animal pairs to achieve coordination and a sense of timing and finesse which makes their performances seem effortless. Sport psychology helps athletes from Olympians to weekend enthusiasts achieve compatibility with their animals for competition and companionship.

Elizabeth D. Schafer

intrinsically motivated to complete a task, that person is moved by internal factors such as feelings of competence or an interest in the task itself. Persons who are extrinsically motivated are driven by external rewards, such as money, trophies, or praise from coaches and parents. Ideally, children should become involved in sports for intrinsic reasons, and most do become involved as a result of such motives. When intrinsically motivated children are given external rewards for their performance, however, the result can be a reduced overall motivation to participate in sports. That is, when children believe that they are no longer participating simply because of an inherent enjoyment of sports, they tend to become less interested.

SELF-ESTEEM

The desire to maintain positive levels of self-esteem continues to be a primary motivational force for both adolescent and adult athletes. For these persons, participation in athletics allows them the opportunity to feel good about themselves by helping to fulfill their need for achievement and status. Successful athletic performance provides them with a feeling of accomplishment and mastery.

In addition to motivating the participants, a desire to feel good about oneself serves as a motiva-

tional force for sports spectators. Although spectators do not personally accomplish performance goals as do the athletes, feelings of satisfaction and accomplishment can be experienced by the fans. Sports fans report elation following their team's victory and sorrow after their team's defeat, with levels of intensity similar to those of the players. When one's favorite team is successful, feelings of pride and increased self-esteem are the result. Thus, spectators can improve their self-concept without requiring any special athletic skills.

Nyla Branscombe and Daniel Wann performed a series of studies showing that spectators may experience increases in self-esteem even if their favorite team is not of championship caliber. Fans of the local team, regardless of the success of that team, tend to have higher self-esteem, experience fewer negative emotions, and report greater life satisfaction than do persons who are not fans of the team. Such high self-esteem seems to be caused by feelings of belonging and the social support gained through interactions with other fans. Supporting the local team allows one the opportunity to affiliate with others similar to oneself and to belong to something greater than oneself.

The desire to affiliate with, and belong to, certain groups also motivates sports participants. Humans are social animals and usually enjoy being members of various groups and organizations. As adolescents begin to detach themselves from their families, social groups involving their peers become increasingly important. A primary source of peer-group memberships is sports teams. Membership in such teams permits adolescents to be accepted by their peers, extends their social network, gives them a sense of belonging, and helps establish their social identity. Adults also may satisfy their need for affiliation and belonging by playing in recreational sports leagues.

EUSTRESS

A third factor shown to motivate both the athlete and the spectator is a desire for positive levels of stress. Unlike the negative stress that often accompanies academic or work endeavors, positive stress, called eustress, is reflective of people's desire to find stimulation in life. For both participants and spectators, an athletic event involving their chosen team can be very stimulating. Hearts begin to race, people may feel nervous, and, in general, the event can be quite arousing—much like a roller-coaster ride. This stimulation is actively sought by many people, and involvement in sports is an easy way to obtain it.

ATTRIBUTION, IDENTIFICATION, AND STIMULATION

The motivational forces described above help to explain a wide variety of the behaviors exhibited by athletic participants and spectators. For example, the importance of maintaining a positive self-concept has been used to explain the self-serving attributions of both players and fans. Attributions are the explanations that people give when explaining why certain events occur. Attributions can be either external (the "A" grade was attributable to luck or easy questions) or internal (the "A" on a test was attributable to intelligence or intensive studying). Because of the desire for a positive self-concept, people tend to use external attributions to explain their failures (thereby protecting their self-concept) while forming internal attributions concerning their successes (thereby enhancing their self-concept). This self-serving attributional bias can be found in many areas, including athletics. Research has demonstrated that when a participant or a spectator's team has failed a competition, people tend to form external attributions as a means of explaining

the defeat. For example, when asked to explain why they lost, athletes often blame the officials, bad luck, or the opponents' dirty play. They do not perceive the failure to be internal (attributable to a lack of skill or ability on their part); hence, their self-concept is protected. Conversely, when victorious, athletes tend to assign internal, not external, causes for their success. That is, when the match was won, they state that it was attributable to their skill rather than to luck.

This pattern of self-serving attributions is also found among sports spectators. When their favorite team is successful, sports fans tend to give internal attributions similar to those of the players. When their team loses, spectators choose external attributions to explain the defeat. This bias, used most frequently by the highly allegiant or identified fans, is driven by a desire to maintain the belief that the groups with which they are associated are good. Spectators can increase their self-esteem through a related process, called "basking in reflected glory" by Robert Cialdini and his colleagues. Cialdini has found that spectators enhance their self-esteem by increasing their association with successful teams and protect their self-esteem by decreasing their association with failing teams. In one study, students at a large university were telephoned and asked to describe the most recent game of the university's football team. When the team had won, people tended to give statements such as "We won" or "We were victorious." When the team had lost, however, the typical reply was "They lost" or "They were defeated." In a second study, the day after their college team played, more students wore clothing that identified their university affiliation following a victory compared to when the team had been defeated. The most allegiant fans, however, tend to continue showing support for their team even when it loses over long periods of time. This is consistent with observation of some sports fans (such as members of the Chicago Cubs Die-Hard Fan Club) who continue supporting teams even though they have a long history of losing.

The findings on the intrinsic-extrinsic motivational dichotomy have been used to help individuals who are trying to establish youth sports leagues. In the early stages of a league, intrinsic motives should be emphasized. Increases in extrinsic motivation via rewards and trophies will probably result in a reduction of intrinsic motivation and decrease of interest in the activity. In fact, simply having children come to expect their parents' praise can reduce intrinsic motivation. Unexpected praise and rewards are less likely to reduce intrinsic motivation. In general, it is probably best to take a "hands off" approach to children's athletic games. Less structure and parental influence will most likely result in greater enjoyment of the activity by children.

Coaches often try to increase the motivation of athletes as a means of increasing their performance. For example, by increasing a player's motivation to achieve a specific goal, a coach will probably increase that player's performance; however, increasing the player's motivation is only one method of enhancing performance. Another popular technique, called imagery, involves having the athlete mentally rehearse the athletic situations occurring in a competition. For example, prior to shooting the ball, a basketball player might form a mental image of himself or herself taking the correct stances, completing the correct follow-through, and so on. The results of research investigating the impact of imagery on performance have been quite positive. For example, L. Verdelle Clark had varsity and junior varsity high school basketball players practice their free-throw shooting through either mental imagery or physical practice. The results indicated that the mental practice technique was almost as effective as the physical practice method.

The final factor motivating sports participants and spectators is eustress, or an individual's need for positive stimulation. The notion that people attend or participate in athletics to become aroused has important implications for their aggressive behavior. Considerable literature has noted that higher levels of arousal often result in increases in aggression. Thus, as either the players or the fans become excited (and many become involved with that purpose in mind), they are more likely to act aggressively toward either the players or the spectators of the opposing team. Consequently, at many sporting events, the stage is set for violence.

PROFESSIONAL DEVELOPMENT

Sport psychology is a relatively young specialty area within psychology. Pioneers, such as Coleman R. Griffith of the University of Illinois's Athletic Research Laboratory, expressed interest in sport psychology in the early twentieth century. Griffith published *Psychology of Coaching* (1926) and *Psychology of*

Athletics (1928). The field did not develop at that time. In fact, most of the national and international professional organizations designed to examine issues in sport psychology were founded no earlier than the 1970's, and it was not until 1986 that the American Psychological Association (APA) recognized sport psychology as the separate academic Division 47 (http://www.psyc.unt.edu/apadiv47/). Organizations promoting professionalism include the North American Society for the Psychology of Sport and Physical Activity (http://www.naspspa.org/) and the International Society of Sport Psychology (http://nimbus.ocis.temple.edu/~msachs/issp.html).

Sport psychologists can receive certification from the Association for the Advancement of Applied Sport Psychology (http://www.aaasponline.org/) or by completing continuing education courses offered by the American Board of Sport Psychology (http://www.AmericanBoardofSportPsychology.org). Sport psychologists train in many ways and pursue varied treatment methods. Some sport psychologists analyze how social environments influence the behavior of athletes, while others focus on cognitive aspects which evaluate how thoughts shape athletic behavior. Others focus on psychophysiology, which correlates how brain chemistry affects behavior. Motor development interests many sport psychologists. In addition to traditional forms of counseling, biofeedback, hypnosis, and neurofeedback are utilized. Certified sport psychologists can register with the United States Olympic Committee and National Collegiate Athletic Association to assist elite and student athletes fine-tune their performances and develop coping and psychological skills to deal with demanding, high-profile lives.

MOTIVATION RESEARCH

The topic of motivation is one of the major areas of emphasis within the discipline of sport psychology, and it has attracted considerable research and theoretical attention. Increased interest in the factors underlying the motivation of sports participants and spectators has been driven by the fact that sports are among the most popular leisure-time activities. The vast majority of individuals living in the United States are involved in sports in some form or another, many on a daily basis. In fact, families who share an interest in sports are almost twice as likely to express satisfaction with their leisure time as are persons who are not actively involved with sports.

Furthermore, satisfaction with leisure-time activities greatly influences other areas of an individual's life, such as school or work.

Questions such as why some individuals are motivated to become involved in athletics, why some discontinue their involvement, and what the effects of sport involvement are should receive additional research attention in the future. Many of the initial questions examined in this area focused on ways of assisting athletic coaches in improving athletes' motor performance. Research into casual sports participation, and spectatorship in particular, has become a major focus of sport psychologists since the 1990's.

Understanding the motivations of sport spectators and participants is important for several reasons. First, most individuals begin their involvement with sports at a young age, usually by early adolescence. As a consequence of the large impact of peer relations on the development of young persons' personalities, insight into these relationships is important; comprehension can be gained by studying athletic team formation and cohesion. Second, because self-esteem plays such a critical role in determining whether individuals will become involved in sports, the positive emotional impact of athletics may be used for therapeutic purposes. For example, a clinical psychologist might suggest to clients that they become involved in sports as one means of improving their self-concepts. Third, professional sports is a very big business with many millions of dollars at stake. If an individual's performance could be increased by increasing motivation, the result could be quite profitable. In fact, many professional sports organizations, as well as the United States Olympic Committee, have their own sport psychologists on staff to help players with motivational issues, adjustment difficulties, and stress. As sports gain more cultural significance, sport psychology will prove essential to improve and understand the roles of professional and amateur athletes, coaches, trainers, physical therapists, affiliated personnel, and fans.

SPECIALITIES AND APPLICATIONS

Sport psychology research has expanded as psychologists develop specialties within the field to explore both familiar and emerging concerns. Technological developments offer new sport psychology methods such as virtual reality to practice performances. The Internet provides sport psychology resources for experts, athletes, and related personnel worldwide to network and share insights to advance research investigating universal issues. Many therapists address aging-related concerns, especially as celebrity athletes attempt to lengthen professional careers and amateur athletes seek recreational exercise during retirement. Some researchers evaluate how athletes' age, gender, and ethnicity affect development of psychological skills which aid athletic performances. They also study how grief and terrorism affect athletes of all ages.

Some sport psychologists focus on individual athletes, while others study the dynamics of teams and how members communicate to achieve effective cohesiveness. Investigators collect data concerning athletes' perceptions of sport psychology and subsequent acceptance of or resistance to such efforts to improve their performances. Sport psychologists and physicians study athletes' psychological responses to injuries and illnesses, particularly those medical conditions which halt high-profile athletic careers. They also examine psychological factors involved in rehabilitation and how athletes endure pain, adjust to their new nonparticipant status, and commit to physical therapy. Health professionals are also interested in learning more about athletes who engage in substance abuse or eating disorders or suffer mental illnesses.

Most sport psychologists are concerned with ethical issues that regulate who is qualified to identify themselves and practice as sport psychologists. Leaders in the field attempt to improve graduate and certification programs which offer sport psychology education and training. Sport psychology also incorporates studies of how exercise is psychologically beneficial to nonathletes throughout their lives. Some sport psychologists apply techniques used for athletes to nonsport situations. As consultants to corporations, sport psychologists can improve employees' performance by teaching them cognitive restructuring and visualization methods to cope with stressful situations such as presentations. Private patients benefit from learning to focus on process instead of outcome and to relax with breathing methods to achieve better job performances both on and off athletic fields.

SOURCES FOR FURTHER STUDY

Andersen, Mark B., ed. *Doing Sport Psychology.* Champaign, Ill.: Human Kinetics, 2000. A text focusing on applied sports psychology which provides practical examples, transcripts from sessions, and details describing how athletic personnel use such sports psychology techniques as evaluating personalities to enhance performances.

Hill, Karen Lee. *Frameworks for Sports Psychologists: Enhancing Sports Performance.* Champaign, Ill.: Human Kinetics, 2001. Presents case studies of how athletic activities can be improved by applying therapeutically five theoretical models: psychodynamic, behavioral, cognitive, humanistic, and neuro-linguistic.

Jarvis, Matt. *Sport Psychology.* New York: Routledge, 1999. A volume in the Routledge Modular Psychology Series which differentiates between academic and applied sport psychology. Author discusses such research topics as attitude, memory and learning, anxiety and stress, types of participation, and the process of skill acquisition. He describes how such knowledge can benefit athletes, ranging from ballerinas to football players.

Murphy, Shane M., ed. *Sport Psychology Interventions.* Champaign, Ill.: Human Kinetics, 1995. Edited by the first U.S. Olympic Committee sport psychologist and a former Division 47 president who advocates a zone of mental harmony to achieve athletically, this collection includes essays and case studies which address diverse intervention issues to aid athletes. Topics include injuries, drug and alcohol abuse, burnout, weight and body image, career changes, gender, family and team relationships, ethics, and student athletes.

Roberts, Glyn C., ed. *Advances in Motivation in Sport and Exercise.* Champaign, Ill.: Human Kinetics, 2001. Contributors present social cognitive views of motivational behavior and explore why people are or are not motivated to exercise and participate in sports. Authors discuss the roles of goals, self-determination, and athletes' perceptions of competence and control while engaging in physical activities.

Silva, John M., III, and Diane E. Stevens, eds. *Psychological Foundations of Sport.* Boston: Allyn & Bacon, 2002. Silva, the founding president of the AAASP and handball coach, and Stevens present essays which discuss how the psychological dynamics of sports influence athletes, coaches, and spectators. The book's significant sections address gender, aggression, teamwork, confidence, and youth athletes.

Singer, Robert N., Heather A. Hausenblas, and Christopher M. Janelle, eds. *Handbook of Sport Psychology.* 2d ed. New York: John Wiley & Sons, 2001. A comprehensive collection which incorporates both theoretical and practical sport psychology information for mental health professionals, athletes of all competency levels, and coaches to condition minds in addition to bodies. Subjects, activities, and exercises include psychological skill development for managing pain, increasing self-confidence, and gauging improvement.

Van Raalte, Judy L., and Britton W. Brewer, eds. *Exploring Sport and Exercise Psychology.* 2d ed. Washington, D.C.: American Psychological Association, 2002. The editors, psychology associate professors and coaches at Springfield College, compiled a guide of insights from experts explaining how to become a sport psychologist, improve athletes' physical and mental health, and apply interventions such as intensity regulation and modeling.

Wann, Daniel L. *Sport Fans: The Psychology and Social Impact of Spectators.* New York: Routledge, 2001. This book focuses on the role played by spectators, such as how they affect athletes' self-esteem and the psychological impact of sports on observers. Wann emphasizes that sports tend to benefit fans' mental health but admits a small percentage suffer athletic addictions which interfere with their lives.

Weinberg, Robert S., and Daniel Gould. *Foundations of Sport and Exercise Psychology.* 2d ed. Champaign, Ill.: Human Kinetics, 1999. A basic sport psychology text which explains fundamental psychological aspects that can be appropriated for therapy, coaching, sports medicine, and exercise education. Authors address the role of personalty, motivation, social dynamics, and development of psychological skills to advance athletic talent. Aggression, addictions, and other self-defeating behaviors are discussed.

Williams, Jean M., ed. *Applied Sport Psychology: Personal Growth to Peak Performance.* 4th ed. Mountain View, Calif.: Mayfield, 2001. This anthology thoroughly presents both basic and advanced information to assist students and coaches learn about sport and exercise psychology. Authors explain why intervention is necessary in sport psychology and how to achieve desired behavioral changes.

Nyla R. Branscombe and Daniel L. Wann; updated by Elizabeth D. Schafer

SEE ALSO: Achievement motivation; Affiliation motive; Aggression: Reduction and control; Attributional biases; Crowd behavior; Groups; Intergroup relations; Motivation; Self-esteem.

Stanford-Binet test

DATE: 1910 forward
TYPE OF PSYCHOLOGY: Intelligence and intelligence testing; learning
FIELDS OF STUDY: Ability tests; General issues in intelligence; intelligence assessment

The Stanford-Binet test represented the first widespread method for evaluation of intelligence. Later, the score on the test was adapted into the concept of an intelligence quotient (IQ).

KEY CONCEPTS
- Binet-Simon
- intelligence quotient (IQ)
- mental age
- Wechsler scale

INTRODUCTION

The origin of the idea that intelligence could be tested can be found as early as the 1860's, following the publication of British naturalist Charles Darwin's work *On the Origin of Species by Means of Natural Selection* (1859). Among the concepts addressed in this book, and in his "sequel," *The Descent of Man* (1871), was the idea that the intelligence of animals, including man, could be understood and measured through scientific investigation.

Sir Francis Galton, a British scientist and explorer, who was also Darwin's cousin, was among the first to adopt Darwin's ideas for testing. Galton maintained a laboratory in London, England, where visitors could undergo assorted physical or sensory tests. A subject could be observed on the basis of, for instance, ability to interpret musical pitch. Galton believed such physical or sensory abilities reflected intelligence.

THE BINET-SIMON TEST

In 1904, the Commission for the Education of Retarded Children was established in Paris, France, for the purpose of developing a test that could accurately measure levels of intelligence. The concern was that children were being labeled as retarded not on the basis of mental capacity, but because of behavioral problems. An intelligence test could be used to avoid such incorrect labeling.

Alfred Binet believed that what was recognized as intelligence actually represented a combination of factors, including both knowledge gained from school and knowledge obtained from general observations and interactions with others. The Stanford-Binet test represented the first attempt at determining the mental age of a subject as a means of separating retarded children from those who were normal. The basis of such testing consisted of a series of mental tasks of increasing difficulty. Children of various ages were assumed to have a certain level of knowledge in dealing with such tasks. The number of correct responses to these questions resulted in the assignment of a certain "mental age" to the child.

As originally developed in 1905 by Binet and his colleague Théodore Simon, the test, known as the Binet-Simon test, consisted of thirty tasks which ranged from manual dexterity to the ability to remember general facts or concepts. Binet initially screened fifty children considered of average intelligence and developed a series of norms, now called the 1905 scale. Children were tested in this manner and received a score reflecting what Binet and Simon considered their mental age.

TERMAN'S REFINEMENTS

In 1912, psychologist William Stern adapted Binet's work by calculating what became known as the intelligence quotient, or IQ. The IQ score was calculated by dividing the mental age by the chronological age and multiplying by 100. For example, a mental age of ten and a chronological age of ten resulted in an IQ of 100, considered average. A mental age of twelve in a child of ten would result in an IQ of 120, considered somewhat above average.

Experience with administration of the test to thousands of children over many decades has demonstrated that distribution of scores resembles a symmetrical pattern, a "normal distribution" or bell-shaped curve. Most children (approximately two-thirds) fall within the middle of the curve, with the remaining children distributed more or less equally in higher or lower ranges.

The test as originally devised by Binet consisted primarily of verbal reasoning, reflecting the purpose of the test as a means to separate retarded children from normal counterparts. In 1916, Lewis Terman of Stanford University increased the length of the test and extended the range of age among the children who served as subjects. The result was the normal distribution of scores which are now characteristic of the results. What now became known as the Stanford-Binet test replaced its predecessor, the Binet-Simon. Terman's adaptation has undergone several revisions in the ensuing decades.

The most recent version of the Stanford-Binet test, developed in 1985, consists of both verbal and nonverbal items. The verbal portion involves asking the child to explain or define the use of specific objects. The nonverbal portion contains questions which attempt to examine concepts such as quantitative and abstract reasoning, and memory.

SOURCES FOR FURTHER STUDY

Binet, Alfred, and Theodore Simon. *The Development of Intelligence in Children*. Manchester, N.H.: Ayer, 1983. Reprint of the original 1916 articles by Binet on the subject.

Gould, Stephen Jay. *The Mismeasure of Man*. New York: W. W. Norton, 1996. A highly controversial book by one of modern science's most forceful proponents of evolution. Gould traces the use and, in great depth, abuse of intelligence testing.

Hernnstein, Richard, and Charles Murray. *The Bell Curve*. New York: Simon & Schuster, 1995. The authors address the question of whether the genetics and heritability of intelligence can be reflected both in IQ and in subsequent social success. The authors' conclusions resulted in significant discussion and controversy about the topic.

Minton, Henry. *Lewis M. Terman: Pioneer in Educational Testing*. New York: New York University Press, 1990. Biography of the man most noted for adaptation of the modern Stanford-Binet test.

Santrock, John. *Child Development*. 9th ed. New York: McGraw-Hill, 2001. A general text on the subject of child development. Several chapters discuss and apply methods of intelligence testing in children. Example questions for the Stanford-Binet are included.

Richard Adler

SEE ALSO: Ability tests; Assessment; Career and personnel testing; College entrance examinations; Cre-

ativity: Assessment; General Aptitude Test Battery (GATB); Human resource training and development; Intelligence tests; Peabody Individual Achievement Test (PIAT); Race and intelligence; Scientific methods; Survey research: Questionnaires and interviews; Testing: Historical perspectives; Wechsler Intelligence Scale for Children-Third Edition (WISC-III).

State-Trait Anxiety Inventory

DATE: 1970 forward
TYPE OF PSYCHOLOGY: Personality; psychopathology
FIELDS OF STUDY: Anxiety disorders; personality assessment

The State-Trait Anxiety Inventory, developed in 1970, is the most widely used questionnaire to measure anxiety in the late twentieth century. It is brief (twenty items), and it is widely used in clinical and research settings.

KEY CONCEPTS
• anxiety
• psychological inventories
• state anxiety
• trait anxiety

INTRODUCTION

The State-Trait Anxiety Inventory is a very widely used measure of anxiety. It was developed by American psychologist Charles D. Spielberger, who first produced it in collaboration with Richard L. Gorsuch, Robert Lushene, Peter R. Vagg, and Gerald A. Jacobs in 1970. It is copyrighted by Consulting Psychologists Press.

The State-Trait Anxiety Inventory comprises twenty items about the person's feelings of anxiousness (such as "I am presently worrying over possible misfortunes") that are answered on a four-point scale ranging from 1 ("Not at all") to 4 ("Very much so"). Some of the items are worded positively ("I feel calm"); others are worded negatively ("I am tense"). The positive items are reverse-scored, so that higher scores indicate more anxiety. Frequently abbreviated as the STAI, the inventory has two forms: state form and trait form. In the state form (also called Y-1), the items are about feelings at the present time; in the trait form (also called Y-2), the items are about general feelings overall. The STAI has cut-off scores; a score over this point indicates clinically relevant anxiety symptoms. The original form of the STAI was called Form X.

The STAI has been revised so that it can be used with many different kinds of people. The children's version has twenty items that the child rates on a three-point scale. There is a short version that contains only six items. There is a version for parents to complete about their children that has the usual twenty items, an additional six items. There are versions in many different languages, including Arabic, Amharic, Chinese, Czech, Dutch, French, German, Hindi, Italian, Japanese, Norwegian, Polish, Portuguese, Spanish, and Thai.

USES

The STAI has clinical uses: It can be administered before and after therapy or before and after medication for anxiety. For example, in one report, a woman had distressing a vocal tic, which meant that she involuntarily made repeated sounds, words and coughing in particular. A vocal tic is similar to stuttering. She received therapy that included awareness training, a review of situations and of how inconvenient the habit was, relaxation training, the learning of competing responses, and social support. The therapist measured whether she improved by videotaping her and counting the number of vocal tics and having her complete the STAI to measure her anxiety. She improved in having fewer vocal tics and less anxiety.

The STAI is widely used in research with both adults and children. In a citation analysis of six commonly used measures of anxiety, it ranked first. The reason it is so widely used is that it is a reliable and valid research instrument. One type of reliability is test-retest reliability, which means that people typically describe themselves the same way on the STAI from one time to another. Another type of reliability is internal consistency, which means that all of the STAI questions are measuring the same thing. In terms of validity, the STAI is correlated with other measures of anxiety. Also, people who describe themselves as anxious or who are diagnosed with anxiety disorders score higher on the STAI than people who describe themselves as calm or who are not diagnosed with anxiety disorders. For research purposes, questionnaires must be reli-

able and valid to be useful, and the STAI meets both criteria.

An example of a research project using the STAI with adults was a study of 147 cancer patients (mean age 57.6 years). They completed the STAI and interviews before and after discussions with their cancer physician. Patients who did not like their physician's communication style had higher anxiety following the discussion. Further, after the discussion, patients' anxiety levels remained low, even among those patients with unfavorable examination results, when the patients liked their physician's communication style.

An example of a research project using the STAI with children is a study of ninety children with spina bifida who attended a one-week summer camp. They completed the STAI before and after camp. By the end of the camp, their anxiety was lower than it had been at the beginning.

SOURCES FOR FURTHER STUDY

Briery, Brandon G., and Brian Rabian. "Psychosocial Changes Associated with Participation in a Pediatric Summer Camp." *Journal of Pediatric Psychology* 24, no. 2 (1999): 183-190. This study is a good example of research using the State-Trait Anxiety Inventory for Children.

Fuata, Patricia, and Rosalyn A. Griffiths. "Cognitive Behavioural Treatment of a Vocal Tic." *Behavior Change* 9, no. 1 (1992): 14-18. This article describes how the State-Trait Anxiety Inventory might be used in a clinical situation.

Spielberger, Charles D., Sumner J. Sydeman, Ashley E. Owen, and Brian J. Marsh. "Measuring Anxiety and Anger with the State-Trait Anxiety Inventory (STAI) and the State-Trait Anger Expression Inventory (STAXI)." In *The Use of Psychological Testing for Treatment Planning and Outcomes Assessment*, edited by Mark E. Maruish. 2d ed. Mahwah, N.J.: Lawrence Erlbaum, 1999. This chapter describes the development of the STAI and the State-Trait Anger Scale.

Takayama, Tomoko, Yoshihiko Yamazaki, and Noriyuki Katsumata. "Relationship Between Outpatients' Perceptions of Physicians' Communication Styles and Patients' Anxiety Levels in a Japanese Oncology Setting." *Social Science and Medicine* 53, no. 10 (2001): 1335-1350. This study is a good example of research using the State-Trait Anxiety Inventory with adults.

Lillian M. Range

SEE ALSO: Anxiety disorders; Beck Depression Inventory (BDI); California Psychological Inventory (CPI); Children's Depression Inventory (CDI); Clinical interviewing, testing, and observation; Depression; Diagnosis; *Diagnostic and Statistical Manual of Mental Disorders* (DSM); Minnesota Multiphasic Personality Inventory (MMPI); Personality: Psychophysiological measures; Personality interviewing strategies; Personality rating scales; Thematic Apperception Test (TAT).

Statistical significance tests

TYPE OF PSYCHOLOGY: Psychological methodologies
FIELDS OF STUDY: Methodological issues

Statistical significance tests are techniques that help assess the importance of research findings; they are crucial in helping to determine what inferences can be drawn from the data gathered from a psychological study.

KEY CONCEPTS
- mean
- normal distribution
- null hypothesis
- probability
- significance level
- standard deviation
- T-test

INTRODUCTION

Psychological researchers make extensive use of statistical methods in the analysis of data gathered in their research. Statistical methods serve two primary functions: descriptive, to provide a summary of large sets of data so that the important features are readily apparent, and inferential, to evaluate the extent to which the data support the hypothesis being studied as well as the extent to which the findings can be generalized to the population as a whole. It is this second function that makes use of statistical significance tests.

Researchers may employ these tests either to ascertain whether there is a significant difference in the performance of different groups being studied or to determine whether different variables (charac-teristics) of subjects have a strong relationship to one another. For example, in conducting an experiment to test the effect of a particular treatment on behavior, the experimenter would be interested in testing the differences in performance between the treatment group and a control group. Another researcher might be interested in looking at the strength of the relationship between two variables—such as scores on the Scholastic Aptitude Test (SAT) and college grade-point average. In both cases, statistical significance tests would be employed to find out whether the difference between groups or the strength of the relationship between variables was statistically significant.

LAWS OF PROBABILITY

The term "statistically significant" has a specific meaning based on the outcome of certain statistical procedures. Statistical significance tests have their basis in the laws of probability, specifically in the law of large numbers and conditional probability. Primarily, the law of large numbers states that as the number of events with a certain probabilistic outcome increases, the frequencies of occurrence that are observed should come closer and closer to matching the frequencies that would be expected based on the probabilities associated with those events. For example, with a coin flip, the probability associated with "heads" is .50 (50 percent), as is the probability associated with "tails." If a person flipped a coin ten times, it would not be too startling if he or she got eight heads; if the coin were flipped ten thousand times, however, the observed frequencies of heads and tails would be about 50 percent each. Thus, with large numbers of probabilistic events, the expected outcomes can be predicted with great precision.

Conditional probability refers to the probability of a second event, given that a certain first event has occurred. For example, if someone has already pulled one ace from a deck of cards, what is the probability of pulling a second ace on that person's next attempt (without replacing the first card)? The probability of pulling the first ace was four (the number of aces in the deck) out of fifty-two (the number of cards in the deck). The second draw has a conditional probability created by what happened on the first pick. Since an ace was drawn first, there are now three left in the deck, and since the card was not replaced, there are now fifty-one cards left in the deck. Therefore, the probability of pulling the second ace would be three out of fifty-one.

ESTABLISHING AND TESTING HYPOTHESES

Armed with these two concepts, it is now possible to understand how statistical significance tests work. Researchers are always investigating hypothetical relationships between variables through experiments or other methodologies. These hypotheses can be about how strongly related two variables are or about differences between the average performance between groups—for example, an experimental and a control group. One possible hypothesis is that the variables have no relationship, or that the groups are not different in their performance. This is referred to as the null hypothesis (from the Latin *nullus*, meaning "none"), and it plays an important role in establishing statistical significance. A second possible hypothesis is that there is a relationship between variables, or that there is a difference between the mean (the average value of a group of scores) performances of groups. This is referred to as the alternative hypothesis, and it is the hypothesis truly of interest to the researcher. It is not possible, however, to test this hypothesis directly; it is possible to test the null hypothesis. Since these two hypotheses are both mutually exclusive and exhaustive (only one can be true, but one *must* be true), if it can be shown from the data gathered that the null hypothesis is highly unlikely, then researchers are willing to accept the alternative hypothesis.

This works through a conditional probability strategy. First, one assumes that the null hypothesis is true. Then one looks at the data gathered during the research and asks the question, "How likely is it that we would have gotten this particular sample data if the null hypothesis were true?" In other words, researchers evaluate the probability of the data given the null hypothesis. If they find, after evaluation, that the data would be very unlikely if the null hypothesis were true, then they are able to reject the null hypothesis and accept the alternative hypothesis. In such a case, it can be said that the results were statistically significant.

Arbitrarily, the standard for statistical significance is usually a conditional probability of less than .05 (5 percent). This probability value required to reject the null hypothesis is referred to as the significance level. This criterion is set at a stringent level because science tends to be conservative; it does not want

to reject old ideas and accept new ones too easily. The significance level actually represents the probability of making a certain type of error—of rejecting the null hypothesis when it is in fact true. The lower the significance level, the higher the confidence that the data obtained would be very unlikely if the null hypothesis were true and the observed effects are reliable.

EVALUATION OF CONDITIONAL PROBABILITY

Statistical significance tests are the procedures that allow one to evaluate the conditional probability of the data, given the null hypothesis. The data from one's study are used to compute a test statistic. This is a number whose size reflects the degree to which the data differ from what would be expected if the null hypothesis were true. Some commonly encountered test statistics are the t-ratio, the F-ratio, and the critical (Z) ratio. The probability associated with the test statistic can be established by consulting published tables, which give the probability of obtaining a particular value of the test statistic if the null hypothesis is true. The null hypothesis is rejected if the probability associated with the test statistic is less than a predetermined "critical" value (usually .05). If the probability turns out to be greater than the critical value, then one would fail to reject the null hypothesis; however, that does not mean that the null hypothesis is true. It could simply be that the research design was not powerful enough (for example, the sample size may have been too small, like flipping the coin only ten times) to detect real effects that were there, like a microscope that lacks sufficient power to observe a small object that is nevertheless present.

DIFFERENCES IN SIGNIFICANCE

There is sometimes a difference between statistical significance and practical significance. The size of most test statistics can be increased simply by increasing the number of subjects in the sample that is studied. If samples are large enough, any effect at all will be statistically significant no matter how small that effect may be. Statistical significance tests tell researchers how reliable an effect is, but not whether that effect has any practical significance. For example, a researcher might be investigating the effectiveness of two diet plans and using groups of one thousand subjects for each diet. Upon analyzing the data, the researcher finds that subjects following diet A have a significantly greater weight loss than subjects following diet B. This is practically significant. If, however, the average difference between the two groups was only one-tenth of a pound, this difference would be statistically significant, but it would have no practical significance whatsoever.

T-TEST

Statistical significance tests provide a measure of how likely it is that the results of a particular research study came about by chance. They accomplish this by putting a precise value on the confidence or probability that rerunning the same study would produce similar or stronger results. A specific test, the t-test, can provide an example of how this works in practice. The t-test is used to test the significance of the difference between the mean performance of two groups on some measure of behavior. It is one of the most widely used tests of significance in psychological research.

Suppose a professor of psychology is interested in whether the more "serious" students tend to choose the early-morning sections of classes. To test this hypothesis, the professor compares the performance on the final examination of two sections of an introductory psychology course, one that met at 8:00 A.M., and one that met at 2:00 P.M. In this example, the null hypothesis would state that there is no difference in the average examination scores for the two groups. The alternative hypothesis would state that the average score for the morning group will be higher. In calculating the mean scores for each of the two groups, the professor finds that the early-morning class had an average score of 82, while the afternoon class had an average score of 77. Before reaching any conclusion, however, the professor would have to find out how likely it is that this difference could be attributable to chance, so a t-test would be employed.

INFLUENTIAL FACTORS

There are three factors that influence a test of significance such as the t-test. One is the size of the difference between the means. In general, the larger the measured difference, the more likely that the difference reflects an actual difference in performance and not chance factors. A second factor is the size of the sample, or the number of measurements being tested. In general, differences based on large numbers of observations are more likely to be significant than the same differences based on fewer observations (as in the coin-flipping example). This is true because with larger samples, random factors within a group (such as the presence of a "hot-shot" student, or some students who were particularly sleepy on exam day) tend to be canceled out across groups. The third factor that influences a measure of statistical significance is the variability of the data, or how spread out the scores are from one another. If there is considerable variability in the scores, then the difference (variability) in the group means is more likely to be attributable to chance. The variability in the scores is usually measured by a statistic called the standard deviation, which could loosely be thought of as the average distance of a typical score from the mean of the group. As the standard deviation of the groups gets smaller, the size of the measure of statistical significance, such as the t, will get larger.

Knowing these three things—the size of the difference of the two groups, the number of scores for each group, and the standard deviations of the test scores of the two groups—the professor can calculate a t-statistic and then draw conclusions. The actual calculation of the t is beyond the scope of this article, but with a difference of mean test scores of five points, fifty students in each class, and standard deviations of 3.5 in the first class and 2.2 in the second, the value of t would be 1.71. To determine whether this t is significant, the professor would go to a published statistical table that contains the minimum values for significance of the t statistic based on the number of subjects in the calculation (more technically, the degrees of freedom, which is the total number of subjects minus the number of groups—in this case, 100 minus 2, or 98). If the computed value of t is larger than the critical value published in the table, the professor can reject the null hypothesis and conclude that the performance of the early morning class was significantly better than that of the afternoon class.

COMPLEX DESIGNS

Many research studies in psychology involve more complex designs than simple comparisons between two groups. They may contain three or more groups and evaluate the effects of more than one treatment or condition. This more complex evaluation of statistical significance is usually carried out through a procedure known as the analysis of variance (or F-test). The details of this procedure are also beyond the scope of this article; but, like the t-test, the F-test is calculated based on the size of the group differences, the sizes of the groups, and the standard deviation of the groups.

Other tests of statistical significance are available, and the choice of the appropriate technique is determined by such factors as the kind of scale on which the data are measured, the number of groups, whether one is interested in assessing a difference in performance or the relationship between subject characteristics, and so on. One should bear in mind, however, that statistical significance tests are only tools and that numbers can be deceptive. It is important to remember that even the best statistical analysis means nothing if a research study is designed poorly.

EVOLUTION OF PRACTICE

Tests of statistical significance have been important in psychological research since the early 1900's. Pioneers such as Sir Francis Galton, Karl Pearson, and Sir Ronald A. Fisher were instrumental in both developing and popularizing these methods. Galton was one of the first to recognize the importance of the normal distribution (the bell-shaped curve) for organizing psychological data. The properties of the normal distribution are the basis for many of the probabilistic judgments underlying inferential statistics. Pearson, strongly influenced by Galton's work, was able to develop the chi-squared "goodness of fit" test around 1900. This was the first test that enabled the determination of the probability of discrepancies between the observed number of occurrences of categories of phenomena and what would be expected by chance.

It was the publication of Fisher's book *Statistical Methods for Research Workers* in 1925, however, that popularized the method of hypothesis testing and the use of statistical significance tests. Even though he was not the first to suggest it, Fisher, in this book, established the .05 level of significance as the standard for scientific research. Fisher's second book, *The Design of Experiments* (1935), brought his theory of hypothesis testing to a wider audience, and he believed that he had developed the "perfectly rigorous" method of inductive inference. Among Fisher's accomplishments was the development of the method of analysis of variance for use with complex experimental designs (the F-test was named for Fisher). Prior to Fisher's work, the evaluation of whether the results of research were "significant" was based either on a simple "eyeballing" of the data or on an informal comparison of mean differences with standard deviations. Through the efforts of Fisher and some of his followers, hypothesis testing using statistical significance tests soon became an indispensable part of most scientific research. In particular, between 1940 and 1955, statistical methods became institutionalized in psychology during a period that has been called the "inference revolution." Many researchers believed that these techniques provided scientific legitimacy to the study of otherwise abstract psychological constructs.

PROBLEMS WITH APPROACH

There have been some problems, however, with the statistical revolution in psychological research. Many researchers routinely misinterpret, for example, the meaning of rejecting the null hypothesis. Employing statistical significance tests can only tell the probability of the data, given the null hypothesis. It cannot tell the probability of a hypothesis (either the null or the alternative), given the data. These are two different conditional probabilities. Yet many researchers, and even some textbooks in psychology, claim that the level of significance specifies the probability that the null hypothesis is correct or the probability that the alternative hypothesis is wrong. Often the quality of research is measured by the level of significance, and researchers are often reluctant to submit, and journal editors reluctant to publish, research reports in which there was a failure to reject the null hypothesis. This tendency has led over the years to the publication of many statistically significant research results that have no practical significance and to the withholding by researchers of reports of worthwhile studies (that might have had practical significance) because of a failure to reject the null hypothesis.

Statistical significance tests are valuable techniques for the analysis of research results, but they must be applied correctly and analyzed properly in order to serve their intended function.

SOURCES FOR FURTHER STUDY

Cowles, M., and C. Davis. "On the Origins of the .05 Level of Statistical Significance." *American Psychologist* 37, no. 5 (1982): 553-558. Traces the historical development of the .05 criterion for statistical significance. It discusses many of the earlier standards that were applied informally by statisticians and researchers and discusses Fisher's role in formalizing and popularizing the .05 level.

Gigerenzer, Gerd, and David J. Murray. *Cognition as Intuitive Statistics.* Hillsdale, N.J.: Lawrence Erlbaum, 1987. A somewhat technical but readable account of the emergence of statistical inference in psychological research. The first chapter not only chronicles the important events in this revolution but also gives a very clear discussion of the misinterpretation and misuse of statistical significance tests.

Howell, David C. *Fundamental Statistics for the Behavioral Sciences.* 4th ed. Pacific Grove, Calif.: Duxbury, 1998. An excellent text designed for an introductory statistics course in the behavioral sciences. It does not require a mathematics background beyond high school algebra, and it emphasizes the logic of statistical procedures rather than their mathematical derivation.

Phillips, John L. *How to Think About Statistics.* 6th ed. New York: W. H. Freeman, 1999. Takes a common-sense approach to the logic behind statistical analysis and problem solving. Not a textbook, it focuses more on the thinking behind the numbers than on computations. It also emphasizes the application of statistics, with numerous examples from psychology, education, politics, and sociology.

Pyrczak, Fred. *Statistics with a Sense of Humor.* 2d ed. Los Angeles: F. Pyrczak, 1998. This is a workbook that provides an excellent supplement to any statistics text. The author has a real gift for presenting statistical concepts in a clear manner, and his humorous examples and riddle format tend to make the principles easier to understand.

Rowntree, Derek. *Statistics Without Tears.* New York: Charles Scribner's Sons, 1981. Another excellent introduction to the main concepts and terminology of statistics. Concepts are presented through words and diagrams rather than by means of formulas and equations, which tends to reduce the impact of "math phobia."

Oliver W. Hill, Jr.

SEE ALSO: Data description; Hypothesis development and testing; Sampling; Scientific methods; Survey research: Questionnaires and interviews.

Stepfamilies

TYPE OF PSYCHOLOGY: Developmental psychology; social psychology

FIELDS OF STUDY: Adolescence; coping; infancy and childhood; interpersonal relations; stress and illness

Stepfamilies, created when adults with children marry, remarry, or cohabit, constitute a family form that differs in several ways from the nuclear family. Children in stepfamilies may evidence different levels of social adjustment than children in nuclear families, and there are several perspectives to understand these differences.

KEY CONCEPTS

- child abuse
- developmental stages
- effects on stepchildren
- family system perspective
- family stress perspectives
- nuclear families
- parenting
- (step)parent involvement or style rationales

INTRODUCTION

Social scientists have coined a number of terms for the new social unit that is created when adults with children marry, remarry, or cohabit and form a new family: stepfamilies, blended families, binuclear families, remarried families, subsequent families, and reconstituted families. Historically, there has been some social stigma attached to these terms, and some scholars believe that any structure other than the nuclear family is deficient. Other scholars note the increasing number of stepfamilies and the challenges faced by stepfamilies as they suggest constructive and therapeutic means to assist them.

According to the U.S. Bureau of the Census, nearly one-half of marriages each year in the United States involve a remarriage for one or both parties. Slightly more than half of all divorces involve children under the age of eighteen. Approximately 75 percent of divorced people remarry, on average within four years of the divorce, with 30 percent remarried within one year. The result is that approximately 15 percent of children currently live with a parent and a stepparent, and about one in three children will live with a stepparent at some point before age nineteen. Patterns of marriage, divorce, and remarriage vary by race, ethnicity, and gender. For example, African Americans and Latinos remarry at lower rates than whites. Some groups are more likely to cohabit than remarry after divorce, but this still introduces a new partner into the family dynamic. Stepfamilies also include never-married parents who later marry a person who is not the child's biological parent. Finally, approximately half of all women in remarriages give birth to at least one child in the new relationship. Because of the variety of formation of these families, they are not a homogenous group; tremendous variations exist between stepfamilies.

EXPLANATORY MODELS

According to a review of the literature conducted by Marilyn Coleman, Lawrence Ganong, and Mark Fine of the University of Missouri, the primary models for understanding stepfamily issues and effects on children include family stress perspectives and (step)parent involvement or style rationales. Other scholars note the importance of the developmental stages of the stepfamily and the entire family system perspective.

Family stress models focus on the changes and transitions faced by stepfamilies, such as moving into a different home, learning new rules and routines, and adapting to new family members. These challenges may increase levels of distress, reduce parenting competencies, or result in more conflict in stepfamilies than in nuclear families. The age of children in stepfamilies may impact the amount of conflict, because studies show that adolescent stepchildren report more conflict with stepparents than adolescents in nuclear families.

(Step)parent involvement and style models suggest that biological parents and stepparents may have less time and energy to devote to interactions with stepfamily children because they need to devote those resources to building the new marital relationship or to their children from prior relationships. This is illustrated in the fact that the parents in stepfamilies spend less time with their children on schoolwork and school activities than parents in nuclear families, sometimes resulting in lower academic achievement and behavior problems. Research consistently finds that stepparents interact with their stepchildren less than the biological parents do, and that stepparents are more disengaged

and show less affection to stepchildren. The role of genetic relationship to children is understood to impact parenting style, but it is also a major explanation for the fact that children who reside in a household with an adult who is not their biological parent are more at risk for physical and sexual abuse than children who live in a nuclear household. However, research does not show clearly that the stepparent always commits the abuse; it may be committed by another adult, such as a step-grandparent. It is clear that the same types of authoritative parenting processes, such as warmth and control, which are positive in other types of families, are effective styles in stepfamilies.

Mark A. Fine and Lawrence A. Kurdek note that stepfamilies evolve through several developmental stages: dating and courtship with the eventual spouse, cohabitation (more likely in remarriage situations, but may not occur), early remarriage (the first two years), middle remarriage (two to five years), and late remarriage (over five years). They suggest that premarital relations between the adults who will marry establish the foundation and procedures for later definition of roles and relationships in the stepfamily. The early stage often focuses on management of the transitions and stress of remarriage, while the middle stage concentrates on relationship issues and achieving family consensus about roles.

The family system perspective views the stepfamily as an interactive system in which all members mutually influence each other regarding emotions, relations, and behavior. The system is understood to include people who do not live in the stepfamily household, such as the noncustodial biological parent, the new spouse of the noncustodial parent, or siblings who live with the other parent. This perspective recognizes real-life implications of the complex factors influencing stepfamily relations.

EFFECTS ON STEPCHILDREN

Research on children in stepfamilies has demonstrated a number of differences between them and children in first-marriage families. In academics, stepchildren on average had lower grades, lower scores on achievement tests, lower school attendance, higher drop-out rates, and greater likelihood to receive a General Education Degree (GED) rather than to graduate from high school. Regarding conduct, stepchildren were more likely to have problems with drugs and alcohol, to have sexual relations or conceive a child outside of marriage, and to be arrested. In emotional adjustment, stepchildren on average evidence more emotional problems. However, it is important to recognize that the differences found in the research were relatively small. Many stepchildren do not have conduct or emotional problems, and they do well in school. More research is needed to determine what factors lead to success and positive adjustment.

Psychologist James H. Bray at Baylor College of Medicine conducted research with stepchildren at three periods after remarriage: six months, two and a half years, and five to seven years. He found that children often experience a period of calm and apparent adjustment to the divorce and remarriage prior to a new eruption of problems during adolescence. He suggests that the adolescent task of achieving autonomy and individuality may be complicated by the absence of one biological parent. Many adolescents in stepfamilies experience a renewed interest in their noncustodial parent and about 20 percent of adolescents changed residence from their mother's home to their father's home. These findings may indicate that it is especially difficult to create a stepfamily when one or more children are adolescents. Bray notes that young children accept stepparents more rapidly than do adolescents.

Sociologist Jean Giles-Sims researched the literature on child abuse in stepfamilies and found that a higher percentage of stepchildren than children from nuclear families are included in severe cases of abuse that have been reported and confirmed. She warns against the assumption that all stepchildren are at risk, however, and notes that further research must be conducted to determine the specific factors that contribute to the likelihood of abuse in some stepfamilies.

Parenting in Stepfamilies

Researchers report that parenting in stepfamilies is difficult and stressful. Certain conditions improve the interaction with biological children and stepchildren in the stepfamily. First, it is important to recognize the developmental stage of the stepfamily and the child(ren). At the beginning of stepfamily formation, even positive, normally successful parenting behaviors may be rejected by stepchildren. Emily B. Visher and John S. Visher, founders of the Stepfamily Association of America, recommend that stepparents build a friendly relationship with stepchildren before focusing on discipline. After a positive, nurturing relationship is established over several months, discipline is more likely to be accepted and respected. However, Bray notes that children and stepparents may define friendly affection differently. Children in stepfamilies report that they prefer praise and compliments to hugs and embraces as signs of affection.

Biological parents may have a difficult time with child discipline by the stepparent, even when the biological parent has encouraged the stepparent to be involved. Loyalty to one's own children may create a reaction to discipline from the new spouse. Visher and Visher suggest that the biological parent may need to be the primary disciplinarian initially, but that both adults do need to support each other's authority in the household. However, stepparenting that is too strict or lacking in warmth is consistently connected with more behavior problems and poorer social adjustment in children, no matter how long the remarriage has been in place.

Other Issues

Several other issues are noted in the literature on stepfamilies as common occurrences. Difficulties between the former spouses (biological parents) after one or both have remarried may complicate the functioning of the stepfamily. Visitation with the noncustodial parent, or lack of consistent visitation, may cause tensions and loyalty problems for children. Child support payments or lack of payment of prescribed child support can cause conflict with the ex-spouse and/or marital tension in the new relationship.

Stepsibling relationships may also complicate stepfamily life. Problems may occur if there is too much conflict between stepbrothers and stepsisters, or if adolescent stepsiblings experience sexual attraction or engage in sexual behavior toward each other.

Finally, the lack of clear role definitions for stepfamily members in American society appears to complicate the formation and conduct of stepfamilies. The most common difficulty is the attempt to superimpose roles and understandings from the nuclear onto the stepfamily. Clinicians such as the Vishers suggest that open discussion and dialog about expectations is important in stepfamilies to avoid misperceptions and missed expectations.

SOURCES FOR FURTHER STUDY

Coleman, Marilyn, Lawrence Ganong, and Mark Fine. "Reinvestigating Remarriage: Another Decade of Progress." *Journal of Marriage and the Family* 62 (2000): 1288-1307. This article provides a review of research during the 1990's on stepfamilies. It summarizes key ideas and trends and provides a thorough reference list.

Hetherington, E. Mavis, ed. *Coping with Divorce, Single Parenting, and Remarriage: A Risk and Resiliency Perspective.* Mahwah, N.J.: Lawrence Erlbaum, 1999. This book is written by researchers in a format intended to be accessible to nonresearchers, so complex data analyses are not presented, but the results of research are provided. Part 4 contains four chapters concerning family functioning and child adjustment in stepfamilies.

Levin, Irene, and Martin B. Sussman, eds. *Stepfamilies: History, Research, and Policy.* New York: Haworth Press, 1997. Chapters in this book address various aspects of stepfamilies from an American and international perspective.

Pasley, Kay, and Marilyn Ihinger-Tallman, eds. *Stepparenting: Issues in Theory, Research, and Practice.* Westport, Conn.: Praeger, 1994. This book presents findings from research on stepfamilies that is intended to be helpful to therapists, educators, lawyers, and others who work with stepfamilies.

Teyber, Edward. *Helping Children Cope with Divorce.* Rev. ed. San Francisco: Jossey-Bass, 2001. This is a practical book, written by an experienced clinical psychologist, for parents who want to help their children as they transition from a divorced family system to a stepfamily. Chapter 11 addresses common issues in forming stepfamily relationships.

Visher, Emily B., and John S. Visher. *How to Win as a Stepfamily.* 2d ed. New York: Brunner/Mazel, 1991. The founders of the Stepfamily Association of America provide insight and guidance to stepfamilies about handling all the adjustments in blended family life. This book is written for stepfamily members.

_____. *Old Loyalties, New Ties: Therapeutic Strategies with Stepfamilies.* New York: Brunner/Mazel, 1988. This book is written by a couple who have specialized in working therapeutically with stepfamilies. They provide basic theoretical concepts, therapeutic strategies for working with stepfamilies, and ways to deal with the major areas of difficulty in the formation of a stepfamily identity. Written primarily for professionals.

Mark Stanton

SEE ALSO: Family life: Adult issues; Family life: Children's issues; Father-child relationship; Mother-child relationship; Parental alienation syndrome; Parenting styles; Separation and divorce: Adult issues; Separation and divorce: Children's issues; Sibling relationships.

Strategic family therapy

TYPE OF PSYCHOLOGY: Psychotherapy
FIELDS OF STUDY: Group and family therapies

Strategic theory and interventions have been highly influential in the founding of modern family therapy. Strategic family therapy focuses on influencing family members by carefully planned interventions and the issuance of directives for resolving problems. At times, these directives may appear to be in direct opposition to the goals of treatment (an approach referred to as paradox). Strategic therapy is one of the most widely studied, taught, and emulated approaches to treating family (and individual) dysfunction.

KEY CONCEPTS
- agoraphobia
- double bind
- paradoxical intervention
- reframing
- restraining strategies
- symptom prescription

INTRODUCTION

Families engage in complex interactional sequences that involve both verbal and nonverbal (for example, gestures, posture, intonation, volume) patterns of communication. Family members continually send and receive complicated messages. Strategic family approaches are designed to alter psychological difficulties which emerge from problematic interactions between individuals. Specifically, strategic therapists view individual problems (for example, depression, anxiety) as manifestations of disturbances in the family. Psychological symptoms are seen as the consequences of misguided attempts at changing an existing disturbance. For example, concerned family members may attempt to "protect" an agoraphobic patient from anxiety by re-arranging activities and outings so that the patient is never left alone; unfortunately, these efforts only serve to foster greater dependency, teach avoidant behaviors, and maintain agoraphobic symptoms. From a strategic viewpoint, symptoms are regarded as communicative in nature. That is, symptoms have distinct meanings within families and usually appear when a family member feels trapped and cannot break out of the situation via nonsymptomatic ways.

COMMUNICATION MODELS
The strategic model views all behavior as an attempt to communicate. In fact, it is impossible not to communicate, just as it is impossible not to act. For example, an adolescent who runs away from home sends a message to his or her parents; similarly, the parents communicate different messages in terms of how they react. Frequently, the intended message behind these nonverbal forms of communication is difficult for family members to discern. Moreover, when contradictions appear between verbal and nonverbal messages, communication can become incongruent and clouded by mixed messages.

Gregory Bateson, who was trained as an anthropologist and developed much of the early theory behind strategic approaches, worked with other theorists to develop the double-bind theory of schizophrenia. A double-bind message is a particularly problematic form of mixed communication that occurs when a family member sends two messages, requests, or commands that are logically inconsistent, contradictory, or impossible. For example, problems arise when messages at the content level ("I love you" or "Stay close to me") conflict with nonverbal messages at another level ("I despise you" or "Keep your distance"). Eventually, it is argued, a child who is continually exposed to this mixed style of communication, that is, a "no-win" dilemma, may feel angered, helpless, and fearful, and responds by withdrawing.

Since Bateson's early work in communication theory and therapy, the strategic approach has undergone considerable revision. At least three divisions of strategic family therapy are frequently cited:

the original Mental Research Institute (MRI) interactional view, the strategic approach advocated by therapists Jay Haley and Cloe Madanes, and the Milan systemic family therapy model. There is considerable overlap among these approaches, and the therapy tactics are generally similar.

FAMILY THERAPY TYPES
The MRI interactional family therapy approach shares a common theoretical foundation with the other strategic approaches. In addition to Bateson, some of the prominent therapists who have been associated with the institute at one time or another are Don Jackson, Jay Haley, Virginia Satir, and Paul Watzlawick. As modified by Watzlawick's writings, including *The Invented Reality* (1984), the MRI model emphasizes that patients' attempts to solve problems often maintain or exacerbate difficulties. Problems may arise when the family either overreacts or underreacts to events. For example, ordinary life difficulties or transitions (for example, a child beginning school, an adult dealing with new work assignments) may be associated with family overreactions. Similarly, significant problems may be treated as no particular problem. The failure to handle such events in a constructive manner within the family system eventually leads to the problem taking on proportions and characteristics which may seem to have little similarity to the original difficulty. During family therapy, the MRI approach employs a step-by-step progression of suggested strategies toward the elimination of a symptom. Paradoxical procedures, which are described later, represent a mainstay of the MRI approach.

Haley and Madanes's approach to strategic family therapy argues that change occurs through the process of the family carrying out assignments (to be completed outside therapy) issued by the therapist. As described in Madanes's *Strategic Family Therapy* (1981), strategic therapists attempt to design a therapeutic strategy for each specific problem. Instead of "suggesting" strategies, as in the MRI approach, therapists issue directives which are designed deliberately to shift the organization of the family in order to resolve the presenting problem. Problems are viewed as serving a function in the family and always involve at least two or three individuals. As detailed in Haley's *Leaving Home: The Therapy of Disturbed Young People* (1980) and *Ordeal Therapy: Unusual Ways to Change Behavior* (1984), treatment includes intense involvement, carefully planned interventions designed to reach clear goals, frequent use of therapist-generated directives or assignments, and paradoxical procedures.

The Milan systemic family therapy model is easily distinguished from other strategic approaches because of its unique spacing of therapeutic sessions and innovative team approach to treatment. The original work of therapists Mara Selvini-Palazzoli, Luigi Boscolo, Gianfranco Cecchin, and Guiliana Prata has been described as "long brief" family therapy and was used to treat a wide variety of severe problems such as anorexia and schizophrenia. The first detailed description of the Milan group's approach was written by the four founding therapists and called *Paradox and Counterparadox: A New Model in the Therapy of the Family in Schizophrenic Transition* (1978). The original Milan approach incorporated monthly sessions for approximately one year. The unusual spacing of sessions was originally scheduled because many of the families seen in treatment traveled hundreds of miles by train to receive therapy. Later, however, the Milan group decided that many of their interventions, including paradox, required considerable time to work. Thus, they continued the long brief model. Another distinguishing factor of the Milan group was its use of therapist-observer teams who watched treatment sessions from behind a two-way mirror. From time to time, the therapist observers would request that the family therapist interrupt the session to confer about the treatment process. Following this discussion, the family therapist would rejoin the session and initiate interventions, including paradox, as discussed by the team of therapist observers who remained behind the mirror. In 1980, the four originators of the Milan group divided into two smaller groups (Boscolo and Cecchin; Selvini-Palazzoli and Prata). Shortly thereafter, Selvini-Palazzoli and Prata continued pursuing family research separately. The work of Boscolo and Cecchin is described in *Milan Systemic Family Therapy* (1987), while Selvini-Palazzoli's work is presented in *Family Games* (1989), which she wrote with several new colleagues.

THE IMPORTANCE OF FAMILY

Jay Haley argued that conventional mental health approaches were not providing effective treatment. Based on his work with schizophrenics, he observed that patients typically would improve during their hospitalizations, return home, and then quickly suffer relapses. He also suggested that if the patient did improve while away from the hospital, then a family crisis would often ensue, resulting in the patient's eventual rehospitalization. Thus, effective treatment from a strategic framework often required family members to weather crises and alter family patterns of communication so that constructive change could occur.

Related to Haley's work with hospitalized patients was his treatment of "disturbed" young adults who exhibited bizarre behavior and/or continually took illegal drugs. In *Leaving Home: The Therapy of Disturbed Young People* (1997), Haley suggests that it is best to assume that the problem is not an individual problem, but a problem of the family and the young person separating from each other. That is, young adults typically leave home as they succeed in work, school, or career and form other intimate relationships. Some families, however, become unstable, dysfunctional, or distressed as the son or daughter attempts to leave. In order to regain family stability, the young adult may fail in attempts to leave home (often via abnormal behavior). Furthermore, if the family organization does not shift, then the young adult may be destined to fail over and over again.

Haley's approach to treating such cases includes several stages of strategic therapy. First, the entire family attends the initial interview, and the parents are put in charge of solving their child's problems. During treatment, the parents are told that they are the best therapists for their child's problems. Because the family is assumed to be in conflict (as shown by the patient's problems), requiring the family to take charge and become active in the treatment of the identified patient allows for greater opportunities to intervene around the conflict. In particular, it is assumed that the hierarchy of the family is in confusion and that the parents must take an active role in shifting the family's organization. Also, all family members are encouraged to adopt a position in which they expect the identified patient's problems to become normal.

As the identified patient improves, the family will often experience a crisis and become unstable again. A relapse of the identified patient would follow the usual sequence for the family and return stability (and familiarity) to the system. Unfortunately, a relapse would only serve to perpetuate the dysfunction. Therefore, the therapist may further assist the family by dealing with concerns such as parental conflicts and fears, or attempt to assist the young adult by providing opportunities away from therapy sessions that foster continued growth. Eventually, termination is planned, based on the belief that treatment does not require the resolution of all family problems, but instead those centered on the young adult.

PARADOXICAL PROCEDURES

Strategic therapists share a common belief in the utility of paradoxical procedures. In fact, the history of modern paradoxical psychotherapy is frequently credited as beginning with the MRI group, although paradoxical techniques have been discussed by various theorists from other orientations. Paradox refers to a contradiction or an apparent inconsistency that defies logical deduction. That is, strategic paradox is employed as a means of altering behavior through the use of strategies in apparent opposition to treatment goals. The need for paradoxical procedures is based on the assumption that families are very resistant to change and frequently attempt to disrupt the therapist's effort to help them. Thus, if the therapist suggests common therapeutic tactics (for example, communication homework, parenting suggestions), then the family may resist (for example, may "forget" to do the homework, sabotaging the exercise) and fail to improve. On the other hand, if the therapist tells the family to do what they are already doing, then the family may resist by getting better.

A variety of explanations have been offered to explain the manner in which paradox works. In *Change: Principles of Problem Formation and Problem Resolution* (1974), written by Watzlawick and his colleagues, paradox is described as producing a special type of change among family members. That is, there are two levels of change: first-order and second-order change. First-order change is change within a family system (for example, a parent increasing punishment as the child's behavior becomes more disruptive). First-order change is typically conducted in a step-by-step fashion and involves the uses of problem-solving strategies. On the other hand, second-order change refers to changing the family system itself, and it typically occurs in a sudden and radical manner. The therapist attempts to change the system by unexpected, illogical, or abrupt methods. Paradoxi-

cal procedures are designed to effect second-order change. A paradoxical approach might be to encourage the child to act out every time he or she believes that the parents are about to have a fight. In such a case, the family system may be transformed by family members receiving important feedback about the manner in which they operate, by increased understanding of one another's impact on the system, and by efforts to discard "old family rules" by initiating new procedures for effective family living.

Several different classes of paradoxical interventions are highlighted in Gerald Weeks and Luciano L'Abate's book *Paradoxical Psychotherapy: Theory and Practice with Individuals, Couples, and Families* (1982). These include reframing, prescribing the symptom, and restraining.

REFRAMING, RESTRAINING, AND RELAPSING

Reframing refers to providing an alternative meaning or viewpoint to explain an event. A common example of reframing is Tom Sawyer, who described the boredom of whitewashing a fence as pleasurable and collected cash from his peers for the opportunity to assist him. Reframing provides a new framework from which to evaluate interactions (for example, "Mom is smothering" versus "Mom is caring and concerned").

Prescribing the symptom refers to encouraging or instructing patients to engage in the behavior that is to be eliminated or altered. Symptom prescription is the most common form of paradox in the family therapy literature. Following the presentation of an appropriate rationale to the family (for example, to gain more assessment information), the therapist offers a paradoxical instruction to the family, typically as part of the week's homework. For example, a child who frequently throws temper tantrums may be specifically instructed to engage in tantrums, but only in certain locations at scheduled times. Another common use of paradox involves symptom prescription for insomniacs. A patient with onset insomnia (difficulty falling asleep) may be encouraged to remain awake in order to become more aware of his or her thoughts and feelings before falling asleep. As might be guessed, anxiety is often associated with onset insomnia, and such an intervention serves to decrease anxiety about failing to fall asleep by introducing the idea that the patient is supposed to stay awake. Frequently, patients describe difficulty completing the homework because they "keep falling asleep too quickly."

Restraining strategies include attempts to discourage, restrain, or even deny the possibility of change; the therapist might say, "Go slow" or "The situation appears hopeless" or "Don't change." The basis for restraining strategies is the belief that many patients may not wish to change. Why would patients seek treatment and spend money toward that end if they do not wish to improve? All change involves risk, and with risk comes danger and/or uncertainty. Moreover, the future may be less predictable following change. In fact, it is possible to conceive of most recurring patterns of family dysfunction or individual difficulties as a heavy overcoat. At times, the heavy overcoat serves a useful purpose by protecting one from harsh weather. As time passes, however, the overcoat becomes uncomfortable as the weather becomes warmer. Still, many people dread taking off the overcoat because they are used to it, it has become familiar, and the future seems uncertain without it. From the patient's viewpoint, discomfort may be more acceptable than change (and the uncertainty it brings).

Perhaps the most common restraining strategy is predicting a relapse. In predicting a relapse, the patient is told that a previous problem or symptom will reappear. By so doing, the therapist is in a no-lose situation. If the problem reappears, then it was predicted successfully by the therapist, is understood by the therapist, and can be dealt with by the therapist and patient. If the problem does not reappear, then the problem is being effectively controlled by the patient.

THEORETICAL EVOLUTION

Strategic approaches, based on communication theories, developed from research conducted at the Mental Research Institute (MRI) in Palo Alto, California, in the 1950's. In contrast to psychodynamic approaches, which emphasize the importance of past history, trauma, and inner conflicts, strategic therapies highlight the importance of the "here and now" and view psychological difficulties as emerging from problematic interactions between individuals (family members or married partners). Moreover, strategic therapists tend to follow a brief model of treatment, in contrast to many individual and family therapy approaches.

The effectiveness of family therapy approaches, including strategic approaches, is difficult to measure. Although there has been a clear increase in research evaluating the efficacy of family interventions since about 1980, the results are less than clear because of difficulties with research methodologies and diverse research populations. For example, psychodynamic therapists prefer to use case studies rather than experimental designs to determine effectiveness. Strategic therapists have conducted only a handful of research studies, but these results are encouraging. A structural-strategic approach developed by psychologist M. Duncan Stanton has demonstrated effectiveness in the treatment of drug abuse. Also, the Milan approach has been found to be effective for a variety of problems identified by families who participated in a three-year research program. Further research is warranted, however, before definitive conclusions about the empirical effectiveness of strategic approaches can be reached.

In conclusion, strategic family therapy has shaped the field of family therapy. Innovative approaches such as paradox have been associated with strategic therapy for years, and advances continue to be seen from the respective groups of strategic therapists. Although strategic approaches such as paradoxical directives are frequently regarded as controversial and perhaps risky, the importance of some strategic contributions to the field of family therapy—in particular, the recognition of multiple levels of communication, and of subtle nuances of power struggles in relationships—is widely accepted.

SOURCES FOR FURTHER STUDY

Goldenberg, Irene, and Herbert Goldenberg. *Family Therapy: An Overview.* 5th ed. Belmont, Calif.: Wadsworth, 1999. An updated review of the major family therapy approaches, including strategic family therapy. Also provides a background on family development, and highlights issues in family therapy research and training.

Haley, Jay. *Leaving Home: The Therapy of Disturbed Young People.* 2d ed. New York: Brunner/Mazel, 1997. Presents a treatment program for disturbed young people and their families. Describes the use of intense involvement and rapid disengagement with such families. Haley is one of the foremost theorists and therapists in strategic approaches.

Madanes, Cloe. *Strategic Family Therapy*. 1981. Reprint. San Francisco: Jossey-Bass, 1991. Provides an overview of strategic family therapy from one of the primary therapists in the field. Describes the philosophy and common approaches employed by strategic therapists in the treatment of a variety of presenting problems.

Stanton, M. Duncan. "Strategic Approaches to Family Therapy." In *Handbook of Family Therapy*, edited by Alan S. Gurman and David P. Kniskern. New York: Brunner/Mazel, 1981. Summarizes the strategic family therapy approach and highlights the central components of the MRI group, Milan school, and other notable strategic therapists. Also highlights the dimensions of healthy and dysfunctional families from a strategic model. Finally, briefly outlines some research on the effectiveness of the model in treating a variety of disorders.

Weeks, Gerald R., and Luciano L'Abate. *Paradoxical Psychotherapy: Theory and Practice with Individuals, Couples, and Families*. New York: Brunner/Mazel, 1982. Provides an overview of paradoxical approaches and details a variety of considerations in using paradox in treatment. Presents a compilation of paradoxical methods and describes some of the theories underlying these methods.

Gregory L. Wilson

SEE ALSO: Behavioral family therapy; Couples therapy; Family life: Adult issues; Family life: Children's issues; Observational learning and modeling therapies; Parenting styles; Play therapy; Psychotherapy: Children; Separation and divorce: Adult Issues; Separation and divorce: Children's issues.

Stress

TYPE OF PSYCHOLOGY: Stress
FIELDS OF STUDY: Coping; critical issues in stress; stress and illness

The stress response consists of physiological arousal, subjective feelings of discomfort, and the behavioral changes people experience when they confront situations that they appraise as dangerous or threatening. Because exposure to extreme situational or chronic stress causes emotional distress and may impair physical functioning, it is important to learn effective stress coping strategies.

KEY CONCEPTS
- cognitive appraisal
- emotion-focused coping
- learned helplessness
- problem-focused coping
- stressor

INTRODUCTION

In the past, the term "stress" designated both a stimulus (a force or pressure) and a response (adversity, affliction). More recently, it has usually been used to denote a set of changes that people undergo in situations that they appraise as threatening to their well-being. These changes involve physiological arousal, subjective feelings of discomfort, and overt behaviors. The terms "anxiety" and "fear" are also used to indicate what people experience when they appraise circumstances as straining their ability to cope with them.

The external circumstances that induce stress responses are called stressors. Stressors have a number of important temporal components. Exposure to them may be relatively brief with a clear starting and stopping point (acute stressors) or may persist for extended periods without clear demarcation (chronic stressors). Stressors impinge on people at different points in their life cycles, sometimes occurring "off time" (at times that are incompatible with personal and societal expectations of their occurrence) or at a "bad time" (along with other stressors). Finally, stress may be induced by the anticipation of harmful circumstances that one thinks one is likely to confront, by an ongoing stressor, or by the harmful effects of stressors already encountered. All these factors affect people's interpretations of stressful events, how they deal with them, and how effective they are at coping with them.

Although there are some situations to which almost everyone responds with high levels of stress, there are individual differences in how people respond to situations. Thus, though most people cringe at the thought of having to parachute from an airplane, a substantial minority find this an exciting, challenging adventure. Most people avoid contact with snakes, yet others keep them as pets. For most people, automobiles, birds, and people with deep voices are largely neutral objects, yet for others they provoke a stress reaction that may verge on panic.

The key concept is cognitive appraisal. Situations become stressors for an individual only if they are construed as threatening or dangerous by that individual. As demonstrated in a study of parachuters, by psychologists Walter D. Fenz and Seymour Epstein, stress appraisals can change markedly over the course of exposure to a stressor, and patterns of stress arousal differ as a function of experience with the stressor. Fenz and Epstein found that fear levels of veteran jumpers (as evaluated by a self-report measure) were highest the morning before the jump, declined continuously up to the moment of the jump, and then increased slightly until after landing. Fear levels for novice jumpers, in contrast, increased up to a point shortly before the jump and then decreased continuously. For both groups, the peak of stress occurred during the anticipatory period rather than at the point of the greatest objective danger (the act of jumping).

MEASURING STRESS

Stress reactions are measured in three broad ways: by means of self-report, through behavioral observations, and on the basis of physiological arousal. The self-report technique is the technique most commonly used by behavioral scientists to evaluate subjective stress levels. The State Anxiety Scale of the State-Trait Anxiety Inventory, developed by psychologist Charles Spielberger, is one of the most widely used self-report measures of stress. Examples of items on this scale are "I am tense," "I am worried," and "I feel pleasant." Subjects are instructed to respond to the items in terms of how they currently feel.

Self-report state anxiety scales may be administered and scored easily and quickly. Further, they may be administered repeatedly and still provide valid measures of momentary changes in stress levels. They have been criticized by some, however, because they are face valid (that is, their intent is clear); therefore, people who are motivated to disguise their stress levels can readily do so.

Overt behavioral measures of stress include direct and indirect observational measures. Direct measures focus on behaviors associated with stress-related physiological arousal such as heavy breathing, tremors, and perspiration; self-manipulations such as nail biting, eyeblinks, and postural orienta-

tion; and body movement such as pacing.

Speech disturbances, both verbal (for example, repetitions, omissions, incomplete sentences, and slips of the tongue) and nonverbal (for example, pauses and hand movements), have been analyzed intensively, but no single measure or pattern has emerged as a reliable indicant of stress. Another way in which people commonly express fear reactions is by means of facial expressions. This area has been studied by psychologists Paul Ekman and Wallace V. Friesen, who concluded that the facial features that take on the most distinctive appearance during fear are the eyebrows (raised and drawn together), the eyes (open, lower lid tensed), and the lips (stretched back).

Indirect observational measures involve evaluating the degree to which people avoid feared objects. For example, in one test used by clinical psychologists to assess fear level, an individual is instructed to approach a feared stimulus (such as a snake) and engage in increasingly intimate interactions with it (for example, looking at a caged snake from a distance, approaching it, touching it, holding it). The rationale is that the higher the level of fear elicited, the earlier in the sequence the person will try to avoid the feared stimulus. Other examples include asking claustrophobics (people who are fearful of being closed in) to remain in a closed chamber as long as they can and asking acrophobics (people who fear heights) to climb a ladder and assessing their progress.

Physiological arousal is an integral component of the stress response. The most frequently monitored response systems are cardiovascular responses, electrodermal responses, and muscular tension. These measures are important in their own right as independent indicants of stress level, and in particular as possible indices of stress-related diseases.

ULCERS AND LEARNED HELPLESSNESS

The concept of stress has been used to help explain the etiology of certain diseases. Diseases that are thought to be caused in part by exposure to stress or poor ability to cope with stress are called psychophysiological or psychosomatic disorders. Among the diseases that seem to have strong psychological components are ulcers and coronary heart disease. The role of stress in ulcers was highlighted in a study by Joseph V. Brady known as the "executive monkey" study. In this study, pairs of monkeys were yoked together in a restraining apparatus. The monkeys received identical treatment except that one member of each pair could anticipate whether both of them would be shocked (he was given a warning signal) and could control whether the shock was actually administered (if he pressed a lever, the shock was avoided). Thus, one monkey in each pair (the "executive monkey") had to make decisions constantly and was responsible for the welfare of both himself and his partner. Twelve pairs of monkeys were tested, and in every case the executive monkey died of peptic ulcers within weeks, while the passive member of each pair remained healthy. This experiment was criticized because of flaws in its experimental design, but it nevertheless brought much attention to the important role that chronic stress can play in the activation of physiological processes (in this case, the secretion of hydrochloric acid in the stomach in the absence of food) that can be damaging or even life threatening.

Although being in the position of a business executive who has to make decisions constantly can be very stressful, research indicates that it may be even

more damaging to be exposed to stress over long periods and not have the opportunity to change or control the source of stress. People and animals who are in aversive situations over which they have little or no control for prolonged periods are said to experience learned helplessness. This concept was introduced by psychologist Martin E. P. Seligman and his colleagues. In controlled research with rats and dogs, he and his colleagues demonstrated that exposure to prolonged stress that cannot be controlled produces emotional, motivational, and cognitive deficits. The animals show signs of depression and withdrawal, they show little ability or desire to master their environment, and their problem-solving ability suffers.

Learned helplessness has also been observed in humans. Seligman refers to Bruno Bettelheim's descriptions of some of the inmates of the Nazi concentration camps during World War II, who, when faced with the incredible brutality and hopelessness of their situation, gave up and died without any apparent physical cause. Many institutionalized patients (for example, nursing home residents and the chronically ill) also live in environments that are stressful because they have little control over them. Seligman suggests that the stress levels of such patients can be lowered and their health improved if they are given maximum control over their everyday activities (such as choosing what they want for breakfast, the color of their curtains, and whether to sleep late or wake up early).

STRESS AND CONTROL

Research findings have supported Seligman's suggestions. For example, psychologists Ellen Langer and Judith Rodin told a group of elderly nursing home residents that they could decide what they wanted their rooms to look like, when they wanted to go see motion pictures, and with whom they wanted to interact. A second comparable group of elderly residents, who were randomly assigned to live on another floor, were told that the staff would care for them and try to keep them happy. It was found that the residents in the first group became more active and reported feeling happier than those in the second group. They also became more alert and involved in different kinds of activities, such as attending movies and socializing. Further, during the eighteen-month period following the intervention, 15 percent of the subjects in the first

Studies show that stress, and the accompanying health risks, can be lessened through contact with pets. (Digital Stock)

group died, whereas 30 percent of the subjects in the second group died.

Altering people's perception of control and predictability can also help them adjust to transitory stressful situations. Studies by psychologists Stephen Auerbach, Suzanne Miller, and others have shown that for people who prefer to deal with stress in active ways (rather than by avoiding the source of stress), adjustment to stressful surgical procedures and diagnostic examinations can be improved if they are provided with detailed information about the impending procedure. It is likely that the information enhances their sense of predictability and control in an otherwise minimally controllable situation. Others, who prefer to control their stress by "blunting" the stressor, show better adjustment when they are not given detailed information.

REACTION TO STRESS

Physiologist Walter B. Cannon was among the first scientists to describe how people respond to stressful circumstances. When faced with a threat, one's body mobilizes for "fight or flight." One's heart rate increases, one begins to perspire, one's muscles tense, and one undergoes other physiological changes to prepare for action either to confront the stressor or to flee the situation.

Physician Hans Selye examined the fight-or-flight response in more detail by studying physiological changes in rats exposed to stress. He identified three stages of reaction to stress, which he collectively termed the general adaptation syndrome (GAS). This includes an initial alarm reaction, followed by a stage of resistance, and finally by a stage of exhaustion, which results from long-term unabated exposure to stress and produces irreversible physiological damage. Selye also brought attention to the idea that not only clearly aversive events (for example, the death of a spouse or a jail sentence) but also events that appear positive (for example, a promotion at work or meeting new friends) may be stressful because they involve changes to which people must adapt. Thus, these ostensibly positive events (which he called eustress) will produce the nonspecific physiological stress response just as obviously negative events (which he called distress) will.

How an individual cognitively appraises an event is the most important determinant of whether that event will be perceived as stressful by that person. Psychologist Richard S. Lazarus has delineated three

important cognitive mechanisms (primary appraisals, secondary appraisals, and coping strategies) that determine perceptions of stressfulness and how people alter appraisals. Primary appraisal refers to an assessment of whether a situation is neutral, challenging, or potentially harmful. When a situation is judged to be harmful or threatening, a secondary appraisal is made of the coping options or maneuvers that the individual has at his or her disposal. Actual coping strategies that may be used are problem focused (those that involve altering the circumstances that are eliciting the stress response) or emotion focused (those that involve directly lowering physiological arousal or the cognitive determinants of the stress response). Psychologists have used concepts such as these to develop stress management procedures that help people control stress in their everyday lives.

SOURCES FOR FURTHER STUDY

Goldberger, Leo, and Shlomo Breznitz, eds. *The Handbook of Stress: Theoretical and Clinical Aspects.* 2d ed. New York: Free Press, 1993. A wide-ranging collection of essays on the diagnosis and treatment of stress. A good starting point for investigating the field.

Greenberg, Jerrold S. *Comprehensive Stress Management.* 7th ed. New York: McGraw-Hill, 2001. An easy-to-read text giving an overview of psychological and physiological stress responses and stress-management techniques. Separate sections on applications to occupational stress, the college student, the family, and the elderly.

Janis, Irving Lester. *Psychological Stress.* New York: John Wiley & Sons, 1958. Describes some of Janis's early investigations evaluating relationships between stress and behavior. The focus is on his pioneering study evaluating the relationship between preoperative stress levels in surgical patients and their ability to adapt to the rigors of the postoperative convalescent period.

Monat, Alan, and Richard S. Lazarus, eds. *Stress and Coping.* 2d ed. New York: Columbia University Press, 1985. This anthology consists of twenty-six brief readings under the headings of effects of stress, stress and the environment, coping with the stresses of living, coping with death and dying, and stress management.

Rabin, Bruce S. *Stress, Immune Function, and Health: The Connection.* New York: Wiley-Liss, 1999. A psychoneurimmunological approach to the physiological effects of stress.

Sapolsky, Robert. *Why Zebras Don't Get Ulcers: An Updated Guide to Stress, Stress-Related Diseases, and Coping.* New York: W. H. Freeman, 1998. An entertaining comparison of the physiology of stress in humans and other mammals, written by a neuroscientist. Argues that the human nervous system evolved to cope with short-term stressors, and that contemporary stress-related diseases, such as heart disease and diabetes, are the result of living in an environment that produces long-term stress instead.

Silver, R. L., and C. Wortman. "Coping with Undesirable Life Events." In *Human Helplessness,* edited by Judy Garber and Martin E. P. Seligman. New York: Academic Press, 1980. Silver and Wortman examine the behavioral consequences of encountering and adjusting to cataclysmic stressful events such as a disabling accident, a serious illness, or the death of a loved one.

Stephen M. Auerbach

SEE ALSO: Coping: Strategies; General adaptation syndrome; Post-traumatic stress disorder; Stress: Behavioral and psychological responses; Stress: Physiological responses; Stress: Theories; Stress-related diseases.

Stress

Behavioral and psychological responses

TYPE OF PSYCHOLOGY: Stress
FIELDS OF STUDY: Coping; critical issues in stress; stress and illness

Stress is an adaptive reaction to circumstances that are perceived as threatening. It motivates people and can enhance performance. Learning to cope with adversity is an important aspect of normal psychological development, but exposure to chronic stress can have severe negative consequences if effective coping mechanisms are not learned.

KEY CONCEPTS
- circumplex model
- coping strategies
- daily hassles
- phobias
- state anxiety
- trait anxiety

INTRODUCTION

The term "stress" is used to designate how human beings respond when they confront circumstances that they appraise as dangerous or threatening and that tax their coping capability. Stressful events (stressors) elicit a wide range of responses in humans. They not only bring about immediate physiological changes but also affect one's emotional state, the use of one's intellectual abilities and one's efficiency at solving problems, and one's social behavior. When experiencing stress, people take steps to do something about the stressors eliciting the stress and to manage the emotional upset they are producing. These maneuvers are called coping responses. Coping is a key concept in the study of the stress process. Stress-management intervention techniques are designed to teach people the appropriate ways to cope with the stressors that they encounter in their everyday lives.

ANXIETY AND PHOBIAS

The emotional state most directly affected by stress is anxiety. In fact, the term "state anxiety" is often used interchangeably with the terms "fear" and "stress" to denote a transitory emotional reaction to a dangerous situation. Stress, fear, and state anxiety are distinguished from trait anxiety, which is conceptualized as a relatively stable personality disposition or trait. According to psychologist Charles Spielberger, people high in trait or "chronic" anxiety interpret more situations as dangerous or threatening than do people who are low in trait anxiety, and they respond to them with more intense stress (state anxiety) reactions. Instruments that measure trait anxiety ask people to characterize how they usually feel, and thus they measure how people characteristically respond to situations. Measures of trait anxiety (such as the trait anxiety scale of the State-Trait Anxiety Inventory) are especially useful in predicting whether people will experience high levels of stress in situations involving threats to self-esteem or threat of failure at evaluative tasks.

The recently developed two-dimensional circumplex model (see the figure "Circumplex Model") has been adopted as a model for illustrating how

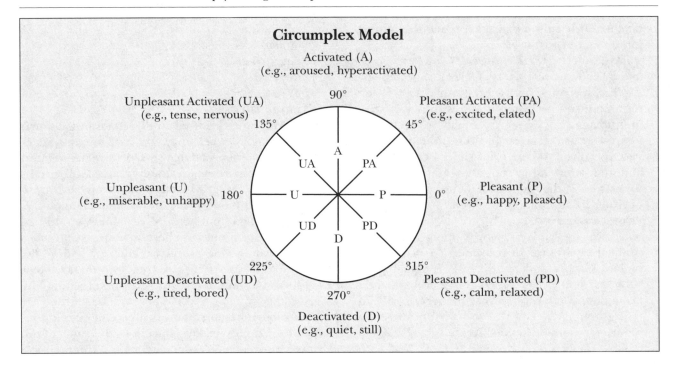

Circumplex Model

Activated (A)
(e.g., aroused, hyperactivated)

Unpleasant Activated (UA)
(e.g., tense, nervous)

Pleasant Activated (PA)
(e.g., excited, elated)

Unpleasant (U)
(e.g., miserable, unhappy)

Pleasant (P)
(e.g., happy, pleased)

Unpleasant Deactivated (UD)
(e.g., tired, bored)

Pleasant Deactivated (PD)
(e.g., calm, relaxed)

Deactivated (D)
(e.g., quiet, still)

emotion relates to stress. The activation-deactivation dimension of the circumplex relates to how much the emotion invokes a sense of alertness, energy, and mobilization, in contrast to the deactivation end of the continuum that connotes drowsiness and lethargy. The second dimension of the circumplex relates to the degree of pleasantness/unpleasantness associated with the emotion. For example, perceived stress and anxiety relate to unpleasant activation. In contrast, serenity is associated with deactivation and positive affect. Richard Lazarus has argued that the relational meaning of a stressful event determines the particular emotion associated with the event. For example, the relational meaning of anger is "a demeaning offense against me and mine." The relational meaning of anxiety is "facing an uncertain or existential threat." The relational meaning of fright is "facing an immediate, concrete, and overwhelming physical danger." Coping alters the emotion by either changing reality (problem-focused coping) or changing the interpretation of the event (emotion-focused coping).

Common phobias or fears of specific situations, however, especially when the perceived threat has a strong physical component, are not related to individual differences in general trait anxiety level. Measures of general trait anxiety are therefore not good predictors of people's stress levels when they are confronted by snakes, an impending surgical operation, or the threat of electric shock. Such fears can be reliably predicted only by scales designed to evaluate proneness to experience fear in these particular situations.

Seemingly minor events that are a constant source of irritation can be very stressful, as can more focalized events that require major and sometimes sudden readjustments. Psychologists Richard Lazarus and Susan Folkman have dubbed these minor events "daily hassles." The media focus attention on disasters such as plane crashes, earthquakes, and epidemics that suddenly disrupt the lives of many people, or on particularly gruesome crimes or other occurrences that are likely to attract attention. For most people, however, much of the stress of daily life results from having to deal with ongoing problems pertaining to jobs, personal relationships, and everyday living circumstances.

People often have no actual experience of harm or unpleasantness regarding things that they come to fear. For example, most people are at least somewhat uneasy about flying on airplanes or about the prospect of having a nuclear power plant located near them, though few people have personally experienced harm caused by these things. Although people tend to pride themselves on how logical they are, they are often not very rational in appraising how dangerous or risky different events actually are. For example, there is great public concern about the safety of nuclear reactors, though they in fact have caused very few deaths. The same general public that smokes billions of cigarettes (a proved carcinogen and risk factor for heart disease), which cause over 400,000 deaths per year, also supported banning an artificial sweetener because of a minuscule chance that it might cause cancer.

POSITIVE STRESS

People tend to think of stress as being uniformly negative—something to be avoided or at least minimized as much as possible. Psychologists Carolyn Aldwin and Daniel Stokols point out, however, that studies using both animals and humans have indicated that exposure to stress also has beneficial effects. Being handled is stressful for rats, but rats handled as infants are less fearful, are more exploratory, are faster learners, and have more robust immune systems later in life. In humans, physical stature as adults is greater in cultures that expose children to stress (for example, circumcision, scarification, sleeping apart from parents) than in those that are careful to prevent stress exposure—even when nutrition, climate, and other relevant variables are taken into account. Although failure experiences in dealing with stressful circumstances can inhibit future ability to function under stress, success experiences enable learning of important coping and problem-solving skills that are then used to deal effectively with future stressful encounters. Such success experiences also promote a positive self-concept and induce a generalized sense of self-efficacy that in turn enhances persistence in coping with future stressors.

Psychologists Stephen Auerbach and Sandra Gramling note that stress is a normal, adaptive reaction to threat. It signals danger and prepares people to take defensive action. Over time, individuals learn which coping strategies are successful for them in particular situations. This is part of the normal process of personal growth and maturation. Stress can, however, cause psychological problems if the demands posed by stressors overwhelm a person's coping capabilities. If a sense of being overwhelmed and unable to control events persists over a period of time, one's stress signaling system ceases to work

in an adaptive way. One misreads and overinterprets the actual degree of threat posed by situations, makes poor decisions as to what coping strategies to use, and realizes that one is coping inefficiently; a cycle of increasing distress and ineffective coping may result. Some people who have experienced high-level stress for extended periods or who are attempting to deal with the aftereffects of traumatic stressors may become extremely socially withdrawn and show other signs of severe emotional dysfunction.

In severe cases where these symptoms persist for over a month, a psychological condition known as post-traumatic stress disorder (PTSD) may develop. Common symptoms of PTSD include reliving the traumatic event, avoiding anything that reminds the person of the event, insomnia, nightmares, wariness, poor concentration, chronic irritability resulting in angry or aggressive outbursts, and a numbing of emotions. The symptom of numbing of emotions has been referred to as alexithymia, a condition where the person lacks the ability to define and express their emotions to themselves and others. James Pennebaker believes that although alexithymics cannot express their emotions, their emotions are still present in an unconscious cycle of rumination; this suppression and rumination of negative thoughts is associated with increased psychological and physiological arousal. That is, it takes a lot of work to inhibit one's emotions.

Although anxiety is the most common emotion associated with stress, chronic stress may induce chronic negative emotions such as hostility and depression. Chronic hostility and depression have been shown to have damaging effects on social relationships and physical health. The known physical costs of chronic stress include poor immune functioning, not engaging in health-promoting activities (such as exercise and following the advice of a physician), and a shortened life expectancy.

When people are faced with a stressful circumstance that overwhelms their coping mechanisms, they may react with depression and a sense of defeat and hopelessness. According to Martin Seligman, learned helplessness is the result of a person coming to believe that events are uncontrollable or hopeless, and it often results in depression.

ASSESSING AND MEASURING STRESS

The fact that stress has both positive and negative effects can be exemplified in many ways. Interpersonally, stress brings out the "worst" and the "best" in people. A greater incidence of negative social behaviors, including less altruism and cooperation and more aggression, has generally been observed in stressful circumstances. Psychologist Kent Bailey points out that, in addition to any learning influences, this may result from the fact that stress signals real or imagined threats to survival and is therefore a potent elicitor of regressive, self-serving survival behaviors. The highly publicized murder of Kitty Genovese in Queens, New York, in 1964, which was witnessed by thirty-eight people (from the safety of their apartments) who ignored her pleas for help, exemplifies this tendency, as does the behavior during World War II of many Europeans who either did not stand up for the Jews and other minorities who were oppressed by the Nazis or conveniently turned their heads. Everyone has heard, however, of selfless acts of individual heroism being performed by seemingly ordinary people who in emergency situations rose to the occasion and risked their own lives to save others. After the terrorist attack on the World Trade Center on September 11, 2001, firemen continued to help victims and fight fires after more than two hundred of their fellow firemen had been killed in the buildings' collapse. In addition, in stressful circumstances in which cooperation and altruism have survival value for all concerned, as in the wake of a natural disaster, helping-oriented activities and resource sharing are among the most common short-term reactions.

Stress may enhance as well as hinder performance. For example, the classic view of the relationship between stress and performance is represented in the Yerkes-Dodson inverted-U model, which posits that both low and high levels of arousal decrease performance, whereas intermediate levels enhance performance. Although this model has not been unequivocally validated, it seems to be at least partially correct, and its correctness may depend upon the circumstances. On one hand, psychologists Gary Evans and Sheldon Cohen concluded that, in learning and performance tasks, high levels of stress result in reduced levels of working-memory capacity and clearly interfere with performance of tasks that require rapid detection, sustained attention, or attention to multiple sources of input. On the other hand, psychologist Charles Spielberger found that in less complex tasks, as learning progresses, high stress levels may facilitate performance.

Psychologist Irving Janis examined the relationship between preoperative stress in surgical patients and how well they coped with the rigors of the postoperative convalescent period. He found that patients with moderate preoperative fear levels adjusted better after surgery than those with low or high preoperative fear. He reasoned that patients with moderate fear levels realistically appraised the situation, determined how they would deal with the stressful aspects of the recovery period, and thus were better able to tolerate those stressors. Patients low in preoperative fear engaged in unrealistic denial and thus were unprepared for the demands of the postoperative period, whereas those high in preoperative fear became overanxious and carried their inappropriately high stress levels over into the recovery period, in which that stress continued to inhibit them from realistically dealing with the demands of the situation. Janis further found that giving people information about what to expect before the surgery reduced their levels of fear and stress and allowed them to recover from surgery more quickly.

BENEFITS OF CONTROL

Research by Judith Rodin and others has shown that interventions designed to increase the predictability of and perceived control over a stressful event can have dramatic effects on stress and health. In one control-enhancing intervention study, nursing home residents were told by the hospital administrator to take responsibility for themselves, were asked to decide what activities to participate in, and were told what decisions they were responsible for. Patients who received the control-enhancing intervention reported being happier in the nursing home, and the death rate was half of that among nursing home residents who were told that it was the staff's responsibility to care for them. Dr. Rodin's research has been replicated by other researchers. More intensive stress reduction interventions have even been shown to increase survival rates among patients with breast cancer.

The negative effect of unrealistically low fear levels is also exemplified in the description by psychologists Walter Fenz and Seymour Epstein of two first-time sky divers who surprised everyone with their apparent total lack of concern during training and on the morning of their first jump. Their reactions changed dramatically, however, once they entered the aircraft. "One began vomiting, and the other developed a coarse tremor. Both pleaded for the aircraft to be turned back. Upon leaving, they stated that they were giving up jumping."

Janis's investigation was particularly influential because it drew attention to the question of how psychologists can work with people to help them cope with impending stressful events, especially those (such as surgery) that they are committed to confronting and over which they have little control. Findings by psychologists Thomas Strentz and Stephen Auerbach indicate that in such situations it may be more useful to teach people emotion-focused coping strategies (those designed to minimize stress and physiological arousal directly) than problem-focused strategies (those designed to change the stressful situation itself). In a study with volunteers who were abducted and held hostage for four days in a stressful simulation, they found that hostages who were taught to use emotion-focused coping techniques (such as deep breathing, muscular relaxation, and directed fantasy) adjusted better and experienced lower stress levels than those who were taught problem-focused techniques (such as nonverbal communication, how to interact with captors, and how to gather intelligence).

In a series of studies, Dr. Pennebaker and others have found that writing for just twenty minutes a day for three or four consecutive days about the most stressful experience one has ever experienced has widespread beneficial effects that may last for several months. In a series of studies, he found that his writing task improved immune functioning, reduced illness and perceived stress, and even improved students' grade point averages. He believes that his writing task may help people to release their inhibited emotions about past stressful events. This release of emotions decreases physiological arousal and psychological anxiety associated with repressing negative past events.

ADAPTIVE AND MALADAPTIVE FUNCTIONS

Stress has many important adaptive functions. The experience of stress and learning how to cope with adversity is an essential aspect of normal growth and development. Coping strategies learned in particular situations must be generalized appropriately to new situations. Exposure to chronic stress that cannot be coped with effectively can have severe negative consequences. Work by pioneering stress re-

searchers such as Hans Selye brought attention to the physiological changes produced by exposure to chronic stress, which contribute to diseases such as peptic ulcers, high blood pressure, and cardiovascular disorders. Subsequent research by psychiatrists Thomas Holmes and Richard Rahe and their colleagues indicated that exposure to a relatively large number of stressful life events is associated with the onset of other diseases, such as cancer and psychiatric disorders, which are less directly a function of arousal in specific physiological systems.

Studies by these researchers have led psychologists to try to understand how best to teach people to manage and cope with stress. Learning to cope with stress is a complex matter because, as Richard Lazarus has emphasized, the stressfulness of given events is determined by how they are cognitively appraised, and this can vary considerably among individuals. Further, the source of stress may be in the past, the present, or the future. The prospect of an impending threatening encounter (such as a school exam) may evoke high-level stress, but people also experience stress when reflecting on past unpleasant or humiliating experiences or when dealing with an immediate, ongoing danger. Sometimes, people deal with past, present, and future stressors simultaneously.

It is important to distinguish among present, past, and future stressors, because psychological and behavioral responses to them differ, and different kinds of coping strategies are effective in dealing with them. For example, for stressors that may never occur but are so aversive that people want to avoid them if at all possible (for example, cancer or injury in an automobile accident), people engage in preventive coping behavior (they stop smoking, or they wear seat belts) even though they are not currently experiencing a high level of anxiety. In this kind of situation, an individual's anxiety level sometimes needs to be heightened in order to motivate coping behavior.

When known stressors are about to affect one (for example, a surgical operation the next morning), it is important for one to moderate one's anxiety level so that one can function effectively when actually confronting the stressor. The situation is much different when one is trying to deal with a significant stressor (such as sexual assault, death of a loved one, or a war experience) that has already occurred but continues to cause emotional distress.

Important aspects of coping with such stressors include conceptualizing one's response to the situation as normal and rational rather than "crazy" or inadequate, and reinstating the belief that one is in control of one's life and environment rather than subject to the whims of circumstance.

SOURCES FOR FURTHER STUDY

Auerbach, Stephen M. "Assumptions of Crisis Theory and Temporal Model of Crisis Intervention." In *Crisis Intervention with Children and Families*, edited by Stephen M. Auerbach and Arnold L. Stolberg. Washington, D.C.: Hemisphere, 1986. This chapter examines some basic issues pertaining to psychological responses to extremely stressful events, including the role of the passage of time, individual differences, and previous success in dealing with stressful events. Crisis intervention and other stress-management programs are also reviewed.

_____. "Temporal Factors in Stress and Coping: Intervention Implications." In *Personal Coping: Theory, Research, and Application*, edited by B. N. Carpenter. Westport, Conn.: Praeger, 1991. Focuses on how behavioral and psychological stress responses differ depending on whether the stressor is anticipated, is currently ongoing, or has already occurred. The types of coping strategies that are likely to be most effective for each kind of stressor are described, and many examples are given.

Davis, Martha, Elizabeth Eshelman, and Matthew McKay. *The Relaxation and Stress Reduction Workbook*. 5th ed. Oakland, Calif.: New Harbinger, 2000. An overview of techniques used to reduce stress. Sections include body awareness, progressive relaxation, visualization, biofeedback, coping skills training, job stress management, and assertiveness training.

Janis, Irving Lester. *Stress and Frustration*. New York: Harcourt Brace Jovanovich, 1971. Describes some of Janis's early investigations evaluating relationships between stress and behavior. The focus is on his pioneering study evaluating the relationship between preoperative stress levels in surgical patients and their ability to adapt to the rigors of the postoperative convalescent period.

Lazarus, Richard S. "From Psychological Stress to the Emotions: A History of Changing Outlooks." *Annual Review of Psychology* 44 (1993): 1-21. Discusses the history of the study and treatment of stress. Discusses his recent research that has involved the cognitive-mediational approach to the appraisal and coping processes that cause stress.

Miller, Todd, Timothy Smith, Charles Turner, Margarita Guijarro, and Amanda Hallet. "A Meta-analytic Review of Research on Hostility and Physical Health." *Psychological Bulletin* 119, no. 2 (1996): 322-348. Reviews over sixty studies on hostility and health to show that cynical people consistently have shorter life expectancies. In addition, those who display signs of anger are at increased risk for heart disease.

Pennebaker, James W. *Opening Up: The Healing Power of Expressing Emotions*. Rev. ed. New York: Guilford Press, 1997. Presents evidence that personal self-disclosure not only benefits emotional health but also boosts physical health. Explains how writing about problems can improve one's physical and psychological health.

Rodin, Judith, and Christine Timko. "Control, Aging and Health." In *Aging, Health, and Behavior*, edited by Marcia Ory, Ronald Abeles, and Paula Lipman. Newbury Park, Calif.: Sage Publications, 1992. Reviews research on the relationship between stress, control and health.

Russell, James A., and Lisa F. Barrett. "Core Affect, Prototypical Emotional Episodes, and Other Things Called Emotion: Dissecting the Elephant." *Journal of Personality and Social Psychology* 76 (1999): 805-819. This article discusses the validation of the circumplex model of emotion.

Silver, R. L., and C. Wortman. "Coping with Undesirable Life Events." In *Human Helplessness*, edited by Judy Garber and Martin E. P. Seligman. New York: Academic Press, 1980. Silver and Wortman examine the behavioral consequences of encountering and adjusting to cataclysmic stressful events such as a disabling accident, a serious illness, or the death of a loved one. They review different theoretical formulations of reactions to stressful events and examine whether people's actual emotional and behavioral reactions are consistent with theories. They emphasize social support, the ability to find meaning in the outcome of the event, and experience with other stressors as important factors that determine how well people adjust.

Stephen M. Auerbach;
updated by Todd Miller

SEE ALSO: Coping: Strategies; General adaptation syndrome; Post-traumatic stress disorder; Stress; Stress: Physiological responses; Stress-related diseases; Type A behavior pattern.

Stress

Physiological responses

TYPE OF PSYCHOLOGY: Stress
FIELDS OF STUDY: Biology of stress; critical issues in stress; stress and illness

The human body contains a number of regulatory mechanisms that allow it to adapt to changing conditions. Stressful events produce characteristic physiological changes that are meant to enhance the likelihood of survival. Because these changes sometimes present a threat to health rather than serving a protective function, researchers seek to determine relations between stressors, their physiological effects, and subsequent health.

KEY CONCEPTS
- fight-or-flight response
- general adaptation syndrome
- homeostasis
- parasympathetic nervous system
- stress response
- stressor
- sympathetic nervous system

INTRODUCTION

Although the term "stress" is commonly used (if not overused) by the general population to refer to various responses to events that individuals find taxing, the concept involves much more. For centuries, scientific thinkers and philosophers have been interested in learning more about the interactions between the environment (stressful events), emotions, and the body. Much is now known about this interaction, although there is still much left to discover. In the late twentieth century, particularly, much has been learned about how stressful events affect the activity of the body (or physiology); for example, it has been established that these physiological responses to stressors sometimes increase the risk of development or exacerbate a number of diseases. In

order best to understand the body's response to stressful events (or stressors), the general sequence of events and the specific responses of various organ systems must be considered.

Almost all bodily responses are mediated at least partially by the central nervous system: the brain and spinal cord. The brain takes in and analyzes information from the external environment as well as from the internal environment (the rest of the body), and it acts to regulate the activities of the body to optimize adaptation or survival. When the brain detects a threat, a sequence of events occurs to prepare the body to fight or to flee the threat. Walter B. Cannon, in the early twentieth century, was the first to describe this "fight-or-flight" response of the body. It is characterized by generalized physiological activation. Heart rate, blood pressure, and respiration increase to enhance the amount of oxygen available to the tissues. The distribution of blood flow changes to optimize efficiency of the tissues most needed to fight or flee: Blood flow to the muscles, brain, and skin increases, while it decreases in the stomach and other organs less important for immediate survival. Increased sweating and muscle tension help regulate the body's temperature and enhance movement if action is needed. Levels of blood glucose and insulin also increase to provide added energy sources, and immune function is depressed. Brain activity increases, resulting in enhanced sensitivity to incoming information and faster reactions to this information.

Taken together, these physiological changes serve to protect the organism and to prepare it to take action to survive threat. They occur quite rapidly and are controlled by the brain through a series of neurological and hormonal events. When the brain detects a threat (or stressor), it sends its activating message to the rest of the body through two primary channels, the sympathetic nervous system (SNS) and the pituitary-adrenal axis. The SNS is a branch of the nervous system that has multiple, diffuse neural connections to the rest of the body. It relays activating messages to the heart, liver, muscles, and other organs that produce the physiological changes already described. The sympathetic nervous system also stimulates the adrenal gland to secrete two hormones, epinephrine and norepinephrine (formerly called adrenaline and noradrenaline), into the bloodstream. Epinephrine and norepinephrine further activate the heart, blood vessels, lungs, sweat glands, and other tissues.

Also, the brain sends an activating message through its hypothalamus to the pituitary gland, at the base of the brain. This message causes the pituitary to release hormones into the bloodstream that circulate to the peripheral tissues and activate them. The primary "stress" hormone that the pituitary gland releases is adrenocorticotropic hormone (ACTH), which in turn acts upon the adrenal gland to cause the release of the hormone cortisol. The actions of cortisol on other organs cause increases in blood glucose and insulin, among many other reactions.

In addition to isolating these primary stress mechanisms, research has demonstrated that the body secretes naturally occurring opiates—endorphins and enkephalins—in response to stress. Receptors for these opiates are found throughout the body and brain. Although their function is not entirely clear, some research suggests that they serve to buffer the effects of stressful events by counteracting the effects of the SNS and stress hormones.

GENERAL ADAPTATION SYNDROME

One can see that the human body contains a very sophisticated series of mechanisms that have evolved to enhance survival. When stressors and the subsequent physiological changes that are adaptive in the short run are chronic, however, they may produce long-term health risks. This idea was first discussed in detail in the mid-twentieth century by physiologist Hans Selye, who coined the term "general adaptation syndrome" to describe the body's physiological responses to stressors and the mechanisms by which these responses might result in disease.

Selye's general adaptation syndrome involves three stages of physiological response: alarm, resistance, and exhaustion. During the alarm stage, the organism detects a stressor and responds with SNS and hormonal activation. The second stage, resistance, is characterized by the body's efforts to neutralize the effects of the stressor. Such attempts are meant to return the body to a state of homeostasis, or balance. (The concept of homeostasis, or the tendency of the body to seek to achieve an optimal, adaptive level of activity, was developed earlier by Walter Cannon.) Finally, if the resistance stage is prolonged, exhaustion occurs, which can result in

illness. Selye referred to such illnesses as diseases of adaptation. In this category of diseases, he included hypertension, cardiovascular disease, kidney disease, peptic ulcer, hyperthyroidism, and asthma.

Selye's general adaptation syndrome has received considerable attention as a useful framework within which to study the effects of stressors on health, but there are several problems with his theory. First, it assumes that all stressors produce characteristic, widespread physiological changes that differ only in intensity and duration. There is compelling evidence, however, that different types of stressors can produce very different patterns of neural and hormonal responses. For example, some stressors produce increases in heart rate, while others can actually cause heart rate deceleration. Thus, Selye's assumption of a nonspecific stress response must be questioned.

Also, Selye's theory does not take into account individual differences in the pattern of response to threat. Research during the later twentieth century demonstrated that there is considerable variability across individuals in their physiological responses to identical stressors. Such differences may result from genetic or environmental influences. For example, some studies have demonstrated that normotensive offspring of hypertensive parents are more cardiovascularly responsive to brief stressors than individuals with normotensive parents. Although one might conclude that the genes responsible for hypertension have been passed on from the hypertensive parents, these children might also have different socialization or learning histories that contribute to their exaggerated cardiovascular reactivity to stressors. Whatever the mechanism, this research highlights the point that individuals vary in the degree to which they respond to stress and in the degree to which any one organ system responds.

STRESS AND ILLNESS

Coinciding with the scientific community's growing acknowledgment that stressful events have direct physiological effects, much interest has developed in understanding the relations between these events and the development and/or maintenance of specific diseases. Probably the greatest amount of research has focused on the link between stress and heart disease, the primary cause of death in the United States. Much empirical work also has focused on gastrointestinal disorders, diabetes, and pain (for example, headache and arthritis). Researchers are beginning to develop an understanding of the links between stress and immune function. Such work has implications for the study of infectious disease (such as flu and mononucleosis), cancer, and acquired immunodeficiency syndrome (AIDS).

A number of types of research paradigms have been employed to study the effects of stressors on health and illness. Longitudinal studies have identified a number of environmental stressors that contribute to the development or exacerbation of disease. For example, one study of more than four thousand residents of Alameda County, California, spanning two decades, showed that a number of environmental stressors such as social isolation were significant predictors of mortality from all causes. Other longitudinal investigations have linked stressful contexts such as loud noise, crowding, and low socioeconomic status with the onset or exacerbation of disease.

A major drawback of such longitudinal research is that no clear conclusions can be made about the exact mechanism or mechanisms by which the stressor had its impact on health. Although it is possible, in the Alameda County study, that the relationship between social isolation and disease was mediated by the SNS/hormonal mechanisms already discussed, individuals who are isolated also may be less likely to engage in health care behaviors such as eating healthy diets, exercising, and maintaining preventive health care. Thus, other research paradigms have been used to try to clarify the causal mechanisms by which stressors may influence particular diseases. For example, laboratory stress procedures are used by many scientists to investigate the influence of brief, standardized stressors on physiology. This type of research has the advantage of being more easily controlled. That is, the researcher can manipulate one or a small number of variables (for example, noise) in the laboratory and measure the physiological effects. These effects are then thought to mimic the physiological effects of such a variable in the natural environment.

This research primarily is conducted to ask basic questions about the relations between stressors, physiology, and subsequent health. The findings also have implications, however, for prevention and intervention. If a particular stressor is identified that increases risk of a particular disease, prevention efforts could be developed to target the populations exposed to this stressor. Prevention strategies might involve either modifying the stressor, teaching people ways to manage more effectively their responses to it, or both.

During the last two or three decades, applied researchers have attempted to develop intervention strategies aimed at controlling the body's physiological responses to stress. This work has suggested that a number of stress management strategies can actually attenuate physiological responsivity. Most strategies teach the individual some form of relaxation (such as deep muscle relaxation, biofeedback, hypnosis, or meditation), and most of this work has focused on populations already diagnosed with a stress-related disease, such as hypertension, diabetes, or ulcer. The techniques are thought to produce their effects by two possible mechanisms: lowering basal physiological activation (or changing the level at which homeostasis is achieved) and/or providing a strategy for more effectively responding to acute stressors to attenuate their physiological effects. Research has not proceeded far enough to make any statements about the relative importance of these mechanisms. Indeed, it is not clear whether either mechanism is active in many of the successful intervention studies. While research does indicate that relaxation strategies often improve symptoms of stress-related illnesses, the causal mechanisms of such techniques remain to be clarified.

THE MIND-BODY CONNECTION

The notion that the mind and body are connected has been considered since the writings of ancient Greece. Hippocrates described four bodily humors (fluids) that he associated with differing behavioral and psychological characteristics. Thus, the road was paved for scientific thinkers to consider the interrelations between environment, psychological state, and physiological state (that is, health and illness). Such considerations developed most rapidly in the twentieth century, when advancements in scientific methodology permitted a more rigorous examination of the relationships among these variables.

In the early twentieth century, as noted already, Walter B. Cannon was the first to document and discuss the "fight or flight response" to threatening events. He also reasoned that the response was adaptive, unless prolonged or repeated. In the 1940's, two physicians published observations consistent with Cannon's of an ulcer patient who had a gastric fistula, enabling the doctors to observe directly the contents of the stomach. They reported that stomach acids and bleeding increased when the patient was anxious or angry, thus documenting the relations between stress, emotion, and physiology. Shortly after this work was published, Selye began reporting his experiments on the effects of cold and fatigue on the physiology of rats. These physical stressors produced enlarged adrenal glands, small thymus and lymph glands (involved in immune system functioning), and increased ulcer formation.

Psychiatrists took this information, along with the writings of Sigmund Freud, to mean that certain disease states might be associated with particular personality types. Efforts to demonstrate the relationship between specific personality types and physical disease endpoints culminated in the development of a field known as psychosomatic medicine. Research, however, does not support the basic tenet of this field, that a given disease is linked with specific personality traits; thus, psychosomatic medicine has not received much support from the scientific community. The work of clinicians and researchers in psychosomatic medicine paved the way for late twentieth century conceptualizations of the relations between stress and physiology. Most important, biopsychosocial models that view the individual's health status in the context of the interaction between his or her biological vulnerability, psychological characteristics, and socio-occupational environment have been developed for a number of physical diseases.

Future research into individual differences in stress responses will further clarify the mechanisms by which stress exerts its effects on physiology. Once these mechanisms are identified, intervention strategies for use with patients or for prevention programs for at-risk individuals can be identified and implemented. Clarification of the role of the endogenous opiates in the stress response, for example, represents an important dimension in developing new strategies to enhance individual coping with stressors. Further investigation of the influence of stressors on immune function should open new doors for prevention and intervention, as well.

Much remains to be learned about why individuals differ in their responses to stress. Research in this area will seek to determine the influence of genes, environment, and behavior on the individual, elucidating the important differences between stress-tolerant and stress-intolerant individuals. Such work will provide a better understanding of the basic mechanisms by which stressors have their effects, and should lead to exciting new prevention and intervention strategies that will enhance health and improve the quality of life.

SOURCES FOR FURTHER STUDY

Craig, Kenneth D., and Stephen M. Weiss, eds. *Health Enhancement, Disease Prevention, and Early Intervention: Biobehavioral Perspectives.* New York: Springer, 1990. Includes, among other chapters of interest, an excellent chapter by Neal Miller (the "father of biofeedback") on how the brain affects the health of the body.

Feist, Jess, and Linda Brannon. *Health Psychology: An Introduction to Behavior and Health.* 4th ed. Belmont, Calif.: Wadsworth, 1999. Written for undergraduate students. A very readable overview of the field of health psychology. Provides the reader with chapters on stress and health, and various stress-related diseases.

Fuller, M. G., and V. L. Goetsch. "Stress and Stress Management." In *Behavior and Medicine,* edited by Danny Wedding. New York: Mosby-Year Book, 1990. Provides an overview of the field, focusing particularly on the physiological response to stress.

Jacobson, Edmund. *You Must Relax.* New York: McGraw-Hill, 1934. A rare classic which may be available in the special collections section of the library. Jacobson is considered the father of modern relaxation training. This book is worth seeking for the pictures of Jacobson's patients after undergoing his relaxation procedure as well as for Jacobson's thoughtful insights.

Ornstein, Robert, and D. S. Sobel. "The Brain as a Health Maintenance Organization." In *The Healing Brain: A Scientific Reader,* edited by Robert Ornstein and Charles Swencionis. New York: Guilford Press, 1990. Discusses the body's responses to stressors from an evolutionary perspective.

Selye, Hans. *The Stress of Life.* 2d ed. New York: McGraw-Hill, 1978. First published in 1956. A thoroughly readable account of Selye's work and thinking about stress and health. Available at most bookstores, a must for those interested in learning more about stress.

Virginia L. Goetsch and Kevin T. Larkin

SEE ALSO: Biofeedback and relaxation; Emotions; Endocrine system; General adaptation syndrome; Meditation and relaxation; Nervous system; Psychosomatic disorders; Stress: Behavioral and psychological responses; Stress-related diseases; Stress: Theories; Type A behavior pattern.

Stress-related diseases

TYPE OF PSYCHOLOGY: Stress
FIELDS OF STUDY: Stress and illness

As a person experiences stress, physical responses occur that have been associated with a host of physical diseases. Understanding the stress-disease relationship, including how to control and lower stress levels, is important in maintaining a healthful life.

KEY CONCEPTS
- biofeedback
- endorphin
- general adaptation syndrome
- locus of control
- psychoneuroimmunology
- relaxation response
- stressor
- Type A personality
- Type B personality

INTRODUCTION
The term "stress," as it is used in the field of psychology, may be defined as the physical or psychological disturbance an individual experiences as a result of what that individual perceives to be an adverse or challenging circumstance. Four observations concerning this definition of stress should be made. First, stress is what the individual experiences, not the circumstance causing the stress (the stressor). Second, individuals differ in what they perceive to be stressful. What may be very stressful for one individual may not be at all stressful for another. Hans Selye, the researcher who did more than anyone else to make the medical community and the general population aware of the concept and consequences of stress, once noted that, for him, spending the day on the beach doing nothing would be extremely stressful. This difference in people's perceptions is behind the familiar con-

cept that events do not cause stress. Instead, stress comes from one's perception or interpretation of events.

Third, stress occurs in response to circumstances that are seen as negative, but stress may also arise from challenging circumstances, even positive ones. The well-known Social Readjustment Rating Scale developed by Thomas Holmes and Richard Rahe includes both positive and negative life events. A negative event, such as the death of a spouse, is clearly stressful; however, marriage, generally viewed as a positive life event, can also be stressful. Fourth, stressors can lead to stress-related disturbances that are psychological, physiological, or both. The psychological response is rather unpredictable. A given stressor may result in one individual responding with anger, another with depression, and another with a new determination to succeed.

GENERAL ADAPTATION SYNDROME
The physiological response is more predictable. Beginning in the 1930's, Selye began studying the human response to stressors. Eventually he identified what he termed the general adaptation syndrome (GAS) to describe the typical pattern of physical responses. Selye divided the GAS into three stages: alarm, resistance, and exhaustion.

The first stage begins when an individual becomes frightened, anxious, or even merely concerned. The body immediately undergoes numerous physical changes to cope with the stressor. Metabolism speeds up. Heart and respiration rates increase. The hormones epinephrine, norepinephrine, and cortisol are secreted. Sugar is released from the liver. The muscles tense. Blood shifts from the internal organs to the skeletal musculature. These and a host of other changes are aimed at helping the body cope, but the price paid for this heightened state of arousal typically includes symptoms such as headache, upset stomach, sleeplessness, fatigue, diarrhea, and loss of appetite. The body's increase in alertness and energy is accompanied by a lowered state of resistance to illness.

Obviously, people cannot remain in the alarm stage for long. If the stressor is not removed, the body enters the resistance stage—a stage which may last from minutes to days or longer. During this stage, the body seeks to adapt to the stressor. The physical changes that occurred during the alarm stage subside. Resistance to illness is actually increased to above-normal levels. Because the body is still experiencing stress, however, remaining in this stage for a long period will eventually lead to physical and psychological exhaustion—the exhaustion stage.

Selye has noted that over the course of life, most people go through the first two stages many, many times. Such is necessary to adapt to the demands and challenges of life. The real danger is found in not eliminating the stressor. During the exhaustion stage, the body is very vulnerable to disease and in extreme cases may suffer collapse and death. Although newer research has found subtle differences in the stress response, depending on the stressor involved, the basic findings of Selye have continued to be supported. In addition to the direct physiological effects of stress on the body, indirect effects may also lead to illness. For example, stress may cause or exacerbate behavioral risk factors such as smoking, alcohol use, and overeating.

HEART DISEASE AND IMMUNE EFFECTS
Specific illnesses can also be caused or promoted by stress. For many years Americans have been aware of

the relationship between stress and heart disease. The biochemical changes associated with stress lead to higher blood pressure, an increased heart rate, and a release of fat into the bloodstream. If the fat is completely consumed by the muscles through physical activity (for example, defending oneself from an attacker), no serious health consequences follow. If, however, a person experiences stress without engaging in physical activity (a more common scenario in Western culture), the fat is simply deposited on the walls of the blood vessels. As these fatty deposits accumulate, life is threatened.

The work of two cardiologists, Meyer Friedman and Ray Rosenman, is of particular importance to a discussion of heart disease and stress. Friedman and Rosenman demonstrated, based originally on personal observation and subsequently on clinical research, that there is a personality type that is particularly prone to heart disease. The personality type that is at the greatest risk was found to be one which is highly stressed—impatient, hostile, hard-driving, and competitive. They termed this a Type A personality. The low-risk person, the Type B personality, is more patient, easygoing, and relaxed.

Numerous studies have examined health based on the Type A-Type B concept. Virtually all have supported Friedman and Rosenman's conclusions. One major report, however, did not; subsequent analysis of that report and other research generally has indicated that the aspects of the Type A personality which are threatening to one's health are primarily the hostility, cynicism, and impatience, not the desire to achieve.

A newer area of research that is even more fundamental to understanding how stress is related to disease involves the immune system. As the physiological changes associated with stress occur, the immune system is suppressed. The immune system has two primary functions: to identify and destroy hazardous foreign materials called antigens (these include bacteria, viruses, parasites, and fungi) and to identify and destroy the body's own cells that have undergone changes associated with malignancy. Thus, if the immune system is suppressed, the body is less able to detect and defend against a host of diseases. An

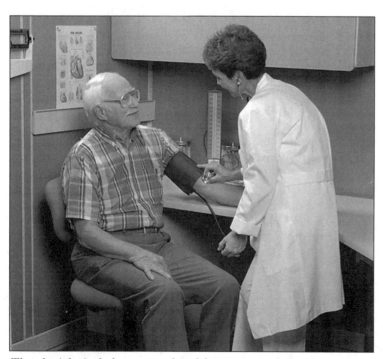

The physiological changes produced by exposure to chronic stress can contribute to diseases such as high blood pressure, peptic ulcers, and cardiovascular disorders. (Digital Stock)

example of this effect again involves research with laboratory rats. One such investigation involved placing tumor cells in the bodies of rats. Some of the rats were then exposed to an abundance of stress. Those that were given this treatment were less resistant to the cancer. Their tumors were larger, and they developed sooner than those found in the "low-stress" rats.

The recent growth of the field of psychoneuro-immunology focuses specifically on the chemical bases of communication between mind and body. Research in this area provides evidence that the body's immune system can be influenced by psychological factors which produce stress. One study, for example, showed that during students' examination periods, the levels of students' antibodies that fight infections were lowest. Thus they were most vulnerable to illness at that most stressful time. Health centers confirm that students tend to report more illness during examination times.

As research continues, the number of specific diseases that can be linked to stress grows. A partial listing of stress-related diseases and disorders for which recent research is available would include acne, asthma, cancers (many types), colds, coronary thrombosis, diabetes mellitus, gastric ulcers, herpes simplex (types 1 and 2), human immunodeficiency virus (HIV) infection, hyperlipidemia, hypertension, infertility, irritable bowel syndrome, migraine headache, mononucleosis syndrome, rheumatoid arthritis, streptococcal infection, stroke, systemic lupus erythematosus, and tuberculosis.

Research has shown that stress may also play a role in depression, sleep disturbances, ovulation, and brain atrophy associated with Alzheimer's disease. Stress as a cause of stomach ulcers has been essentially negated, with the discovery that these ulcers are generally caused by the bacterium *Helicobacter pylori*, which can be treated with antibiotics. However, stress may still play a role in decreasing the mucous lining of the stomach, which makes it more vulnerable to ulcer formation. Some experts feel that there is no illness that is not in some way influenced by stress.

It should be emphasized that few, if any, of these physical problems are caused solely by stress. Many other factors influence risk, including genetic composition, gender, race, environmental conditions, nutritional state, and so forth. Nevertheless, stress is frequently an important factor in determining initial resistance as well as the subsequent course of a given disease.

STRESS REDUCTION AND COPING

Why is it that some individuals who appear to live with many stressors generally avoid physical and psychological illness? Understanding the answer to that question is important, because it can provide insight as to what the average person can and should do to lower stress levels. Dispositional factors (optimistic versus pessimistic, easygoing versus hard-driving, friendly versus hostile) are probably most important in determining one's stress level. The Type A-Type B research noted above is an example of research demonstrating the influence of dispositional factors.

Research with twins has found that temperament is largely inborn; however, any individual can choose to be more optimistic, generous, and patient. Norman Cousins is often cited as an example of a person who decided to change his outlook and mental state in order to preserve his life. He had read Selye's *The Stress of Life* (1956), which describes how negative emotions can cause physical stress and subsequent disease. Cousins, who had a rare and painful illness from which he was told he would likely never recover, decided that if negative emotions could harm one's health, then positive emotions could possibly return one's health.

As Cousins describes his experience in *Anatomy of an Illness as Perceived by the Patient* (1979), he left his hospital room for a more pleasant environment, began trading massive doses of drugs for massive doses of vitamin C and a steady diet of television comedies and laughter, and decided to stop worrying. To the surprise of his medical team, his recovery began at once. Though this now-classic example is only anecdotal, the research on disposition and stress would support the assumption that Cousins's decision to change his mental state and stop worrying—not his avoidance of traditional medical care—was a truly important influence.

A related area of research has investigated how psychological hardiness helps people resist stress. Studies by Suzanne Kobasa and her colleagues examined business executives who all had an obvious abundance of stressors in their lives. In comparing those hardy individuals who handled the stressors well with the nonhardy individuals, the researchers found that the two groups differed in three important but basic ways.

The first was commitment. Stress-resistant executives typically possessed a clear sense of values. They had clear goals and a commitment to those goals. Less hardy executives were more likely to feel alienation. The second was challenge. The hardy executives welcomed challenges and viewed change rather than stability as the norm in life. Their less healthy counterparts viewed change with alarm. The third factor was control. The hardy executives felt more in control of their lives. This aspect of Kobasa's research overlaps with research conducted since the 1960's involving a concept known as the "locus of control." People with an internal locus of control are those individuals who believe they are influential rather than powerless in controlling the direction of their lives. This area of research has also found that such a belief lowers stress.

Many years ago it was estimated that more than a thousand studies had been completed that examined the relationship between physical fitness and mental health. What has emerged from this heavily researched area is a clear conclusion: Exercise can lower stress levels. Though regular, sustained aerobic exercise is generally advocated, research has found that even something as simple as a daily ten-minute walk can have measurable beneficial effects. During exercise, there is a release of chemical substances, including neurotransmitters called endorphins. Endorphins act to decrease pain and produce feelings of well-being, somewhat like an opiate. Exposure to stress has been shown to increase the level of endorphins in the body. For example, studies were conducted with runners, one group using naloxone, a substance which blocks effects of opiates, and the other group a placebo which had no effect on the body. After strenuous runs, those taking the placebo reported feelings of euphoria, sometimes known as "runners' high." Those taking naloxone reported no such feelings. Other chemicals are released during exercise as well, and include dopamine, which is thought to act as an antidepressant. Thus there is abundant evidence of the stress-reducing benefits of exercise.

Another approach to reducing stress involves learning to evoke a physical "relaxation response," a term coined by Harvard Medical School cardiologist Herbert Benson. Benson became intrigued by the ability of some people who practice meditation to lower their blood pressure, heart rate, and oxygen consumption voluntarily. He discovered that the process is not at all mystical and can be easily taught. The process involves getting comfortable, closing the eyes, breathing deeply, relaxing muscles, and relaxing one's mind by focusing on a simple word or phrase.

Others are helped by using an electronic device which closely monitors subtle physiological changes. By observing these changes (typically on a monitor), a person can, for example, learn to slow down a heart rate. This is known as biofeedback training. Many other techniques and suggestions arising from research as well as common sense can lower stress. A strong social support system has been found to be very important; disciplining oneself not to violate one's own value system is essential. Even having a pet that needs love and attention has been found to lower stress.

RESEARCH AND THE FUTURE

A general recognition that a relationship exists between mind and body is at least as old as the biblical Old Testament writings. In the book of Proverbs, for example, one reads, "A cheerful heart is good medicine,/ but a crushed spirit dries up the bones" (Proverbs 17:22). Hippocrates (460-377 B.C.E.), generally considered the "father of medicine," sought to understand how the body could heal itself and what factors could slow or prevent this process. He clearly perceived a relationship between physical health and what is now termed "stress," though his understanding was shallow.

Several physiologists of the nineteenth century made contributions; however, it was not until the twentieth century that the classic studies of American physiologist Walter B. Cannon proved the link scientifically. Cannon and his student Phillip Bard began their analysis of stress and physiological arousal to disprove the idea espoused by others, that emotion follows physiological arousal.

Cannon found a variety of stressors that led to the release of the hormones adrenaline and noradrenaline (or, properly now, epinephrine and norepinephrine). Heat, cold, oxygen deprivation, and fright all led to hormonal changes as well as a number of additional physiological adaptations. Cannon was excited about this discovery and impressed with the body's remarkable ability to react to stressors. All these changes were aimed at preparing the body for what Cannon termed the "fight-or-flight" response. It was Selye's task to build on Cannon's work. His description of the reaction subsequently termed the general adaptation syndrome first appeared in a scientific journal in 1936. As knowledge of the stress concept began to spread, interest by the public as well as the research community increased.

Literally tens of thousands of stress research studies conducted throughout the world were completed during the last half of the twentieth century. Of particular importance was the discovery by three American scientists that the brain produces morphinelike antistress substances. The discovery of these substances, named endorphins, won the 1977 Nobel Prize for the scientists involved and opened a whole new area of research.

Research has shown that the brain itself produces neuropeptides, or brain message transmitters which may also be produced by macrophages—white blood cells that attack viruses and bacteria. Since some forms of stress-reduction such as relaxation also seem to result in production of neuropeptides, if the brain could be caused to produce more of these substances, the immune system could be strengthened. The hope remains that someday an endorphin-type drug could be used to counter some of the unhealthy effects of stress, ensuring better health and longer lives. Better health and longer lives are available even today, however, for all people who are willing to make lifestyle changes based on current knowledge.

BIBLIOGRAPHY

Benson, Herbert, and Eileen Stuart. *The Wellness Book.* New York: Simon & Schuster, 1992. Written by a physician and author of *The Relaxation Response,* a nurse, and associates of the Mind/Body Medical Institute of the New England Deaconess Hospital and Harvard Medical School, this is a self-help book on stress-related illness, very informative about mind-body interactions and the role of stress in illness.

Brown, Barbara B. *Between Health and Illness.* Boston: Houghton Mifflin, 1984. One of many books available for the nonprofessional who simply wants an overview of stress and its consequences. This easy-to-read book is full of accurate information and practical suggestions.

Greenberg, Jerrold S. *Comprehensive Stress Management.* 6th ed. New York: WCB/McGraw-Hill, 1999. This is an excellent source which includes numerous self-tests, explains the scientific foundations of stress, and offers methods and techniques used to reduce stress in a variety of life situations. Written in an introductory yet comprehensive textbook format, this book is informative and easy to read.

Leonard, Brian, and Klara Miller, eds. *Stress, the Immune System, and Psychiatry.* New York: John Wiley & Sons, 1995. This book contains difficult reading, with detailed studies from the field of psychoneuroimmunology. The focus is on the immune system as related to various aspects of stress, including discussions of depressive illness, schizophrenia, multiple sclerosis, and food allergies.

Managing Stress: From Morning to Evening. Alexandria, Va.: Time-Life Books, 1987. A very good introduction to understanding and managing stress. Written in clear, simple language and widely available, it provides an overview of the sources of stress, the physiological changes associated with stress, the effects of stress on the immune system, the way to assess one's own stress level, and suggestions for numerous approaches to managing stress. Full of illustrations and photographs. A weakness is that the book fails to address adequately the importance of dispositional factors, focusing too heavily on some stress-reduction techniques that few are likely to use.

Pelletier, Kenneth R. *Mind as Healer, Mind as Slayer.* New York: Dell Books, 1977. This well-known work examines how stress contributes to heart disease, cancer, arthritis, migraine, and respiratory disease. Sources of stress, evaluation of personal stress levels, profiles of unhealthy personality traits, and means of preventing stress-related diseases are addressed.

Selye, Hans. *The Stress of Life.* Rev. ed. New York: McGraw-Hill, 1976. Originally published in 1956, this is the most influential book ever written about stress. It focuses on the relationship between a stressful life and subsequent illness, but it is very technical. Those wanting a less difficult introduction to Selye's writings and work should read his *Stress Without Distress.*

Wedding, Danny, ed. *Behavior and Medicine.* 2d ed. St. Louis: Mosby Year Book, 2001. This is a large volume which covers an extensive area of behavior and medicine, with a strong focus on stress, although it covers much additional territory. In addition to stress-related issues, including substance abuse, stress management, pain, placebos, AIDS, cardiovascular risk, and adherence to medical regimens, sections include assessment of patients, foundations of behavioral science, love and work, and developmental issues from infancy to death, dying and grief. The style is quite readable and combines illustrations, relevant poetry, bibliographies, summaries, and study questions at the end of each article.

Timothy S. Rampey;
updated by Martha Oehmke Loustaunau

SEE ALSO: Biofeedback and relaxation; Endocrine system; Endorphins; General adaptation syndrome; Nervous system; Stress: Behavioral and psychological responses; Stress: Physiological responses; Type A behavior pattern.

Stress

Theories

TYPE OF PSYCHOLOGY: Stress
FIELDS OF STUDY: Critical issues in stress

Stress generally involves emotional and physiological responses to circumstances which an individual views as threatening. Most theories of stress claim that stress involves the interaction between problems people face and their resources for dealing with them. A wide range of theories emphasize physiological responses, environmental circumstances, cognitions, personal coping skills, personal characteristics, or some combination of these factors.

KEY CONCEPTS
- biological theories of stress
- coping
- fight-or-flight response
- general adaptation syndrome
- interactionist approach to stress
- psychological theories of stress
- stress appraisal
- tend-and-befriend response
- Type A personality
- Type B personality

INTRODUCTION
How can thoughts and feelings be translated to changes in the body? Can prolonged stress alter health in life-threatening ways? These questions are new versions of much older ones that for centuries have addressed the dichotomy between mind and body. Unlike most areas within psychology, the study of stress did not begin until well into the twentieth century. Theories of stress began to play an important role as the potential relationships between stress and illness were systematically investigated

BIOLOGICAL THEORIES OF STRESS
The first important theorist who attempted to account for stress was Walter B. Cannon. He claimed that the sympathetic nervous system is activated by signals from the brain when a person is exposed to an emotionally arousing stimulus. This produces a series of physiological reactions which includes increases in heart rate, blood pressure, and respiration. This "fight-or-flight" response prepares the person for potential vigorous physical activity. According to Cannon, the confrontation with an arousing stimulus produces both the feelings and physiological reactions that are associated with stress. While the contributions of Cannon were important, they did not take into consideration the role played by psychological and behavioral factors in the overall stress response.

The work of Cannon paved the way for the efforts of the most renowned stress theorist, Hans Selye, who has claimed that stress is nonspecifically induced and can be caused by diverse stimuli. It does not matter if the event is a major disaster, an uncooperative colleague, or a disobedient child. The important point to remember is that if the event is stressful for a person, the person's bodily reaction remains the same. Selye has labeled the body's response to stress the general adaptation syndrome (GAS). This process occurs in three stages. Stage one is the alarm reaction, during which the body activates in order to handle the perceived danger at hand. This activation resembles Cannon's fight-or-flight response. Blood is diverted to the skeletal muscles in order to prepare them for action. The second phase of the general adaptation syndrome is the resistance stage. During this stage, the person either adapts to or resists the source of stress. The longer this stage lasts, the greater is the danger to the person. If the individual accepts the source of stress as a necessary part of life, the stressor may persist indefinitely. The person then gradually becomes more susceptible to a wide range of stress-related problems and diseases including fatigue, headaches, ulcers, hypertension, certain forms of cancer, and cardiovascular disease. These are but a few of the physical problems which are potentially related to stress. The third stage is the exhaustion stage. This demonstrates the finite nature of the body's ability to battle or adapt to stress. If the stressor is extremely intense and persists over a long period of time, the exhaustion stage sets in and the risk of emotional and physical problems increases. In Selye's system, the precise nature of the source of the stress is unimportant. The reaction is hypothesized to be the same in the face of physiological and psychological stressors.

INTERACTIONIST APPROACH TO STRESS

Cannon and Selye clearly focus on stress as a person's biological response to a wide range of stimuli. Selye emphasizes the nonspecific nature of the stress response. This position has been criticized by John Mason, who maintains that while the general adaptation syndrome does exist, responses differ according to the stimuli. He views stress as dependent upon emotional responses to situations. It is the nature of a person's emotional response that will play an important role in the probability that stress will lead to disease. People who are not psychologically aware of the existence of a potentially stressful event are least likely to experience a stress response. Mason believes that Selye's approach is too simplistic and does not provide ample opportunities to explain why some people develop stress-related disorders and others do not.

In 2000, Shelley Taylor and her colleagues proposed that, although "fight-or-flight" may characterize the primary physiological responses to stress for both males and females, behaviorally females' responses are more marked by a pattern of "tend-and-befriend." Tending, or the nurturing activities that protect the self and offspring, promotes safety and reduces distress; befriending is the creation and maintenance of social networks that may aid in this process. The brain-behavior mechanism that underlies the tend-and-befriend pattern appears to draw on the attachment-caregiving system. Evidence from animal and human studies suggests that the neuropeptide oxytocin, in conjunction with female reproductive hormones and endogenous opioid peptide mechanisms, may be at its core of this previously unexplored stress regulatory system.

PSYCHOLOGICAL THEORIES OF STRESS

The theories of Cannon and Selye emphasize biological factors, while Mason's theory is typically described as an interactionist approach to stress. The psychological approach to stress is best represented by the work of Richard S. Lazarus. He claims that the key to a stress response cannot be found in either the nature of a specific stressful event or the person's psychological response to that event. Rather, the most important factors are cognitive ones. Lazarus believes that it is the person's perception of an event that is crucial. This perception involves a combination of the person's perception of the potential danger of an event and his or her perceived ability to cope with that event. Stress will occur in those circumstances in which the person perceives that he or she does not have the ability or resources needed to cope with the situation.

Clearly, an important factor within the stress equation provided by Lazarus is appraisal of the situation. Along with his colleague Susan Folkman, Lazarus has described three types of appraisal of a potentially stressful situation. The first to occur is the primary appraisal. When a person is exposed to a new event such as a spouse returning to work, the situation can be judged as irrelevant, positive, or potentially stressful. The key to the stress is the person's appraisal of the situation, rather than the situation itself. Next in the appraisal process is the secondary appraisal. It is at this point that the person determines his or her ability to control, handle, or cope with the new situation. During this process, the person examines potential options for dealing with an event which has been judged as potentially stressful. This is followed by an analysis of his or her ability to make use of one or more of these options and a consideration of the success potential of each option, that is, whether the person is likely to be successful in making this option work for himself or herself. The final type of appraisal is reappraisal. During this process, the person reevaluates the stressful potential of a situation based on access to new thoughts and information. This can lead to an increase or decrease in stress. For example, the man who might have been mildly stressed by his wife's return to work may experience a decrease in stress as the family finances improve and he learns that many domestic tasks which he must now perform are less noxious than he originally thought. On the other hand, his stress may increase if he determines that he has less free time and that the cost of babysitters has removed the potential for financial improvement associated with his wife's return to work outside the home.

An alternative to the appraisal-based conception of stress and coping developed by Lazarus and Folkman is the resource-based approach to the stress process first proposed by S. E. Hobfoll in the late 1980's. Resources were defined as those things that people value or that act as a means to obtaining that which they value and include social, personal, object, and condition resources. The conservation of resource theory has been applied, for example, to assess the impact of resource losses and gains that occur in women's lives. One study found that resource losses better predicted postpartum anger and depression than resource gains (in the opposite direction).

Whether they support a biological, interactionist, or psychological approach to stress, all theorists agree that stress has the capability of increasing the risk of suffering various forms of illness. In addition, many theorists believe that important relationships exist between stress, personality, and susceptibility to disease.

FACTORS AFFECTING RESPONSE TO STRESS

Potentially stressful events occur in everyone's life. Many people, however, never develop stress-related symptoms and illnesses. This may result in part from issues pertaining to lifestyle and personality. One interesting approach to this problem has been provided by Suzanne Kobasa. She found that several personality factors are helpful in people's efforts to avoid illness in the face of stress. These factors are control, commitment, and challenge. When faced with difficult events, one can view the situation either as hopeless or as one over which one has a degree of control. In a situation where a man is notified that the factory in which he works is going to close in three years, it is normal initially to treat the news with shock and disappointment, but it is the worker's long-term response which is critical. On one hand, he can continue to report for work during the next three years and commiserate with his colleagues. He can make the statement that the fac-

tory is going to close and there is nothing he can do about it. This response is likely to lead to gradual increases in stress and susceptibility to illness. On the other hand, he could take control of the situation by looking for other work, entering a job retraining program, or returning to school on a part-time basis. This approach is likely to decrease his risk of stress-related illness.

The second factor, commitment, involves one's dedication to and involvement with people, activities, institutions, and oneself. Some people have nowhere to turn in the presence of a stressful event. They have no friends, family ties have been severed, and they are loners who have no goal in life other than to wake up the next morning. These individuals will find it extremely difficult to cope with a stressful event such as the death of a parent or loss of a job. They may feel that they have nowhere to turn in the face of adversity; they lack the social supports that help one cope with stressful situations. These people are highly susceptible to those illnesses that are associated with stress. Conversely, a person with many friends, strong family ties, and a sense of purpose in life will be better able to cope with significant stress.

The final factor, challenge, relates to a person's view of changes in his or her life. For example, a secretary who is transferred from one department at work to another, and who views this change as presenting interesting and new challenges, is likely to remain healthy. However, if she views the new position as a threat which should be avoided at all costs, she is likely to become ill. The three factors of control, commitment, and challenge make up an overall factor known as hardiness. The person who maintains high levels of these three factors has a high level of hardiness and is not a likely candidate for stress-related illnesses.

PERSONALITY TYPES

Perhaps the most talked-about and researched personality factor that has been related to stress is the Type A personality. The Type A person is one who is always on the go and is extremely driven. He or she walks fast, talks fast, is impatient with others, and is easily angered. The Type A person is a workaholic who measures life in numbers. He or she is concerned about money earned and saved, hours worked, praise received, and clients served. He or she always has a sense of time urgency. The Type B person is just the opposite. He or she is the relaxed and easygoing person who never seems in a hurry to do anything.

Research on the topic of the Type A personality, spearheaded by Meyer Friedman and Ray Rosenman, has traditionally maintained that the Type A personality is associated with increased stress and, more important, an increased risk of heart disease. This finding has been supported in at least forty research studies. For many years, the notion that Type A behavior was a risk factor for heart disease was taken for granted by many health professionals; however, several studies have failed to support this relationship. Researchers have attempted to account for these discrepancies. The mystery appears to have been solved in that it has been discovered that not all Type A behaviors are associated with increased risk of heart disease. The key factors appear to be anger and hostility. It is those Type A persons who are angry and hostile who are likely to convert potentially stressful situations into disease. The best advice that can be given to the typical Type A angry person is to learn to respond to situations without anger. This does not mean that anger which is felt should be held inside. Rather, the person should learn to respond to situations with feelings and emotions other than anger.

There is also increasing evidence that stress can influence the immune response, the body's defense against many types of illness. Research with animals has demonstrated the direct impact of various stressors on the immune system and, consequently, on infectious, malignant, and autoimmune diseases. Human studies also suggest that stress can adversely affect the body's immune response.

People must learn to cope with situations in ways which do not lead to increased stress and increased risk of disease. The good news is that many such strategies have proved to be very effective in helping people deal with those potentially stressful situations that seem to occur in the lives of everyone. The work of pioneers such as Cannon and Selye and more recent research by Rosenman and Friedman, Lazarus, and Taylor has opened up many new avenues of research related to stress and stress management. The potential role of stress in a wide range of diseases including cancer is being explored. It can be anticipated that the future will bring to light many new and unexpected relationships between stress and health.

SOURCES FOR FURTHER STUDY

Fink, George, ed. *Encyclopedia of Stress.* 3 vols. San Diego, Calif.: Academic Press, 2000. A compilation of the latest information on stressors, stress responses, and the disorders that can result. Containing nearly four hundred articles, these volumes cover a wide range of stress-related topics, from stress in the workplace and post-traumatic stress disorder to stress-related diseases and approaches to treatment. Each article is supplemented with a glossary and further reading list. Will appeal to a wide audience seeking information on topics within and outside their areas of expertise

Kaplan, Howard B., ed. *Psychosocial Stress: Perspectives on Structure, Theory, Life-Course, and Methods.* San Diego, Calif.: Academic Press, 1996. Research on stress increased dramatically during the 1980's and 1990's. This book updates the reader on the many facets of this research, including the factors, situations, and personality variables that elicit and mediate stress; theoretical perspectives in the study of stress; life-course perspectives on stress; and the methodology used in stress research.

Lazarus, Richard S., and Susan Folkman. *Stress, Appraisal, and Coping.* New York: Springer, 1984. Provides a thorough analysis of Lazarus's views on stress. Includes his comments on the three types of appraisal and approaches to coping with stress. An excellent book which provides thorough research support for the theoretical positions which are taken.

Lovallo, William R. *Stress and Health: Biological and Psychological Interactions.* Thousand Oaks, Calif.: Sage Publications, 1997. This book examines the biological links between thoughts and feelings and the potential health changes that can result from stress. Also discusses how individual differences in physiology and in perceptions and evaluations of events can have physical and long-term health consequences. A minimal understanding of brain mechanisms and physiology is assumed of the reader.

Selye, Hans. *The Stress of Life.* New York: McGraw-Hill, 1956. The classic book in the field. Includes Selye's original analysis of stress and his development of the general adaptation syndrome. Also includes a thorough analysis of the proposed relationships between stress and various forms of disease.

Taylor, Shelley E., Laura C. Klein, Brian P. Lewis, Tara L. Gruenewald, Regan A. Gurung, and John A. Updegraff. "Biobehavioral Responses to Stress in Females: Tend-and-Befriend, Not Fight-or-Flight." *Psychological Review* 107, no. 3 (2000): 411-429. Proposes an alternative response to stress—"tend-and-befriend"—generally experienced by females rather than males.

Lawrence A. Fehr;
updated by Allyson Washburn

SEE ALSO: Emotions; General adaptation syndrome; Stress; Stress: Behavioral and psychological responses; Stress: Physiological responses; Stress-related diseases; Type A behavior pattern.

Strong Interest Inventory (SII)

DATE: 1974

TYPE OF PSYCHOLOGY: Intelligence and intelligence testing

FIELDS OF STUDY: Ability tests; intelligence assessment

The Strong Interest Inventory (SII) is one of the most empirically sound interest surveys. The survey is relatively easy to administer, requires at least a six-grade reading level, and requires a computer for scoring. There are twenty-three basic occupational scales and the results are mainly applicable for use by persons who are oriented toward professional, semiprofessional, or managerial occupations that attract college students.

KEY CONCEPTS
- career
- interest inventory
- job choice

INTRODUCTION

The Strong Interest Inventory (SII) replaced the well-known Strong-Campbell Interest Inventory in 1985 and was based on several decades of compiling empirical data. The empirical nature of the studies developed by E. K. Strong, Jr., is grounded in his observation of the specific interest patterns of workers in the occupational groups and careers he studied. He suggested that an individual who has interests that are similar to those of persons working in a given occupation is more likely to find satisfaction in that particular occupation than is a person who does not have common interests with those workers.

The SII contains 325 test items that measure a respondent's interests in a wide range of occupations, occupational activities, hobbies, leisure activities, school subjects, and types of people. Most test takers can complete the interest inventory in about thirty minutes; the reading level is sixth grade. The survey is appropriate for use by people with an approximate age range of thirteen years through adulthood. The SII has been translated for administration into several foreign languages.

The scores can also be converted to a common reporting system developed by John Holland relating to a general occupational grouping or a job choice. The Holland system consists of six concepts arranged in a hexagon indicating relative positioning. The nomenclature for the Holland system consists of Realistic (R), Investigative (I), Artistic (A), Social (S), Enterprising (E), and Conventional (C) (also referred to as the R-I-A-S-E-C sequence).

TECHNICAL ASPECTS

The SII has been well researched in relation to other inventories by Strong and others. The stability of the SII is well documented and reliability and validity studies suggest that the SII is well suited for career development, counseling, and review. The strength of the SII is the variety of data generated on an interpretive report. This information is useful in providing information that is usually not found on interest inventory profiles.

Interpreting the SII develops from a review of the general occupational theme scores. These provide three phases of review from the scores: first, a general overview of interest patterns; second, specific basic interest scores; and third, interests in specific occupations or jobs. The SII profiles are structured around Holland's six occupational styles. Each of the six themes is reported and indicates whether the interest level is considered very low, low, average, high, or very high.

The basic interest scales focus on subdivisions of the six occupational themes from which career groups or clusters of occupations can be derived. Ten administrative indices are reported on the SII, including an infrequent response index, an academic comfort scale indicating the degree to which a person likes academic work, and an introversion-extroversion (IE) index indicating whether a person likes working with people or things. To make maximum use of the information on the SII profile, a systematic evaluation is recommended by a professional who can develop a complete evaluation of the responses.

CRITIQUE

Needs and interests have been found to be closely related. The relationship between needs, occupational interests, and personality identification has been demonstrated carefully. Holland's research has also demonstrated that inner-directed and other-directed personalities differ in their occupational interests, as do persons who are decided and undecided. The relative importance of interests to vocational decisions has also been extensively studied. Certain occupations evidently satisfy specific needs, and these needs are related to interests. With respect to career maturity, high scores on the SII correspond to other career inventory scores.

To make maximum use of the information on the SII profile, a systematic evaluation is recommended. For these purposes, an SII summary evaluation is devised from the total number of responses. Several steps are outlined for evaluation of SII scores along with the available interpretations. Comparing the interests of African Americans, Mexican Americans, Asian Americans, and Native Americans, it was found that Holland's theory of six occupational groupings adequately represents the interests of these groups.

In order for individuals to enter an appropriate career, they must begin to identify specific interests and relative importance of those interests. Some individuals will need little guidance in making career choices; others will need to guidance of a survey instrument like the SII. Millions of people have received important information from it to use in decision making. Caution is always expressed by the authors of these inventories that no decision should be made solely on the basis of the results determined by one inventory alone. The SII is one of eighty interest inventories currently in use.

SOURCES FOR FURTHER STUDY

Herr, E. L., and Stanley H. Cramer. *Career Guidance and Counseling Through the Life Span.* 5th ed. Read-

ing, Mass.: Addison-Wesley, 1996. An overview of career counseling and guidance needs and resources for people from elementary school through adulthood.

Power, P. W. *A Guide to Vocational Assessment.* 3d ed. Austin, Tex.: Pro-ed, 2000. Useful guide for those both administering and creating vocational assessment tools.

Sharf, R. S. *Applying Career Development Theory to Counseling.* 3d ed. Pacific Grove: Calif.: Brooks/ Cole, 2002. Covers theory and practice, with numerous case examples.

Zunker, V. G., and Debra Osborn. *Using Assessment Results for Career Development.* 6th ed. Belmont, Calif.: Wadsworth, 2001. A workbook for career counselors, focused on what assessment results mean in practical terms for their clients.

Daniel L. Yazak

SEE ALSO: Ability tests; Assessment; Career and personnel testing; Career Occupational Preference System (COPS); College entrance examinations; Creativity: Assessment; General Aptitude Test Battery (GATB); Human resource training and development; Intelligence tests; Interest inventories; Kuder Occupational Interest Survey (KOIS); Peabody Individual Achievement Test (PIAT); Race and intelligence; Scientific methods; Stanford-Binet test; Survey research: Questionnaires and interviews; Testing: Historical perspectives; Wechsler Intelligence Scale for Children-Third Edition (WISC-III).

Structuralism and functionalism

DATE: 1879-1913

TYPE OF PSYCHOLOGY: Origin and definition of psychology

FIELDS OF STUDY: General constructs and issues; thought

Structualism and functionalism represent early schools of thought in psychology. While the structuralists were devoted to discovering the elements of consciousness, the functionalists believed that psychology should focus on understanding how consciousness is useful or functional.

KEY CONCEPTS

- applied psychology
- evolution
- imageless thought
- introspection
- stimulus error
- stream of consciousness
- voluntarism

INTRODUCTION

Structuralism and functionalism were two of the earliest schools of thought in psychology. To understand these early perspectives, it is important to consider the sociohistorical context in which they developed. Psychology as an independent scientific discipline was founded in 1879 by German scholar Wilhelm Wundt (1832-1920) at the University of Leipzig. Wundt was a medically trained physiologist appointed to the department of philosophy at Leipzig. In 1879, he established the first-ever laboratory devoted solely to the experimental study of psychological issues. The German *Zeitgeist* was conducive to this development. For example, the education reform movement encouraged the development of university research and promoted academic freedom. Furthermore, German scholars at the time accepted a broader definition of science compared to their counterparts in many other European countries.

Wundt defined psychology as the scientific study of conscious experience, and organized it into two broad areas: experimental psychology (the study of sensation and perception, reaction time, attention, and feelings) and *Völkerpsychologie* (cultural psychology, which included the study of language, myth, and custom). Wundt made an important distinction between immediate and mediate experiences. Mediate experiences involve an interpretation of sensory input ("I see an apple"), whereas an immediate experience consists of pure and unbiased sensory experiences ("I see a roundish, red object"). Wundt emphasized the process of organizing and synthesizing the elemental components of consciousness (the immediate experiences) into higher-level thoughts. Because this process of apperception was considered to be an act of will or volition, he often referred to his system as voluntarism.

One of Wundt's students, Edward Bradford Titchener (1867-1927), an Englishman who earned his Ph.D. under Wundt in 1892, ascended to prominence by establishing the structural school of thought in psychology as a professor at Cornell University. Functionalism soon arose as a school of thought that opposed structuralism.

Titchener, it should be noted, considered structuralism to be a refined extension of and largely compatible with Wundt's work. Because Titchener was the main translator of Wundt's work into English and was widely considered to be a loyal and accurate representative of Wundt's system, the term "structuralism" at the time was used as a label for both Titchener's and Wundt's work. This interpretative error, which is still propagated in some textbooks, was not fully realized until the mid-1970's, when scholars started to examine Wundt's original work in detail. There are some important differences between Titchener's structuralism and Wundt's system of voluntarism. First, Titchener rejected the idea of a branch of cultural psychology. Second, structural psychology neglected the study of apperception and focused almost exclusively on the identification of the elements of consciousness. Finally, in a structuralist framework, the elements of consciousness themselves were of utmost importance; mediate and immediate experiences were considered the same event simply viewed from different vantage points. There was no need for a volitional process.

STRUCTURALISM

For Titchener, psychology was the study of consciousness. Whereas physics was said to be concerned with assessing environmental events from an objective, external standard, psychology was concerned with examining how humans experience such events subjectively. For example, an hour spent listening to a boring speech and an hour spent playing an enjoyable game last exactly the same length of time—3,600 seconds—but, psychologically, the second event goes by more quickly.

In structuralism, consciousness is defined as the sum total of experiences at any given moment, and the mind is defined as the sum of experiences over the course of a lifetime. In order to understand consciousness and thus the mind, psychology, according to structuralism, must be concerned with three primary questions: First, what are the most basic elements of consciousness? Just as chemists break down physical substances into their elemental components, psychologists should identify the basic components of consciousness. Second, how are the elements associated with one another? That is, in what ways do they combine to produce complex experiences? Third, according to Titchener, what underlying physiological conditions are associated with the elements? Most of Titchener's work was devoted to the first goal of identifying the basic elements of consciousness. The primary methodology used toward this end was systematic experimental introspection.

INTROSPECTION

A primary goal for structuralism was to identify the basic elements of consciousness. Titchener reasoned that any science requires an observation of its subject matter, and psychology was no different. As detailed in Titchener's classic work, *Experimental Psychology: A Manual of Laboratory Practice* (4 vols., 1901-1905), introspection involved the systematic analysis and reporting of conscious experiences by highly trained researchers. Such individuals were trained to report on the most basic of sensory experiences and to avoid the stimulus error of reporting perceptual interpretations. For example, to report seeing "an apple" or having "a headache" would be a stimulus error. It would be more accurate, psychologically, to report seeing a "roundish, red object" or experiencing a "throbbing sensation of moderate intensity in the lower right part of the head." This methodology was utilized by Wundt, but Wundt emphasized quantitative judgments (such as size, weight, duration, or intensity), whereas in Titchener's system, descriptive reports were emphasized.

Titchener concluded that there were three basic elements of consciousness: sensations, images, and feelings. Sensations were the most fundamental and were the building blocks of all perceptions. In his *An Outline of Psychology* (1896), Titchener listed more than forty-four thousand elementary sensations, including approximately thirty-two thousand visual, twelve thousand auditory, and four taste sensations. It was held that these indivisible sensations could be combined in any number of ways to produce unique perceptions and ideas. Images are the building blocks for ideas and reflect previous sensory experiences. It is possible to have an image of an apple only because of past experiences with a particular combination of sensations. All feelings were viewed as reducible to experiencing a degree of pleasantness or unpleasantness. (In contrast, Wundt postu-

lated two other dimensions: strain/relaxation and excitement/calmness.) A feeling, when combined with certain sensations, can give rise to a complex emotional state, such as love, joy, disgust, or fear.

Later in his career, Titchener asserted that each element of consciousness could be characterized with regard to five basic dimensions: quality, intensity, protensity (duration), attensity (clearness), and extensity (space). Quality refers to the differentiation of sensations (an apple may be red or green; the water may be hot or cold). Intensity refers to the strength or magnitude of the quality (the extent to which the apple is red or the water is cold). Protensity refers to the duration or length of a sensory experience. Attensity refers to the clarity or vividness of the experience and reflects the process of attention (sensations are clearer when they are the focus of attention). Some sensations, especially visual and tactile ones, can also be characterized in terms of extensity (that is, they take up a certain amount of space). Feelings were characterized only in terms of quality, intensity, and protensity. Titchener believed that feelings dissipated when they were the subject of focused attention and therefore could not be experienced with great clarity.

EVALUATION

Structuralism faded away after Titchener's death in 1927. However, the basic tenets of structuralism had been under attack for years. First, there were serious problems with introspection as a scientific methodology. The results of such studies were frequently unreliable and there was no way of objectively verifying the content of someone's consciousness. The controversy over imageless thought was important. One group of researchers, most notably a former follower of Wundt, Oswald Külpe (1862-1915), at the University of Würzburg, concluded, using introspection methodology, that some thoughts occurred in the absence of any mentalistic sensations or images. This was completely at odds with structuralism, and researchers loyal to the structuralist position were not able to replicate the findings. On the other hand, researchers sympathetic to the Würzburg school were able to replicate the findings. Obviously, a theoretical bias was driving the results. It was widely concluded that introspection was lacking the objectivity needed to sustain a scientific discipline. Other methodologies were discouraged by structuralists in part because of the limited scope of psychology they practiced. In essence, structural psychology was limited to the study of the elements of consciousness in the healthy adult human. There was no place for the use of nonhuman animals as subjects, no child psychology, and no concern with the psychology of physical or mental illness. In addition, Titchener was against applied research, that is, conducting research to help resolve practical problems. He felt that this would detract from the objectivity of the study, and that academic researchers should be devoted to advancement of pure knowledge. Finally, structuralism was criticized for focusing almost exclusively on the elements of consciousness without taking into serious consideration the idea that consciousness is experienced as a unified whole, and that this whole is different from the sum of the elements.

Today, two major contributions of structuralism are recognized. The first is the strong emphasis that Titchener and his followers placed on rigorous laboratory research as the basis for psychology. While other methods are utilized by contemporary psychologists (such as case studies and field research), the emphasis on experimentation in practice and training remains dominant. Second, structuralism provided a well-defined school of thought and set of ideas that others could debate and oppose, with the ultimate result being the development of new and different schools of thought. The most prominent opposition to structuralism was functionalism.

FUNCTIONALISM

Unlike structuralism, functionalism was not a formal school of psychological thought. Rather, it was a label (originally used by Titchener) applied to a general set of assumptions regarding the providence of psychology, and a loosely connected set of principles regarding the psychology of consciousness. In many respects, functionalism was defined in terms of its opposition or contrast to structuralism. For example, functionalists believed that psychology should focus on the functions of mental life (in contrast to the structuralist focus on elemental components); be concerned with using psychology for practical solutions to problems (structuralists were, at best, indifferent to this concern); study not only healthy adult humans (the main focus of attention of structuralists) but also nonhuman animals, children, and nonhealthy individuals; employ a wide range of methodologies to investigate psychologi-

cal issues (structuralists relied almost totally on introspection); and examine individual differences, rather than being solely concerned, like the structuralists, with the establishment of universal (nomothetic) principles.

While structuralism was imported to the United States by a British scholar (Titchener) who received his psychological training in Germany (under Wundt), functionalism had a distinctly American flair. The American *Zeitgeist* at the time emphasized pragmatism and individuality. Such qualities made American psychologists especially receptive to the revolutionary work of Charles Darwin (1809-1882) on evolution and its subsequent application (as "social Darwinism") by anthropologist Herbert Spencer (1820-1903) to education, business, government, and other social institutions. Other important developments that influenced functionalism include work by Sir Francis Galton (1822-1911) on individual differences in mental abilities and the work on animal psychology by George Romanes (1848-1894) and C. Lloyd Morgan (1852-1936).

WILLIAM JAMES

William James (1842-1910) is considered the most important direct precursor of functional psychology in the United States, and one of the most eminent psychologists ever to have lived. James earned his M.D. from Harvard University in 1869 and subsequently became keenly interested in psychology. Despite his severe bouts with depression and other ailments, he accepted a post at Harvard in 1872 to teach physiology. Shortly thereafter, in 1875, James taught the first psychology course offered in the United States, "The Relations Between Physiology and Psychology," and initiated a classroom demonstration laboratory.

James published the two-volume *The Principles of Psychology* in 1890. This work was immediately a great success and is now widely regarded as the most important text in the history of modern psychology. Given the expansiveness of *Principles*—more than thirteen hundred pages arranged in twenty-eight chapters—it is impossible to summarize fully, but it includes such topics as the scope of psychology, functions of the brain, habit, methods of psychology, memory, the consciousness of self, sensation, perception, reasoning, instinct, emotions, will, and hypnotism. In this text James presented ideas that became central to functionalism. For example, in the chapter "The Stream of Consciousness," James criticized the postulate of structural psychology that sensations constitute the simplest mental elements and must therefore be the major focus of psychological inquiry. In contrast, James argued that conscious thought is experienced as a flowing and continuous stream, not as a collection of frozen elements. In critiquing introspection, the methodology championed by the structuralists, James asserted,

> The rush of the thought is so headlong that it almost always brings us up at the conclusion before we can arrest it. . . . The attempt at introspective analysis in these cases is in fact like seizing a spinning top to catch its motion, or trying to turn up the gas quickly enough to see how darkness looks.

With this new, expansive conceptualization of consciousness, James helped pave the way for psychologists interested in broadening the scope and methods of psychology. What was to emerge was the school of functionalism, with prominent camps at the University of Chicago and Columbia University.

THE CHICAGO SCHOOL

The Chicago school of functionalism is represented by the works of American scholars John Dewey (1859-1952), James Rowland Angell (1869-1949), and Harvey A. Carr (1873-1954). Functionalism was launched in 1896 with Dewy's *Psychological Review* article, "The Reflex Arc Concept in Psychology." Here Dewey argued against reducing reflexive behaviors to discontinuous elements of sensory stimuli, neural activity, and motor responses. In the same way that James attacked elementalism and reductionism in the analysis of consciousness, Dewey argued that it was inaccurate and artificial to do so with behavior. Influenced by Darwin's evolutionary theory of natural selection, Dewey asserted that reflexes should not be analyzed in terms of their component parts, but rather in terms of how they are functional for the organism—that is, how they help an organism adapt to the environment.

Angell crystalized the functional school in his 1907 *Psychological Review* paper, "The Province of Functional Psychology." In this work, three characteristics of functionalism were identified: Functional psychology is interested in discerning and portraying the typical operations of consciousness under actual life conditions, as opposed to analyzing and describing the elementary units of consciousness.

Functional psychology is concerned with discovering the basic utilities of consciousness, that is, how mental processes help organisms adapt their surroundings and survive. Functional psychology recognizes and insists upon the essential significance of the mind-body relationship for any just and comprehensive appreciation of mental life itself.

Carr's 1925 textbook *Psychology: A Study of Mental Activity* presents the most polished version of functionalism. As the title suggests, Carr identified such processes as memory, perception, feelings, imagination, judgment, and will as the topics for psychology. Such psychological processes were considered functional in that they help organisms gain information about the world, retain and organize that information, and then retrieve the information to make judgments about how to react to current situations. In other words, these processes were viewed as useful to organisms as they adapt their environments.

THE COLUMBIA SCHOOL

Another major camp of functionalism was at Columbia University and included such notable psychologists as James McKeen Cattell (1860-1944), Robert Sessions Woodworth (1869-1962), and Edward Lee Thorndike (1874-1949).

In line with the functionalist's embrace of applied psychology and the study of individual differences, Cattell laid the foundation for the psychological testing movement that would become massive in the 1920's and beyond. Under the influence of Galton, Cattell stressed the statistical analysis of large data sets and the measurement of mental abilities. He developed the order of merit methodology, in which participants rank-order a set of stimuli (for instance, the relative appeal of pictures or the relative eminence of a group of scientists) from which average ranks are calculated.

Woodworth is best known for his emphasis on motivation in what he called dynamic psychology. In this system, Woodworth acknowledged the importance of considering environmental stimuli and overt responses but emphasized the necessity of understanding the organism (perceptions, needs, or desires), representing therefore an early stimulis-organism-response (S-O-R) approach to psychology.

Thorndike represented a bridge from functionalism to behaviorism, a new school of thought that was led by John Broadus Watson (1878-1958) and emerged around 1913. Thorndike was notable for his use of nonhuman subjects, a position consistent with Darwin's emphasis on the continuity among organisms. He is also famous for his puzzle box research with cats, which led to his Law of Effect, which states that when an association is followed by a satisfying state of affairs, that association is strengthened. This early operant conditioning research was later expanded on by the famous behaviorist psychologist B. F. Skinner (1904-1990).

EVALUATION

Functionalism paved the way for the development of applied psychology, including psychological testing, clinical psychology, school psychology, and industrial-organizational psychology. Functionalism also facilitated the use of psychological research with a wide variety of subjects beyond the healthy adult male, including infants, children, the mentally ill, and nonhuman animals. Finally, functional psychologists utilized a wide variety of methods beyond that of introspection, including field studies, questionnaires, mental tests, and behavioral observations. These developments were responsible, in part, for the United States becoming the world center for psychological study by 1920. The term "functional psychology" faded from usage as it became clear that, by default, being simply a psychologist in the United States meant being a functional psychologist. The shift in psychological thought instigated by functionalism set the stage for the next major evolutionary phase in American psychology, behaviorism.

SOURCES FOR FURTHER STUDY

Behnamin, Ludy T., Jr. "The Psychology Laboratory at the Turn of the Twentieth Century." *American Psychologist* 55 (2000): 318-321. This is a nontechnical and brief introduction to laboratory research in psychology from 1879 to 1900. The author discusses the importance of the laboratory for establishing psychology as a scientific discipline separate from philosophy.

Boring, E. G. *A History of Experimental Psychology.* 2d ed. New York: Appleton-Century-Crofts, 1950. This is the classic text on the history of psychology, written by one of Titchener's students. The first edition of 1925 is also widely available.

Donnelly, M. E. *Reinterpreting the Legacy of William James.* Washington, D.C.: American Psychological Association, 1992. This book explores how James's masterwork might have been revised in light of his later pluralistic, pragmatic approach to psychology and philosophy. A distinguished group of psychologists, philosophers, and historians contribute twenty-three chapters that probe this and other questions in a broad-based collection focused on the contemporary relevance of the works of James.

Hergenhahn, B. R. *An Introduction to the History of Psychology.* 4th ed. Belmont, Calif.: Wadsworth/ Thomson Learning, 2001. Another excellent standard textbook on the history of psychology. Written for college students; includes in-depth chapters on structuralism and functionalism.

Leys, R., and R. B. Evans. *Defining American Psychology: The Correspondence Between Adolf Meyer and Edward Bradford Titchener.* Baltimore: The Johns Hopkins University Press, 1990. Adolf Meyer was a highly influential psychiatrist who exchanged a series of letters with Titchener in 1909 and again in 1918. This book represents an interesting first-hand look at how the new science of psychology was being discussed and situated among other disciplines.

Shultz, D. P., and S. E. Shultz. *A History of Modern Psychology.* 7th ed. Fort Worth, Tex.: Harcourt College Publishers, 1999. A clear, well-organized history of modern psychology, placing schools of thought within their social contexts.

Watson, R. I., and R. B. Evans. *The Great Psychologists: A History of Psychological Thought.* 5th ed. New York: HarperCollins, 1991. Psychologists and schools of psychology from ancient Greek times to the present. Chapters 19 and 20 specifically focus on structuralism and functionalism.

Jay W. Jackson

SEE ALSO: Behaviorism; Madness: Historical concepts; Psychoanalytic psychology; Psychology: Definition; Psychotherapy: Historical approaches; Skinner, B. F.; Thorndike, Edward L.; Watson, John B.

Stuttering

TYPE OF PSYCHOLOGY: Psychopathology
FIELDS OF STUDY: Childhood and adolescent disorders

Stuttering is the most common speech disorder among adolescents and adults, and it has profound consequences for self-esteem. Its origins appear in early childhood, as a result of both biological influences and learning processes; modern therapy most often focuses on the latter.

KEY CONCEPTS

- communication environment
- desensitization techniques
- distraction techniques
- learning theory
- neurosis
- psychoanalyst
- psychotherapy
- speech disrupters
- stuttering
- verbal disfluencies

INTRODUCTION

All people sometimes hesitate when they speak or repeat the starting sound or syllable of a word when they are nervous. These are examples of normal verbal disfluencies. Stutterers are different from normal speakers primarily because of the frequency of their problem, not because their speech problem is by itself unusual. Stuttering is a problem of the timing and rhythms of speech, not of articulation. Thus, it is quite different from other common speech defects. It is also the most common speech problem to affect teens or adults.

Stuttering is a universal phenomenon, affecting people of every society and language group on earth. It is about four times as common in boys as in girls. It typically begins in the preschool years (almost always before age six) and, unless outgrown by adolescence, becomes progressively more pronounced. As the problem worsens, the stutterer is likely to show other, related behavior problems such as nervous twitches or slapping himself when trying to stop stuttering. Self-esteem usually suffers; teens, especially, are self-conscious about this speech problem. This can lead to avoidance of speaking or to more pronounced social withdrawal.

POSSIBLE CAUSES

There are several possible causes of stuttering. Scientists do not seek to know which of these causes is "correct"; for different stutterers, different causes may apply. In addition, in any individual case, more

than one cause may be relevant. For example, stuttering tends to run in families, suggesting a genetic contribution. This contribution may only make an individual more likely to develop the stuttering problem, given the right (or wrong) circumstances. About the only cause which has been ruled out is imitation. There is no evidence that stuttering develops from a child's exposure to another stutterer.

A variety of physical differences between stutterers and nonstutterers have been investigated, with all aspects of the mouth and airways involved in speech production taken into account. Hearing problems should be considered, although stuttering is actually less common among the deaf. Nevertheless, partial hearing losses can influence confidence in learning to speak, and, in fact, the onset of the stuttering problem often corresponds with the earliest use of sentences. In the treatment of any speech defect, a check for hearing problems is an important preliminary step. Brain damage can also lead to stuttering, although this is not the usual cause.

While stress certainly aggravates stuttering for a stutterer, it is not usually the cause of the speech disorder. Most stuttering problems develop gradually, and parents typically cannot pinpoint when the problem began. Extremely stressful events have, however, been known to cause stuttering directly.

Most stuttering probably develops gradually during the time when children are beginning to speak in sentences and engage in conversation. As stated earlier, everyone shows verbal disfluencies; young children are even more likely to do so. Wendell Johnson argues that the difference between stuttering and nonstuttering preschoolers is not in the children, but in the perceptions of their parents. By overreacting to normal disfluencies, parents may impair a young child's self-confidence, instigating a truly vicious cycle: Low self-confidence creates more disfluency, which further lowers self-confidence. The cycle continues until the child is, in fact, a "stutterer."

The difficulty with this line of reasoning is that it imposes an unfair burden of guilt on the parents. In effect, concerned parents are accused of causing the problem by expressing their concern. While parental behavior may contribute to stuttering, most experts believe that the genetic evidence and the preponderance of boys among stutterers suggest a physical contribution as well. Moreover, treatment of speech disorders is most effective when begun early, and the social impact of stuttering makes early treatment even more critical; thus, parents of stutterers may not know whether they will do more harm by calling attention to the problem (thus making it worse) or by ignoring it.

TREATMENT APPROACHES

The best advice to parents is to maintain patient but watchful concern. First, it is important to remember that all speakers show disfluencies and show more of them under stress. The child learning to speak may require patience from the adult listener. Parents should not pressure a child who is attempting to express what, to the child, may be a complex idea. Parents should not finish a child's sentences. If a child's stuttering problem does not disappear with time, if it appears without obvious stressful circumstances, or if accompanying nervous behaviors develop, it is time to seek help. Patience and lack of pressure are that much more important with a diagnosed stutterer. The most helpful role for the parent at this point is to provide unconditional emotional support and to cooperate with the therapist.

Current approaches to the treatment of stuttering emphasize controlling the problem rather than eliminating it. Stutterers are often advised to slow down their speaking and simply to stop and take a deep breath if stuttering begins. They may be advised to sigh before any speech attempt. Therapy is also concerned with self-esteem problems and with the social avoidance of stutterers, treating these as results, not causes, of stuttering.

Stutterers often develop their own control techniques. Some find, for example, that singing is easier than talking and take advantage of this to modify the pitch of their speech when a problem occurs. The best advice may simply be to do whatever works for any individual.

The decision to treat or not treat stuttering is complicated by the similarity of speech between early stutterers and nonstutterers and by the resulting difficulty in pinpointing the origin of the problem. Edward G. Conture has pointed out that therapists deal both with parents who are overconcerned about normal disfluency and with parents who are underconcerned about a real problem. Moreover, Conture has noted, the nature of treatment depends considerably on the age of the stutterer.

Younger stutterers offer the best hope for treatment, before the complications created by social stigma occur or worsen. On the other hand, they present greater problems in diagnosis, as well as a need to counsel parents who are themselves experiencing stress related to the stuttering. For example, parents of stutterers frequently have great difficulty looking at their child when the child stutters. They feel their child's pain, but their own pained response may not be helpful. Additionally, young children may not understand instructions for speech exercises or may lack the patience to practice techniques. Teens are better able to cooperate with the activities of speech therapy, which involve following directions and practice. On the other hand, they may be uncooperative for a number of reasons: past negative therapy experience, fear of peer reactions to being in speech therapy, and normal adolescent resistance to adults.

Adult stutterers have the least likelihood of overcoming the problem but are highly motivated (although they also may have had bad experiences with past therapy efforts) and have the freedom to structure their own environments. This last point is

---

DSM-IV-TR Criteria for Stuttering (DSM code 307.0)

Disturbance, inappropriate for age, in the normal fluency and time patterning of speech

Characterized by frequent occurrences of one or more of the following:

- sound and syllable repetitions
- sound prolongations
- interjections
- broken words (such as pauses within a word)
- audible or silent blocking (filled or unfilled pauses in speech)
- circumlocutions (word substitutions to avoid problematic words)
- words produced with an excess of physical tension
- monosyllabic whole-word repetitions

Fluency disturbance interferes with academic or occupational achievement or with social communication

If speech-motor or sensory deficit is present, speech difficulties exceed those usually associated with these problems

important, because a stutterer's relationship with parents often is a complication for younger stutterers. The adult's greater freedom—not only from parents but also from peer pressure—can make psychotherapy for self-esteem problems more successful. On the other hand, the adult continues to face a tremendous social stigma, which can even take the form of job discrimination. Moreover, stuttering by this time has become ingrained as part of a stutterer's identity and is thus more resistant to change.

SPEECH THERAPY

Specific speech therapy techniques are varied. Distraction techniques aim to distract the stutterer from the speech problem. They have their basis in the fact that self-consciousness about speech aggravates stuttering. One example that has been used is asking the stutterer to speak while crawling on the floor. These techniques most often provide only temporary success. One obvious problem is that it is hard to generalize the use of such methods to real-life situations.

Desensitization techniques focus on training the stutterer to deal with situations that provoke stuttering. This requires analyzing all situations that produce stuttering (such as interruptions or being asked to hurry one's speech). After a stress-free therapy environment is created, the "speech disrupters" are reintroduced one at a time, with the aim of strengthening the individual's tolerance for disruption.

Therapy is most effective when parents are involved. They are very important for their role in promoting self-esteem. They may require counseling themselves, both to deal with their own frustrations and to understand the impact of their own and others' reactions on the stuttering child. In addition, they are the most important members of the child's communication environment. The parents' roles, not only in their responses to the child's speech but also in their own manner of speaking with the child, largely structure that environment. It has been found, for example, that when parents slow down their own speech to a stuttering child, the child's stuttering is reduced.

The individual's self-esteem is central to effective therapy. Psychotherapy frequently deals with the psychological damage created by the stigma of stuttering. There are also many books on stuttering, many with a focus on self-help. Several authors advise stutterers of the needs, first, to increase their self-confidence, and second, to refrain from avoiding social interaction. For example, Wendell Johnson specifically emphasizes concentrating on one's "normal" speech instead of on one's stuttering. The idea is that the stutterer's overconcern with stuttering has served to maintain and worsen the problem.

A common tactic in the self-help literature is to cite famous stutterers. Jock A. Carlisle composed an impressive list, including Moses, Aristotle, Thomas Jefferson, Winston Churchill, Charles Darwin, and Marilyn Monroe. Many famous stutterers have been known for their writing, and some have sufficiently coped to allow public speaking or even acting. This success may help to inspire a stutterer; it should at least enhance a stutterer's self-esteem to know that stutterers have succeeded in such a variety of fields. Self-confidence is the common thread, whether a result of self-help, speech therapy, psychotherapy, or unconditional parental support.

CONTEMPORARY THEORIES

Descriptions of the treatment of stuttering can be found throughout recorded history. Charles Van Riper has listed several of the prescientific approaches, some dating to ancient Greece and Rome: speaking with pebbles in the mouth (an ancient use of a distraction technique), exorcism, hot substances applied to the tongue, and blood-letting. The beginning of the modern era saw the development of tongue exercises and even surgery that deformed the tongue.

In the late nineteenth century, stuttering was for the first time described as a neurosis, or disorder caused by anxiety. This theme was elaborated by twentieth century psychoanalysts in their treatment of stutterers; through the first half of the twentieth century, the psychoanalytic view dominated theoretical views and treatment of stuttering. According to this view, stuttering is the result of an unconscious conflict between the desire to speak and a preference to remain silent. The obvious tension experienced by stutterers, as well as their avoidance of speaking, supported this interpretation.

While some therapists remain influenced by psychoanalytic views, most contemporary therapists view the observed tension to be a result of, not the cause of, stuttering. They are more influenced by learning theory—that is, they view stuttering as the result of a process of learned reactions to specific environmental influences. Johnson's research on the similarities between preschool stutterers and nonstutterers, along with the differences among those same children's parents' perceptions, strongly supports this interpretation. Most theorists and therapists also accept the role of genetic disposition in determining who is more likely to develop a stuttering disorder. In this view, therapy relies on relearning on the part of the stutterer and on control of the communication environment, especially the speech and reactions of the parents. Psychotherapy remains important not because psychological problems are seen as the cause of stuttering but because they appear to result from stuttering—from the social stigma involved as well as from the frustrations in communicating with others.

The recent shift in views may in part be attributed to the growing role in research of people who themselves have or have had a stuttering problem. Charles Van Riper was such an individual, and he devoted his entire career to research and treatment of stuttering. The value of his personal experience is found in his own solution: He became fluent when he stopped trying to hide his problem. Stuttering is a learned speech problem, with tremendous emotional consequences; stutterers are simply normal people coping with this problem.

SOURCES FOR FURTHER STUDY

Carlisle, Jock Alan. *Tangled Tongue: Living with a Stutter.* Toronto: University of Toronto Press, 1985. A comprehensive review of the causes of and treatments for stuttering, written by a stutterer. Besides general information for and identification with the reader, it provides useful appendices on self-help and consumer organizations as well as organizations involved in stuttering therapy and research.

Conture, Edward G. *Stuttering: Its Nature, Diagnosis, and Treatment.* Boston: Allyn & Bacon, 2000. A basic text aimed at speech therapy students. Emphasis is on evaluation and treatment, highlighting important treatment differences related to the age of the stutterer. Includes a wealth of clinical examples throughout and a full case study in an appendix.

Glauber, I. Peter. *Stuttering: A Psychoanalytic Understanding.* New York: Human Sciences Press, 1982. Presents the psychoanalytic view of stuttering as the result of unconscious conflicts. Not the dominant view, but one that should be considered for a full understanding of stuttering. The first of two parts presents the basic interpretation. The second part requires more familiarity with psychoanalytic concepts and concerns.

Johnson, Wendell. *Stuttering: And What You Can Do About It.* Minneapolis: University of Minnesota Press, 1961. Aimed at parents of stutterers; very readable as well as comprehensive. Johnson presents his own research comparing stuttering and nonstuttering children as well as their parents, and he emphasizes the importance of parental expectations as well as the child's self-concept in both the cause and treatment of stuttering.

Starkweather, C. Woodruff, and Janet Givens-Ackerman. *Stuttering.* Austin, Tex.: Pro-ed, 1997. Aimed at speech therapy students. Presents a readable and thorough summary of current research, with a particular sensitivity to the variability of the problem and to problems in defining stuttering. Emphasizes a client-centered approach to therapy.

Nancy E. Macdonald

SEE ALSO: Language; Linguistics; Self-esteem; Speech disorders.

Substance use disorders

TYPE OF PSYCHOLOGY: Biological bases of behavior; motivation; psychopathology; stress

FIELDS OF STUDY: Biological treatments; coping; critical issues in stress; motivation theory; nervous system; stress and illness; substance use

Substance use disorders include the formal medical diagnoses of substance abuse and substance dependence for many types of drugs of abuse, including alcohol and prescription drugs. These disorders are characterized by recurrent problems in everyday life and/or physical or emotional distress and impairment that are caused or exacerbated by the use of the substances of abuse.

KEY CONCEPTS
- hallucinogens
- inhalants
- opioids
- psychological dependence

- sedatives/hypnotics
- self-medication
- stimulants
- tolerance
- withdrawal

INTRODUCTION

Substance use is studied in psychology from personality, social, and biological perspectives. Social and personality studies of individuals with substance use disorders have produced a variety of theories. These theories have focused on issues such as difficulties people might have with tolerating stress, being unable to delay gratification, developing social skills, being socially isolated or marginalized, being attracted to taking risks, and having difficulties regulating one's own behavior. Additionally, environmental issues, such as poverty or high levels of stress, have been linked to substance use problems. Biological theories of these disorders suggest that genetic and conditioned sensitivities to substances of abuse and their effects may predispose individuals to acquire these disorders. For instance, people who have increased needs to seek relief from pain or have an increased need to seek pleasure or euphoria might be at greater risk for developing such problems. Pain is broadly defined as any feeling of dysphoria. Because both pain and euphoria can be produced by psychosomatic or somatopsychic events, these two biological categories can subsume most of the stated nonbiological correlates of substance abuse.

There are several forms of substance use disorders including abuse and dependence. These should be contrasted to normal experimentation, normal use without problems, and limited instances of misuse that are more appropriately attributed to situational factors than an underlying psychiatric disorder.

There are several types of substances of abuse, and some of these are not typically viewed as problematic. Major categories include sedatives/hypnotics; alcohol; nicotine; marijuana; opioids, such as heroin; stimulants, including amphetamine, cocaine, crack, and caffeine; inhalants, such as glue, paint, nitrous oxide (laughing gas), and shoe polish; hallucinogens, including phencyclidine (PCP or "angel dust"), LSD ("acid"), MDMA (an amphetamine-like drug with hallucinogenic effects, also known as X or ecstasy); anabolic steroids; and even some types of prescription drugs, such as Valium.

When diagnoses are given for substance use disorders, diagnoses should be given in terms of a specific type of substance. A diagnosis of "substance abuse" would be too general, because it does not specify the substance causing the problem. Having problems with one substance does not automatically mean that a person has problems with all substances. Thus, any diagnosis for a substance use disorder should be substance-specific; examples might include alcohol abuse, inhalant abuse, marijuana dependence, marijuana abuse, cocaine dependence, or stimulant abuse.

For the substance abuse category, the key features of the disorder are patterns of repeated problems in individual functioning in terms of roles at work, school, or home; legal status; use of the substance in hazardous situations, or the consequences of the use on interpersonal relationships. For the substance dependence category, the key features of the disorder are patterns of repeated problems in several areas that are distinct from those considered for abuse. Diagnosis of dependence relies on factors such as tolerance; withdrawal; new or worsened physical or emotional problems directly resulting from the use of the substance; loss of control over the use of the substance; unsuccessful efforts to cut down or quit coupled with intense desire to quit; excessive periods of time spent obtaining, using, or recovering from using the substance; and the displacement of social or occupational activities in order to use the substance.

PAIN AND EUPHORIA

The experience of pain or the seeking of euphoria as causes of substance use disorders can be measured physically or can be perceived by the individual without obvious physical indicators. The relative importance of pain and euphoria in determining the development and maintenance of substance use disorders requires consideration of the contributions of at least five potential sources of behavioral and physical status: genetic predisposition, dysregulation during development, dysregulation from trauma at any time during the life span, the environment, and learning. Any of these can result in or interact to produce the pain or feelings of euphoria that can lead to substance use disorders.

The key commonality in pain-induced substance use disorders is that the organism experiences pain that it does not tolerate. Genetic predisposers of pain include inherited diseases and conditions that interfere with normal pain tolerance. Developmental dysregulations include physical and behavioral arrests and related differences from developmental norms. Trauma from physical injury or from environmental conditions can also result in the experience of pain, as can the learning of a pain-producing response.

Several theories of pain-induced substance use disorders can be summarized as self-medication theories. In essence, these state that individuals misuse substances in order to correct an underlying disorder that presumably produces some form of physical or emotional distress or discomfort. Self-medication theories are useful because they take into account the homeostatic (tendency toward balance) nature of the organism and because they include the potential for significant individual differences in problems with pain.

Relief from pain by itself does not account entirely for drug use that goes beyond improvement in health or reachievement of normal status and certainly cannot account entirely for drug use that becomes physically self-destructive. Thus, the use of substances to achieve positive effects such as euphoria or pleasure are also important to consider as causes of these disorders. Associative conditioning and operant conditioning effects play an important role as well. This type of substance misuse can be distinguished from the relief caused by substance use to decrease pain because the substance use does not stop when such relief is achieved, but continues until the person experiences the pleasurable effects.

Euphoria-induced substance use, or pleasure seeking, is characteristic of virtually all species tested. Some theorists have proposed that pleasure seeking is an innate drive not easily kept in check even by socially acceptable substitutes. Other theorists believe that these types of substance use disorders related to the positively reinforcing aspects of the substances may have developed as a function of biological causes such as evolutionary pressure and selection. For example, organisms that could eat rotten, fermented fruit (composed partly of alcohol) may have survived to reproduce when others did not; people who could tolerate or preferred drinking alcohol instead of contaminated water reproduced when those who drank contaminated water did not.

SUBSTANCE USE DISORDER RESEARCH

Laboratory studies of the biological bases of substance abuse and dependence involve clinical (human) and preclinical (animal) approaches. Such research has demonstrated that there are areas of the brain that can provide powerful feelings of euphoria when stimulated, indicating that the brain is primed for the experience of pleasure. Direct electrical stimulation of some areas of the brain, including an area first referred to as the medial forebrain bundle, produced such strong addictive behaviors in animals that they ignored many basic drives including those for food, water, mating, and care of offspring.

Later research showed that the brain also contains highly addictive analgesic and euphoriant chemicals that exist as a normal part of the neural milieu. Thus, the brain is also predisposed to aid in providing relief from pain and has coupled such relief in some cases with feelings of euphoria. It is not surprising, therefore, that substance abuse, dependence, and other behaviors with addictive characteristics can develop so readily in so many organisms.

The effects of typical representatives of the major categories of abused substances can be predicted. Alcohol can disrupt several behavioral functions. It can slow reaction time, movement, and thought processes and can interfere with needed rapid eye movement (REM) sleep. It can also produce unpredictable emotionality, including violence. Those who abuse alcohol may go on to develop the symptoms of physiological dependence (a condition where tolerance or withdrawal are present) and may go on to develop the full diagnosis of alcohol dependence, and it is important to note that the symptoms of alcohol withdrawal can be life-threatening. Heroin, an opioid, has analgesic (pain-killing) and euphoriant effects. It is also highly addictive, but withdrawal seldom results in death. Marijuana, sometimes classified as a sedative, sometimes as a hallucinogen, has many of the same behavioral effects as alcohol.

Stimulants vary widely in their behavioral effects. Common to all is some form of physiological and behavioral stimulation. Some, such as cocaine and the amphetamines (including crystal methamphetamine, or "ice"), are extremely addictive and seriously life-threatening and can produce violence. Others, such as caffeine, are relatively mild in their

Substance-Related Disorders in DSM-IV-TR

- Substance Use Disorders:
  Dependence; Abuse
- Substance-Induced Disorders:
  Intoxication; Withdrawal; Anxiety Disorder; Persisting Amnestic Disorder; Intoxication Delirium; Persisting Dementia; Mood Disorder; Psychotic Disorder; Sexual Dysfunction; Sleep Disorder; Withdrawal Delirium
- Alcohol-Related Disorders:
  Abuse; Dependence; Anxiety Disorder; Intoxication; Intoxication Delirium; Mood Disorder; Persisting Amnestic Disorder; Persisting Dementia; Psychotic Disorder; Sexual Dysfunction; Sleep Disorder; Withdrawal; Withdrawal Delirium; Alcohol-Related Disorder Not Otherwise Specified
- Amphetamine- (or Amphetamine-like) Related Disorders:
  Abuse; Anxiety Disorder; Intoxication Delirium; Dependence; Intoxication; Psychotic Disorder; Mood Disorder; Sexual Dysfunction; Sleep Disorder; Withdrawal; Amphetamine-Related Disorder Not Otherwise Specified
- Caffeine-Related Disorders:
  Anxiety Disorder; Intoxication; Sleep Disorder; Caffeine-Related Disorder Not Otherwise Specified
- Cannabis-Related Disorders:
  Abuse; Anxiety Disorder; Intoxication; Dependence; Intoxication Delirium; Psychotic Disorder; Cannabis-Related Disorder Not Otherwise Specified
- Cocaine-Related Disorders:
  Abuse; Anxiety Disorder; Dependence; Intoxication; Intoxication Delirium; Mood Disorder; Psychotic Disorder; Sleep Disorder; Withdrawal; Cocaine-Related Disorder Not Otherwise Specified
- Hallucinogen-Related Disorders:
  Abuse; Anxiety Disorder; Dependence; Intoxication; Intoxication Delirium; Mood Disorder; Persisting Perception Disorder; Psychotic Disorder with Delusions; Hallucinogen-Related Disorder Not Otherwise Specified
- Inhalant-Related Disorders:
  Abuse; Anxiety Disorder; Dependence; Intoxication; Intoxication Delirium; Mood Disorder; Persisting Dementia; Psychotic Disorder; Inhalant-Related Disorder Not Otherwise Specified
- Nicotine-Related Disorders:
  Dependence; Withdrawal; Nicotine-Related Disorder Not Otherwise Specified
- Opioid-Related Disorders:
  Abuse; Intoxication Delirium; Dependence; Intoxication; Mood Disorder; Psychotic Disorder; Sleep Disorder; Sexual Dysfunction; Withdrawal; Opioid-Related Disorder Not Otherwise Specified
- Phencyclidine- (or Phencyclidine-like) Related Disorders:
  Abuse; Anxiety Disorder; Intoxication Delirium; Dependence; Intoxication; Mood Disorder; Psychotic Disorder; Phencyclidine-Related Disorder Not Otherwise Specified
- Sedative-, Hypnotic-, or Anxiolytic-Related Disorders:
  Abuse; Persisting Amnestic Disorder; Anxiety Disorder; Persisting Dementia; Dependence; Intoxication; Intoxication Delirium; Mood Disorder; Psychotic Disorder; Withdrawal; Withdrawal Delirium; Sexual Dysfunction; Sleep Disorder; Sedative-, Hypnotic-, or Anxiolytic-Related Disorder Not Otherwise Specified
- Polysubstance-Related Disorder:
  Dependence
- Other (or unknown) Substance-Related Disorders:
  Other (or unknown) Substance Use Disorders; Other (or unknown) Substance-Induced Disorders

euphoriant effects. Withdrawal from stimulants, especially the powerful forms, can result in profound depression.

Hallucinogens are also a diverse group of substances that can produce visual, auditory, tactile, olfactory, or gustatory hallucinations, but most do so in only a small percentage of the population. Some, such as PCP, can produce violent behavior, while others, such as lysergic acid diethylamide (LSD), are not known for producing negative emotional

outbursts. Inhalants usually produce feelings of euphoria; they are most often used by individuals in their adolescent years who cannot afford to buy other types of drugs such as marijuana, as well as by adult individuals who have easy access to these substances in their work environments or social circles.

BRAIN CHEMISTRY

It is noteworthy that some of the pharmacological effects of very different drugs are quite similar. Marijuana and alcohol affect at least three of the same brain biochemical systems. Alcohol can become a form of opiate in the brain following some specific chemical transformations. These similarities raise an old and continuing question in the substance use field: Is there a fundamental addictive mechanism common to everyone that differs only in the level and nature of expression? Older theories of drug-abuse behavior approached this question by postulating the "addictive personality," a type of person who would become indiscriminately addicted as a result of his or her personal and social history. With advances in neuroscience have come theories concerning the possibility of an "addictive brain," which refers to a neurological status that requires continued adjustment provided by drugs.

An example of the workings of the addictive brain might be a low-opiate brain that does not produce normal levels of analgesia or normal levels of organismic and behavioral euphoria (joy). The chemical adjustment sought by the brain might be satisfied by use or abuse of any drug that results in stimulation of the opiate function of the brain. As discussed above, several seemingly unrelated drugs can produce a similar chemical effect. Thus, the choice of a particular substance might depend both on brain status and on personal or social experience with the effects and availability of the drug used.

The example of the opiate-seeking brain raises at least two possibilities for prevention and treatment, both of which have been discussed in substance-use literature: reregulation of the brain and substitution. So far, socially acceptable substitutes or substitute addictions offer some promise, but reregulation of the dysregulated brain is still primarily a hope of the future. An example of a socially acceptable substitute might be opiate production by excessive running, an activity that can produce some increase in opiate function. The success of such a substitution procedure, however, depends upon many variables that may be quite difficult to predict or control. The substitution might not produce the required amount of reregulation, the adjustment might not be permanent, and tolerance to the adjustment might develop. There are a host of other possible problems.

FUTURE POSSIBILITIES
Use of psychoactive substances dates from the earliest recorded history and likely predates it. Historical records indicate that many substances with the po-

tential for abuse were used in medicinal and ceremonial or religious contexts, as tokens in barter, for their euphoriant properties during recreation, as indicators of guilt or innocence, as penalties, and in other practices.

Substance use disorders are widespread in virtually all countries and cultures, and can be extremely costly, both personally and socially. There is no doubt that most societies would like to eliminate substance use disorders, as many efforts are under way to prevent and treat their occurrence. It is obvious that economic as well as social factors contribute both to substance use disorders and to the laws regulating substance use, and possibly create some roadblocks in eliminating abuse and dependence.

In psychology, the systemic and popular study of substance use became most extensive as the field of pharmacology blossomed and access to substances of abuse increased. The creation of the National Institute of Alcohol Abuse and Alcoholism and the National Institute on Drug Abuse helped to fuel research in this area in the 1970's and later. During the 1980's and 1990's, there was an increase in exploration of the biological mechanisms underlying substance use disorders and the possibility that pharmacological interventions might be useful to prevent and treat substance use disorders. The 1990's also brought an increase in awareness among the research and clinical communities that attention to specific demographic characteristics, such as age, gender, and ethnicity, was also important for understanding the etiology, prevention, and treatment of substance use disorders. As research progresses, these factors and the impact of the environment on behavior are increasingly the focus of study, and attention to the diagnosis of abuse is increasing.

Future research on substance use disorders is likely to focus on biological determinants of the problem for the purposes of prevention and treatment, environmental circumstances related to problem development, the interaction of culture and gender as they relate to substance use disorders and treatments, and how other mental illnesses can compound problems related to substance use. Many people erroneously consider biological explanations of problematic behaviors to be an excuse for such behaviors. In fact, discoveries regarding the neural contributions to such behaviors are the basis on which rational therapies for such behaviors can be developed. Recognizing that a disorder has a basis in the brain can enable therapists to address the disorder with a better armamentarium of useful therapeutic tools. In this way, simple management of such disorders can be replaced by real solutions to the problems created by substance abuse.

SOURCES FOR FURTHER STUDY

Gitlow, Stuart. *Substance Use Disorders: A Practical Guide.* Philadelphia: Lippincott, Williams & Wilkins, 2001. Provides basic explanations for different diagnoses of substance use disorders and explains other diagnostic terms.

Hardman, Joel G., and Lee E. Limbard, eds. *Goodman and Gilman's "The Pharmacological Basis of Therapeutics."* 10th ed. New York: Macmillan, 2001. A standard reference for students interested in an overview of the pharmacological aspects of selected addictive drugs. Of greater interest to those interested in pursuing the study of substance abuse from a neurological and physiological perspective.

Inaba, Daryl. *Uppers, Downers, All Arounders: Physical and Mental Effects of Psychoactive Drugs.* 4th ed. Ashland, Oreg.: CNS Productions, 2000. An easy-to-read, practical book on what substance use disorders look like to the everyday person, as well as a description of related problems and concerns.

Julien, Robert M. *A Primer of Drug Action.* Rev. ed. New York: W. H. Freeman, 2001. An introductory treatment of types and actions of many abused and therapeutic substances. A useful, quick reference guide for psychoactive effects of drugs used in traditional pharmacological therapy for disorders and abused substances. Contains good reference lists and appendices that explain some of the anatomy and chemistry required to understand biological mechanisms of substance abuse.

Weil, Andrew, and Winifred Rosen. *From Chocolate to Morphine: Everything You Need to Know About Mind Altering Drugs.* Rev. and updated ed. Boston: Houghton Mifflin, 1998. This classic, popular text discusses mind-altering substances, from foods that alter moods to illicit drugs of abuse.

Rebecca M. Chesire;
updated by Nancy A. Piotrowski

SEE ALSO: Addictive personality and behaviors; Alcohol dependence and abuse; Codependency; Endorphins; Motivation; Optimal arousal theory.

Suicide

TYPE OF PSYCHOLOGY: Psychopathology
FIELDS OF STUDY: Depression

Suicide is the intentional taking of one's own life; roughly 12 per 100,000 Americans commit suicide annually. Suicide rates are higher for males than females and increase with age; risk for suicide also increases with clinical depression, so suicide may be considered the most severe consequence of any psychological disorder.

KEY CONCEPTS
- altruistic suicide
- anomie
- egoistic suicide
- epidemiological research
- psychological autopsy
- suicidal gesture

INTRODUCTION

Suicide is the intentional taking of one's own life. Psychologists have devoted much effort to its study, attempting to identify those at greatest risk for suicide and to intervene effectively to prevent suicide.

Sociologist Émile Durkheim introduced what has become a well-known classification of suicide types. Altruistic suicides, according to Durkheim, are those that occur in response to societal demands (for example, the soldier who sacrifices himself to save his comrades). Egoistic suicides occur when the individual is isolated from society and so does not experience sufficient societal demands to live. The third type is the anomic suicide. Anomie is a sense of disorientation or alienation which occurs following a major change in one's societal relationships (such as the loss of a job or the death of a close friend); the anomic suicide occurs following such sudden and dramatic changes.

Research supports Durkheim's ideas that suicide is associated with social isolation and recent loss. Many other variables, both demographic and psychological, have also been found to be related to suicide. Numerous studies have shown that the following demographic variables are related to suicide: sex, age, marital status, employment status, urban/rural dwelling, and race. Paradoxically, more females than males attempt suicide, but more males than females commit suicide. The ratio in both cases is about three to one. The difference between the sex ratios for attempted and completed suicide is generally explained by the fact that males tend to employ more lethal and less reversible methods than do females (firearms and hanging, for example, are more lethal and less reversible than ingestion of drugs).

Age is also related to suicide. In general, risk for suicide increases with increasing age; however, even though suicide risk is higher in older people, much attention has been devoted to suicide among children and adolescents. This attention is attributable to two factors. First, since 1960, there has been an increase in the suicide rate among people under twenty-five years of age. Second, suicide has become one of the leading causes of death among people under twenty-one, whereas suicide is surpassed by many illnesses as a cause of death among older adults. Other demographic variables are related to suicide. Suicide risk is higher for divorced than married people. The unemployed have a higher suicide rate than those who are employed. Urban dwellers have a higher suicide rate than rural dwellers. Caucasians have a higher suicide rate than African Americans.

In addition to these demographic variables, several psychological or behavioral variables are related to suicide. Perhaps the single best predictor of suicide is threatening to commit suicide. Most suicide victims have made some type of suicide threat (although, in some cases, the threat may be veiled or indirect, such as putting one's affairs in order or giving away one's belongings). For this reason, psychologists consider seriously any threat of suicide. A related index of suicide risk is the detailedness or clarity of the threat. Individuals who describe a suicide method in detail are at greater risk than those who express an intent to die but who describe the act only vaguely. Similarly, the lethality and availability of the proposed method provide additional measures of risk. Suicide risk is higher if the individual proposes using a more lethal method and if the individual has access to the proposed method.

Another useful indicator of suicide risk is previous suicide attempts. People who have made prior attempts are at higher risk for suicide than people who have not. The lethality of the method used in the prior attempt is a related indicator. An individual who survives a more lethal method (a gunshot to the head) is considered at higher risk than one

Studies show that women who attempt suicide are more likely to choose nonviolent and less lethal methods, such as pills, rather than violent and more lethal methods, such as guns. (PhotoDisc)

who survives a less lethal attempt (swallowing a bottle of aspirin).

Suicide risk is associated with particular behavioral or psychological variables: depression, isolation, stress, pain or illness, recent loss, and drug or alcohol use. These factors may help explain why certain of the demographic variables are related to suicide. For example, people who are unemployed may experience higher levels of stress, depression, and isolation than people who are employed. Similarly, divorced people may experience more stress and isolation than married people. The elderly may experience more isolation, depression, and pain or illness than younger people.

Although the demographic and psychological variables summarized above have been found to be related to suicide, the prediction of suicide remains extremely difficult. Suicide is a statistically rare event; according to basic laws of probability, it is very difficult to predict such rare occurrences. What happens in actual attempts to predict suicide is that, in order to identify the "true positives" (individuals who actually attempt suicide), one must accept a very large number of "false positives" (individuals who are labeled suicidal but who in fact will not attempt suicide).

RESEARCH AND PREVENTION

Several methods have been used to study the psychology of suicide. Epidemiological research determines the distribution of demographic characteristics among suicide victims. Another method is to study survivors of suicide attempts. This enables psychologists to examine intensively their psychological characteristics. A third method is to analyze suicide notes, which may explain the individual's reasons for suicide. A final method is the psychological autopsy. This involves interviewing the victim's friends and family members and examining the victim's personal materials (such as diaries and letters) in an attempt to identify the psychological cause of the suicide.

Although all these approaches have been widely used, each has its limitations. The epidemiological method focuses on demographic characteristics and so may overlook psychological influences. Studying survivors of suicide attempts has limitations because survivors and victims of suicide attempts may differ significantly. For example, some suicide attempts are regarded as suicidal gestures, or "cries for help," the intent of which is not to die but rather to call attention to oneself to gain sympathy or assistance. Thus, what is learned from survivors may not generalize to successful suicide victims. The study of suicide notes is limited by the fact that, contrary to popular belief, most suicide victims do not leave notes. For example, in a study of all suicides in Los Angeles County in a single year, psychologists Edwin Shneidman and Norman Farberow found that only 35 percent of the males and 39 percent of the females left notes. Finally, the psychological autopsy is limited in that the vic-

tim's records and acquaintances may not shed light on the victim's thought processes.

In 1988, Harry Hoberman and Barry Garfinkel conducted an epidemiological study to identify variables related to suicide in children and adolescents. They examined death records in two counties in Minnesota over an eleven-year period for individuals who died at age nineteen or younger. Hoberman and Garfinkel examined in detail the death records of 225 suicide victims. They noted that 15 percent of their sample had not been identified as suicides by the medical examiner but had instead been listed as accident victims or as having died of undetermined causes. This finding suggests that official estimates of suicide deaths in the United States are actually low.

Consistent with other studies, Hoberman and Garfinkel found that suicide was related to both age and sex. Males accounted for 80 percent of the suicides, females for only 20 percent. Adolescents aged fifteen to nineteen years composed 91 percent of the sample, with children aged fourteen and under only 9 percent. In addition, Hoberman and Garfinkel found that a full 50 percent of the sample showed evidence of one or more psychiatric disorders. Most common were depression and alcohol and drug abuse. Finally, Hoberman and Garfinkel found that a substantial number of the suicide victims had been described as "loners," "lonely," or "withdrawn." Thus, several of the indicators of suicide in adults also are related to suicide in children and adolescents.

Warning Signs for Suicide

No suicide attempt should be dismissed or treated lightly

The following can be warning signs:
- verbal threats such as "You'd be better off without me" or "Maybe I won't be around anymore . . ."
- Expressions of hopelessness and/or helplessness
- Previous suicide attempts
- Daring and risk-taking behavior
- Personality changes (such as withdrawal, aggression, moodiness)
- Depression
- Giving away prized possessions
- Lack of interest in the future

Source: National Mental Health Association (NMHA) factsheet "Suicide: General Information."

ASSESSING RISK

Psychiatrist Aaron Beck and his colleagues developed the Hopelessness Scale in 1974 to assess an individual's negative thoughts of self and future. In many theories of suicide, an individual's sense of hopelessness is related to risk for suicide. Beck and others have demonstrated that hopelessness in depressed patients is a useful indicator of suicide risk. For example, in 1985, Beck and his colleagues reported a study of 207 patients who were hospitalized because of suicidal thinking. Over the next five to ten years, fourteen patients committed suicide. Only one demographic variable, race, differed between the suicide and nonsuicide groups: Caucasian patients had a higher rate of suicide (10.1 percent) than African American patients (1.3 percent). Of the psychological variables assessed, only the Hopelessness Scale and a measure of pessimism differed between suicide victims and other patients. Patients who committed suicide were higher in both hopelessness and pessimism than other patients. Beck and his colleagues determined the Hopelessness Scale score which best discriminated suicides from nonsuicides. Other mental health professionals can now use this criterion to identify those clinically depressed patients who are at greatest risk for suicide.

Several approaches have been developed in efforts to prevent suicide. Shneidman and Farberow developed what may be the most well-known suicide-prevention program, the Los Angeles Suicide Prevention Center. This program, begun in 1958, helped popularize telephone suicide hotlines. Staff members are trained to interact with individuals who are experiencing extreme distress. When an individual calls the center, staff members immediately begin to assess the caller's risk for suicide, considering the caller's demographics, stress, lifestyle, and suicidal intent. Staff members attempt to calm the caller, so as to prevent an immediate suicide, and to put the person into contact with local mental health agencies so that the individual can receive more extensive follow-up care.

Psychologists William Fremouw, Maria de Perczel, and Thomas Ellis published a useful guide for those who work with suicidal clients. Among their suggestions are to talk openly and matter-of-factly about suicide, to avoid dismissing the client's feelings or motives in a judgmental or pejorative way, and to adopt a problem-solving approach to dealing with the client's situation.

Suicide-prevention programs are difficult to evaluate. Callers may not identify themselves, so it is difficult to determine whether they later commit suicide. Still, such programs are generally thought to be useful, and suicide-prevention programs similar to that of Shneidman and Farberow have been developed in many communities.

SOCIAL AND CULTURAL CONTEXTS

Suicide is one of the most extreme and drastic behaviors faced by psychologists. Because of its severity, psychologists have devoted considerable effort to identifying individuals at risk for suicide and to developing programs that are effective in preventing suicide.

Psychological studies of suicide have shown that many popular beliefs about suicide are incorrect. For example, many people erroneously believe that people who threaten suicide never attempt suicide; that all suicide victims truly wish to die; that only the mentally ill commit suicide; that suicide runs in families; and that there are no treatments that can help someone who is suicidal. Because of these and other popular myths about suicide, it is especially important that psychological studies of suicide continue and that the results of this study be disseminated to the public.

Suicide risk increases in clinically depressed individuals. In depressed patients, suicide risk has been found to be associated with hopelessness: As one's sense of hopelessness increases, one's risk for suicide increases. Since the 1970's, Beck's Hopelessness Scale has been used in efforts to predict risk for suicide among depressed patients. Although the suicide rate has been relatively stable in the United States since the early twentieth century, the suicide rate of young people has increased since the 1960's.

For this reason, depression and suicide among children and adolescents have become major concerns of psychologists. Whereas childhood depression received relatively little attention from psychologists before the 1970's, psychologists have devoted considerable attention to this condition since then. Much of this attention has concerned whether biological, cognitive, and behavioral theories of the causes of depression and approaches to the treatment of depression, which were originally developed and applied to depressed adults, may generalize to children. In the 1980's, psychologists developed several innovative programs that attempt to identify youths who are depressed and experiencing hopelessness, and so may be at risk for suicide; evaluations and refinements of these programs will continue.

SOURCES FOR FURTHER STUDY

Durkheim, Émile. *Suicide*. Reprint. Glencoe, Ill.: Free Press, 1951. In this work, originally published in 1897, Durkheim introduced his classification system of suicide types—altruistic, egoistic, and anomic suicides—and examined the relationship of suicide to isolation and recent loss.

Fremouw, William J., Maria de Perczel, and Thomas E. Ellis. *Suicide Risk: Assessment and Response Guidelines*. New York: Pergamon, 1990. This book presents useful guidelines, based on both research and clinical practice, for working with suicidal individuals.

Hawton, Keith. *Suicide and Attempted Suicide Among Children and Adolescents*. Beverly Hills, Calif.: Sage Publications, 1986. This work overviews research results concerning the causes of youth suicide and treatment programs for suicidal youngsters.

Holinger, Paul C., and J. Sandlow. "Suicide." In *Violent Deaths in the United States*, edited by Paul C. Holinger. New York: Guilford Press, 1987. This chapter presents epidemiological information on suicide in the United States, from 1900 to 1980. It also addresses demographic variables and their relationship to suicide.

Lann, Irma S., Eve K. Moscicki, and Ronald Maris, eds. *Strategies for Studying Suicide and Suicidal Behavior*. New York: Guilford Press, 1989. This book examines the various research methods used to study suicide. Considers the relative strengths and weaknesses and offers examples of each method.

Lester, David, ed. *Current Concepts of Suicide*. Philadelphia: Charles Press, 1990. A useful overview of research results on the possible causes of suicide and on programs designed both to prevent suicide and to treat suicidal patients.

Peck, Michael L., Norman L. Farberow, and Robert E. Litman, eds. *Youth Suicide*. New York: Springer, 1985. A useful overview of the psychological influences on youth suicide and on the treatment and prevention programs that have been used with suicidal youths.

Shneidman, Edwin S., Norman L. Farberow, and Robert E. Litman. *The Psychology of Suicide*. New York: Science House, 1970. This is a collection of articles, some of which are now regarded as classics in the study of suicide.

Stengel, Erwin. *Suicide and Attempted Suicide*. Rev. ed. Harmondsworth, England: Penguin Books, 1973. This classic work summarizes the demographic and psychological variables that were known at the time to be associated with suicide.

Michael Wierzbicki

SEE ALSO: Bipolar disorder; Clinical depression; Death and dying; Depression; Drug therapies; Teenage suicide.

Sullivan, Harry Stack

BORN: February 21, 1892, in Norwich, New York
DIED: January 14, 1949, in Paris, France
IDENTITY: American psychiatrist and social analyst
TYPE OF PSYCHOLOGY: Personality; psychotherapy
FIELDS OF STUDY: Interpersonal relations; personality theory; psychodynamic and neoanalytic models; schizophrenias

Sullivan created an interpersonal psychiatry using an integration of experience, development, pathology, culture, and system.

Harry Stack Sullivan was an American physician who studied psychopathology and psychiatry. He was born of Irish-Catholic stock in Chenango County, south central New York State. After a troubled early life, he entered the psychiatric world at St. Elizabeths Hospital in Washington, D.C., in 1920. Influenced by Swiss psychiatrist Adolf Meyer and analyzed by American psychiatrist Clara Thompson, he joined Karen Horney (1885-1952) and Erich Fromm (1900-1980) in promoting a social (interpersonal) form of psychoanalysis. He was an inspiring teacher, which brought him a loyal following. He worked clinically with varied groups, including schizophrenics. He never married.

Sullivan took an eclectic and interpersonal approach to understanding personality that later influenced British psychoanalyst R. D. Laing (1927-1989). Sullivan provided an integration in self theory between the social role orientation and mirroring approach of philosopher George H. Mead (1863-1931) and the psychoanalytic view of unconscious processes pioneered by Sigmund Freud (1856-1939). In creating a unique mixture, Sullivan added his own view of development, a view which came out of his own experience in growing up and his diagnostic and therapeutic work with severely disturbed patients. His ideas about developmental eras predate an American focus on cognitive development as articulated by Swiss psychologist Jean Piaget (1896-1980) and the American response of Jerome Bruner and others. Consideration of a developmental mode of functioning—prototaxic, parataxic, and syntaxic—added to his description of experience. He viewed the self as a system which included significant others, especially their anxiety, before psychiatrist Murray Bowen introduced the notion of system into family therapy. His contacts with cultural anthropologists such as Edward Sapir (1884-1939) and Ruth Benedict (1887-1948) led him to views that prefigured social constructionism, the postmodern view that society exclusively shapes the self.

Sullivan's approach has been synthesized with that of Piaget by James Youniss, who has applied this integrated approach to the study of social development, looking at ways of understanding friendship, kindness, and reciprocity in youth.

As cofounder and editor of the journal *Psychiatry*, Sullivan wrote a number of short articles and editorials. His several books were assembled and published after his death. His 1939 lectures are summed up in *Conceptions of Modern Psychiatry* (1953), and his 1948 notes for lectures were edited and published in *The Interpersonal Theory of Psychiatry* (1953).

SOURCES FOR FURTHER STUDY

Monte, Christopher F. *Beneath the Mask: An Introduction to Theories of Personality.* 6th ed. New York: Harcourt Brace, 1999. The chapter on Harry Stack Sullivan and interpersonal theory integrates theory and significant events with his life history.

Mullahy, Patrick, ed. *The Contributions of Harry Stack Sullivan: A Symposium on Interpersonal Theory in Psychiatry and Social Science.* New York: Humanities Press, 1952. Contemporaries of Sullivan view his contributions as clinician and social scientist. Contains a bibliography of works published until 1952.

Perry, Helen Swick. *Psychiatrist of America: The Life of Harry Stack Sullivan.* Cambridge, Mass.: Harvard University Press, 1981. A sympathetic and complete biography by the editor of Sullivan's posthumous papers.

Everett J. Delahanty, Jr.

SEE ALSO: Social psychological models: Erich Fromm; Social psychological models: Karen Horney.

Support groups

TYPE OF PSYCHOLOGY: Cognition; emotion; language; learning; memory; motivation; personality; psychological methodologies; psychopathology; psychotherapy; social psychology; stress

FIELDS OF STUDY: Adolescence; adulthood; aggression; aging; anxiety disorders; attitudes and behavior; behavioral therapies; childhood and adolescent disorders; cognitive therapies; coping; critical issues in stress; depression; group and family therapies; group processes; interpersonal relations; motivation theory; personality disorders; prejudice and discrimination; problem solving; prosocial behavior; schizophrenias; sexual disorders; sleep; social motives; social perception and cognition; stress and illness; substance abuse

The history of support groups in modern times begins with the formation of the Oxford Group in 1908 and the subsequent development of Alcoholics Anonymous. For the participants, support groups reduce feelings of isolation, offer information, instill hope, provide feedback and social support, and teach new social skills. At the opening of the twenty-first century, support groups exist for persons suffering from all kinds of medical and psychological conditions to support for victims of violent crime.

KEY CONCEPTS

• cohesion
• exchange theory
• group dynamics
• networks
• norms
• roles
• social facilitation

- social inhibition
- social learning
- sociobiology

INTRODUCTION

Humans are social animals—they live in groups. These networks among people are powerful in shaping behavior, feelings, and judgments. Groups can lead to destructive behavior, such as mob violence and aggression, but they can also encourage loyalty, nurturing of others, and achievement, as found in cancer-support groups. Scientific investigation of how groups affect human behavior began as early as 1898, but the main body of research on group functioning began only in the 1940's and 1950's. The study of groups is still a major topic of scientific enquiry.

D. R. Forsyth defined a group as "two or more individuals who influence each other through social interaction." A group may be permanent or temporary, formal or informal, structured or unstructured. Those groups known as "support groups" may share any of these characteristics.

Why do human beings seek out groups? Social learning theorists believe that humans learn to depend on other people because most are raised within families, where they learn to look to other people for support, validation, amusement, and advice. Exchange theorists, on the other hand, reason that groups provide both rewards (such as love and approval) and costs (such as time and effort). Membership in a group will "profit" the individual if the rewards are greater than the costs. Yet another set of theorists, the sociobiologists, argue that humans form groups because this has a survival benefit for the species. They hypothesize a genetic predisposition toward affiliation with others. It is within groups that the fittest have the greatest chance of survival.

Whatever the reason for forming groups, all groups have important characteristics that must be addressed in seeking to understand why support groups work. First of all, group size is important. Larger groups allow more anonymity, while smaller groups facilitate communication, for example. Group structure includes such elements as status differences, norms of conduct, leaders and followers, and subgroups. Individuals in groups develop social roles—those expected behaviors associated with the individual's position within the group. Roles are powerful in influencing behavior and can

cause individuals even to act contrary to their private feelings or their own interests. These roles carry varying degrees of status within the group—who is influential and respected and who is less so. Groups may have subgroups, based on age, residence, roles, interests, or other factors. These subgroups may contribute to the success of the whole or may become cliquish and undermine the main group's effectiveness.

Groups also have varying degrees of cohesion. Cohesion reflects the strength of attachments within the group. Sometimes cohesion is a factor of how well group members like one another, sometimes a factor of the need to achieve an important goal, and sometimes a factor of the rewards that group membership confers. All groups have communication networks, or patterns of openness and restrictions on communication among members.

Group norms are those attitudes and behaviors that are expected of members. These norms are needed for the group's success because they make life more predictable and efficient for the members. Leadership may be formal or informal, may be task oriented or people oriented, and may change over time. Finally, all groups go through fairly predictable stages as they form, do their work, and conclude. The comprehensive term for the way a group functions is "group dynamics."

HOW GROUPS INFLUENCE INDIVIDUALS

Researchers have found that for all animals, including human beings, the mere presence of other members of the same species may enhance performance on individual tasks. This phenomenon is known as social facilitation. However, with more complex tasks the presence of others may decrease performance. This is known as social inhibition or impairment. It is not clear whether this occurs because the presence of others arouses the individual, leads individuals to expect rewards or punishments based on past experience, makes people self-conscious, creates challenges to self-image, or affects the individual's ability to process information. Most theorists agree that the nature of the task is important in the success of a group. For example, the group is more likely to succeed if the individual members' welfare is closely tied to the task of the group.

Groups provide modeling of behavior deemed appropriate in a given situation. The more similar the individuals doing the modeling are to the individual who wants to learn a behavior, the more powerful the models are. Groups reward members for behavior that conforms to group norms or standards and punish behaviors that do not conform. Groups provide a means of social comparison—how one's own behavior compares to others' in a similar situation. Groups are valuable sources of support during times of stress. Some specific factors that enhance the ability of groups to help individuals reduce stress are attachment, guidance, tangible assistance, and embeddedness. Attachment has to do with caring and attention among group members. Guidance may be provision of information or it may be advice and feedback provided by the group to its members. Tangible assistance may take the form of money or of other kinds of service. Embeddedness refers to the sense the individual has of belonging to the group. Some researchers have shown that a strong support system actually increases the body's immune functioning.

ALCOHOLICS ANONYMOUS

The most well-known support group is Alcoholics Anonymous (AA), formed in Akron, Ohio, in the late 1930's. AA groups now number in the tens of thousands and are found across the globe. What is less well known is that AA is an outgrowth of the Oxford Group, an evangelical Christian student and athlete group formed at Oxford University in England in 1908. The Oxford Group's ideals of self-examination, acknowledgment of character defects, restitution for harm done, and working with others directly influenced the steps to recovery practiced by members of AA and other so-called twelve-step groups, including Al-Anon, Narcotics Anonymous, Smokers Anonymous, and many others.

For addicts, support groups are important for a number of reasons. They provide peer support for the effort to become "clean and sober." They provide peer pressure against relapsing into substance use. They assure addicts that they are not alone—that others have suffered the destruction brought about by drinking or drugging. Addicts in twelve-step groups learn to interact with others on an emotional level. Importantly, members of AA and other support groups for addicts are able to confront the individual's maladaptive behaviors and provide models for more functional behavior. The norm for AA is sobriety, and sobriety is reinforced by clear directions on how to live as a sober person. Another important aspect of AA is the hope that it is able to inspire in persons who, while using, saw no hope for the future. This hope comes not only from seeing individuals who have successfully learned to live as sober persons but also from the group's emphasis on dependence on a higher power and the importance of one's spiritual life.

OTHER SUPPORT GROUPS

Not all support groups are for addicts. Support groups exist for adoptive parents, children who have been adopted, persons with acquired immunodeficiency syndrome (AIDS), caregivers for patients with Alzheimer's disease, amputees—and that is just the beginning. Why are these groups so popular? Some writers believe that Americans have turned away from the "rugged individualism" that has characterized the national psyche in the past and are searching for meaning in groups to replace the extended families found in other societies. However, this does not explain why support groups are also popular in other parts of the world. The answer probably lies in the characteristics of groups.

Support groups are generally composed of small numbers of people who are facing similar challenges in their lives. They meet, with or without a trained facilitator, to explore their reactions, problems, solutions, feelings, frustrations, successes, and needs in relation to those challenges. They build bonds of trust. Members show compassion to one another. Groups may provide material support or simply assure the individual member he or she is not alone. They help minimize stress and maximize coping. They model strategies for dealing with the given challenge. They provide information. They nurture their members. They encourage application of new learning. Through this sharing, each member grows, and through individual growth, the group matures.

Support groups have traditionally met "in person," but the World Wide Web has altered this expectation. Many support groups now meet on-line. These may take the form of synchronous or asynchronous chat groups, bulletin boards, listservs, Web sites with multiple links to information sources, referrals, and collaboration with professionals. These groups, while not well studied, seem to serve the same purposes as in-person groups. In addition, they provide a possible advantage: The anonymity of the Web makes it possible to observe and to learn from observing without actually participating until one is comfortable doing so.

Support groups may not be sufficient in and of themselves to solve individual problems. They are probably most effective as a part of an integrated plan for addressing the challenge in the individual's life that involves other resources as appropriate. For example, the caregiver of a person with Alzheimer's disease may also need social services support, adult daycare or respite care facilities, medical assistance for control of problem behaviors, and home health services to deal successfully with the day-to-day challenges of dealing with the patient. The support group can facilitate access to these other resources in addition to serving as an important stress reducer and support system for the caregiver.

SOURCES FOR FURTHER STUDY

Carlson, Hannah. *The Courage to Lead: Start Your Own Support Group—Mental Illnesses and Addictions.* Madison, Conn.: Bick, 2001. A complete how-to manual for creating small groups for persons striving against addiction or to overcome mental illnesses.

Ferguson, Tom. *Health Online: How to Find Health Information, Support Groups, and Self-Help Communities in Cyberspace.* Reading, Mass.: Addison-Wesley, 1996. A comprehensive guide to information on diseases and illnesses. Explains how to locate on-line medical journals and interpret articles. Includes commercial on-line services, Internet, World Wide Web, electronic bulletin boards, and National Institutes of Health databases.

Kauth, Bill. *A Circle of Men: The Original Manual for Men's Support Groups.* New York: St. Martin's Press, 1992. Covers finding the right members, running meetings, training in listening, creating rituals, and dealing with problems within the group.

Kelly, Pat. *Living with Breast Cancer: A Guide for Facilitating Self-Help Groups.* Lewiston, N.Y.: B. C. Drecker, 2000. A guide to starting and running a member-managed self-help group. Provides a good list of resources.

Klein, Linda L. *The Support Group Sourcebook: What They Are, How You Can Find One, and How They Can Help You.* New York: John Wiley & Sons, 2000. The most comprehensive guide to how groups work and develop, and how they assist people. Good advice on how to start or find a group.

O'Rourke, Kathleen, and John C. Worzbyt. *Support Groups for Children.* Washington, D.C.: Accelerated Development, 1996. Helpful description of how to find an appropriate support group for children.

Shaffer, Carolyn R., and Kristin Anundsen. *Creating Community Anywhere: Finding Support and Connection in a Fragmented World.* New York: Penguin Putnam, 1993. Focuses on how to find or create intentional communities.

Wuthnow, Robert. *Sharing the Journey: Support Groups and America's New Quest for Community.* New York: Free Press, 1994. Examines the shift from extended family through the isolation of the nuclear family and the present movement toward intentional communities.

Rebecca Lovell Scott

SEE ALSO: Coping: Social support; Group therapy; Groups; Internet psychology; Social networks.

Survey research
Questionnaires and interviews

TYPE OF PSYCHOLOGY: Psychological methodologies
FIELDS OF STUDY: Descriptive methodologies; experimental methodologies; methodological issues

Psychologists use survey research techniques, including questionnaires and interviews, to evaluate specific attitudes about social or personal issues and to find out about people's behaviors directly from those people. Questionnaires are self-administered and in written form; interviews entail the psychologist asking questions of a respondent. There are strengths along with limitations for both of these data collection methods.

KEY CONCEPTS
• attitudes
• demographics
• interview
• population
• questionnaire
• respondent
• sample

INTRODUCTION

Survey research is common in both science and daily life. Almost everyone in today's society has been exposed to survey research in one form or another. Researchers ask questions about the political candidate one favors, the television programs one watches, the soft drink one prefers, whether there should be a waiting period prior to purchasing a handgun, and so on.

There are many ways to obtain data about the social world; among them are observation, field studies, and experimentation. Two key methods for obtaining data—questionnaires and interviews—are survey research methods. Most of the social research conducted or published involves these two data collection methods.

In general, when using survey methods, the researcher gets information directly from each person (or respondent) by using self-report measurement techniques to ask people about their current attitudes, behaviors, and demographics (statistical features of populations, such as age, income, race, and marital status), in addition to past experiences and future goals. In questionnaires, the questions are in written format and the subjects write down their answers. In interviews, there is one-to-one verbal communication, either face-to-face or by means of a telephone, between the interviewer and respondent. Both techniques are flexible and adaptable to the group of people being studied and the particular situation. Both can range from being highly structured to highly unstructured.

STRENGTHS AND LIMITATIONS

Questionnaires can be completed in groups or self-administered on an individual basis. They can also be mailed to people. They are generally less expensive than conducting interviews. Questionnaires also allow greater anonymity of the respondents. One drawback is that a questionnaire requires that the subjects understand exactly what the questions are asking. Also, there may be a problem of motivation with the filling out of questionnaires, because people may get bored or find it tedious to fill out the forms on their own. The survey researcher must therefore make sure that the questionnaire is not excessively long or complex.

In contrast, with an interview there is a better chance that the interviewer and subject will have good communication and that all questions will be understood. Telephone interviews are less expensive than face-to-face interviews; still, questionnaires tend to be less costly. In an interview, the respondent is presented with questions orally, whereas in the questionnaire, regardless of type or form, the respondent is presented with a written question. Each data collection device has pros and cons. The decision to use questionnaires versus interviews depends on the purpose of the study, the type of information needed, the size of the sample (the number of people who participate in a study and are part of a population), the resources for conducting the study, and the variable(s) to be measured. Overall, the interview is probably the more flexible device of the two.

DESIGNING BIAS-FREE QUESTIONS

When creating a questionnaire, the researcher must give special thought to writing the specific questions. Researchers must avoid questions that would lead people to answer in a biased way, or ones that might be easily misinterpreted. For example, the questions "Do you favor eliminating the wasteful excesses in the federal budget?" and "Do you favor reducing the federal budget?" might well result in different answers from the same respondent.

Questions are either closed- or open-ended, depending on the researcher's choice. In a closed-ended question, a limited number of fixed response choices are provided to subjects. With open-ended questions, subjects are able to respond in any way they like. Thus, a researcher could ask, "Where would you like a swimming pool to be built in this town?" as opposed to "Which of the following locations is your top choice for a swimming pool to be built in this town?" The first question allows the respondent to provide any answer; the second provides a fixed number of alternative answers from which the person must choose. Use of closed-ended questions is a more structured approach, allowing greater ease of analysis because the response alternatives are the same for everyone. Open-ended questions require more time to analyze and are therefore more costly. Open-ended questions, however, can provide valuable insights into what the subjects are actually thinking.

CLINICAL INTERVIEW

A specialized type of interview is the clinical, or therapeutic, interview. The specific goal of a particular clinical interview depends on the needs and the condition of the individual being interviewed. There is a distinction between a therapeutic interview, which attempts both to obtain information and to remedy the client's problem, and a research interview, which attempts solely to obtain information about people at large. Because the clinical interview is a fairly unstructured search for relevant information, it is important to be aware of the factors that might affect its accuracy and comprehensiveness. Research on hypothesis confirmation bias suggests that it is difficult to search for unbiased and comprehensive information in an unstructured setting such as the clinical interview. In the context of the clinical interview, clinicians are likely to conduct unintentionally biased searches for information that confirms their early impressions of each client. Research on self-fulfilling prophecies suggests a second factor that may limit the applicability of interviews in general: The interviewer's expectations may affect the behavior of the person being interviewed, and respondents may change their behavior to match the interviewer's expectations.

ROLE OF SCIENTIFIC METHOD

Knowing what to believe about research is often related to understanding the scientific method. The two basic approaches to using the scientific method, the descriptive and the experimental research approaches, differ because they seek to attain different types of knowledge. Descriptive research tries to describe particular situations; experimental research tries to determine cause-and-effect relationships. Independent variables are not manipulated in descriptive research. For that reason, it is not possible to decide whether one thing causes another. Instead, survey research uses correlational techniques, which allow the determination of whether behaviors or attitudes are related to one another and whether they predict one another. For example, how liberal a person's political views are might be related to that person's attitudes about sexuality. Such a relationship could be determined using descriptive research.

Survey research, as a widely used descriptive technique, is defined as a method of collecting standardized information by interviewing a representative sample of some population. All research involves sampling of subjects. That is, subjects must be found to participate in the research whether that research is a survey or an experiment. Sampling is particularly important when conducting survey research, because the goal is to describe what a whole population is like based on the data from a relatively small sample of that population.

KINSEY GROUP RESEARCH

One famous survey study in the mid-1930's was conducted by Alfred Kinsey and his colleagues. Kinsey studied sexual behavior. Until that time, most of what was known about sexual behavior was based on what biologists knew about animal sex, what anthropologists knew about sex among indigenous peoples in non-Western, nonindustrialized societies, or what Freud learned about sexuality from his emotionally disturbed patients. Kinsey and his colleagues were the first psychological researchers to interview volunteers from mainstream American society about their sexual behaviors. The research was hindered by political investigations and threats of legal action. In spite of the harassment encountered by the scientists on the project, the Kinsey group published *Sexual Behavior in the Human Male* in 1948 and *Sexual Behavior in the Human Female* in 1953.

The findings of the Kinsey group have benefited the public immensely. As a result, it is now known that the majority of people (both males and females) interviewed by the Kinsey group masturbated at various times, but that more males than females said they masturbated. Data collected by the Kinsey group on oral-genital sexual practices have allowed researchers to discover that, since the 1930's, attitudes toward oral-genital sex have become more positive. Their research also shocked the nation with the discovery that the majority of brides at that time were not virgins.

When scientific sampling techniques are used, the survey results can be interpreted as an accurate representation of the entire population. Although Kinsey and his associates helped to pave the way forfuture researchers to be able to investigate sexual behaviors and attitudes, there were some problems with the research because of its lack of generalizability. The Kinsey group's research is still the largest study of sexual behavior ever completed. They interviewed more than ten thousand people; however, they did not attempt to select a random or representative sample of the population of the United States, which meant that the responses of middle-class, well-educated Caucasians were overrepresented. There is also a problem with the accuracy of the respondents' information, because of memory errors, exaggerations, or embarrassment about telling an interviewer personal, sensitive information. Despite these limitations, the interviewing conducted by Kinsey and associates made great strides for the study of sexuality and great strides for psychology in general.

IMPORTANCE OF SAMPLING PROCEDURES

When research is intended to reveal very precisely what a population is like, careful sampling procedures must be used. This requires defining the population and sampling people from the population in a random fashion so that no biases will be introduced into the sample. In order to learn what elderly people think about the medical services available to them, for example, a careful sample of the elderly population is needed. Obtaining the sample only from retirement communities in Arizona would bias the results, because these individuals are not representative of all elderly people in the population.

Thus, when evaluating survey data, a researcher must examine how the responses were obtained and what population was investigated. Major polling organizations such as the Gallup organization typically are careful to obtain representative samples of people in the United States. Gallup polls are frequently conducted to survey the voting public's opinions about the popularity of a presidential candidate or a given policy. Many other surveys, however, such as surveys that are published in popular magazines, have limited generalizability because the results are based on people who read the particular magazine and are sufficiently motivated to complete and mail in the questionnaire. When *Redbook*, for example, asks readers to write in to say whether they have ever had an affair, the results may be interesting but would not give a very accurate estimate of the true extent of extramarital sexual activity in the United States. An example of an inaccurate sampling technique was a survey by *Literary Digest* (a now defunct magazine) sampling almost ten million people in 1936. The results showed that Alfred Landon would beat Franklin D. Roosevelt by a landslide in that year's presidential election. Although it was large, the sample was completely inaccurate.

EARLY SURVEY METHODS

One of the earliest ways of obtaining psychological information using descriptive techniques was through clinical interviewing. The early interviews conducted by Sigmund Freud in the late 1800's were based on question-and-answer medical formats, which is not surprising, considering that Freud was originally a physician. Later, Freud relied on the less structured free-association technique. In 1902, Adolf Meyer developed a technique to assess a client's mental functioning, memory, attention, speech, and judgment. Independent of the style used, all the early clinical interviews sought to get a psychological portrait of the person, determine the source of the problem, make a diagnosis, and formulate a treatment. More detailed studies of interviews were conducted in the 1940's and 1950's to compare and contrast interviewing styles and determine how much structure was necessary. During the 1960's, much research came about as a result of ideas held by Carl Rogers, who emphasized the interpersonal elements he thought were necessary for the ideal therapeutic relationship; among them are warmth, positive regard, and genuineness on the part of the interviewer.

In the 1800's and early 1900's, interviews were used mainly by psychologists who were therapists helping people with problems such as fear, depression, and hysteria. During that same period, experimental psychologists had not yet begun to use survey research methods. Instead, they used introspection to investigate their own thought processes. For example, experimental psychologist Hermann Ebbinghaus gave himself lists of pronounceable nonsense syllables to remember; he then tested his own memory and attempted to improve it methodically. Many experimental psychologists during this period relied upon the use of animals such as dogs and laboratory rats to conduct behavioral research.

EVOLUTION OF QUESTIONNAIRES

As mentioned above, one of the first attempts by experimental psychologists to study attitudes and behaviors by means of the interview was that of the Kinsey group in the 1930's. At about that same time, Louis Thurstone, an experimental social psychologist, formalized and popularized the first questionnaire methodology for attitude measurement. Thurstone devised a set of questionnaires, or scales, that have been widely used for decades. He is considered by many to be the father of attitude scaling. Soon thereafter, Rensis Likert made breakthroughs in questionnaire usage with the development of what are known as Likert scales. A Likert scale provides a series of statements to which subjects can indicate degrees of agreement or disagreement. Using the Likert technique, the respondent answers by selecting from predetermined categories ranging from "strongly agree" to "strongly disagree." It is fairly standard to use five categories (strongly agree, agree, uncertain, disagree, strongly disagree), but more categories can be used if necessary. An example of a question using this technique might be, "Intelligence test scores of marijuana users are higher on the average than scores of nonusers." The respondent then picks one of the five categories mentioned above in response. Likert scales have been widely used and have resulted in a vast amount of information about human attitudes and behaviors.

Sources for Further Study

Bordens, Kenneth S., and Bruce B. Abbott. *Research Design and Methods: A Process Approach.* 5th ed. Mountain View, Calif.: Mayfield, 2001. Places the techniques of surveys, interviews, and questionnaires for collecting data in the context of conducting research as a process from start to finish. A well-received textbook in psychology.

Converse, Jean M., and Stanley Presser. *Survey Questions: Handcrafting the Standardized Questionnaire.* Beverly Hills, Calif.: Sage Publications, 1986. Provides explicit, practical details which would be of use to a person who needs to put together a questionnaire for any of a variety of reasons. Stresses the art of questionnaire creation.

Cozby, Paul C. *Methods in Behavioral Research.* 7th ed. Mountain View, Calif.: Mayfield, 2000. Examines the importance of survey research in the context of conducting experiments and doing research in psychology in general. Allows the reader to understand the research process from a broader perspective.

Judd, Charles M., Louise H. Kidder, and Eliot R. Smith. *Research Methods in Social Relations.* 6th ed. Pacific Grove, Calif.: International Thomson, 1991. A popular book whose writing style is exceptionally clear. Offers thorough information that introduces the reader to the process of doing research in psychology, including how to get an idea for a research topic, how to collect the information, how to be ethical with subjects, and

how to report the results. Detailed information is provided on questionnaires and interviews.

Stewart, Charles J., and William B. Cash, Jr. *Interviewing Principles and Practices.* 9th ed. Boston: McGraw-Hill College, 2000. A hands-on introduction to interviewing which provides practical suggestions and tips along with background information.

Deborah R. McDonald

See also: Behavioral assessment; Case-study methodologies; Clinical interviewing, testing, and observation; Complex experimental designs; Data description; Personality interviewing strategies; Personality rating scales; Quasi-experimental designs; Sampling; Statistical significance tests; Within-subject experimental designs.

Synaptic transmission

Type of psychology: Biological bases of behavior
Fields of study: Nervous system

A neuron transmits chemical or electrical signals to other cells and controls their functions through an intercellular space called synaptic cleft. Synaptic transmission is a key to understanding various normal and abnormal behavioral and physiological phenomena as well as the effects of various neuroactive drugs.

Key concepts
- agonist
- antagonist
- neuropsychopharmacology
- neurotransmitter
- receptor
- synaptic cleft
- synaptic transmission
- vesicle

Introduction

Transmission refers to the transferring of signals from a source to a receiving end through or across a medium. Synaptic transmission specifically refers to the transferring of a signal from a neuron (a nerve cell) across a space called the synaptic cleft to a target cell. The nerve impulse is generated in the cell body of the neuron and is related to the movement of sodium ions across the cell membrane of the axon (the axon is an extension of the neuron cell body). This impulse is known as an action potential. When the impulse reaches the axon terminal, this presynaptic signal either remains as an electrical signal or is converted to a chemical signal; either way, it is then transmitted through this space and exerts an influence on the target cell. The synapse contains three areas: the presynaptic terminal, the synaptic cleft, and the postsynaptic membrane.

Physical activity and behavior involve neuronal activities and the resulting contractions and relaxations of many muscles. The winking of an eye, for example, involves the control of contraction and relaxation of eyelid muscles. The axon terminals of the motor neurons must synapse with the eyelid muscles. A synapse between neuron and muscle cells is called a neuromuscular junction. The axon terminal releases a neurochemical that acts on the receptors embedded in the cell membrane of the postsynaptic muscle cells, resulting in muscle contraction. The synaptic area is a key to the control of neural effects; most chemicals that affect the nervous system vary physiological and behavioral responses at this site.

ELECTRICAL AND CHEMICAL MODES

Two distinct modes of synaptic transmission have been delineated, one electrical and the other chemical. At an electrical synapse, the presynaptic current spreads across the intercellular gap to the target cell. In order for this spreading to occur, a low-resistance pathway is required; this is achieved by a close apposition of cells with a gap of about 2 nanometers (one nanometer is one-billionth of a meter). This type of coupling is called a gap junction. In electrical transmission, unlike chemical transmission, an impulse in the presynaptic terminal is transmitted to the postsynaptic terminal with little attenuation (lessening) and with no time delay. Electrical synapses are very common in the nervous systems of invertebrates, lower vertebrates, and embryonic animals.

At a chemical synapse, the gap is about 20 to 30 nanometers. The high resistance does not allow spreading of the presynaptic current to the postsynaptic current to occur. Upon arrival of impulses, a presynaptic terminal releases chemicals termed neurotransmitters. These molecules then diffuse through the cleft and interact with receptors, complex protein molecules embedded in the postsynaptic membrane. The neurotransmitter molecules are stored in vesicles. The wall of the vesicle becomes fused to the presynaptic membrane because of the influx of calcium ions upon arrival of the impulse; this results in release of the molecules. The interaction between neurotransmitter and receptor results in certain electrical and chemical events in the target cell. In chemical transmission, the signals are attenuated, and the process takes more time than electrical transmission—about 0.3 millisecond, which is termed the synaptic delay. Neurotransmitters secreted by the presynaptic terminals include acetylcholine, dopamine, epinephrine, norepinephrine, serotonin, certain amino acids (gamma-aminobutyric acid, glutamate, glycine, aspartate), and many peptides.

Neurons come in various shapes and possess varying numbers of branches. Basically, however, each consists of the dendrites, the soma (cell body), and the axon. Synapses are classified in terms of the nature of the presynaptic terminal and the postsynaptic end. The presynaptic terminal is usually an axon; however, it has been found that dendrites may communicate with other dendrites directly at a synapse termed a dendrodendritic synapse. Three types of synapses between neurons are axodendritic, axosomatic, and axoaxonic. An axodendritic synapse couples an axon terminal to a dendrite of another neuron and usually produces a depolarization or excitatory postsynaptic potential (EPSP). An axosomatic synapse couples an axon terminal to the soma of another neuron, and it may produce a hyperpolarization or inhibitory postsynaptic potential (IPSP) as well as an EPSP. An axoaxonic synapse couples an axon terminal to another axon terminal, which results in reduction of EPSP in the target neuron of the second neuron, so the net effect is inhibitory. When an axon terminal is coupled to a muscle cell or a glandular cell, the synapse is called a neuromuscular junction or a neuroeffector junction. The EPSP occurring in the muscle is called end-plate potential. When the sum of those potential changes reaches the threshold of firing, an action potential is generated, resulting in a propagating impulse or muscular contraction.

STUDYING THE NERVOUS SYSTEM

The release of a neurotransmitter substance, the binding of neurotransmitter molecules to receptors, and the termination of neurotransmitter activities are among the key considerations in understanding the regulation of the effects of the nervous system. The synthesis and storage (in vesicles) of these substances are also important. The magnitude and duration of many physiological and behavioral responses are jointly determined by various neuronal effects. Neuroactive drugs are crucial tools, and various ones manipulate different phases of transmission, synthesis, storage, release, binding, and termination of neurotransmitters. These drugs may be used to study the functions of various neurochemicals as well as to control synaptic transmission for therapeutic purposes.

Neuroactive drugs and chemicals are classified in terms of their facilitating or inhibitory effects. Agonists are those that enhance the effects of a neurotransmitter; antagonists inhibit the effects. For example, curare, a compound extracted from a vine by South American Indians for use as an arrow posion to paralyze animals, is an antagonist of the neurotransmitter acetylcholine at the neuromuscular junction. Curare interferes with synaptic transmission at this junction, resulting in muscle paralysis.

A lock-and-key analogy is often employed to explain how synaptic transmission works. The neurotransmitter molecule represents the key, and the receptor molecule represents the lock. Just as the correct key is needed to open the lock on a door, the appropriate chemical "key" is needed to start the effect. The molecular lock has the recognition site and the active site as well as the support structure, just as the door has the keyhole with specific notch configurations, as well as other parts. A neurotransmitter may be able to open several different locks, termed receptor subtypes, which are named for the chemical compounds specific to each subtype. (In this sense, a neurotransmitter is like a submaster key that will fit several doors, while a subtype-specific compound is the key for only one door.) The neurotransmitter acetylcholine, for example, acts on two receptor subtypes—nicotinic and muscarinic. The nicotinic receptor is so named because it reacts specifically to nicotine, a substance found in tobacco. This receptor subtype is found in the smooth and cardiac muscles; the muscarinic subtype, on the other hand, is abundant in the brain.

Nicotine and muscarine, in other words, each affect only one subtype, but acetylcholine affects both; thus, acetylcholine and nicotine are both nic-

otinic receptor agonists, and acetylcholine and muscarine are both muscarinic receptor agonists. To return to the example of curare, it is a subtype-specific blocker that acts on the nicotinic receptor to block the effect of acetylcholine, causing paralysis of the skeletal muscles. Chemical variants of curare are used clinically to cause muscle relaxation before surgery.

Atropine is a muscarinic receptor blocker, so the cholinergic effects that are mediated by this subtype are antagonized. This drug is used to reduce motion sickness, to induce pupillary dilation for retinal examination, and to fight the sickening effects of certain gases used in chemical warfare. It is because those gases often involve cholinergic agonists that atropine is an appropriate antidote. There are many other compounds that can affect cholinergic effects through interfering with the release, receptor binding, and termination mechanisms. For example, the venom of the black widow spider facilitates the release of acetylcholine, whereas botulinum food poison inhibits its release. Physostigmine, a compound obtained from the Calabar bean in West Africa, enhances acetylcholine effects. Physostigmine is used to treat glaucoma and to help control the forgetfulness of Alzheimer's disease patients.

SYNTHETIC NEUROTRANSMITTERS

The potency and efficacy of a drug are presumably related to the degree of fit between the drug molecule and the receptor molecule; a potent drug is one with a good fit to a receptor or subtype. The pharmaceutical industry is constantly working to synthesize variants of neurotransmitters and neuroactive compounds to make the effects of the drug both potent and specific, thus reducing undesirable side effects.

Since acetylcholine in the brain is known to be related to learning and memory, and since Alzheimer's disease involves memory loss, it is theorized that the disease may involve cholinergic subfunctioning. Indeed, cholinergic neurons have been found to be lacking in Alzheimer's patients' brains. Thus, drugs that could alleviate the symptoms are cholinergic agonists of various kinds, such as physostigmine, and various cholinomimetics, drugs that mimic acetylcholine. Many cholinomimetics are so-called nootropic drugs, compounds that may be able to improve learning, memory, and cognitive functions. Dopamine, another neurotransmitter in the brain, has been found to be involved with the hallucinations and delusions of schizophrenics, and dopamine antagonists are used as antipsychotic drugs. Amphetamine is known to induce those psychotic symptoms; this type of drug promotes the release of dopamine.

Furthermore, a lack of dopamine activity has been linked to the symptoms of Parkinson's disease, so anti-Parkinson's drugs tend to be dopamine agonists. Depression has been found to be related to reduced activity of norepinephrine in the brain, so some antidepressants are norepinephrine agonists. Morphine is a well-known pain reducer; in the body, there are chemically similar compounds known as endorphins (from "endogenous morphine"). They are released by neurons within the spinal cord, resulting in a reduction of the release of the neurotransmitter (called substance P) related to pain signaling, thus suppressing pain. Arousal is known to be related to acetylcholine and norepinephrine in the brain; dreaming has also been related to norepinephrine. The action of the tranquilizer Valium (diazepam), the most commonly prescribed drug in the United States, is related to the activity of an inhibitory neurotransmitter, gamma-aminobutyric acid. Neuropsychopharmacology is the area of study that explores the relationships among neurophysiology, neuroanatomy, and pharmacology. Neurotransmission is an important key to discovering these relationships. Beyond the importance of such research efforts, however, it must also be remembered that behavior, both normal and abnormal, is inextricably related to the effects of synaptic transmission.

DISCOVERING NEW NEUROTRANSMITTERS

In the earliest years of the twentieth century, neurotransmission was thought to be solely electrical. The discovery of the synaptic cleft, however, made neuroscientists wonder whether an electrical current could jump a gap of this magnitude. The chemical hypothesis of neurotransmission was then proposed, although it was not until 1921 that convincing evidence of chemical transmission was obtained. Otto Loewi, a German physiologist, electrically stimulated the parasympathetic vagus nerve of a frog and recorded the effect on the frog's heart. He then transferred the liquid from the stimulated heart to an unstimulated frog heart and observed that the recipient heart reacted as if it were stimulated. The effect of the vagal stimulation—decreasing the heart rate—was transferred to the unstimu-

lated heart via the liquid from the stimulated heart. This transferral could only occur if the electrical stimulation of the vagus had resulted in the release of a chemical into the heart and this chemical was transferred to the new heart, thus inducing the same effect. Loewi called this substance *Vagusstoff,* since it was released from the vagus nerve. Later chemical analysis revealed the substance to be acetylcholine, the first neurotransmitter to be identified.

No fewer that fifty neurotransmitter substances have been identified, and researchers are still discovering new ones. In order to classify a substance as a neurotransmitter, a scientist needs to show that it fulfills a number of conditions. The substance (referred to as a putative neurotransmitter) should be found in the presynaptic terminals. Exogenous applications of the substance should mimic the effect of endogenously released substance when the presynaptic neurons are electrically stimulated. The drug effect should be the same as the effect of the exogenously applied substance and the same as the effect of the endogenously released transmitter substance. A mechanism must exist for the synthesis of the substance in the presynaptic neuron. A mechanism must also exist for the termination of the transmitter activity of the substance. As can be seen, it is not easy to identify and define a new neurotransmitter substance.

The United States Public Health Service proclaimed the 1990's to be the "decade of the brain." The synthesis of drugs that may be related to brain functions is still an area of intense research activity. Neuropsychopharmacological studies test the effects of various compounds; the new compounds are also used to test for specific neuronal bases of brain functions. New drugs not only increase the possibilities for controlling neuronal function but also reduce the undesirable side effects of drug therapy by making the effects specific to receptor subtypes. Better, more effective drugs will undoubtedly continue to be produced.

SOURCES FOR FURTHER STUDY

Adelman, George, ed. *Encyclopedia of Neuroscience.* 2 vols. 2d ed. New York: Elsevier, 1999. A very comprehensive source of information on neuroscience. Eleven topics cover the synapses specifically.

Feldman, Robert Simon, and Linda F. Quenzer. *Fundamentals of Neuropsychopharmacology.* Sunderland,

Mass.: Sinauer Associates, 1984. This is a popular text addressing much information related to drugs and behavior. It covers major neurochemical systems in terms of how the synthesis, release, and fate of each neurotransmitter may be controlled by various neuroactive compounds, and it looks at the ensuing behavioral changes.

Julien, Robert M. *A Primer of Drug Action.* Rev. ed. New York: W. H. Freeman, 2001. This paperback book describes how synaptic transmission can be manipulated by drugs to effect physiological and psychological responses. Historical episodes about drugs and coverage of various "street" compounds make this interesting reading.

Nicholls, John G., A. Robert Martin, Bruce G. Wallace, and Paul A. Fuchs. *From Neuron to Brain.* 4th ed. Sunderland, Mass.: Sinauer Associates, 2000. The authors are well-known researchers. This widely used neuroscience text covers historical and modern approaches to neurophysiology in general and synaptic transmission in particular.

Shepherd, Gordon M. *Neurobiology.* 3d ed. New York: Oxford University Press, 1997. The author is an authority in sensory physiology at Yale University. The text covers the nervous system from molecular to system levels, with synaptic transmission regarded as a major link.

Siegel, George J., Bernard W. Agranoff, R. Wayne Albers, and Perry B. Molinoff, eds. *Basic Neurochemistry.* 6th ed. Philadelphia: Lippincott, Williams & Wilkins, 1999. The book covers forty-eight topics, each discussed by one or more authoritative researchers in the respective fields. Thirteen topics are addressed under "Synaptic Function," covering the major neurotransmitter systems. Useful as a text or reference source; it has a helpful glossary and an index.

Sigmund Hsiao

SEE ALSO: Inhibitory and excitatory impulses; Nervous system; Neurons; Reflexes.

Synesthesia

TYPE OF PSYCHOLOGY: Biological bases of behavior; sensation and perception
FIELDS OF STUDY: Auditory, chemical, cutaneous, and body senses; vision

Synesthesia, from a Greek word meaning "to perceive together," is the experience of two or more sensations occurring simultaneously. People with synesthesia may hear, smell, taste, or feel in color, while others may taste shapes. The most common form of synesthesia is colored hearing, in which sounds are also experienced as colors.

KEY CONCEPTS
- color
- sensation
- sensory systems

INTRODUCTION

The first medical reference to synesthesia, the experience of two or more sensations simultaneously, was circa 1710, when an English ophthalmologist described a case of a blind man who described colored vision in response to auditory stimulation. Although there are a number of other isolated accounts of this condition, a sharp rise in publications on synesthesia occurred in the 1880's. At least twenty-seven articles on this topic appeared from 1882 to 1892.

Several key findings emerged from the classical studies of synesthesia: Colored hearing seems to be the most common form. Other forms, such as colored taste and pain are reported but are apparently quite rare. People who experience synesthesia report that they have experienced it for as long as they can remember and often report that family members have the same condition. In cases of colored hearing, merely reading is insufficient to elicit synesthesia; the words must be heard.

At the beginning of the twentieth century, there was a marked drop in research attention. This drop continued until the 1960's. This period in which synesthesia was relatively ignored by researchers coincides with the behavioral era, in which U.S. psychologists limited their studies to observable behaviors rather than to mental processes that can only be measured indirectly and subjectively. The cognitive revolution in psychology in the 1960's allowed internal mental processes, such as synesthesia, to become objects of study. What followed was a slow increase of research on this phenomenon.

STRONG SYNESTHESIA

Many researchers distinguish between strong and weak synesthesia. Strong synesthesia tends to run in families, is more common in women than in men, and is relatively rare. Scientists estimate that it occurs in approximately one person in two thousand. Strong synesthesia is typically noticed in early childhood. The connection between the two sensations seems to be actually experienced and is not just a metaphorical description created by the person.

The most common form of strong synesthesia is colored hearing, in which sounds, music, or voices are perceived as colors. People with strong synesthesia (often referred to as synesthetes) may hear, smell, taste, feel pain, or experience written language in color, while others may taste shapes. In one account, a woman described that, as a little girl, she had problems writing the letter *R*. She remembered that it eventually dawned on her that all she had to do was make the letter *P* and draw a line down from the loop. She then commented to her father that she had just "turned a yellow letter into an orange letter." For as long as she could remember, each letter of the alphabet elicited an experience of color.

Nineteenth century researcher Sir Francis Galton, who is thought to have been a strong synesthete, wrote, "Each word is a distinct whole. I have always associated the same colors with the same letters, and no amount of effort will change the color of one letter. Occasionally, when uncertain how a word should be spelt, I have considered what color it ought to be and have decided in that way."

In his book *The Man Who Tasted Shapes* (1998), Richard Cytowic, a neurologist who has done extensive study of strong synesthesia, described how Michael, the subject of the book, invited him to dinner. Michael said, as he cooked a roast chicken, that "there aren't enough points on the chicken." When questioned by Cytowic, Michael explained that "flavors have shape" and that he wanted the "chicken to be a pointed shape, but it came out round." Upon further inquiry, Michael stated,

Nobody's ever heard of this. They think I'm on drugs or that I'm making it up. That's why I never intentionally tell people about my shapes. Only when it slips out. It's perfectly logical that I thought everybody felt shapes when they ate. If there's no shape, there's no flavor.

In some cases, the induced sensation in a strong synesthete is so vivid that it becomes distracting. Neuropsychologist Aleksandr Luria wrote, in his book *The Mind of a Mnemonist* (1968), that "S" described "crumbly and yellow" images that flowed from a speaker's mouth. His experience of this image was so strong that it diminished his capacity to attend to what the speaker was saying. "S" was often quite distressed about his inability to separate such strong sensory experiences. "S" described to Luria how the induced visual images were so troubling that he tried describing them in writing and then destroying what he had written in an effort to rid himself of the intrusive experiences.

His experience also exemplifies another general principle of strong synesthesia—that the induced sensory experience is often visual, while inducing stimuli are often auditory, tactile, or gustatory (relating to taste). The underlying reason for this pattern is unknown.

POSSIBLE CAUSES OF STRONG SYNESTHESIA

Many researchers currently believe that strong synesthesia is biologically based, automatic, and unlearned. It is also different from hallucinations or metaphoric descriptions of experience. Various theories have been proposed to explain synesthesia. The "sensory leakage" theory suggests that synesthesia is caused by an overabundance of neural connections in the brain. Ordinarily, the different sensory systems are assigned to separate areas in the brain during development, which results in distinct sensory experiences. In the synesthete's brain, stronger neural connections among these areas may blur the separation of sensory experiences.

Other researchers have speculated that all people are born with the neural connections that may cause synesthesia, but that these connections are weeded out during normal brain development.

Some scientists, however, object to defining synesthesia as an abnormality. In the brains of nonsynesthetes, higher-level neural connections in the brain that mediate the experience of sensory integration may have feedback connections to the single sensory systems, which gives rise to distinct sensory experiences. In the brains of synesthetes, however, such connections may not be inhibited as they are in the brains of nonsynesthetes. Evidence that supports this explanation is the fact that hallucinogenic drugs can lead to synesthetic experiences. Such drugs may temporarily disinhibit the feedback connections between the brain areas that process multisensory integration and those that mediate distinct sensory experiences.

In the late 1980's, a research team asked people with synesthesia to describe the color perceptions triggered by each of one hundred words. When they repeated the test a year later, the synesthetes described the same associations between the words and colors with over 90 percent accuracy.

The availability of brain imaging techniques, such as positron emission tomography (PET), allows researchers to directly observe synesthesia at work in the brain. PET scans of synesthetes with colored hearing show increased activation in the visual areas of the brain in response to sounds.

Weak Synesthesia

There is considerable evidence that many people can create, identify, and appreciate less vivid cross-sensory experiences. These abilities are often referred to as weak synesthesia. An example of such associations is found in common metaphorical language (for example, a "sweet smell" or a "warm person").

Weak synesthesia is also evident in the experience of music, such as an association between certain pitches and colors. Laboratory experiments have shown that when people are presented with a set of notes of varying pitch and a set of colors varying in lightness, they will systematically pair lighter colors with higher pitches. This common experience is distinguished from that of strong synesthetes in one important way—in weak synesthesia, the associations are highly influenced by context, so that the lightest color always corresponds to the highest pitch.

Thus, in weak synesthesia, sensory associations are contextual, while those in strong synesthesia cut across time and situations. Another distinction is that in weak synesthesia, both sensory stimuli are perceived simultaneously, while in strong synesthetic experiences, one sensation is perceived and then another (typically visual) is induced.

Researchers have studied the experience of weak synesthesia by measuring a person's ability to respond to a stimulus while receiving simultaneous input from a different, unattended sensory modality. If the unattended stimulus impairs the person's ability to respond to the attended one, then the two stimuli are thought to compete in the processing of information.

In one such experiment, participants were asked to classify the pitch of a sound (low versus high) in the presence of a color. The results showed a pattern of high-pitched tones being classified faster in the presence of a light color and low-pitched tones being associated with darker colors. This pattern is known as the congruence effect, which suggests that there is cross-sensory interaction (unattended signals can affect responses to an attended one) and that these cross-sensory associations are often bidirectional (unlike in strong synesthesia, which is commonly unidirectional).

Possible Causes of Weak Synesthesia

Two explanations for weak synesthesia predominate. The sensory hypothesis is consistent with the sensory leakage theory in strong synesthesia. Congruence effects may involve absolute neural connections between areas in the brain that process different sensory experiences.

The semantic-encoding hypothesis is another explanation of weak synesthesia. The term "semantic" refers to meaning, while "encoding" refers to the process in which sensory stimulation from the world is transformed into a mental representation, such as a memory. Information is encoded more easily when the stimulus is meaningful to the person.

The semantic-encoding hypothesis includes several claims. First, cross-sensory associations occur at a perceptual rather than at a sensory level. According to cognitive information processing theory, there is a one-to-one correspondence between a physical stimulus and the way it is encoded in the sensory areas of the brain. Perception, however, is a higher-level process that involves the interpretation of sensory information.

Second, perceptions of various sensory stimuli are strongly influenced by language. For example, four-year-old children match pitch and brightness systematically, but not pitch and visual size. However, by age twelve, such matches are performed as well as they are by adults.

Third, corresponding sensory stimuli are recoded from distinct, one-to-one sensory experiences to an abstract, integrated perception. This suggests that the integration of sensory experiences occurs at a higher level in the brain in which meaning is constructed.

Synesthesia is not a single phenomenon but represents a broad range of cross-sensory experiences, from weak to strong. The two extremes of synesthetic experience also seem to have different theoretical explanations.

SOURCES FOR FURTHER STUDY

Cytowic, Richard E. *The Man Who Tasted Shapes.* Cambridge, Mass.: MIT Press, 1998. This book is a highly readable narrative of synesthetic experiences, based on a fascinating case study.

Duffy, Patricia L. *Blue Cats and Chartreuse Kittens: How Synesthetes Color Their Worlds.* New York: Henry Holt, 2001. This book describes the personal, inner experiences of different synesthetes.

Harrison, John. *Synesthesia: The Strangest Thing.* New York: Oxford University Press, 2001. This book is a scholarly, yet accessible, account of the history and science of synesthesia.

Cathy J. Bogart

SEE ALSO: Hallucinations; Hearing; Sensation and perception; Senses; Smell and taste; Touch and pressure; Vision: Brightness and contrast; Vision: Color; Visual system.

T

Taste aversion

TYPE OF PSYCHOLOGY: Learning
FIELDS OF STUDY: Biological influences on learning; instrumental conditioning; Pavlovian conditioning

Taste aversion occurs when an animal or person eats a food, becomes ill, and subsequently develops a distaste for the food that motivates avoidance. Most often considered a form of Pavlovian conditioning, taste aversion learning has several unusual characteristics that have made it an important topic in the literature of learning theory.

KEY CONCEPTS
- avoidance conditioning
- equipotentiality
- instrumental conditioning
- interstimulus interval
- Pavlovian conditioning
- preparedness

INTRODUCTION

When an animal eats a food, especially one with which it has had little experience, and then becomes ill, the food acquires a nauseating or aversive quality and will subsequently be avoided. This phenomenon is called bait shyness, food aversion, or, most commonly, taste aversion, although the odor and sometimes even the sight of the food also become aversive.

When confronted with a new food, rats will investigate it thoroughly by sniffing. If the odor is unfamiliar, and familiar food is available elsewhere, the rats may pass by the novel food without eating it. If sufficiently hungry, the rats may sample the new food by nibbling at it and then withdrawing to wait for adverse effects. If none occurs, the new food may be accepted, but if the rats become ill the food will be avoided; even the trails or runways where the new food is located may be abandoned. This cautiousness toward novel foods makes rats notoriously difficult to poison.

STIMULUS AND RESPONSE

Taste-aversion learning has been construed both as instrumental avoidance learning and as Pavlovian conditioning. Clearly, elements of both are involved. Development of the aversion itself, in which the food takes on a negative motivational quality, is seen by most learning theorists as Pavlovian conditioning. Subsequent avoidance of the food is learned by instrumental conditioning.

In development of the aversion, the smell or taste of the food clearly serves as the conditioned stimulus; however, there has been some confusion in the literature as to what constitutes the unconditioned stimulus in taste-aversion conditioning. In a typical experiment, rats are presented with water that contains a distinctive flavor, such as saccharin or almond extract. After drinking the flavored water, the rats are treated in some way that makes them ill. Illness treatments have been as diverse as X-ray irradiation and spinning on a turntable, but the preferred method is injection of a toxic drug such as lithium chloride or apomorphine. As a result of the treatment-produced illness, the rats subsequently avoid the flavored water.

Most frequently, "illness" is cited as the unconditioned stimulus in these experiments, but one also sees references to "poisoning" or to the "illness treatment" in this regard. These latter references actually make more sense and are more consistent with other research in which a drug treatment (the unconditioned stimulus) is seen as producing an innate drug effect (the unconditioned response).

In 1927, Ivan Pavlov described experiments with morphine and apomorphine in which the drug injection, the drug itself, or "changes in the internal environment due to alteration in the composition of the blood" were construed as the unconditioned stimulus. The drug effects, including salivation, nausea, vomiting, and sleep, were construed as unconditioned responses. Pavlov even described an experiment in which tying off the portal vein led to development of an aversion to meat in dogs because of buildup in the blood of toxic substances derived from the digestion of the meat. The implication was that the smell and taste of meat were conditioned stimuli and the toxins (or the alterations in blood chemistry) were unconditioned stimuli.

In taste-aversion conditioning, the smell or taste (and sometimes the sight) of food serves as the conditioned stimulus. This stimulus signals the presence of a toxin, which acts as the unconditioned stimulus by altering body chemistry, which in turn produces nausea, illness, or vomiting, the unconditioned response. Through conditioning, nausea or "aversion" develops as the conditioned response to presentation of the taste, smell, or sight of the food. This aversion then motivates an instrumental avoidance response; that is, because of the conditioned aversion, the animal does not eat the food.

LEARNING AVERSIONS

Taste aversion plays an important adaptive role in the everyday life of animals, especially those that eat a diversity of foods. Food preferences are learned early in the lives of such animals—they eat what they see their mothers eating or, even earlier, they come to prefer foods with flavors encountered previously in mothers' milk. To cope with a variable environment, however, animals must often adopt a new food. Animals with no mechanism for learning to accept safe foods while rejecting toxic ones would soon perish.

Nor is taste aversion learning seen only in laboratory animals. Humans, too, learn food aversions quickly and convincingly. Martin E. P. Seligman, a prominent learning theorist, has supplied his own autobiographical account of taste aversion learning. Six hours after eating filet mignon flavored with béarnaise sauce, Seligman became violently ill with the stomach flu. "The next time I had sauce béarnaise, I couldn't bear the taste of it," he relates. He did not, however, develop an aversion to the steak, to the white plates from which it had been eaten, or to the opera that he attended during the six-hour interstimulus interval.

Seligman's experience exemplifies several peculiarities of taste-aversion learning that have made it an important topic in the literature of learning the-

ory: A strong conditioned response develops in a single learning trial, the conditioned response develops even when the conditioned and unconditioned stimuli are separated by long interstimulus intervals, the aversion develops selectively to some stimuli but not to others, and the conditioned response is irrational in the sense that it is not much affected by conscious knowledge that the food was not tainted or is not likely to be tainted in the future.

NATURAL AVERSIONS

In nature, taste-aversion learning is a common event. Animals that do not specialize on one or a few foods must be able to reject toxic foods. Rats especially have a problem in this regard, since they do not vomit and therefore cannot expel poisons once they have ingested them. When rats have access to many foods, their behavior is marvelously adapted to detecting toxins. They eat only one or two different food types at a time and may eat these exclusively for days. Then they shift to concentration on another food type. If illness develops, the rats know immediately which type of food is probably to blame and subsequently avoid it. If the rats had eaten a variety of foods all the time, such discrimination would not be possible.

Human infants may adopt a similar strategy when allowed to eat without supervision. In the 1920's, Clara Davis gave infants the opportunity to eat any of a variety of nutritious foods, none of which alone supplied a balanced diet. The infants specialized on one or two foods for days at a time before shifting to another food. Although daily diets were certainly not nutritionally balanced, the infants did, over the long run, eat a balanced, healthy diet. The behavior of one infant was particularly interesting. This child voluntarily consumed cod-liver oil, a vile-tasting fluid usually rejected by children. This child, however, had a vitamin D deficiency, and the cod-liver oil supplied the necessary vitamin. After the deficiency was eliminated, the infant stopped eating cod-liver oil and never went back to it.

The idea that the infant's behavior may be related to taste learning was shown by Paul Rozin, who found that rats fed a thiamine-deficient diet subsequently chose a food laced with thiamine supplements even though thiamine itself is tasteless. The rats apparently were able to use the taste of the food as a discriminative stimulus for its nutritive properties. Thus, the phenomenon is the opposite of taste-aversion learning—the development of specific hungers for foods with nutritive qualities, foods that promote health or recovery from illness. Anecdotal reports suggest that humans sometimes also suddenly develop tastes for foods that contain needed nutrients.

Thus, taste aversion is apparently only one side of the story of food selection and rejection in nature. Both appetitive and avoidance behaviors can be predicated on taste cues. In some cases, these behaviors are innate responses to the taste. Bitter tastes usually indicate the presence of toxic alkaloids and are often rejected by young animals that have had no prior experience with them. Human infants do the same. In other cases, the response to taste cues must be learned. Thus, specific hungers and taste aversions both represent examples of appropriate behaviors that are cued by discriminative taste stimuli.

Lincoln Brower has described a classic example of taste-aversion learning in nature. Blue jays, he noted, typically avoid preying on monarch butterflies. If hungry enough, however, jays will take and eat monarchs. The caterpillars of these butterflies eat milkweed, which contains a poison to which the butterflies are immune but birds are not. Enough of the poison remains concentrated in the tissues of adult monarchs to make a bird that eats one quite sick. The jays subsequently reject monarchs after a brief taste, and eventually the distinctive orange and black insects are rejected on sight.

INDUCED AVERSIONS

In more applied settings, Carl Gustavson and John Garcia have described the use of taste-aversion conditioning in wildlife management. On the western ranges where large flocks of sheep are left relatively unprotected, ranchers often face the threat of predation by coyotes, wolves, and mountain lions. One response has been wholesale shooting and poisoning of these wild predators, but this is a less than ideal solution. Gustavson and Garcia found that predators, such as coyotes, that scavenge a lamb carcass laced with a sublethal dose of lithium chloride will subsequently develop a strong aversion to lamb and may even avoid areas where lamb and sheep are grazing. The authors proposed a scheme for reducing predation on sheep using taste-aversion conditioning that would drastically reduce the need for

shooting and the use of indiscriminate lethal poisons.

In humans, many medical conditions are accompanied by loss of appetite and weight loss. Although this is often attributable to chemical changes within the body, it can also be caused by taste-aversion learning. Ilene Bernstein investigated the loss of appetite, or anorexia, that frequently accompanies cancer chemotherapy and found that, in all likelihood, it was attributable to aversive conditioning caused by the cancer medications, which often induce nausea and vomiting. Bernstein and her colleague, Soo Borson, investigated other anoretic syndromes and found the same possibility. In an important review article published in 1986, they proposed that taste-aversion learning may play a significant role in such conditions as cancer anorexia, tumor anorexia, anorexia nervosa, and the anorexias that accompany clinical depression and intestinal surgery.

On the other hand, taste-aversion learning is intentionally induced in some types of aversion therapy for maladaptive behaviors. Alcoholics are sometimes given a drug called Antabuse (disulfiram) that interferes with alcohol metabolism in the liver. Drinking alcohol after taking this drug results in a very unpleasant illness that conditions an aversion to alcohol. Subsequently, the taste, smell, or even the thought of alcohol can induce nausea. Cigarette smoking has been treated similarly.

EXPERIMENTAL AVERSIONS

Before 1966, psychologists believed that learning obeyed the law of equipotentiality. In Pavlovian conditioning, the nature of conditioned and unconditioned stimuli was seen as unimportant—if they were paired appropriately, learning would occur with equal facility for any stimulus pair. In instrumental conditioning, psychologists believed that any reinforcer would reinforce any behavior.

Equipotentiality had been challenged. Ethologists insisted that each species of animal is unique in what it learns, that learning is an evolutionary adaptation, and that species are not interchangeable in learning studies. Nikolaas Tinbergen, in *The Study of Instinct* (1951), wrote of the innate disposition to learn. Keller and Marian Breland, who trained animals for commercial purposes, discovered that animals drifted toward species-specific food-related behaviors when their arbitary instrumental responses were reinforced with food.

In 1966 John Garcia, Robert Koelling, and Frank Ervin published their research on taste-aversion learning. In an article called "Relation of Cue to Consequence in Avoidance Learning," they described an experiment in which rats received aversive consequences for licking water from a drinking spout. In the "tasty water" condition of the experiment, the water was flavored with saccharin, while in the "bright-noisy water" condition, licking the spout activated a flashing lamp and a clicking relay. Half the animals from each condition were made sick after drinking. The other half received a mild but disruptive electric shock after licking the spout. In the tasty water condition, animals that were made sick, but not those that were shocked, avoided drinking. In the bright-noisy water condition, animals that were shocked, but not those that were made sick, avoided drinking. Thus, light and noise were easily associated with shock, and taste was easily associated with illness, but the contrary associations were much more difficult to establish.

In a second article, called "Learning with Prolonged Delay of Reinforcement," Garcia, Ervin, and Koelling demonstrated that taste aversion developed even when the taste and illness treatment were separated by seventy-five minutes. Learning with such prolonged delays had been regarded as impossible, and it could not be reproduced in shock-avoidance experiments. These results were quickly replicated in other laboratories. Similar effects were demonstrated in other types of learning experiments, including traditional avoidance paradigms and even in mazes and Skinner boxes. The fact that something was wrong with traditional learning theory and equipotentiality was soon evident.

The doctrine of prepared learning replaced equipotentiality. Preparedness is the idea that evolution equips animals to learn things that are important to their survival. Examples of prepared learning already existed in the literature, but until 1966 their significance was not widely recognized among psychologists. Ethologists, however, pointed to studies of imprinting, food recognition, song learning, and place learning in a variety of animals, all illustrating prepared learning. Psychologists quickly included language learning and the learning of some phobias under the umbrella of preparedness. It was even proposed that human cognition evolved to cope with widely divergent situations that require unprepared learning. Taste-aversion learning, however, which is strongly prepared apparently even in humans, seems relatively immune to such ratiocination.

SOURCES FOR FURTHER STUDY

Bernstein, Ilene L., and Soo Borson. "Learning Food Aversion: A Component of Anorexia Syndromes." *Psychological Review* 93, no. 4 (1986): 462-472. A review of some of the issues relevant to development of clinically significant food aversions in humans. The authors discuss tumor anorexia, cancer anorexia, anorexia nervosa, and anorexia following intestinal surgery. Technical, but interesting and important.

Bolles, Robert C. *Learning Theory*. 2d ed. Pacific Grove, Calif.: International Thomson, 1979. One of the most concise and readable textbooks on learning theory; it reads almost like a mystery story in places. Details learning theory both before and after the discovery of the Garcia effect and includes a discussion of learning in its evolutionary context. Chapter 9 is almost entirely on taste aversion and its implications.

Braveman, Norman S., and Paul Bronstein, eds. *Experimental Assessments and Clinical Applications of Conditioned Food Aversions*. New York: New York Academy of Sciences, 1985. This is volume 443 in the Annals of the New York Academy of Sciences, and it reprints papers presented at a 1984 conference. Many of the articles, by experts in the field, deal with the medical relevance of food aversions in humans. Many of the articles are quite technical, but some are accessible to the general reader with some background.

Brower, Lincoln Pierson. "Ecological Chemistry." *Scientific American* 220 (February, 1969): 22-29. An excellent and enjoyable description of taste-aversion learning in nature. Brower describes how birds become averted to insects, such as monarch butterflies, that feed on plants containing chemical toxins. Some of the evolutionary implications of this phenomenon are discussed.

Bures, Jan, Federico Bermudez-Rattoni, and Takashi Yamamoto. *Conditioned Taste Aversion: Learning of a Special Kind*. New York: Oxford University Press, 1998. A comprehensive and up-to-date summary of research into the neuroanatomy, pharmacology, electrophysiology, and functional morphology of conditioned taste aversion.

Gustavson, Carl R., and John Garcia. "Pulling a Gag on the Wily Coyote." *Psychology Today* 8 (August,

1974): 68-72. Very entertaining article describing the research on averting wild predators to sheep as a way of limiting predation on ranchers' herds without destroying the predators themselves. The authors convincingly show that shooting and poisoning coyotes are unnecessary and undesirable.

Seligman, Martin E. P., and Joanne L. Hager, eds. *Biological Boundaries of Learning.* New York: Appleton-Century-Crofts, 1972. Almost a history of the revolution in learning theory brought about by taste aversion, this volume contains reprints of and commentaries on many of the original research articles, including those by Garcia cited in the text. Difficult in places but necessary reading for a complete understanding of taste aversion.

William B. King

SEE ALSO: Conditioning; Defense reactions: Species-specific; Learning; Pavlovian conditioning; Preparedness.

Teaching methods

TYPE OF PSYCHOLOGY: Learning; motivation
FIELDS OF STUDY: Biological influences on learning; cognitive learning

Teaching methods are techniques to induce students to learn. There are six classes of complementary methods: information-providing, inquiry-oriented, active or performance-based, cooperative, mastery-based, and creativity-inducing. Excellent instruction depends not upon how well any one method is implemented, but rather upon how well all the techniques can be coordinated to complement one another.

KEY CONCEPTS
- active or performance-based methods
- cooperative methods
- creativity-inducing methods
- information-providing methods
- inquiry-oriented methods
- mastery-based methods
- responsibility for learning

INTRODUCTION
Teaching methods are techniques to induce students to do what they need to do to learn a specific content, skill, or thinking strategy. Two underlying features of this definition—responsibility for learning and the quest for one best method—deserve further consideration.

Regarding responsibility, there is little doubt that, if learners did what they needed to do, teachers would be unnecessary. However, few learners are sufficiently self-motivated or capable of diagnosing what they need. Enter teachers: It is they who can—and must—structure a task so that students are willing to do what they do not yet understand, diagnose errors or misconceptions, provide feedback on how to improve, and encourage or motivate as needed.

Current thinking on the responsibilities of teachers can probably be traced to the book by philosopher and educator John Dewey, *How We Think* (1933), in which Dewey specifically equated the teaching-learning process with selling-buying. Teaching activities which do not culminate in student achievement are every bit as unsuccessful as merchant activities which do not result in a sale. The analogy is not perfect, however, because merchants succeed by selling to only a portion of their customers; teachers are held accountable for each student. Virtually all models of instruction since Dewey make learning a shared or reciprocal responsibility between teacher and student.

Regarding the "one best method" mentality, all models recommend that teachers learn and employ a wide variety of techniques so that, first, students can find different ways to engage the material and, second, students cannot overemphasize one learning strategy and allow others to atrophy. An aphorism makes the point more dramatically: If a child has only a hammer, everything looks like a nail. To get past that narrow perception requires that the child begin to use other tools. Tools of teaching are therefore most profitably conceived as ways to expand the teacher's repertoire, which increases the probability of inducing students to do what they need to do to learn.

TYPES OF TEACHING METHODS
Teaching methods can be classified in a number of ways, none of which is entirely satisfactory because of considerable overlap of purposes and procedures. For example, although lectures can be straight presentation of information with little or no active involvement by an audience, since the 1970's teachers have increasingly woven opportunities for

active participation into lectures, even in very large classes. As another example, mastery learning, which requires students to demonstrate competence individually, is often successfully combined with cooperative teams.

Recognizing that overlaps exist, one can divide methods into categories according to whether they are primarily information-providing, inquiry-oriented, active or performance-based, cooperative, mastery-based, or creativity-inducing.

INFORMATION-PROVIDING METHODS

Prime exemplars of information-providing methods are lectures and demonstrations in which authoritative information is presented or a skill or process modeled. Strengths of the lecture are not only that much information, including data too recent to be published, can be presented in a relatively short period of time, but also that an expert's ways of thinking about the topic can be displayed. Also on display is the lecturer's excitement about the topic, as well as implicit or explicit concern for ethical issues. While many facts can be embedded in a lecture, they will better be remembered by other methods; thus, the lecture is better used to convey how an expert reflects on the chain of logic used to draw inferences about the data or events which constitute the topic.

Demonstrations have many of the same features as lectures—indeed, a lecture could be considered a demonstration of reasoning—but they display skills and performances in modalities beyond the verbal. These include physical skills, artistic performances, and scientific experiments in which experts can model effective, efficient, and/or aesthetic techniques.

Lectures and demonstrations are often combined to great effect, and they have the advantage of being locally recordable for later viewing or transmission to distant or very large audiences. Conversely, professionally developed videos of actual or simulated research or events—such as space exploration or an experiment involving deoxyribonucleic acid (DNA)—can be made available to students anywhere in the world. Using similar technology, teachers can present complex skills or ideas, dissecting a sports or musical performance, or even a chemical reaction.

The primary weakness of information-providing methods is, ironically, that they are not very efficient for learning specific information. A popular saying conveys the problem: I hear, I forget; I see, I remember; I do, I understand. Research on verbal and visual elaborations in memory confirms the point that demonstrations provide imagery, which improves memory beyond that of simple verbal processing. To understand and use, which implies beginning to become truly competent, learners must construct their own examples, organize their knowledge, and practice their skills. Thus, lectures and demonstrations are most effective if they are accompanied by other methods.

INQUIRY-ORIENTED METHODS

In general, the word "inquiry" implies some systematic examination of a topic in search of information, or discovery of the truth. Hence, inquiry and discovery are often used as synonyms for techniques that require students not only to solve problems but also to pose them, not only to conduct investigations but also to plan them, not only to draw inferences from data but also to elucidate the chain of logic they are using. These are higher levels of thinking, requiring such cognitive processes as planning, critical analysis, organization, and synthesis, as well as such metacognitive processes as self-reflection on "what I know and how I know it."

Case studies—real or simulated—in which illnesses are diagnosed, problems are identified, and alternative solutions or treatments are compared and evaluated are excellent illustrations of inquiry methods. So is the search for historical antecedents or consequences of a scientific finding, sociopolitical event, or ethical/moral debate. Inquiry is integral to progress in science and the social sciences and, if education is preparation for such fields, students need to have such discovery experiences to understand these fields.

Weaknesses of inquiry/discovery learning include the extended time required, the fact that breadth of coverage of a field is sacrificed in favor of in-depth study of only a few topics, and that every student must be involved in all stages of the investigation to reap the benefit (and receive teacher feedback). In practice, therefore, teachers often use inquiry methods in combination with other techniques. For example, they save time by demonstrating an experiment or by having teams of students doing different phases of the research. To the extent that students are excluded from responsibility for various phases, however, their experience with inquiry is diluted.

Still, some practice with inquiry may be better than none, and thus it may be possible to place specific inquiry/discovery methods on a continuum from complete to none. A teacher demonstration followed by students searching for alternative explanations would be a legitimate, if partial, inquiry experience. The other end of the continuum might be a concept attainment lesson, in which elementary students are shown objects or pictures of objects and must decide why they are alike or different, and thereby discover symmetry, even before they know the concept label.

ACTIVE OR PERFORMANCE-BASED METHODS

Active methods are those in which students are continually participating in the lesson, sometimes "hands-on," or overtly, when they are performing, always "minds-on," or covertly, because they may be called upon to contribute at any moment. Such methods are usually contrasted with passive learning, in which students just listen for extended periods of time or wait until it is their turn to perform. Examples of passive methods—which active methods were invented to supplement—include long lectures or demonstrations; classroom recitations in which, for example, one student translates a sentence from one language to another or performs a song, while other students wait their turn in sequence; and procedures in which only volunteers participate.

Active methods have long been used to supplement lectures and demonstrations, as well as to monitor learning in performance-based fields such as music or sports. In these fields, information may be provided via brief lectures or demonstrations, following which students practice with feedback and coaching. For academic subjects, lectures or demonstrations could likewise be broken into ten- to twenty-minute segments, followed by such techniques as learning by teaching, in which the teacher demonstrates, say, three concepts and each member of a three-person team teaches one of those concepts to the other two persons (perhaps also inventing their own examples); think-pair-share, in which the lecture is interrupted with a question designed to make individuals process or apply the content, which is then discussed with a partner and subsequently share with the whole class; one-minute papers, in which students must summarize the main points or central inference to be drawn from the presentation, which can then be discussed further in class (or turned in

anonymously as feedback to the instructor); or short quizzes, in which the teacher asks a few true-false, multiple-choice, or short-answer questions to be scored and discussed immediately.

To substitute for recitations in which only the performer is active, it is more desirable to ask questions of, or invent an activity for, the whole class before any individual is called upon to respond. Thus, for language translation, all students may be asked to translate the sentence, then compare translations or call on two or three students. For a recital, the student audience may be assigned to assess the difficulty of the piece, find one exemplary aspect of the performance, and make one positive suggestion for improving. (Even if these are not shared with the performer, such exercises give students practice with the higher levels of thinking involved in evaluation of performances.)

Discussions can also be active methods, but not if they are dominated by only the few individuals who are willing to volunteer. At the other extreme is an inquisition-like atmosphere in which the teacher dominates by asking question after question. Somewhere between these extremes is an optimal active method, which may use techniques from other methodologies as precursors to the whole class discussion.

The main weakness of active methods is probably that, in trying to keep them brief enough to fit into the limited class time available, they tend to overemphasize lower-level thinking skills or initial performances. Thus, they need to be supplemented by other information-providing techniques and inquiry projects which can provide experiences with problem posing and sustained reasoning.

COOPERATIVE METHODS

Cooperative methods should also be included in repertoire of active methods, but what makes them a unique category is that they were explicitly designed to teach collaborative skills as well as traditional academic objectives. They do this through what David and Roger Johnson, pioneers in cooperative teaching methods, in 1975 called cooperative goal structures. In contrast to individualistic or competitive approaches, cooperative goals require individuals to coordinate their efforts to achieve an instructional objective, so that individuals succeed only when all succeed. This is accomplished by two features which both define cooperative teams and distinguish them from the kinds of groups most people have experienced: individual accountability and positive interdependence.

Individual accountability means that, despite having a group assignment or product to complete, all students will be assessed, first, on what each was responsible for doing and, second, on their comprehension of the whole task. Positive interdependence means, first, that each student will have a unique role that complements the others' roles, and, second, that each student has an incentive for assuring that all students succeed in fulfilling their roles and comprehending the material.

Using different role assignments, a math or science teacher might identify a leader, researcher, and presenter as roles for three-person teams (with different assignments on other days). Leaders will help define the task, distribute responsibilities, keep the group on task, and maintain records of the group's work; researchers will bring class notes, organize and calculate data, or consult the teacher; and presenters will organize the report and present findings to the class.

Other ways of assuring positive interdependence in many subject areas were developed in the 1980's by Robert Slavin and his colleagues. For example, in jigsaw, each member of the team becomes responsible for one aspect of a complex topic and meets with corresponding members of other teams. That is, each team member is given a number from one to four; then the ones get together to study one component of the topic, the twos another, and so on. Following acquisition of expertise in this topic, they return to their groups and teach their team members.

To assure individual accountability in these approaches, the teacher must still provide incentive for each student to care that all learn. This can be done, for example, by giving a bonus to the whole team when each member individually passes a quiz or mastery test on the material. Alternatively, the teacher can assess individual students' fulfillment of their responsibilities, which might also include students' self-ratings or (if done properly) students rating one another.

MASTERY-BASED METHODS
Both a philosophy and a collection of methods, mastery learning seeks to ensure that each student achieves at least the minimum standard of knowledge or performance for each required objective. Such competencies can be defined formally, as when students will eventually be accountable for professional certifications as lawyers, physicians, and psychologists, or less formally, as in demonstrating mastery of multiplication tables, rules of grammar, or reading comprehension. In any case, the concern of mastery methods is to teach and monitor the progress of each student's competence in a criterion-referenced fashion—that is, in relation to established standards for the instructional objectives.

To implement mastery learning, one must divide the curriculum into critical and enrichment objectives. The former are basic concepts or skills which must be attained by all to prepare for more advanced study in the course or discipline. These critical objectives need to be divided into manageable units, perhaps two to four weeks in length, and learned to a high level (75 percent correct or higher) on conventional tests. Demonstrating mastery, whether by test or performance, is only the initial acquisition of new material and, as such, the material will surely be forgotten. Unlike poorly learned basics, however, material and skills initially mastered can be relearned quickly when needed in subsequent lessons, providing considerable savings in time overall. For students who do not demonstrate mastery, remedial instruction and retesting must be provided.

Because mastery is conceived as initial acquisition and not expert status, even perfect scores on the test must be graded as the beginning levels of skill. People pass a driver's test or learn a new tennis strike to begin to drive or play tennis, not because they are finished learning. Thus, people need enrichment objectives, which provide advanced study and application of the mastered material. These are optional assignments that can be done in different ways and that carry the incentive of raising course grades above basic passing. For example, in science or history, enrichment exercises might be inquiry assignments; in English, writing a poem or critiquing an essay or book; in music, arranging a piece for the instruments just studied; in any field, tutoring students who need help with initial mastery.

Weaknesses of mastery methods are that, in emphasizing basic skills, instruction tends to be at the lowest levels of thinking and to go at the rate of the slowest learners. To avoid this, mastery must be used in combination with other methods, and only for material that all students must know to be certified as competent or to assure that prerequisite knowledge has been attained.

CREATIVITY-INDUCING METHODS

While any teaching method has potential for encouraging creativity, it is easy to become dominated by the established logic and ways of thinking in a field. Edward deBono, a longtime advocate of creativity training, calls such approaches "vertical thinking" to emphasize their sensible, top-to-bottom structure. While logic is necessary to solve problems and organize thinking, it is often insufficient to generate a wide variety of alternative, uncommon, and even bizarre ideas which can later be evaluated logically. He called this approach "lateral thinking."

Similar to William Gordon's synectics, lateral thinking has specific techniques for forcing familiar concepts to seem strange so that knowledge—or assumptions—may be reconsidered. For example, one may consider what life would be like if people were born old and became younger every year (deBono's reversibility method) or what it feels like to be the bull in a bullfight (personal analogy in synectics). While these ideas may not lead to new theories, they may help spice up essays on developmental psychology or dysfunctional families, respectively, if used as warm-up exercises.

Like brainstorming, the rules include suspending judgment during the idea-generating phase. Finding fault with an idea shuts out further thinking in that direction, while praising an idea reinforces similar thinking. Evaluation comes later, when the goal shifts from generating ideas to deciding which ones to use. As deBono made explicit in his 1985 *Six Hat Thinking* curriculum, people need to learn to put on different thinking caps for different purposes. Each type has weaknesses. Creative thinking is not logical, by definition, and is therefore a method to be used in combination with other methods. Furthermore, while these techniques can stimulate truly novel inventions, when used in classrooms creativity is defined as behavior or thinking that is novel for this student. Thus, the goal is to encourage each student to avoid habitual or rigidifying thinking through exercises which expand their thinking.

SOURCES FOR FURTHER STUDY

Block, James H., Helen E. Efthim, and Robert B. Burns. *Building Effective Mastery Learning in Schools.* New York: Longman, 1989. Beginning with John Carroll's redefinition of aptitude as "time needed to learn," the authors describe the logical and empirical bases for mastery learning, along with suggestions for implementing mastery in various fields and levels of schooling.

Bonwell, Charles C., and James A. Eisen. *Active Learning: Creating Excitement in the Classroom.* Washington, D.C.: School of Education and Human Development, George Washington University, 1991. Aimed at teachers in higher education, this book clearly describes practical methods for involving students, even in large lecture classes.

Johnson, David W., Roger T. Johnson, Edythe J. Holubec, and Patricia Roy. *Circles of Learning: Cooperation in the Classroom.* Alexandria, Va.: Association for Supervision and Curriculum Development, 1984. This practical book makes the case for cooperative methods, as well as how to teach the collaborative skills and establish the procedures for maximizing their effectiveness.

Joyce, Bruce R., Marsha Weil, and Beverly Showers. *Models of Teaching.* 4th ed. Englewood Cliffs, N.J.: Prentice-Hall, 1992. This book presents dozens of instructional methods from various theoretical approaches: from behavioral to cognitive, from individual to cooperative, from didactic to creative.

Rosenshine, Barak, and Robert Stevens. "Teaching Functions." In *Handbook of Research on Teaching,* edited by Merlin C. Wittrock. 3d ed. New York: Macmillan, 1986. This review of the literature analyzes the effectiveness of various things teachers do, particularly regarding review and homework, lecture presentations, feedback, and practice.

J. Ronald Gentile

SEE ALSO: Concept formation; Creativity and intelligence; Educational psychology; Intelligence; Learning; Learning disorders; Problem-solving stages; Problem-solving strategies; Thought: Inferential; Thought: Study and measurement.

Teenage suicide

TYPE OF PSYCHOLOGY: Developmental psychology
FIELDS OF STUDY: Adolescence

Teenage suicide is a profoundly tragic and unsettling event. The rise in adolescent suicide has been so dramatic since the 1960's that it cannot be ignored as a passing problem; attention has been directed toward gaining insight into the myths, causes, warning signs, treatments, and preventive measures of adolescent suicide.

KEY CONCEPTS

- behavioral psychology
- cognitive limitations
- cognitive psychology
- depression
- psychodynamic orientation
- suicide
- suicide attempt

INTRODUCTION

The statistics on teenage suicide are shocking. Suicide is the fifth leading cause of death for those under age fifteen, and it is the second leading cause of death for those ages fifteen to twenty-four.

In 1960, the suicide rate among fifteen- to nineteen-year-olds was 3.6 per 100,000. By 1990, 11.1 out of every 100,000 teenagers fifteen and older committed suicide, according to the U.S. Centers for Disease Control and Prevention (CDC). In 1997, about 9 percent of suicides in the United States were committed by people aged nineteen or younger. Perhaps even more disturbing are the statistics regarding the classification of attempted suicides. Although it is difficult to determine accurately, it is estimated that for every teenager who commits suicide there are approximately fifty teenagers who attempt to take their own lives.

Females attempt suicide at higher rates than males but are less successful in actually dying. Males are much more likely to use violent and lethal methods for trying to kill themselves, such as shooting or hanging. Females are more likely to use passive means to commit suicide; the use of drugs and poisons, for example, is more prevalent among females than males.

As alarming as these facts may be, it should be noted that suicide is still rare among the young. Nevertheless, preventing suicide would save thousands of adolescent lives each year. The problem of suicide is complex, and studying it has been especially difficult because suicidal death is often denied by both the medical professional and the victim's family. The whole subject of suicide is carefully avoided by many people. As a result, the actual suicide rate among adolescents may be significantly higher than the official statistics indicate.

CONTRIBUTING FACTORS

There are no simple answers to explain why adolescents attempt suicide, just as there are no simple solutions that will prevent its occurrence; however, researchers have discovered several factors that are clearly related to this drastic measure. These include family relations, depression, social interaction, and the adolescent's concept of death.

Family factors have been found to be highly correlated with adolescent suicide. A majority of adolescent suicide attempters come from families in which home harmony is lacking. Often there is a significant amount of conflict between the adolescent and his or her parents and a complete breakdown in communications. Many suicidal youths feel unloved, unwanted, and alienated from the family. Almost every study of suicidal adolescents has found a lack of family cohesion.

Most adolescents who attempt suicide have experienced serious emotional difficulty prior to their attempt. For the majority, this history involves a significant problem with depression. The type of chronic depression that leads some adolescents to commit suicide is vastly different from the occasional "blues" most people experience from time to time. When depression is life-threatening, adolescents typically feel extremely hopeless and helpless, and believe there is no way to improve their situation. These feelings of deep despair frequently lead to a negative self-appraisal in which the young person questions his or her ability to cope with life.

Further complicating the picture is the fact that clinically depressed adolescents have severe problems with relating to other people. As a result, they often feel isolated, which is a significant factor in the decision to end one's life. They may become withdrawn from their peer group and develop the idea that there is something wrong with society. At the same time, they lack the ability to recognize how their inappropriate behavior adversely affects other people.

Another factor that may contribute to suicidal thoughts is the adolescent's conception of death. Because of developmental factors, a young person's cognitive limitations may lead to a distorted, incomplete, or unrealistic understanding of death. Death may not be seen as a permanent end to life and to all contact with the living; suicide may be viewed as a way to punish one's enemies while maintaining the ability to observe their anguish from a different dimension of life. The harsh and unpleasant reality of death may not be realized. Fantasy, drama, and "magical thinking" may give a picture of death that is appealing and positive. Adolescents' limited ability to comprehend death in a realistic manner may be further affected by the depiction of death in the songs they hear, the literature they read, and the films they watch. Frequently death is romanticized. Often it is presented in euphemistic terms, such as "gone to sleep" or "passed away." At other times it is trivialized to such an extent that it is the stimulus for laughter and fun. Death and violence are treated in a remarkably antiseptic fashion.

PREVENTION ATTEMPTS

Suicide is a tragic event for both the victim and the victim's family. It is also one of the most difficult problems confronting persons in the helping professions. In response, experts have focused their attention on trying to understand better how to prevent suicide and how to treat those who have made unsuccessful attempts to take their own lives.

It is believed that many suicides can be prevented if significant adults in the life of the adolescent are aware of various warning signals that often precede a suicide attempt. Most adolescents contemplating suicide will emit some clues or hints about their serious troubles or will call for help in some way. Some of the clues are easy to recognize, but some are very difficult to identify.

The adolescent may display a radical shift in characteristic behaviors related to academics, social habits, and relationships. There may be a change in sleeping habits; adolescents who kill themselves often exhibit difficulty in falling asleep or maintaining sleep. They are likely to be exhausted, irritable, and anxious. Others may sleep excessively. Any deviation from a usual sleep pattern should be noted. The individual may experience a loss of appetite with accompanying weight loss. A change in eating habits is often very obvious.

A pervasive feeling of hopelessness or helplessness may be observed. These feelings are strong indicators of suicide potential. Hopelessness is demonstrated by the adolescent's belief that his or her situation will never get better. It is believed that current feelings will never change. Helplessness is the belief that one is powerless to change anything. The more intense these feelings are, the more likely it is that suicide will be attempted. The adolescent may express suicidal thoughts and impulses. The suicidal adolescent may joke about suicide and even outline plans for death. He or she may talk about another person's suicidal thoughts or inquire about death and the hereafter. Frequently, prized possessions will be given away. Numerous studies have demonstrated that drug abuse is often associated with suicide attempts. A history of drug or alcohol abuse should be considered in the overall assessment of suicide potential for adolescents.

A variable that is often mentioned in suicide assessment is that of recent loss. If the adolescent has experienced the loss of a parent through death, divorce, or separation, he or she may be at higher risk. This is especially true if the family is significantly destabilized or the loss was particularly traumatic. A radical change in emotions is another warning sign. The suicidal adolescent will often exhibit emotions that are uncharacteristic for the individual. These may include anger, aggression, loneliness, guilt, grief, and disappointment. Typically, the emotion will be evident to an excessive degree.

Any one of these factors may be present in the adolescent's life and not indicate any serious suicidal tendency; however, the com-

---

Warning Signs for Teenage Suicide

Four out of five teenagers who attempt suicide have given clear warnings, such as some of the following signs:
- suicide threats, direct and indirect
- obsession with death
- poems, essays, and drawings that refer to death
- dramatic change in personality or appearance
- irrational, bizarre behavior
- overwhelming sense of guilt, shame, or reflection
- changed eating or sleeping patterns
- severe drop in school performance
- giving away belongings

Source: National Mental Health Association (NMHA) factsheet "Suicide: Teen Suicide," 1997.

bination of several of these signs should serve as a critical warning and result in some preventive action.

TREATMENT

The treatment of suicidal behavior in young people demands that attention be given to both the immediate crisis situation and the underlying problems. Psychologists have sought to discover how this can best be done. Any effort to understand the dynamics of the suicidal person must begin with the assumption that most adolescents who are suicidal do not actually want to die. They want to improve their lives in some manner, they want to overcome the perceived meaninglessness of their existence, and they want to remove the psychological pain they are experiencing.

The first step in direct intervention is to encourage talking. Open and honest communication is essential. Direct questions regarding suicidal thoughts and/or plans should be asked. It simply is not true that talking about suicide will encourage a young person to attempt it. It is extremely important that the talking process include effective listening. Although it is difficult to listen to an individual who is suicidal, it is very important to do so in a manner that is accepting and calm. Listening is a powerful demonstration of caring and concern.

As the adolescent perceives that someone is trying to understand, it becomes easier to move from a state of hopelessness to hope and from isolation to involvement. Those in deep despair must come to believe that they can expect to improve. They must acknowledge that they are not helpless. Reassurance from another person is very important in this process. The young person considering suicide is so overwhelmed by his or her situation that there may seem to be no other way of escape. Confronting this attitude and pointing out how irrational it is does not help. A better response is to show empathy for the person's pain, then take a positive position which will encourage discussion about hopes and plans for the future.

Adolescents need the assurance that something is being done. They need to feel that things will improve. They must also be advised, however, that the suicidal urges they are experiencing may not disappear immediately and that movement toward a better future is a step-by-step process. The suicidal young person must feel confident that help is avail-able and can be called upon as needed. The adolescent contemplating suicide should never be left alone.

If the risk of suicide appears immediate, professional help is indicated. Most desirable would be a mental health expert with a special interest in adolescent problems or in suicide. Phone-in suicide prevention centers are located in virtually every large city and many smaller towns, and they are excellent resources for a suicidal person or for someone who is concerned about that person. In order to address long-term problems, therapy for the adolescent who attempts suicide should ideally include the parents. Family relationships must be changed in order to assist the young person in feeling less alienated and worthless.

SUICIDAL PERSONALITIES

Suicide has apparently been practiced to some degree since the beginning of recorded history; however, it was not until the nineteenth century that suicide came to be considered a psychological problem. Since that time, several theories which examine the suicidal personality have been developed.

Émile Durkheim was one of the first to offer a theoretical explanation for suicidal behavior. In the late nineteenth century he conducted a now-classic study of suicide and published his book *Le Suicide: Étude de sociologie* (1897; *Suicide: A Study in Sociology*, 1951). He concluded that suicide is often a severe consequence of the lack of group involvement. He divided suicide into three groupings: egoistic, altruistic, and anomic suicides.

The egoistic suicide is representative of those who are poorly integrated into society. These individuals feel set apart from their social unit and experience a severe sense of isolation. He theorized that people with strong links to their communities are less likely to take their lives. Altruistic suicide occurs when individuals become so immersed in their identity group that group goals and ideals become more important than their own lives. A good example of this type of suicide would be the Japanese kamikaze pilots in World War II: They were willing to give up their lives in order to help their country. The third type, anomic suicide, occurs when an individual's sense of integration in the group has dissolved. When caught in sudden societal or personal change that creates significant alienation or confusion, some may view suicide as the only option available.

Psychologists with a psychodynamic orientation explain suicide in terms of intrapsychic conflict. Emphasis is placed on understanding the individual's internal emotional makeup. Suicide is viewed as a result of turning anger and hostility inward. Sigmund Freud discussed the life instinct versus the drive toward death or destruction. Alfred Adler believed that feelings of inferiority and aggression can interact in such a way as to bring a wish for death in order to punish loved ones. Harry Stack Sullivan viewed suicide as the struggle between the "good me," "bad me," and "not-me."

Other areas of psychology offer different explanations for suicidal behavior. Cognitive psychologists believe that suicide results from the individual's failure to utilize appropriate problem-solving skills. Faulty assessment of the present or future is also critical and may result in a perspective marked by hopelessness. Behavioral psychologists propose that past experiences with suicide make the behavior an option which may be considered; other people who have taken their lives may serve as models. Biological psychologists are interested in discovering any physiological factors that are related to suicide. It is suggested that chemicals in the brain may be linked to disorders which predispose an individual to commit suicide.

Research in the area of suicide is very difficult to conduct. Identification of those individuals who are of high or low suicidal risk is complex, and ethical considerations deem many research possibilities questionable or unacceptable. Theory construction and testing will continue, however; the crisis of adolescent suicide demands that research address the causes of suicide, its prevention, and treatment for those who have been unsuccessful in suicide attempts.

SOURCES FOR FURTHER STUDY

Friedman, Myra. *Buried Alive: The Biography of Janis Joplin.* Updated ed. New York: Harmony Books, 1992. A powerful biography of a famous rock singer who died of a heroin overdose. It poignantly describes how insecurity and acute loneliness played a significant role in her death. An interesting and informative book which is appropriate for adolescents and adults. Contains photographs.

Hyde, Margaret O., and Elizabeth Held Forsyth. *Suicide: The Hidden Epidemic.* Rev. ed. New York: Franklin Watts, 1991. A book written for grades nine through twelve. Discusses the misconceptions of suicide, self-destructive patterns, and motivation theories. Includes a chapter that specifically addresses teenage suicide. Contains a list of suicide prevention centers located across the nation.

Peck, Michael L., Norman L. Farberow, and Robert E. Litman, eds. *Youth Suicide.* New York: Springer, 1985. Provides a comprehensive overview of adolescent suicide. Written especially for the individual who is interested in working with suicidal youth, but an excellent resource for all who want to increase their understanding of this topic. Contains information on the psychodynamics of suicide, the impact of social change, the role of the family, and intervention strategies.

Petti, T. A., and C. N. Larson. "Depression and Suicide." In *Handbook of Adolescent Psychology,* edited by Vincent B. Van Hassett and Michel Herson. New York: Free Press, 1995. A well-written chapter that makes the complicated factors involved in depression and suicide accessible to the general audience. The authors discuss the causes of both depression and suicide, as well as how the two are related. Addresses how to help the suicidal adolescent. Very readable and informative.

Robbins, Paul R. *Adolescent Suicide.* Jefferson, N.C.: McFarland, 1997. Covers racial and gender differences, methods used in the study of suicidal behavior, associated behavioral problems such as drugs and alcohol, psychological profiles, precipitating events for suicide attempts, teenage suicide clusters, the effects of suicide on family and friends, the treatment of suicidal adolescents, and strategies for intervention and prevention.

Doyle R. Goff

SEE ALSO: Adolescence: Cognitive skills; Clinical depression; Community psychology; Coping: Social support; Death and dying; Depression; Identity crises; Suicide.

Temperature

TYPE OF PSYCHOLOGY: Sensation and perception
FIELDS OF STUDY: Auditory, chemical, cutaneous, and body senses

Thermoreceptors are specialized to detect a particular physical change in the environment—the flow of heat, detected as a change in temperature—and to convert this information into nerve impulses that can be integrated and processed by the central nervous system to allow an appropriate compensating response.

KEY CONCEPTS
- adaptation
- circadian temperature rhythm
- cold thermoreceptor
- hyperthermia
- hypothalamus
- hypothermia
- pyrogen
- thermoreceptor
- warm thermoreceptor

INTRODUCTION

Humans have thermoreceptors that can detect the flow of heat energy. These specialized sensory receptors can detect the flow of heat, which is detected as a change in temperature, and convert this information into nerve impulses. Conversion into nerve impulses places the information into a form that can be processed by the central nervous system, allowing a compensating response, if required, to be initiated.

Humans and other mammals have two kinds of thermoreceptors. One type, called the warm thermoreceptor, becomes active in sending nerve impulses when the body surroundings or an object touched reaches temperatures above 30 degrees Celsius. Nerve impulses from the warm thermoreceptors increase proportionately in frequency as the temperature rises to about 43 degrees Celsius; past this temperature, impulses from the warm thermoreceptors drop proportionately in frequency until they become inactive at about 50 degrees Celsius.

The second type of thermoreceptor becomes active in generating nerve impulses at temperatures below about 43 degrees Celsius. Nerve impulses from these receptors, called cold thermoreceptors, increase proportionately as temperatures fall to about 25 degrees Celsius. Below this temperature, the frequency of nerve impulses generated by the receptors drops proportionately; as temperatures fall to about 5 to 10 degrees Celsius, activity of the cold thermoreceptors falls to zero. The activity of cold and warm thermoreceptors overlaps between temperatures of about 30 and 40 degrees Celsius. Within this range, the sensation of heat or cold results from an integration in the brain of nerve impulses generated by both cold and warm receptors.

At temperatures below about 15 degrees and above about 45 degrees Celsius, pain receptors become active and increase proportionately in activity as temperatures rise or fall beyond these levels. There is a narrow range of overlap of the limits of pain receptors and thermoreceptors, so that temperatures between about 5 and 15 degrees Celsius are felt as both cold and pain (or as "freezing cold") and temperatures between about 43 and 50 degrees Celsius are felt as both heat and pain (or "burning hot"). Temperatures beyond the 5-degree and 50-degree limits for the thermoreceptors stimulate only the pain receptors and are felt primarily or exclusively as pain. Curiously, the cold receptors become active as pain receptors as the temperature rises above about 45 degrees Celsius. The dual activity of the cold thermoreceptors may account for the fact that freezing cold and burning heat may produce a similar sensation.

ADAPTATION PROCESS

Both types of thermoreceptors adapt quickly as the temperature stabilizes. Adaptation refers to the fact that as a stimulus is maintained at a constant level, the nerve impulses generated by a receptor drop in frequency. In effect, the receptor undergoes a reduction in sensitivity if the stimulus remains constant. If the stimulus changes, the receptor again generates nerve impulses at a frequency proportional to the intensity of the stimulus. The ability of receptors to adapt makes them sensitive to a change in stimulus, which is often the factor of greatest importance to an appropriate response.

The rapid adaptation of thermoreceptors is part of common experience. In going from the outdoors into a warm room on a cold day, one immediately detects the warmer temperature and has a resultant strong sense of a temperature change. After a few minutes, one no longer notices the temperature difference, as one's thermoreceptors adapt and reduce their generation of nerve impulses. If the temperature of the room changes by only a degree or so, however, the generation of impulses by the thermoreceptors increases again, and one becomes aware of the change.

SPATIAL SUMMATION AND RECEPTOR LOCATION

Thermoreceptors also show strong spatial summation. If only a very small region of the body is stimulated, one has difficulty discerning whether a temperature change has been experienced, or even whether the stimulus is hot or cold. As the surface area stimulated increases, impulses arriving in the brain from thermoreceptors are summed, so that perception of the change increases proportionately. If only a square centimeter of skin is stimulated by a warm or cold probe, for example, one might not be able to detect a temperature change smaller than about 1 degree Celsius. If the entire body surface is stimulated, as in total immersion in water, one becomes exquisitely sensitive to changes in temperature. Summation of information from all surface thermoreceptors may allow detection of temperature changes as small as a hundredth of a degree Celsius.

Thermoreceptors in humans are most numerous at the body surface, where they are located immediately under the skin. Each thermoreceptor can detect temperature changes over an area of about 1 millimeter in diameter. Cold thermoreceptors occur in greater numbers at the body surface than warm receptors—depending on the body region, there may be as many as three to ten cold thermoreceptors for each warm thermoreceptor. Thermoreceptors of both types are particularly densely distributed in the skin of the tongue and lips. In these regions, there may be as many as twenty to thirty or more thermoreceptors per square centimeter of surface. About a third as many thermoreceptors occur in the skin of the fingertips. In other parts of the body surface, only a few thermoreceptors occur per square centimeter.

PHYSICAL AND CHEMICAL MECHANISMS

Although the locations of cold and heat receptors can be pinpointed on the body surface by touching the skin with a warm or cold probe, it has proved difficult to detect particular structures responsible for thermoreception. One group of cold thermoreceptors, however, has been identified as branched nerve endings that terminate near the inner surfaces of cells in the skin. Presumably, other cold thermoreceptors and the warm thermoreceptors are little more than naked nerve endings that cannot be distinguished from pain and some touch receptors, which have a similar appearance.

Little is understood about the physical and chemical mechanisms underlying thermoreception; however, it is considered likely that the reception mechanism depends on increases and decreases in chemical reaction rates in the receptor cells as the temperature rises and falls. In general, chemical reaction rates approximately double for each 10-degree increase in temperature or are halved for each 10-degree fall. Thermoreceptors probably respond to these increases or decreases in chemical reaction rates rather than directly detecting the changes heat flow responsible for changes in temperature. The thermoreceptors responsible for detecting heat are also sensitive, to some degree, to chemicals. This explains why spices such as red peppers give the sensation of heat when placed on the tongue or rubbed into the skin. Other chemicals, such as menthol, feel cold on the tongue or skin.

BODY TEMPERATURE MAINTENANCE

Thermoreception has two primary functions in warm-blooded animals such as humans. One is detection of extreme temperatures, so that a person can respond to avoid tissue damage by burning or freezing. The second is maintenance of normal body temperature of 37 degrees Celsius.

Maintenance of body temperature involves both conscious and automated responses. At temperatures not too far above and below the range of comfort (about 22 to 24 degrees Celsius), one feels consciously warm or cool and responds by one or more voluntary methods to decrease or increase skin temperature, such as donning or removing clothing. The automated responses maintaining body temperature are complex and involve a variety of systems. Changes in internal temperature are detected by thermoreceptors in the body interior, particularly in the hypothalamus—a brain structure containing the center that detects and regulates internal body temperature. The thermoreceptors of the hypothalamus are extremely sensitive to shifts from the normal body temperature of 37 degrees Celsius. If such changes occur, the hypothalamus triggers involuntary responses that adjust body temperature.

If the internal body temperature rises above 37 degrees, sweat glands in the skin are stimulated to release their secretion, which evaporates and cools the body surface. Heat loss is also promoted by dilation of the peripheral vessels, which increases blood flow to the body surface. Blood cooled at the surface is carried to the body interior by the circulatory system, where it removes heat from internal regions and causes a drop in body temperature. In addition to these cooling mechanisms, release of thyroxin from the thyroid gland is inhibited. The resulting reduction in the concentration of this hormone in the circulation slows the rate at which body cells oxidize fuel substances and diminishes the amount of heat released by these reactions in the body.

If the internal body temperature falls below 37 degrees Celsius, a series of automated responses with opposite effects are triggered. Peripheral blood vessels contract, reducing the flow of blood to the body surface. The output of thyroxin from the thyroid gland increases; the increased thyroxin concentration stimulates body cells to increase the rate at which fuel substances are oxidized to release heat within the body. Although the effect of the response in humans is not pronounced, a drop in internal temperature also stimulates contraction of small muscles at hair roots over the body. The contraction, which is felt as "goose bumps," raises body hairs and increases the dead-air space at the surface of the body. If the drop in internal temperature becomes more extreme, shivering caused by rhythmic contractions of voluntary muscles is induced. Shivering increases body temperature through the heat released by the muscular contractions.

ROLE OF THE HYPOTHALAMUS

The hypothalamus has been identified as the region of the brain regulating body temperature through observations of the effects of injuries and electrical stimulation. Damage to the hypothalamus can inhibit such temperature-regulating responses as sweating and dilation or constriction of peripheral blood vessels. Conversely, experimental electrical stimulation of the hypothalamus can induce the regulatory responses. These observations indicate that the primary temperature-regulating center of the hypothalamus is in its anterior or preoptic region. The automated responses triggered by the hypothalamus in addition to conscious responses allow humans to maintain an almost constant body temperature in the face of a wide variety of environmental conditions. These combined automated and conscious responses allow humans to survive and remain active in a wider range of environmental conditions than any other animal.

The body temperature maintained by the thalamus is not actually set perfectly and constantly at 37 degrees. For most persons, the internal body temperature varies over a range of about 0.6 degree, with the lowest temperatures in the early morning and the highest point at about four to six in the afternoon. This daily variation in body temperature is called the circadian temperature rhythm.

Although the body temperature is normally set at 37 degrees, the set point can be adjusted upward to produce fever as a part of the body's response to infection by invading organisms. Raising the body temperature above 37 degrees results from the same automated responses that normally raise internal temperatures—shivering, constriction of peripheral blood vessels, and an increase in the rate of metabolic reactions.

FEVER

Several types of bacteria secrete substances that can directly stimulate the hypothalamus to raise its set point and induce fever. Substances of this type, capable of inducing fever, are termed pyrogens. Other substances derived through the breakdown of infecting bacteria, or from substances released through the breakdown of body tissues in disease, particularly fragments of some body proteins, can indirectly trigger the hypothalamus to raise its set point. These substances are engulfed by certain types of white blood cells, including macrophages. On engulfing the breakdown substances, the white blood cells release a powerful pyrogen called interleukin-1. This substance stimulates the secretion of a type of hormone, the prostaglandins, which in turn induces the hypothalamus to raise its temperature set point above 37 degrees. The advantage that fever provides to the body in fighting infection is unclear. Aspirin and corticosteroids are able to reduce fever by inhibiting the secretion of prostaglandins.

When the body's ability to regulate temperature is exceeded, resulting in extreme hyperthermia or hypothermia, the results can be extremely serious. Fevers above about 41 to 42 degrees Celsius, or about 106 to 108 degrees Fahrenheit, can cause severe or fatal damage if the body temperature is not quickly lowered by treatments such as water or alcohol sponging of the skin. The high temperatures injure or kill body cells, particularly in the brain, liver, and kidneys, and cause internal bleeding. Damage to brain cells from extremely high fever is essentially irreversible and may cause permanent impairment or even death within minutes.

Hyperthermia and Hypothermia

Under some conditions, as on hot and humid days or when the body is immersed in hot water, the normal physiological reactions regulating body temperature are ineffective and body temperature may rise uncontrollably. If the air temperature rises above about 38 degrees Celsius on days in which the humidity approaches 100 percent, for example, temperature regulation by sweating and dilation of peripheral blood vessels is ineffective. Under such conditions, internal body temperature may rise to damaging levels, particularly if physical exercise is attempted. The resulting reaction, known as hyperthermia or heat stroke, may include dizziness and abdominal distress or pain in milder cases; more severe heat stroke may produce delirium or even death. Hyperthermia differs fundamentally from fever in that the set point of the hypothalamus remains at 37 degrees. Another difference is that the circadian temperature rhythm is maintained during fever, but not in hyperthermia. In addition to high environmental heat and humidity, hyperthermia may be caused by cocaine and psychedelic drugs.

Low environmental temperatures can also exceed the body's capacity to regulate its internal temperature. Heat loss attributable to accidental or intentional immersion in ice water, for example, induces a steady drop in internal body temperature that cannot be effectively reversed by shivering, constriction of peripheral blood vessels, or increases in chemical reaction rates. The effects of extreme cold in lowering body temperature are magnified by impairment of the regulatory function of the hypothalamus. At body temperatures below about 34 degrees Celsius, the function of the hypothalamus in temperature regulation becomes severely impaired. Shivering usually stops below 32 degrees. At internal temperatures below about 28 degrees Celsius, the temperature regulation centers of the hypothalamus cease to function entirely. Below this temperature, internal body temperature falls rapidly, breathing slows greatly or arrests, and the heart may develop an irregular beat or stop beating entirely. Death follows quickly if breathing or the hearbeat stops. Any fall of body temperature below 35 degrees is known as hypothermia.

Surgical Applications

For some surgical procedures, body temperature is deliberately reduced by administering a drug that inhibits activity of the hypothalamus. The body is then immersed in ice water or surrounded by cooling blankets until internal temperatures reach levels of 30 degrees or below. At these temperatures, the heart can be stopped temporarily without significant damage to the brain or other body tissues. Induced reduction of body temperatures in this manner is routinely used in heart surgery.

Sources for Further Study

Berne, Robert M., and Matthew N. Levy, eds. *Physiology.* 4th ed. St. Louis: C. V. Mosby, 1998. The chapter on the somatosensory system in this standard college physiology text outlines the anatomy and physiology of the cells and nerve tracts in the spinal column and brain involved in the sensation of temperature and other body sensations. Although the text is intended for students at the college level, it is clearly written and should be accessible to high school readers.

Coren, Stanley. *Sensation and Perception.* 5th ed. Pacific Grove, Calif.: International Thomson, 1999. This simply written text provides an easily understood discussion of the senses, sensory cells, and the routes traveled by sensory information through the spinal cord to the brain. A clear and interesting description is provided of the basics of perception in the cerebral cortex.

Guyton, Arthur C., and John E. Hall. *Textbook of Medical Physiology.* 10th ed. Philadelphia: W. B. Saunders, 2000. Chapter 50, "Somatic Sensations II: Pain, Visceral Pain, Headache, and Thermal Sensations," in this readable and clearly written text includes an excellent discussion of thermoreceptors, the role of the hypothalamus in regulation of body temperature, and medical implications of fever, hyperthermia, and hypothermia. Chapter 48, "Sensory Receptors and Their Basic Mechanisms of Action," provides a general description of the structure and function of receptors. Although intended for college and medical students, the text can be easily understood by readers at the high school level.

Schmidt-Nielsen, Knut. *Animal Physiology: Adaptation and Environment.* New York: Cambridge University Press, 1997. This standard college text, by one of the greatest animal physiologists, provides a deeply perceptive comparison of sensory systems in humans and other animals. Chapters 6 and 7 describe temperature effects and temperature regulation. The text is remarkable for its lucid and entertaining descriptions of animal physiology.

Stephen L. Wolfe

SEE ALSO: Nervous system; Neurons; Pain; Sensation and perception; Senses; Signal detection theory; Touch and pressure.

Testing

Historical perspectives

TYPE OF PSYCHOLOGY: Intelligence and intelligence testing

FIELDS OF STUDY: Ability tests; intelligence assessment

Current psychological tests have been historically influenced by French researchers, who emphasized clinical observation; by German researchers, who emphasized experimentation; by British researchers, who were interested in individual differences; and by American researchers, who have been more pragmatic in their approach.

KEY CONCEPTS
- genius
- individual differences
- reaction time
- sensory
- test

INTRODUCTION

Tests are an intrinsic part of people's lives. They are tested as children to determine when they will enter school and how much they will learn in school. They are tested as young adults to determine whether they should receive a high school diploma, whether they should enter college, how much they can learn, or whether they can participate in some specialized training. People are tested if they seek admission to law school or medical school, if they want to practice a profession, and if they want to work for a specific company or show proficiency in a particular talent.

Tests have been used for quite some time. In China around 2000 B.C.E., public officials were examined regularly and were promoted or dismissed on the basis of these examinations. The direct historical antecedents of contemporary testing go back slightly more than one hundred years and reflect contributions made by many individuals representing four historical traditions: the French clinical tradition, the German scientific tradition, the British emphasis on individual differences, and the American practical orientation.

EUROPEAN TRENDS

The French clinical tradition emphasized clinical observation. That is, the French were very interested in the mentally ill and mentally retarded, and a number of French physicians wrote excellent descriptions of patients they had studied. They produced very perceptive and detailed descriptions, or case studies, and thereby contributed the notion that the creation of a test must be preceded by careful observations of the real world. To develop a test to measure depression, for example, one must first carefully observe many depressed patients. The French also produced the first practical test of intelligence: Alfred Binet, a well-known French psychologist, in 1905 devised the Binet-Simon test (with Théodore Simon) to be used with French schoolchildren in order to identify those who were retarded and hence needed specialized instruction.

A second historical trend that affected testing was the scientific approach promulgated by German scientists in the late 1800's. Perhaps the best-known name in the field was Wilhelm Wundt, who is considered to be the founder of experimental psychology. He was particularly interested in reaction time, the rapidity with which a person responds to a stimulus. To study reaction time, Wundt and his students carried out systematic experimentation in a laboratory, focused mostly on sensory functions such as vision, and developed a number of instruments to be used to study reaction time. Although Wundt was not interested in tests, his scientific approach and his focus on sensory functions did influence later test developers, who saw testing as an experiment in which standardized instructions needed to be followed and strict control over the

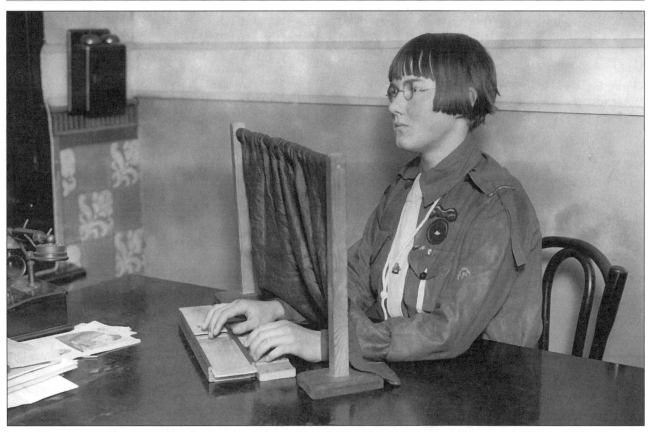

A member of the Girl Guides undergoes a psychological test in 1926. (Hulton Archive)

testing procedure needed to be exercised. They even took the measurement of sensory processes such as vision to be an index of how well the brain functioned, and therefore of how intelligent the person was.

Whereas the Germans were interested in discovering general laws of behavior and were trying to use reaction time as a way of investigating the intellectual processes that presumably occur in the brain, the British were more interested in looking at individual differences. The British viewed these differences not as errors, as Wundt did, but as a fundamental reflection of evolution and natural selection, the ideas that had been given a strong impetus by the work of Charles Darwin. In fact, it was Darwin's cousin, Sir Francis Galton, who is said to have launched the testing movement on its course. Galton studied eminent British men and became convinced that intellectual genius was fixed by inheritance: One was born a genius rather than trained to be one. Galton developed a number of tests to measure

various aspects of intellectual capacity, tested large numbers of individuals who visited his laboratory, and developed various statistical procedures to analyze the test results.

AMERICAN PERSPECTIVES

It was in the United States, however, that psychological testing really became an active endeavor. In 1890, psychologist James McKeen Cattell wrote a scientific paper that for the first time used the phrase "mental test." In this paper, he presented a series of ten tests designed to measure a person's intellectual level. These tests involved procedures such as the subject's estimating a ten-second interval, and measurement of the amount of pressure exerted by the subject's grip. Cattell had been a pupil of Wundt, and these tests reflected Wundt's heavy emphasis on sensory abilities. The tests were administered to Columbia University students, since Cattell was a professor there, to see if the results predicted grade point average. They did not; nevertheless, the practice of testing students to predict their college performance was born.

Lewis Terman, a professor at Stanford University, took the French test that Binet had developed and created a new, English version, called the Stanford-Binet test; thus, intelligence testing became popular in America. When the United States entered World War I in 1917, there was a great need in the military to screen out recruits whose intellectual capabilities were too limited for military service, as well as a need to identify recruits who might be given specialized training or admitted to officer training programs. Several tests were developed to meet these needs and, when the war was over, they became widely used in industry and schools. By World War II, testing had become quite sophisticated and widespread and was again given impetus by the need to make major decisions about military personnel in a rapid and efficient manner. Thus, not only intellectual functioning but also problems of adjustment, morale, and psychopathology all stimulated interest in testing.

As with any other field of endeavor, advances in testing were also accompanied by setbacks, disputes, and criticisms. In the late 1930's and early 1940's, for example, there was a rather acrimonious controversy between researchers at Iowa University and those at Stanford University over whether the intelligence quotients (IQs) of children could be increased through enriched school experiences. In the 1960's, tests were severely criticized, especially the multiple-choice items used in tests to make admission decisions in higher education. Many books were published that attacked testing, often in a distorted and emotional manner. In the 1970's, intelligence tests again came to the forefront, in a bitter controversy about whether whites are more intelligent than blacks. Many school districts eliminated the administration of intelligence tests, both because the tests were seen as tools of potential discrimination and because of legal ramifications.

Tests are still criticized and misused, but they have become much more sophisticated and represent a useful set of tools that, when used appropriately, can help people make more informed decisions.

TESTING SKILLS

In the everyday world, there are a number of decisions that must be made daily. For example, "Susan" owns a large manufacturing company and has openings for ten lathe operators. When she advertises these positions, 118 prospective employees apply. How will Susan decide which ten to hire? Clearly, she wants to hire the best of the applicants, those who will do good work, who will be responsible and come to work on time, who will follow the expected rules but also be flexible when the nature of the job changes, and so on. She would probably want to interview all the applicants, but it may be physically impossible for her to do so since it would require too much time, and perhaps she may realize that she does not have the skills to make such a decision. An alternative, then, would be to test all the applicants and to use the test information with other data, such as letters from prior employers, to make the needed decision. A test, then, can be looked upon as an interview, but one that is typically more objective, since the biases of the interviewer will be held in check; more time effective, since a large number of individuals can be tested at one sitting, whereas interviews typically involve one candidate at a time; more economical, since a printed form will typically cost less than the salary of an interviewer; and, usually, more informative, since a person's results can be compared to the results of others, whereas one's performance in an interview is a bit more difficult to evaluate.

In fact, historically, most tests have been developed because of pressing practical needs: the need to identify schoolchildren who might benefit from specialized instruction, the need to identify army recruits with special talents or problems, or the need to identify high school students with particular interest in a specific field such as physics. As testing has grown, the applications of testing have also expanded. Tests are now used to provide information about achievement, intellectual capacity, potential talents, career interests, motivation, and hundreds of other human psychological concerns. Tests are also developed to serve as tools for the assessment of social or psychological theories; for example, measures of depression are of interest to social scientists investigating suicide, while measures of social support are useful in studies of adolescents and the elderly.

TESTING POETENTIAL

Another way of thinking about tests is that a test represents an experiment. The experimenter, in this case usually a psychologist or someone trained in testing, administers a set of carefully specified procedures and just as carefully records the subject's responses or performance on these procedures. Thus, a psychologist who administers an intelligence test to a schoolchild is interested not simply in computing the child's IQ but also in observing how the child goes about solving new problems, how extensive the child's vocabulary is, how the child reacts to frustration, the facility with which the child can solve word problems versus numerical problems, and so on. While such information could be derived by carefully observing the child in the classroom over a long period of time, using a specific test procedure not only is less time-consuming but also allows for a more precise comparison between a particular child's performance and that of other children.

There are, then, at least two ways, not mutually exclusive, of thinking about a test. Both of these ways of thinking are the result of the various historical emphases: the French emphasis on the clinical symptoms exhibited by the individual, the German emphasis on the scientific procedure, the British interest in individual differences, and the American emphasis on practicality—"Does it work, and how fast can I get the results?"

To be sure, tests are only one source of information, and their use should be carefully guided by a variety of considerations. In fact, psychologists who use tests with clients are governed by two very detailed sets of rules. One set has to do with the technical aspects of constructing a test, with making sure that indeed a particular test has been developed according to scientific guidelines. A second set has to do with ethical standards, ensuring that the information derived from a test is to be used carefully for the benefit of the client.

Because the use of tests does not occur in a vacuum, but rather in a society that has specific values and expectations, that emphasizes or denies specific freedoms, and in which certain political points of view may be more or less popular, the use of tests is often accompanied by strong feelings. For example, in the 1970's, Americans became very concerned about the deteriorating performance of high school seniors who were taking the Scholastic Aptitude Test (SAT) for entrance into college. From 1963 to 1977, the average score on the SAT verbal portion declined by about 50 points, and the average score on the SAT mathematics section declined by about 30

points. Rather than seeing the SAT as simply a nationwide "interview" that might yield some possibly useful information about a student's performance at a particular point in time, the SAT had become a goal in itself, a standard by which to judge all sorts of things, including whether high school teachers were doing their job.

TESTING PSYCHOLOGY
Tests play a major role in most areas of psychology, and the history of psychological testing is in fact intertwined with the history of psychology as a field. Psychology is defined as the science of behavior, and tests are crucial to the experimentation that is at the basis of that science. Especially with human subjects, studies are typically carried out by identifying some important dimension, such as intelligence, depression, concern about one's health, or suicide ideation, and then trying to alter that dimension by some specific procedure, such as psychotherapy to decrease depression, education to increase health awareness, a medication designed to lessen hallucinations, and so on. Whether the specific procedure is effective is then assessed by the degree of change, typically measured by a test or questionnaire.

Psychology also has many applied aspects. There are psychologists who work with the mentally ill, with drug abusers, with college students who are having personal difficulties, with spouses who are not getting along, with business executives who wish to increase their leadership abilities, or with high school students who may not be certain of what career to pursue. All these situations can involve the use of tests, to identify the current status of a person (for example, to determine how depressed the person is), to make predictions about future behavior (for example, to determine how likely it is that a person will commit suicide), to identify achievement (for example, to assess how well a person knows elementary math), or to identify strengths (for example, to gauge whether someone is a people-oriented type of person)—in other words, to get a more objective and detailed portrait of the particular client.

The wide and growing use of computers has also affected the role of tests. Tests can be administered and scored by computer, and the client can receive feedback, often with great detail, by computer. Computers also allow tests to be tailored to the individual. Suppose, for example, a test with one hundred items is designed to measure basic arithmetic knowledge in fifth-grade children. Traditionally, all one hundred items would be administered and each child's performance scored accordingly. By using a computer, however, a test can present only selected items, with subsequent items being present or absent depending on the child's performance on the prior item. If, for example, a child can do division problems quite well, as shown by his or her correct answers to more difficult problems, the computer can be programmed to skip the easier division problems.

Clearly, tests are here to stay. The task is to use them wisely, as useful but limited tools to benefit the individual rather than facilitate political manipulations.

SOURCES FOR FURTHER STUDY

Anastasi, Anne. *Psychological Testing.* 6th ed. New York: Macmillan, 1988. An excellent though somewhat technical introduction to psychological testing. Often required reading for students of psychology. Chapter 1 gives an overview of the history of psychological testing.

Ballard, Philip Boswood. *Mental Tests.* London: Hodder & Stoughton, 1920. A fascinating little book, written for schoolteachers, that covers the development of mental tests, the measurement of intelligence, and school-related activities such as reading, spelling, and arithmetic. Gives the English translation of the Binet-Simon test of intelligence, as well as a number of tests the author developed. Should be read for historical context; most of the book's contents are clearly outdated, but certainly give a flavor of what testing was like in the 1920's.

Garrett, Henry Edward, and Matthew R. Schneck. *Psychological Tests, Methods, and Results.* New York: Harper & Brothers, 1933. A textbook for courses in psychological testing as given in the 1930's. A book to be read in its historical context.

Gregory, Robert. *Psychological Testing: History, Principles, and Applications.* Boston: Allyn & Bacon, 1997. A good summary of the history of psychological testing in the United States.

Office of Strategic Services. Assessment Staff. *Assessment of Men: Selection of Personnel for the Office of Strategic Services.* New York: Rinehart, 1948. A fascinating book that describes the Office of Strategic Services (the OSS, the forerunner of the Central Intelligence Agency) program during World War II to select potential spies and saboteurs.

Sacks, Peter. *Standardized Minds: The High Price of America's Testing Culture and What We Can Do to Change It.* Cambridge, Mass.: Perseus, 2001. Covers current controversies in standardized testing.

Sokal, Michael M., ed. *Psychological Testing and American Society, 1890-1930.* New Brunswick, N.J.: Rutgers University Press, 1987. This book had its genesis in a symposium given in 1984 at the 150th national meeting of the American Association for the Advancement of Science. Consists of eight chapters, written by seven different authors, which place testing in a historical perspective. For example, chapter 2 talks about James McKeen Cattell and how his tests came to be.

Wise, Paula Sachs. *The Use of Assessment Techniques by Applied Psychologists.* Belmont, Calif.: Wadsworth, 1989. Introduces the reader to the ways in which assessments are conducted in real settings by professional psychologists, especially clinical, counseling, organizational, and school psychologists. Well written, with a minimum of technical detail and many examples. Covers assessment in its broad aspects, rather than simply discussing psychological testing.

George Domino

SEE ALSO: Ability tests; Assessment; Career and personnel testing; Career Occupational Preference System (COPS); College entrance examinations; Creativity: Assessment; General Aptitude Test Battery (GATB); Human resource training and development; Intelligence tests; Interest inventories; Kuder Occupational Interest Survey (KOIS); Peabody Individual Achievement Test (PIAT); Race and intelligence; Scientific methods; Stanford-Binet test; Strong Interest Inventory (SII); Survey research: Questionnaires and interviews; Wechsler Intelligence Scale for Children-Third Edition (WISC-III).

Thematic Apperception Test (TAT)

DATE: 1935 forward
TYPE OF PSYCHOLOGY: Personality
FIELDS OF STUDY: Personality assessment

The Thematic Apperception Test (TAT) is one of the most popular personality assessment instruments. It consists of pictures of ambiguous social situations; the subject makes up a story about each picture. These stories are interpreted by a trained clinician to reveal important aspects of the subject's personality.

KEY CONCEPTS
- apperception
- personality assessment instruments
- projective techniques
- psychological testing

INTRODUCTION

The kind of psychological testing concerned with the affective, or nonintellectual, aspects of behavior is called personality assessment. Personality tests refer to measures of such characteristics as emotional states, motivation, attitudes, interests, and interpersonal relations. There are two general types of personality assessment instruments. Objective assessment instruments require a specific response such as "true" or "false," while projective techniques require that the client respond to a relatively unstructured task that permits a variety of possible responses. Methods for eliciting and interpreting stories told about pictured scenes are one type of projective technique. The most widely used set of pictures is the one introduced in 1935 by Henry Murray of the Harvard Psychological Clinic. This set is titled the Thematic Apperception Test (TAT).

Apperception is more than just the recognition or perception of an object based on sensory experience. It is also the addition of meaning to what is perceived. Thus, telling stories about pictured scenes is an apperceptive task requiring the interpretation of what is pictured to discern character's motives, intentions, and expectations. The TAT shows the actual dynamics of interpersonal relationships. It reveals the testing subject's relationship to peers of both sexes, male and female authority figures, and specific family relationships such as the relationship between a mother and her son.

The TAT set comprises thirty pictures and one blank card. These cards are organized into four parallel sets of twenty pictures according to the age and gender of the test subject. Thus, these cards are numbered from 1 to 20 and are designated suitable for boys (B), girls (G), males over fourteen (M), females over fourteen (F), or combinations of those groups (MF, BG, BM, GF). Cards with no letters following their numbers are suitable for all subjects. The cards are achromatic and lack racial diversity. However, adaptations of these cards for specialized populations do not result in richer, more productive stories than does the traditional TAT. The primary advantage of the TAT set is that the pictures portray situations conveying unfinished business and are ambiguous, thus allowing many possible interpretations.

ADMINISTRATION AND INTERPRETATION

Generally, the clinician selects eight to twelve of the cards to administer to the client. Leopold Bellak, the author of the most widely used book on the TAT, has suggested certain cards for standard use. For example, Card 1 is recommended for all subjects. It depicts a boy seated at table looking down at a violin resting on the table. The stimulus requires an explanation for the boy's facial expression in relation to the violin.

Instructions are given to the client to make up a story for each picture shown. They are told to tell what has happened before the event in the picture, to describe what is happening at the moment, what the characters are thinking and feeling, and what the outcome is. Exact wording of the instructions can vary depending on the age and intellectual level of the subject. Approximately five minutes for storytelling per picture is typical. In the standard procedure, the examiner will write the stories down as the test is given individually. After all the stories are given, the examiner may inquire about any specific dates, places, or names of people. It is also feasible to use self-administration with written instructions, and group administration in which the pictures are projected onto a screen and each person writes down a story.

As indicated in the name "Thematic Apperception Test," the clinician examines themes that emerge across all the stories generated by the client. These themes may involve cognition (that is, logic or realism), emotion (and how to cope with emotion), and motivation (what motivates individuals to act and how they pursue goals). A common theme for Card 1 depicting the boy and violin is that of achievement motivation. Various methods of interpreting the TAT have been developed and some are fairly structured. Generally, clinicians prefer to use the TAT as a flexible tool for eliciting information that they would interpret based on their professional training and experience.

SOURCES FOR FURTHER STUDY

Anastasi, Anne. *Psychological Testing.* 6th ed. New York: Macmillan, 1988. An excellent overview on psychological testing by one of the pioneers in the field. Chapters include basics in assessment, including the origins of psychological testing and types of tests, including a chapter on projective techniques. The section on the TAT and related instruments is clear and concise.

Bellak, Leopold. *The T.A.T., C.A.T., and S.A.T. in Clinical Use.* 5th ed. Boston: Allyn & Bacon, 1993. The most comprehensive text on the TAT by one of the pioneering investigators in the field and developer of the CAT (for young children) and SAT (for older adults). While this book is primarily for students in psychology and professions, the general reader will find the chapter devoted to analyzing themes from literary products such as the short stories of Somerset Maugham particularly interesting.

Teglasi, Hedwig. *Essentials of TAT and Other Storytelling Techniques Assessment.* New York: John Wiley & Sons, 2001. An exceptionally clear and well-written presentation of the TAT and related assessment instruments. Discusses administration, scoring, interpretation, and reporting results. This book is conveniently formatted for rapid reference and provides numerous examples, advice on common pitfalls, and self-tests at the end of each chapter. An excellent book for students and professionals, as well as nonprofessional readers.

Karen D. Multon

SEE ALSO: Beck Depression Inventory (BDI); California Psychological Inventory (CPI); Children's Depression Inventory (CDI); Clinical interviewing, testing, and observation; Depression; Diagnosis; *Diagnostic and Statistical Manual of Mental Disorders* (DSM); Minnesota Multiphasic Personality Inventory (MMPI); Personality: Psychophysiological measures; Personality interviewing strategies; Personality rating scales; State-Trait Anxiety Inventory.

Thirst

TYPE OF PSYCHOLOGY: Motivation
FIELDS OF STUDY: Endocrine system; motivation theory; physical motives

Thirst, along with hunger, is one of the basic biological drives; it motivates humans to drink in order to ensure their survival.

KEY CONCEPTS
- antidiuretic hormone (ADH)
- cellular dehydration thirst
- drive
- hypothalamus
- hypovolemic thirst
- motivation

INTRODUCTION

The range of human motivation is quite broad in controlling behaviors. Motivation can be defined as a condition that energizes and directs behavior in a particular manner. Different aspects of motivation can be attributed to instinctive behavior patterns, the need to reduce drives, or learned experiences.

Thirst is one of many biologically based motivational factors; among other such factors are those that involve food, air, sleep, temperature regulation, and pain avoidance. Biologically based motivational factors help humans and other organisms to maintain a balanced internal environment. This is the process of homeostasis. Deviations from the norm, such as hunger, excessive water loss, and pain, will cause an organism to seek out whatever is lacking.

Biologically based motivational factors, such as thirst, have been explained by the drive-reduction theory proposed by Clark Hull in 1943. The lack of some factor, such as water or food, causes the body to feel unpleasant. This is turn motivates one to reduce this feeling of unpleasantness, thus reducing the drive. Thirst is considered what is called a primary drive. Primary drives, which are related to biologically based needs such as hunger, thirst, and sleepiness, energize and motivate one to fulfill these biological needs, thus helping the body to maintain homeostasis. Secondary drives fulfill no biological need.

One may wonder what it is that makes one thirsty and how one knows when one has had enough to drink. Seventy-five percent of a human's weight is water. The maintenance of water balance is an on-going process. In an average day, a person will lose approximately 2.5 liters of water; 60 percent of the water loss occurs through urination, 20 percent is lost through perspiration, and the remainder is lost through defecation and exhalation from the lungs. These 2.5 liters of water must be replaced.

What is the stimulus that motivates one to drink when one is thirsty? The simplest hypothesis, which was proposed by Walter Cannon in 1934, is the dry mouth hypothesis. According to Cannon, it is a dry mouth that causes one to drink, not the need for water. This hypothesis has not held up under scrutiny. Research has shown that neither the removal of the salivary glands nor the presence of excess salivation in dogs disrupts the animals' regulation of water intake. Studies have indicated that the amount of water consumed is somehow measured and related to the organism's water deficit. This occurs even before the water has been replaced in the person's tissues and cells. Thus, dry mouth is a symptom of the need for water.

WATER REGULATION PROCESS

When a human being's water intake is lower than its level of water loss, two bodily processes are set in motion. First, the person becomes thirsty and drinks water (provided it is available). Second, the kidneys start to retain water by reabsorbing it and concentrating the urine. Thus, the kidneys can conserve the water that is already in the body. These processes are set in motion by the central nervous system (CNS).

The CNS responds to two primary internal bodily mechanisms. One is cellular dehydration thirst, and the other is hypovolemic thirst (a change in the volume of water in the body). In order to understand these mechanisms, one must realize that the body contains two main supplies of water. One supply, the intracellular fluid, is in the cells; the other supply consists of the extracellular fluid surrounding the cells and tissues and the fluid in the circulatory system. Water moves between these two areas by means of a process called osmosis, which causes it to move from an area of higher concentration to an area of lower concentration.

A person who is deprived of water will experience cellular dehydration thirst as a result of water loss caused by perspiration and excretion through the urine. This increases the salt concentration in the extracellular fluid, thereby lowering the water concentration. Thus, the cells lose their water to the surrounding extracellular fluid. The increasing salt concentration triggers specialized osmoreceptors located in the hypothalamic region of the brain. Two events occur: First, drinking is stimulated; second, antidiuretic hormone (ADH) is secreted from the pituitary gland in the brain. The ADH helps to promote the reabsorption of water into the kidneys.

The second kind of thirst, hypovolemic thirst, occurs when there is a decrease in the volume of the extracellular fluid as a result of bleeding, diarrhea, or vomiting. This produces a decrease in the salt concentration of the extracellular fluid, which lowers the blood pressure, which in turn stimulates the kidney cells to release a chemical. Eventually, the thirst receptors in the hypothalamus are stimulated; these cause the organism to consume water. In addition, ADH is secreted in this process, which promotes the conservation of water.

The regulation of water intake in humans is thus related to a number of factors and is quite complex. Though cellular dehydration thirst and hypovolemic thirst play a role, it appears that in humans, peripheral factors such as dry mouth play an even larger role. Humans can drink rapidly, replacing a twenty-four-hour water deficit in two to three minutes. This occurs even before the cellular fluid has replaced the water, which takes approximately eight to twelve minutes.

MOTIVATIONAL FACTOR

Thirst is a strong motivational factor. The importance of replacing lost water is underscored by the fact that a person can survive for a month without food but for only several days without water. It appears that both thirst processes help to promote drinking. Researchers have estimated that 64 to 85 percent of the drinking following water loss is caused by cellular dehydration thirst. Hypovolemic thirst accounts for 5 to 27 percent of the drinking, and the remainder is caused by peripheral factors.

The two types of thirst are independent of each other. The receptors for both thirsts are located in the hypothalamic region of the brain, but they are at different locations. Research has shown that lesions in one region will have no effect on thirst regulation in the other region.

Although the motivation to drink in humans is under conscious control by peripheral factors, unconscious control does exert a large influence. A study of cellular dehydration thirst using goats showed that the injection of a saline solution that has a salt concentration of more than 0.9 percent salt (body fluids have a salt concentration of 0.9 percent salt) into the area in which the osmoreceptors are located will produce a drinking response within sixty seconds. Similar results have been found regarding hypovolemic thirst; injecting angiotensin II (a converted protein found in the blood) into the hypothalamus causes a drinking response. This occurs even in animals that are fully hydrated. These animals will consume in direct proportion to the amount of angiotensin II injected into the hypothalamus.

Diet can have a profound effect on water balance in humans. Eating salty foods will produce cellular dehydration thirst despite adequate fluid levels, because water will flow out of the cells into the extracellular fluid. In contrast, salt-free diets will produce hypovolemic thirst by causing water to flow into the cells. Other factors also cause thirst. As stated previously, diarrhea, vomiting, and blood loss will cause hypovolemic thirst as a result of the loss of extracellular fluid. Therefore, significant blood loss will cause a person to become thirsty.

IMPACT OF DISEASES

Diseases can also have an impact on thirst. An interesting example of such a disease is diabetes. Diabetes is a condition in which the body cannot process blood glucose (a type of sugar) properly. Improper diet or medication can cause diabetic ketoacidosis, which causes the levels of glucose and ketone bodies (derivatives from fat) in the blood to rise. This creates a major shift in the water balance of the body. Water leaves the cells and enters the blood system, causing the volume of blood to increase. This extra fluid (along with potassium and sodium) is excreted from the body in the urine, which causes the body to suffer dehydration and triggers a tremendous thirst. Since fluid is lost from both cells and extracellular fluid, this causes both types of thirst. Excessive thirst is still a symptom of diabetes, but it has become rare as a result of education and improved treatment.

IMPACT OF EXERCISE

Thirst motivation also operates during exercise. In short-term exercise, thirst motivation does not come into play because the body usually maintains its temperature. During long-term exercise, however, water intake at intervals facilitates athletic performance by helping to maintain body temperature. The motivation to drink occurs as a result of sweating, which causes the salt concentration in the body to rise during exercise, thereby causing cellular dehydration thirst. Interestingly, voluntary thirst and peripheral factors do not motivate one to take in water during prolonged exercise in the heat until it is too late. Thus, coaches should insist that athletes drink water as they perform.

SOURCES FOR FURTHER STUDY

Carlson, Neil. *Foundations of Physiological Psychology.* 5th ed. Boston: Allyn & Bacon, 2001. An introductory college textbook. Thirst is covered in the chapter on ingestive behavior.

Levinthal, Charles F. "Chemical Senses and the Mechanisms for Eating and Drinking." In *Introduction to Physiological Psychology.* 3d ed. Englewood Cliffs, N.J.: Prentice-Hall, 1990. A very good chapter on the thirst drive. It is quite detailed, but the clarity of the writing makes it easy to read.

Mader, Sylvia S. *Biology.* 7th ed. Boston: McGraw-Hill, 2001. An easy-to-read introductory textbook on biology that provides a good background on hormones, water regulation, and kidney function, with many fine diagrams and figures. A good basis for understanding physiological psychology.

Lonnie J. Guralnick

SEE ALSO: Drives; Endocrine system; Hormones and behavior; Hunger; Pituitary gland.

Thorndike, Edward L.

BORN: August 31, 1874, in Williamsburg, Massachusetts
DIED: August 9, 1949, in Montrose, New York
IDENTITY: American psychologist
TYPE OF PSYCHOLOGY: Cognition; learning
FIELDS OF STUDY: Behavioral and cognitive models; cognitive development; cognitive processes

Thorndike, an early behaviorist, was an important contributor to the study of the psychology of learning.

Thorndike was born in Williamsburg, Massachusetts, in 1874. His family traced its roots back to colonial America. Thorndike's father was a Methodist minister who held up high standards for all of his children. Thorndike took his bachelor's degree at Wesleyan University in Connecticut. While he was an undergraduate student, he read William James's two-volume *Principles of Psychology* (1890). Thorndike was so taken with James's work that he decided to pursue graduate study with him at Harvard. While he was at Harvard, Thorndike had to work part-time. Columbia University made him an irresistible offer, to come to New York and devote himself full-time to studying. Thorndike placed his two brightest chickens (part of animal experiment) in a basket, got on the train, and went to Columbia.

After Thorndike finished his doctorate, he taught at Columbia for forty years. During his long and distinguished career, Thorndike made a number of significant contributions to educational research. He is credited with having devised two experimental procedures, the maze and the puzzle box. He also laid the groundwork for educational measurement. Thorndike devised intelligence tests, rating scales, reading tests, composition tests, geography tests, arithmetic tests, and college entrance tests. His dictionaries were used by millions of public-school children.

Thorndike was a pioneer in applying experimental procedures to the study of learning. His work with kittens in puzzle boxes convinced him learning was a trial-and-error procedure. The kittens were not able to escape from the puzzle boxes by using either reason or instinct. As they dashed madly around the boxes, the kittens—quite by accident—tripped devices that allowed them to escape. They were caught and returned to their boxes. Through repeated trial-and-error procedures, stimulus (S) and response (R) bonds were stamped into the kittens' neural pathways.

Thorndike was committed to the scientific study of education. He formulated three laws of learning. The Law of Readiness holds that when an organism is ready to act, satisfaction will follow action. The Law of Effect asserts that when an action is followed by satisfaction, that action will be more likely to be repeated in the future. The Law of Exercise contends that stimulus and response bonds are strengthened by repetition.

Edward L. Thorndike. (Library of Congress)

Thorndike collected data that refuted two widely accepted doctrines in education, formal discipline and faculty psychology. Formal discipline held that Latin disciplined the mind. Faculty psychology maintained the mind was composed of separate faculties such as memory, reason, and creativity. These faculties, like muscles, could be strengthened through exercise. Latin improved memory; geometry heightened reasoning; and music furthered creativity. Thorndike's data indicated these doctrines were faulty. Latin did not discipline the mind, and mental faculties could not be strengthened through exercise. Generalized transfer simply did not exist. If teachers wished their students to transfer information from one area to another, they would have to show them the identical elements that the two subjects shared in common.

SOURCES FOR FURTHER STUDY

Clifford, Geraldine. *Edward L. Thorndike: The Sane Positivist.* Middletown, Conn.: Wesleyan University Press, 1968. A biography of Thorndike and explanation of his work.

Stanley D. Ivie

SEE ALSO: Behaviorism; Cognitive psychology; Learning; Structuralism and functionalism.

Thought
Inferential

TYPE OF PSYCHOLOGY: Cognition
FIELDS OF STUDY: Thought

An argument is a process that takes assertions as inputs and produces conclusions as outputs; to go beyond the information given and get from the inputs to the outputs is to draw inferences. Formal inferences include deduction and induction. Inferential thought of a formal and informal nature is essential to both scientific reasoning and reasoning in daily life.

KEY CONCEPTS
- argument
- assertion
- belief
- categorical syllogism
- deductive inference
- formal logic
- induction
- pragmatic inferences
- premise
- presupposition

INTRODUCTION
Psychologists are only beginning to understand how human thought processes operate, but there is no doubt that thinking is a critical skill. Reasoning is but one of many types of thought. Others include decision making and concept formation. Reasoning is unique in that it involves drawing inferences from current knowledge and beliefs. Reasoning has multiple components, including the production and evaluation of arguments, the drawing of inferences, and the generation and testing of hypotheses.

The process of inference involves the exploration of alternatives, using evidence. Evidence is information that helps determine the degree to which

a possibility achieves a goal. Basically, using inference, each possibility for choice is made stronger or weaker, considering that goal. The process can be done well or poorly. Without the ability to make inferences, there would be no science, mathematics, or even laws.

Almost every statement a person says or writes leads the listener or reader to make inferences. A presupposition is knowledge upon which one draws in order to understand a statement or assertion. Once the assertion is understood, an inference can be drawn. Certain types of inferences, known as logical inferences, *must* follow from what was said. Logical inferences are, in a sense, demanded by the assertions. For example, the statement "Jack's heart problems forced his doctor to put him on a strict diet" logically implies that Jack was put on a diet.

INDUCTION AND DEDUCTION
There are two basic forms of formal, logical inference: induction and deduction. An induction is a judgment that something is probably true on the basis of experience. It involves generalization—that is, reasoning from a few to all, or from the particular to the general. People infer that they should avoid all bees, having been stung by only one or two up to that time. The inductive inference allows one to go beyond the data at hand and draw a useful conclusion (*all* bees will sting people) that cannot be proved, because it cannot be exhaustively tested. Induction can extend the content of the assertions at the cost of introducing uncertainty.

In contrast, deductive inference achieves absolute certainty, if performed correctly, at the cost of sacrificing innovation. It requires that two or more separate assertions be integrated in order to deduce a new assertion as a necessary consequence. Deductive inference deals with the validity, or form, of the arguments, providing methods and rules for restating given information so as to make what is implicit explicit. All valid deductive arguments reformulate knowledge already given in the assertions. They typically utilize key terms, such as quantifiers (such as "all," "some," "none"), connectives (such as "and," "or," "if-then"), and comparatives (such as "more," "less").

INFERRING SENTENCE MEANING
An experiment published in 1972 by John D. Bransford, J. Richard Barclay, and Jeffrey J. Franks

illustrated that people could not distinguish sentences that were actually presented from inferences they made in the process of comprehending those sentences. Subjects saw sentences such as "Three turtles rested on a floating log and a fish swam beneath it." Subjects were then given memory tests to see if they recognized logically implied sentences such as "Three turtles rested on a floating log and a fish swam beneath them" that were new, so to speak, because they had not actually been seen by the subjects before the recognition test. A large number of the subjects claimed that they had seen the new sentences, which suggests that the logical inferences were formed and stored at the time when the original sentences were initially presented.

Not all inferences are demanded by formal logic, however; the majority of inferences are *invited* by the assertion, and they are known as pragmatic inferences. A pragmatic inference does not need to follow from an assertion, but rather is reasonable, considering world knowledge. For example, to say that "Albert and Rae were looking at wedding rings" in no way demands the inference that Albert and Rae are to be married; however, that inference is certainly reasonable, given what is known about the world. A large number of experiments have been reported which demonstrate that pragmatic inferences also are remembered as part of the original event.

As a further illustration, additional research by Bransford and other colleagues in 1973 presented subjects with sentences such as "John was trying to fix the birdhouse. He was pounding the nail when his father came out to watch him and to help him do the work." The assertions imply, but do not logically demand, that John was using a hammer. Subjects later falsely recognized the sentence "John was using a hammer to fix the birdhouse when his father came out to watch him and help him do the work." Like the logical inference, the pragmatic inference is usually remembered as if it had actually been presented.

SHORTCOMINGS OF INFERENCE

Experimental investigations of thinking have revealed a wide range of shortcomings in human inference. Both deductive and inductive reasoning can go astray and produce incorrect conclusions, often either because one of the premises from which the conclusion was drawn is false or because the

rules of deductive inference were violated. Many inferential judgments are based on imperfect information, and that means mistakes are unavoidable; however, the shortcomings are not simply errors. Instead, the ones that psychologists have identified involve the way in which information is used to draw the inference. For example, relevant information is sometimes ignored and sometimes relied upon too heavily. In addition, multiple pieces of information are often not combined as they should be.

In order to understand human communication, it is necessary to recognize the prevalence and power of inferential processing. Much of what is communicated is actually left unsaid. Speakers instead rely on listeners to draw appropriate inferences. The ability to communicate without explicitly saying everything one is trying to convey enormously increases efficiency; however, as with other thought processes, increased efficiency comes at the cost of increased error. Everyone occasionally says things in such a way that a listener will infer information that may not be quite accurate. To determine whether a speaker is actually being dishonest, the speaker's intentions need to be discovered, which is a difficult thing to do if the actual assertion is accurate. As a result, it is easy to mislead—either when sufficient information to evaluate an assertion is intentionally withheld or when care in drawing inferences is not taken.

IMPLIED MESSAGES OF ADVERTISING

Real-world situations such as advertising copy and courtroom testimony provide interesting examples of the use of potentially misleading information. For example, the Federal Trade Commission was established to make decisions about what constitutes deceptive advertising, but deciding exactly what is deceptive is complex. The decision becomes especially difficult if a claim is not blatant but instead is implied. Consider the following commercial: "Aren't you tired of sneezing and having a red nose throughout the winter? Aren't you tired of always feeling under the weather? Get through the entire winter without colds. Take NuPills as directed."

Notice that the commercial does not directly state that NuPills will get one through the entire winter without colds. The commercial only implies it. In order to test whether people can distinguish between asserted and implied claims, John Harris, in a study published in 1977, presented people with a series of twenty fictitious commercials, half of which asserted claims and half of which implied claims. The subjects in the experiment were told to rate the claims as true, false, or of indeterminate truth value, based on the presented information. Some of the people made their judgments immediately after hearing each commercial, and others made their judgments after hearing all the commercials. Half the people were given instructions that warned them to take care not to interpret implied claims as asserted ones.

The results were that the subjects responded "true" more often to assertions than to implications, and instructions did help to reduce the number of implications accepted as true. Overall error rates, however, were high. Even in the group that gave an immediate judgment after hearing each commercial, people mistakenly accepted about half the implied statements as asserted ones. Finally, when the judgments were delayed until all commercials were presented, people accepted about as many implied statements as true as they did direct statements, even when they had been specifically warned about implied statements.

COURTROOM TESTIMONY

In the context of how information can be misleading in courtroom testimony, Elizabeth Loftus published an article in 1975 that described how she showed subjects ("witnesses") a film of a multiple-car accident. Immediately afterward, the witnesses completed a questionnaire that included questions such as "Did you see a broken headlight?" Half the witnesses, however, were given a question that was worded "Did you see *the* broken headlight?" When the word "the" is used, the question encourages the subject/witness to assume that there was a broken headlight and seems to be asking whether he or she happened to see it. The word "a" does not presuppose the existence of a broken headlight. Questions with "the" more often led to reports that the witness had seen the broken headlight than questions with "a." This was the case regardless of whether the object (a broken headlight) had actually appeared in the film. Thus, in a courtroom situation, attorneys can intentionally or inadvertently influence the memories of witnesses by using leading words that entail presuppositions in their questions, leading to inaccurate inferences.

Regardless of the source of the information, the elaborative nature of comprehension can be and is

used to imply potentially inaccurate information. Yet through knowledge of influence, one can be in the position to protect oneself by directly questioning assertions and carefully analyzing one's own inferences.

EVOLUTION OF STUDY

In ancient Greece, the philosopher Aristotle was the main creator of a formal inferential system. Historically, however, the scientific study of inference began fairly recently. Psychologists such as Robert S. Woodworth and S. B. Sells first began publishing articles in the 1930's on errors people made in the process of inferring conclusions. Woodworth and Sells were interested in how a reasoner's personal attitudes toward the conclusion of a syllogistic argument could bias the ability to draw inferences. They, along with other psychologists during the next three decades or so, studied formal inference and mainly looked at logical arguments called categorical syllogisms. As time passed, psychologists began to study other forms of deductive arguments and, later, inductive ones.

In 1962, Mary Henle encouraged psychologists to consider the difference between formal and practical reasoning. Henle attempted to clarify the heated controversy between the psychologists who thought formal logic was largely irrelevant to the thinking process, those who believed the mind contained a formal logic, and those who thought the mind contained other systems of logic that were more practical for day-to-day thinking. Henle pointed out that mathematical logic was never intended to be a direct description of how people think. For example, formal reasoning makes two demands not made in everyday reasoning. First of all, the reasoner must restrict the information to that contained in the premises. Second, the reasoner needs to discover the minimum commitments of the assertions as they are worded, which is not typical of ordinary comprehension. In ordinary comprehension, many inferences are invited that are unacceptable in formal deductive logic.

Linguists have also helped to promote research on inference. A long-standing question posed by linguists is how logic relates to actual conversation and argumentation. In conversation, most utterances have multiple functions. For example, the same utterance could be a description, a persuasion, an emotional expression, or even a warning. Numerous functions can arise, because the speaker may have one of a variety of intentions in mind when making the utterance.

It has been argued by Philip Johnson-Laird, in work he began publishing in 1978, that what subjects use to understand text is a mental model of the textual statements. He claims that people construct representations of models when they read a text. Rather than relying on formal logic in the interpretation of the material, Johnson-Laird believes, people manipulate the models they have formed. He thinks that the psychology of reasoning should describe the degree of competence that people display when it comes to inference, but that the mental processes underlying them—inferential performance— also need to be investigated. Given the increasing interest in the relationship of inference to linguistics, especially considering the applications that can be made in the area of artificial intelligence, such as getting computers to understand speech and to translate from one human language to another, the psychology of inferential thought will undoubtedly continue to be important research.

Sources for Further Study

Baron, Jonathan. *Thinking and Deciding.* 3d ed. New York: Cambridge University Press, 2001. An excellent book that emphasizes the factors that keep people from thinking effectively and provides information to help the reader improve thinking and decision-making skills. The book is clearly written, but many of the ideas are complex. The author describes the role that thinking plays in relationship to learning, intelligence, and creativity.

Evans, Jonathan St. B. T. *Bias in Human Reasoning: Causes and Consequences.* Hillsdale, N.J.: Lawrence Erlbaum, 1989. Almost everyone interested in inferential thought should find this short book (slightly more than a hundred pages) a pleasure to read. The book is in an extended essay. Classifies the types of bias and puts them in a general theoretical framework, while considering practical applications. Suggestions, based on research, are provided to help the reasoner avoid bias as much as possible. There are also suggestions for educators.

_____. *The Psychology of Deductive Reasoning.* Boston: Routledge & Kegan Paul, 1982. The author reviews the available research in the area.

He has published numerous journal articles on reasoning and is one of the top experts in the area of the psychology of reasoning.

Nickerson, Raymond S. *Reflections on Reasoning.* Hillsdale, N.J.: Lawrence Erlbaum, 1986. This brief book is an adaptation of a report that the author prepared under a project sponsored by the National Institute of Education. It clearly describes reasoning and factors that can impede reasoning, and it provides practical chapters on how to improve one's own reasoning ability and how to use reasoning to win disputes of all kinds.

Deborah R. McDonald

See also: Artificial intelligence; Cognitive ability: Gender differences; Cognitive development: Jean Piaget; Computer models of cognition; Concept formation; Decision making; Intelligence tests; Logic and reasoning; Thought: Study and measurement

Thought
Study and measurement

Type of psychology: Cognition
Fields of study: Cognitive processes; thought

The study of thought is probably as old as thought itself. Although the measurement of thought did not originate in psychology, cognitive psychology is primarily dedicated to the study and measurement of thought processes.

Key concepts
- cognitive psychology
- Ebbinghaus forgetting curve
- higher mental functions
- information processing model
- parallel processing
- percent savings
- personal equation
- serial processing
- subtraction technique

Introduction

Cognitive psychologists study many processes basic to human nature and everyday life. Mental processes are central to who people are, what they do, and how they survive. In cognitive psychology, the study of thought necessitates its measurement. For example, much effort has been put forth in cognitive psychology to study how people understand and process information in their environment. One popular approach is to use the idea of a human information-processing system, analogous to a computer. Computers are information-processing devices that use very specific instructions to achieve tasks. A computer receives input, performs certain internal operations on the data (including memory operations), and outputs certain results. Cognitive psychologists often use the information-processing metaphor in describing human operations. People must "input" information from the environment; this process includes sensory and perceptual systems, the recognition of certain common patterns of information, and attention processes.

Once this information has entered the "system," a vast number of operations can be performed. Much of the work by cognitive psychologists has centered on the storage of information during this process—that is, on memory. While memory processes have been of interest since ancient times, it was not until the 1880's that scientists, notably Hermann Ebbinghaus, first systematically and scientifically studied memory. Scientists studying memory today talk about concepts such as short-term and long-term memory as well as about the distinction between episodic and semantic memory systems. The function of memory is essential to human thought and ultimately to the measurement of thought.

In terms of measuring what happens to incoming information, more than memory storage occurs; people manipulate these data. They make decisions based on the information available, and they have capabilities (often referred to as higher mental processes) that in many ways differentiate humans from other animals. Some of the functions commonly studied and measured include reasoning, problem solving, logic, decision making, and language development and use. The information-processing analogy is completed with the "output" of information. When a person is asked a question, the response is the output; it is based on the information stored in memory, whether those items be personal experiences, knowledge gained from books, or awareness of social customs. People do these things so effortlessly, day in and day out, that it is difficult to stop,

appreciate, and comprehend how thoughts work. Psychologists have pondered these questions for many years and are only beginning to discover the answers.

MEASURING THOUGHTS

Some of the earliest systematic studies of thought and the accompanying desire to measure it came from astronomy, not psychology or philosophy. From this beginning, Dutch physiologist Frans C. Donders set out specifically to measure a sequence of mental process—thought—in the middle of the nineteenth century. His technique was simple yet elegant in its ability to measure how much time mental processes consume; the procedure developed by Donders is typically referred to as the subtraction technique.

The subtraction technique begins with the timing and measurement of a very basic task. For example, a person might be asked to press a button after hearing a tone. Donders realized that it was fairly easy to time accurately how long subjects took to perform this task. He believed that two cognitive (thought) processes would be operating: perception of the tone and the motor response of pressing the button. Once the time of this simple task was known, Donders would make the task more difficult. If a discrimination task were added, he believed, the time taken to complete the task would increase compared to the basic perception-motor response sequence. In this discrimination task, for example, Donders might tell a person to press the button only after hearing a high-pitched sound. That person is now faced with an added demand—to make a decision about pitch. Donders believed that with this discrimination stage, the processing of the information would require more mental effort and more time; he was right. More important, Donders could now measure the amount of extra thought required for the decision by subtracting the simple-task time from the discrimination-task time. In a general sense, Donders had a method for measuring thought.

Donders also had the ability to measure and manipulate specific components of the thought process. He even added another component to the sequence of tasks, what he called choice time. For example, the task could be changed so that for a high tone the subject should press the right button, and for a low tone, press the left button. By subtracting the discrimination time from this new choice time, he could estimate how long the added choice contributed to the overall thought process. By means of these ingenious methods, Donders inspired generations of cognitive psychologists to study thought in terms of the time it takes to think.

EBBINGHAUS ON LEARNING AND FORGETTING

The first recognized work done in psychology on the measurement of thought processes was Hermann Ebbinghaus's work on memory capacity and forgetting. Working independently in the 1880's in Germany, Ebbinghaus set out to study memory processes, particularly the nature of forgetting. Being the first psychologist to study the issue, he had no precedent as to how to proceed, so Ebbinghaus invented his own procedures for measuring memory. To his credit, those procedures were so good that they are still commonly used. Before describing his measurement of memory, Ebbinghaus made two important decisions about methods for studying memory. First, he studied only one person's memory—his own. He believed he would have better control over situational and contextual variables that way.

Second, Ebbinghaus decided that he could not use everyday words in his memory studies, because they might have associations that would make them easier to study. For example, if one were memorizing a poem, the story and the writing style might help memory, and Ebbinghaus was interested in a pure measure of memory and forgetting. To achieve this, Ebbinghaus pioneered the use of nonsense syllables. He used three-letter combinations of consonant-vowel-consonant so that the items were pronounceable but meaningless. Nonsense syllables such as "geb," "fak," "jit," "zab," and "buh" were used.

Ebbinghaus used a vigorous schedule of testing and presented himself with many lists of nonsense syllables to be remembered at a later time. In fact, he spent five years memorizing various lists until he published his seminal work on the topic, *Über das Gedächtnis* (1885; *Memory: A Contribution to Experimental Psychology*, 1913). He systematically measured memory by memorizing a list, letting some time pass, and testing himself on the list. He devised a numerical measurement for memory called percent savings. Percent savings was a measure of the degree of forgetting that occurred over time. For example, it might take him ten minutes to memorize a list

perfectly. He would let forty-eight hours pass, then tell himself to recall the list. Forgetting occurs during that time, and only some items would be remembered. Ebbinghaus would then look at the original list and rememorize it until he knew it perfectly; this might take seven minutes or so. He always spent less time rememorizing the list. Said another way, there was some savings from the earlier experience forty-eight hours before. This percent savings was his measure of memory. The higher the percentage of savings, the more items remembered (or the less forgotten), and Ebbinghaus could remember the list in less time.

Ebbinghaus then varied the time between original list learning and later list recall. He found that percent savings drops over time; that is, the longer one waits to remember something, the less one saves from the prior experience, so the more time he had to spend rememorizing the list. Ebbinghaus found fairly good percent savings two or nine hours later, but percent savings dropped dramatically after two or three days. Plotted on a graph, this relationship looks like a downward sloping curve, and it is called the Ebbinghaus forgetting curve. Simply stated, it means that as time passes, memories become poorer. Although this effect is not surprising today, Ebbinghaus was the first (in 1885) to demonstrate this phenomenon empirically.

STERNBERG ON SPEED

Another example of the work in the area of cognitive psychology comes from the studies of Saul Sternberg in the 1960's at Bell Laboratories. Sternberg examined how additional information in memory influences the speed of mental operations in retrieving information stored in memory. Sternberg's task was fairly simple. He presented people with a list of numbers; the list might range from one to six numbers. After the people saw this initial list, a single number (called a probe) was presented. People were asked to identify whether the probe number was on the initial list of numbers. The list might be 2, 3, 9, and 5, for example, and the probe might be 3.

Sternberg's primary interest was in studying how the length of the initial list affected the time it took to make the required yes-or-no decision. Two possibilities typically emerge when people consider this problem. The concept called serial processing holds that the comparison of the probe to each number in the initial list takes time, so that the more items in the initial list, the longer the memory search takes. An alternative idea, parallel processing, suggests that people instantaneously scan all the items in the memory set, and the number of items in the initial list does not make a difference. Another way of saying this is that all the items are scanned at once, in parallel fashion. Sternberg found that people search their memories using the technique of serial processing. In fact, he was able to calculate precisely the amount of additional search time needed for each added item in the memory set—38 milliseconds (a millisecond is a thousandth of a second). Although the search may seem fast, even instantaneous, the more there is to think about, the more time it takes to think.

COGNITIVE PSYCHOLOGY

The study of thought, and particularly its measurement, is a relatively recent development. For centuries, the thinking processes of humans were believed to be somewhat mystical, and certainly not available for scientific inquiry. Most philosophers were concerned more with the mind and its relationship to the body or the world than with how people think. The study of thought, although it was generally considered by the ancient Greek philosophers, did not merit serious attention until the emergence of the "personal equation" by astronomers and the realization that thought processes are indeed measurable and can be measured accurately and precisely.

The story of the first recorded measurements of thought begins with the royal astronomer to England, Nevil Maskelyne, and his assistant, David Kinnebrook, in 1794. Astronomers of the day were mostly concerned with stellar transits (measuring the movement of stars across the sky). Using telescopes and specialized techniques, the astronomer sought to measure the time it took for a particular star to move across a portion of the telescopic field. Using a complicated procedure that involved listening to a beating clock and viewing the sky, astronomers could measure the transit time of a star fairly accurately, to within one-tenth or two-tenths of a second. These measurements were particularly important because the clocks of that period were based on stellar transits.

Maskelyne and Kinnebrook often worked together in recording the movement of the stars. While Kinnebrook had no problems during 1794, in 1795 Maskelyne began to notice that Kinnebrook's times varied from his own by as much as one-half of a second—considered a large and important difference. By early 1796, the difference between the astronomers' times had grown to eight-tenths of a second. This was an intolerable amount of error to Maskelyne, and he fired his assistant Kinnebrook.

About twenty years later, a German astronomer named Friedrich Bessel came across the records of these incidents and began to study the "error" in the differing astronomers' measurements. He believed that the different measurements were attributable in part to differences between people and that this difference was not necessarily an error. He found that even the most famous and reliable astronomers of the day differed from one another by more than two-tenths of a second.

This incident between Maskelyne and Kinnebrook, and its later study by Bessel, led to some important conclusions. First, measurements in astronomy would have to consider the specific person making the measurement. Astronomers even went to the lengths of developing what became known as the personal equation. The personal equation was a verified, quantified account of how each astronomer's thought processes worked when measuring stellar transits. In essence, the personal equation was a measurement of the thought process involved and a recognition of differences between people. Second, if astronomers differ in their particular thought processes, then many people differ in other types of thinking processes as well. Finally, and perhaps most important in the long run, this incident laid the groundwork for the idea that thought could be measured accurately and the information could be put to good use. No longer was thinking a mystical or magical process that was unacceptable for study by scientists.

It is from this historical context that the field of cognitive psychology has emerged. Cognitive psychology is chiefly concerned with the thought processes and, indeed, all the general mental processing of organisms (most often humans). The interests of a cognitive psychologist can be quite varied: learning, memory, problem solving, reasoning, logic, decision making, linguistics, cognitive development in children, and other topics. Each area of specialization continues to measure and examine how people think, using tasks and procedures as ingenious as those of Donders, Ebbinghaus, and Sternberg. The study and measurement of thought (or, more generally, the field of cognitive psychology) will continue to play an important and vital role. Not many questions are more basic to the study of human behavior than how people think, what processes are involved, and how researchers can scientifically study and measure these processes.

SOURCES FOR FURTHER STUDY

Anderson, John R. *Cognitive Psychology and Its Implications.* 5th ed. New York: Worth, 1999. This text is a long-standing leader in the field of cognitive psychology. Provides a wonderful overview of the fundamental issues of cognitive psychology, including attention and perception, basic principles of human memory, problem solving, the development of expertise, reasoning, intelligence, and language structure and use.

Ashcraft, Mark H. *Human Memory and Cognition.* 2d ed. Upper Saddle River, N.J.: Prentice Hall, 1994. A cognitive psychology textbook that heavily emphasizes the human information-processing metaphor. Arranged differently from Anderson's text, it too provides good coverage of all the basic areas of cognitive psychology.

Boring, Edwin G. *A History of Experimental Psychology.* 2d ed. Englewood Cliffs, N.J.: Prentice-Hall, 1950. This text is the foremost authority on the development and history of psychology up to 1950. Contains detailed accounts of the work of early philosophers and astronomers who contributed to the study of thought, and even contains an entire chapter devoted to the personal equation. This can be a difficult text to read, but it is the authoritative overview of the early history of psychology.

Goodwin, C. James. *A History of Modern Psychology.* New York: John Wiley & Sons, 1998. A readable and understandable treatment of the history of psychology from René Descartes in the Renaissance to the present.

Lachman, Roy, Janet L. Lachman, and Earl C. Butterfield. *Cognitive Psychology and Information Processing: An Introduction.* Hillsdale, N.J.: Lawrence Erlbaum, 1979. One of the earliest texts that adequately captures the coming importance and influence of cognitive psychology. There are outstanding chapters that trace the influences of other disciplines and traditions on what is now known as cognitive psychology. Topic areas within the field are discussed as well.

Mayer, Richard E. *Thinking, Problem Solving, and Cognition.* 2d ed. New York: W. H. Freeman, 1992. A book primarily dedicated to the topic of problem solving, which is unusual. The format is interesting and creative, covering the historical perspective of problem solving, basic thinking tasks, information-processing analysis, and implications and applications. The focus on thought and its measurement is seen throughout, especially in sections discussing mental chronometry.

R. Eric Landrum

SEE ALSO: Artificial intelligence; Cognitive maps; Cognitive psychology; Computer models of cognition; Language; Learning; Logic and reasoning; Memory: Empirical studies; Thought: Inferential.

Thyroid gland

TYPE OF PSYCHOLOGY: Biological bases of behavior
FIELDS OF STUDY: Endocrine system

The thyroid gland is responsible for the production of three hormones important for proper growth and development: thyroxine and triiodothyronine, which regulate the basal metabolic rate of the body, and calcitonin, which lowers blood calcium levels. Disorders associated with the thyroid may result from either underactivity (hypothyroidism) or overactivity (hyperthyroidism) of the gland.

KEY CONCEPTS

- calcitonin
- endocrine glands
- goiter
- hyperthyroidism
- hypothyroidism
- metabolism
- pituitary gland
- thyroid-stimulating hormone (TSH)
- thyroxine
- triiodothyronine

INTRODUCTION

The thyroid gland is the largest endocrine gland in the human body. It is located on the upper portion of the trachea (windpipe) near the junction between the larynx (voice box) and the trachea. The thyroid gland is made up of a right lobe and a left lobe, which are joined by a narrow band of tissue called the isthmus, which lies across the trachea.

The thyroid gland is classified as an endocrine gland because it is made up of epithelial cells which are specialized for the production and secretion of specific hormones. Hormones produced by endocrine glands are specialized organic molecules that regulate biological activity by affecting certain cells of the body called target cells. Once the hormones have been produced by the gland, they are released into the bloodstream and carried by the blood throughout the body. The target cells have receptors on their surfaces to which the hormones attach; attachment of the hormone initiates cellular activities that lead to the observed effects of the hormone on body processes.

Internally, the thyroid gland is composed of hollow groups of cells called follicles. The cells are bound together by connective tissue and surround an inner region which contains a protein substance called colloid. It is in the colloid that the hormones produced by the thyroid gland are stored until their release into the bloodstream. The thyroid gland is different from all other endocrine glands in this respect, since the other endocrine glands of the human body store their hormones within the cells of the gland.

The thyroid gland produces the hormones triiodothyronine (T_3), thyroxine (tetraiodothyronine or T_4), and calcitonin. Triiodothyronine and thyroxine contain iodine, which is obtained from the diet and actively taken up from the bloodstream by the follicle cells. Within the follicle cells, iodine is attached to an amino acid called tyrosine to form a molecule called monoiodotyrosine (MIT). A second iodine may then be attached to form diiodotyrosine (DIT). Thyroxine is produced by coupling two DIT molecules; triiodothyronine is produced by coupling an MIT with a DIT. The thyroid hormones thyroxine T_4 and T_3 are then stored extracellularly in the colloid surrounded by the ball of follicle cells. Normally the thyroid produces 10 percent T_3 and 90 percent T_4.

The release of thyroid hormones is controlled by the anterior lobe of the pituitary gland, a small pea-shaped gland located at the base of the brain. The pituitary gland produces a hormone known as thyrotropin, or thyroid-stimulating hormone (TSH),

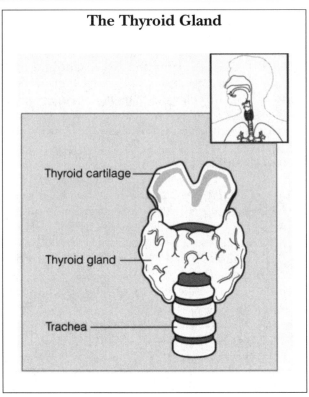

The Thyroid Gland

Thyroid cartilage

Thyroid gland

Trachea

(Hans & Cassidy, Inc.)

which controls the production and secretion of the thyroid hormones. The release of TSH from the anterior pituitary is in turn regulated by thyrotropin-releasing hormone (TRH), a hormone produced by the hypothalamus. TRH is transported by way of a capillary system to the anterior pituitary, where it stimulates the release of TSH. TSH then travels via the bloodstream to the thyroid, where it stimulates the production and release of the thyroid hormones. When the thyroid is stimulated by TSH to secrete its hormones, T_3 and T_4 are taken into the follicle cells from the colloid by a process called endocytosis. T_3 and T_4 then enter the bloodstream from the follicle cells. While traveling in the bloodstream, the thyroid hormones are bound to thyroid-binding globulin (TBG), a plasma protein. Once the hormones reach the target cells, most of the T_4 is converted to T_3, indicating that T_3 is the major active form of the thyroid hormones at the cellular level.

The thyroid hormones influence the metabolic rate of the body primarily by controlling the rate of cell respiration. Most tissues of the body are responsive to the influence of these hormones; exceptions include the testes, uterus, spleen, and brain. T_3 and T_4 cause a calorigenic effect on the body—they promote oxygen usage and heat production by the tissues. They promote the synthesis of proteins from amino acids and stimulate the synthesis, mobilization, and degradation of lipids. Thyroid hormones increase the utilization of carbohydrates, promoting their breakdown and the subsequent release of energy, and they increase the rate by which glucose is absorbed from the intestine. T_3 and T_4 promote the uptake of glucose from the blood by adipose tissue and muscle, and stimulate a process known as gluconeogenesis, whereby carbohydrates are produced from noncarbohydrate molecules. The effects of thyroid hormones on carbohydrate metabolism are modified by other hormones, especially insulin, epinephrine, and norepinephrine.

Although normal quantities of thyroid hormone stimulate the production of proteins, excessive amounts cause muscle wasting and weakness, especially in the heart and eye muscles. High levels of T_3 and T_4 also cause an increase in the breakdown of lipids and a decreased amount of cholesterol and phospholipids in the blood plasma.

In addition to T_3 and T_4, the thyroid produces and secretes calcitonin. This hormone is produced by parafollicular cells, which are located adjacent to the thyroid follicle cell. Structurally, calcitonin is a polypeptide made up of a chain of thirty-two amino acids. When calcitonin is released into the bloodstream, it primarily affects bone cells, causing them to increase bone formation and suppress bone resorption. As a result, the amount of calcium and phosphate in the blood is lowered. Release of calcitonin is regulated by the amount of calcium ions in the blood plasma; when the concentration of calcium increases, calcitonin production and secretion by the thyroid is stimulated. Some hormones released by the digestive tract during the digestion and absorption of food also promote the secretion of calcitonin from the thyroid. This aids the body's conservation of calcium from the diet by preventing a rapid surge in the amount of calcium in the blood, which could lead to increased excretion of calcium in the urine by the kidneys.

Thyroid dysfunction is a common endocrine condition which demonstrates neuropsychiatric symptoms. Both hyperthyroidism and hypothyroidism occur more often in women and can present with psychiatric symptoms including anxiety, depression, and psychosis.

HYPOTHYROIDISM

The psychiatric manifestations of hypothyroidism have been observed for nearly two hundred years. In 1873, British physician William Gull first described the neuropsychiatric manifestations of hypothyroidism and its characteristic clinical picture of mental and physical slowing. It was his fellow Briton William Ord who introduced the term "myxedema" in 1878 and postulated that the overall apathy, fatigue, and weariness of the patients was due to a "jelly-like" swelling of connective tissues. In the later part of nineteen century, the Clinical Society of London released a classic report which revealed that insanity, manifested by delusions and hallucinations, was seen in more than one-third of the 109 cases of myxedema. Dementia was also found in a significant number of patients, and mental slowing was noticed in all but 3 of 109 patients.

Hypothyroidism has an overall prevalence of 0.5 to 1.0 percent of the total population, increasing to 2 to 4 percent in the elderly. Overt hypothyroidism occurs in 2 percent of women compared with 0.1 percent percent of men. Many patients suffering from hypothyroidism frequently present with neuropsychiatric symptoms such as apathy, anxiety, suicidal ideation, depression, diminished libido, delusions, memory impairment, and overall slowing. These neuropsychiatric symptoms commonly manifest before the onset of other recognizable symptoms and signs of hypothyroidism—cold intolerance, husky voice, constipation, excessive menstrual bleeding, and muscle cramps, or dry, coarse skin, goiter, mild edema, and slow heart rate. A rapid onset of severe hypothyroidism is sometimes accompanied by delirium with psychotic features (myxedema madness). In most cases of hypothyroidism, the neuropsychiatric symptoms remit with appropriate replacement hormone resulting in euthyroidism. There is evidence that in some patients with long-standing hypothyroidism, neuronal death may occur and resulting in persistence of neuropsychiatric manifestations even after adequate hormonal replacement.

More controversial, less well understood, and far more easily missed is the diagnosis of subclinical hypothyroidism, which is more common in women. Subclinical forms of hypothyroidism may present with few if any nonpsychiatric signs or symptoms. In one study, the researchers found that the prevalence of depression is three times higher among those with subclinical hypothyroidism compared to those with normal thyroid function. In the psychiatric populations, one should not forget that lithium, used in the treatment of mania, could well cause hypothyroidism.

In women, thyroid dysfunction has been described during pregnancy, after childbirth or abortion, before menstruation and at menopause. Hypothyroidism is more common in women after delivery and may cause a constellation of symptoms resembling major depressive disorder. Researchers have found a positive correlation between postpartum depression and postpartum thyroiditis, a frequently recognized thyroid disorder among women after the childbirth. Postpartum thyroiditis (as defined by the presence of thyroid autoantibodies) is caused by the combination of heightened immune activity, postpartum, in at-risk individuals. One study found that 38 percent of the women with postpartum thyroiditis experienced either major or minor depression as compared with 9.5 percent of women in a matched control group. Hence it is important to recognize postpartum depression and exclude any organic disease. In the absence of universal screening, numerous cases of thyroid disorders including the thyroiditis will remain undiagnosed and untreated.

HYPERTHYROIDISM

Caleb Parry, a physician at the health resort of Bath, England, first described hyperthyroid state in 1835, attributing the condition to traumatic fear. In 1835, Irish physician Robert Graves also suggested that a patient's psychological state could play a role in the development of hyperthyroidism, linking it in particular to globus hystericus in women. Since then the relationship between psychological state and hyperthyroidism has gained much attention in the scientific community. Graves' disease, an autoimmune disorder, is more common in women. In Graves' disease, an autoantibody to the thyroid stimulating hormone receptor on the thyroid follicular cell causes stimulation of the receptor and eventually thyrotoxicosis.

Many common symptoms of hyperthyroidism are behavioral—such as nervousness, irritability, restlessness, insomnia, mood lability, and poor attention—and could mislead a clinician into making a diag-

nosis of anxiety or mood disorder, or even stimulant intoxication. In general, the presentation is similar to that seen in agitated depression, panic disorder, and anxiety states. Interestingly, the hyperthyroid patient may show several symptoms of anxiety or depression but may not report feeling dysphoric or anxious. Frequently, the behavioral and psychiatric manifestations of hyperthyroidism lead patients to seek medical attention. In the rare form of thyrotoxicosis, the "thyroid storm," the psychiatric features may be more marked and include psychosis and profound agitation. Many of the neuropsychiatric complaints of hyperthyroidism are probably due to the central effects of thyroid hormones. Several of the neuropsychiatric features appear to be consistent with prefrontal lobe dysfunction.

In the elderly individuals who suffer from the apathetic form of thyrotoxicosis, features of depression and severe slowing of mental and bodily activities predominate and such a clinical picture may be mistaken for a major depression. When hyperthyroidism is suspected, clinical clues that include heat intolerance, diaphoresis, warm skin, weight loss (despite increased appetite), palpitations, and faster heart rates are helpful to establish the clinical diagnosis. However, the biochemical thyroid function tests help to confirm the diagnosis.

Hyperthyroidism can exacerbate chronic psychotic disorders or precipitate manic episodes in susceptible individuals. Psychotic patients may poorly communicate common hallmark signs and symptoms of hyperthyroidism, thereby further obscuring the diagnosis. One should be aware of transient elevations of thyroid hormone levels, which have been reported, especially at the height of psychiatric illness or at the time of hospitalization. This possibility of false-positive results from laboratory testing makes diagnosis of hyperthyroidism especially difficult in psychiatric populations.

In most patients successful treatment of the hyperthyroidism itself is effective in reducing the neuropsychiatric symptoms. Sometimes beta-blockers in conjunction with antithyroid medications ameliorate many of the symptoms of anxiety. Adjunctive antipsychotic therapy may pose risks. Tricyclic antidepressant medications may increase the risk of central toxicity. Lithium is generally avoided in Graves' disease because of the possibility of exacerbating the exophthalmos. Haloperidol has been found to result in neurotoxicity and possibly the initiation of thyroid storm. However, some of the neurocognitive deficits may be irreversible inpatients with long-standing hyperthyroidism.

In summary, thyroid disorders are important endocrine abnormalities that are common in women and frequently present with neuropsychiatric symptoms. It is important to realize that many of the neuropsychiatric manifestations of both hypothyroid and hyperthyroid states are reversible if the underlying thyroid disturbance is diagnosed and treated in a timely manner.

SOURCES FOR FURTHER STUDY

Braverman, Lewis E., and Robert D. Utiger. *Werner and Ingram's "The Thyroid: A Fundamental and Clinical Text."* 8th ed. Philadelphia: Lippincott, Williams & Wilkins, 2001. Compiles information regarding the thyroid from many diverse sources. The book is designed for clinical as well as laboratory use. The text is thorough and detailed, suitable for college students. Extensive reference sections are provided at the end of each chapter.

Corbett, Nancy Sickles. "The Endocrine System." In *Hole's Human Anatomy and Physiology.* 9th ed. Boston: McGraw-Hill, 2001. Presents a well-organized discussion of the endocrine glands, including pertinent information on clinical aspects (such as pathological disorders) and laboratory techniques associated with each gland. The text is suitable for high school and college students, as the writing is easy to read and rather informal.

Fox, Stuart I. "The Endocrine System." In *Perspectives on Human Biology.* Boston: McGraw-Hill, 1991. This textbook is an excellent source for introductory biology information. Student aids such as chapter outlines, lists of objectives, and keys to pronunciation are included as well as clinical and practical applications of the material presented. Illustrations are outstanding.

Larson, David E., ed. *Mayo Clinic Family Health Book.* 2d ed. New York: William Morrow, 1996. Excellent text on human diseases and disorders; includes symptoms, diagnosis, treatment, and medication. The authors explain concepts clearly. Can be readily understood by high school and college students.

Stern, A. Robert, and Arthur J. Prange. "Neuropsychiatric Aspects of Endocrine Disorders." In *Kaplan and Sadock's Comprehensive Textbook of Psychiatry,* edited by Benjamin J. Sadock and Virginia A. Sadock. 7th ed. 2 vols. Philadelphia: Lippincott, Williams & Wilkins, 2000. An exhaustive reference for medical and psychological professionals.

Debra Zehner;
updated by Krishna Bhaskarabhatla and
Kausalya Chennapragada

SEE ALSO: Adrenal gland; Endocrine system; Hormones and behavior; Nervous system; Pituitary gland; Stress: Physiological responses.

Touch and pressure

TYPE OF PSYCHOLOGY: Sensation and perception
FIELDS OF STUDY: Auditory, chemical, cutaneous, and body senses

Receptors of touch and pressure are mechanoreceptors that convert mechanical energy into the electrical energy of nerve impulses. Touch receptors detect objects coming into light contact with the body surface and allow a person to reconstruct the size, shape, and texture of objects even if they are unseen; pressure receptors detect heavier contacts, weights, or forces and provide a sense of the position of body parts.

KEY CONCEPTS
- adaptation
- expanded-tip tactile receptor
- free nerve ending
- hair end organ
- mechanoreceptor
- Meissner's corpuscle
- Pacinian corpuscle
- proprioception
- Ruffini's end organ
- somatic sensory cortex

INTRODUCTION
The human body is supplied with an abundance of sensory receptors that detect touch and pressure. These receptors are members of a larger group called mechanoreceptors; they are able to detect energy in mechanical form and convert it to the energy of nerve impulses. Mechanoreceptors occur both on body surfaces and in the interior, and they

detect mechanical stimuli throughout the body. Touch receptors are located over the entire body surface; pressure receptors are located only under the skin and in the body interior. The two sensations are closely related. A very light pressure on the body surface is sensed by receptors in the skin and is felt as touch. As the pressure increases, mechanoreceptors in and immediately below the skin and at deeper levels are stimulated, and the sensation is felt as pressure.

TYPES OF MECHANORECEPTORS

Several different types of mechanoreceptors are located in the skin and primarily detect touch. One type, known as free nerve endings, consists simply of branched nerve endings without associated structures. Although located primarily in the skin, some mechanoreceptors of this type are also found to a limited extent in deeper tissues, where they detect pressure.

A second mechanoreceptor type, termed Meissner's corpuscles, consists of a ball of nerve endings enclosed within a capsulelike layer of cells. These mechanoreceptors, which are exquisitely sensitive to the lightest pressure, occur in nonhairy regions of the skin, such as the lips and fingertips.

A third mechanoreceptor type, the expanded-tip tactile receptor, occurs in the same nonhairy regions as Meissner's corpuscles and, in smaller numbers, in parts of the skin that are covered with hair. These mechanoreceptors often occur in clusters that are served by branches of the same sensory nerve cell. Meissner's corpuscles and the expanded-tip tactile receptors, working together in regions such as the fingertips, are primarily responsible for a person's ability to determine the size, surface texture, and other tactile features of objects touched.

A fourth type of mechanoreceptor consists of a network of nerve endings surrounding the root of a hair. The combined nerve-hair root structure, called a hair end organ, is stimulated when body hairs are displaced. These mechanoreceptors, because hairs extend from the body surface, give an early warning that the skin of a haired region of the body is about to make contact with an object. The remaining mechanoreceptors of this group are located in deeper regions of the body; because of their location, they detect pressure rather than touch.

Pacinian corpuscles, which occur just under the skin and in deeper regions of the body, consist of a

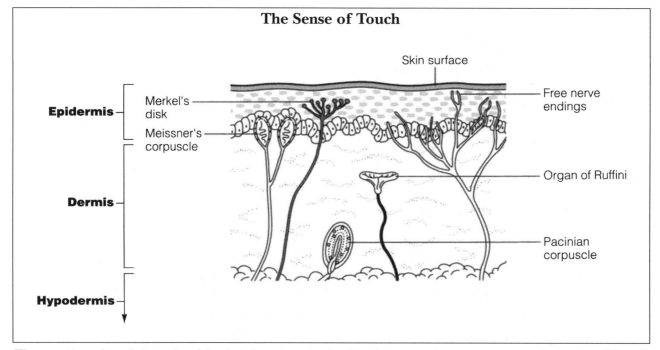

The sensation of touch is produced by special receptors in the skin that respond to temperature and pressure. (Hans & Cassidy, Inc.)

single sensory nerve ending buried inside a fluid-filled capsule. The capsule is formed by many layers of connective tissue cells, which surround the nerve ending in concentric layers, much like the successive layers of an onion. Pressure displaces the capsule and deforms its shape; the deforming pressure is transmitted through the capsule fluid to the surface of the sensory nerve ending. In response, the sensory nerve generates nerve impulses.

The remaining type of pressure receptor, Ruffini's end organ, consists of a highly branched group of nerve endings enclosed in a capsule. These mechanoreceptors occur below the skin, in deeper tissues, and in the connective tissue capsules surrounding the joints. They detect heavy pressures on the body that are transmitted to deeper layers, and, through their locations in the joints, contribute to proprioception—the sense of the position of the body's limbs.

The various types of mechanoreceptors are believed to convert mechanical energy into the electrical energy of nerve impulses by essentially the same mechanism. In some manner, as yet incompletely understood, the mechanical forces deforming the cell membranes of sensory nerve endings open channels in the membranes to the flow of ions. The ions, which are electrically charged particles, produce the electrical effects responsible for generating nerve impulses.

MECHANORECEPTOR ADAPTATION

The different mechanoreceptor types exhibit the phenomenon of adaptation to varying degrees. In adaptation, the number of nerve impulses generated by a sensory receptor drops off with time if the stimulus remains constant. In the Pacinian corpuscle, for example, which is highly adaptive, adaptation results from flow of the capsule fluid. If pressure against the corpuscle is held at steady levels, deforming the capsule in one direction, the fluids inside the capsule flow in response to relieve the pressure. The new fluid distribution compensates for the applied pressure, and the nerve impulses generated by the Pacinian corpuscle drop in frequency. Any change in the pressure, however, is transmitted through the fluid to the sensory nerve ending before the fluid has a chance to shift in response. As a result, a new volley of nerve impulses is fired by the sensory neuron on a change of pressure until the fluid in the corpuscle shifts again to com-

pensate for the new pressure. In Pacinian corpuscles, compensating movements of the fluid take place within hundredths or even thousandths of a second. Meissner's corpuscles and the hair end organs also adapt quickly.

The expanded-tip tactile receptors and Ruffini's end organs adapt significantly more slowly than the other mechanoreceptors. Expanded-tip tactile receptors adapt initially to a steady touch or pressure, but reach a base level at which they continue to generate nerve impulses under steady pressure. The Ruffini's end organs adapt only to a limited extent. The continuing nerve impulses arriving from these mechanoreceptors provide continuous monitoring of a constant stimulus. Thus, some of the mechanoreceptors are specialized to detect changes in touch or pressure and some to keep track of constant stimuli.

MECHANOSENSORY ABILITIES

The combined effects of touch and pressure receptors, along with the varying degrees of adaptation of different receptor types, allow the detection of a range of stimuli, varying from the lightest, most delicate, glancing touch, through moderate pressures, to heavy pressures that stimulate both the body surfaces and interior. People can explore the surface, texture, and shape of objects and can interpret the various levels of touch and pressure so well that they can reconstruct a mental image of objects touched by the fingers with their eyes closed.

Much of this mechanosensory ability depends on the degree to which the different receptor types adapt. The rapid adaptation of Meissner's corpuscles and the hair end organs explains why, if a steady, light to moderate pressure (not heavy enough to cause pain) is maintained on the body surface, the sensation of pressure quickly diminishes. If the pressure is heavy enough to cause pain, a person continues to be aware of the painful sensation, because pain receptors are very slow to adapt. If the degree or location of the pressure is altered, a person again becomes acutely aware of the pressure.

Awareness of continued touch depends primarily on the expanded-tip tactile receptors, which initially adapt but then continue to send nerve impulses when a light surface pressure is held constant. This allows a person to continue to be aware, for example, that some part of the body surface is touching an object. The limited adaptation of Ruffini's corpuscles keeps a person aware of stronger pressures that are felt deeply in the body. Through their locations in joints, these slow-adapting mechanoreceptors also help keep a person continually aware of the positions of the limbs.

The sensory effects of the fast-and slow-adapting mechanoreceptors can be demonstrated by a simple exercise such as pinching the skin on the back of the hand with a steady pressure only strong enough to cause slight pain. The feeling of pressure dissipates rapidly; however, one remains aware of the touch and pain. The rapid dissipation of the sensation of pressure is caused by the fast adaptation of Meissner's corpuscles and any Pacinian corpuscles that may have been stimulated. Some degree of touch sensation is maintained, however, by residual levels of nerve impulses sent by the expanded-tip tactile receptors. The sensation of pain continues at almost steady levels because, in contrast to most of the mechanoreceptors, pain receptors adapt very little. If the pressure is released, the pain stops, and another intense sensation of pressure is felt as all the receptor types fire off a burst of nerve impulses in response to the change.

Mechanoreceptors located at deeper levels keep a person constantly aware of the positions of body parts and the degree of extension of the limbs with respect to the trunk. Ruffini's and Pacinian corpuscles located within the connective tissue layers covering the bones, and within the capsules surrounding the joints, keep track of the angles made by the bones as they are pulled to different positions by the muscles. Ruffini's and Pacinian corpuscles are among the most important mechanoreceptors keeping track of these movements.

MUSCLE SPINDLES AND GOLGI TENDON ORGANS

Touch and pressure receptors represent only a part of the body's array of mechanoreceptors. Other mechanoreceptors located more deeply in the body help monitor the position of body parts and detect the degree of stretch of body cavities.

In addition to the Ruffini's and Pacinian corpuscles detecting the positions of the bones and joints, two further types of mechanoreceptors constantly track the tension developed by the muscles moving the limbs. One is buried within the muscle itself, and one is in the tendons connecting the muscles to the bones. The mechanoreceptors buried within muscles, called muscle spindles, consist of a special-

ized bundle of five to twelve small muscle cells enclosed within a capsule of connective tissue. Sensory nerve endings surround the muscle cells in a spiral at the midpoint of the capsule and also form branched endings among the muscle cells of the capsule. Because of their position within the muscle spindle, the nerve endings are stretched, and generate nerve impulses, when the surrounding muscle tissue contracts.

The mechanoreceptors of tendons, called Golgi tendon organs, are formed by nerve endings that branch within the fibrous connective tissue cells forming a tendon. The nerve endings of Golgi tendon organs detect both stretch and compression of the tendon as the muscles connected to them move and place tension on the limbs. The combined activities of the deeply located mechanoreceptors keep a person aware of posture, stance, and positions of the limbs. They also allow a person to perform feats such as bringing the thumbs or fingers together behind the back, or touching the tip of the nose with the forefinger with the eyes closed.

SOMATIC SENSES

Mechanoreceptors are one of five different types of sensory receptors that also include thermoreceptors, which detect changes in the flow of heat to or from the body; nociceptors, which detect tissue damage and whose nerve impulses are integrated and perceived in the brain as pain; chemoreceptors, which detect chemicals in locations such as the tongue, where they are responsible for the sense of taste, and in the nasal cavity, where they contribute to the sense of smell; and photoreceptors, which detect light. The mechanoreceptors, thermoreceptors, and nociceptors together form what are known as the somatic or body senses.

Sensory nerve tracts originating from mechanoreceptors, particularly those arising from the body surfaces, and their connecting neurons within the spinal cord and the brain are held in highly organized register with one another. Sensory fibers and their connecting nerves originating from the hand, for example, are located in a position near those originating from the wrist. In the cerebral cortex, the organization is retained, so that there is a projection of the body parts over a part of the cerebrum called the somatic sensory cortex. In this region, which occupies a band running from the top to the lower sides of the brain along anterior segments of the parietal lobes, segments corresponding to major body parts trace out a distorted image of the body from the top of the brain to the sides, with the genitalia, feet, and legs at the top, the arms and hands at the middle region, and the head, lips, tongue, and teeth at the bottom. Sensory information from the right side of the body is received and integrated in the somatic sensory cortex on the left side of the brain, and information from the left side of the body is received and integrated on the right side of the brain. The area of the somatic sensory cortex integrating signals from various body regions depends on the numbers of touch and other sensory receptors in the body regions. The lips and fingers, for example, which are generously supplied with sensory receptors, are represented by much larger areas in the somatic sensory cortex than the arms and legs. Reception and integration of signals in the somatic sensory cortex are partly under conscious control; a person can direct attention to one body part or another and concentrate on the signals arriving from the selected region. The activities of touch, pressure, and other sensory receptors, integrated and interpreted in the somatic sensory cortex, supply people's link to the world around them and supply the information people require to survive and interact with the environment.

SOURCES FOR FURTHER STUDY

Berne, Robert M., and Matthew N. Levy, eds. *Physiology*. 4th ed. St. Louis: C. V. Mosby, 1998. The chapter on the somatosensory system in this standard college physiology text outlines the anatomy and physiology of the cells and nerve tracts in the spinal column and brain involved in the sensation of temperature and other body sensations. Although the text is intended for students at the college level, it is clearly written and should be accessible to high school readers.

Coren, Stanley. *Sensation and Perception*. 5th ed. Pacific Grove, Calif.: International Thomson, 1999. This simply written text provides an easily understood discussion of the senses, sensory cells, and the routes traveled by sensory information through the spinal cord to the brain. A clear and interesting description is provided of the basics of perception in the cerebral cortex.

Guyton, Arthur C., and John E. Hall. *Textbook of Medical Physiology*. 10th ed. Philadelphia: W. B. Saunders, 2000. Chapter 50, "Somatic Sensations

II: Pain, Visceral Pain, Headache, and Thermal Sensations," in this readable and clearly written text includes an excellent discussion of thermoreceptors, the role of the hypothalamus in regulation of body temperature, and medical implications of fever, hyperthermia, and hypothermia. Chapter 48, "Sensory Receptors and Their Basic Mechanisms of Action," provides a general description of the structure and function of receptors. Although intended for college and medical students, the text can be easily understood by readers at the high school level.

Schmidt-Nielsen, Knut. *Animal Physiology: Adaptation and Environment*. New York: Cambridge University Press, 1997. This standard college text, by one of the greatest animal physiologists, provides a deeply perceptive comparison of sensory systems in humans and other animals. Chapters 6 and 7 describe temperature effects and temperature regulation. The text is remarkable for its lucid and entertaining descriptions of animal physiology.

Stephen L. Wolfe

SEE ALSO: Hearing; Neurons; Sensation and perception; Senses; Signal detection theory; Smell and taste; Temperature; Visual system.

Tourette's syndrome

TYPE OF PSYCHOLOGY: Psychopathology
FIELDS OF STUDY: Nervous system, organic disorders

Tourette's syndrome is a neurologic disorder which is characterized by motor tics of the face, head, and other extremities. The onset of the disorder is in childhood, with most patients developing symptoms before twenty-one years of age. The syndrome is not a progressive disorder and symptoms seem to appear and disappear during the patient's lifetime. Symptoms are usually controlled quite effectively with the use of a drug or a combination of drugs. Haloperidol is the single most effective medication.

KEY CONCEPTS
• attention-deficit hyperactivity disorder (ADHD)
• coprolalia

- copropraxia
- echolalia
- incomplete penetrance
- multiple tics
- obsessive-compulsive disorder
- variable expressivity

INTRODUCTION

Tourette's syndrome is named for Gilles de la Tourette, the French physician who described the syndrome extensively in 1885. Tourette described many of the symptoms that are still associated with the syndrome, including multiple tics, echolalia (the repetition of what is said by other people as if the patient was producing an echo of their speech), and coprolalia (the use of obscene and vulgar language, often in a sexual context). The syndrome is considered to be rare, with a rate of perhaps 1 in 2,500 (0.4 percent), but accurate estimates are difficult because of the variability of expression of the condition in different individuals and the occurrence of multiple tics due to other causes. The incidence of Tourette's syndrome is ten times higher in children than in adults. A similar discrepancy is found in the incidence of Tourette's syndrome in males and females, with three to four times more males than females having the condition in adulthood, but nine to ten times more males than females being affected in childhood.

The onset of Tourette's syndrome usually occurs in childhood, with some patients developing symptoms before entering school, even as early as two years of age, and the majority of patients showing signs during the early to middle school years. One of the first signs occurs when a previously attentive, "good" student appears to lose focus and has difficulty paying attention in class. Most people affected with Tourette's syndrome develop features before twenty-one years of age.

Although the basis of genetics and inheritance was not known at the time the syndrome was characterized in 1885, Tourette described symptoms in multiple members of a single family. The genetic basis of Tourette's syndrome is still not completely understood, but family studies have indicated that biological relatives of patients appear to have significantly greater risk of developing the syndrome than do relatives of unaffected persons.

Although there is no cure yet for Tourette's syndrome, medications have been found to be useful in reducing tics and some of the associated abnormal behaviors.

CLINICAL FEATURES

The American Psychiatric Association's *Diagnostic and Statistic Manual of Mental Disorders: DSM-IV-TR* (rev. 4th ed., 2000) lists the diagnostic criteria for Tourette's syndrome. Both multiple motor and one or more vocal tics have been present at some time during the illness, although not necessarily concurrently. The tics occur many times during a day (usually in bouts), nearly every day or intermittently throughout a period of more than a year. The anatomic location, number, frequency, complexity, and severity of the tics may change over time. Onset occurs before age eighteen. Occurrence is not exclusively during psychoactive substance intoxication or due to known central nervous system disease, such as Huntington chorea and postviral encephalitis.

The tics that are associated with Tourette's syndrome may be motor tics if movements are involved or they may be vocal tics if sound is produced. The syndrome commonly begins with facial tics such as blinking, grimacing, and nose twitching. Other involuntary movements may involve head shaking, arm flapping, and foot movements. Head-banging and other forms of self-abuse may occur. Tics may be simple and involve relatively simple motors—eye blinking, for example—or they may be complex and involve a number of muscle groups—jumping up and down, for example, or imitating movements of another person. It is likely that simple tics over time will be replaced by complex tics, and there is also a tendency for the severity and frequency of tics to wax and wane over time. Tics tend to worsen under conditions of stress and tend to subside when the patient is concentrating on some task or activity. Some people with Tourette's syndrome have been able to have successful careers as actors and professional athletes.

The most severe aspects of Tourette's syndrome, from a social point of view, are coprolalia and copropraxia. Although it is a common conception, it is not correct to think that coprolalia and copropraxia (an involuntary use of obscene gestures) are found in nearly all people with Tourette's syndrome. In fact, coprolalia is found in less than one-third of the cases and copropraxia is far less common. Attention-deficit hyperactivity disorder (ADHD) and obsessive-compulsive disorder also may be associated with Tourette's syndrome, but the exact cause of the relationship is not known.

Although Tourette's syndrome is a chronic disorder, symptoms are usually much more severe in childhood and tend to improve or disappear entirely in more than half of affected adults.

ETIOLOGY

The cause of Tourette's syndrome is not known. The syndrome is classified with other disorders that have involuntary movements as a major feature, such as Huntington's disease. For much of its history, Tourette's syndrome was considered primarily a psychiatric disorder because of the bizarre forms of the motor and vocal tics and other bizarre behaviors often associated with the syndrome. Psychiatric comorbidity does appear to be a primary feature of Tourette's syndrome, but it is often a secondary consequence of the emotionally disabling physical features. As effective treatment with medications came into use, it became apparent that there was an underlying biochemical basis for the syndrome. The drug haloperidol, which is a dopamine receptor blocker, gave good results in controlling tics, indicating that somehow there was an increased sensitivity of the dopamine system in patients with Tourette's syndrome. Other studies have found some evidence of subtle structural abnormalities in the basal ganglia of the brain. There have been surprisingly few autopsies to study Tourette's syndrome patients. Both gross and fine anatomical studies have not yielded conclusive findings, but results indicate that multiple structures of the brain may be involved in the syndrome.

Although a familial association of Tourette's syndrome has long been known, two problems have contributed to the difficulty of genetic studies: the problem of variable expressivity, and the problem of incomplete penetrance. With variable expressivity, there is a range of phenotypes resulting from a given genotype, and this is very characteristic of Tourette's syndrome, where clinical features range from very mild to very severe. In incomplete penetrance, a genotype that should give rise to a certain expression or phenotype is not expressed at all, and

---

DSM-IV-TR Criteria for Tourette's Syndrome

TOURETTE'S DISORDER (DSM CODE 307.23)

Both multiple motor and one or more vocal tics (sudden, rapid, recurrent, nonrhythmic, stereotyped motor movements or vocalizations) at some time during the disorder, although not necessarily concurrently

Tics occur many times a day (usually in bouts) nearly every day or intermittently throughout a period of more than one year; during this period, no tic-free periods of more than three consecutive months

Onset before age eighteen

Disturbance not due to direct physiological effects of a substance (such as stimulants) or a general medical condition (such as Huntington's disease or postviral encephalitis)

---

this seems to be true of Tourette's syndrome also. In addition, there is no universal agreement as to what is the Tourette syndrome phenotype. In spite of the limitations, considerable progress has been made in the understanding of the inheritance of Tourette's syndrome.

The agreement between Tourette's syndrome exhibited by both members of monozygotic twins is about 50 percent, compared to 10 percent for dizygotic twins. Since the value for monozygotic twins is less than 100 percent, this indicates also that nongenetic and environmental factors play a role in etiology.

Most family studies indicate that Tourette's syndrome is probably due to an autosomal dominant gene with incomplete penetrance. Although simple tics do not seem to have a familial relationship, severe tics do show such a relationship, with relatives of a patient being at an increased risk for tics, if not necessarily severe tics. Relatives of patients also are at increased risks for ADHD and obsessive-compulsive disorder, indicating a possible genetic relationship of the disorders. Although the human genome has been scanned, no single gene has been found that is associated with Tourette's syndrome.

TREATMENT

No medication has been found to eliminate the symptoms of Tourette's syndrome completely. Good progress has been made in using medications in controlling and improving motor and vocal tics and some of the behavioral symptoms. Haloperidol acts as a depressant of the central nervous system and is successful in helping to suppress symptoms in many patients. Side effects of haloperidol include drowsiness and alterations in mood and may be severe enough to limit its use. Also, the effectiveness of haloperidol tends to diminish over time in many patients. Other drugs in use may have fewer side effects than haloperidol, but all drugs may have side effects. If behavioral disorders such as obsessive-compulsive symptoms and ADHD present problems, other medications may need to be prescribed.

Since the symptoms of Tourette's syndrome may change over time, it is critical to monitor the levels of medications employed. It cannot be overemphasized that since Tourette's syndrome is such a chronic and potentially a socially debilitating disorder, supportive psychotherapy should be available not only for patients but for their families as well. Until the inheritance of Tourette's syndrome is understood more fully, genetic counseling will continue to be difficult. General information about recurrence risks and gender differences in the incidence of Tourette's syndrome may be transmitted. It also is essential to inform family members and patients of the variability of expression of the disorder in different patients and how symptoms may change over time in the same individual.

SOURCES FOR FURTHER STUDY

Brunn, Ruth Davling, and Bertel Brunn. *A Mind of Its Own: Tourette's Syndrome, a Story and a Guide.* New York: Oxford University Press, 1994. The authors present the symptoms, diagnosis, biochemistry, genetics, and treatment of Tourette's syndrome. The book is directed toward patients and their families and is enhanced by utilization of a composite case history.

Hayden, Michael R., and Berry Kremer. "Basal Ganglia Disorders." In *Emery and Rimoin's Principles and Practice of Medical Genetics*, edited by David L. Rimoin, J. Michael Connor, and Reed E. Pyeritz. 3d ed. New York: Churchill Livingstone Press, 1996. This is an excellent review article of basal ganglia disorders that involve involuntary movement syndromes. In addition to Tourette's syndrome, the article has basic information on other syndromes including Parkinson's disease, Huntington's disease, and dystonias.

Hyde, Thomas M., and Daniel R. Weinberger. "Tourette's Syndrome: A Model Neuropsychiatric Disorder." *The Journal of the American Medical Association* 273, no. 6 (1995): 498-501. An overview of Tourette's syndrome with useful information on a case report, genetics, environmental-genetic interactions, and treatment.

Kushner, Howerd I. *A Cursing Brain? The Histories of Tourette Syndrome.* Cambridge, Mass.: Harvard University Press, 1999. The book examines the history of Tourette's syndrome with exceptionally interesting historical details. There is information concerning the etiology, progression, and treatment of the disorder from the nineteenth century up to the 1980's.

Leckman, James F., and Donald J. Cohen, eds. *Tourette's Syndrome—Tics, Compulsions: Developmental Psychopathology and Clinical Care.* New York: John Wiley & Sons, 1999. A useful book for doctors, students, and families of persons affected with Tourette's syndrome. The book combines basic information and clinical care from neurobiological, developmental, and psychodynamic perspectives.

Rubio, Gwyn Hyman. *Icy Sparks.* New York: Viking Press, 2001. This book is a fictional account of a ten-year-old girl with Tourette's syndrome. The plot of the story is interesting, and the author does an excellent job of describing the physical and emotional problems faced by a young person growing up with the syndrome.

Donald J. Nash

SEE ALSO: Brain structure; Nervous system; Obsessive-compulsive disorder; Parkinson's disease.

Transactional analysis

TYPE OF PSYCHOLOGY: Psychotherapy
FIELDS OF STUDY: Cognitive therapies; humanistic therapies; interpersonal relations

Transactional analysis (TA) is a school of psychotherapy and personality theory. Many of TA's key concepts, such as therapeutic contracts, games, and life scripts, have been accepted in the general psychotherapy community.

KEY CONCEPTS
- adult
- child

- decision
- ego state
- games
- life script
- parent
- racket
- stroke

INTRODUCTION

Transactional analysis (TA) is a theory of personality and social interaction originated by Eric Berne in the mid-1950's. TA's popularity has been primarily as a form of psychotherapy and a method for improving social interactions between people in almost any setting—from the group therapy room to business and industry. Berne rejected psychoanalytic therapy, which he considered a type of game called "archaeology," in favor of his own short-term, action-oriented, commonsense approach to psychotherapy. Before entering a group psychotherapy session, Berne would ask himself, "How can I cure everyone in this room today?" In 1964, Berne's book *Games People Play* created a popular interest in a theory of personality and psychotherapy unequaled in the history of psychology; the book sold more than a million copies.

The basic concepts of transactional analysis describe an individual personality and the individual's repetitive patterns of interacting with others. Three distinct ego states compose the individual personality: "parent," "adult," and "child." Berne observed these as distinct phases in his patients' self-presentations. The child ego state within each individual is defined by the feeling, creative, and intuitive part within the person. The child ego state may be approval-seeking or defiant. The fun-loving or "free" side of the child state is curious, spontaneous, and impulsive. Parental discipline, when too harsh or inconsistent, often damages this spontaneous and free child; the adapted child is what then results. The adapted child can have a broken or rebellious spirit and may develop depression or addictions. In either case, the individual, authentic self becomes distorted because of an excessively compliant or defiant adaptation.

The adult ego state is objective and, in a sense, resembles a computer. The adult retrieves, stores, and processes data about physical and social reality. Problem solving and task-oriented behavior are the domain of the adult. If one were trying to build a bridge or do homework, the adult ego state would serve best; however, many problems require the assistance of the intuitive and creative child to be solved most effectively.

The parent ego state is an internalization of one's biological parents or other substitute authority figures in early childhood. The parent state judges, criticizes, and blames. This harsh side of the parent state is the critical parent. In contrast, Berne also recognized the nurturing parent that soothes, encourages, and gently supports the individual. The nurturing parent calls forth the free child, while the critical parent conditions the adapted child. The parent ego state is like a tape recording of the "do's and don'ts" of one's family of origin and culture; it may contain obsolete information. When in the parent state, one may point or shame with an extended index finger or disapproving scowl.

ROLE OF TRANSACTIONS

Transactions are basic units of analysis for the TA therapist. A transaction occurs when one individual responds to the behavior of another. Transactions are called complementary when both persons interact from compatible ego states. For example, a feverish child asks her parent for a glass of water, and the parent complies. A crossed transaction occurs when individuals in incompatible ego states interact. For example, a whining and hungry child asks a parent for an ice cream cone, and the parent (speaking from her adult ego state) reminds the child that it would not be nutritious. The child cannot incorporate the adult data. Another important type of transaction is the ulterior one. An ulterior transaction occurs when the spoken message is undercut by a hidden agenda. To exemplify this, Berne cited a cowboy who asks a woman to leave the dance and go look at the barn with him. The face value of his adult-to-adult question is subtly undercut by a child-to-child sexual innuendo.

Ulterior transactions, when not clearly understood by both parties, lead to "games." A game by definition is a social transaction in which either both or one member of the duo ends up feeling "bad." This bad feeling is experienced as a payoff by the game perpetrator; the game pays off by confirming the player's existential life position. For example, the game that Berne called "blemish" involves an existential life position of "I am not OK, you are not OK." In this game, the player exhaustively searches his or her partner for some defect, such as a personality quirk or physical imperfection. Once this defect or blemish is found, the player can hold it up as proof that others are not OK. One thus avoids examining one's own blemish while providing that "others are no good." An example of this can be seen in the chronic bachelor who cannot find a woman who measures up to his perfectionistic standards for marriage.

RACKET FEELINGS AND LIFE SCRIPTS

"Rackets" are the negative feelings that one experiences after a game. Racket feelings are chronic and originate in the early stroking patterns within one's family of origin. In the game of blemish, the player will ultimately feel lonely and sad, while the victim may feel hurt and rejected. Berne compared rackets to stamp collecting: When one collects ten books of brown stamps from playing blemish, they can be cashed in for a divorce or suicide.

Life scripts emerge through repetitive interactions with one's early environment. Messages about what to expect from others, the world, and self become ingrained. A script resembles an actor's role in a drama. An important outcome of one's early scripting is the basic decision one makes about one's existential position. Specifically, the basic identity becomes constellated around feelings of being either OK (free child) or not OK (adapted child). Coping strategies are learned that reinforce the basic decision. Life scripts can often be discovered by asking individuals about their favorite games, heroes, or stories from their childhood. Once individuals become aware of their life scripts, they can be presented with the option of changing them. If a script does not support a person's capacity to be an authentic winner in life, the TA therapist will confront it. TA holds that people are all born to win.

USE IN PSYCHOTHERAPY

Transactional analysis has been applied to the areas of individual and group psychotherapy, couples and family relationship problems, and communication problems within business organizations. This widespread application of TA should not be surprising, since TA's domain is wherever two human beings meet. Berne believed that the playing of games occurs everywhere, from the sandbox to the international negotiation table. Consequently, wherever de-structive patterns of behavior occur, TA can be employed to reduce dysfunctional transactions.

TA's most common application is in psychotherapy. The TA therapist begins by establishing a contract for change with his client. This denotes mutual responsibilities for both therapist and client and avoids allowing the client to assume a passive spectator role. The therapist also avoids playing the rescuer role. For example, Ms. Murgatroyd (Berne's favorite hypothetical patient name), an attractive thirty-two-year-old female, enters therapy because her boyfriend refuses to make the commitment to marry her. Her contract with the therapist and group might be that she either will receive a marriage commitment from her boyfriend or will end the relationship. As her specific games and life script are analyzed, this contract might undergo a revision in which greater autonomy or capacity for intimacy becomes her goal.

During the first session, the therapist observes the client's style of interacting. The therapist will be especially watchful of voice tone, gestures, and mannerisms and will listen to her talk about her current difficulties. Since games are chronic and stereotypical ways of responding, they will appear in the initial interview. For example, her dominant ego state might be that of a helpless, whining child looking for a strong parent to protect her. Ms. Murgatroyd may describe her boyfriend in such bitter and negative terms that it is entirely unclear why a healthy adult would want to marry such a man. Discrepancies of this sort will suggest that a tragic script may be operating.

During the first few interviews, the transactional analysis includes game and script analysis. This might require some information about Ms. Murgatroyd's early childhood fantasies and relationships with parents, but would eventually return to her present behavior and relationship. The early history would be used primarily to help the therapist and client gain insight into how these childhood patterns of interacting are currently manifesting. Once the games and script have been clearly identified, the client is in a much better position to change.

After several interviews, in which Ms. Murgatroyd's past and recent history of relationships is reviewed, a pattern of her being rejected is evident. She acknowledges that her existential position is "I am not OK, you are not OK." Her repeated selection of men who are emotionally unavailable maintains her racket feelings of loneliness and frustration. She begins to see how she puts herself in the role of victim. Armed with this new awareness, she is now in a position to change her script. Through the support of the therapist and group, Ms. Murgatroyd can learn to catch herself and stop playing the victim.

THERAPIST TECHNIQUES

Berne believed that the original script could best be changed in an atmosphere of openness and trust between the client and therapist. Hence the TA therapist will at all times display respect and concern for his or her client. At the appropriate time in therapy, the therapist delivers a powerful message to the client which serves to counteract the early childhood messages that originally instated the script. Ms. Murgatroyd's therapist, at the proper time, would decisively and powerfully counterscript her by telling her, "You have the right to intimacy!" or "You have the right to take care of yourself, even if it means leaving a relationship." Since the existential life position is supported by lifelong games and scripts, which resist change, TA therapists often employ emotionally charged ways of assisting a client's script redecision.

To catalyze script redecision, a client is guided back in time to the original scene where the destructive message that started the losing life script was received. Simply being told differently by a therapist is not always strong enough to create an emotionally corrective experience that will reverse a life script. Once in the early childhood scene, the client will spontaneously enter the child ego state, which is where the real power to change lies. This time, during the therapeutic regression, the choice will be different and will be for the authentic self.

Ms. Murgatroyd, who is struggling to change an early message, "Don't be intimate," needs to reexperience the feeling she had at the time she first received this message and accepted it from her adapted child ego state. In the presence of the therapist and group, she would role-play this early scene and would tell herself and the significant parent that she *does* have the right to be intimate. These words would probably be spoken amid tears and considerable emotional expression. The parent(s) would be symbolically addressed by her speaking to an empty chair in which she imagines her significant parent sitting: "Whether you like it or not, I'll

be intimate!" She would tell herself that it is OK to be intimate. This time she will make a new decision about her script based on her authentic wants and needs, rather than on faulty messages from early childhood. Ms. Murgatroyd's further TA work might involve new contracts with the therapist and group as she integrates her new script into her daily life.

INFLUENCES OF OTHER APPROACHES

The general thesis of TA that current behavior is premised on responses to emotional trauma of early childhood is generally agreed upon by most psychologists. Early life experience teaches people a script, a behavioral pattern, which they then repetitively act out in adulthood. Behavioral and humanistic schools alike recognize the formative role that early experiences play in adult behavior patterns; these ideas are not original to TA. TA's contribution is to have created a vocabulary that demystifies many of these ideas and provides a readily learned method of psychotherapy.

Transactional analysis evolved as a form of short-term psychotherapy beginning in the mid-1950's. Eric Berne's early work in groups as a major in the Army during World War II helped him identify the need for both group and short-term therapy. The human growth and potential movement of the 1960's added momentum to the transactional analysis approach. TA's recognition of the innate goodness of the free child prior to the damage of early parental injunctions and self-defeating scripts was consistent with the then-emerging humanistic schools of psychology. Berne began using TA as an adjunct to psychoanalysis, but he eventually rejected the psychoanalytic idea of the dynamic unconscious. Berne's move away from the unconscious and Freudian system paralleled developments in other schools of psychology. Both behavioral psychologists and the cognitive school wished to move away from what they saw as "depth psychology" fictions.

Most of the TA jargon and concepts can be readily seen to correspond to equivalent ones used by other psychologists. Sigmund Freud's constructs of the superego, ego, and id bear a noteworthy similarity to Berne's parent, adult, and child. The superego as the internalized voice of parental and societal values to regulate behavior nearly coincides with Berne's parent ego state. Freud's ego and the adult ego state similarly share the responsibility of solving the individual's problems with a minimum of emotional bias. Freud's id as the instinctual, spontaneous part of the personality shares many characteristics with Berne's child ego state.

Berne's concept of a game's "payoff" is clearly what the behaviorists call a reinforcer. The idea of scripts corresponds to the notion of family role or personality types in other personality theories. For example, an individual with a dominant child ego state would be labeled an orally fixated dependent type in Freudian circles.

INTEREST IN DYSFUNCTIONAL FAMILIES

The psychological role of dysfunctional families has become a topic of conversation for many nonspecialists. The explosion of twelve-step self-help groups has evidenced growing concern about America's mental health; the prominent role of shame and abandonment experiences in early childhood is receiving widespread interest. This surge of interest in making mental health services available to all society is a continuation of what TA practitioners pioneered. It is likely that future developments in the mental health field will draw upon the rich legacy of TA.

RESCRIPTING METHODS

Finally, pure transactional analysis as practiced by Berne in the 1960's right before his death has been modified by TA therapists who combine it with emotive and experiential techniques. Many TA therapists found that life scripts failed to change when their clients merely executed new adult decisions. Powerful therapeutic experiences in which the individual regresses and relives painful experiences were necessary. These enable the client to make script redecisions from the child ego state, which proved to be an effective source of change. Future TA therapists are likely to continue enhancing their methods of rescripting by eclectically drawing upon new methods of behavior change that go beyond traditional TA techniques. The intuitive child ego state, upon which TA therapists freely draw, promises creative developments in this school of psychotherapy.

SOURCES FOR FURTHER STUDY

Berne, Eric. *Games People Play.* 1964. Reprint. New York: Ballantine, 1996. A national bestseller that provides a highly readable introduction to the basic ideas of TA and games. Provides an interesting catalog of the most common games played in groups of many kinds. The reader will find that he or she can immediately apply the ideas contained here.

_____. *What Do You Say After You Say Hello?* New York: Grove Press, 1972. This is another excellent primary source for the reader who wants to apply TA to everyday life. Focuses on games and on Berne's final development of his script theory shortly before his death.

Corey, Gerald. *Theory and Practice of Counseling and Psychotherapy.* 6th ed. Belmont, Calif.: Wadsworth, 2000. TA is covered in a brief twenty-five pages but is treated with excellent scholarship. Ideal for the reader who would like a sound overview of TA before moving on to the particular works of Berne. A two-page bibliography is included.

Dusay, J., and K. Dusay. "Transactional Analysis." In *Current Psychotherapies*, edited by Raymond J. Corsini and Danny Wedding. 4th ed. Itasca, Ill.: Peacock, 1989. This forty-two-page article contains five pages of bibliography and is cowritten by a leading TA therapist and writer. Thorough and scholarly. The Dusays go into considerable depth in explaining Berne's ideas. Egograms, the drama triangle, and many more key TA concepts are excellently covered. Recommended for the reader who wants a serious introduction to TA.

Goulding, Mary McClure, and Robert L. Goulding. *Redecision Therapy.* Rev. ed. New York: Grove, 1997. This three-hundred-page book is written by the two therapists who pioneered the integration of TA with Gestalt therapy. Both Gouldings studied directly with Berne and Fritz Perls. An overview of TA, contracts, and stroking is covered. The clinical use of TA with depression, grieving, and establishing "no suicide contracts" is handled with many case examples and some transcripts of actual sessions. Recommended for the advanced student of TA.

James, Muriel, and Dorothy Jongeward. *Born to Win.* 1971. Reprint. Cambridge, Mass.: Perseus, 1996. Another TA work that became a best-seller. An optimistic and humanistic version of TA mixed with Gestalt experiments gives the reader a rich firsthand experience of TA. Contains many experiential and written exercises that enable readers to diagnose their own scripts and rackets. A practical program in how to apply the ideas of TA immediately to improve one's life is provided.

Paul August Rentz

SEE ALSO: Affiliation and friendship; Cognitive therapy; Ego, superego, and id; Existential psychology; Group therapy; Rational-emotive therapy; Self.

Type A behavior pattern

TYPE OF PSYCHOLOGY: Stress
FIELDS OF STUDY: Stress and illness

The Type A behavior pattern has been related to coronary artery disease; individuals who exhibit the Type A behavior pattern have been shown to be at a greater risk of coronary artery disease in some studies.

KEY CONCEPTS
- hard-driving behavior
- hurry sickness
- job involvement
- speed and impatience
- stress

INTRODUCTION

The Type A behavior pattern, often simply called the Type A personality, identifies behaviors which have been associated with coronary artery disease. Although these behaviors appear to be stress related, they are not necessarily involved with stressful situations or with the traditional stress response. Instead, the behaviors are based on an individual's thoughts, values, and approaches to interpersonal relationships. In general, Type A individuals are characterized as ambitious, impatient, aggressive, and competitive. Individuals who are not Type A are considered Type B. Type B individuals are characterized as relaxed, easygoing, satisfied, and noncompetitive.

Cardiologists Meyer Friedman and Ray H. Rosenman began work on the Type A behavior pattern in the mid-1950's. It was not until the completion of some retrospective studies in the 1970's, however, that the concept gained credibility. During the 1950's, it was noticed that younger and middle-aged people with coronary artery disease had several characteristics in common. These included a hard-driving attitude toward poorly defined goals; a continuous need for recognition and advancement; aggressive and at times hostile feelings; a desire for competition; an ongoing tendency to try to accomplish more in less time; a tendency to think and act faster and faster; and a high level of physical and mental alertness. These people were classified as "Pattern A" or "Type A."

CORRELATION TO HEART DISEASE

Following their work on identifying the characteristics of the Type A personality or behavior pattern, Friedman and Rosenman began conducting studies to determine if it might actually cause coronary artery disease. First they conducted several correlational studies to determine if there was a relationship between the Type A behavior pattern and metabolic function in humans. They found that healthy persons with the Type A behavior pattern had elevated levels of fat in the blood (serum cholesterol and triglycerides), decreased blood-clotting time, increased catecholamine secretion (which increases heart contractility) during normal work hours, and decreased blood flow to some tissues. These studies indicated that the Type A behavior pattern may precede coronary artery disease.

Following these studies, Friedman, Rosenman, and their research team initiated the Western Collaborative Group Study in 1960. This large study, which went on for more than eight years, attempted to determine if the presence of the Type A behavior pattern increased the risk of coronary artery disease. The results of Rosenman and Friedman's study in 1974 indicated that the subjects with the Type A pattern had more than twice the incidence of the disease than subjects with the Type B pattern. More specifically, Type A individuals (when compared to Type B individuals) were twice as likely to have a fatal heart attack, five times more likely to have a second heart attack, and likely to have more severe coronary artery disease (of those who died). These results were found when other known risk factors, such as high blood pressure, smoking, and diet, were held constant. This study was followed by numerous other studies which linked coronary artery disease to the Type A behavior pattern. In 1978, the National Heart, Lung, and Blood Institute sponsored a conference on the Type A behavior pattern. As a result of the Review Panel on Coronary-Prone Behavior and Coronary Heart Disease, a document was released in 1981 which stated that the Type A behavior pattern is related to increased risk of coronary artery disease.

IDENTIFYING TYPE A BEHAVIOR

Another product of the Western Collaborative Group Study was a method for assessing the Type A behavior pattern, developed by Rosenman in 1978. This method was based on a structured interview. A predetermined set of questions were asked of all participants. The scoring was based on the content of the participants' verbal responses as well as their nonverbal mannerisms, speech style, and behaviors during the interview process. The interview can be administered in fifteen minutes. Since the interview was not a traditional type of assessment, however, many interviewers had a difficult time using it.

In an effort to simplify the process for determining Type A behavior, many self-report questionnaires were developed. The first developed and probably the most-used questionnaire is the Jenkins Activity Survey, which was developed by C. David Jenkins, Stephen Zyzanski, and Rosenman in 1979. This survey is based on the structured interview. It gives a Type A score and three related subscores. The subscores include speed and impatience, hard driving, and job involvement. The Jenkins Activity Survey is a preferred method, because the questionnaire responses can be tallied to provide a quantitative score. Although this instrument is easy to use and provides consistent results, it is not considered as good as the structured interview because many believe the Type A characteristics can best be identified by observation.

The Type A behavior pattern continues to be studied, but research appears to have reached a peak in the late 1970's and early 1980's. Researchers are challenging the whole concept of coronary-prone behavior, because many clinical studies have not shown high correlations between the Type A behavior pattern and the progression of coronary artery disease. Other risk factors for coronary artery disease, such as smoking, high blood pressure, and high blood cholesterol, have received increasing attention.

BIOCHEMICAL AND PHYSIOLOGICAL MECHANISMS

The Type A behavior pattern, or personality, has been used to explain in part the risk of coronary artery disease; however, many risk factors for the disease have been identified. Since the various risk factors interact with one another, it is difficult to understand any one risk factor clearly.

Efforts have been made to explain the mechanism by which the Type A behavior pattern affects coronary artery disease. It has been theorized that specific biochemical and physiological events take place as a result of the emotions associated with Type A behavior. The neocortex and limbic system of the brain deliver emotional information to the hypothalamus. In a situation that arouses the Type A characteristics, the hypothalamus will cause the pituitary gland to stimulate the release of the catecholamines epinephrine and norepinephrine (also known as adrenaline and noradrenaline) from the adrenal glands, as well as other hormones from the pituitary itself. These chemicals will enter the blood and travel throughout the body, causing blood cholesterol and fat to increase, the ability to get rid of cholesterol to decrease, the ability to regulate blood sugar levels to decrease (as with diabetics), and the time for the blood to clot to increase. This response by the body to emotions is normal. The problem with Type A individuals arises because they tend to maintain this heightened emotional level almost continually, and the constant release of pituitary hormones results in these negative effects on the body being continuous as well.

The connection between Type A behavior and coronary artery disease actually results from the continuous release of hormones controlled by the pituitary gland. Through complex mechanisms, the constant exposure to these hormones causes several problems. First, cholesterol is deposited on the coronary artery walls as a result of the increase in blood cholesterol and the reduced ability to rid the blood of the cholesterol. Second, the increased ability of the blood to clot results in more clotting elements being deposited on the arterial walls. Third, clotting elements can decrease blood flow through the small capillaries which feed the coronary arteries, resulting in further complications with the cholesterol deposits. Fourth, increased insulin in the blood further destroys the coronary arteries. Therefore, the reaction of the pituitary gland to the Type A behavior pattern is believed to be responsible for the connection with coronary artery disease.

MODIFICATION TECHNIQUES

Fortunately, it is believed that people with the Type A behavior pattern can modify their behavior to reduce risk of coronary artery disease. As with many health problems, however, denial is prevalent.

Therefore, it is important that Type A individuals become aware of their problem. In general, Type A individuals need to focus on several areas. These include hurry sickness, speed and impatience, and hostility.

Type A individuals try to accomplish more and more in less and less time (hurry sickness). Unfortunately, more is too often at the expense of quality, efficiency, and, most important, health. Type A individuals need to make fewer appointments related to work, and they need to schedule more relaxation time. This includes not starting the day in a rush by getting out of bed barely in time to get hurriedly to work. Finally, Type A individuals need to avoid telephone and other interruptions when they are working, because this aggravates hurry sickness. Therefore, it is recommended that individuals who suffer from hurry sickness avoid scheduling too much work; take more breaks from work (relaxation), including a lunch hour during which work is not done; and have calls screened in order to get blocks of working time.

Type A individuals typically do things rapidly and are impatient. For example, they tend to talk rapidly, repetitiously, and narrowly. They also have a hard time with individuals who talk slowly, and Type A individuals often hurry these people along by finishing their sentences. Additionally, Type A individuals try to dominate conversations, frequently focusing the discussion on themselves or their interests. In an effort to moderate speed and impatience, Type A individuals need to slow down, focus their speech in discussions to the specific problem, and cut short visits with individuals who waste their time. They should spend more time with individuals who enhance their opportunities.

The other area is hostility, or harboring destructive emotions. This is highly related to aggressiveness. Aggressive Type A individuals must learn to use their sense of humor and not look at situations only as challenges set up to bother or upset them. One way to accomplish this is for them consciously to attempt to socialize with Type B individuals. Obviously, this is not always possible, since Type A individuals have certain other individuals with whom they must associate, such as colleagues at work and certain family members. Nevertheless, Type A individuals must understand their hostilities and learn to regulate them. In general, Type A individuals must learn to control their feelings and relation-

ships. They must focus more attention on being well-rounded individuals rather than spending most of their time on work-related successes. Type A individuals can learn the Type B behavior pattern, resulting in a lower risk for coronary artery disease.

BEHAVIOR PATTERN VERSUS PERSONALITY

Since Friedman and Rosenman defined the Type A behavior pattern in the 1950's, many researchers have studied the Type A behavior pattern. Initially, most of the researchers were cardiologists. Gradually, more and more psychologists have become involved with Type A research.

Since the concept of relating coronary heart disease with human behavior was developed by cardiologists instead of psychologists, it was initially called the Type A behavior pattern rather than the Type A personality. "Personality" relates to an individual's inner traits, attitudes, or habits and is very complex and generally studied by psychologists. As Type A was defined, however, it only related specific behaviors with disease and was observed openly. Therefore, it seemed appropriate to label Type A a behavior pattern. Over the years, Type A has been assumed to be a personality; technically, this is not accurate, although many people now refer to it as the Type A personality.

Another reason Type A is most accurately considered a behavior pattern rather than a personality relates to the way it is assessed. Whether the structured interview or the written questionnaire is utilized, a predetermined set of questions and sequence are used. While this approach can assess a behavior pattern adequately, different skills, which allow the interviewer to respond appropriately to an individual's answers and probe specific responses further, are needed to assess personality.

CONTRIBUTIONS AND FUTURE RESEARCH

The Type A behavior pattern was originally identified as a risk factor for coronary artery disease. The original need for this idea was not psychologically based. Instead, it was based on a need to understand further the factors that are involved with the development of coronary artery disease, a major cause of death. Therefore, the role of the Type A behavior pattern in psychology has been limited. Nevertheless, Type A studies have benefitted humankind's understanding of an important disease and, to a certain extent, the understanding of psychology.

The future study of the Type A behavior pattern is in question. Research continually shows conflicting results about its role in coronary artery disease. As more research is conducted by both medical clinicians and psychologists, the true value of the Type A behavior pattern will become evident. Until then, health care professionals will continually have to evaluate the appropriateness of using the Type A behavior pattern as an identifier of the risk of artery or heart disease.

SOURCES FOR FURTHER STUDY

Chesney, Margaret A., and Ray H. Rosenman, eds. *Anger and Hostility in Cardiovascular and Behavior Disorders.* Washington, D.C.: Hemisphere, 1985. Integrating psychology and the Type A behavior pattern, this book provides in-depth information on the technical aspects of behavior. Although some portions of the book are technical, the introductions to each chapter provide historical and nontechnical information related to the broader topic of behavior.

Friedman, Meyer. *Type A Behavior: Its Diagnosis and Treatment.* New York: Plenum, 1996. The physician who first identified Type A behavior and its relation to cardiovascular illnesses provides an overview of the treatments he has used in his Recurrent Coronary Prevention Program.

Houston, B. Kent, and C. R. Snyder, eds. *Type A Behavior Pattern: Research, Theory, and Intervention.* New York: John Wiley & Sons, 1988. Contains thirteen chapters by various authors. The first three chapters nicely introduce the topic in relatively simple terms. Subsequent chapters tend to be more technical and require a better background for understanding. A wealth of references are listed throughout.

Price, Virginia Ann. *Type A Behavior Pattern.* New York: Academic Press, 1982. A good technical resource for Type A behavior. Very comprehensive. The introductory chapters provide the nontechnical reader with valuable, understandable information. More than three hundred references are listed at the end of the book.

Bradley R. A. Wilson

SEE ALSO: Aggression; Aggression: Reduction and control; Biofeedback and relaxation; Coping: Social support; Environmental psychology; Fight-or-flight response; General adaptation syndrome; Health psychology; Stress; Stress: Physiological responses; Stress-related diseases.

V

Violence and sexuality in the media

TYPE OF PSYCHOLOGY: Social psychology
FIELDS OF STUDY: Aggression

The American mass media, especially films and television, contain high levels of violence. In some pornography, violence is presented in a sexual context. The consensus among social scientists, based on both laboratory experiments and field studies, is that nonsexual and sexual violence causes aggressive behavior in the audience but that nonviolent pornography does not.

KEY CONCEPTS
- aggression machine
- aggressive cues
- arousal
- catharsis hypothesis
- desensitization
- disinhibition
- excitation transfer
- imitation
- mean world syndrome
- priming
- rape myths
- script

INTRODUCTION

The world of the American mass media is much more violent than the real world. Communication researcher George Gerbner has found that approximately 80 percent of television programs contain some violence, for an average of almost ten violent acts per hour. Some prime-time television programs and R-rated action films contain as many as 50 to 150 violent acts per hour. Cartoons average 25 violent acts per hour. It has been estimated that by the age of eighteen, the average American has witnessed 100,000 acts of violence, including 25,000 killings, on television alone. There are many cases of direct copying of media violence. For example, at least twenty-eight people have killed themselves in apparent imitation of the Russian roulette scene in the film *The Deer Hunter* (1978). Reactions to such anecdotal evidence, however, must be tempered by the knowledge that many millions of people have seen these programs and films.

In the early 1960's, psychologist Leonard Berkowitz devised a laboratory procedure to study the effects of filmed violence on aggressive behavior. In a typical experiment, subjects are made angry by a confederate or accomplice of the experimenter. They then watch a ten-minute film clip containing a high level of violence (a boxing match) or an equally exciting control film (a foot race). Finally, subjects are permitted to evaluate the confederate's work using an "aggression machine," an apparatus that they think delivers electric shocks to the confederate. Results of these studies consistently show that subjects who have seen a violent film deliver longer and more intense shocks than control subjects do. This experiment has been repeated at least 150 times with the same results, making its findings among the most reliable in social psychology. Similar effects have been found with other measures of verbal and physical aggression.

Four variables have been shown to influence the amount of imitation of media violence. First, the more realistic the portrayal of violence, the greater the imitation. The same violence is more effective when presented as a real event than as fiction. "Aggression cues," or points of similarity between the filmed violence and the subject's real-life experience, such as a weapon or a character's name, can increase aggression. Second, more imitation occurs when violence is presented as justified. Violence committed by the hero in revenge for previous harm produces greater imitation than violence that is unfair to the victim. Third, imitation increases when violence is effective—that is, when aggressors are rewarded with wealth, happiness, and social approval. Fourth, imitation is more likely when the viewer is in a psychological state of readiness to aggress—for example, when he or she is emotionally aroused or angry. Anger, however, is not a necessary condition for imitation of violence.

Critics have argued that laboratory studies of aggression are so different from everyday experience that the results are not generalizable to the real world. This skepticism produced a second generation of studies using field research methodologies. These included correlational studies in which subjects' exposure to violent programs was related to ratings of their aggressiveness by parents, teachers, or peers; field studies in which the exposure of institutionalized boys to media violence was controlled and physical and verbal aggression was observed; "natural experiments" in which communities or nations that were slow to receive television were compared with others that received it sooner; and archival studies of the effects of highly publicized suicides or homicides on the suicide or homicide rate. Although the results of these studies are not as clear as those of laboratory experiments, they have generally supported the hypothesis.

In summary, there is substantial evidence from studies using a variety of research methods converging on the conclusion that filmed and televised violence increases aggression. Although any single study can be criticized on methodological grounds, there are no convincing alternative explanations for all of them.

Media violence can affect attitudes as well as behavior. The prevalence of crime and violence on television appears to cultivate a "mean world syndrome." For example, heavy viewers are more likely than infrequent viewers to overestimate the frequency of crime. It is not clear, however, whether television causes these attitudes or pessimistic and fearful people are more attracted to television.

This drawing made by a Palestinian child reveals the impact of watching violent media coverage about the conflict in his homeland. (AP/Wide World Photos)

Pornography Effects

Laboratory research on the effects of pornography has used procedures similar to those of aggression research. In several studies, male subjects were angered by a female confederate. They watched either violent pornography (a sexually explicit rape scene) or a control film. The men who saw the rape film showed more violence against women than did control subjects. Violent pornography, however, contains two distinct variables that might plausibly be related to aggression—violence and sexual explicitness. To determine whether either or both contribute to aggression, it is necessary to compare four conditions: sex plus violence (a sexually explicit rape scene), violence only (a nonexplicit rape scene), sex only (sexually explicit but with willing participants), and a control film. Researchers who have made this comparison find that the sex-plus-violence and violence-only conditions increase aggression toward women (to about the same degree), but nonviolent pornography does not usually produce any more aggression than a control film. This suggests that the effect of violent pornography is a special case of the well-established effect of filmed violence. Nonviolent pornography does not increase aggression. This is important, because only a small percentage of pornography—for example, about 15 percent of pornography videotapes—contains violence.

Studies show that men exposed to violent (and, in some cases, nonviolent) pornography in laboratory experiments show undesirable changes in attitude. They are more likely to endorse rape myths, such as the belief that women secretly enjoy being raped. They recommend less severe punishment for the defendant in a hypothetical rape trial, suggesting that they regard rape as a less serious crime. There is no evidence, however, that these attitudes are directly related to the likelihood of raping someone. It should be noted that these attitude changes are small and temporary and that similar effects have been obtained with nonpornographic violence, such as R-rated "mad slasher" films.

Field research on the effects of pornography falls into two categories. Some researchers have examined the relationship between the availability of pornography and the incidence of reported rape in various locales. Others have interviewed convicted sex offenders to see whether they differ from nonoffenders in their history of exposure to pornography. Both approaches have produced mixed results, suggesting that, at most, pornography plays a minor role in sexual assault once alternative explanations have been removed.

An Ongoing Debate

The effects of media violence have been vigorously debated for several decades. Televised violence is of special concern because of its vivid and realistic nature and its easy accessibility to children. The most extensive government investigation of the effects of television on chilpdren was the 1972 Surgeon General's Scientific Advisory Committee on Television and Social Behavior, which conducted forty scientific studies. It concluded that television can cause aggression, but the committee's report contained so many qualifications that it was widely perceived as indicating that television is not really an important cause of aggressive behavior. This ambiguity may have resulted from the fact that the television networks were allowed to appoint five of the twelve commissioners and to blackball several proposed members. A 1982 update by the National Institute of Mental Health stated more directly that television violence is indeed a cause of aggression. In spite of these investigations and the lobbying of pressure groups such as Action for Children's Television, the amount of violence on television has changed little since the late 1960's. The television networks believe (with some justification) that violent programs are more popular, and they have considerable power to resist governmental regulation.

Pornography in all media, from print to film to the Internet, has also been an issue of great concern to the American public. The country's ambivalence about media sexuality is illustrated by the contrasting recommendations of two government commissions. The 1970 Commission on Obscenity and Pornography consisted primarily of social scientists. It funded nineteen original studies (all of nonviolent pornography) and concluded that pornography had no proven harmful effects. Political reaction to the report was primarily negative. In 1986, President Ronald Reagan appointed the Attorney General's Commission on Pornography (the Meese Commission), consisting primarily of antipornography activists with little social scientific background. The Meese Commission came to the following conclusions: Violent pornography causes aggression toward women and harmful attitude change; nonviolent pornography that is degrading to women (although the report was not very clear about what "degrading" means) does not cause aggressive behavior but produces harmful attitude change; and nonviolent and nondegrading pornography has no specific negative effects, although certain moral and aesthetic harms were claimed. In spite of the different effects attributed to each type, the commission concluded that all pornography should be banned and proposed ninety-two recommendations for doing so. Social scientists criticized the Meese Commission for failing to define categories of pornography clearly, for biased selection and presentation of research, for not distinguishing between low- and high-quality evidence, and for obscuring differences between the effects of violent and nonviolent pornography.

Attempts to regulate media violence and pornography would appear to be in conflict with the First Amendment to the United States Constitution, which states that "Congress shall make no law . . . abridging the freedom of speech, or of the press." The courts have historically permitted many exceptions to the First Amendment, however, and there is a long history of legal censorship of news and entertainment media. Social scientists disagree on whether there is enough evidence of antisocial effects of violence or pornography to justify censorship. Many social scientists would insist, however, that the Constitution places a strong burden of proof on the censor, that a much stronger case could be made for censorship of violence (including violent pornography) than of nonviolent pornography, and that attempts to censor media content because it is alleged to produce "bad attitudes" are in conflict with the free marketplace of ideas model assumed by the Constitution.

While social scientists see media violence as more harmful than pornography, the American public favors censorship of nonviolent pornography more than of violence. This suggests that people underestimate the effects of media violence, overestimate the effects of nonviolent pornography, or object to pornography for reasons other than its alleged harmful effects.

PSYCHOLOGICAL MODELS

Two early psychological approaches to the study of aggression made different predictions about the effects of media violence. Instinct and drive theories of aggression suggested that watching media violence would provide a "catharisis," or release of aggressive energy, which would reduce the likelihood of subsequent aggression. Social learning theory proposed that much of one's knowledge of how to behave comes from observing and sometimes imitating the behavior of others. Exposure to media violence would be expected to increase aggression. The majority of research has supported the social learning theory position.

There are several contemporary explanations for the effects of media violence. The imitation approach emphasizes the direct transmission of information about when, why, and how to commit aggressive behaviors. This theory accounts for copycat aggression but has difficulty explaining more general effects. The disinhibition approach points out that adults already know how to aggress, and that media violence reduces restraints that would normally cause people to inhibit their aggressive impulses by suggesting that aggression is socially acceptable. The arousal and desensitization approaches suggest that watching violence will have different short- and long-term effects. In the short run, violence is exciting and increases physiological arousal, which can spill over and energize real aggressive behavior. This effect would appear to be temporary. In the long run, each exposure produces progressively less arousal, called desensitization. This implies that a steady diet of media violence can make people indifferent to the pain and suffering of victims and increase their tolerance of real violence.

In the 1970's and 1980's, cognitive theories became more popular in psychology. The cognitive priming approach proposes that media violence increases the availability of aggressive thoughts in the viewer for as long as several days, and these thoughts increase the probability of aggressive behavior. A related approach suggests that media portrayals contribute to the formation and maintenance of aggressive behavioral scripts, which are later activated by real situations similar to those observed in the media.

The effects of violent pornography can be explained by the same theories that explain the effects of general film violence. Those who claim that nonviolent pornography causes aggression are faced with the problem of explaining how nonaggressive content (sexuality) can activate aggressive behavior. A variation on arousal theory, the excitation transfer theory, suggests that the physiological arousal caused by pornography can subsequently be confused with anger and can energize aggression. Any source of arousal, such as music or exercise, can have this effect if the timing is right. This theory predicts very subtle, temporary effects of exposure to pornography, and as noted, research does not consistently support it.

Effects of aggression and pornography on attitudes can be explained on the basis of theories of attitude change, which show that, not surprisingly, almost any media presentation produces small, temporary changes of attitude in the direction advocated by its author. Resistance to attitude change occurs when the audience has the information and the motivation to argue with the media effectively.

SOURCES FOR FURTHER STUDY

Donnerstein, Edward I., Daniel Linz, and Steven Penrod. *The Question of Pornography*. New York: Free Press, 1987. Review of laboratory research on effects of pornography. Distinguishes between the proven antisocial effects of violent pornography and the more speculative claims against nonviolent pornography. Accessible to the general reader.

Huesmann, L. Rowell, and Neil M. Malamuth. "Media Violence and Antisocial Behavior." *Journal of Social Issues* 42, no. 3 (1986): 125-139. This article is in a special issue of a psychological journal containing eleven articles that summarize the effects of media violence and pornography.

Joy, Leslie A., Meredith M. Kimball, and Merle L. Zabrack. "Television and Children's Aggressive Behavior." In *The Impact of Television*, edited by Tannis MacBeth Williams. Orlando, Fla.: Academic Press, 1986. Presents a study of the effects of the introduction of cable television in an isolated community in western Canada on the aggressive behavior of its children.

Liebert, Robert M., and Joyce Sprafkin. *The Early Window: Effects of Television on Children and Youth*. 3d ed. Elmsford, N.Y.: Pergamon, 1988. Excellent overview of the socializing effects of television. Discusses the effects of televised violence and the politics of governmental regulation of television content.

Signorelli, Nancy, and George Gerbner, comps. *Violence and Terror in the Mass Media: An Annotated Bibliography*. New York: Greenwood Press, 1988. Citations and paragraph-length summaries of 784 studies of violent media content and its effects. Very helpful when doing a literature survey.

Zillmann, Dolf, and Jennings Bryant, eds. *Pornography: Research Advances and Policy Considerations*. Hillsdale, N.J.: Lawrence Erlbaum, 1989. Fifteen papers dealing with the content and effects of pornography and the legal debate over pornography regulation. Papers are sometimes difficult but are generally rewarding.

Lloyd K. Stires

SEE ALSO: Aggression; Aggression: Reduction and control; Attitude-behavior consistency; Attitude formation and change; Sexism; Social learning: Albert Bandura; Social schemata.

Violence by children and teenagers

TYPE OF PSYCHOLOGY: Developmental psychology; emotion; personality; psychopathology; social psychology

FIELDS OF STUDY: Adolescence; aggression; attitudes and behavior; childhood and adolescent disorders; infancy and childhood; interpersonal relations; personality disorders; social perception and cognition; substance abuse

Some children and teenagers commit acts of violence on their families, peers, authority figures, or strangers. Such antisocial behavior may result from psychiatric disorders or social catalysts.

KEY CONCEPTS
- aggression
- antisocial behavior
- predatory violence
- psychopathological violence
- relational violence
- situational violence

INTRODUCTION

Some children and teenagers prey on vulnerable people, exhibiting antisocial behavior, neurological dysfunctions, and mental illnesses. These youths may assault other children or adults for a variety of reasons, ranging from invoking fear as a form of entertainment to causing bodily harm as retribution for perceived wrongs such as social ostracism.

Youth crimes doubled during the late 1980's and early 1990's and included shocking crimes that exceeded those committed by previous generations. Although homicide rates for teenage perpetrators began to decline in the United States by 1997, youth violence remained an urgent issue. By the beginning of the twenty-first century, violent youths were committing callous acts at increasingly younger ages. They also behaved more extremely with regard to weapons used or number of victims attacked during violent sprees. Crimes such as school shootings targeted individuals both known and unfamiliar to perpetrators.

WHO IS VIOLENT?

Violent youths represent varying social classes and ethnicities, living in both rural and urban areas. Young males are twice as likely to act violently outside the home than are young females, but both genders are equally likely to be violent toward their families. Violent tendencies sometimes emerge when children are toddlers. Aggressive children may fight with other youngsters, act up in class, challenge authority figures, or steal. Some sadistically abuse animals. Such aberrant behaviors can intensify during adolescence.

Researchers offer contrasting theories about why some youths become violent. Violent youths may suffer from severe mental illnesses, display disruptive behavior disorders or antisocial personalities, or have experienced brain damage. Some researchers suggest that brain circuits containing the neurotransmitter serotonin have malfunctioned in violent youths. A few researchers speculate that some infants have innate repressed violent characteristics that develop when the child encounters biological or psychological triggers, such as sexual or physical abuse, illegal substances, or peer pressure.

Authorities agree that many violent children and teenagers have been exposed to violence in their homes or communities. Inadequate or abusive parenting can prevent children from learning appropriate values of right and wrong. Neglected or abused children can feel emotionally abandoned and become self-centered. Egocentric youths are more likely to lack consciences and to be incapable of feeling empathy or compassion for others. Emotions such as depression, frustration, rage, and

shame can intensify a child's perceived inadequacies. Many violent youths are alienated from emotional support systems and feel isolated and discriminated against. They may become desensitized to violence or emotionally numb and seek excitement through violence. Some are suicidal and resigned to accepting and participating in violence.

HOW VIOLENCE IS COMMITTED

Youth violence can be categorized into four major types. Situational violence, one of the most common types of violence committed by children and teenagers, is sparked by an event that upsets or enrages the victimizer. For example, a student might assault a teacher who gave a failing grade. Relational violence occurs when a child or teenager is violent toward a relative or friend with whom he or she has a personal dispute. Dating violence is one of the most prevalent forms of this type of violence, as when a teenage boy attacks a girl who terminates their relationship. Predatory violence describes thefts and muggings involving violence or violent activities carried out to prove loyalty and ensure acceptance by a group. Violence connected to competition, drug dealing, riots, and gang fights and the use of concealed weapons with intent to maim or murder is considered predatory. Less than 1 percent of juvenile cases involve psychopathological violence, which involves perpetrators who probably are neurologically damaged or mentally ill and who commit extremely violent acts. These individuals require pharmaceutical and management therapy. Other violent acts that may be committed by youths include hate crimes, vandalism, bombings, or activism such as ecoterrorism. Some violent youths are attention seekers who believe that they will become celebrities through their acts.

While engaged in violent acts, youths may be disassociated from what they are doing and may feel as if they are experiencing a dreamlike or fantastical state instead of reality. Violent youths may verbally antagonize and ridicule their victims, who are often people whom the perpetrators view as weak, such as young children, the elderly, and handicapped individuals. Sometimes, groups of youths plan assaults to surround and attack one person. Preteens have raped or murdered children their own age or younger. A notorious case of youth violence occurred in England in 1993, when two ten-year-olds kidnapped and beat to death a two-year-old. Some children

Teenagers without a sense of hope, power, or self-esteem may turn to the violent life of gangs for identity. (CLEO Photography)

who commit violent acts are not sufficiently mature, intellectually and morally, to realize that their actions can hurt other people. In 2000, a six-year-old who shot a classmate at a Michigan school expressed confusion when she died.

INTERVENTION

Mental health professionals stress that children who display violent behaviors should be identified as young as possible so that intervention measures can be implemented to prevent them from harming other youths. Facilities that treat violent juvenile offenders include boot camps, detention centers, wilderness programs, and group or private psychotherapy sessions. Both public and private schools attempt to identify emotionally disturbed students who might interfere with the learning process of other students by disrupting classes and challenging faculty members.

Violent youths who are mentally ill should receive counseling and medication. Other options are available to those whose behavior has social and emotional roots. These youths may be enrolled in programs that promote self-esteem, emotional resilience, and self-control. Parents can teach their children appropriate coping techniques to prevent violence. Communities and churches can provide children with supervised recreational activities during afternoons, which are the hours when youths are most likely to act violently. Mentoring programs can demonstrate alternatives to destructive behavior. Peer counseling has been shown to be an effective deterrent to violence. Violence prevention curricula can teach children to resolve conflicts creatively and help them develop skills to control emotional outbursts.

SOURCES FOR FURTHER STUDY

Eron, Leonard D., Jacquelyn H. Gentry, and Peggy Schlegel. *Reason to Hope: A Psychosocial Perspective on Violence and Youth.* Washington, D.C.: American Psychological Association, 1994. Discusses youth violence as a form of juvenile delinquency and social handicap which can be rehabilitated.

Garbarino, James. *Lost Boys: Why Our Sons Turn Violent and How We Can Save Them.* New York: Free Press, 1999. Focuses on why young males are more likely to commit extremely antisocial acts such as school shootings.

Holden, Constance. "The Violence of the Lambs." *Science* 289 (July 28, 2000): 580-581. Commentary on the various risk factors that investigators suggest cause children to become violent. This issue of the American Association for the Advancement of Science's magazine is devoted to scientific research concerning violence in humans and animals.

Katch, Jane. *Under Deadman's Skin: Discovering the Meaning of Children's Violent Play.* Boston: Beacon Press, 2001. Explores how violence is learned and displayed by children through games and in social groups.

Kellerman, Jonathan. *Savage Spawn: Reflections on Violent Children.* New York: Ballantine, 1999. Analyzes the psychopathology exhibited by children with conduct disorders.

Richman, Jack M., and Mark W. Fraser, eds. *The Context of Youth Violence: Resilience, Risk, and Protection.* Westport, Conn.: Praeger, 2001. Examines personality traits associated with violence in children and teenagers.

Shafii, Mohammad, and Sharon Lee Shafii, eds. *School Violence: Assessment, Management, Prevention.* Washington, D.C.: American Psychiatric Press, 2001. Comprehensive study addressing why children and teenagers target their peers for victimization.

Elizabeth D. Schafer

SEE ALSO: Aggression; Aggression: Reduction and control; Anger; Conduct disorder; Juvenile delinquency; Law and psychology; Misbehavior; Psychotic disorders; Suicide; Teenage suicide; Violence and sexuality in the media.

Virtual reality

DATE: The early 1990's forward

TYPE OF PSYCHOLOGY: Cognition; learning; memory; psychological methodologies; psychotherapy; sensation and perception; social psychology; stress

FIELDS OF STUDY: Anxiety disorders; attitudes and behavior; behavioral therapies; cognitive therapies; experimental methodologies; problem solving

Virtual reality is a form of computer-generated technology that offers innovative alternative therapies through human-machine interactions to treat psychological disorders by creating environments for people to address and confront factors that cause stress, fear, or other unwanted behaviors.

KEY CONCEPTS
- artificiality
- environments
- graphics
- immersion
- interactive
- phobia
- real-time
- simulators

INTRODUCTION

After World War II, computer scientists and engineers developed technology, such as flight simula-

tors, that provided a foundation for virtual reality through digitization, real-time graphics, and interactive and pointing devices. By the early 1980's, medical and computer science professionals collaborated to integrate their specialties. Some medical professionals incorporated virtual reality as a tool to learn and practice medical procedures, especially surgery, by manipulating virtual organs. Virtual reality underwent a transition from laboratories to hospitals. Physicians reported that virtual reality eased the pain that burn patients felt, when they became distracted and unaware of their real world while immersed in alternative environments such as snowy landscapes, which convinced patients they felt coolness.

Virtual reality techniques were appropriated for psychological applications by the early 1990's to influence people's perceptions and psychological processes. Computer hardware and software were developed to simulate specific situations for therapeutic sessions. As a result, computer technology can enable phobic patients to interact safely with situations that arouse fear. Phobic patients often prefer virtual reality therapy because they can encounter their fears in private instead of in public situations. In 1998, *CyberPsychology and Behavior: The Leading Psychology Journal for Internet, Multimedia and Virtual Reality Research* began providing a centralized forum to advance virtual reality as a therapeutic tool. Software improvements enable the creation of more virtual environments to meet therapeutic demands.

METHODOLOGY

Six types of virtual reality therapies have been tested. They rely on convincing people that they are experiencing an environment that is realistic to their senses of sight, hearing, and touch. The desktop method involves patients interacting with images on a computer screen by using pointing devices. Projected virtual reality casts the patient's image on an artificial setting. Cave virtual reality displays images on the walls of a small room and several people can participate in therapy simultaneously. Telepresence is the delivery of a setting in another place on a video screen that the patient observes. Augmented virtual reality utilizes objects that enhance the setting for specific therapies.

Immersive virtual reality is used most frequently and includes aspects of other virtual reality types. In contrast to two-dimensional computer images, virtual reality creates a three-dimensional environment composed of computer graphics. People believe they are immersed in and participating in the simulation. This illusion is enabled by devices that participants wear that aid them to interact with and manipulate the virtual setting.

A head-mounted visor has a stereoscopic optical display. The scenery is adjusted by motion-tracking sensors attached to people's heads and limbs, and the experience seems more realistic because graphics respond convincingly to movement. Additional sensors in datagloves improve the illusion by suggesting that the participant is interacting with items located in the virtual world and navigating through the setting.

VIRTUAL FEAR

Many psychologists are skeptical whether virtual reality can be advantageous for therapeutic use. The expense associated with equipment and operation is considered prohibitive by many professionals, who dismiss virtual reality as an irrelevant technology more suitable for entertainment than therapy. Many mental health professionals view virtual reality as an experimental therapy that needs additional research. Gradually, the benefits of virtual reality have secured the approval of some mental health practitioners, many of whom admit to being surprised at patients' successful improvement due to virtual reality exposure (VRE) therapy.

Phobia treatment has been virtual reality's most frequent psychological application. For treatment of phobias, VRE therapy parallels traditional therapy in which patients are gradually exposed to a situation or object stimuli that arouse acute fear and anxiety. Such exposure is either in vivo (actually experienced by the patient) or in vitro (imagined by the patient). The degree of exposure is deliberately increased over time. Individuals become conditioned and desensitized, learn not to panic, and develop more receptive attitudes.

Virtual reality creates a safe, private environment for patients to confront their fears without being publicly embarrassed or risking physical harm. Compared with most real settings and props, such as airplanes and animals, necessary for conventional phobia therapy, virtual reality is inexpensive and more controllable. Multiple stimuli can be presented. Specific stimuli can be isolated, and distractions can be eliminated. Virtual reality also allows

therapists to develop settings not easily located in their communities.

Patients can face frightening situations and objects virtually that they could not initially handle in person. These computer settings are more realistic at depicting genuine dangerous conditions than most patients would imagine. Virtual reality enables people to overcome the limitations of their imagination and memory. Active interaction with anxiety-arousing stimuli cause patients to feel more in control, confident, and capable than undergoing more passive observational and listening therapies. Virtual reality allows people in remote places to experience settings and fears that would otherwise not be easily arranged.

In 1992, a team of psychological and computer science researchers at Emory University and Georgia Institute of Technology began investigating the use of virtual reality technology to treat psychological disorders. By 1995, Larry F. Hodges and Barbara Rothbaum had published peer-reviewed results of the first controlled study of VRE exposure therapy. Their data concluded that virtual reality therapy significantly lowered the anxiety and avoidance of people suffering acrophobia (fear of heights).

In additional experimental test cases of individuals and groups conducted by other researchers, virtual reality proved effective in countering claustrophobia (fear of enclosed spaces), agoraphobia (fear of open spaces), and arachnophobia (fear of spiders). Hodges and Rothbaum initiated virtual reality airplane settings to combat aerophobia (fear of flying). Concurrently, Ralph Lamson, a San Rafael, California, psychologist, tested acrophobes in a virtual environment. At the University of Washington Medical Center's Human Interface Technology Laboratory, researchers developed virtual spiders.

Patients with social phobias such as fear of public speaking can practice skills with virtual reality to interact more comfortably with people. Researchers are developing models for virtual humans for future study of attachment theories about human relationships, such as parent and child, for possible use in clinical practices. Research teams are also considering the possibilities of patients and therapists being immersed in virtual reality settings together.

VIRTUAL TRAUMA

Psychologists use virtual reality to aid patients suffering from chronic post-traumatic stress disorder

(PTSD). At the Georgia Institute of Technology's College of Computing, Hodges studied how virtual reality therapy aided a group of Vietnam veterans suffering PTSD. During virtual reality sessions, therapists encouraged veterans to narrate their experiences while serving in the military. The veterans were asked to reiterate their stories many times to bolster their memories. Although many veterans were reticent to share their stories in traditional therapy, virtual reality freed them to become more talkative and physical as they interacted with virtual comrades and enemies in a setting that included combat sounds.

Such experiences helped the veterans deal with guilt about such things as being sole survivors of attacks. While PTDS was not eliminated, many veterans did not suffer as severely after they revisited their memories via virtual reality. Veterans hospitals have incorporated virtual reality equipment for chronic anxiety disorders therapy. Hodges established Virtually Better, Incorporated, to develop clinical virtual reality systems. He created standardized virtual scenarios such as helicopter transportation across an open field near a jungle that would be common to most Vietnam veterans.

MEASUREMENT AND NEUROSCIENCE

Some researchers use virtual reality to measure patients' cognitive capacities. Giuseppe Riva of the Applied Technology for Neuro-Psychology Laboratory in Verbania, Italy, conducts European virtual reality psychological research for neuroscience applications. He has studied how virtual reality environments enable patients unable to function in normal settings to respond to stimuli presented in real time so that neuroscientists can gauge individuals' cognitive abilities. Virtual reality has proven effective to rehabilitate some individuals who are cognitively impaired due to brain injuries or diseases such as Alzheimer's. Patients are tested with virtual reality scenarios that researchers can control and adjust as needed to assess how well individuals function.

Virtual settings offer people with neurological impairments the opportunity to interact with an environment to which they would otherwise lack physical access in order to enrich their sensory and motor skills. Virtual reality classrooms have been designed to evaluate and measure the cognitive abilities of children who possibly have attention-deficit hyperactivity disorder (ADHD). Most cognitive researchers

consider virtual reality tests less biased than traditional tools. They do not consider its lack of realism, comparable to a photograph, problematic.

SELF-IMPROVEMENT

Virtual reality has been used therapeutically for patients' self-improvement. Mythseeker software, developed by the MYTHSEEKER Institute at Eagle Rock, California, offers virtual reality for psychotherapy. Patients use this software system to explore their aspirations and beliefs in a virtual setting to achieve better self-expression.

Eating disorders have been successfully treated with virtual reality methods that often supplement traditional forms of therapy. The virtual-reality-based experiential cognitive treatment of obesity and binge-eating disorders assists people to modify their flawed body perceptions. Improved body awareness obtained through an integration of virtual environments and traditional cognitive-behavioral and visual-motorial therapies results in awareness of latent feelings, decreased problematic eating, and displays of more normal social behavior.

The Virtual Environment for Body Image Modification (VEBIM) has six zones in which patients initially develop skills concerning food choice and eating by encountering objects and having a virtual weight which reflects choices made in the first two zones. Next, patients alter their body experience with guided imagery of models and can only proceed into other zones by selecting passages appropriate to their size. The final zone has imaging tools for patients to shape an ideal image of their bodies.

SIDE EFFECTS

Virtual reality is limited by its costs, complexity, technology, and reliability, as well as the technical proficiency of users. Time delays, noise, and distortions (particularly in body image sessions) can impede therapy. In order to improve techniques, virtual reality researchers investigate human-computer interaction with clinical tests. They are interested in how people perceive and accept or reject computer-generated worlds as a mental health treatment method. Researchers evaluate whether virtual reality therapy is more time- and cost-effective than traditional techniques.

Some patients experience simulation sickness, which is a form of motion sickness, and nausea. Careful design of virtual scenarios and screening of patients can minimize such adverse reactions. Some people's neck muscles are too weak to support heavy virtual reality helmets, and many claustrophobic patients are reluctant to wear the bulky helmets. Some users experience depth perception problems. Sometimes virtual reality confuses patients and virtual experiences replace real experiences in memories. Many patients, however, seem receptive to virtual reality techniques.

SOURCES FOR FURTHER STUDY

Carlin, Alvin S., H. G. Hoffman, and S. Weghorst. "Virtual Reality and Tactile Augmentation in the Treatment of Spider Phobia: A Case Study." *Behavior Research and Therapy* 35 (1997): 153-158. Describes the innovative development of virtual spiders at Washington University and their therapeutic effectiveness.

Hodges, Larry F., Barbara O. Rothbaum, Rob Kooper, Dan Opdyke, Thomas Meyer, Max M. North, J. J. de Graaff, and James S. Williford. "Virtual Environments for Treating the Fear of Heights." *IEEE Computer* 28, no. 7 (1995): 27-34. An early study about the potential of virtual reality to treat specific fears.

North, Max M., Sarah M. North, and Joseph R. Coble. *Virtual Reality Therapy: An Innovative Paradigm.* Colorado Springs, Colo.: IPI Press, 1996. One of the first texts describing the potential of virtual reality to provide alternative treatments for a variety of psychological disorders.

Riva, Giuseppe, ed. *Virtual Reality in Neuro-psychophysiology: Cognitive, Clinical, and Methodological Issues in Assessment and Rehabilitation.* Amsterdam: ISO Press, 1997. Focuses on the advantages and limitations of virtual reality environments to diagnose and treat people with cognitive impairments.

Riva, Giuseppe, Brenda K. Wiederhold, and Enrico Molinari, eds. *Virtual Environments in Clinical Psychology and Neuroscience: Methods and Techniques in Advanced Patient-Therapist Interaction.* Amsterdam: ISO Press, 1998. Pioneer researchers in the field of virtual reality therapy describe specific topics, compare virtual reality versus traditional methods, and discuss the roles of humans and technology in mental health.

Rothbaum, Barbara O., and Larry F. Hodges. *Virtually Better: Therapist Manual for Fear of Flying.* Atlanta: Virtually Better, 1997. Guide based on authors' research, which promotes computer-generated techniques to prepare patients for experiences aboard airplanes.

Rothbaum, Barbara O., Larry F. Hodges, Rob Kooper, Dan Opdyke, James S. Williford, and Max M. North. "Effectiveness of Computer-Generated (Virtual Reality) Graded Exposure in the Treatment of Acrophobia." *American Journal of Psychiatry* 152, no. 4 (1995): 626-628. The report of the first controlled study of VER therapy to treat a psychological disorder.

Schultheis, Maria T., and Albert A. Rizzo. "The Application of Virtual Reality Technology in Rehabilitation." *Rehabilitation Psychology* 46, no. 3 (August, 2001): 296-311. Concludes that virtual reality presents alternatives unavailable in traditional therapy but needs additional research to become fully integrated as an accepted method.

Elizabeth D. Schafer

SEE ALSO: Artificial intelligence; Aversion, implosion, and systematic desensitization; Computer models of cognition; Phobias.

Vision

Brightness and contrast

TYPE OF PSYCHOLOGY: Sensation and perception
FIELDS OF STUDY: Cognitive processes; vision

Brightness refers to one's perception of the intensity of light reflected from a surface; contrast refers to one's perception of differences in light reflected from two surfaces. Contrast enhances perception of intensity differences, thereby accentuating lines, colors, and borders; it makes a dark area appear darker and a bright area appear brighter when they are juxtaposed.

KEY CONCEPTS
- assimilation
- complementary color
- contrast sensitivity function
- hue
- retina
- simultaneous contrast
- successive contrast

INTRODUCTION

Brightness is the perception of intensity of light. Roughly, the more intense a light is, the brighter it seems to be. Intensity refers to the physical energy of light, as measured by a photometer. Brightness, however, is a perceptual phenomenon: It cannot be measured by physical instruments. It is a basic perception, difficult if not impossible to describe; it must be experienced. Measurements of brightness are generally observers' reports of their experience viewing lights of different intensities. Only in living systems—only in the eye of the perceiver—is the term "brightness" relevant.

The brightness of a spot of light, although related to the intensity of light reflected from that spot, is also influenced by other factors. It varies with the intensity of light reflected from the immediately surrounding area at any given time and at immediately preceding times. In general, a spot appears brighter if the surrounding areas are dark or are stimulated with light perceived as complementary in color; it also appears brighter if the eye has become accustomed to the dark ("dark-adapted"). These factors contribute contrast, the perception of differences in light intensity, which enhances brightness. Brightness and contrast are perceptually linked.

INFLUENCES ON PERCEPTION

A light of a given physical intensity may appear quite bright when viewed with an eye that has been dark-adapted, perhaps by being covered for ten to fifteen minutes. That same light may seem dim in comparison to an eye exposed to bright light for the same time period. This is largely attributable to the fact that a dark-adapted eye has more photopigment available to respond to incoming light; when this pigment has been exposed, it becomes bleached and needs time to regenerate. The enhancement of differences in brightness by an adapting light or other stimulus preceding the test light is called successive contrast and is primarily attributable to the state of adaptation of the retina.

Simultaneous contrast can also affect brightness perception. In this case, a spot of light at one place on the retina can be made to appear brighter or dimmer depending only on changes in the lighting of adjacent retinal locations. A small gray paper square placed on a sheet of black paper appears brighter than an identical square on a sheet of white paper. This is mostly a result of lateral inhibition, or photoreceptors stimulated by the white background inhibiting the receptors stimulated by the square so it appears less dazzling on white than on black. In general, differences are enhanced when the stimuli are side by side.

Sensitivity to contrast also varies with the detail of the object being viewed. Reading a book involves attending to high spatial frequencies, closely spaced lines, and minute detail. Recognizing a friend across the room or finding one's car in a parking lot involves attention to much broader spatial frequencies; that is, the lines important for recognition are much farther apart. The visual system handles low, moderate, and high spatial frequencies, although not equally well. A contrast sensitivity function may be plotted to show which spatial frequencies are most easily detected—that is, to which frequencies the eye-brain system is most sensitive.

The peak of this function, the highest sensitivity to spatial frequency, is within the midrange of detectable frequencies. At this peak, it takes less physical contrast (a smaller intensity difference) for an observer to report seeing the border between areas of different frequency. At higher and lower spatial frequencies, sensitivity drops off, so greater intensity differences must be made for perception in those ranges.

While perceptual systems exaggerate physical contrast, they fail to notice lack of contrast, change, or movement. Changes in brightness, for example, can be made so gradually that no notice of them is taken at all. In fact, the visual system, while signaling changes well, does not respond to seemingly constant stimulation. When an image, a bright pattern of light projected on the retina, is stabilized so it does not move at all, the observer reports first seeing the image and then, in a few seconds, its fading from view. The field does not turn gray or black or become empty; it simply ceases to exist. A border circumscribing a pattern within another pattern, perhaps a red-filled circle within a green-filled one, may be stabilized on the retina. In this case, the inner border disappears completely: The observer continues to see an unstabilized green-filled circle with no pattern in it. The area that formerly appeared red—and which indeed does reflect long-wavelength light—is perceived only as a part of the homogeneous green circle. Thus, while borders and movement creating physical contrast are exaggerated in perception, a stimulus signaling no change at all is simply not perceived.

COLOR PERCEPTION

Brightness and contrast are especially well illustrated in color perception. In the retina, three different cone pigments mediate color perception. Each pigment maximally absorbs light of certain wavelengths: One maximally absorbs the short lengths that are perceived as blue, one the medium wavelengths perceived as green, and one the red or long-wavelength region of the spectrum. The outputs of the cones interact with one another in the visual system in such a way that reds and greens stand in opposite or complementary roles, as do blues and yellows, and black and white. A gray square reflects light of all wavelengths equally. It has no hue, or color. Yet when it is placed on a red background, it appears greenish; if placed on a blue background, that same gray square appears yellowish. In each case, the neutral square moves toward the complement of its background color. The background has induced the perception of hue, tinting the gray with the color of its complement. Brightness of the background can also affect hue. A royal-blue square against a moderately white background can appear deep navy when the background intensity is increased, or seem to be a powder blue when it is decreased. The same color in two different settings or under two different brightness conditions is not the same color.

The appearance of color is not a simple property of the color pigment itself but is defined in its relationship to others. Simultaneous color contrast can be quite startling, depending on the color relationships chosen. For example, if two squares of different hues but the same brightness are juxtaposed, colors appear very strong and exaggerated. One's attention goes immediately to the contrast. If they are complementary colors such as red and green, the contrast is heightened. If they are close to the complements of each other, they are perceived in the direction of complementarity.

Yet not all colors are contrasting. A color configuration that does not move toward contrast moves toward assimilation—toward being united with the major color present. For example, a painting's central blue feature may bring out subtly blue features elsewhere in the painting. Whenever colors show enough similarity to one another, they approach one another, emphasizing similarity rather than contrast. Both color contrast and assimilation are beautifully illustrated in Josef Albers's book *Interaction of Color* (1987).

THE PULFRICH PHENOMENON

Another visual demonstration of brightness effects is the Pulfrich pendulum effect, or the Pulfrich phenomenon. To observe this, tie a pendulum bob to a two-foot length of string. Swing this in a plane normal to the line of sight, moving it back and forth as a pendulum. Then observe this continuing motion while wearing glasses, one lens of which is darkened or covered with a sunglass cover. Suddenly the pendulum appears to move in an ellipse instead of an arc. This illusion is a brightness effect. The shaded or sunglass-covered eye does not receive as much light as the other eye at any given time. It takes this eye longer to integrate the light information it does receive and so, by the time it sends location information to the brain, the other eye is sending its information of another location. The brain interprets disparity, this difference in the locations, as depth. Therefore the pendulum appears to move closer and farther away from the observer in elliptical depth and not constantly in a single plane. Intriguingly, switching the covered eye changes the elliptical path from clockwise rotation to counterclockwise or vice versa.

The Pulfrich phenomenon is a demonstration of changes in perception with changes in brightness; such changes have very practical effects. Driving at dusk, for example, can be dangerous, because light levels are suddenly lower than expected. Although the eye gathers the available light for form, distance, and depth perception, it takes a longer period of time to do so. Unaware of this, a driver may find reaction time to be longer than in the middle of the day and not allow enough braking distance. Similarly, an umpire may halt an evening soccer game earlier than the spectators think is necessary because of low light levels. The spectators can see well enough, as they gather the light needed to perceive what is happening. The players, on the other hand, notice that their reaction times are extended and that they are having trouble localizing the ball.

For a third application, the fact that contrast sensitivity shows peaks in particular spatial frequencies bears explanatory if not practical value. Robert Sekule, Lucinda Hutman, and Cynthia Owsley showed, in a 1980 study, that as one grows older, sensitivity to low spatial frequencies decreases. This may partly explain why older people may show greater difficulty recognizing faces or locating an automobile than the young even though the two groups may be equally able to discriminate fine structural details. Making an older person aware of this change in sensitivity may be of assistance in defining the difficulty and in providing assurance that this is not a memory problem or a sign of decreasing cognitive ability.

SENSATION AND PERCEPTION

In the late nineteenth century, much of the early development of psychology as a science came about through work in sensation and perception. As empirical evidence grew, theories of contrast perception took shape. Two of the most notable are those of Hermann von Helmholtz and Ewald Hering.

Helmholtz had a psychological theory—a cognitive theory that explained color and brightness changes with contrast as errors in judgment. Errors were attributed to lack of practice in making brightness judgments, not in any physiological change in the neural input. Something suddenly looked brighter simply because it was misinterpreted, probably because one was focusing on some other aspect.

At the same time, Hering insisted and provided convincing demonstrations that contrast involves no error in judgment but has a physiological base. The neural response of any region of the retina, he argued, is a function not only of that region but also of neighboring regions. These neighboring sensations were postulated as having an effect opposite in brightness, or in the complementary color, of the region being viewed. Hering showed with successive contrast and simultaneous contrast studies that the outputs of different places on the retina could be modified by one another.

In 1890, William James described this controversy and gave, in *The Principles of Psychology*, his support to Hering's physiological position. With some modifications, it may be supported today. Yet the Helmholtz theory has some supportive evidence as well. For example, John Delk and Samuel Fillenbaum showed in 1956 that an object's characteristic color influences an observer's perception of that object's color. In this way, for example, an apple cut out of red paper is identified as redder than it actually is. This line of evidence would support Helmholtz in his theory of errors in judgment.

Almost any modern consideration of contrast includes a discussion of brightness changes at borders, commonly called Mach bands. This dates to 1865, when Ernst Mach, an Austrian physicist, described borders as places where differences in brightness are shown side by side. One way to observe these is to create a shadow by holding a book or other object with a sharp edge between a light source and the surface it illuminates. The border of the shadow is not crisp; in fact, it seems to be made of several lines. On the inside there is a dark stripe, darker than the central shaded object that separates it from the unshaded region. Adjacent to this, on the bright side of the shadow, is another stripe that appears brighter than the rest of the illuminated surface. These additional bands are an example of brightness contrast at a border where the physical contrast between shadow and light is exaggerated in perception. As true brightness phenomena, Mach bands do not exist in the physics of the situation (that is, in the distribution of light intensity). They are purely a perceptual phenomenon, their brightness depending not only on the intensity of an area but also on the intensity of surrounding areas.

SOURCES FOR FURTHER STUDY

Albers, Josef. *Interaction of Color*. Rev. ed. New Haven, Conn.: Yale University Press, 1987. Albers, an artist and teacher, presents commentary on form and color in addition to his paintings. Many of his works illustrate simultaneous contrast, successive contrast, assimilation, and other brightness effects. They are especially intriguing in that they were not designed to support psychological theories but to be viewed as art.

Bloomer, Carolyn M. *Principles of Visual Perception*. New York: Van Nostrand Reinhold, 1976. Bloomer interweaves visual perception and art theory in an easily comprehensible explanation of perceptual principles complete with illustrations from the fine arts. She includes a full chapter on color, including illustrations of contrast and suggestions for making one's own demonstrations. Annotated bibliography.

Gregory, Richard L. *Eye and Brain: The Psychology of Seeing*. 5th ed. Princeton, N.J.: Princeton University Press, 1997. An introduction to the basic phenomena of visual perception that was clearly written to be read and enjoyed by general readers as well as serious students. Gregory gives a full chapter on seeing brightness, including an excellent discussion of the eye's sensitivity to light. Well illustrated.

Palmer, Stephen. *Vision Science*. Cambridge, Mass.: MIT Press, 1999. A groundbreaking textbook covering all areas of visual perception, reflecting an integrated computational approach to the subject. Presents theoretical approaches and then places empirical data within that framework.

Bonnie S. Sherman

SEE ALSO: Depth and motion perception; Pattern recognition; Pattern vision; Sensation and perception; Vision: Color; Visual system.

Vision
Color

TYPE OF PSYCHOLOGY: Sensation and perception
FIELDS OF STUDY: Vision

Color vision depends on three types of photoreceptors in the retina of the eye. Each photoreceptor type absorbs light maximally at a wavelength corresponding to one of the three primary colors. The colors perceived in the brain result from integration of the degree to which each photoreceptor type is stimulated by light at given wavelengths.

KEY CONCEPTS
- chlorolabe
- cone
- cyanolabe
- dark adaptation
- deuteranope
- erythrolabe
- photoreceptor
- protanope
- rod
- tritanope

INTRODUCTION

Light is a form of radiant energy that is absorbed by sensory cells in the retina of the eye. The absorbing cells, the photoreceptors, convert light into the electrical energy of nerve impulses. The impulses generated by photoreceptors travel along the optic nerves to the optic lobes of the brain, where they are integrated into perception of a visual image.

The energy of light follows a wave path through space. The distance from crest to crest in a wave path is called the wavelength; the wavelengths of light that are visible to humans fall between about 400 nanometers (seen as blue light) and 750 nanometers (seen as red light). Wavelengths outside this range are invisible to humans because human photoreceptors are not "tuned" to receive and convert them to electrical energy.

The cornea and lens of the eye, acting together, focus light rays reflected from objects in the environment into a picturelike image that falls on the retina of the eye. The retina contains the photoreceptors of the eye, called rods and cones because of their elongated shapes. The cones, which are shorter in length than rods and conically shaped at their outer tips, are the photoreceptor type responsible for color vision. The retina contains about 110 to 120 million rods and 6 million cones. More than half the cones are concentrated in the fovea, where rods are completely absent.

CONES

There are three types of cones in the retina. Each type absorbs light maximally at a different wavelength. One absorbs maximally at 445 nanometers (blue light), one at 535 nanometers (green light), and one at 570 nanometers (yellow light near the border of the spectrum with orange). The absorption maxima at these wavelengths depend on three types of pigment molecules that absorb light in the cones. One pigment, cyanolabe, absorbs maximally at blue wavelengths; the second, chlorolabe, absorbs maximally at green wavelengths; and the third, erythrolabe, absorbs maximally at yellow wavelengths.

Each type of cone cell contains only one of the three pigments. As a result, there is one population of cones in the retina that absorbs blue light maximally, one population absorbing green, and one absorbing yellow. The three types of cones are mixed intimately in the fovea, the region of clearest vision in the retina.

The 445-, 535-, and 570-nanometer wavelengths are the colors absorbed most efficiently by each type of cone; however, each photoreceptor type also absorbs other wavelengths near their absorption maxima, although less efficiently. For example, the cone type absorbing maximally at yellow wavelengths actually absorbs wavelengths beginning at about 460 nanometers and extending to nearly 700. As wavelengths are encountered farther from the absorption maximum, light absorption becomes progressively less efficient. The pattern produces a smooth absorption curve that starts near zero on either side and peaks at the 570-nanometer wavelength.

The total ranges absorbed by the three cone types overlap, so that light at any wavelength in the visible range is likely to be absorbed by, and stimulate, at least two of the three photoreceptor types. For example, orange light at 580 nanometers is absorbed by and stimulates both the green and yellow cone types, but not the blue photoreceptors. The green and yellow photoreceptor types, however, are stimulated to a different extent: At 580 nanometers, the yellow photoreceptors would be stimulated almost maximally, but the green photoreceptors would be stimulated to only about 40 percent of their maximum.

COLOR PERCEPTION

This difference in the absorption and stimulation of cones by light of a given wavelength is considered to underlie human perception of color. For example, when light stimulates the yellow photoreceptors at 99 percent, the green photoreceptors at 40 percent, and the blue photoreceptors at 0 percent, the color is perceived as orange. A wavelength stimulating the blue and green photoreceptors at 50 percent of their maxima, and yellow photoreceptors at 5 percent, is perceived as a blue-green color.

Light at wavelengths above about 620 nanometers stimulates only the yellow photoreceptors at or below 70 percent of their maximum; these wavelengths are perceived as red colors. For this reason, the photoreceptors absorbing maximally in the yellow wavelengths are often identified as red rather than yellow cones. Similarly, light at about 420 nanometers stimulates only the blue photoreceptors and is perceived as a deep blue. Light stimulating all three cone types equally is perceived as white. White is strictly a perceived color; there is no wavelength of light corresponding to white.

In response to absorbing light at various levels nearer or farther from their maxima, the photoreceptors generate nerve impulses. When absorbing

at its maximum, a photoreceptor generates impulses at the highest frequency; at levels farther from the maximum, the frequency of impulses is proportionately reduced. The impulses sent by the three types of cones at various frequencies are partially integrated into color perception in the complex nerve circuitry of the retina, which may be considered as an extension of the brain into the eye, and partly in the optic lobes at the rear of the cerebral cortex. When objects are viewed in bright light, the total integration reconstructs the image focused in the fovea of the retina as a full-color perception of the scene viewed.

Each cone in the fovea has essentially a straight-line connection through neurons to the optic lobes. As a result, each detail of light, shade, and color in the image is likely to register as differences in stimulation between neighboring cones in the fovea, and to be registered and transmitted separately to the visual area of the brain. This arrangement specializes the cones in the fovea for the detection of minute details in full color.

DARK ADAPTATION

Color reception by the cones is most efficient in bright light. As light intensity falls during and after sunset, stimulation of the cones drops off rapidly. (The cones have relatively little ability to adapt to dark as compared to the rods of the retina.) The yellow photoreceptors drop out first, so that colors in the yellow, orange, and red wavelengths fade and, in deep twilight, appear gray or black. The blue and green photoreceptors still retain some sensitivity at twilight, so that blues and greens can still be perceived. In deepest twilight, only the blue photoreceptors are stimulated, so that if any color can be perceived at all, the scene appears blue-black. The shift in color sensitivity toward the greens and blues in reduced light also explains why green fields and trees look so rich in color, and reds and yellows seem dull, on overcast or rainy days.

Adaptation to darkness occurs through an increase in the amount of pigment molecules in both the cone and rod photoreceptors. The ability of the cone cells to increase their quantities of pigment molecules is limited as compared to the rods, which can greatly increase their pigment quantities and their sensitivity to light. As a result, as light intensity decreases, visual perception shifts from the cones to the rods, which detect light but are not stimulated differentially by different wavelengths. This produces the perception of images of grays and blacks rather than color in light that is too dim to stimulate the cones. Because the rods are outside the region of sharp vision in the fovea, objects are perceived only as relatively unfocused, fuzzy images in light of very low intensity.

The rods are completely insensitive to red light. Therefore, it is possible to become completely dark-adapted even if relatively bright red light is used as a source of illumination. For this reason, persons who must work under conditions of reduced light, such as pilots flying at night, commonly use red light for required illumination.

COLOR BLINDNESS

Individuals who are color-blind carry gene mutations that reduce or inhibit the synthesis of one or more of the three color-absorbing pigments of the cones in the retina. A protanope, an individual who carries a mutation inhibiting synthesis of the erythrolabe, or yellow-absorbing pigment, is insensitive to red, orange, and yellow wavelengths and perceives all these colors as the same gray or greenish hue. Typically, such individuals cannot distinguish between green and red. A deuteranope, a person lacking the chlorolabe, or green-absorbing pigment, is also unable to distinguish between red, orange, yellow, and green. Since their inability to distinguish between red, orange, yellow, and green is similar, both protanopes and deuteranopes are classified as red-green color-blind. A tritanope, an individual deficient in the cyanolabe, or blue-absorbing pigment, cannot distinguish between blue and green. Persons deficient in all three pigments cannot perceive color and see the world only in shades of gray. Mutations affecting synthesis of the chlorolabe and erythrolabe pigments, producing green and red color blindness, are most common. About 2 percent of men are deficient in the erythrolabe pigment, and about 6 percent of men are deficient in the chlorolabe pigment, giving a total of about 8 percent of men who are red-green color-blind. The total red-green color blindness among women is about 2 percent. Blue color blindness is relatively rare in the human population; only about one in as many as 65,000 people is deficient in the blue-absorbing pigment.

Color blindness affects males more often than females—about twenty times more frequently—because it is a sex-linked, recessive trait. A color-blind father cannot pass the trait to any of his sons. A color-blind mother married to a man with normal vision will pass the trait to all of her sons. Her daughters will have normal vision but will be carriers of the trait. The sons of a female carrier of the trait married to a man with normal vision have a 50 percent chance of being color-blind; all the daughters are expected to have normal vision. Half of the daughters, however, will be carriers of the trait. Deficiencies in color vision are presently uncorrectable.

COLOR COMMENTARY

The beginnings of an understanding of color vision go back to 1801, when the English physicist Thomas Young proposed that the human eye has only three different kinds of receptors for color. According to Young, an ability to sense the hundreds of different colors that humans can recognize depends on an interaction between the three receptor types. Young based his idea on the fact that painters can mix any color by starting from only three: the red, blue, and yellow primary colors. Orange, for example, can be mixed from equal quantities of red and yellow. Young's highly perceptive explanation for this was that wavelengths in the orange range are not actually produced when light is reflected from mixed red and yellow pigments. Instead, he proposed that the mixture of red and yellow stimulates red and yellow receptors in the eye equally. This equal stimulation is summed and interpreted in the brain as the color orange. Young proposed that the sensation of white, which can be mixed from pigments by adding equal quantities of red, yellow, and blue, is produced through equal stimulation of all three receptors. Young's proposals, which turned out to be essentially correct, were later expanded by the German physicist and physiologist Hermann von Helmholtz into what is now known as the Young-Helmholtz trichromatic theory of color vision.

Two lines of more contemporary research revealed that there are only three types of color photoreceptors in the eye, as Young and Helmholtz proposed. One series of experiments, carried out in the 1960's by Paul K. Brown and George Wald at Harvard University, and Edward F. MacNichol, William H. Dobelle, and William B. Marks at The Johns Hopkins University, measured the wavelengths of light stimulating individual cones to generate nerve impulses. This work revealed that there are actually only three different types of cones, each absorbing light maximally at the blue (445-nanometer), green (535-nanometer), or yellow-orange (570-nanometer) wavelength. These colors differ to some extent from the red, blue, and yellow photoreceptors proposed by Young and Helmholtz, whose ideas were derived primarily from the results obtained by mixing painter's pigments; however, they are exactly the colors used if colored lights rather than painter's pigments are used to mix additional colors from three primary colors.

The second line of major supporting evidence came from experiments carried out by George Wald, William A. H. Rushton, and others, identifying and isolating the pigments responsible for light absorption in the eye. Some of these experiments were done by the simple but elegant technique of shining a white or colored light into the eye and then analyzing the light reflected from the retina. The reflected light was missing the colors absorbed by the pigments in the eye; the colors absorbed in the eye were those absorbed by the pigments in rod cells. Only three different pigments were detected in the cones—the cyanolabe, chlorolabe, and erythrolabe pigments—by these experiments, as predicted by Young and Helmholtz so many years ago.

SOURCES FOR FURTHER STUDY

Albers, Josef. *Interaction of Color.* Rev. ed. New Haven, Conn.: Yale University Press, 1987. Albers, an artist and teacher, presents commentary on form and color in addition to his paintings. Many of his works illustrate simultaneous contrast, successive contrast, assimilation, and other brightness effects. They are especially intriguing in that they were not designed to support psychological theories but to be viewed as art.

Ball, Philip. *Bright Earth: Art and the Invention of Color.* New York: Farrar, Straus and Giroux, 2002. Primarily a history of art, but covers subjects such as the physiology of color perception and the cultural factors, such as the range of color vocabulary, that influence color perception.

Berne, Robert M., Matthew N. Levy, Bruce M. Keoppen, and Bruce A. Stanton. *Physiology.* 4th ed. St. Louis: C. V. Mosby, 1998. The chapter on the visual system in this standard college physiology text outlines the anatomy and physiology of the human organ systems integrated in the detection and perception of vision, including the eye and the optic lobes of the brain, and the nerve tracts connecting them. Intended for students at the college level, but written clearly enough so that it should be accessible to high school readers.

Gegenfurtner, Karl R., and Lindsey T. Sharpe, eds. *Color Vision: From Genes to Perception.* New York: Cambridge University Press, 2000. A multidisciplinary textbook on color vision, ranging from the physiology of perception to the cognitive psychology of color. Contains twenty review essays written by thirty-five internationally renowned experts in the field.

Palmer, Stephen. *Vision Science.* Cambridge, Mass.: MIT Press, 1999. A groundbreaking textbook covering all areas of visual perception, reflecting an integrated computational approach to the subject. Presents theoretical approaches and then places empirical data within that framework.

Stephen L. Wolfe

SEE ALSO: Brain structure; Depth and motion perception; Pattern recognition; Pattern vision; Sensation and perception; Vision: Brightness and contrast; Visual system.

Visual system

TYPE OF PSYCHOLOGY: Sensation and perception
FIELDS OF STUDY: Biological influences on learning; vision

The visual system allows perception of an object's form, color, size, movement, and distance. In seeing, light passes through a transparent lens in each eye, is focused, enters the inner eye, and falls on the retina. The resultant nerve impulses move to the brain through the optic nerve to create sight.

KEY CONCEPTS
- blindness
- cornea
- fovea centralis
- night blindness
- peripheral vision
- photopic and scotopic vision
- retina
- rods and cones

- sclera
- vision defects

INTRODUCTION

The visual system is one of the primary means by which humans are aware of and monitor their environment. The visual system provides information on the form, color, size, movement, and distance of any object in sight range. Its importance is seen in the fact that sight loss (blindness) is much more debilitating than any other sensory deprivation. The anatomy of the eye is quite complex. Each eye sits in a protective, bony skull cavity, an eye socket. The human eye is roughly spherical and about one inch in diameter. Six muscles, attached at one end to the eyeball and at the other end to the eye socket, control the directional movements of each eye.

The semiliquid eyeball interior is surrounded by three tissue layers. Outermost is the tough and protective sclera, made up of fibrous tissue. The sclera, or "white of the eye," has at its front a circular cornea. This sclera segment is modified to allow light rays to enter the eye and to aid in the focusing of light reflected from objects seen. At the front of each eye, paired eyelids protect the sclera's outer surface, removing dirt and lubricating with tears by blinking. The eyelids also close reflexively for protection when an object comes close to an eye.

The middle and inner tissue layers of the eye are the choroid and the retina. The choroid holds all the blood vessels that feed the eye and a muscular ciliary body that alters the shape of the eye lens in order to help to focus light. The retina lines most of the eyeball interior, except at its front. Retinal tissue converts light energy to nerve impulses carried to the brain. Choriod blood vessels extend throughout the retina, except at its front. There, a hole, the pupil, allows light entry into the eye. A circular iris around the pupil gives each eye its color.

The retina translates light energy into nerve impulses, using rod cells, cone cells, bipolar cells, and ganglion cells. Rods and cones are light-sensitive, yielding nerve impulses when they are struck by light. Bipolar cells transfer the acquired information to the brain via ganglion cell fibers in the optic nerve at the rear of the eye. The rods, sensitive to tiny amounts of light, enable dim light vision. Cones enable the perception of color and detail. Rods and cones hold the pigment rhodopsin (RO, or visual purple). When it interacts with light, RO decom-

poses to a protein (opsin) and a form of vitamin A called retinal$_1$. More RO must be made before a rod's next operation. Unless the diet provides vitamin A (as retinol$_1$) in amounts enabling this, an afflicted person has night blindness (nyctalopia). Nyctalopics cannot see well in dim light.

A small region in the retina's center, the fovea centralis, contains cones but no rods, and cone number per unit of retinal area decreases as the front edge of the retina—near the pupil—is approached from the fovea. In contrast, the relative number of rods increases as the number of cones diminishes. Humans see most clearly in daylight, using the fovea almost exclusively. At night, vision is accomplished mostly by using a retina region at the side of each eye.

A blind spot in the visual field occurs when objects cast images on the retina's optic disk. This disk, the point where the optic nerve leaves the eye, lacks both rods and cones. The optic nerves from the two eyes pass through the optic chiasma. Fibers from the inner half of each retina cross to the opposite side of the brain. Those from the outer half remain on the same side of the brain. This causes the right visual field, which stimulates the left half of each retina to activate the left half of the thalamus and visual cortex. The left visual field affects the right half of the brain, a situation similar to that of the other human sensory systems.

The visual cortex includes the occipital lobe of each cortical hemisphere, and there is a point-for-point correspondence between the retinas and the cortex. This yields a "map," whose every point represents a point on the retina and visual space seen by each eye. Vision simultaneously depicts object color, shape, location, movement, and orientation in space. Seeking a model to explain the overall brain action in vision, neurophysiologists have identified various cortical cell types, each involved selectively in these features. Retinal maps from each eye merge in a cortical projection area, which allows images from the two eyes to yield stereoscopic vision. Other brain regions also participate in vision; for instance, the cortex appears to be involved in perceiving form and movement.

LENSES AND VISION TYPES

Just behind the cornea, a transparent, elastic lens is attached to a ligament which controls its shape. Lens shape focuses light reflected from an object

The Anatomy of the Human Eye

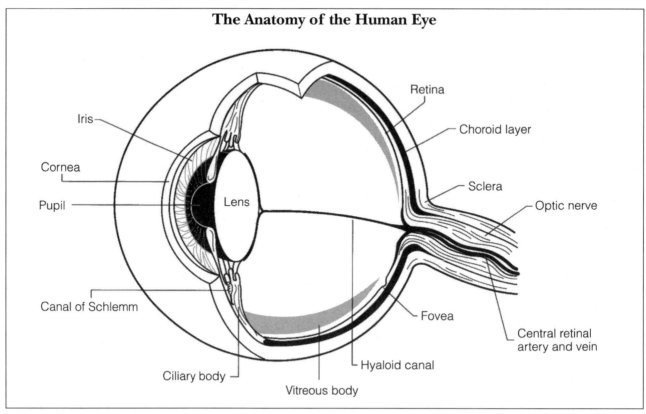

(Hans & Cassidy, Inc.)

and forms on the retina the sharpest possible visual image. The eyes regulate the amount of light reaching retinal rods and cones by contracting or expanding the pupil by means of the iris. These involuntary responses are controlled by brain reflex pathways. The lens also divides the eye into two compartments. The small compartment in front of the lens holds watery aqueous humor. The much larger rear compartment between lens and retina is full of jellylike vitreous humor. This humor maintains the eye's shape.

Usable visible (380- to 730-nanometer) light enters the eye through the pupil and excites color sensations by interacting with retinal cones. Light reflected from an object passes through the lens to form a focused retinal image, similar to what a camera forms on film. Focusing a visual image also requires regulation of the amount of light passing through the pupil by making the iris larger or smaller. The eye lens produces an inverted retinal image, interpreted in the brain right-side-up. Binocular vision enables accurate depth perception. Each

eye gets a slightly different view of any object, and the two retina images are interpreted by the brain as a three-dimensional view.

Nocturnal animals see in low-light environments with black-and-white (scotopic) vision. Diurnal (day-living) animals have photopic vision, which needs much more light in order to perceive colors and textures. Humans have both photopic and scotopic vision. Scotopic vision uses the rods as well as photosensitive RO. RO is bleached by bright light, so scotopic animals are almost blind by day. Humans suffer brief blindness on walking indoors on bright days. Then, by dark adaptation, scotopic vision quickly begins to function. Faulty dark adaptation (night blindness) occurs in humans who lack rods or are vitamin A deficient. Afflicted individuals cannot find their way around at night without artificial light. Photopic vision mostly uses the fovea, so it is due to cones, the only foveal visual cells. In the central fovea there are approximately 100,000 cones per square millimeter of retinal surface. Each cone associates with nerve cells that process the incoming visual data, convey it to the brain cortex, and provide detailed information on objects whose images fall in the fovea.

Peripheral vision occurs outside of the fovea, as may be seen by looking directly at one letter on a page. That letter and a few others, nearby, look very sharp and black because they are seen by foveal vision. The rest of the page, seen by peripheral vision, blurs. The clarity of foveal vision versus peripheral vision is due to the increasing scarcity of cones in retinal areas farther and farther from the fovea. Also, the nerve connections in the retinal periphery result in each optic nerve fiber being activated by hundreds of rods. This shared action is useful in detecting large or dim objects at night. However, it prevents color vision, which requires the brain to differentiate between many signals.

VISUAL DEFECTS AND THEIR SYMPTOMS

Human eyes can have numerous vision defects. The most common of these defects are small, opaque bodies (floaters) in the eye humors. Usually, floaters are only an inconvenience. Much more serious are lens opacities called cataracts. They develop for several reasons, including advancing age and diabetes. Opacity of the cornea can also cause obscured vision. It can be repaired through the transplantation of a section of clear cornea from another person. Three very dangerous eye diseases that can cause blindness are detached retinas (retina rips), glaucoma (eye pressure buildup due to blocked tear ducts), and macular degeneration (destruction of the retinal areas responsible for sight).

Six serious, but relatively easily treated, vision problems are myopia, hyperopia, presbyopia, astigmatism, diplopia, and strabismus. They are due to incorrect eyeball length, to lens defects, or to external eye muscle weakness. In myopia (near-sightedness) the eyeball is too long. Light from nearby objects will focus well on the retina. Distant rays focus before it, yielding blurry images. Conversely, farsightedness (hyperopia) occurs because the eyeball is too short. As a result, the light from distant objects focuses on the retina, but that from nearby objects focuses behind it and makes them blurry. An eye can also lose the ability to adapt quickly from far vision to near vision. This problem, presbyopia, usually happens after age forty. In an astigmatism, uneven curvature of an eye lens causes retinal images to be made up of short lines, not sharp points.

Weakness or paralysis of external eyeball muscles may cause diplopia (double vision) and strabismus (squint).

Blindness, the most serious vision problem, is much more debilitating than any other sensory deprivation. It occurs in many forms. Some are temporary, mild, and readily treated. Others are severe and untreatable. Color blindness is an incurable lack of some or all color vision. This congenital form of blindness is attributed to genetic defects in the retina or some part of the optic tract. It is mild, causing, at worst, no color perception and a life spent in a black-and-white world. Amblyopia, weak vision without apparent structural eye damage, is another type of acquired blindness, due to toxic drugs, alcoholism, or hysteria. Blindness may also be caused by diseases such as iritis and trachoma.

Blindness varies in extent, from inability to distinguish light from darkness (total blindness) to inability to see well enough to do any job requiring use of the eyes (economic blindness) to vocational and educational blindness: inability to work in a job done before becoming blind, and inability to become educated by methods commonly used in school, respectively. Most severe blindness is permanent and incurable. There are about two blind people per thousand in industrialized nations and two per hundred in underdeveloped countries. The causes of blindness include genetic abnormalities of components of the eye or brain, pressure on the optic nerve from a brain tumor, detachment of the retina from the choriod, damage to the eyes or brain by excess light, or severe head trauma.

TREATMENT OPTIONS FOR VISION PROBLEMS

Visual defects are most often identified by ophthalmologists who prescribe eye treatments such as the use of eyeglasses, contact lenses, or surgery. Detached retinas and glaucoma can both be repaired by surgery, and most night blindness is cured by adding sufficient vitamin A to the diet to allow optimal cone and rod operation. Amblyopia is treated by psychologists or psychiatrists who identify its basis and work with afflicted individuals to reassure them or apply pharmacological treatment of the problem. Some kinds of structurally based blindness may be cured by surgery (such as removing brain tumors). However, in a great many cases the blindness is incurable. Where blindness is acquired by sighted people (adventitious blindness) it can be important to receive the help of a mental health professional to gain the ability to live with it successfully. This is most crucial early in the adventitious blindness, when afflicted individuals are least likely to be able to cope with being cut off from a major source of their contact with the world.

The adjustments that must be made upon occurrence of adventitious blindness are so extensive that the blind person eventually becomes a different individual from the sighted person he or she once was. Usually, the initial response to adventitious blindness is apathy and severe depression. These symptoms are followed by the return of interest in living and coping with the practical problems caused by blindness. The function of a psychologist or a psychiatrist is the careful combination of psychotherapy and pharmacological treatment—varied, individually, in its length and scope—to ready each afflicted individual to function well in a sighted world. After an adventitiously blind individual is capable of coping well with being blind, there are several federal and private agencies aimed at teaching such individuals to operate well and engaging in their training so as to allow them to reachieve gainful employment.

SOURCES FOR FURTHER STUDY

Chalkley, Thomas. *Your Eyes.* 3d ed. Springfield, Ill.: Charles C Thomas, 1995. Thoroughly covers the human eye; light and vision; diseases such as cataracts, glaucoma, and strabismus; how eyes and brain relate; and eye changes due to general disease and injury.

De Valois, Karen K., ed. *Seeing.* 2d ed. San Diego, Calif.: Academic Press, 2000. This work has chapters on vision, physiological aspects of vision, color perception, binocular vision processes, and motion perception. It includes a bibliography.

Hollins, Mark. *Understanding Blindness: An Integretive Approach.* Hillsdale, N.J.: Lawrence Erlbaum, 1989. A well-done book, covering blindness, its causes, and its psychological aspects. It also has a complete bibliography.

Hubel, David H. *Eye, Brain, and Vision.* New York: W. H. Freeman, 1995. Thoroughly covers the eye, the brain's function in vision, and vision. Includes a bibliography.

Rodieck, Robert W. *The First Steps in Seeing.* Sunderland, Mass.: Sinauer Associates, 1998. Covers vision, the physiology of vision and the eye, and the anatomy and histology of the eye. Good bibliography.

Schwartz, Steven H. *Visual Perception.* 2d ed. Stamford, Conn.: Appleton & Lange, 1999. Covers many aspects of vision, including the retina, functional retinal physiology, the cortex, color vision and its anomalies, depth perception, and the anatomy of the eye. Has a good bibliography.

Tovee, Martin J. *An Introduction to the Visual System.* New York: Cambridge University Press, 1996. Covers many vision topics, including the eye and image formation, color vision, organization of the visual system, the visual cortex, object perception and recognition, and motion perception.

Sanford S. Singer

SEE ALSO: Brain structure; Depth and motion perception; Hearing; Pattern recognition; Pattern vision; Sensation and perception; Smell and taste; Touch and pressure; Vision: Brightness and contrast; Vision: Color.

W

Watson, John B.

BORN: January 9, 1878, in Greenville, South Carolina

DIED: September 25, 1958, in New York City

IDENTITY: American psychologist

TYPE OF PSYCHOLOGY: Learning; origin and definition of psychology; psychological methodologies

FIELDS OF STUDY: Anxiety disorders; infancy and childhood

Watson founded a school of psychology known as behaviorism.

John Broadus Watson was born into a strict religious family. When sixteen years old, he entered Furman University and eventually received a master's degree. He then enrolled at the University of Chicago, where he became the youngest student ever at the university to earn a Ph.D.

Watson was an instructor at Chicago for four years before becoming a professor at The Johns Hopkins University. When the department chairman resigned, Watson replaced him and also assumed editorship of *Psychological Review,* a respected journal. In 1913, he published "Psychology as the Behaviorist Views It" in the journal; this launched a new school of psychology. In the paper, Watson rejected the introspective techniques of the school of structuralism and declared that psychology must become the science of behavior by examining overt behavior in an objective fashion. Mentalistic concepts must be replaced by empirical study of observable behavior only. In 1915, Watson was elected president of the American Psychological Association and used this position to promote behaviorism.

Watson's behaviorism incorporated a strong form of environmentalism; he argued that there were no genetic influences on behavior and that humans were simply a product of their environment. In one famous demonstration, he and his graduate assistant Rosalie Rayner used Pavlovian conditioning to instill a phobia in a young boy. "Little Albert," an eleven-month-old infant, was conditioned to fear a rat after the animal's appearance was paired with a loud noise. The boy also cried when shown other furry objects, such as a rabbit and fur coat, even though these objects had not been paired with the noise. The boy's fear had generalized to objects similar to the rat. Watson argued, therefore, that phobias are simply learned behavior and not the result of unconscious sexual conflict, as Sigmund Freud had claimed.

Unfortunately, Watson's academic career ended unexpectedly in 1920. He was having an affair with

John B. Watson. (Hulton Archive)

Rayner and was forced to resign after his wife began divorce proceedings. Watson moved to New York and began a successful career in advertising. Throughout the 1920's, he continued to promulgate his ideas through several books, most notably *Behaviorism* (1924), and numerous articles. Many of these writings were read by general audiences and solidified behavioristic views in the United States.

By emphasizing the study of overt behavior, Watson's behaviorism moved psychology away from its philosophic roots and helped fashion it into a science. In many areas, such as learning, behaviorism dominated American psychology throughout much of the twentieth century. B. F. Skinner, one of the most famous twentieth century American psychologists, was a strong advocate of behaviorism.

Sources for Further Study

Buckley, Kerry W. *Mechanical Man: John Broadus Watson and the Beginnings of Behaviorism.* New York: Guilford Press, 1989. Provides a comprehensive examination of how Watson's personal and scientific lives affected each other.

Cohen, David. *J. B. Watson, the Founder of Behaviourism: A Biography.* London: Routledge & Kegan Paul, 1979. Persuasively demonstrates the breadth of Watson's psychological contributions and vision.

Fancher, Raymond E. *Pioneers of Psychology.* New York: W. W. Norton, 1979. Includes a chapter on Watson and Pavlov's contributions in making psychology the science of behavior.

Charles H. Evans

SEE ALSO: Behaviorism; Learning; Radical behaviorism: B. F. Skinner; Skinner, B. F.

Wechsler Intelligence Scale for Children-Third Edition (WISC-III)

DATE: Originally devised in 1949; revised in 1974 and 1991

TYPE OF PSYCHOLOGY: Intelligence and intelligence testing

FIELDS OF STUDY: Intelligence assessment

The Wechsler Intelligence Scale for Children-Third Edition (WISC-III) is an individually administered test battery developed to measure the intellectual ability of children aged six years through sixteen years, eleven months. The WISC-III is commonly used for the psychoeducational, neurological, and clinical assessment of school-aged children, and for the diagnosis of mental retardation, learning disabilities, brain injury, and giftedness.

KEY CONCEPTS
- culture bias
- intelligence test
- performance subtests
- psychoeducational assessment
- verbal subtests

INTRODUCTION

The Wechsler Intelligence Scale for Children-Third Edition (WISC-III) retains the essential content and structure of the original Wechsler Intelligence Scale for Children (WISC), published in 1949, and its 1974 revision (WISC-R). The third edition, however, provides current representative normative data, updated test items that attempt to minimize culture bias and gender bias, more contemporary and visually appealing testing materials, and clearer administrative procedures, factor structure rules, and scoring rules. These improvements make the test more interesting and fairer for the child and more user-friendly for the examiner.

HISTORY OF DEVELOPMENT

David Wechsler defined intelligence as the overall capacity of an individual to act purposefully, think rationally, and deal effectively with the environment. He believed intelligence to be a general concept that is multidetermined and multifaceted, rather than a specific trait or type of intellectual ability. An intelligence test is a device that assesses an individual's potential for purposeful and useful behavior. To measure intelligence at the adult level, he selected eleven subtests from a wide range of existing standardized tests and published the Wechsler-Bellevue Intelligence Scale in 1939. This assessment became the Wechsler Adult Intelligence Scale in 1955 and is currently the Wechsler Adult Intelligence Scale-Third Edition (WAIS-III), published in 1998.

In 1949, to provide an instrument to measure the intelligence of children as young as five years old, he developed the Wechsler Intelligence Scale for Children by designing easier items appropriate for children and adding them to the original scales. Due to suspected ethnic and socioeconomic bias in the standardization sample, the test was revised in 1974 to establish normative data that were more representative of ethnic minorities and children from lower socioeconomic levels. The present form, the Wechsler Intelligence Scale for Children-Third Edition, was published in 1991.

Description of the Test

The WISC-III consists of thirteen subtests organized into two groups: the verbal subtests and the performance subtests. The verbal subtests require language to administer the items and the child must provide a verbal response. These subtests and the behaviors assessed include information (knowledge of general information), similarities (abstract and conceptual thinking), arithmetic (arithmetic knowledge and short-term memory), vocabulary (general vocabulary knowledge and long-term memory), comprehension (social judgment), and digit span (short-term auditory memory). The performance subtests consist of perceptual-motor items that also must be administered verbally but require minimal or no verbal response. The performance subtests and behaviors measured are picture completion (perceptual discrimination), coding (visual-motor coordination), picture arrangement (visual perception), block design (abstract visual-spatial reasoning), object assembly (visual-motor coordination and integration), mazes (visual planning ability), and a new item labeled symbol search (perceptual discrimination). Subtests are reported as scaled (standard) scores with a mean of 10 and a standard deviation of 3.

The performance on each of these subtests yields three composite intelligence quotient (IQ) scores, which are also reported as scaled scores. The sum of the scaled scores on the verbal subtests yields the verbal IQ score and the sum of the scaled scores on the performance subtests results in the performance IQ scores. The verbal and performance subtests are then added to compute the full-scale IQ. The mean of each IQ is 100 and the standard deviation is 15. The WISC-III also provides four new index scores that are composites of subtests identified by a previous factor analytic study that reported the existence of four factors. The verbal comprehension index, perceptual organization index, freedom from dis-

tractibility index, and processing speed index also have a mean of 100 and a standard deviation of 15.

Standardization, Reliability, and Validity

The WISC-III was standardized on groups considered representative of the United States population of children according to 1988 census data. A stratified sampling plan was used to select children in representative proportions according to age, gender, race/ethnicity, geographic region, and parent education. A total of 2,200 children in eleven age groups ranging from six years to sixteen years, eleven months of age were selected, with 200 children (100 males and 100 females) in each group. Both public and private schools were sampled, and students receiving special services in school settings were included if they could speak and understand English. Thus, 7 percent of the sample consisted of students identified as having a learning disability, speech/language impairment, emotional disorder, physical disability, or reading challenge that qualified them for Chapter 1 programs. Also, 5 percent of the sample consisted of students identified as gifted and/or talented.

Split-half reliability coefficients reported in the manual for the verbal, performance, and full-scale IQ scores range from an average of .91 to .96. Due to the considerable overlap of test items, as well as the acceptable IQ score correlations and subtest correlations between the WISC-R and the WISC-III (.42 to .90), the validity research on the WISC-R was generalized to the WISC-III. The findings from these studies supported the construct, concurrent and predictive validity of the WISC-R.

Applications of the WISC-III

The WISC-III is commonly used for the psycho-educational assessment, neurological assessment, and clinical assessment of school-aged children. As a psychoeducational tool, the WISC-III is often part of the assessment battery used for the diagnosis of mental retardation and giftedness, and for the appropriate placement in special school-based programs. Moreover, the separation of verbal and performance subtests allows the examiner to select portions of the test that can be successfully completed by children with hearing impairments, visual impairments, and orthopedic handicaps. Studies have shown that responses to WISC-III subtests have provided information useful for the diagnosis and remediation of learning disabilities, brain injury, and other cognitive deficits.

SOURCES FOR FURTHER STUDY

Cooper, Shawn. *The Clinical Use and Interpretation of the Wechsler Intelligence Scale for Children.* 3d ed. Springfield, Mass.: Charles C Thomas, 1995. The author describes the history and development of the WISC-III and provides detailed information and advice on the administration, analysis and interpretation of the test. He offers a number of alternative approaches to the intellectual assessment of children and adolescents.

Groth-Marnat, Gary. *Handbook of Psychological Assessment.* 3d ed. New York: John Wiley & Sons, 1997. The author dedicates a chapter to a thorough overview of the measurement of intelligence as a construct, as well as the development of the Wechsler Intelligence Scales. The sections describing assessment of brain damage and special populations of school-age children are particularly interesting and useful to clinicians and educators.

Newmark, Charles S. *Major Psychological Assessment Instruments.* 2d ed. Boston: Allyn & Bacon, 1996. The author describes the psychometric properties of the WISC-III, the specific abilities measured by each of the subtests, and the sources of IQ scores and index scores. The book provides very clear descriptions of the clinical uses of the test, approaches to interpret test results, and the assets and liabilities of the test.

Sattler, Jerome M. *Assessment of Children.* 3d ed. San Diego, Calif.: Author, 1992. Three chapters in this textbook are devoted to a highly detailed description of the development, characteristics, subtests, and interpretation of the WISC-R. The writing style is directed toward students and professionals who might not have a strong background in tests and measurements.

_____. *WISC-III and WPPSI-R Supplement to Assessment of Children.* San Diego, Calif.: Author, 1992. This supplement to *Assessment of Children* compares the WISC-R and the WISC-III, and describes the WISC-III in detail. The supplement was designed to be more readable and comprehensive than the main text. However, according to the author, the supplement should be used in conjunction with the main text in order to have all the tables and guidelines needed to interpret the WISC-III.

Wechsler, David. *Manual for the Wechsler Intelligence Scale for Children.* 3d ed. New York: Psychological Corporation, 1991. The technical manual that was published with the WISC-III provides information on the development and application of the test, standardization procedures, administration and scoring procedures, and statistical information on reliability and validity. Chapter 2 provides a detailed description of the changes made to update and improve the WISC-R.

"The Wechsler Intelligence Scale for Children-Third Edition." In *The Twelfth Mental Measurement Yearbook,* edited by Jane C. Conoley and James C. Impara. Lincoln: University of Nebraska Press, 1995. Technical information about the WISC-III is provided and 409 references are listed that relate to the development, psychometric quality, and use of the test. Two independent reviews of the test by measurement specialists describe the characteristics, updates, changes, strengths, and weaknesses of the test.

Woodrich, David L. *Children's Psychological Testing: A Guide for Nonpsychologists.* 3d ed. Baltimore: Brooks, 1997. This resource describes the reasons for psychological testing, explains the principles of assessment, and provides a nontechnical overview of the WISC-III. The writing style is very appropriate for nonprofessional readers.

Lyn T. Boulter

SEE ALSO: Ability tests; Assessment; Career and personnel testing; Career Occupational Preference System (COPS); College entrance examinations; Creativity: Assessment; General Aptitude Test Battery (GATB); Human resource training and development; Intelligence tests; Interest inventories; Kuder Occupational Interest Survey (KOIS); Peabody Individual Achievement Test (PIAT); Race and intelligence; Scientific methods; Stanford-Binet test; Strong Interest Inventory (SII); Survey research: Questionnaires and interviews; Testing: Historical perspectives.

Within-subject experimental designs

TYPE OF PSYCHOLOGY: Psychological methodologies
FIELDS OF STUDY: Experimental methodologies

Within-subject designs are experimental plans in which each participant in the experiment receives every level of the independent variable. Such designs are powerful, because individual differences cannot confound the effects of the independent variable.

KEY CONCEPTS

- balanced Latin square
- between-subject designs
- carryover effects
- confounding
- counterbalancing
- dependent variable
- independent variable
- reversal design
- small-*n* designs

INTRODUCTION

In an experiment, a particular comparison is produced while other factors are held constant. For example, in order to investigate the effects of music on reading comprehension, an experimenter might compare the effects of music versus no music on the comprehension of a chapter from a history textbook. The comparison that is produced—music versus no music—is called the independent variable. An independent variable must have at least two levels or values so that a comparison can be made. The behavior that is observed or measured is called the dependent variable, which would be some measure of reading comprehension in the example.

Presumably, any changes in reading comprehension during the experiment depend on changes in the levels of the independent variable. The intent of an experiment is to hold everything constant except the changes in the levels of the independent variable. If this is done, the experimenter can assume that changes in the dependent variable were caused by changes in the levels of the independent variable.

ROLE OF INDEPENDENT VARIABLE

Experimental design concerns the way in which the levels of the independent variable are assigned to experimental subjects. This is a crucial concern, because the experimenter wants to make sure that it is the independent variable and not something else that causes changes in behavior. Between-subject designs are plans in which different participants receive the levels of the independent variable. There-

fore, in terms of the example already mentioned, some people would read with music playing and other people would read without music. Within-subject designs are plans in which each participant receives each level of the manipulated variable. In a within-subject design, each person would read a history chapter both while music is playing and in silence. Each of these designs has unwanted features that make it difficult to decide whether the independent variable caused changes in the dependent variable.

Because different subjects receive each level of the independent variable in a between-subject design, the levels of the independent variable vary with the subjects in each condition. Any effect observed in the experiment could result from either the independent variable or the characteristics of the subjects in a particular condition. For example, the people who read while music is playing might simply be better readers than those who read in silence. This difference between the people in the two groups would make it difficult to determine whether music or reading ability caused changes in comprehension. When something other than the independent variable could cause the results of an experiment, the results are confounded. In between-subject designs, the potential effects of the independent variable are confounded with the different subjects in each condition. Instead of the independent variable, individual differences, such as intelligence or reading ability, could account for differences between groups. This confounding (the variation of other variables with the independent variable of interest, as a result of which any effects cannot be attributed with certainty to the independent variable) may be minimized by assigning participants to conditions randomly or by matching the different subjects in some way, but these tactics do not eliminate the potential confounding. For this and other reasons, many experimenters prefer to use within-subject designs.

Because each subject receives each level of the independent variable in within-subject designs, subjects are not confounded with the independent variable. In the example experiment, this means that both good and bad readers would read with and without music. Yet the order in which a subject receives the levels of the independent variable is confounded with the levels of the independent variable. Therefore, determining whether a change in the dependent variable occurred because of the independent variable or as a result of the timing of the administration of the treatment might be difficult. This kind of confounding is called a carryover effect. The effects of one value of the independent variable might carry over to the period when the next level is being tested. Just as likely, an unwanted carryover effect could result because the subject's behavior changes as the experiment progresses. The subject might become better at the task because of practicing it or worse because of boredom or fatigue. Whatever the source of the carryover effects, they represent serious potential confounding.

COUNTERBALANCING

Carryover effects can be minimized by counterbalancing. Counterbalancing means that the order of administering the conditions of an experiment is systematically varied. Consider the reading experiment: One condition is reading with music (M), and the comparison level is reading in silence (S). If all subjects received S before M, order would be confounded with condition. If half the subjects had M before S and the remaining subjects had S before M, the order of treatments would not be confounded with the nature of the treatments. This is so because both treatment conditions occur first and second equally often.

Complete counterbalancing is done when all possible orders of the independent variable are administered. Complete counterbalancing is easy when there are two or three levels of the independent variable. With four or more levels, however, complete counterbalancing becomes cumbersome because of the number of different orders of conditions that can be generated. With more than three levels, experimenters usually use a balanced Latin square to decide the order of administering conditions. In a balanced Latin square, each condition occurs at the same time period on average and each treatment precedes and follows each other treatment equally often. Imagine an experiment with four levels of the independent variable, called A, B, C, and D. One might think of these as four different types of music that are being tested in the reading-comprehension example. Suppose there are four subjects, numbered 1, 2, 3, and 4. In a balanced Latin square, the following would be the orders for the four subjects: subject 1, A, B, D, C; subject 2, B, C, A, D; subject 3, C, D, B, A; subject 4, D, A, C, B.

Notice that across subjects each treatment occurs first, second, third, and fourth. Notice also that each treatment precedes and follows each other treatment. Although these four orders do not exhaust the possibilities for four treatments (there are a total of twenty-four), they do minimize the confounding from carryover effects.

INFERENTIAL STATISTICS AND TESTING SUBJECTS

Another feature favoring within-subject designs concerns inferential statistics. Because each participant serves in all conditions in within-subject designs, variability associated with individual differences among subjects has little influence on the statistical significance of the results. This means that within-subject designs are more likely than between-subject designs to yield a statistically significant result. Experimenters are more likely to find an effect attributable to the independent variable when its levels vary within subjects rather than between them.

A final reason within-subject designs are preferred to between-subject ones is that they require fewer subjects for testing. To try to minimize the confounding effects of individual differences in between-subject designs, experimenters typically assign many subjects randomly to each condition of the experiment. Since individual differences are not a hindrance in within-subject designs, fewer subjects can be tested, and there is a corresponding savings in time and effort.

REVERSAL DESIGN

Experimenters in all areas of psychology use within-subject designs. These designs are used whenever the independent variable is unlikely to have permanent carryover effects. Thus, if the characteristics of the subjects themselves are the variable of interest (such as place of birth or reading ability), those variables must be varied between subjects. If permanent carryover effects are of interest (such as learning to type as a function of practice), however, experimenters use within-subject plans.

Many experiments undertaken to solve practical problems use within-subject designs. These experiments are often small-n designs, which means that the number of subjects (n) is small—sometimes only one. Consider an experiment conducted by Betty M. Hart and her associates. They wanted to decrease the amount of crying exhibited by a four-year-old boy in nursery school. They observed his behavior for several days to find the baseline rate of crying episodes. During a ten-day period, the boy had between five and ten crying episodes each day that lasted at least five seconds. Hart and her associates noted that the teacher often tried to soothe the boy when he began crying. The researchers believed that this attention rewarded the crying behavior. Therefore, in the second phase of the experiment, the teacher ignored the boy's crying unless it resulted from an injury. Within five days, the crying episodes had decreased and remained at no more than one per day for a week. To gain better evidence that it was the teacher's attention that influenced the rate of crying, a third phase of the experiment reinstated the conditions of the baseline phase. The teacher paid attention to the boy when he whined and cried, and in a few days the level of crying was back to six or seven episodes per day.

The small-*n* design used by Hart and her associates is an example of a reversal design. In a reversal design, there is first a baseline phase, then a treatment phase, and finally a return to the baseline phase to make sure that it was the treatment that changed the behavior. Hart's experiment had a fourth phase in which the teacher again ignored the boy's crying, because the purpose of the treatment was to reduce the crying. In the fourth phase, the level of crying dropped to a negligible level.

When there is only one subject in an experiment, counterbalancing cannot be used to minimize carryover effects. Thus, the experience in the treatment phase of a reversal design might carry over into the second baseline phase. Experimenters seek an approximate return to the original behavior during the second baseline phase, but the behavior is seldom exactly as it was before the treatment period. Therefore, deciding about the effectiveness of the treatment introduced in the second phase may be difficult. This means that the reversal design is not a perfect experimental design. It has important applications in psychology, however, especially in clinical psychology, where practical results rather than strict experimental control are often very important.

TRAPPERS CASE STUDY

Lise Saari conducted an experiment that used a more conventional within-subject design. Saari wanted to assess the effect of payment schedule on the performance and attitudes of beaver trappers.

The trappers received an hourly wage from a forest-products company while they participated in the following experiment.

Initially, trapping performance was measured under the ordinary hourly payment plan. Later, the trappers worked under two incentive plans manipulated in a within-subject design. In the continuous-reward condition, trappers received an additional dollar for each animal that was trapped. In the second condition, trappers received a reward of four dollars when they brought in a beaver. They obtained the four dollars only if they correctly predicted twice whether the roll of a die would yield an even or an odd number. In this variable-ratio condition, the trapper could guess the correct roll one out of four times by chance alone. In summary, the trappers always received a one-dollar reward in the continuous-reward condition. In the variable-ratio condition, however, the payment of four dollars occurred once every four times on average. Therefore, the trappers averaged an extra dollar for each beaver in each condition.

To minimize carryover effects, counterbalancing the order of treatments occurred as follows. The trappers were split into two groups, which alternated between the two schedules, spending a week at a time on each. This weekly alternation of experimental payment continued for the entire trapping season.

Compared to the amount of trapping that occurred under the hourly wage, the results showed that beaver trapping increased under both the continuous and the variable-payment scheme. The increase was, however, much larger under the variable payment plan than under the continuous one. In addition, Saari found that the trappers preferred to work under the variable-ratio scheme. Since both plans yielded the same amount of extra money on average, the mode of giving the payment (continuous or variable) seems crucial.

The experiment by Saari has obvious important practical implications concerning methods of payment. Still, it is equally important that the design of the experiment was free of confounding. The counterbalancing scheme minimized the possibility of confounding the payment scheme with order. Thus, Saari could conclude that the change in attitudes and the increased trapping performance resulted from the variable payment plan, not from some confounding carryover effect.

USE IN PSYCHOLOGY

Within-subject designs have a long history of use in psychology. The psychophysics experiments conducted by Ernst Weber and Gustav Fechner in the nineteenth century were among the first within-subject experiments in psychology. The tradition of obtaining many observations on a few subjects started by Weber and Fechner continues in modern psychophysical scaling and signal-detection experiments.

One of the most famous small-*n* experiments in psychology is that reported by Hermann Ebbinghaus in his book *Über das Gedächtnis* (1885; *Memory: A Contribution to Experimental Psychology*, 1913). Ebbinghaus tested himself in a series of memory experiments. In his work on remembering nonsense syllables and poetry, he discovered many laws of retaining and forgetting. These laws are now firmly established. Numerous modern experiments with larger numbers of experimental participants and various verbal materials have yielded results confirming Ebbinghaus's work. Among the most important findings are the shape of the curve of forgetting over time, the important role of practice in improving retention, and the benefits of distributing practice as opposed to cramming it.

B. F. Skinner pioneered the use of small-*n* designs for laboratory experiments on rats and pigeons in the 1930's. Skinner's work on schedules of reinforcement is among the most frequently cited in psychology. In his work, Skinner insisted on making numerous observations of few subjects under tightly controlled conditions. His ability to control the behavior of experimental subjects and obtain reliable results in within-subject plans such as the reversal design has led to the wide acceptance of within-subject plans in laboratory and applied experimental work.

Developmental psychologists regularly use a variant of the within-subject design. This is the longitudinal design, in which repeated observations are made as the subject develops and grows older. In a typical longitudinal experiment, a child first might receive a test of problem solving when he or she is three years old. Then the test would be repeated at ages five and seven.

CROSS-SECTIONAL PLAN

The longitudinal design inherently confounds age or development with period of testing, since age cannot be counterbalanced for an individual. An alternative developmental design is the cross-sectional plan. In this design, subjects of different ages are tested at the same time. Since participants of different ages have grown up in different time periods with different people, age is confounded with generation of birth in the cross-sectional design. Thus, the cross-sectional plan is between subjects and cannot control for individual differences. Although the longitudinal design confounds age with time of testing, individual differences do not confound the results. Therefore, the longitudinal design is a valuable research tool for the developmental psychologist.

Because of their control, efficiency, and statistical power, within-subject designs are popular and important in psychology. All areas of applied and basic scientific psychology rely heavily on within-subject designs, and such designs are likely to remain important in the field.

SOURCES FOR FURTHER STUDY

Gescheider, George A. *Psychophysics: Method and Theory.* 2d ed. Hillsdale, N.J.: Lawrence Erlbaum, 1984. This is a standard work on psychophysical methods. Gescheider describes the many experimental plans used to examine the sensory judgments that people make. The student will find the discussion of method more valuable than the sections that deal with the theories of psychophysics.

Gravetter, Frederick J., and Larry B. Wallnau. *Essentials of Statistics for the Behavioral Sciences.* 4th ed. Belmont, Calif.: Wadsworth, 2001. This accessible statistics text shows the strength of within-subject designs. The authors do not assume that the reader has a sophisticated mathematical background, but understanding the statistical analysis of within-subject designs may require some effort.

Kantowitz, Barry H., David G. Elmes, and Henry L. Roediger III. *Experimental Psychology: Understanding Psychological Research.* 7th ed. Belmont, Calif.: Wadsworth, 2000. A standard textbook on all aspects of research in psychology. Chapters focus on experimental design, detail methods of counterbalancing, and small-*n* designs besides the reversal design. Can be understood by college students and sophisticated high school students.

Martin, David W. *Doing Psychology Experiments.* 5th ed. Belmont, Calif.: Wadsworth, 2001. Chapters 5 and 6 of this book examine many issues considered in this article. Martin presents humorous examples that may help the reader comprehend the important principles of experimental design.

Reis, Harry T., and Charles M. Judd, eds. *Handbook of Research Methods in Social and Personality Psychology*. New York: Cambridge University Press, 2000. A very thorough overview of psychological research methods. Within-subject experimental design is discussed at several points throughout.

David G. Elmes

SEE ALSO: Complex experimental designs: Developmental methodologies; Experimentation: Independent, dependent, and control variables; Sampling; Scientific methods; Signal detection theory; Statistical significance tests.

Women's psychology
Carol Gilligan

TYPE OF PSYCHOLOGY: Social psychology
FIELDS OF STUDY: Adolescence; classic analytic themes and issues; general constructs and issues; social motives

Carol Gilligan's theories of girls' and women's different moral voice and development led many researchers to examine the ways boys and girls, men and women develop morality, and has been instrumental in drawing attention to the importance of the study of the lives of girls and women.

KEY CONCEPTS
- ethic of care
- ethic of justice
- moral orientation
- relational self
- voice

INTRODUCTION
Within the fields of the moral psychology and the psychology of women, Carol Gilligan, a developmental psychologist, has raised a number of important questions about moral psychology and has generated a great deal of research on girls and their development. Her theory about the "different voice" of girls and women, described in her 1982

book, *In a Different Voice: Psychological Theory and Women's Development*, has been used to explain gender differences in such diverse fields as children's play, the speech of children, adult conversation, women in academia, leadership style, career choice, war and peace studies, the professions of law, nursing, and teaching, and theories about women's epistemologies or ways of knowing.

Originally Gilligan's work was conducted in the field of moral psychology. She followed a tradition of social scientists and moral philosophers who associated moral development with cognitive development. Gilligan argued that boys and men apply rational, abstract, or objective thought to moral questions; as a result they are likely to appeal to the principle of justice when describing their thinking about moral issues. In contrast, Gilligan asserted, girls and women are more likely than boys and men to focus on the relationships between people and the potential for human suffering and harm. When this thinking is applied to moral issues, girls and women appeal to the ethic of care. The ethic of care, she claims, reflects women's "different voice."

In the preface written to the 1993 edition of her book, Gilligan describes "voice" as the core of the self. She calls it "a powerful psychological instrument and channel, connecting inner and outer worlds . . . a litmus test of relationships and a measure of psychological health." Gilligan and colleagues in the Harvard Project on Women's Psychology and the Development of Girls designed an interview and qualitative scoring method to study moral orientation and voice. They interviewed, held focus groups, and used sentence completion measures to examine female adolescent and adult development. They argued that girls "lose voice" in adolescence; they dissociate from their real selves, a loss that puts them at risk for depression and anxiety.

DEVELOPMENT OF THE ETHIC OF CARE AND VOICE
Gilligan offers two explanations regarding how the ethic of care and women's different voice develop. The first draws from the psychoanalytic theory of Nancy Chodorow. According to Chodorow, from infancy both boys and girls develop a strong attachment to their mothers, which is the basis for their relational selves. However, during the Oedipal period (about age five), boys must separate from their mothers and must form an autonomous and separate identity as a male. This leads them to repress

their relational selves and identify with their fathers. For girls, it is not necessary to detach themselves psychologically from their mothers in order to develop a gender role identity as a female; their attachment to their mothers is not repressed and girls maintain a strong relational self.

Gilligan claimed to find a developmental pattern in her study of women facing a decision to have an abortion, described in her 1982 book. The first level, called "orientation to individual survival," focused on caring for oneself. The second level, called "goodness as sacrifice" focused on care of self. The third level, "the morality of nonviolence," is a morality of care for both self and others. Gilligan's levels have not been validated in any subsequent studies, raising questions about whether the ethic of care is a developmental construct.

Socialization also affects women's sense of self and is connected with the development of voice. According to Gilligan, society reinforces the male/female gender roles, rewarding boys and men for being autonomous, independent, and rational while their relational voices are silenced. In contrast, girls' independent autonomous voices are silenced during adolescence when they experience a conflict. If they become "good women" by conforming to societal stereotypes, they risk losing their authentic (independent) self, or voice. However, if girls resist social pressures to conform to an ideal of femininity, they risk damaging their connections to others. Most girls do not resist and, as a consequence, learn to doubt their true selves.

HISTORICAL CONTEXT FOR GILLIGAN'S THEORY

Gilligan's theory of moral development was an attempt to correct psychological theories that overlooked the experiences of women or discredited women's moral psychology. For example, Sigmund Freud (1856-1939), the "father" of psychoanalysis, had claimed that women and men differ in their moral capacity because girls' superegos are less developed than those of boys. While Freud found women's morality inferior to men's, Gilligan claimed that women's moral thinking was different from men's but of great, if not greater, moral value.

Gilligan's theory drew from the developmental work of Lawrence Kohlberg (1927-1987) but corrected what she claimed was a gender bias in Kohlberg's theory. Kohlberg's theory of moral development was based on six stages of moral thinking that

develop universally in an invariant sequence as a result of maturation and experience. In 1969, Kohlberg published results comparing men's and women's moral reasoning and reported that women typically scored at stage three, "mutual interpersonal expectations, relationships, and conformity," while men typically scored at stage four, "social system and conscience maintenance." Since developmental theories such as Kohlberg's assume that higher stages are more adequate, this was tantamount to saying that the moral reasoning of women was less well developed than that of men. However, Kohlberg made no claim regarding gender differences in moral reasoning. It is likely that in the 1960's, when his study was conducted, his sample of working men and their wives had very different life experiences and that these differences account for his findings.

Gilligan's influential book *In a Different Voice* entered the field of the psychology of women at an important time. In the 1960's and 1970's, researchers who were studying the psychology of women had argued that empirical evidence shows that psychological differences between men and women are small, and, if they exist at all, gender differences are due to socialization and experience. If no relevant differences exist, there is no basis for assigning men and women to different spheres; gender cannot be used to exclude women from education, political life, or work.

Androgyny theorists in the 1960's and 1970's sought to discredit claims of gender differences that denigrate women or bar them from educational or career opportunities. They argued that with proper gender-role socialization, boys and girls, men and women would be equal in psychological attributes. However, by the late 1970's, feminist psychologists began pointing out that androgyny theory contained its own problems: the qualities of competitiveness, aggression, independence, and autonomy, which characterized the masculine norm, might not be the best ideal for either men or women. Some feminist psychologists, such as Jean Baker Miller, sought a new norm for human development, an ideal that celebrated the alternative, feminine virtues of care, concern for others, and the ability to maintain strong relationships with others.

In this postandrogyny period, Carol Gilligan's theory was hailed as a corrective to psychological studies based on male samples that posited masculinity as normative. Gilligan called attention to the study of adolescent girls and claimed to map a new psychological theory that begins with the experience of girls and women and reveals women's different voice.

RESEARCH ON MORAL REASONING, MORAL ORIENTATION, AND VOICE

Research on moral psychology shows that children are concerned with moral issues at a very early age. They care about "what's fair" and they are disturbed when someone has been hurt, suggesting that both justice and care orientations can be identified early in life. Research also shows that in Western culture, girls and women are expected to be more concerned with relationships and more in tune with their feelings than boys. However, a great deal of research since the 1970's has shown that girls and boys are not as different in moral reasoning and voice as Gilligan claims.

Studies using the Kohlbergian Moral Judgment Interview (MJI) reveal that males and females at same age and educational levels are equally able to resolve moral dilemmas by appealing to justice principles. Similar results have been obtained with the Defining Issues Test (DIT) the most frequently used objective test of comprehension of and preference for moral issues. Meta-analysis on DIT scores reveals that education is 250 times more powerful than gender in predicting principled moral reasoning. Narrative and longitudinal studies also have shown that women are as likely as men at the same educational level to advance in the sequential order of development predicted from Kohlberg's theory. In sum, evidence does not support the assertions that, compared with females, males are more principled in their moral reasoning, more concerned with conflicts resulting from conflicting claims about rights, or more capable of using abstract principles of justice in their moral reasoning. Evidence does not support the claim that Kohlberg's theory or measure of moral reasoning is biased against girls or women.

Are women more caring or more relational than men? Are they more likely to be silenced, silence themselves, or lose their voice than men? The evidence to support or refute Gilligan's assertion that the ethic of care characterizes female morality or voice is inconclusive. In part, this is because there are so many different ways that care and voice as psychological constructs are measured; it is difficult to compare across studies that operationalize the constructs differently. Different researchers view the ethic of care as a moral theory, an interpersonal orientation, a perceptual focus, or an epistemological theory. Voice is understood variously as a theory of self, a moral perspective, or a defensive posture. Furthermore, most of Gilligan's qualitative studies of girls' development only present girls' voices and gender differences cannot be tested.

Research on the ethic of care suggests that the majority of people, both males and females, can and do use both care and justice orientations. Some studies, particularly those conducted using Gilligan's qualitative interview, report that females tend to focus on the care orientation and males on the justice orientation, particularly in self-identified moral dilemmas. While qualitative research is very important in developing theory and understanding a construct, testing specific hypotheses (such as that there are gender differences in voice) requires quantitative studies. Most such studies fail to support Gilligan's theory of gender differences in moral orientation.

Some researchers have found that whether someone uses an ethic of care or an ethic of justice depends on the type of moral dilemma they discuss. Lawrence J. Walker and his colleagues found that when participants talk about their own moral dilemmas, females were more likely to identify interpersonal dilemmas, whereas males were more likely to choose impersonal dilemmas. If respondents focus on people and their relationships (a friend who betrays another friend), they are more likely to see that the ethic of care has been violated. If respondents focus on issues in which the rights of others are violated or societal rules are transgressed (breaking a law), they are more likely to be concerned about justice. Interpersonal conflicts elicit a care orientation, while issues of conflicting rights elicit a justice orientation for both men and women. However, when asked to think about an issue differently, both boys and girls are able to change and use either justice or care reasoning.

Gilligan's studies of adolescent girls' voices, using her methods of interview, focus groups, and open-ended sentence completion measures, depict a conflicted adolescence, loss of voice, and growing dissociation from what girls know. While some girls resist, most strive to retain their relationships, and thus seek to please others even if it means developing an inauthentic self.

Research conducted by Susan Harter using more standardized measures and large samples of both boys and girls indicates that adolescence is a challenging time for girls, and that they are concerned about their relationships. Girls feel silenced by others and they silence themselves, but not more so than adolescent boys. Harter's studies of loss of voice indicate there are not gender differences in voice, that girls do not have lower levels of voice than boys, and voice does not decline with age.

GENDER DIFFERENCE RESEARCH

Given the empirical results that gender differences, when they exist, are small and usually attributable to different socialization, why do such claims persist? In part the answer lies in the methodology that is used in research on gender. Gilligan and her colleagues' work, particularly their research using qualitatively analyzed interviews, leads to the conclusion that there are large differences in the ways boys and girls view moral issues, think, react emotionally, and commit to relationships. However, studies that use standardized measures to compare men and women reveal more similarities than differences. Either conclusion has important implications.

Rachel Hare-Mustin and Jeanne Marecek claim that since knowledge in the social sciences is always incomplete, interpretation of events, including research findings, is always subject to bias. They suggest two forms of bias influence beliefs about gender differences. Alpha bias is the tendency to emphasize gender difference; beta bias is the tendency to emphasize similarity. In beta bias, underemphasizing gender differences can lead to ignoring the different resources men and women need. In contrast, alpha bias, overestimating differences, can lead one to advocate different roles for men and women. If women are more caring, ought they be the caregivers? If men are more justice oriented, ought they be judges? If there is no difference in moral orientation between boys and girls, ought all children be taught to use both principles? Ought care and justice be expected from all adults?

GILLIGAN'S CONTRIBUTION

Gilligan raised important questions in the field of the psychology of morality and in so doing drew attention to the ethic of care. While the gender differences that she originally asserted have not been found, her work draws on the experience of girls and women in ways that value that experience. Her insistence that studying the lives of girls is as important as studying the lives of boys brought a good deal of research attention that can lead to new knowledge and new ways to promote the well-being of all boys and girls, men and women.

SOURCES FOR FURTHER STUDY

Brown, Lyn Mikel, and Carol Gilligan. *Meeting at the Crossroads: Women's Psychology and Girls' Development.* Cambridge, Mass.: Harvard University Press, 1992. This book describes interviews conducted at the Laurel School, a private day school for girls. The authors describe the listener's guide, a method of listening to girls' thoughts and feelings. The interviews demonstrate that relationships are central concerns for middle and high school girls.

Chodorow, Nancy. *The Reproduction of Mothering: Psychoanalysis and the Sociology of Gender.* Berkeley: University of California Press, 1978. Chodorow draws on psychoanalytic theory to describe how women's mothering is reproduced across culture and across time. The book requires a fairly good background in psychoanalytic theory.

Freud, Sigmund. "Some Psychical Consequences of the Anatomical Distinction Between the Sexes." In *The Standard Edition of the Complete Psychological Works of Sigmund Freud.* Vol 19. Translated and edited by James Strachey. London: The Hogarth Press, 1961. Freud claimed that because of anatomical differences, girls do not have an Oedipal conflict as emotionally strong as that of boys. As a consequence, boys develop a stronger superego, the structure of the psyche responsible for morality.

Gilligan, Carol. *In a Different Voice: Psychological Theory and Women's Development.* Reprint. Cambridge, Mass.: Harvard University Press, 1993. The theory of ethic of care and girls' and women's different moral voice is described. This often cited book launched a great deal of discussion and prompted many studies of adolescent girls. Gilligan describes her theory of gender differences in moral orientation and of women's voice as different from men's voice.

Gilligan, Carol, Annie G. Rogers, and Deborah L. Tolman. *Women, Girls, and Psychotherapy: Reframing Resistance.* New York: Harrington Park Press, 1991. This collection of essays describes the social pressures that silence girls' voices and demonstrates girls' resistance to being silenced.

Gilligan, Carol, Jamie Victoria Ward, and Jill McLean Taylor, with Betty Bardige, eds. *Mapping the Moral Domain: A Contribution of Women's Thinking to Psychological Theory and Education.* Cambridge, Mass.: Harvard Graduate School of Education, 1988. These essays describe research on gender and morality and include a chapter on the origins of gender differences in moral orientation. Many of the chapters were previously published as journal articles or book chapters.

Gilligan, Carol, Nona Lyons, and Trudy Hanmer, eds. *Making Connections: The Relational Worlds of Adolescent Girls at Emma Willard School.* Cambridge, Mass.: Harvard University Press, 1990. The voice of girls and their resistance to imposed silencing of their voices are described through interviews conducted at the Emma Willard School, a private day and boarding school for girls.

Hare-Mustin, Rachel, and Jeanne Marecek, eds. *Making a Difference: Psychology and the Construction of Gender.* New Haven, Conn.: Yale University Press, 1990. The essays describe how gender differences are socially constructed and includes Hare-Mustin and Marecek's discussion of alpha and beta bias, a distinction that is useful in interpreting findings of gender differences.

Harter, Susan. *The Construction of the Self: A Developmental Perspective.* New York: Guilford Press, 1999. Harter describes her theory and measurement of the self from a developmental perspective. This book includes an important summary and discussion of her research on gender differences in voice.

Miller, Jean Baker. *Toward a New Psychology of Women.* 2d ed. Boston: Beacon Press, 1986. Miller draws on her clinical experience with women to describe and value a relational self, as defined through connections and relationships with others. This is an essential text for understanding relational theories about women's psychology.

Walker, Lawrence J. "Sex Differences in the Development of Moral Reasoning: A Critical Review." *Child Development* 55 (1984): 677-691. Walker's first meta-analysis revealed no gender differences in moral reasoning among men and women. Subsequent studies conducted by Walker and associates have confirmed these initial findings.

Mary Brabeck

SEE ALSO: Feminist psychotherapy; Moral development; Women's psychology: Karen Horney; Women's psychology: Sigmund Freud.

Women's psychology
Karen Horney

TYPE OF PSYCHOLOGY: Personality
FIELDS OF STUDY: Classic analytic themes and issues; personality theory

Karen Horney's theories emphasize the effects of cultural influences on women's personality development. Her theories modified classical psychoanalytic views and provided new insights into women's interpersonal relationships.

KEY CONCEPTS
• biological influences
• classical psychoanalysis
• cultural influences
• instinct
• neo-Freudians
• sexual instinct
• unconscious

INTRODUCTION

Karen Horney (1885-1952) considered people to be products of their environment as well as of biology. She stressed the ways in which cultural influences affect women's personality development. These cultural influences include interpersonal relationships and society's attitudes about women.

Cultural influences are overlooked by classical psychoanalysis—a system of psychology based on Freudian doctrine and procedure that seeks the root of human behavior in the unconscious, a region of the mind that is the seat of repressed impulses and experiences of which the conscious mind is unaware. Unconscious motivation and conflict, particularly sexual conflict, according to Horney, play an important role in women's development. She viewed women as living in a male-oriented world in which they are judged by men according to male standards. Women have come to believe that these male-based standards represent their true nature. As a result, according to Horney, women live with the dilemma of having to choose between fulfilling their ambitions and meeting their needs for love by adhering to the passive role that society assigns to them. These circumstances contribute to depression and low self-esteem.

Horney described three basic patterns of behavior by which people relate to others: moving toward (or self-effacing), moving away from (or distancing), and moving against (or expanding). The moving-toward behavior involves dependency and taking care of others as well as self-effacement. Women have been conditioned since birth to relate to others in this manner, according to Horney.

RELATIONSHIP TO FREUDIAN THEORY

Horney's theories were modifications of classical psychoanalytic beliefs. Her theories are best understood when viewed in relation to the Freudian concepts that were prevalent during her lifetime. According to Sigmund Freud, who founded classical psychoanalysis during the late nineteenth century, biological influences determine human behavior. Of these biological factors, sexual instincts are the strongest motivators of human behavior. Neurosis, or mental disorder, was considered by Freud to be the result of unconscious sexual conflicts which began in early childhood.

Horney was grounded in psychoanalytic thinking and agreed with many of Freud's concepts. She disagreed radically, however, with the heavy sexual content of Freudian theory. A major point of departure was the Freudian concept of penis envy. Freud essentially viewed all psychological problems in women to be the result of the woman's inherent wish to be a man. Freud maintained that girls are not born with a natural sense of their femininity and regard themselves as inferior, castrated boys. As a result of penis envy, the female rebels against her biological inferiority. The consequences, according to Freud, are resentment, devaluation of her "negative sexual endowments," envy of the opposite sex, and a constant search for compensation.

Horney considered penis envy to be contrary to biological thinking. She maintained that little girls are instinctively feminine and aware of their femaleness in early childhood. Thus, girls are not programmed to feel inferior. Women may envy men the power and freedom they have in their private and professional lives, but women do not envy men's genitals. The behaviors which Freud associated with penis envy—including greed, envy, and ambition—Horney attributed to the restrictions society places on females.

Horney also disagreed with the Freudian theory that viewed frigidity and masochism as biologically determined aspects of woman's nature. Frigidity, or the inability of a woman to experience sexual desire, is neither a normal condition for a woman nor an illness, according to Horney. She considered frigidity to be a symptom of an underlying psychological disturbance, such as chronic anxiety. Frequently, it is caused by tensions between marital partners. Powerful forces in society restrict a woman in the free expression of her sexuality. Custom and education promote female inhibitions. Men's tendency to view their wives as spiritual partners and to look for sexual excitement with prostitutes or others whom they do not respect may also cause frigidity in wives.

Masochistic tendencies, wherein a woman seeks and enjoys pain and suffering, particularly in her sexual life, result from special social circumstances, Horney maintained. Freudian theory, holding that women are biologically programmed for masochism, is associated with the Freudian concept of the female as having been rendered less powerful than the male through castration. Horney, on the other hand, believed that society encourages women to be masochistic. Women are stereotyped as weak and emotional, as enjoying dependence, and these qualities are rewarded by men. Masochistic tendencies, according to Horney, are a way of relating by which a woman tries to obtain security and satisfaction through self-effacement and submission.

Karen Horney's theories stressed the positive aspects of femininity. As her ideas developed, she became more influenced by social scientists of her period. Her theories placed increasing emphasis on interpersonal and social attitudes in determining women's feelings, relations, and roles. Her ideas about the development of women's sexuality were focused on adolescent girls, rather than on young children, as in Freudian theory. According to Horney, adolescents develop attitudes to cope with sexual conflict, and these attitudes carry over into adulthood.

NEW APPROACH TO WOMEN AND RELATIONSHIPS

Horney's theories opened the door for new ways of understanding women's personalities and relationships. In a 1984 study of women's reaction to separation and loss, psychotherapist Alexandra Symonds found Horney's theories to be relevant to what she encountered in her female patients. Writing in the *American Journal of Psychoanalysis*, Symonds reported female reaction to separation and loss to be a frequent motivation for women to enter therapy. In contrast, she found that men come into therapy in these circumstances mainly because of pressure from a wife or girlfriend. According to Symonds, women are more eager than men to create relationships, and women express more feeling when the relationships end.

Symonds considered these behaviors from the viewpoint of the three basic patterns of behavior described by Horney: moving toward, moving away from, and moving against. Symonds viewed the moving-toward, self-effacing type of behavior as love oriented, or dependent; the moving-away-from, detached type as freedom oriented; and the moving-against, expansive type as power oriented. According to Symonds's views, society assigns the love-oriented, dependent pattern to women, while men are encouraged to develop power- and/or freedom-oriented patterns. She described a frequent combination in a couple to be a detached, expansive, power-oriented male married to a dependent, self-effacing, love-oriented female. Relationships often develop between the silent, strong, withdrawn, noncommunicative male and the loving, dependent woman who always wants to talk about feelings.

As people develop character patterns, such as love-oriented and dependent, they suppress feelings that cause inner conflicts, such as aggressiveness, according to Symonds. By contrast, power-oriented people suppress dependent feelings. People idealize their self-values and feel contempt for what is suppressed; thus, the power-oriented person views dependency and need as contemptible weaknesses. This contempt is conveyed to those who are aware of their dependency needs. Women then add self-hate for needing others to the anxiety they feel when a relationship ends.

Extremely dependent, self-effacing women often stay in poor and even abusive relationships rather than separate, according to Symonds. They are victims of a culture that considers a woman nothing unless attached to a man. Symonds found these women to be coming from two different backgrounds: either having been held close by mother and/or father during childhood and adolescence, thus having no

opportunity for healthy growth; or having separated prematurely from parents in childhood in an effort to become self-sufficient at an early age, often having developed a façade of self-sufficiency with deep, unresolved dependency needs.

UNDERSTANDING FEAR OF SUCCESS

Horney's theories predicted the anxiety women feel about their own ambition and the ways in which women sabotage their competence and success. In the book *Women in Therapy* (1988), psychotherapist Harriet Goldhor Lerner discusses female work inhibition in the light of Horney's theories. Lerner views work inhibition as an unconscious attempt to preserve harmony within a relationship as well as to allay fears of being unfeminine. Women often fear success because they fear they will pay dearly for their accomplishments. Women frequently equate success, or the wish for it, with the loss of femininity and attractiveness, loss of significant relationships, loss of health, or even loss of life. Feelings of depression and anxiety are ways women either apologize for their competence and success on the one hand or ensure the lack of success on the other hand, according to Lerner. She views self-sacrifice or self-sabotage to be other common ways women react to their feelings of guilt and anxiety about becoming successful.

When faced with the choice (real or imagined) of sacrificing the self to preserve a relationship or strengthening the self at the risk of threatening a relationship, women often choose the former, according to Lerner. She applies Horney's views to the situation of a thirty-year-old married woman who entered therapy because of personal distress and marital tension over her desire to enroll in graduate school and embark on a career. Lerner found that multigenerational guilt on the part of the woman was involved, as well as fears of destroying her marriage. The woman's husband was opposed to his wife's enrolling in graduate school. In addition, the woman was the first female in her family to aspire to graduate school. In the face of these circumstances, she put aside her ambitions in order to preserve harmony in her relationships. The woman's work inhibition involved profound anxiety and guilt over striving for things previous generations of women in her family could not have. Work inhibition also may result when a woman perceives her strivings as "too masculine," a perception Lerner sees as reinforced by society. Being labeled "masculine" triggers deep guilt and anxiety in women.

BACKGROUND AND ACCOMPLISHMENTS

Horney's theories on female psychology developed from a series of papers she wrote over a thirteen-year period in response to Freud's views on female sexuality. The last paper was published after Horney emigrated to America from Germany at a highly productive point in her career.

One of the first women admitted to medical school in Berlin, she had completed her psychiatric and psychoanalytic training there by 1913. By that time, Freud had passed the peak of his greatest creative years. Horney was thirty years younger than Freud and a product of the twentieth century. Her views were more in tune with the relatively open structure of twentieth century science than with the more closed science of Freud's period. Horney was influenced greatly by sociologists of her time. She and other neo-Freudians, such as Harry Stack Sullivan, Alfred Adler, and Erich Fromm, were the first psychoanalysts to emphasize cultural influences on personality development.

Horney's theories grew out of a need for a feminine psychology different from male psychology. She believed that women were being analyzed and treated according to a male-oriented psychology that considered women to be biologically inferior to males. She did not find these male theories supported by what she observed in her female patients or in her own life experience.

Horney was the first female doctor to challenge male theory and went on to take a position in the foreground of the psychoanalytic movement. In so doing, she became a role model for women in general and professional women in particular. She was a controversial figure, and her career involved many disputes with the established psychoanalytic world. She and her followers eventually were ostracized by the establishment, and for a time her name disappeared from the psychoanalytic literature. Her biographers attribute this to a fear on the part of some Freudians of being contaminated by association with her ideas.

MODERN-DAY IMPACT

A growing interest in her work occurred during the women's liberation movement in the 1970's. The feminist movement brought her name back into the literature as a pioneer in upgrading women's status. Her name began appearing more frequently in literature associated with women's therapy. The series of important books which she had written throughout her career remain popular and continue to be used as textbooks.

An independent thinker, Horney is considered an individual who was always ahead of her time. Her work anticipated a revival of interest in the narcissistic personality. Her theories predicted popular trends in psychology, although she often is not credited for her ideas. One of these trends is the increasing emphasis on social and cultural factors as causes of emotional illness. Systems theory is another popular trend related to Horney's concepts. Systems theory, which includes a type of psychology called family therapy, emphasizes the continuous interaction between cultural conditions, interpersonal relations, and inner emotional experience.

SOURCES FOR FURTHER STUDY

Horney, Karen. *Feminine Psychology*. 1967. Reprint. New York: W. W. Norton, 1993. A collection of all of Horney's writings on feminine psychology. Gives a flavor of Horney's personality and force as a psychoanalyst and educator. Includes an informative introduction by Harold Kelman, one of Horney's colleagues. Available through college libraries.

Lerner, Harriet Goldhor. *Women in Therapy*. Reprint. New York: HarperCollins, 1989. Discusses women and their psychotherapists from a psychoanalytic perspective, with references to Horney's theories. Illustrates how Horney's theories apply to many themes and issues in women's psychology.

Paris, Bernard. *Karen Horney: A Psychoanalyst's Search for Self-Understanding*. New Haven, Conn.: Yale University Press, 1996. A biography of Horney that places her theories squarely within the context of her life history. Written by the editor of the papers unpublished during Horney's lifetime (*The Unknown Karen Horney*, 2000).

Quinn, Susan. *A Mind of Her Own: The Life of Karen Horney*. Reading, Mass.: Addison-Wesley, 1988. This biography is an excellent source of information about Horney's personal and professional life. Much of it is devoted to her female psychology. Easy to read; contains photographs, biographical essays, extensive source notes, and a complete list of Horney's work.

Rubins, Jack L. *Karen Horney: Gentle Rebel of Psychoanalysis.* New York: Dial Press, 1978. The first biography of Karen Horney. Thorough and well documented; includes detailed discussions of Horney's theories on women. Lengthy but well organized. Can be read by the college or high school student.

Symonds, Alexandra. "Separation and Loss: Significance for Women." *American Journal of Psychoanalysis* 45, no. 1 (1985): 53-58. Discusses women's feelings about separation and loss. Important illustration of how Horney's theories help explain women's role in interpersonal relationships. Available in college libraries.

Margaret M. Frailey

SEE ALSO: Abnormality: Psychological models; Consciousness; Dreams; Feminist psychotherapy; Instinct theory; Penis envy; Psychoanalysis; Psychoanalytic psychology; Psychoanalytic psychology and personality: Sigmund Freud; Psychosexual development; Social psychological models: Karen Horney; Women's psychology: Carol Gilligan; Women's psychology: Sigmund Freud.

Women's psychology

Sigmund Freud

TYPE OF PSYCHOLOGY: Personality
FIELDS OF STUDY: Classic analytic themes and issues; personality theory

Sigmund Freud, the first person to develop a comprehensive theory of personality, thought that women undergo distinct experiences in the development of their personalities. He believed that traumatic events during the phallic stage (from approximately three to five years of age) were likely to hinder normal female development, the results being a failure of same-sex identification and a diminished superego or moral capacity.

KEY CONCEPTS
- free association
- id
- identification
- instincts
- Oedipus complex
- penis envy
- psychosexual stages of development
- superego

INTRODUCTION

Two central concepts underlie Sigmund Freud's theory of personality development. The first is the notion of the unconscious; the second concept has to do with the role of infantile sexuality. Freud believed that consciousness could be viewed as a continuum of experience, with one pole being the familiar one of acute awareness of one's thoughts, feelings, and behaviors and the other pole being a state of profound unconsciousness in which one's feelings, thoughts, and wishes are completely beyond one's awareness. Midway between these poles is the preconscious, which Freud believed contained material or mental life from both the conscious and the unconscious and could, with effort, be made totally conscious. Freud believed that the bulk of mental life is represented in the unconscious, with only a small portion, "the tip of the iceberg," being conscious awareness.

Operating from the depths of the unconscious, a structure of personality known as the id operates to seek pleasure, to avoid pain at all costs, and to accomplish solely selfish aims. The id is the source of all psychic energy, including both sexual and aggressive instincts.

PSYCHOSEXUAL STAGES OF DEVELOPMENT THEORY

Freud proposed that the sexual instincts are critical and that personality develops over time as the individual responds to these instincts. He believed that a number of component instincts arise from various regions of the body. These instincts strive for satisfaction in what he calls organ pleasure. Each of these organs is the focus of a phase or stage of development, the first of which is the oral stage. The oral stage begins at birth and continues through the first year, as the infant seeks pleasure through the mouth and the mouth becomes the source of all gratification. Milk from the mother's breast or a bottle is devoured, just as, later, any object that the child can reach will be manipulated and explored orally. The child takes in physical nourishment in the same way that he or she takes in, in a very rudimentary way, the behaviors, values, and beliefs of others, beginning the basis for later identification with others.

Sigmund Freud in London in 1938, a year before his death at age eighty-three. (Library of Congress)

The second psychosexual stage of development is the anal stage, which Freud believed revolved around the pleasure associated with elimination. During the second year of life, the child begins taking control of urination and defecation, trying to do so within parental and societal limits.

Freud believed that both boys and girls proceed through the oral stage in essentially the same manner. For both, the mother is the primary love object. Sometime after the third year, however, Freud believed that the sexes diverge. In the third, or phallic, stage of development, both boys and girls discover the pleasurable nature of the genitals. For boys, the stage is centered on the Oedipus complex, in which they develop strong sexual feelings toward their mothers. These feelings are accompanied by others, such as anger and jealousy, as fathers are perceived as competitors for mothers' affection and attention. As sexual desires heighten, the boy begins to perceive competition and hostility from the father. The sense of peril becomes located in the physical source of the boy's feelings for his mother, the pe-

nis, and the result is a phenomenon that Freud called castration anxiety—the fear that the father will retaliate. Over time, fear of castration motivates the boy to give up the mother as a love object and turn toward the father in same-sex identification. According to Freud, this strengthening identification with the father is essential for the development of a solid superego, which, in turn, empowers the male, making possible major contributions to culture and society.

Unlike the male's experience, the onset of the phallic stage for females entails a major trauma: the realization that she does not have a penis. Often, the realization is accompanied by the notion that the mother is responsible for her own and her daughter's castrated state. Here the little girl turns away from her mother as the primary love object and turns toward her father, limiting her future chances for same-sex identification. Feelings of inferiority pervade, and she falls victim to penis envy, a chronic wish for the superior male organ. Freud believed that, as a result of this trauma, the remaining course of female development would be difficult at best and that the accomplishment of same-sex identification was questionable. The girl's life is thus spent in search of a substitute penis, which Freud thought might be a husband or a child, particularly a male child. Indeed, Freud believed that the single most rewarding relationship in a woman's life would be her relationship with her son, regarding which her feelings would be totally unambivalent.

Freud believed that the foundations of personality were in place by the end of the phallic stage. He described the post-Oedipal period, beginning with the latency stage, as a period when children repress, or make unconscious, the sexual conflicts of the Oedipal period. Females during this time are said to be more passive and less aggressive than boys, but, like boys, they tend to seek out same-sex play groups.

The final psychosexual stage of development is the genital stage. Unlike the previous, more self-centered periods of stimulation and gratification, the genital stage marks a period of sexual attraction to others and a time during which social activities and career goals become important before marriage. The child is thus transformed into an adult. Freud believed that, in some cases, failure to resolve the female Oedipus complex results in neurosis, which he often observed in his practice with female patients. He believed that in other cases the lack of resolution caused a masculinity complex in which women attempt to succeed in traditionally male endeavors (he offered this explanation to his contemporary female analysts for their behavior). Freud believed that the female's failure to unite with her mother in post-Oedipal identification, and her subsequent diminished superego capacity, caused her to have a tendency toward negative personality traits and an inability to apply objective standards of justice.

CRITICISMS

Several of Freud's contemporaries, including some female analysts, were critical of Freud's views on the psychology of women. Among his critics was Karen Horney, who rejected the idea that penis envy is central to normal female development. She acknowledged, however, that from a cultural point of view, envy of the male role might explain some of Freud's clinical observations better than the biological notion of penis envy. In addition, after many years of analyzing female patients, Horney began

analyzing males; from her observations, she concluded that males often exhibit an intense envy of pregnancy, childbirth, and motherhood, as well as of the breasts and of the act of suckling.

FREE INTERPRETATION AND DREAM ANALYSIS

Historically, psychoanalysis has represented a method of psychological observation, a set of theoretical constructs or ideas, and an approach to psychotherapy. When Freud began psychoanalysis, it was a method of observation intended to broaden the knowledge of human behavior. Believing that the unconscious is the major clue to solving problems of human behavior, Freud used two processes to understand it: free association and dream interpretation. Free association, the reporting of what comes to mind in an unedited fashion, was an important tool used to discover the contents of the unconscious. Freud believed that all thoughts are connected in some fashion and that therefore the spontaneous utterances of the patient are always meaningful clues to what has been repressed or buried in the unconscious. Freud also believed that the unconscious can be clarified by means of dream interpretation. Those thoughts and impulses that are unacceptable to the conscious mind are given symbols in dreams.

An interesting study conducted by Calvin Hall in 1964 illustrates how the interpretation of dreams has been used in research—in this case, to test Freud's observation that the female superego is not as strong as it appears to be in males. Hall reasoned that a person with a strong internalized superego would be independent of external agents, whereas a person who has a less internalized superego would tend to disown his or her own guilt and blame external authority figures. Hall further made the assumption that dreams in which the dreamer was the victim of aggression were expressions of an externalized superego, whereas dreams in which the dreamer was the victim of misfortune (accident, circumstance) were expressions of an internalized superego. It was hypothesized that females would be more likely to dream of themselves as victims of aggression and males would be more likely to dream of themselves as victims of misfortune. Careful content analysis of more than three thousand dreams of young adults was performed. Results supported the hypotheses, although Hall cautioned that additional hypotheses should be tested and more diverse data collected to support thoroughly Freud's theory of the differences between the male and the female superego.

TRANSFERENCE AND THE UNCONSCIOUS

Freud was also the first to understand and describe the concept of transference, the patient's positive or negative feelings that develop toward the therapist during the long, intimate process of analysis. These feelings often relate to earlier ones that the patient has had for significant others: namely, mother, father, or sibling. The analysis of transference has become extremely important to neo-Freudian analysts, particularly as it relates to the treatment of borderline and other personality disturbances.

Another aspect of Freud's legacy involves the many theoretical constructs that psychoanalysis has generated. Among these is the concept of the unconscious. Freud provided many everyday examples of the operation of the unconscious as he described slips of the tongue and other phenomena. He was convinced that such slips, now known as "Freudian slips," were not accidental at all, but somehow expressed unconscious wishes, thoughts, or desires. For example, the woman who loses her wedding ring wishes she had never had it.

MENTAL ILLNESS THERAPY

Finally, psychoanalysis also represents a method of therapy that Freud and later analysts used to treat the symptoms of mental illness. Practicing for many years, Freud refined his technique, using free association and dream interpretation to help patients gain insight into themselves by recognizing their unconscious patterns and to help them work through the unconscious conflicts that affect everyday life. Many of Freud's patients were women, and it was from these women's recollections in analysis that Freud built his theory of female development. Some of Freud's critics argue that building a theory of normal development from the observation of pathology or abnormality represents an inappropriate conceptual leap.

SEXUAL BASIS OF NEUROSIS

During years of analysis, Freud became convinced of the sexual basis of neurosis. He believed that sexual experiences occurring prior to puberty and stored in the unconscious as memories produced conflict that later caused certain neurotic condi-

tions. These ideas, often referred to as Freud's seduction theory, were used to explain hysterical symptoms such as paralysis, blindness, inability to understand the spoken word (receptive aphasia), and sexual dysfunction as the result of sexual abuse probably occurring before ages six to eight. It is important to note, however, that Freud later revised his thinking on infantile sexuality and concluded that it is the thought or psychic reality of the individual that counts more than the physical reality of events. In other words, a person might fantasize a seduction, store the fantasy in unconscious memory (repress it), and have that conflictual memory cause neurosis just as readily as the memory of an actual seduction. Some recent critics have suggested that Freud's reformulation represented a form of denial of his inability to recognize the prevalence of sexual abuse at that time.

FREUD'S BACKGROUND AND IMPACT

Born in 1856 to Jewish parents, Freud lived and practiced most of his life in Vienna. He was graduated from medical school in 1881 and practiced as a clinical neurologist for several years before becoming interested in the "talking cure" that his colleague, Josef Breuer, had developed as a means of dealing with his patients' emotional symptoms. Freud's writings and lectures on the subject of hysteria and its sexual roots led him to be ostracized by most of his medical colleagues. His medical training and the influence of the work of Charles Darwin were largely responsible for his emphasis on sexual and aggressive instincts as the basis for behavior.

Freud's theory was important because it was the first of its kind and because it was controversial, generating further research into and theorizing about the female personality.

CHALLENGES TO FREUDIAN THEORY

Over the years, many aspects of Freudian theory have been challenged. Freud's notion that penis envy is a primary motivator in the female personality was challenged by Karen Horney, who believed that, if it existed, a woman's envy was related to the male's privileged role in society. Freud's idea that the clitoral orgasm is immature and must be surrendered for the vaginal orgasm at puberty spurred work by William Masters and Virginia Johnson, who concluded, after much rigorous research, that orgasm is a reaction of the entire pelvic area.

Freud's theory has forced critics to determine what is uniquely female about personality. In *Toward a New Psychology of Women* (1976), Jean Baker Miller attempted to show how traditional theories of female behavior have failed to acknowledge the essence of the female personality. Miller suggested that affiliation is the cornerstone of the female experience and that it is in response to her relationships with others that a woman's personality grows and develops.

In her book *In a Different Voice* (1982), Carol Gilligan disputes Freud's notion that females show less of a sense of justice than males and have weak superegos. She argues that morality involves respect for the needs of self balanced with respect for the needs of others; thus, it is not that females lack the justice principle, but rather that they have different expressions of justice and different internal and external demands.

Heavily influenced by Freud, many object-relations theorists continue to make contributions in the area of psychotherapy with clients whose early relationships have been disturbed or disrupted. This work will continue to constitute the basis for decisions made by courts, adoption agencies, and social-service agencies regarding the placement of children.

Freud's views on the origins of neurosis may continue to play a role in the understanding of multiple personality disorder and its roots in early sexual abuse. The concept of body memory, the physical memory that abuse has occurred, may well bridge the gap between Freud's concepts of repressed psychic memory and repressed actual memory of early sexual abuse; it may streamline the treatment of this condition. Finally, Freud's theory will no doubt continue to generate controversy, motivating both theory and research in the area of women's personality development.

SOURCES FOR FURTHER STUDY

Freud, Sigmund. *New Introductory Lectures on Psychoanalysis.* New York: W. W. Norton, 1933. This volume contains seven lectures or papers that Freud wrote toward the end of his career. Among them is "The Psychology of Women," in which Freud attempts to explain some fundamental differences between the sexes. Freud describes female behavior and the Oedipus complex for males and females, and he elaborates on the role of penis envy in female development. The volume also contains lectures on dreams, on the structure of personality, and on anxiety and the instincts.

_____. *The Standard Edition of the Complete Psychological Works of Sigmund Freud.* Edited by James Strachey. London: Hogarth Press, 1953-1974. Volume 7 in this collection of Freud's works contains a detailed case history of a woman named Dora, whom Freud treated over a period of years. This case history illustrates Freud's ideas about the causes of neurosis and hysterical symptoms. The work also contains three essays on sexuality, including sexual aberrations, infantile sexuality, and puberty.

Gilligan, Carol. *In a Different Voice.* Cambridge, Mass.: Harvard University Press, 1982. Traditional theories of development have tried to impose male thinking and values on female psychology. Gilligan discusses the importance of relationship as well as female conceptions of morality, challenging Freud's views on female superego development.

Horney, Karen. *Feminine Psychology.* Edited by Harold Kelman. New York: W. W. Norton, 1967. A collection of some of Karen Horney's early works in which she describes Freudian ideas on the psychology of women and offers her own observations and conclusions. Horney disputes Freud's notion of penis envy and in later essays explores such topics as distrust between the sexes, premenstrual tension, and female masochism.

Miller, Jean Baker. *Toward a New Psychology of Women.* 1976. 2d ed. Boston: Beacon Press, 1987. Miller proposes that traditional theories of female development have overlooked a critical ingredient in female behavior—affiliation—which she believes is a cornerstone of female psychology.

Miller, Jonathan, ed. *Freud: The Man, His World, His Influence.* Boston: Little, Brown, 1972. Miller has edited a series of essays that put Freud's work in historical, social, and cultural perspective. One essay, by Friedrich Heer, describes the impact of Freud's Jewish background on his life and work in Vienna. Another, by Martin Esslin, describes Vienna, the exciting and culturally rich background for Freud's work.

Rychlak, Joseph F. *Introduction to Personality and Psychotherapy.* 2d ed. Boston: Houghton Mifflin, 1981. This introductory personality text carefully reviews the work of several leading psychologists and psychotherapists, including Sigmund Freud.

Rychlak describes the gradual development of Freud's structural hypothesis, and he reviews Freud's ideas about the instincts, dynamic concepts such as defense mechanisms, and the development of the Oedipus complex for males and females, noting the concerns of modern feminists who have found Freud's work offensive.

Ruth T. Hannon

SEE ALSO: Abnormality: Psychological models; Consciousness; Dreams; Feminist psychotherapy; Instinct theory; Penis envy; Psychoanalysis; Psychoanalytic psychology; Psychoanalytic psychology and personality: Sigmund Freud; Psychosexual development; Women's psychology: Carol Gilligan; Women's psychology: Karen Horney.

Work motivation

TYPE OF PSYCHOLOGY: Motivation
FIELDS OF STUDY: Motivation theory; social motives

Work motivation theories describe the psychological processes that affect people's choices regarding their work-related behaviors; the theories provide managerial guidelines for increasing worker productivity.

KEY CONCEPTS
- expectancy theory
- extrinsic motivation
- goal setting
- hierarchy of needs theory
- intrinsic motivation
- job enrichment
- scientific management

INTRODUCTION

Motivation is the psychological process that directs people's choices regarding the type and intensity of their behavior. A common misconception among managers is that motivation is merely the desire to work hard. Consequently, managers often think that only productive workers possess motivation. In contrast, psychologists define motivation as a general process that influences virtually all behavior. Thus, psychologists believe that all workers are motivated. Some workers are motivated to work hard; other workers are motivated to stay home.

A basic principle that underlies most modern theories of motivation is that motivated behavior is performed to obtain pleasurable outcomes. Based on this principle, motivational theorists have defined two types of motivation: intrinsic motivation and extrinsic motivation. A behavior is intrinsically motivated if the valued or pleasurable outcome associated with the behavior is in the behavior itself. The intrinsically motivated employee works because the work itself is enjoyable. A behavior is extrinsically motivated if the valued outcome associated with the behavior is performed only as a means to obtain the outcome. The extrinsically motivated worker works not because the work is pleasurable but because working leads to a pleasurable outcome external to the job, such as money, status, security, or friendship.

EXPECTANCY THEORY

The most popular and widely accepted theory of work motivation is the expectancy theory. Originally proposed by Victor Vroom, this model has been elaborated on by a large number of researchers. The expectancy theory describes the decision-making process that people experience when they choose which behavior to perform. It suggests that a person's motivation to perform some behavior is a function of three components: expectancy, instrumentality, and valence.

"Expectancy" refers to a person's beliefs about his or her ability to perform a behavior. "Instrumentality" refers to a person's beliefs about the likelihood that a number of outcomes will occur if the behavior is performed. "Valence" refers to how positively or negatively a person values these outcomes. The expectancy theory suggests that when people are deciding which of a number of behaviors they will perform, they consider the three components associated with each behavior and choose the behavior that is most likely to lead to positive outcomes.

For example, a worker is given an opportunity to receive a bonus for completing a project early. The employee's motivation to work on the project is a function of the worker's beliefs about her ability to get the project done early (expectancy), her beliefs about the likelihood that she will actually receive a bonus for completing the project early (instrumentality), and the degree to which she values the bonus (valence). To the extent that the worker values the bonus, is certain that the bonus will be awarded if the project is completed early, and is certain that she is capable of completing the project, the worker will be motivated to complete the project early. Whether the worker attempts to complete the project, however, is influenced by her competing motivation to perform other behaviors. While the worker may be motivated to complete the project, she may also feel that other activities, such as going on vacation or calling in sick, are more likely to lead to equally or more pleasurable outcomes than the bonus.

MASLOW'S HIERARCHY OF NEEDS

The expectancy theory is considered a cognitive model. The theory proposes that behavior is guided by choices based on beliefs and values. The theory describes the process of decision making. "Needs models" are another type of motivation model. Needs models complement the process-oriented cognitive models by suggesting the categories of outcomes that people typically value. Needs models also provide insight into how the values of outcomes change.

The most widely known needs model is the hierarchy of needs theory, proposed by Abraham Maslow. Maslow suggested that all people have five categories of needs, which are arranged in a hierarchy. From lowest level to highest level, these needs include physiological needs, safety needs, social needs, esteem needs, and self-actualization needs. Maslow argued that a person's first concern is to fulfill the lowest level of unsatisfied need. When a need is not satisfied, opportunities to fill the need gain value. As the need is met, opportunities to fill the satisfied need lose value, and opportunities to satisfy the next higher level of need gain value. For example, once a worker has enough air, water, and food, thus satisfying his or her physiological needs, the worker will become less concerned about these needs and will value opportunities to fill safety needs. The process of unsatisfied needs gaining value and satisfied needs losing value continues up the hierarchy through safety, social, and esteem needs. When all the lower-level needs are reasonably well satisfied, people will most highly value opportunities for self-actualization. Self-actualization can be thought of as the process of developing one's physical and mental skills to the limit of one's potential.

Maslow's theory helps define the distinction between extrinsic and intrinsic motivation. Extrinsic motivation usually involves performing a job as a way to meet physiological, safety, and social needs. Intrinsic motivation typically occurs when a job offers opportunities to meet higher-level needs. That is, the work itself becomes enjoyable when performance of the job leads to greater self-esteem and self-actualization.

ROLE OF A SUPERVISOR

The supervisor's job is to increase a subordinate's motivation to be productive. The supervisor does this by defining productivity and establishing a contingency between productive behavior and the attainment of an outcome the worker values. That valued outcome can be either in the job itself, involving intrinsic motivation, or external to the job, involving extrinsic motivation. The expectancy theory offers a number of guidelines for helping supervisors establish productivity-outcome contingencies.

First, a supervisor must make certain that the employee believes she or he can be productive. That is, the supervisor must heighten the employee's expectancy beliefs. For example, the supervisor must clearly explain to the employee what behaviors or levels of performance constitute productivity. The supervisor may then need to provide training, giving the employee the skills necessary to meet the performance criteria. Additionally, the supervisor may need to coach the employee, convincing the employee that he or she has the potential to be productive.

Next, a supervisor must make certain that the employee believes that productive performance will lead to positive outcomes. (The supervisor must strengthen the employee's instrumentality beliefs.) In doing this, the supervisor must clearly explain the potential benefits of productive behavior, including any organizational policies regarding compensation and promotion. Finally, a supervisor must make certain that the employee values the outcome associated with productive behavior—that is, the supervisor must heighten the valence of productive performance. If the supervisor wants to increase intrinsic motivation, the supervisor must make certain that the employee can find the job itself enjoyable. If the supervisor wants to increase extrinsic motivation, he or she must offer a performance reward that the employee enjoys.

ENHANCING EMPLOYEE MOTIVATION

The expectancy theory provides useful theoretical guidelines for shaping employee motivation. Over the years, researchers have developed a number of specific techniques for increasing employee motivation to be productive. Two of the most useful techniques involve goal setting and job enrichment.

Goal setting involves assigning specific objectives for employee performance. For example, goal setting might be applied to the job of a computer disk-drive assembler in the following way. The assembler would meet with his or her supervisor. Using information about the worker's past performance, the supervisor and assembler would set a challenging goal regarding the number of disk drives to be assembled per week. The supervisor and assembler would then negotiate rewards for completing the goal on time. Each day, the supervisor would give the worker feedback by posting a running total of the number of disk drives assembled. At the end of the week, the worker's production would be reviewed and appropriate rewards would be given.

Edwin Locke and Gary Latham have studied goal setting extensively. They found that goals will lead to greater productivity if the goals are specific, difficult, and set with time deadlines. Further, goal setting programs will be more effective if the employee receives frequent feedback, allowing the employee to monitor his or her progress toward goal attainment. Additionally, goal setting will increase productivity if the employee is highly committed to the goal; giving employees the opportunity to participate in setting goals is one way to increase goal commitment. Finally, the effects of goal setting may be improved by establishing rewards for meeting goals on time. Other popular motivational techniques that involve goal setting include management by objectives (MBO) and organizational behavior modification (often called OBMod).

Job enrichment, a technique designed specifically to increase intrinsic motivation, was introduced by Frederick Herzberg. Herzberg argued that people will find a job enjoyable if the job provides opportunities to learn, to be responsible, and to experience a sense of achievement. For example, job enrichment might also be applied to the assembler's job. To enrich the job of the disk-drive assembler, the supervisor might change the job so that the assembler assembles a whole computer rather than only the disk drives. This would require greater knowledge and skills. The assembler could be given greater responsibility and be made accountable for the quality of each of the computers he or she assembles. Additional responsibility could be given to the assembler by providing the assembler a budget and requiring the assembler to order all the parts needed for assembly. Finally, the assembler might be given the opportunity to schedule his or her own hours.

Herzberg, like Maslow, argued that people have an innate need to grow psychologically and develop their skills. Herzberg enriched the jobs of mechanics, secretaries, janitors, managers, and assembly-line workers. He found that giving workers challenging and interesting work, personal accountability for success and failures, control over organizational resources, and opportunities to self-schedule increased production quantity, improved production quality, and heightened job satisfaction.

THEORETICAL EVOLUTION

Modern work motivation theories span three eras. The first period was the scientific management era, which began around the beginning of the twentieth century, when Frederick Winslow Taylor applied scientific methodology to the study of worker efficiency. Taylor assumed that workers were basically lazy and incapable of self-direction. He proposed that the best way to motivate workers was to simplify the worker's job as much as possible, to determine empirically the most efficient movements the worker needed to perform the job, and to make pay contingent on job performance. Taylor applied the principles of scientific management to steelworkers and was able to increase productivity dramatically. The result of scientific management was that managers treated employees as if they were simply part of the production machinery. By making jobs specialized and repetitive, the manager could structure and fine-tune a worker's performance. Job routinization, coupled with the assumption that employees were naturally uninterested in work, led managers to use extrinsic motivation techniques.

The next period of work motivation theory was the human relations era. This period began in the 1930's, with a classic study by Elton Mayo, Fritz Roethlisberger, and William Dickson at the Hawthorne Western Electric Plant. These researchers conducted numerous experiments and interviews that led them to question the fundamental assumptions of scientific management. The researchers found that workers were strongly influenced by social norms and that peers could have as much influence on productivity as rules and incentives. They also found that workers expressed a strong desire to have their opinions heard and to make decisions regarding their jobs. The outcome of the human relations era was that managers began to show greater concern for employees' opinions and social needs. Managers assumed that the best way to motivate employees was to alleviate employee morale problems and to improve social relations on the job.

It was not until the human potential movement that managers and psychologists began to emphasize intrinsic motivation. This period began in the 1960's, with a growing concern over job satisfaction. Attracted to the work of Maslow and Herzberg, managers began to recognize employees' needs for psychological growth. Managers thus assumed that the best way to motivate workers was to give workers more opportunities to learn and experience responsibility.

Beginning in the 1970's, motivational theorists and researchers became less concerned about finding the one best way to motivate employees. Instead, they took a more eclectic approach, elaborating on and integrating established motivation theories. For example, researchers have become interested in the degree to which extrinsic motivational strategies, such as performance bonuses, interfere with or supplement intrinsic motivation.

As work roles become more central to people's identity, as world economic competition increases, and as telecommunications and the Internet change the dynamics of work and the workplace, work motivation should remain a popular area of research. Managers will continue to find motivation theories useful in improving job satisfaction and increasing worker productivity.

SOURCES FOR FURTHER STUDY

Doyle, Christine E. *Work and Organizational Psychology: An Introduction with Attitude.* New York: Psychology Press, 2002. A cutting-edge introduction to work psychology. Covers work motivation as well as other topics relevant to organizational and work psychology. Suitable for undergraduate and graduate students.

Hodson, Christine. *Psychology and Work.* New York: Routledge, 2001. Chapter 3 covers a number of topics related to work motivation, including overviews of Maslow's heirarchy of needs and McClelland's research on the need for achievement.

Maslow, Abraham H. *Toward a Psychology of Being.* 3d ed. New York: John Wiley & Sons, 1998. Maslow describes his needs hierarchy model of motivation and presents an interesting discussion of self-actualization.

Smither, Robert D., ed. *The Psychology of Work and Human Performance.* Reading, Mass.: Addison Wesley, 1998. Chapter 7 covers work motivation, with emphasis on understanding individual differences among employees in motivation and performance.

Taylor, Frederick Winslow. *The Principles of Scientific Management.* New York: W. W. Norton, 1967. This management classic, originally published in 1911, describes Taylor's studies at the Midvale Steel Mill. Taylor was one of the first authors to discuss such concepts as wage incentives, time and motion studies, employee selection, and planning.

Daniel Sachau

SEE ALSO: Achievement motivation; Affiliation motive; Human resource training and development; Incentive motivation; Industrial and organizational psychology; Motivation; Self-actualization.

GLOSSARY

Absolute threshold: The smallest amount of stimulus that elicits a sensation 50 percent of the time.

Accommodation: In Jean Piaget's theory of development, adjusting the interpretation (schema) of an object or event to include a new instance; in vision, the ability of the lens to focus light on the retina by changing its shape.

Acetylcholine (ACh): A cholinergic neurotransmitter important in producing muscular contraction and in some autonomic nerve transmissions.

Achievement motivation: The tendency for people to strive for moderately difficult goals because of the relative attractiveness of success and repulsiveness of failure.

Acquisition: In learning, the process by which an association is formed in classical or operant conditioning; in memory, the stage at which information is stored in memory.

Action potential: A rapid change in electrical charges across a neuron's cell membrane, with depolarization followed by repolarization, leading to a nerve impulse moving down an axon; associated with nerve and muscle activity.

Actor-observer bias: The tendency to infer that other people's behavior is caused by dispositional factors but that one's own behavior is the product of situational causes.

Actualizing tendency: The force toward maintaining and enhancing the organism, achieving congruence between experience and awareness, and realizing potentials.

Adaptation: Any heritable characteristic that presumably has developed as a result of natural selection and thus increases an animal's ability to survive and reproduce.

Addiction: Physical dependence on a substance; components include tolerance, psychological dependence, and physical withdrawal symptoms.

Adolescence: The period extending from the onset of puberty to early adulthood.

Adrenal glands: The suprarenal glands, small, caplike structures sitting each on top of one kidney; in general, they function in response to stress, but they are also important in regulating metabolic and sexual functions.

Affect: A class name given to feelings, emotions, or dispositions as a mode of mental functioning.

Affective disorders: Functional mental disorders associated with emotions or feelings (also called mood disorders); examples include depression and bipolar disorders.

Afferent: A sensory neuron or a dendrite carrying information toward a structure; for example, carrying sensory stimuli coming into the reticular formation.

Affiliation motive: The motive to seek the company of others and to be with one's own kind, based on such things as cooperation, similarity, friendship, sex, and protection.

Aggression: Behavior intended to harm or injure another person or thing.

Agoraphobia: An intense fear of being in places or situations in which help may not be available or escape could be difficult.

Allele: One of the many forms of a gene; it may be dominant (needing only one copy for the trait to appear) or recessive (needing two copies).

Altruism: A phenomenon in human and animal behaviors in which individuals unselfishly sacrifice their own genetic fitness in order to help other individuals in a group.

Alzheimer's disease: A form of presenile dementia, characterized by disorientation, loss of memory, speech disturbances, and personality disorders.

Amplitude: The peak deviation from the rest state of the movement of a vibrating object, or the ambient state of the medium through which vibration is conducted.

Anal stage: According to Sigmund Freud, the second psychosexual stage of personality development, approximately from ages two to four; sexual energy is focused on the anus and on pleasures and conflicts associated with retaining and eliminating feces.

Analgesia: The reduction or elimination of pain.

Analytical psychology: A school of psychology founded by Carl Jung that views the human mind as the result of prior experiences and the preparation of future goals; it deemphasizes the role of sexuality in psychological disorders.

Androgens: Male sex hormones secreted by the testes; testosterone, the primary mammalian male androgen, is responsible for the development and maturation of male sexual structures and sexual behaviors.

Androgyny: The expression of both traditionally feminine and traditionally masculine attributes.

Anorexia nervosa: An eating disorder characterized by an obsessive-compulsive concern for thinness achieved by dieting; often combined with extreme exercising and sometimes part of a binge-purge cycle.

Anterograde amnesia: An inability to form new memories after the onset of amnesia.

Antidepressants: Drugs that are used in the treatment of depression, many of which affect or mimic neurotransmitters; classes of antidepressants include the tricyclics and monoamine oxidase inhibitors (MAOIs).

Antisocial personality disorder: A personality disorder characterized by a history of impulsive, risk-taking, and perhaps chronic criminal behavior, and by opportunistic interpersonal relations.

Anxiety: A chronic fearlike state that is accompanied by feelings of impending doom and that cannot be explained by an actual threatening object or event.

Aphasia: Partial or total loss of the use of language as a result of brain damage, characterized by an inability to use and/or comprehend language.

Applied research: Research intended to solve existing problems, as opposed to "basic research," which seeks knowledge for its own sake.

Aptitude: The potential to develop an ability with training and/or experience.

Archetypes: In Carl Jung's theory, universal, inherited themes—such as the motifs of the self, hero, and shadow—that exercise an influence on virtually all human beings.

Archival data: Information collected at an earlier time by someone other than the present researcher, often for purposes very different from those of the present research.

Artificial intelligence: The use of computers to simulate aspects of human thinking and, in some cases, behavior.

Assimilation: The interpretation of a new instance of an object or event in terms of one's preexisting schema or understanding; the fit, never perfect, is close enough.

Attachment: An emotional bond between infant and caregiver based on reciprocal interaction patterns.

Attention: The ability to focus mentally.

Attitude: A relatively stable evaluation of a person or thing; it can be either positive or negative, can vary in level of intensity, and has an affective, cognitive, and behavioral component.

Attribution: The process by which one gathers information about the self and others and interprets it to determine the cause of an event or behavior.

Attributional biases: Typical motivational and cognitive errors in the attribution process; tendencies that are shared among people in using information in illogical or unwarranted ways.

Autonomic nervous system: The division of the peripheral nervous system that regulates basic, automatically controlled life processes such as cardiovascular function, digestive function, and genital function.

Availability heuristic: A decision-making heuristic whereby a person estimates the probability of some occurrence or event depending on how easily examples of that event can be remembered.

Aversion therapy: A therapy that involves pairing something negative (such as electric shock) with an undesired behavior (such as drinking alcohol or smoking cigarettes).

Axon: The single fiberlike extension of a neuron that carries information away from the cell body toward the next cell in a pathway.

Beck Depression Inventory (BDI): A brief questionnaire used to measure the severity of depression; developed by Aaron Beck.

Behavior therapy: A branch of psychotherapy narrowly conceived as the application of classical and operant conditioning to the alteration of clinical problems, but more broadly conceived as applied experimental psychology in a clinical context.

Behaviorism: A theoretical approach which states that the environment is the primary cause of behavior and that only external, observable stimuli and responses are available to objective study.

Between-subject designs: Experimental plans in which different participants receive each level of the independent variable.

Bilingual: A person who has enough control of two

languages to function well with both languages in a number of different contexts.

Binocular cues: Visual cues that require the use of both eyes working together.

Biofeedback: A psychophysiological technique in which an individual monitors a specific, supposedly involuntary, bodily function such as blood pressure or heart rate and consciously attempts to control this function through the use of learning principles.

Bipolar disorder: A disorder characterized by the occurrence of one or more manic episodes, usually interspersed with one or more major depressive episodes.

Bottom-up processing: Information processing guided by simple stimulus features of units rather than by a person's general knowledge, beliefs, or expectations.

Brain stem: The lower part of the brain, between the brain and spinal cord, which activates the cortex and makes perception and consciousness possible; it includes the midbrain, pons, medulla, and cerebellum.

Bystander effect: The tendency for an individual to be less likely to help as the number of other people present increases.

Cardinal trait: According to Gordon W. Allport's theory of personality, a single outstanding characteristic that dominates a person's life; few individuals are characterized by a cardinal disposition.

Case study: An in-depth method of data collection in which all available background data on an individual or group are reviewed; typically used in psychotherapy.

Catecholamines: A neurotransmitter group derived from the amino acid tyrosine that includes dopamine, epinephrine, and norepinephrine; they are activated in stressful situations.

Catharsis: A reduction of psychological tension and/or physiological arousal by expressing (either directly or vicariously) repressed aggressive or sexual anxieties.

Central nervous system: The nerve cells, fibers, and other tissues associated with the brain and spinal cord.

Central traits: According to Gordon W. Allport's theory, the relatively few (five to ten) distinctive and descriptive characteristics that provide direction and focus to a person's life.

Cephalocaudal development: A pattern of early physical growth consisting of motor development that proceeds from head to foot.

Cerebellum: The portion of the brain that controls voluntary muscle activity, including posture and body movement; located behind the brain stem.

Cerebral commissures: Fiber tracts, such as the corpus callosum and anterior commissure, that connect and allow neural communication between the cerebral hemispheres.

Cerebral cortex: The outer layer of the cerebrum; controls higher-level brain functions such as thinking, reasoning, motor coordination, memory, and language.

Cerebral hemispheres: Two anatomically similar hemispheres that make up the outer surface of the brain (the cerebral cortex); separated by the cerebral longitudinal fissure.

Cerebrospinal fluid: A fluid, derived from blood, that circulates in and around the ventricles of the brain and the spinal cord.

Cerebrum: The largest and uppermost portion of the brain; the cerebrum performs sensory and motor functions and affects memory, speech, and emotional functions.

Chaining: The process by which several neutral stimuli are presented in a series; they eventually assume reinforcing qualities by being ultimately paired with an innate reinforcer.

Children's Depression Inventory (CDI): A modified version of the Beck Depression Inventory (BDI) that was developed to measure the severity of depression in children; developed by Maria Kovacs.

Chromosomes: Microscopic threadlike bodies in the nuclei of cells; they carry the genes, which convey hereditary characteristics.

Circadian rhythm: A cyclical variation in a biological process or behavior that has a duration of about a day; in humans under constant environmental conditions, the rhythm usually reveals its true length as being slightly more than twenty-four hours.

Classical conditioning: A form of associative learning in which a neutral stimulus, called the conditioned stimulus (CS), is repeatedly paired with a biologically significant unconditioned stimulus (US) so that the CS acquires the same power to elicit response as the US; also called Pavlovian conditioning.

Clinical psychologist: A person with a Ph.D. in psychology, specially trained to assess and treat mental disorders and behavior problems.

Cochlea: The snail-shell-shaped portion of the inner ear, which contains the nerve connections to the auditory nerve.

Code-switching: A speech style used by many bilinguals that is characterized by rapid shifts back and forth between two languages within a single conversation or sentence.

Cognition: Mental processes involved in the acquisition and use of knowledge, such as attention, thinking, problem solving, and perception; cognitive learning emphasizes these processes in the acquisition of new behaviors.

Cognitive appraisal: An assessment of the meaningfulness of an event to an individual; events that are appraised as harmful or potentially harmful elicit stress.

Cognitive behavior therapy: Therapy that integrates principles of learning theory with cognitive strategies to treat disorders such as depression, anxiety, and other behavioral problems (such as smoking or obesity).

Cognitive dissonance theory: Leon Festinger's theory that inconsistencies among one's cognitions cause tension and that individuals are motivated to reduce this tension by changing discrepant attitudes.

Cognitive map: A mental representation of an external area that is used to guide one's behavior.

Cognitive processes: The processes of thought, which include attending to an event, storing information in memory, recalling information, and making sense of information; they enable people to perceive events.

Cognitive psychology: An area of study that investigates mental processes; areas within cognitive psychology include attention, perception, language, learning, memory, problem solving, and logic.

Cognitive science: A multidisciplinary approach to the study of cognition from the perspectives of psychology, computer science, neuroscience, philosophy, and linguistics.

Cohort: An identifiable group of people; in developmental research, group members are commonly associated by their birth dates and shared historical experiences.

Collective unconscious: In Carl Jung's theory, memory traces of repeated experiences that have been passed down to all humankind as a function of evolutionary development; includes inherited tendencies to behave in certain ways and contains the archetypes.

Color: The brain's interpretation of electromagnetic radiation of different wavelengths within the range of visible light.

Color blindness: An inability to perceive certain colors; the most common type is green-minus color blindness, involving a defect in the eyes' green cones.

Compensation: In Alfred Adler's theory, a defense mechanism for overcoming feelings of inferiority by trying harder to excel; in Sigmund Freud's theory, the process of learning alternative ways to accomplish a task while making up for an inferiority—a process that could involve dreams that adjust psychologically for waking imbalances.

Complementary color: Light that complements another light in that their addition produces white light and their juxtaposition produces high contrast.

Compulsions: Ritualistic patterns of behavior that commonly follow obsessive thinking and that reduce the intensity of the anxiety-evoking thoughts.

Concrete operations stage: The third stage of Jean Piaget's theory, during which children acquire basic logical rules and concrete concepts; occurs between the ages of seven and eleven.

Conditioned response (CR): In Pavlovian conditioning, the behavior and emotional quality that occurs when a conditioned stimulus is presented; related to but not the same as the unconditioned response.

Conditioned stimulus (CS): A previously neutral stimulus (a sight, sound, touch, or smell) that, after Pavlovian conditioning, will elicit the conditioned response (CR).

Conditioned taste aversion: An avoidance of a food or drink that has been followed by illness when consumed in the past.

Conditioning: A type of learning in which an animal learns a concept by associating it with some object or by the administration of rewards and/or punishments.

Conditions of worth: In Carl Rogers's theory, externally based conditions for love and praise; the expectation that the child must behave in accordance with parental standards in order to receive love.

Cone: One type of visual receptor found in the retina of the eye; primarily for color vision and acute daytime vision.

Confounding of variables: The variation of other variables along with the independent variable of interest, as a result of which any effects cannot be attributed with certainty to the independent variable.

Consciousness: A level of awareness that includes those things of which an individual is aware at any given moment, such as current ideas, thoughts, accessed memories, and feelings.

Consensual validation: The verification of subjective beliefs by obtaining a consensus among other people.

Consensus information: Information concerning other people's responses to an object; in attribution theory, high consensus generally leads people to attribute situational rather than personal causes to a behavior.

Conservation: In Jean Piaget's theory, understanding that the physical properties (number, length, mass, volume) remain constant even though appearances may change; a concrete-operational skill.

Consistency information: Information concerning a person's response to an object over time. In attribution theory, high consistency implies that behavior is dispositional or typical of a person.

Consolidation: A neural process by which short-term memories become stored in long-term memory.

Construct: A formal concept representing the relationships between variables or processes such as motivation and behavior; may be empirical (observable) or hypothetical (inferred).

Construct validity: A type of validity that assesses the extent to which a test score (variable) correlates with other tests (variables) already established as valid measures of the item.

Consumer psychology: The subfield of psychology that studies selling, advertising, and buying; the goal of its practitioners is generally to communicate clearly and to persuade consumers to buy products.

Context dependence: The phenomenon in which memory functions more effectively when material is recalled in the same environment in which it was originally learned, compared with recall in a different environment.

Contingency: A relationship between a response and its consequence or between two stimuli; sometimes considered a dependency.

Contingency management: A method of behavior modification that involves providing or removing positive rewards in accordance with whether the individual being treated engages in the expected behavior.

Continuous reinforcement: A schedule in which each response is followed by a reinforcer.

Control group: A group of subjects that are like the experimental groups in all ways except that they do not experience the independent variable; used as a comparison measure.

Control variable: An extraneous factor that might influence the dependent variable, making it difficult to evaluate the effect of the independent variable; in an experiment, attempts are made to isolate or control such effects systematically.

Convergence: In perception, the turning of the eyes inward from parallel lines of sight to look at a nearby object; a depth cue.

Convergent thinking: Creative thinking in which possible solutions to a problem are systematically eliminated in search for the best solution; the type of ordinary thinking in which most people generally engage.

Conversion disorder: A psychological disorder in which a person experiences physical symptoms, such as the loss or impairment of some motor or sensory function (paralysis or blindness, for example), in the absence of an organic cause.

Coping: Responses directed at dealing with demands (in particular, threatening or stressful ones) upon an organism; these responses may either improve or reduce long-term functioning.

Correlation: The degree of relatedness or correspondence between two variables, expressed by a coefficient that can range from +1.00 to −1.00; 0.00 signifies no correspondence.

Cortex: The surface (or outer layer) of the brain, which receives sensory input, interprets it, and relates behavior to external stimuli; responsible for perception and conscious thought.

Cortical brain centers: The portions of the brain making up the cerebral cortex and controlling voluntary behavior, higher reasoning, and language skills; they develop rapidly during the first two years of life.

Countertransference: The phenomenon in which an analyst either shifts feelings from his or her past onto a patient or is affected by the client's emotional problems; caused by a patient's perceived similarity to individuals or experiences in the analyst's life.

Creativity: Cognitive abilities in areas such as fluency, flexibility, originality, elaboration, visualization, metaphorical thinking, and problem definition; the ability to originate something that is both new and appropriate.

Criterion group: A group used to validate a measurement instrument; in the case of interest inventories, it refers to persons in a particular occupational group.

Critical period: A time during which the developing organism is particularly sensitive to the influence of certain inputs or experiences necessary to foster normal development; in nonhuman animals, a specific time period during which a certain type of learning such as imprinting must occur.

Cross-sectional design: A design in which subgroups of a population are randomly sampled; the members of the sample are then tested or observed.

Cue-producing response: A response that serves as a cue for other responses; words (speech) can cue behaviors, and thoughts can cue other thoughts.

Cutaneous sense: Relating to the skin sense, as in responses to touch or temperature.

Cyclothymia: A milder version of a cyclical mood disorder in which mood swings can occur but are not as intense as in bipolar disorder.

Daily hassles: Seemingly minor everyday events that are a constant source of stress.

Dark adaptation: An increase in the sensitivity of rods and cones to light through an increase in the concentration of light-absorbing pigments.

Data: A collection of observations from an experiment or survey.

Death instinct: The unconscious desire for death and destruction in order to escape the tensions of living.

Debriefing: Discussing an experiment and its purpose with subjects after its completion; required if the experiment involved deception.

Decay: The disappearance of a memory trace.

Deduction: A type of logic by which one draws a specific conclusion from one or more known truths or premises; often formed as an "if/then" statement.

Defense mechanism: According to Sigmund Freud, a psychological strategy by which an unacceptable sexual or aggressive impulse may be kept from conscious thought or expressed in a disguised fashion.

Deindividuation: The loss of self-awareness and evaluation apprehension that accompanies situations that foster personal and physical anonymity.

Delusion: A symptom of psychosis that consists of a strong irrational belief held despite considerable evidence against it; types include delusions of grandeur, reference, and persecution.

Dementia: Globally impaired intellectual functioning (memory reasoning) in adults as a function of brain impairment; it does not mean "craziness," but a loss or impairment of mental power.

Dendrite: A branching extension of a neuron through which information enters the cell; there may be one or many dendrites on a neuron.

Dependent variable: The outcome measure in a study; the effect of the independent variable is measured by changes in the dependent variable.

Depolarization: A shift in ions and electrical charges across a cell membrane, causing loss of resting membrane potential and bringing the cell closer to the action potential.

Depression: A psychological disorder characterized by extreme feelings of sadness, hopelessness, or personal unworthiness, as well as loss of energy, withdrawal, and either lack of sleep or excessive sleep.

Depth perception: The ability to see three-dimensional features, such as the distance of an object from oneself and the shape of an object.

Descriptive statistics: Procedures that summarize and organize data sets; they include mean, median, range, correlation, and variability.

Desensitization: A behavioral technique of gradually removing anxiety associated with certain situations by associating a relaxed state with these situations.

Determinism: The theory or doctrine that acts of the will, occurrences in nature, or social or psychological phenomena are causally determined by preceding events or natural laws.

Development: The continuous and cumulative process of age-related changes in physical growth, thought, perception, and behavior of people and animals; a result of both biological and environmental influences.

Developmental psychology: The subfield of psychology

that studies biological, social, and intellectual changes as they occur throughout the human life cycle.

Deviancy: The quality of having a condition or engaging in behavior that is atypical in a social group and is considered undesirable.

Diagnosis: The classification or labeling of a patient's problem within one of a set of recognized categories of abnormal behavior, determined with the aid of interviews and psychological tests.

Diagnostic and Statistical Manual of Mental Disorders (DSM): A handbook created by the American Psychiatric Association for diagnosing and classifying mental disorders; used by mental health professionals and insurance companies.

Dichotic listening: A technique in which two different messages are simultaneously played through earphones, with a different message to each ear.

Diffusion of responsibility: The reduction of personal responsibility that is commonly experienced in group situations; diffusion of responsibility increases as the size of the crowd increases.

Discounting: Reducing the role of a particular cause in producing a behavior because of the presence of other plausible causes.

Discrimination: In perception, the ability to see that two patterns differ in some way; in intergroup relations, behavior (usually unfavorable) toward persons that is based on their group membership rather than on their individual personalities.

Discriminative stimulus: A stimulus that signals the availability of a consequence, given that a response occurs.

Dispersion: A statistical measure of variability; a measure (range, semi-interquartile range, standard deviation, or variance) that provides information about the difference among the scores.

Displacement: According to Sigmund Freud, a defense mechanism by which a person redirects his or her aggressive impulse onto a target that may substitute for the target that originally aroused the person's aggression.

Display: A visual dance or series of movements or gestures by an individual or animal to communicate such things as dominance, aggression, and courtship to other individuals.

Display rules: Culturally determined rules regarding the appropriate expression of emotions.

Dispositional: Relating to disposition or personality rather than to situation.

Dissociative disorder: A disorder that occurs when some psychological function, such as memory, is split off from the rest of the conscious mind; not caused by brain dysfunction.

Dissonance: An unpleasant psychological and physiological state caused by an inconsistency between cognitions.

Distal stimulus: An object or other sensory element in the environment.

Distinctiveness information: Information concerning a person's response to an object under given conditions; in attribution theory, high distinctiveness suggests that individuals are behaving uniquely toward a given target/object.

Diurnal enuresis: The presence of enuretic episodes when the individual is awake.

Divergent thinking: Thinking that results in new and different responses that most people cannot, or do not, offer; the type of thinking most clearly involved in creativity.

Domestic violence: Physical, emotional, psychological, or sexual abuse perpetrated by a family member toward another family member; typically the abuse follows a repetitive, predictable pattern.

Dominance hierarchy: An ordered arrangement of dominant to subordinate individuals in an animal population that serves numerous social functions, including protection; a pecking order.

Dopamine: One type of neurotransmitter, a chemical that is released from one nerve cell and stimulates receptors on another, thus transferring a message between them; associated with movement and with treatment of depression.

Double bind: A form of communication that often occurs when a family member sends two messages, requests, or commands that are logically inconsistent, contradictory, or impossible, resulting in a "damned if one does, damned if one doesn't" situation; a hypothesis about the development of schizophrenia.

Double-blind method: A procedure in which neither the experimenter nor the subjects know who is receiving treatment and who is not; this controls for subject and experimenter biases and expectations.

Down syndrome: A chromosomal abnormality that causes mental retardation as well as certain physical defects, such as extra eyelid folds and a thick tongue; caused by an extra (third) chromosome on chromosome pair 21.

Drive: The tendency of a person or animal to engage in behaviors brought about by some change or condition inside that organism; often generated by deprivation (hunger or thirst) or exposure to painful or other noxious stimuli.

Drive reduction hypothesis: The idea that a physiological need state triggers a series of behaviors aimed at reducing the unpleasant state; drive reduction is reinforcing.

Dysfunctional family: A family grouping that is characterized by the presence of disturbed interactions and communications; particularly an abusive, incestuous, or alcoholic family.

Dyslexia: Diffculties in reading, usually after damage to the left cerebral hemisphere.

Dysphoria: A symptom of clinical depression; extreme sadness.

Dysthymic disorder: A form of depression in which mild to moderate levels of depressive symptoms persist chronically.

Early recollections: A projective technique in which the patient attempts to remember things that happened in the distant past; these provide clues to the patient's current use of private logic.

Eating disorders: Afflictions resulting from dysfunctional relationships to hunger, food, and eating.

Echoic memory: Sensory memory for sound.

Echolalia: An involuntary and parrotlike repetition of words or phrases spoken by others.

Eclectic therapy: Therapy in which a combination of models and techniques is employed, rather than a single approach.

Educational psychology: The subfield of psychology that studies the effectiveness of education, usually formal education; educational psychologists seek to develop new educational techniques and to improve the learning process.

Efferent nerve: A motor neuron or an axon carrying information away from a structure; for example, in the transmission of stimuli from the reticular formation to the cerebral cortex.

Ego: In psychoanalytic theory, the part of the personality responsible for perceiving reality and thinking; mediates between the demands of the pleasure-seeking id, the rule-following superego, and reality.

Egocentric thought: A cognitive tendency in childhood in which the child assumes that everyone shares his or her own perspective; the cognitive inability to understand the different perspective of another.

Elaborative rehearsal: Giving meaning to information to enable encoding it in memory.

Electroconvulsive therapy (ECT): A treatment for severe depression in which an electric current is passed through the brain of the patient.

Electroencephalogram (EEG): The graphic recording of the electrical activity of the brain (brain waves).

Electroencephalography: Measurement of the electrical output of the brain, which may then sometimes be brought under voluntary control by biofeedback and relaxation.

Embryonic phase: The period of rapid prenatal change that follows the zygote period; extends from the second to the eighth week after conception.

Emotion: A psychological response that includes a set of physiological changes, expressive behaviors, and a subjective experience.

Empathy: In therapy, the therapist's ability to focus attention on the needs and experience of the client; also refers to the therapist's ability to communicate an understanding of the client's emotional state.

Empirical evidence: Data or information derived objectively from the physical senses, without reliance on personal faith, intuition, or introspection.

Empiricism: A philosophy holding that knowledge is learned through experience and that infants begin life like blank slates, learning about their environment through experience.

Encoding: The transformation of incoming sensory information into a form of code that the memory system can accept and use.

Endocrine gland: A gland that produces one or more hormones and secretes them into the blood so that they can serve as intercellular messengers.

Endocrine system: A system of ductless glands in the bodies of vertebrate animals that secretes hormones which travel through the bloodstream to target tissues, whose functioning is altered by the hormones.

Endogenous behavior: An innate, or inborn, behavior that is established by the animal's inherited genetic code (DNA) and that is not influenced by the animal's experiences or environment.

Endorphins: A group of endogenous, opiate-like neuropeptides of the central nervous system that simulate analgesia and interfere with transmission of pain impulses; the brain's own morphine.

Enkephalins: Peptides containing five amino acids, within the endorphin group, that may act as neurotransmitters; the first of the endorphins to be discovered.

Enmeshment: An excessively close relationship between parent and child in which adult concerns and needs are communicated and in which overdependence on the child is apparent.

Entitlement: The expectation of special or unusually favorable treatment by others; commonly seen among narcissistic personalities.

Entropy: In Carl Jung's analytical theory, a concept maintaining that aspects of a person's psychic energy which are not in balance will tend to seek a state of equilibrium.

Enuresis: The inability to control the release of urine; nocturnal enuresis is also called bed-wetting.

Environmental psychology: The subfield of psychology that studies the relationship between the environment and behavior, particularly the effects of the physical and social environments (such as noise or crowding) on behavior.

Environmental stressor: A condition in the environment, such as crowding, noise, toxic chemicals, or extreme temperatures, that produces stress (bodily or mental tension).

Epilepsy: A disorder of the nervous system in which the cortex produces electrical firing that causes convulsions and other forms of seizures; thought by some to be linked to the reticular formation.

Epinephrine: The neurotransmitter released from the adrenal gland as a result of innervation of the autonomic nervous system; formerly called adrenaline.

Episodic memory: A form of long-term memory involving temporal and spatial information, including personal experiences.

Equipotentiality: In Pavlovian conditioning, the idea that any stimulus paired with an effective unconditioned stimulus will come to elicit a conditioned response with equal facility.

Equity theory: A theory in attraction and work motivation that contends that individuals are motivated to remain in relationships they perceive to be fair, just, and equitable—that is, where one's outcomes are proportional to one's inputs, particularly when contrasted with others in the relationship.

Equivalence: A principle stating that an increase in energy or value in one aspect of the psyche is accompanied by a decrease in another area.

Estradiol: The primary sex hormone of mammalian females, which is responsible for the menstrual cycle and for development of secondary sex characteristics; a primary estrogen, secreted by the corpus luteum.

Ethnocentrism: An attitude of uncritically assuming the superiority of the in-group culture.

Ethology: A branch of zoology that studies animals in their natural environments; often concerned with investigating the adaptive significance and innate basis of behaviors.

Etiology: The factors that are thought to cause or contribute to the development of a particular disorder.

Eustress: Positive arousal or stress, appraised as a challenge rather than as a threat.

Evoked potential: A brain response that is triggered by electroencephalography using discrete sensory stimuli.

Excitation transfer: The theory that arousal from one source can intensify an emotional reaction to a different source (for example, that sexual arousal can increase the response to an aggressive cue).

Existentialism: A philosophical viewpoint emphasizing human existence and the human situation in the world that gives meaning to life through the free choice of mature values and commitment to responsible goals; the critical goal involves finding one's true self and living according to this potential.

Exogenous substances: Substances not normally occurring in the body, present only when administered; exogenous substances include substances such as drugs or synthetic test compounds mimicking endogenous substances.

Expectancy confirmation bias: Interpreting ambiguous information as being supportive of expectations; mistakenly "seeing" what is expected.

Expectancy theory: A cognitive motivation model which proposes that people choose to perform behaviors they believe to be the most likely to lead to positive outcomes; in work theory, workers are more motivated when they perceive congruence between their efforts, products, and rewards.

Experiment: One of several data collection methods; requires systematically manipulating the levels of an independent variable under controlled conditions in order to measure its impact on a dependent variable.

Experimenter bias: Biases introduced into a research study as a result of the expectations of the experimenter.

Expressive aphasia: Difficulties in expressing language, usually after damage to Broca's area in the left frontal lobe of the cerebral cortex.

External validity: The extent to which the results of a research study can be generalized to different populations, settings, or conditions.

Externalization: A defense mechanism in which one experiences unresolved, repressed inner turmoil as occurring outside oneself; holding external factors responsible for one's problems.

Extinction: A process by which the probability of a response is decreased; in classical or Pavlovian conditioning, a process in which the temporal contiguity of the conditioned stimulus and the unconditioned stimulus is disrupted and the learned association is lost; in operant or instrumental conditioning, a process in which undesirable behavior is not followed by reinforcement.

Extraneous variable: A variable that has a detrimental affect on a research study, making it difficult to determine if the result is attributable to the variable under study or to some unknown variable not controlled for; for example, in jury decision making, the effect of defendant attractiveness.

Extrinsic motivation: Motivation to perform an activity only because the activity leads to a valued outcome external to the activity itself.

Extrinsic religion: An immature religious orientation that uses religion for self-serving purposes such as security or a sense of social or economic well-being.

Factor analysis: A statistical technique wherein a set of correlated variables can be regrouped in terms of the degree of commonality they share.

Family therapy: A type of psychotherapy that focuses on correcting the faulty interactions among family members that maintain children's psychological problems.

Farsightedness: An inability to focus clearly on nearby objects that is caused by the point of focus of the lens falling behind the retina.

Feminist analysis: The examination of the ways in which inequality, injustice, or oppression devalues women and/or limits their potential, both individually and collectively.

Fetal phase: The third period of prenatal development, extending from the ninth week of pregnancy until birth.

Fetishism: A sexual behavior in which a person becomes aroused by focusing on an inanimate object or a part of the human body.

Field research: An approach in which evidence is gathered in a "natural" setting, such as the workplace; by contrast, laboratory research involves an artificial, contrived setting.

Fight-or-flight response: A sequence of physiological changes, described by Walter B. Cannon, that occurs in response to threat and prepares the organism to flee from or fight the threat; includes increases in heart rate, blood pressure, and respiration.

Fixation: In psychoanalytic theory, an inability to progress to the next level of psychosexual development because of overgratification or undergratification of desires at a particular stage.

Flashback: A type of traumatic reexperiencing in which a person becomes detached from reality and thinks, feels, and acts as if a previous traumatic experience were happening again.

Flocking: A defensive maneuver in many mammalian and bird species in which a scattered group of individuals implodes into a compact cluster at the approach of a predator.

Flooding: A type of therapy in which a phobic person imagines his or her most-feared situation until fear decreases.

Fluid intelligence: The form of intelligence that reflects speed of information processing, reasoning, and memory capacity rather than factual knowledge (crystallized intelligence); associated with Raymond Cattell.

Forebrain: A developmentally defined division of the brain that contains structures such as the cerebral hemispheres, the thalamus, and the hypothalamus.

Forensic psychology: The application of psychological skills in the legal profession—for example, in jury selection, sanity determination, and assessing competency to stand trial.

Forgetting: The loss of information from memory.

Formal operations: According to Jean Piaget, the fourth stage of cognitive development, reached at adolescence; characterized by the ability to engage in abstract thinking, hypothetical constructs, and unobserved logical possibilities.

Fovea: The central part of the retina, which is densest in cone cells and is therefore the area of sharpest visual acuity.

Free association: The psychoanalytic method in which a patient talks spontaneously without restriction; thought to reveal repressed conflicts of the unconscious.

Frequency: The number of complete back-and-forth movements or pressure changes (cycles) from the rest or ambient state that occur each second; measured in units called hertz.

Frequency distribution: The pairing of a measurement or score with the number of people or subjects obtaining that measurement.

Frontal lobe: The anterior portion of each cerebral hemisphere, containing control of motor areas and most of the higher intellectual functions of the brain, including speech.

Frustration: A psychological state of arousal that results when a person is prevented from attaining a goal.

Frustration-aggression hypothesis: A concept, pioneered by John Dollard, stating that aggressive behavior is born of frustration in attempting to reach a goal.

Fugue state: A flight from reality in which the individual develops amnesia, leaves his or her present situation, travels to a new location, and establishes a new identity.

Function word: A word that has little meaning in itself yet signals grammatical relationships between other words in a sentence, such as an article ("the" or "a") or a preposition (for example, "in," "on," "of").

Functional autonomy: A concept, pioneered by Gordon W. Allport, that many adult motives are independent in purpose from their childhood origins.

Functional disorders: Signs and symptoms for which no organic or physiological basis can be found.

Functional fixedness: An inability to think of novel uses for objects because of a fixation on their usual functions.

Functionalism: An early school of American psychology that argued for the study of the human mind from the standpoint of understanding consciousness in terms of its purpose rather than its elements.

Fundamental attribution error: Underestimating the influence of situations and overestimating the influence of personality traits in causing behavior.

Fundamental frequency: The lowest frequency in a harmonic series of complex overtones; the overtones are integer multiples of the fundamental.

Gamete: A reproductive sex cell; the female cell is known as the ovum, and the male cell is known as the sperm.

Gamma-aminobutyric acid (GABA): The most common neurotransmitter in the brain, derived from the amino acid glutamic acid; an inhibitor that seems to affect mood and emotion.

Gender: Social maleness or femaleness, reflected in the behaviors and characteristics that society expects from people of one biological sex.

Gender identity: A child's accurate labeling of himself or herself by gender; also, a person's inner sense of femaleness or maleness.

Gender schema: A general knowledge framework that organizes information and guides perceptions related to males and females.

Gene: The basic unit of heredity; a segment of a DNA molecule that contains hereditary instructions for an individual's physical traits and abilities and for the cell's production of proteins.

General adaptation syndrome: The three-stage physiological response pattern of the body to stress that was proposed by Hans Selye; the three stages are the alarm reaction, resistance stage, and exhaustion stage.

Generalization: The process by which behavior learned in one situation transfers to new situations.

Generativity: In Erik Erikson's theory of personality, the seventh stage, associated with the desire to leave a legacy; the need to take care of future generations through the experiences of caring, nurturing, and educating.

Genetics: The biochemical basis of inherited characteristics.

Genital stage: In Sigmund Freud's theory, the fifth psychosexual stage, beginning at adolescence and extending throughout adulthood; the individual learns to experience sexual gratification with a partner.

Genotype: The genetic makeup of an individual.

Gestalt: A German word, for which there is no precise translation, that is generally used to refer to a form, a whole, or a configuration.

Gestalt school of psychology: A school of psychology which maintains that the overall configuration of a stimulus array, rather than its individual elements, forms the basis of perception.

Gestalt therapy: A form of psychotherapy, initiated by Fritz Perls, that emphasizes awareness of the present and employs an active therapist-client relationship.

Giftedness: A marked ability to learn more rapidly, perform more intricate problems, and solve problems more rapidly than is normally expected for a given age; operationally defined as an IQ score above 130 on an individually administered test.

Goal setting: A motivational technique used to increase productivity in which employees are given specific performance objectives and time deadlines.

Gray matter: Unmyelinated neurons that make up the cerebral cortex, so called because they lack the fatty covering (myelin) found on neurons of the white matter.

Group dynamics: The study of how groups influence individual functioning.

Gustation: The sense of taste.

Gyrus: A convolution on the surface of the brain that results from the infolding of the cortex (surface).

Habit: An association or connection between a cue and a response, such as stopping (the response) at a red light (the cue).

Habituation: A decrease in response to repeated presentations of a stimulus that is not simply caused by fatigued sensory receptors.

Hallucinogen: A drug that can alter perception (vision and audition, in particular); examples include LSD, PCP, peyote, psilocybin, and possibly marijuana.

Hardiness: A constellation of behaviors and perceptions, characterized by perceptions of control, commitment, and challenge, that are thought to buffer the effects of stress; introduced by Suzanne Kobasa.

Hawthorne effect: A phenomenon that occurs when a subject's behavior changes after the subject discovers that he or she is being studied.

Hedonic: Associated with the seeking of pleasure and the avoidance of pain.

Helplessness: The belief that one has little or no control over the events in one's life; viewed by Martin Seligman as an important cause of depression.

Heredity: The transmission of characteristics from parent to offspring through genes in the chromosomes.

Heuristic: A shortcut or rule of thumb used for decision making or problem solving that often leads to, but does not guarantee, a correct response.

Higher-order conditioning: The linking of successive conditioned stimuli, the last of which elicits the conditioned response; higher-order associations are easily broken.

Hindbrain: A developmentally defined division of the brain that contains the pons, medulla, and cerebellum.

Hippocampus: A structure located in the temporal lobe (lateral cortical area) of the brain that has important memory functions.

Homeostasis: A term referring to the idea that the body tries to maintain steady states—that is, to maintain physiological characteristics within relatively narrow and optimum levels.

Homophobia: A fear, prejudice, or hatred toward homosexuals, usually based upon irrational stereotyping.

Hormone: A chemical "messenger," usually composed of protein or steroids, that is produced and secreted by an endocrine gland and released into the bloodstream; it targets specific genes in certain body tissue cells.

Hostile aggression: Aggressive behavior that is associated with anger and is intended to harm another.

Hue: The chromatic or color sensation produced by a certain wavelength of light.

Humanistic psychology: A branch of psychology that emphasizes the human tendencies toward growth and fulfillment, autonomy, choice, responsibility, and ultimate values such as truth, love, and justice; exemplified by the theories of Carl Rogers and Abraham Maslow.

Hypermetropia: Hereditary farsightedness caused by the length of the eyeball in the anterior-posterior direction being too short.

Hypnagogic hallucination: A vivid auditory or visual hallucination that occurs at the transition from wakefulness to sleep or from sleep to wakefulness; associated with narcolepsy.

Hypnosis: An altered state of consciousness brought on by special induction techniques (usually progressive relaxation instructions) and characterized by varying degrees of responsiveness to suggestions.

Hypnotic susceptibility: A subject's measured level of responsiveness to hypnotic suggestions on standardized scales.

Hypochondriasis: A psychological disorder in which the person is unrealistically preoccupied with the fear of disease and worries excessively about his or her health.

Hypothalamus: A small region near the base of the brain that controls the pituitary gland, autonomic nervous system, and behaviors important for survival, including eating, drinking, and temperature regulation.

Hypothesis: An educated guess about the relationship between two or more variables, derived from inductive reasoning; often tested by an experiment.

Iconic memory: Brief sensory memory for vision.

Id: The part of the psyche that contains the instincts and is directed solely by pleasure seeking; it is the most primitive part of the psyche and was thought by Sigmund Freud to fuel the ego and superego.

Idealized self: Alienation from the real self that is characterized by grandiose, unrealistic conceptions of the self and unattainable standards; part of Karen Horney's psychology.

Identification: The internalization of parental or societal values, behaviors, and attitudes; in Freudian theory, a defense and resolution of incestuous feelings toward the opposite-sex parent that is important in the development of the superego.

Identity: A personal configuration of occupational, sexual, and ideological commitments; according to Erik Erikson, the positive pole of the fifth stage of psychosocial development.

Identity crisis: According to Erik Erikson, the central developmental issue in adolescence; encompasses a struggle between an integrated core identity and role confusion.

Idiographic study: The study of the unique patterns of the individual through methods such as case studies, autobiographies, and tests that examine patterns of behavior within a single person.

Illusions: Beliefs that are unsupported by evidence or that require facts to be perceived in a particular manner.

Imagery: The use of visualization to imagine the physical movements involved in executing a skill.

Imitation: The performance of behaviors that were learned by observing the actions of others.

Immune response: The body's response to invasion by disease-producing organisms; proteins (antibodies) are produced that mark the unwanted cells for destruction.

Immutable characteristics: Physical attributes (such as gender) that are present at birth and that other people assume gives them information as to the kind of person they are seeing.

Implosion therapy: A therapy in which the patient imagines his or her feared situation, plus elements from psychodynamic theory that are related to the fear until fear decreases.

Impression management: The attempt to control the impressions of oneself that others form; synonymous with "self-presentation."

Imprinting: The innate behavioral attachment that a young animal forms with another individual (for example, its mother), with food, or with an object during a brief critical period shortly after birth; especially seen in ducks and chicks.

In-group: A social group to which a person belongs or with which a person is identified, thereby forming part of the self-concept.

In-group bias: The tendency to discriminate in favor of one's own group.

Incentive: A motivating force or system of rewards that is presented to an individual if he or she behaves or successfully performs specified tasks according to the norms of society; a goal object.

Incompetency: The legally established lack of sufficient knowledge and judgment to maintain a given right or responsibility.

Incongruence: In Carl Rogers's theory, inconsistency or distortion between one's real and ideal self; a lack of genuineness.

Independent variable: The factor that is manipulated by the experimenter in order to assess its causal impact on the dependent variable.

Individual psychology: Alfred Adler's school of personality theory and therapy; stresses the unity of the individual and his or her striving for superiority to compensate for feelings of inferiority.

Induction: A type of logic by which one arrives at a general premise or conclusion based on generalization from a large number of known specific cases.

Industrial and organizational psychology: The subfield of psychology that studies behavior in business and industry; practitioners analyze placement, training, and supervision of personnel, study organizational and communication structures, and explore ways to maximize efficiency.

Inflection: An addition to the stem of a word which indicates subtle modulations in meaning, such as plurality (more than one) or tense (present time or past time); in English, inflections are all suffixes.

Information processing model: The approach of most modern cognitive psychologists; it interprets cognition as the flow of information through interrelated stages (input, processing, storage, and retrieval) in much the same way that information is processed by a computer.

Innate: A term describing any inborn characteristic or behavior that is determined and controlled largely by the genes.

Insanity: A legal term for having a mental disease or defect so great that criminal intent or responsibility and punishability are not possible; it renders one incompetent.

Insight: A sudden mental inspiration or comprehension of a problem that was previously unsolved.

Insomnia: Difficulty in falling asleep or in remaining asleep for sufficient periods.

Instinct: An innate or inherited tendency that motivates a person or animal to act in often complex sequences without reasoning, instruction, or experience; in Freudian theory, a biological source of excitation that directs the development of personality into adulthood, such as the life instinct (Eros) and death instinct (Thanatos).

Institutional racism: The behavior patterns followed in organizations and in society at large that produce discrimination against members of racial minorities regardless of the prejudice or lack thereof of individuals.

Instrumental aggression: Aggressive behavior that is a by-product of another activity; instrumental aggression occurs only incidentally, as a means to another end.

Instrumental conditioning: The learning of the relationship between a voluntary action and the reinforcements or punishments that follow that action; also known as operant conditioning.

Integration: The function of most of the neurons of the cerebral cortex; summarizing incoming sensory information and producing a consensus as to what the nervous system will do next.

Intelligence: The ability to perform various mental tasks, including reasoning, knowledge, comprehension, memory, applying concepts, and manipulating figures; thought to reflect one's learning potential.

Intelligence quotient (IQ): A measure of a person's mental ability (as reflected by intelligence test scores) in comparison with the rest of the population at a comparable age.

Intensity: A measure of a physical aspect of a stimulus, such as the frequency of a sound or the brightness of a color.

Interest inventory: A type of test designed to determine areas of interest and enjoyment, often for the purpose of matching a person with a career.

Interference: The loss or displacement of a memory trace because of competing information that is presented.

Intermittent reinforcement: Any reinforcement schedule in which some but not all responses are rewarded; particularly difficult to extinguish.

Internal validity: The extent to which the dependent variable is caused by the independent variable; if relevant plausible rival alternative hypotheses can be ruled out, the study has strong internal validity.

Interneuron: A neuron that receives information from a sensory neuron and transmits a message to a motor neuron; very common in the brain and important in integration.

Interrater reliability: The obtained level of agreement between two observers when scoring the same observations with the same behavioral taxonomy.

Interval schedule: A schedule in which reinforcer delivery is contingent upon performance of a response after a specified amount of time has elapsed.

Intrinsic motivation: Motivation based on the desire to achieve or perform a task for its own sake, because it produces satisfaction or enjoyment, rather than for external rewards.

Introspection: The self-report of one's own sensations, perceptions, experiences, and thoughts; analyses of and reports on the content of one's own conscious experiences.

Irradiation: Nervous excitement generated in a specific brain center by an unconditioned stimulus that spreads to surrounding areas of the cerebral cortex.

Kinesthetic: Related to the sensation of body position, presence, or movement, resulting mostly from the stimulation of sensory nerves in muscles, tendons, and joints.

Korsakoff's syndrome: Alcohol-induced brain damage that causes disorientation, impaired long-term memory, and production of false memories to fill memory gaps.

Latency: In Sigmund Freud's theory, the period between approximately age six and adolescence, when sexual instincts are not strongly manifested; strictly speaking, not a psychosexual stage.

Latent content: According to psychoanalytic theory, the hidden content of a dream, camouflaged by the manifest content.

Lateral geniculate nucleus: A subdivision of the thalamus in the brain, which receives the nerve impulse from the retina; it assembles visual information.

Laterality: Specialization by sides of almost symmetrical structures; speech is lateralized in human brains, because it is mainly controlled by the left hemispheres of almost all right-handed people.

Law of Effect: Thorndike's basic law of instrumental conditioning, which holds that responses followed by certain events will be either more or less likely to recur.

Leakage: Nonverbal behavior that reveals information that a person wishes to conceal; especially useful in deception detection.

Learned helplessness: The hypothesized result of experiences in which behavior performed seems to bear no relationship to the appearance or control of a stressor.

Learning: A modification in behavior as the result of experience that involves changes in the nervous system which are not caused by fatigue, maturation, or injury.

Lesion: Damage or injury to brain tissue that is caused by disease or trauma or produced experimentally using mechanical, electrical, or chemical methods.

Levels-of-processing model: The perspective that holds that how well something is remembered is based on how elaborately incoming information is mentally processed.

Libido: The energy used to direct behavior that is pleasurable either for the self or others; when it is directed toward the self, it results in self-gratification, follows the pleasure principle, and is immature.

Limbic system: An integrated set of cerebral structures (including the amygdala, hypothalamus, hippocampus, and septal area) that play a vital role in the regulation of emotion and motivation.

Linguistic relativity hypothesis: The idea that the structure of particular languages that people speak affects the way they perceive the world.

Linguistics: A field of inquiry that focuses on the underlying structure of language; linguists study phonology (the sound system), syntax (sentence structure), and semantics (meaning), among other topics.

Lipids: Fats and oils.

Lithium carbonate: An alkaline compound that modulates the intensity of mood swings and is particularly effective in the dampening of symptoms of manic excitability.

Loci method: A serial-recall mnemonic consisting of visualizing items to be remembered along a known path of distinct locations.

Locus of control: Beliefs concerning the sources of power over one's life; persons who believe they can generally control the direction of their lives have an internal locus of control, whereas those who believe that their lives are influenced more by fate have an external locus of control.

Long-term memory: A memory system of unlimited capacity that consists of more or less permanent knowledge.

Longitudinal study: A research methodology that requires the testing of the same subjects repeatedly over a specified period of time.

Loudness: The strength of sound as heard; related to sound pressure level but also affected by frequency.

Magnitude estimation: A technique for measuring perceptual experience by having persons assign numbers to indicate the "magnitude" of an experience.

Main effect: A statistically significant difference in behavior related to different levels of a variable and not affected by any other variable.

Major depressive episode: A disorder of mood and functioning, meeting clearly specified criteria and present for at least two weeks, which is characterized by dysphoric mood or apathy.

Mania: A phase of bipolar disorder in which the

mood is one of elation, euphoria, or irritability; a disorder in which manic symptoms occur, including hyperactivity, agitation, restlessness, and grandiosity, and then are followed by a return to a normal mood state.

Manifest content: In Freudian theory, the content of a dream just as it is experienced or recalled; masks the dream's latent content.

Masculine protest: The denying of inferiority feelings through rebelliousness, violence, or maintaining a tough exterior.

Maturation: Development attributable to one's genetic timetable rather than to experience.

Mean: The arithmetic average of all the data measuring one characteristic; it can be used as a descriptive or inferential statistic.

Mechanoreceptor: A sensory receptor that is sensitive to mechanical stimulation, such as touch, movement of a joint, or stretching of a muscle.

Medical model: A view in which abnormality consists of a number of diseases that originate in bodily functions, especially in the brain, and have defined symptoms, treatments, and outcomes.

Medulla oblongata: The bulbous portion of the brain stem that directly connects with the spinal cord; controls cardiac and respiratory activity.

Melatonin: A hormone produced by the pineal gland within the forebrain that is usually released into the blood during the night phase of the light-dark cycle.

Memory: The mental processes that are involved in storing and recalling previously experienced images, information, and events.

Mere exposure: A psychological phenomenon in which liking tends to increase as a person sees more of something or someone.

Meta-analysis: A set of quantitative (statistical) procedures used to evaluate a body of empirical literature.

Metastasis: The transfer of disease from one part of the body to an unrelated part, often through the bloodstream or lymphatic system.

Midbrain: The section of the brain just above the hindbrain; influences auditory and visual processes and arousal.

Midlife crisis: A sense of reevaluation, and sometimes panic, that strikes some individuals during middle age; impulsive behavior, reassessment of goals, and career changes can result.

Mind-body problem: A psychological question originating from philosophy and religion that concerns how to understand the relationship between a physical body or brain and a nonphysical mind or subjective experience.

Mineralocorticoids: The proinflammatory hormones aldosterone and deoxycorticosterone, secreted by the adrenal cortex and having a role in salt metabolism.

Misattribution: Attributing an event to any factor other than the true cause.

Mnemonics: Strategies for improving memory through placing information in an organized context.

Monoamine oxidase inhibitors (MAOIs): A class of antidepressant drugs.

Monoamines: A group of neurotransmitters derived from a single amino acid; they include serotonin and the catecholamines.

Monocular cue: A visual cue available to each eye separately; often used by artists to portray depth.

Monosynaptic reflex: A reflex system that consists of only one synapse, the synapse between the sensory input and motor output.

Monotic: Referring to the stimulation of only one ear.

Morpheme: The smallest part of a word that has a discernible meaning.

Morphology: The rules in a given language that govern how morphemes can be combined to form words.

Motivation: A hypothetical construct used to explain behavior and its direction, intensity, and persistence.

Motor neurons: The cells of the central nervous system responsible for causing muscular activity.

Multiple personality disorder: A rare mental disorder characterized by the development and existence or two or more relatively unique and independent personalities in the same individual.

Myopia: Hereditary nearsightedness caused by the length of the eyeball in the anterior-posterior direction being too long.

Nanometer: A billionth of a meter.

Narcolepsy: A condition in which an individual is prone to fall suddenly into a deep sleep.

Nativism: A philosophy which holds that knowledge is innate and that the neonate enters the world prepared for certain kinds of environmental inputs.

Natural selection: The process by which those characteristics of a species that help it to survive or adapt to its environment tend to be passed along by members that live long enough to have offspring.

Need: A state of an organism attributable to deprivation of a biological or psychological requirement; it is related to a disturbance in the homeostatic state.

Negative reinforcement: The procedure whereby the probability of a response is increased by the contingent removal of an aversive stimulus.

Neo-Freudian: A term for psychoanalysts who place more emphasis on security and interpersonal relations as determining behavior than on the biological theories of Sigmund Freud; Neo-Freudians include Alfred Adler, Carl Jung, Karen Horney, Harry Stack Sullivan, and Erik Erikson.

Nerve impulse: Electrical activity transmitted through a nerve fiber.

Nervous system: An array of billions of neurons (conducting nerve cells) that transmits electrical information throughout the body and thereby controls practically all bodily processes.

Neurologist: A physician who specializes in the diagnosis and treatment of disorders of the nervous system.

Neuron: An individual nerve cell, the basic unit of the nervous system; receives and transmits electrical information and consists of a cell body, dendrites, and an axon.

Neuropsychology: The study of brain-behavior relationships, usually by using behavioral tests and correlating results with brain areas.

Neuropsychopharmacology: The field of study of the relationship among behavior, neuronal functioning, and drugs.

Neurosis: Any functional disorder of the mind or the emotions, occurring without obvious brain damage and involving anxiety, phobic responses, or other abnormal behavior symptoms.

Neurotransmitter: A chemical substance released from one nerve cell that communicates activity by binding to and changing the activity of another nerve cell, muscle, or gland; some stimulate, others inhibit.

Nomothetic study: A research approach that compares groups of people in order to identify general principles; the dominant method of personality research.

Nonparticipant observation: A field technique in which the researcher passively observes the behavior of the subjects, trying not to get involved in the setting.

Nonverbal communication: Communication through any means other than words; includes facial expression, tone of voice, and posture.

Normal distribution: A bell-shaped curve that often provides an accurate description of the distribution of scores obtained in research; it forms the basis of many statistical tests.

Observational learning: Learning that results from observing other people's behavior and its consequences.

Observational study: A research technique in which a scientist systematically watches for and records occurrences of the phenomena under study without actively influencing them.

Obsessions: Intrusive, recurrent, anxiety-provoking thoughts, ideas, images, or impulses that interfere with an individual's daily functioning.

Obsessive-compulsive disorder: A chronic, debilitating anxiety disorder characterized by continuous obsessive thinking and frequent compulsive behaviors.

Occipital lobe: The posterior portion of each cerebral hemisphere, where visual stimuli are received and integrated.

Oedipal complex: In Freudian theory, sexual attraction to the parent of the opposite sex, and jealousy of and fear of retribution from the parent of the same sex; first manifested in the phallic stage (in girls, sometimes called the "Electra complex").

Olfaction: The sense of smell.

Operant: The basic response unit in instrumental conditioning; a response which, when emitted, operates upon its environment and is instrumental in providing some consequences.

Operant conditioning: Learning in which a behavior increases or decreases depending on whether the behavior is followed by reward or punishment; also known as instrumental conditioning.

Operational definition: A description of a measurement or manipulation in terms that are unambiguous, observable, and easily identified.

Opiates: A class of drugs that relieve pain; opiates include morphine, heroin, and several naturally occurring peptides.

Oral stage: In Freudian theory, the first stage of

psychosexual development, from birth to approximately age two; sexual energy focuses on the mouth, and conflicts may arise over nursing, biting, or chewing.

Organic disorder: A symptomatology with a known physiological or neurological basis.

Organizational effects: The early and permanent effects of a hormone; for example, the sex hormones, which produce differentiation in the developing embryo of primordial gonads, internal reproductive structures, and external genitalia.

Ossicle: Any of the three bones of the middle ear (the hammer, anvil, and stirrup) that are involved in conduction of sound into the inner ear.

Out-group: Any social group to which an individual does not belong and which, as a consequence, may be viewed in a negative way.

Overextension: The application of a word to more objects than ordinary adult usage allows; for example, when children refer to all small four-legged animals as "dog."

Overjustification effect: The tendency of external factors that are perceived to be controlling an individual's behavior to undermine the individual's intrinsic motivation to engage in that behavior.

Overtone: One of several sine waves simultaneously generated by most sound sources; these pure tones are all integer multiples of the fundamental.

Papilla: A small bundle of taste receptor cells surrounded by supportive cells and communicating with the exterior through a small pore.

Paradoxical intervention: A therapeutic technique in which a therapist gives a patient or family a task that appears to contradict the goals of treatment.

Parallel distributed processing (PDP): A neurally inspired model in which information is processed in a massively parallel and interactive network; the course of processing is determined by the connection strengths between units of the network.

Paranoia: A psychosis characterized by delusions, particularly delusions of persecution, and pervasive suspiciousness; paranoia rarely involves hallucinations.

Parasympathetic nervous system: A branch of the autonomic nervous system; responsible for maintaining or reestablishing homeostasis.

Parietal lobe: The side and upper-middle part of each cerebral hemisphere and the site of sensory reception from the skin, muscles, and other areas; also contains part of the general interpretive area.

Pavlovian conditioning: Learning in which two stimuli are presented one after the other, and the response to the first changes because of the response automatically elicited by the second; also called classical conditioning.

Penis envy: In Freudian theory, the strong envy that females develop of the male organ because they subconsciously believe they have been castrated; Sigmund Freud proposed that penis envy dominates the female personality.

Perception: The psychological process by which information that comes in through the sense organs is meaningfully interpreted by the brain.

Perceptual constancy: The tendency to perceive figures as constant and stable in terms of shape, color, size, or brightness.

Peripheral nervous system: All the nerves located outside the bones of the skull and spinal cord.

Persona: A major Jungian archetype representing one's public personality; the mask that one wears in order to be acceptable to society at large.

Personality: An individual's unique collection of behavioral responses (physical, emotional, and intellectual) that are consistent across time and situations.

Personality disorder: A disorder involving deep-rooted behavior patterns that are inflexible and maladaptive and that cause distress in an individual's relationships with others.

Personality trait: A stable disposition to behave in a given way over time and across situations.

Phallic stage: In Freudian theory, the third stage of psychosexual development, from approximately age four to age six; sexual energy focuses on the genitals.

Phenomenology: An approach that stresses openness to direct experience in introspective or unsophisticated ways, without using analysis, theory, expectations, or interpretation.

Pheromone: A hormone or other chemical that is produced and released from the tissues of one individual and targets tissues in another individual, usually with a consciously or unconsciously detectable scent.

Phobia: An anxiety disorder involving an intense irrational fear of a particular class of things (such as horses) or a situation (such as heights).

Phoneme: A minimal unit of sound that can signal a difference in meaning.

Phonology: The specification, for a given language, of which speech sounds may occur and how they may be combined, as well as the pitch and stress patterns that accompany words and sentences.

Photoreceptor: A specialized nerve cell that can transform light into a neural message; rods are specialized for black-and-white vision, cones for color vision.

Pineal gland: A light-sensitive endocrine gland that is located toward the back of the brain and that controls reproductive cycles in many mammalian species.

Pitch: The highness or lowness of a sound as heard; related to frequency but also affected by loudness.

Pituitary: An endocrine gland located in the brain that controls several other endocrine glands and that cooperates with the hypothalamus of the nervous system in controlling physiology.

Placebo: A substance or treatment (such as a pill or an injection) that has no intrinsic effect but is presented as having some effect.

Placebo effect: The relief of pain or the causing of a desired behavioral effect as a result of a patient's belief that a substance or treatment which has no known psychological or biological effect will in fact be effective; for example, a sugar pill may relieve a backache if given by a trusted doctor.

Plasticity: The ability of neurons and neural networks to grow into specific patterns based partially upon the organism's genetics and partially upon the organism's learned experience; in the brain, neurons can modify the structural organization in order to compensate for neural damage.

Play therapy: A system of individual psychotherapy in which children's play is utilized to explain and reduce symptoms of their psychological disorders.

Pons: A part of the brain stem that serves as the nerve connection between the cerebellum and the brain stem.

Population: All members of a specified group that a researcher is interested in studying.

Positive reinforcement: A procedure used to increase the frequency of a response by presenting a favorable consequence following the response.

Positron emission tomography (PET): An imaging technique that allows blood flow, energy metabolism, and chemical activity to be visualized in the living human brain.

Post-traumatic stress disorder (PTSD): A pathological condition caused by severe stress such as an earthquake or a divorce; it has an acute stage and a chronic stage, and symptoms involve reexperiencing the traumatic event.

Postsynaptic potential: A chemical stimulus that is produced in a postsynaptic cell; may excite the cell to come nearer to electrical firing, or may inhibit firing.

Power law: A statement of the lawful relationship between two variables that expresses one of them as the other raised to some exponent.

Pragmatism: A philosophical position that provided the framework of functionalism by proposing that the value of something lies in its usefulness.

Prejudice: Liking or disliking of persons based on their category or group membership rather than on their individual personalities; predominantly refers to unfavorable reactions.

Preoperational stage: In Jean Piaget's theory, a transitional stage of the preschool child (ages two to seven, approximately), after mental representations (symbols) are acquired but before they can be logically manipulated.

Preparedness: The idea that, through evolution, animals have been genetically prepared to learn certain things important to their survival.

Presbyopia: Farsightedness resulting from decreased flexibility of the lens of the eye and other age-related factors.

Primacy effect: The tendency for things that are seen or received first to be better recalled and more influential than things that come later.

Primary motive: A motive that arises from innate, biological needs and that must be met for survival.

Primary reinforcer: A stimulus that acts as a natural, unlearned reinforcer.

Primary sex characteristics: The physiological features of the sex organs.

Priming: An increase in the availability of certain types of information in memory in response to a stimulus.

Prisoner's dilemma: A laboratory game used by psychologists to study the comparative strategies of cooperation and competition.

Probability: The proportion of times a particular event will occur; also, the study of uncertainty that is the foundation of inferential statistics.

Progesterone: A female sex hormone secreted by the corpus luteum of the ovary; maintains the lining of the uterus during pregnancy and the second half of the menstrual cycle.

Programmed instruction: A self-paced training program characterized by many small, increasingly difficult lessons separated by frequent tests.

Progressive muscle relaxation: A relaxation technique that systematically works through all the major muscle groups of the body by first tensing, then relaxing each group and paying attention to the changes.

Projective task: Any task that provides an open-ended response that may reveal aspects of one's personality; tasks or tests commonly include standard stimuli that are ambiguous in nature.

Proposition: A mental representation based on the underlying structure of language; a proposition is the smallest unit of knowledge that can be stated.

Prosocial behavior: Behavior intended to benefit another; can be motivated by either egoistic or altruistic concern.

Prototype: A "best example" of a concept—one that contains the most typical features of that concept.

Proxemics: The use of space as a special elaboration of culture; it is usually divided into the subfields of territory and personal space.

Proximo-distal development: Motor development that proceeds from the center of the body to its periphery.

Psychoactive drugs: Chemical substances that act on the brain to create psychological effects; usually classified as depressants, stimulants, narcotics (opiates), hallucinogens, or antipsychotics.

Psychoanalytic theory: A set of theories conceived by Sigmund Freud that see the roots of human behavior and mental disorders in unconscious motivation and in childhood and early adulthood conflict.

Psychobiology: The study of the interactions between biological and psychological processes.

Psychogenic disorder: An illness that is attributable primarily to a psychological conflict or to emotional stress.

Psychometrics: The theory or technique of psychological measurement; the measurement of psychological differences among people and the statistical analysis of those differences.

Psychophysics: The study of the relationship between physical units of a stimulus, such as amplitude, and its sensory, experienced qualities, such as loudness.

Psychophysiology: The study of the interaction between the psyche (mind and emotions) and the physiology (physical processes such as blood pressure and heart rate) of the organism.

Psychosis: A general term referring to a severe mental disorder, with or without organic damage, characterized by deterioration of normal intellectual and social function and by partial or complete withdrawal from reality; includes schizophrenia and mood disorders such as bipolar disorder.

Psychosocial crisis: In Erik Erikson's theory, a turning point in the process of development precipitated by the individual having to face a new set of social demands and new social relationships.

Psychosomatic disorder: A physical disorder that results from, or is worsened by, psychological factors; synonymous with psychophysiological disorder and includes stress-related disorders.

Psychosurgery: Brain surgery conducted to alter an inappropriate or maladaptive behavior.

Psychotherapy: A general category of treatment techniques for mental disorders; most psychotherapy uses talking as a tool and centers on the client-psychotherapist relationship to develop awareness and provide support.

Punishment: The procedure of decreasing the probability of a behavior by the response-contingent delivery of an aversive stimulus.

Pure tone: A sound produced by a vibration of a single frequency, the amplitude of which changes over time as a sinusoidal function; a sine wave.

Quasi-experimental designs: Experimental plans that do not allow subjects to be assigned randomly to treatment conditions.

Random assignment: The most common technique for establishing equivalent groups by balancing subject characteristics through the assigning of subjects to groups through some random process.

Rapid eye movement (REM) sleep: A special stage of sleep that involves desynchronized electrical brain activity, muscle paralysis, rapid eye movements, and narrative dream recall.

Ratio schedule: A reinforcement schedule in which reinforcer delivery is contingent upon the performance of a specified number of responses.

Rational-emotive therapy: A cognitive-based psychotherapy, pioneered by Albert Ellis, that attempts to replace or modify a client's irrational, inappropriate, or problematic thought processes, outlooks, and self-concept.

Realistic conflict theory: A theory from social psychology that suggests that direct competition for scarce or valued resources can lead to prejudice.

Receptive aphasia: Difficulties in comprehending spoken and written material, usually after damage to Wernicke's area in the left temporal lobe of the cerebral cortex.

Receptive field: The region and pattern in space to which a single neuron responds.

Receptor: A specific protein structure on a target cell to which a neurotransmitter binds, producing a stimulatory or inhibitory response.

Recessive gene: A gene whose corresponding trait will not be expressed unless the gene is paired with another recessive gene for that trait.

Reciprocal determinism: An interactional model proposing that environment, personal factors, and behavior all operate as interacting determinants of one another.

Reductionism: An aspect of the scientific method which seeks to understand complex and often interactive processes by reducing them to more basic components and principles.

Reflex: An unlearned and automatic biologically programmed response to a particular stimulus.

Reflex arc: The simplest behavioral response, in which an impulse is carried by a sensory neuron to the spinal cord, crosses a synapse to a motor neuron, and stimulates a response.

Regression: An ego defense mechanism that a person uses to return to an earlier stage of development when experiencing stress or conflict.

Regulators: Facial gestures and expressions by listeners that are informative for speakers; they convey comprehension or acceptance, or indicate when the other person may speak.

Reinforcement: An operation or process that increases the probability that a learned behavior will be repeated.

Reinforcer: A stimulus or event that, when delivered contingently upon a response, will increase the probability of the recurrence of that response.

Relative deprivation: The proposition that people's attitudes, aspirations, and grievances largely depend on the frame of reference within which they are conceived.

Reliability: The consistency of a psychological measure, which can be assessed by means of stability over repeated administrations or agreement among different observers.

Representativeness: A heuristic in which an estimate of the probability of an event or sample is determined by the degree to which it resembles the originating process or population.

Repression: In psychoanalytic theory, a defense mechanism that keeps unacceptable thoughts and impulses from becoming conscious.

Response cost: Negative consequences that follow the commission of an undesired behavior, decreasing the rate at which the misbehavior will recur.

Response hierarchy: An arrangement of alternative responses to a cue, in a hierarchy from that most likely to occur to that least likely to occur.

Resting membrane potential: The maintenance of difference in electrical charges between the inside and outside of a neuron's cell membrane, keeping it polarized with closed ion channels.

Retardation: A condition wherein a person has mental abilities that are far below average; other skills and abilities, such as adaptive behavior, may also be marginal; measured by an IQ score of less than 70.

Reticular formation: A core of neurons extending through the medulla, pons, and midbrain that controls arousal and sleeping/waking, as well as motor functions such as muscle tone and posture.

Retina: The light-sensitive area at the back of the eye, containing the photoreceptors (rods and cones) that detect light.

Retrieval: The process of locating information stored in memory and bringing it into awareness.

Retrograde amnesia: The type of amnesia that involves an inability to remember things that occurred before the onset of the amnesia.

Rhodopsin: The visual pigment in the cells of the rods that responds to light.

Rod: A photoreceptor of the retina specialized for the detection of light without discrimination of color.

Role: A social position that is associated with a set of behavioral expectations.

Rule-governed behavior: Behavior that is under the discriminative control of formalized contingencies.

Sample: A subset of a population; a group of elements selected from a larger, well-defined pool of elements.

Sampling error: The extent to which population parameters deviate from a sample statistic.

Satiety: A feeling of fullness and satisfaction.

Schema: An active organization of prior knowledge, beliefs, and experience which is used in perceiving the environment, retrieving information from memory, and directing behavior (plural, schemata).

Schizophrenia: Any of a group of psychotic reactions characterized by withdrawal from reality with accompanying affective, behavioral, and intellectual disturbances, including illusions and hallucinations.

Schwann cell: A type of insulating nerve cell that wraps around neurons located peripherally throughout the organism.

Script: An event schema in which a customary sequence of actions, actors, and props is specified; for example, behavior at a restaurant.

Seasonal affective disorder (SAD): Bipolar disorder that undergoes a seasonal fluctuation resulting from various factors, including seasonal changes in the intensity and duration of sunlight.

Secondary reinforcement: A learned reinforcer that has acquired reinforcing qualities by being paired with other reinforcers.

Secondary sex characteristics: Physical features other than genitals that differentiate women and men; for example, facial hair.

Self: The unified and integrated center of one's experience and awareness, which one experiences both subjectively, as an actor, and objectively, as a recipient of actions.

Self-actualization: A biologically and culturally determined process involving a tendency toward growth and full realization of one's potential, characterized by acceptance, autonomy, accuracy, creativity, and community; pioneered by Abraham Maslow.

Self-concept: The sum total of the attributes, abilities, attitudes, and values that an individual believes defines who he or she is.

Self-efficacy: The perception or judgment of one's ability to perform a certain action successfully or to control one's circumstances.

Self-esteem: The evaluative part of the self-concept; one's feeling of self-worth.

Self-image: The self as the individual pictures or imagines it.

Self-perception: A psychological process whereby individuals infer the nature of their attitudes and beliefs by observing their own behavior.

Semantic memory: The long-term representation of a person's factual knowledge of the world.

Semicircular canals: The three structures in the inner ear that together signal acceleration of the head in any direction.

Sensation: The process by which the nervous system and sensory receptors receive and represent stimuli received from the environment.

Sensorimotor stage: The first of Jean Piaget's developmental stages, lasting from birth to about two years of age, during which objects become familiar and are interpreted by appropriate habitual, motor, and sensory processes.

Sensory memory: The persistence of a sensory impression for less than a second; it allows the information to be processed further.

Serial processing: A theory concerning how people scan information in memory that suggests that as the number of items in memory increases, so does the amount of time taken to determine whether an item is present in memory.

Set point: An organism's personal homeostatic level for a particular body weight, which results from factors such as early feeding experiences and heredity.

Sex: Biological maleness or femaleness, determined by genetic endowment and hormones.

Sex typing: The process of acquiring traits, attitudes, and behaviors seen as appropriate for members of one's gender; gender-role acquisition.

Sexual instinct: In Sigmund Freud's theory, the innate tendency toward pleasure seeking, particularly through achieving sexual aims and objects.

Shaping: The acquiring of instrumental behavior in small steps or increments through the reinforcement of successively closer approximations to the desired final behavior.

Short-term memory: A memory system of limited capacity that uses rehearsal processes either to retain current memories or to pass them on to long-term memory.

Significance level: The degree of likelihood that research results are attributable to chance.

Skinner box: The most commonly used apparatus for studying instrumental conditioning; manipulation of a lever (for rats, monkeys, or humans) or an illuminated disk (for pigeons) produces consequences.

Social categorization: The classification of people and groups according to attributes that are personally meaningful.

Social cognition: The area of social psychology concerned with how people make sense of social events, including the actions of others.

Social comparison: Comparing attitudes, skills, and feelings with those of similar people in order to determine relative standing in a group or the acceptability of one's own positions.

Social facilitation: The enhancement of a person's most dominant response as a result of the presence of others; for some tasks, such as simple ones, performance is enhanced, while for others, such as novel tasks, performance is impaired.

Social identity theory: A theory maintaining that people are motivated to create and maintain a positive identity in terms of personal qualities and, especially, group memberships.

Social learning theory: The approach to personality that emphasizes the learning of behavior via observations and direct reward; exemplified by the theories of Albert Bandura, Walter Mischel, and Julian Rotter.

Social loafing: The tendency to expend less effort while in the presence of others; most likely to occur on additive tasks in which one's individual effort is obscured as a result of the collective efforts of the group.

Social phobia: A condition characterized by fear of the possible scrutiny or criticism of others.

Social psychology: A subfield of psychology that studies how individuals are affected by environmental factors and particularly by other people.

Social support: The relationships with other people that provide emotional, informational, or tangible resources that affect one's health and psychological comfort.

Socialization: The process of learning and internalizing social rules and standards.

Sociobiology: The application of the principles of evolutionary biology to the understanding of social behavior.

Somatization disorder: A mental syndrome in which a person chronically has a number of vague but dramatic medical complaints that apparently have no physical cause.

Somatoform disorders: A group of mental disorders in which a person has physical complaints or symptoms that appear to be caused by psychological rather than physical factors; for example, hypochondriasis.

Somnambulism: The scientific term for sleepwalking; formerly a term for hypnosis.

Spectrum analysis: The ability of a system, such as hearing, to decompose a complex wave into its sine-wave components and their respective amplitudes.

Spinal cord: The part of the central nervous system that is enclosed within the backbone; conducts nerve impulses to and from the brain.

Spontaneous recovery: The recovery of extinguished behaviors over time in the absence of any specific treatment or training.

Sports psychology: The subfield of psychology that applies psychological principles to physical activities such as competitive sports; frequently concerned with maximizing athletic performance.

Sprouting: A process that occurs when remaining nerve fibers branch and form new connections to replace those that have been lost.

Stage theory of development: The belief that development moves through a set sequence of stages; the quality of behavior at each stage is unique but is dependent upon movement through earlier stages.

Standard deviation: A measure of how variable or spread out a group of scores is from the mean.

Standardization: The administration, scoring, and interpretation of a test in a prescribed manner so that differences in test results can be attributed to the testee.

Statistical significance: Differences in behavior large enough that they are probably related to the subject variables or manipulated variablesdifferences too large to be caused by chance alone.

Stereogram: A two-dimensional image that appears three-dimensional when viewed binocularly, typically consisting of two images of the same scene as viewed from slightly disparate viewpoints; when special glasses are worn, the images are fused into one image with the full three-dimensional effect.

Stereotype: A set of beliefs, often rigidly held, about the characteristics of an entire group.

Stimulants: Drugs that cause behavioral and/or physiological stimulation, including amphetamines, cocaine, and their respective derivatives; caffeine; nicotine; and some antidepressants.

Stimulus: An environmental circumstance to which an organism may respond; it may be as specific as a single physical event or as global as a social situation.

Stimulus generalization: The ability of stimuli that are similar to other stimuli to elicit a response that was previously elicited only by the first stimuli.

Storage: The stage of memory between encoding and retrieval; the period for which memories are held.

Strange situation: A particular experimental technique designed to measure the quality of the mother-infant attachment relationship.

Stress: The judgment that a problem exceeds one's available resources, resulting from a primary appraisal of the problem and a secondary appraisal of the coping resources.

Stressor: Anything that produces a demand on an organism.

Striate cortex: The region of the occipital lobe that reconstitutes visual images for recognition.

Stroke: A vascular accident resulting from either the rupture of a vessel or the blocking of blood flow in an artery.

Structuralism: An early school of psychology that sought to define the basic elements of mind and the laws governing their combination.

Sublimation: According to Sigmund Freud, a defense mechanism by which a person may redirect aggressive impulses by engaging in a socially sanctioned activity.

Suffix: A morpheme that attaches to the end of a word.

Superego: In Freudian theory, the part of the psyche that contains parental and societal standards of morality and that acts to prohibit expression of instinctual drives; includes the conscience and the ego-ideal.

Syllogism: A logical argument constructed of a major premise, a minor premise, and a conclusion, the validity of which is determined by rules of inference.

Symbiotic relationship: An overprotective, often enmeshed relationship between a parent and child.

Sympathetic nervous system: A division of the autonomic nervous system that prepares the organism for energy expenditure.

Synapse: The junction between two neurons over which a nerve impulse is chemically transduced.

Synchronized electroencephalogram: A regular, repetitive brain-wave pattern that is caused by multitudes of neurons firing at the same time and the same rate in a given brain region.

Systematic desensitization: An exposure therapy in which the phobic person is gradually presented with a feared object or situation.

Systems theory: A concept in which the family grouping is viewed as a biosocial subsystem existing within the larger system of society; intrafamilial communications are the mechanisms of subsystem interchange.

Tachistoscope: An experimental apparatus for presenting visual information very briefly to the right or left visual field; sometimes called a T-scope.

Tardive dyskinesia: Slow, involuntary motor movements, especially of the mouth and tongue, which can become permanent and untreatable; can result from psychoactive drug treatment.

Temporal lobe: The lower portion on the side of each cerebral hemisphere, containing the sites of sensory interpretation, memory of visual and auditory patterns, and part of the general interpretive area.

Test-retest reliability: A common way of determining consistency, by administering the same test twice to the same persons.

Testosterone: The principal male sex hormone produced by the testes.

Thalamus: A portion of the diencephalon, located at the base of the forebrain, which receives sensory information from the body and relays these signals to the appropriate regions of the cerebrum.

Thematic Apperception Test (TAT): A personality test in which individuals demonstrate their needs by describing what is happening in a series of ambiguous pictures.

Theory: A model explaining the relationship between several phenomena; derived from several related hypotheses which have survived many tests.

Therapy: The systematic habilitation of a disorder.

Thermoreceptor: A sensory receptor specialized for the detection of changes in the flow of heat.

Threshold: The minimum stimulus intensity necessary for an individual to detect a stimulus; usually defined as that intensity detected 50 percent of the time it is presented.

Thyroxine: The major hormone produced and secreted by the thyroid gland; stimulates protein synthesis and the basal metabolic rate.

Timbre: The sound quality produced by the respective amplitude and frequency of the overtones, or underlying sine waves that make up a complex wave.

Top-down processing: A situation in which a person's perception of a stimulus is influenced by nonstimulus factors such as the person's general knowledge, beliefs, or expectations.

Trait theory: A way of conceptualizing personality in terms of relatively persistent and consistent behavior patterns that are manifested in a wide range of circumstances.

Transduction: The process of changing physical energy, such as light, into neural messages.

Transference: The phenomenon in which a person in psychoanalysis shifts thoughts or emotions concerning people in his or her past (most often parents) onto the analyst.

Transvestite: A person who, for fun or sexual arousal, often dresses and acts like a member of the opposite sex (going "in drag"); most are heterosexual males.

Tricyclics: A class of antidepressant drugs.

Two-factor theory: A behavioral theory of anxiety stating that fear is caused by Pavlovian conditioning and that avoidance of the feared object is maintained by operant conditioning.

Type A personality: A behavior pattern that describes individuals who are driven, competitive, high-strung, impatient, time-urgent, intense, and easily angered; some researchers have associated this pattern with increased risk of heart disease.

Unconditional positive regard: The attempt by a therapist to convey to a client that he or she genuinely cares for the client.

Unconditioned response (UR): An innate or unlearned behavior that occurs automatically following some stimulus; a reflex.

Unconditioned stimulus (US): A stimulus that elicits an unconditioned response; the relation between unconditioned stimuli and unconditioned responses is unlearned.

Unconscious: The deep-rooted aspects of the mind; Sigmund Freud claimed that it includes negative instincts and urges that are too disturbing for people to be aware of consciously.

Unipolar depression: A disorder characterized by the occurrence of one or more major depressive episodes but no manic episodes.

Validity: A statistical value that tells the degree to which a test measures what it is intended to measure; the test is usually compared to external criteria.

Vicarious learning: Learning (for example, learning to fear something) without direct experience, either by observing or by receiving verbal information.

Visual cortex: The top six cell layers in the back of the brain, which are specialized for organizing and interpreting visual information.

Visual dyslexia: The lack of ability to translate observed written or printed language into meaningful terms.

Voyeurism: The derivation of sexual pleasure from looking at the naked bodies or sexual activities of others without their consent.

Wavelength: The distance traveled by a wave front in the time given by one cycle (the period of the wave); has an inverse relation to frequency.

White matter: The tissue within the central nervous system, consisting primarily of nerve fibers.

Within-subject design: An experimental plan in which each subject receives each level of the independent variable.

Working through: A psychoanalytical term that describes the process by which clients develop more adaptive behavior once they have gained insight into the causes of their psychological disorders.

Yerkes-Dodson law: The principle that moderate levels of arousal tend to yield optimal performance.

Zeitgeber: A German word meaning "time giver"; a factor that serves as a synchronizer or entraining agent, such as sunlight in the morning.

BIBLIOGRAPHY

This bibliography is divided into the following categories:

AGGRESSION

Archer, John. *Behavioural Biology of Aggression.* New York: Cambridge University Press, 1988. Archer considers possible chemical and biological determinants of aggressive behavior, particularly in young males.

Bandura, Albert. *Aggression: A Social Learning Analysis.* Englewood Cliffs, N.J.: Prentice-Hall, 1973. This volume in Prentice-Hall's Social Learning Analysis Series considers the roots of violence and the psychological and biological causes of such behavior.

Baron, Robert Alex, and Deborah R. Richardson, eds. *Human Aggression.* 2d ed. New York: Plenum, 1994. The nine essays in this book consider the development of aggressive behavior, aggression in natural settings, the biological sources of aggression, and the prevention and control of human aggression.

Berkowitz, Leonard. *Aggression: Its Causes, Consequences, and Control.* Philadelphia: Temple University Press, 1993. A thorough consideration of aggression in humans and other animals. Berkowitz identifies psychological and biological roots of aggression, the outcomes of aggressive behavior, and its control.

Geen, Russell G., and Edward Donnerstein, eds. *Human Aggression: Theories, Research, and Implications For Social Policy.* San Diego, Calif.: Academic Press, 1998. Among the contributions to this volume are valuable essays on the affects of the mass media on aggressive behavior in young people.

AGING

Abeles, Ronald P., Helen C. Gift, and Marcia G. Ory, eds. *Aging and the Quality of Life.* New York: Springer, 1994. This book's nineteen chapters touch on matters of socioeconomics, helping the aged to remain independent, dealing with health problems that afflict the aging, and sources of social, economic, and medical support for the aged.

Bergeman, Cindy S. *Aging: Genetic and Environmental Influences.* Thousand Oaks, Calif.: Sage Publications, 1997. Considers how different people age differently, the biology and psychology of aging, genetics and aging, and the social implications of aging.

Davey, Basiro, ed. *Birth to Old Age: Health in Transition*. Philadelphia: Open University, 2001. Deals with the development of children, the progression through the aging process, and the problems of old age. Strong discussion of the developmental biology of aging, cradle to grave.

Ebersole, Priscilla. *Geriatric Nursing and Healthy Aging*. St. Louis: Mosby, 2001. Ebersole's twenty-seven chapters deal with a broad spectrum of questions relating to aging, including mobility, families and aging, coping with loss and grief, dealing with bone, joint, and cardiac health problems, and with the need for rest.

Hummert, Mary Lee, and Jon F. Nussbaum, eds. *Aging, Communication, and Health: Linking Research and Practice for Successful Aging*. Mahwah, N.J.: Lawrence Erlbaum, 2001. This volume's eleven essays deal with physician-patient relationships among the aging, the roles of family caregivers, and the responsibility for decision-making as people age.

McFadden, Susan, and Robert C. Atchley, eds. *Aging and the Meaning of Time: An Interdisciplinary Exploration*. New York: Springer, 2001. This book's thirteen essays focus on perspectives of time among the aging, dealing with how personal narratives can be useful in keeping older people alert and interested. Considers the role of religious beliefs among the aging.

ANXIETY DISORDERS

Buss, Arnold H. *Self-Consciousness and Social Anxiety*. San Francisco: W. H. Freeman, 1980. Valuable observations about the relationship of guilt and shame to anxiety disorders. Readable, well researched, and clearly presented.

Crozier, W. Ray, ed. *Understanding Shyness: Psychological Perspectives*. New York: Palgrave, 2001. The chapter on overcoming social anxiety is of special interest. Investigates the nature of shyness. Analyzes its causes genetically and environmentally.

Goodson, Donald W. *Anxiety*. New York: Oxford University Press, 1986. Offers a lucid and accurate overview of the causes and consequences of anxiety. Considers means of coping with this disabling psychological condition.

Leitenberg, Harold, ed. *Handbook of Social and Evaluation Anxiety*. New York: Plenum Press, 1990. Valuable perspectives on the social aspects of anxiety.

Focuses on self-consciousness and bashfulness. Solid overview of the psychological connections of anxiety disorders.

Spielberger, Charles Donald. *Anxiety and Behavior*. New York: Academic Press, 1966. Somewhat dated, but its overall presentation is worthwhile. Deals with both individual and mass anxiety.

ATTITUDES

Allport, Gordon W. *The Nature of Prejudice*. 1954. Reprint. Cambridge, Mass.: Perseus, 1988. A quintessential source outlining the roots and causes of prejudice, linking such attitudes to feelings of personal inadequacy, the lust for power, and aggression born of feelings of inferiority. Considers both the environmental and psychological sources of prejudice.

Baumeister, Roy F., ed. *Self-Esteem: The Puzzle of Low Self-Regard*. New York: Plenum, 1993. The thirteen essays in this volume consider salient aspects of low self-esteem, considering its relationship to clinical depression, its presence in young children and adolescents, and self-esteem resulting from negative and positive life experiences.

Bowser, Benjamin P., and Raymond G. Hunt, eds. *Impacts of Racism on White Americans*. 2d ed. Thousand Oaks, Calif.: Sage Publications, 1996. This collection of twelve essays is strong in assessing the political and economic implications of racism, particularly in corporate America.

Branch, Taylor. *Parting the Waters: America in the King Years, 1954-1963*. New York: Simon & Schuster, 1988. Branch evaluates the psychological factors present in the racial tensions of the 1950's and 1960's that preceded Martin Luther King's assassination.

BEHAVIOR

Bugliosi, Vincent T., and Curt Gentry. *Helter Skelter*. New York: Bantam, 1974. Details the murder of Sharon Tate and others by the followers of Charles Manson, whose psychological control over his followers provides a chilling study of how one magnetic personality influences the behavior of innumerable people.

Burger, Jerry M. *Desire for Control: Personality, Social, and Clinical Perspectives*. New York: Plenum, 1992. Deals effectively with personality assessment and behaviorism. Presented from the practitioner's standpoint.

Carlson, Neil R. *Physiology of Behavior.* Boston: Allyn & Bacon, 1998. Comprehensive overview of the physiological roots of some behaviors with psychological manifestations.

Chagnon, Napoleon A., and W. Irons, eds. *Evolutionary Biology and Social Behavior.* North Scituate, Mass.: Duxbury Press, 1979. Focuses on the biological bases for behaviors common to humans.

Schlenker, Barry R. *The Self and Social Life.* New York: McGraw-Hill, 1985. Deals with the roles of interpersonal interactions in human relationships. Concerned with the self versus the member of the group.

Schroeder, David A., ed. *Social Dilemmas: Perspectives on Individuals and Groups.* Westport, Conn.: Praeger, 1995. The eleven essays in this book deal with various social dilemmas, including the famed Prisoner's Dilemma, and work through them, demonstrating the dynamics of groups solving them.

Skinner, B. F. *The Behavior of Organisms: An Experimental Analysis.* Englewood Cliffs, N.J.: Prentice-Hall, 1938. Well worth reading as an introductory text to the field by the father of behaviorism.

Smith, John L. *The Psychology of Action.* New York: St. Martin's Press, 2000. A strong chapter on enigmas, masochism and suicide, and the weakness of will. Quite specialized.

BRAIN

Berthoz, Alain. *The Brain's Sense Of Movement.* Translated by Giselle Weiss. Cambridge, Mass.: Harvard University Press, 2000. Excellent review of the motor theory of perception. Solid material on the predictive uses of memory and of how coherence evolves.

Davidoff, Jules. *The Brain and Behavior: Critical Concepts in Psychology.* New York: Routledge, 2000. Strong in discussing cognition in relation to mental activity. Somewhat specialized.

Drubach, Daniel. *The Brain Explained.* Upper Saddle River, N.J.: Prentice-Hall, 2000. Lucid presentation of the structure and function of the brain as related to intelligence and language. Quite readable.

Edelman, Gerald M., and Jean-Pierre Changeux, eds. *The Brain.* New Brunswick, N.J.: Transaction Publishers, 2001. Sixteen photographic plates enhance this solid volume that presents an overview of the brain's activities.

Feinberg, Todd E. *Altered Egos: How the Brain Creates the Self.* New York: Oxford University Press, 2001. Imaginative and readable account of the brain's capabilities. Chapter on deconstructing the self is exciting, as are chapters entitled "Missing Pieces, Familiar Places," and "Mything Persons."

Glynn, Ian. *An Anatomy of Thought: The Origin and Machinery of the Mind.* New York: Oxford University Press, 2000. Comprehensive view of neuropsychological aspects of cognition. Compelling philosophy of the mind and the brain's activities.

Ornstein, Robert E., and Richard F. Thompson. *The Amazing Brain.* Boston: Houghton-Mifflin, 1984. Readable account of how the brain functions and of its relationship to consciousness. Not overly technical.

Samples, Bob. *The Metaphoric Mind: A Celebration of Creative Consciousness.* Reading, Mass.: Addison-Wesley, 1976. Written with the layperson in mind, this consideration of the bicameral mind is exciting, informative, and accessible.

CHILDHOOD AND ADOLESCENCE

Belson, William A. *Television Violence and the Adolescent Boy.* Fairborough, Hants, U.K.: Saxon House, 1978. Belson considers the psychological effects violence on television has on teenage boys in the United States.

Bowlby, John. *A Secure Base: Parent-Child Attachment and Healthy Human Development.* New York: Basic Books, 1988. Explores in depth the long-term effects of parent-child relationships.

Byrne, Donn E., and William Fisher. *Adolescents, Sex, and Contraception.* Hillsdale, N.J.: Lawrence Erlbaum, 1983. Well-documented assessment of the sexual habits of adolescents, including those of college age. Their attitudes toward contraception is largely determined by cultural factors.

Clutton-Brock, T. H. *The Evolution of Parental Care.* Princeton, N.J.: Princeton University Press, 1991. The author considers parental care among various animal species and as compared to humans, focusing on how modes of parental care have evolved.

Horne, Arthur M., and Mark S. Kiselica, eds. *Handbook of Counseling Boys and Adolescent Males: A Practitioner's Guide.* Thousand Oaks, Calif.: Sage Publications, 1999. Focuses largely on growing up as a male in America, giving special attention to the question of bullying and its victims.

COGNITION

Bandura, Albert. *Social Foundations of Thought and Action: A Social-Cognitive Theory.* Englewood Cliffs, N.J.: Prentice-Hall, 1986. Emphasizes the social aspects and social perspectives of cognition. Somewhat specialized.

Honeycutt, James M. *Cognition, Communication, and Romantic Relationships.* Mahwah, N.J.: Lawrence Erlbaum, 2001. Investigates the role of memory structures in romantic relationships. The chapter on emotion and cognition in relationships is particularly cogent, as is that on memory structures and decaying relationships.

Rowlands, Mark. *The Body in Mind: Understanding Cognitive Processes.* New York: Cambridge University Press, 1999. Chapters on language, perception, thought, and memory are relevant in the context of cognitive learning.

Solowij, Nadia. *Cannabis and Cognitive Functioning.* New York: Cambridge University Press, 1998. Solowij considers the effects of long-term use of cannabis on cognitive processes. Considers the reversibility of such effects when drug use ceases.

Turner, Mark. *Cognitive Dimensions of Social Science.* New York: Oxford University Press, 2001. Explores the development and use of cognitive processes in relation to all of the social studies, emphasizing their psychological dimensions.

CONSCIOUSNESS

Baars, Bernard J. *A Cognitive Theory of Consciousness.* New York: Cambridge University Press, 1988. Carefully reasoned psychological consideration of how consciousness is intertwined with cognition and with the learning process.

Dodwell, Peter. *Brave New Mind: A Thoughtful Inquiry into the Nature and Meaning of Mental Life.* New York: Oxford University Press, 2000. Deals well with psychological underpinnings of cognitive science. Unique perspectives on representation versus reality.

Hutto, Daniel D. *Beyond Physicality.* Philadelphia: John Benjamins, 2000. Provocative discussion of the pluralism of naturalism compared to absolute idealism. Sharp insights on nonconceptual expression.

Ornstein, Robert E., ed. *The Nature of Human Consciousness: A Book of Readings.* New York: Viking, 1973. Comprehensive overview of the psychophysiological aspects of consciousness. Clear presentation of hemisphericity.

Underwood, Jeffrey, and Robin Stevens. *Aspects of Consciousness.* New York: Academic Press, 1979. Offers valuable information about states of consciousness and their relationship to cognitive development.

DEPRESSION

Bauer, Mark, and Linda McBride. *Structured Group Psychotherapy for Bipolar Disorder: The Life Goals Program.* New York: Springer, 1996. Considers what bipolar disorder is pathologically, biologically, and psychosocially. Outlines the success of the Life Goals Program in treating depression.

Baumeister, Roy F., ed. *Self-Esteem: The Puzzle of Low Self-Regard.* New York: Plenum, 1993. Brett W. Pelham's essay, "On the Highly Positive Thoughts of the Highly Depressed," which deals with how low self-esteem affects clinical depression, is relevant.

Becker, Howard S. *Outsiders.* New York: Free Press, 1963. Considers the effects of social exclusion upon individuals and links such exclusion to psychological depression.

Court, Bryan L., and Gerald E. Nelson. *Bipolar Puzzle Solution: A Mental Health Client's Perspective.* Washington, D.C.: Accelerated Development, 1996. A part of the Psychological Disorders Series, this book provides answers to 187 questions asked by members of a support group for manic-depressive people.

Kendall, Philip C., and David Watson, eds. *Anxiety and Depression: Distinctive and Overlapping Features.* San Diego, Calif.: Academic Press, 1989. Comprehensive view of how anxiety leads to psychological depression. Identifies causes and suggests psychotherapeutic remedies.

DEVELOPMENT

Axelrod, Robert M. *The Evolution of Cooperation.* New York: Basic Books, 1984. Discusses human development from the standpoints of cooperativeness and consensus. Considers egoism. Suggests means of managing conflict.

Baumeister, Roy F., Todd F. Heatherton, and Dianne M. Tice. *Losing Control: How and Why People Fail at Self-Regulation.* San Diego, Calif.: Academic Press, 1994. Considers why people fail to take control of their lives through self-management. Suggests protocols for coping with the problem. Considers addictions and why people feel helpless to control them.

Briggs, Jean L. *Never in Anger: Portrait of an Eskimo Family.* Cambridge, Mass.: Harvard University Press, 1970. Socio-ethnographic study of an Eskimo family. Reveals developmental processes of children within that family.

Parker, Sue Taylor, Jonas Langer, and Michael L. McKinney. *Biology, Brains, and Behavior: The Evolution of Human Development.* Santa Fe, N.M.: School of American Research Press, 2000. Particularly relevant among the ten contributions to this collection are those on the development of primate behavior, the focus of two engrossing chapters.

Schlinger, Henry D., Jr. *A Behavior Analytical View of Child Development.* New York: Plenum, 1995. Provides information about the motor, perceptual, cognitive, language, social, and emotional development of children as they mature.

Unell, Barbara C., and Jerry L. Wyckoff. *The Eight Seasons of Parenthood: How the Stages of Parenting Constantly Reshape Our Adult Identities.* New York: Times Books, 2000. Interesting contrasts between parent-child and parent-adult child relationships and their effect upon people as they mature.

EMOTION

Bar-on, Reuven, and James D. A. Parker, eds. *The Handbook of Emotional Intelligence.* San Francisco: Jossey-Bass, 2000. Assesses emotional intelligence neurologically, psychologically, and socially. Material on purposive behavior and emotional competence is excellent.

Charrochi, Joseph, Joseph P. Forgas, and John D. Mayer. *Emotional Intelligence in Everyday Life: A Scientific Inquiry.* Philadelphia: The Psychological Press, 2001. Focuses on emotional intelligence in intimate relationships and in the workplace. Views emotional intelligence in terms of self-actualization and empathetic accuracy.

Cherniss, Cary, and Daniel Goleman, eds. *The Emotionally Intelligent Workplace: How to Select for, Measure, and Improve Emotional Intelligence in Individuals, Groups, and Organizations.* San Francisco: Jossey-Bass, 2001. Among this volume's dozen essays are those dealing with the development of emotional intelligence and how to bring such intelligence into the workplace. Stresses the economic value of achieving emotional intelligence within corporations.

Saarni, Carolyn. *The Development of Emotional Competence.* New York: Guilford Press, 1999. Considers how to cope with adverse emotions. Links emotional development to overall social development and recommends that people be sensitive to the emotions of others.

Saul, Leon Joseph. *Emotional Maturity: The Development and Dynamics of Personality and Its Disorders.* Philadelphia: J. B. Lippincott, 1971. Deals with the psychopathology that accompanies emotional immaturity and leads to emotional disorders. Suggests ways to overcome this psychopathology and become an emotionally healthy person.

FREUDIAN PSYCHOLOGY

Fordham, Michael. *Freud, Jung, Klein—The Fenceless Field: Essays on Psychoanalysis and Analytical Psychology.* Edited by Roger Hobdell. New York: Routledge, 1995. Sections reviewing major works in psychoanalysis are useful, as is the hundred-page section on analytical psychology.

Gossy, Mary S. *Freudian Slips: Woman, Writing, the Foreign Tongue.* Ann Arbor: University of Michigan Press, 1995. Overview of Freudian psychoanalysis and its relation to feminism is fresh and challenging. Fine study of Freud's views on gender.

Ornstein, Robert E. *The Evolution of Consciousness: Of Darwin, Freud, and Cranial Fire—The Origins of the Way We Think.* New York: Prentice-Hall, 1991. Considers thought processes genetically, biologically, and neuropsychologically. Analysis of Freud's mental processes is revealing.

Sander, Joseph, Ethel Spector Person, and Peter Fonagy. *Freud's "On Narcissism—An Introduction."* New Haven, Conn.: Yale University Press, 1991. English-language version of Freud's *Zur Einführung des Narzissimus.* Presents Freud's feelings about self-love and egoism.

Young-Bruehl, Elisabeth, ed. *Freud on Women: A Reader.* New York: W. W. Norton, 1990. Provides a representative selection of Freud's writing about women. Dated but interesting historically.

GENDER STUDIES

Archer, John. *Sex and Gender.* New York: Cambridge University Press, 2002. Comprehensive assessment of sexual differences, sex roles, and gender considerations in sexual relationships.

Ashmore, Richard D., and Frances K. Del Boca, eds. *The Social Psychology of Female-Male Relations: A Critical Analysis of Central Concepts.* New York: Academic Press, 1986. Presents material on interpersonal relations involving sex roles, identity, and the psychology of both genders.

Beall, Anne E., and Robert J. Sternberg, eds. *The Psychology of Gender.* New York: Guilford Press, 1993. The ten essays in this collection deal with the relationship of gender to biology and environment, a cognitive approach to considering gender, and a social constructionist view of gender.

Brehm, Sharon S. *Seeing Female: Social Roles and Personal Lives.* Westport, Conn.: Greenwood, 1988. This volume in Greenwood's Women's Studies Series assesses the social roles and social conditions of women in the United States during the 1980's.

Burn, Shawn M. *The Social Psychology of Gender.* New York: McGraw-Hill, 1996. Balanced discussion of the motivating forces that shape views of gender and sexual differentiation from a psychological standpoint

Kalbfleish, Pamela J., and Michael J. Cody, eds. *Gender, Power, and Communication in Human Relationships.* Hillsdale, N.J.: Lawrence Erlbaum, 1995. Among the fourteen essays in this volume, those on the role of power in matters of gender, as well as the politics of gender and the presence of nonverbal communication in dealings between men and women are especially relevant.

Keough, Kelli A., and Julio Garcia. *Social Psychology of Gender, Race, and Ethnicity: Readings and Projects.* New York: McGraw-Hill, 2000. Interactive text on sexual differences and on attitudes toward gender. Engaging and informative.

HORMONES

Butt, Wilfrid R. *Hormone Chemistry.* New York: Halsted, 1976. Considers the effects of biogenic amines and steroids neurally and psychologically on those exposed to them.

Conn, P. Michael, and Shlomo Melmed, eds. *Endocrinology: Basic and Clinical Principles.* Totowa, N.J.: Humana, 1997. Among the twenty-seven contributions to this collection are psychologically relevant essays by George P. Chrousos on the effect of hormones on the hypothalamus and by Gregory Brent on thyroid hormones.

Hutchinson, Joseph B., ed. *Biological Determinants of Sexual Behavior.* New York: John Wiley & Sons, 1978. Comprehensive overview of the role hormones play in sexual behavior. Well-balanced collection.

Maisel, Albert Q. *The Hormone Quest.* New York: Random House, 1965. Easily accessible to those not expert in the field. Well written and accurate. Despite its age, it offers valuable information.

Malkinson, A. M. *Hormone Action.* New York: John Wiley & Sons, 1975. Considers in detail the physiology of hormones and their physical and psychological effects on those who take them.

Svare, Bruce B. *Hormones and Aggressive Behavior.* New York: Plenum, 1983. Assesses chemical effects hormones have on certain forms of aggressive behavior, particularly in young males.

INTELLIGENCE

Deary, Ian J. *Intelligence: A Very Short Introduction.* New York: Oxford University Press, 2001. Considers the relationship between genetics and environment in determining intelligence. Speculates that IQs increase overall from generation to generation.

Howe, Michael J. A. *IQ in Question: The Truth about Intelligence.* Thousand Oaks, Calif.: Sage Publications, 1997. Deals in ten well-written chapters with such questions as whether IQ can be increased, relationships between race and intelligence as it is usually measured, and how reliable IQ measurements are. Explodes twelve commonly held beliefs about IQ.

Martinez, Michael E. *Education as the Cultivation of Intelligence.* Mahwah, N.J.: Lawrence Erlbaum, 2000. Sound definition of intelligence considered genetically and experientially. Considers psychometric models of intelligence.

Scheibel, Arnold B., and J. William Schopf, eds. *The Origin and Evolution of Intelligence.* Boston: Jones and Bartlett, 1997. Studies origins of intelligence from prerational intelligence, through intelligence among primates—essentially apes—to that of humans. Steven Pinker's essay on the biology of intelligence is especially challenging.

Sternberg, Robert J. *Handbook of Intelligence.* New York: Cambridge University Press, 2000. Considers biological factors associated with intellect. Presents common theories and frequently used means of measuring intelligence.

LANGUAGE

Brown, Penelope, and Stephen C. Levinson. *Politeness: Some Universals in Language Use.* New York:

Cambridge University Press, 1987. Intriguing assessment of nonverbal aspects of communication and their psychological components. Imaginative approach.

Chomsky, Carol. *The Acquisition of Syntax in Children from Five to Ten.* Cambridge, Mass.: MIT Press, 1969. Brief, compelling study of how children acquire language and of what environmental and psychological forces affect the process.

Chomsky, Noam. *Language and Mind.* New York: Harcourt, Brace and World, 1968. Builds on Chomsky's earlier psycholinguistic approach to language, demonstrating how the mind operates in relation to words, meanings, and syntactic structures.

_____. *Syntactic Structures.* Reprint. New York: Peter Lang, 1975. Brief, landmark volume in which Chomsky establishes the field of transformational-generative grammar that affected directly subsequent theories of language learning.

Pinker, Steven. *The Language Instinct.* New York: William Morrow, 1995. Hypothesizes that all humans are born with a language instinct, so that certain language protocols are inherent rather than learned. Controversial book that stimulates productive thought. Well written. Can be appreciated by nonspecialists.

LEARNING

Amsel, Abram. *Behaviorism, Neobehaviorism, and Cognition in Learning Theory: History and Contemporary Perspectives.* Hillsdale, N.J.: Lawrence Erlbaum, 1989. Presents and evaluates various theories of learning, assessing them historically and contrasting them to earlier theories.

Bandura, Albert. *Social Learning Theory.* Englewood Cliffs, N.J.: Prentice-Hall, 1977. Considers learning as a preparation of people for productive functioning in society. Considers substantive learning in relation to more general forms of learning with social outcomes.

Mowrer, Robert R., and Stephen B. Klein, eds. *Handbook of Contemporary Learning Theories.* Mahwah, N.J.: Lawrence Erlbaum, 2001. Deals with the psychology of learning and the general field of cognition. Accessible to nonspecialists.

Smith, Frank. *The Book of Learning and Forgetting.* New York: Teachers' College Press, 1998. Undermines much traditional learning theory, investigating the immensity of learning in early child-

hood and assessing decreases in learning surges as people age.

Tileston, Donna Walker. *Ten Best Teaching Practices: How Brain Research, Learning Styles, and Standards Define Teaching Competencies.* Thousand Oaks, Calif.: Corwin Press, 2000. Practical book aimed at in-service teachers and those preparing to become teachers. Tileston has a broad knowledge of brain research and applies it effectively to learning styles currently in widespread use.

MEMORY

Berkowitz, Leonard. *Consequences and Causes of Feelings.* New York: Cambridge University Press, 2000. Particularly relevant are Berkowitz's chapters on the influence of feelings on memory and the ways feelings affect memory.

Engel, Susan. *Context Is Everything: The Nature of Memory.* New York: W. H. Freeman, 1999. Explores where memory begins and suggest ways of evoking memory, largely through recalling contexts. Differentiates between remembering things in print and things heard or seen.

Pribram, Karl H., and Donald E. Broadbent, eds. *Biology of Memory.* New York: Academic Press, 1970. Sound presentation of memory psychophysically and biologically, including molecular biological influences on short-term memory.

Richter, Derek. *Aspects of Learning and Memory.* New York: Basic Books, 1966. Explores the relationships between memory and learning, developing a psychologically and biologically based learning theory.

Rose, Steven, ed. *From Brains to Consciousness? The Nature of Memory.* Princeton, N.J.: Princeton University Press, 1998. Striking essays on neurocomputational models of memory, on the physiological basis of memory, and aging from a neurobiological standpoint among the fourteen essays in the collection.

Shank, David R., ed. *Human Memory: A Reader.* New York: St. Martin's Press, 1997. Among the fourteen essays, those on short-term memory, on the reliability of memory, and the neuropsychology of memory are particularly useful.

MENTAL ILLNESS

Andreasen, Nancy C. *Brave New Brain: Conquering Mental Illness in the Era of the Genome.* New York: Oxford University Press, 2001. Valuable for its consideration of how mapping the genome and mapping the mind through neuroimaging may offer hope to those suffering from degenerative forms of mental illness.

Barlow, David H., and Mark Durand. *Abnormal Psychology: An Integrative Approach.* Belmont, Calif.: Wadsworth/Thomson Learning, 2001. Considers among its sixteen clearly presented chapters disorders related to substance abuse, eating and sleeping disorders, problems with anxiety, and a considerable panoply of ills leading to mental illness.

Milt, Harry. *Basic Handbook on Mental Illness.* New York: Charles Scribners' Sons, 1974. Despite its age, still serviceable as a basic guide. It is clear, direct, and, at a mere 125 pages, brief.

Morrison, Michelle. *Foundations of Mental Health Nursing.* St. Louis: Mosby, 1997. Comprehensive consideration of the history of caring for the mentally ill. Considers the ethical and legal issues associated with mental health care and the sociocultural issues affecting such care.

Tessler, Richard, and Gail Gamache. *Family Experiences with Mental Illness.* Westport, Conn.: Auburn House, 2000. This book's thirteen chapters deal with the desirable extent of family involvement, economic and emotional costs to family caregivers, and relationships between professional and family caregivers. Focuses on two Ohio families caring for family members, one from 1989 to 1992, the other from 1995 to 1997.

MOTIVATION

French, Jeffrey A., Alan C. Kamil, and Daniel W. Leger, eds. *Evolutionary Psychology and Motivation.* Lincoln: University of Nebraska Press, 2001. These seven contributions were papers delivered at the Nebraska Symposium on Motivation in 2001. They deal with some of the biological aspects of motivation, notably sexual motivation related to pheromones.

Higgins, E. Tory, and Arie Kruglanski, eds. *Motivational Science: Social and Personality Perspectives.* Philadelphia: Psychology Press, 2000. The twenty-three readings in this volume include excellent material on the dynamics of stressful encounters as they relate to motivation and the cognitive-affective theory of personality.

Lennon, Kathleen. *Explaining Human Action.* La Salle, Ill.: Open Court Press, 1990. Deals with mo-

tivation in relation to intention, reductionism, and functionalism. Specialized approach.

Reeve, Johnmarshall. *Understanding Motivation and Emotions.* Fort Worth, Tex.: Harcourt Brace Jovanovich, 1992. Relates motivation to emotional reactions, positive and negative. Suggests a positive approach results in greater motivation than a negative approach.

NERVOUS SYSTEM

Deutsch, Sid, and Evangelia Micheli-Tzanakou. *Neuroelectric Systems.* New York: New York University Press, 1987. Detailed consideration of the electrophysiology and the neurophysiology of the nervous system.

Leonard, Charles T. *The Neuroscience of Human Movement.* St. Louis: Mosby, 1998. Considers principles of motor control, the neural control of human locomotion, and the role the cerebral cortex plays in movement.

Marshall, Bruce. *The Nervous System: Circuits of Communication.* New York: Torstar Books, 1985. Focuses on neurophysiology and diseases of the nervous system that affect locomotion and communication. Relevant for those concerned with Alzheimer's disease.

Nathan, Peter. *The Nervous System.* New York: Oxford University Press, 1988. One of the best overviews of the nervous system, its functioning and diseases affecting it. Useful eight pages of illustrations.

Willott, James F. *Neurogerontology: Aging and the Nervous System.* New York: Springer, 1999. Excellent presentation of how aging affects the nervous system. Valuable for those interested in Alzheimer's disease.

PAVLOVIAN CONDITIONING

Gray, Jeffrey A. *Ivan Pavlov.* New York: Viking, 1980. Intriguing biography of Pavlov. Directed at nonspecialists. Solid overview of Pavlov's experiments in classical conditioning.

Klein, Stephen B., and Robert R. Mowrer, eds. *Contemporary Learning Theories—Pavlovian Conditioning and the Status of Traditional Learning Theory.* Hillsdale, N.J.: Lawrence Erlbaum, 1989. Presents thorough information about conditioning in laboratory animals and lucid accounts of Pavlov's experiments with dogs.

Martin, Irene, and A. B. Levey. *The Genesis of Classical Conditioned Response.* New York: Pergamon

Press, 1969. Pavlovian conditioning and its relationship to similar theories is emphasized.

Schmajuk, Nestor A., and Peter C. Holland, eds. *Occasion Setting: Associative Learning and Cognition in Animals.* Washington, D.C.: American Psychological Association, 1998. Several of the thirteen contributions to this collection deal with Pavlov's experiments, including a chapter on the real-time theory of Pavlovian conditioning and one on Pavlov's notion of feature-ambiguous discrimination.

PERSONALITY

Allport, Gordon W. *Becoming: Basic Considerations for a Psychology of Personality.* New Haven, Conn.: Yale University Press, 1955. In this brief (106-page) book, the father of the five-factor model of personality clearly and directly sets forth his basic theory.

Craik, Kenneth H., Robert Hogan, and Raymond Wolfe, eds. *Fifty Years of Personality Psychology.* New York: Plenum, 1993. Considerable focus on the psychology of personality set forth by Gordon Allport. Presents current status and contemporary perspectives.

De Raad, Boele. *The Big Five Personality Factors: The Psychological Approach to Personality.* Seattle: Hogrefe and Huber, 2000. Major focus of this well-researched book is personality assessment.

Drapela, Victor J. *A Review of Personality Theories.* Springfield, Ill.: Charles C Thomas, 1993. Overview of work in the field of personality theory. Comprehensive, essentially philosophical.

Mowen, John C. *The 3M Model of Motivation and Personality: Theory and Empirical Applications to Consumer.* Boston: Kluwer Academic, 2000. Comprehensive consideration of personality and human motivation applied to consumer habits. Discusses impulsive and compulsive behavior.

Staats, Arthur W. *Behavior and Personality: Psychological Behaviorism.* New York: Springer, 1996. This book's nine chapters emphasize abnormal personality development and both cognitive and behavioral aspects of personality. Outlines psychological behavioral therapy.

PSYCHOTHERAPY

Bauer, Mark, and Linda McBride. *Structured Group Psychotherapy for Bipolar Disorder: The Life Goals Program.* New York: Springer, 1996. Deals with treating bipolar disorder through psychotherapy. Explains elements of the Life Goals Program that has yielded fruitful results in treating bipolar disorders.

Burns, George W. *101 Healing Stories: Using Metaphors in Therapy.* New York: John Wiley & Sons, 2001. Emphasizes the role of storytelling in psychotherapy, emphasizing the uses of metaphor that permits patients to focus on their own situations without revealing details that they prefer to suppress.

French, Sally, and Julius Sim. *Writing: A Guide for Therapists.* Boston: Butterworth-Heinemann, 1993. Interesting viewed comparatively with the Burns volume (above). Explores composition as a viable means of treating some psychological ills. Emphasizes process in clinical writing. Suggests avoiding using words that create stereotypes.

Hartman, Loren M., and Kirk T. Blankenstein, eds. *Perception of Self in Emotional Disorder and Psychotherapy.* New York: Plenum, 1986. Consideration of the etiology of mental illness and of its treatments through psychotherapy. Emphasizes the role of self-perception in psychotherapy.

Wen-sheng, Tseng, and Jon Stretzer, eds. *Culture and Psychotherapy: A Guide to Clinical Practice.* Washington, D.C.: American Psychological Association, 2001. Tseng Wen-sheng's title article, "Culture and Psychotherapy," provides a splendid overview. The book's seventeen essays are practical guides for psychotherapists.

SCHIZOPHRENIA

Gelman, Sheldon. *Medicating Schizophrenia: A History.* New Brunswick, N.J.: Rutgers University Press, 1999. Traces the history of chemical treatment of schizophrenia and presents valuable material on current chemical treatment of the disorder.

Green, Michael Foster. *Schizophrenia Revealed: From Neurons to Social Interactions.* New York: W. W. Norton, 2001. Discusses the early symptoms of schizophrenia and genetic predispositions for it. The final chapter, following one dealing with interventions, reviews ways of overcoming the condition.

Harrison, Paul J., and Gareth W. Roberts, eds. *The Neuropathology of Schizophrenia: Progress and Interpretation.* New York: Oxford University Press, 2000. A specialized book—not for the beginner. Its thirteen chapters by experts in the field deal accurately and in detail with biological and psychological aspects of the disorder.

Zahavi, Dan, ed. *Exploring the Self: Philosophical and Psychopathological Perspectives on Self-Experience*. Philadelphia: John Benjamins, 2000. Six of the thirteen papers, presented originally at a conference at the University of Copenhagen in May 1999, deal with matters relating to schizophrenia.

SENSATION AND PERCEPTION

Berkowitz, Leonard. *Consequences and Causes of Feelings*. New York: Cambridge University Press, 2000. In seven chapters arranged under four major headings, Berkowitz deals with the psychological effects feelings have on human behavior and the consequences of such feelings.

Classen, Constance. *Worlds of Senses: Exploring the Senses in History and Across Cultures*. New York: Routledge, 1993. An anthropological approach. Considers literacy as anticulture in the Andes. Discusses the words and worlds of the senses.

Gifford, Don. *The Farther Shore: A Natural History of Perception*. New York: Atlantic Monthly Press, 1990. Considers the history of the senses and sensation as well as the history of perception.

Howes, David, ed. *The Varieties of Sensory Experience: A Sourcebook in the Anthropology of the Senses*. Toronto: University of Toronto Press, 1991. Focuses on anthropological considerations of the senses and perception.

Humphrey, Nicholas. *A History of the Mind*. New York: Simon & Schuster, 1992. Presents a history of the senses and sensation, and a history of consciousness, the mind, and body.

Laming, Donald R. J. *The Measurement of Sensation*. New York: Oxford University Press, 1997. Questions whether sensation can be measured effectively. Considers the physiological basis of sensation. Suggests ways of scaling sensation. Shows how to judge relations between sensations.

SEXUALITY

Aron, Arthur, and Elaine N. Aron. *Perspectives on Close Relationships*. Boston: Allyn & Bacon, 1994. Links the success of close relationships to self-understanding and fulfillment in other walks of life.

Buss, David M., and Neil M. Malamuth, eds. *Sex, Power, Conflict*. New York: Oxford University Press, 1996. These twelve essays deal with such questions as sexual aggression, male aggression, the relationship between power and aggression.

Kinsey, Alfred C., and Paul H. Gebhard. *Sexual Behavior in the Human Female*. Philadelphia: W. B. Saunders, 1953. This sequel to *Sexual Behavior in the Human Male* presents the other half of human sexuality.

Kinsey, Alfred C., Wardell B. Pomeroy, and Charles E. Martin. *Sexual Behavior in the Human Male*. Philadelphia: W. B. Saunders, 1948. This landmark study of sexual behavior, based on extensive interviews, changed forever the ways in which Americans viewed human sexuality.

SLEEP

Cooper, Rosemary, ed. *Sleep*. New York: Chapman and Hall, 1994. Considerations of the function of sleep, the classification of sleep disorders, sleep apnea, and such matters as sleeping at high altitudes.

Fosgate, Blanchard. *Sleep Psychologically Considered with Reference to Sensation and Memory*. New York: Da Capo Press, 1982. Considers sleep and dreaming in relation to the unconscious mind. Links sleep with memory. Suggest that dreaming is a form of remembering. Shows how sleep promotes memory by fixing ideas in the mind.

Houvel, Michael. *The Paradox of Sleep: The Story of Dreaming*. Translated by Lawrence Garey. Cambridge, Mass.: MIT Press, 1999. Explores the functions and natural history of dreaming and dream memories. Regards sleep as the guardian of psychological individuality.

Monk, Timothy H., ed. *Sleep, Sleepiness, and Performance*. New York: John Wiley & Sons, 1991. Extremely interesting contribution on circadian rhythms. Material on sleep-wake cycles, effects of sleep deprivation, and several sleep disorders.

Riley, Terrence L., et al., eds. *Clinical Aspects of Sleep and Sleep Disturbance*. Boston: Butterworth, 1985. Somewhat dated. Contains an overview of sleep problems and their effects.

SOCIAL PSYCHOLOGY

Berkowitz, Leonard, ed. *Advances in Experimental Social Psychology*. Orlando, Fla.: Academic Press, 1964-present. This series appears annually and deals with all aspects of experimental social psychology.

Eichelberger, Julia. *Prophets of Recognition: Ideology and the Individual in Novels by Ralph Ellison, Toni Morrison, Saul Bellow, and Eudora Welty*. Baton Rouge:

Louisiana State University Press, 1999. Considers four contemporary American authors from the standpoint of social psychology and documentation.

Farr, Robert M. *The Roots of Modern Social Psychology, 1872-1954.* New York: Basil Blackwell, 1996. Considers social psychology an American phenomenon. Traces its history. Places special emphasis on George Herbert Mead, a leading philosopher and pioneer in modern social psychology.

Gilbert, David T., Susan T. Fiske, and Gardner Lindzey, eds. *Handbook of Social Psychology.* New York: McGraw-Hill, 1998. A serviceable quick reference book in the field of social psychology.

Kotre, John. *Outliving the Self: How We Live on in Future Generations.* New York: W. W. Norton, 1996. Interesting and useful case studies in social psychology, including both children and adults. Considerable emphasis on social psychologist Erik Erikson.

Rickels, Laurence A., ed. *Acting Out in Groups.* Minneapolis: University of Minnesota Press, 1999. Several of this volume's fourteen essays deal with the group dynamics of forms of popular culture such as the talk show. An interesting essay on the trial of host Jenny Jones following a murder resulting from the outing of a gay man on her television show.

STRESS

Bloch, Sidney, and Bruce S. Singh. *Understanding Troubled Minds: A Guide to Mental Illness and Its Treatment.* New York: New York University Press, 1999. Chapter 6 in this twenty-two chapter book is entitled "Coping with Stress." Details ways to handle stress and psychological tensions.

Miley, William M. *The Psychology of Well-Being.* Westport, Conn.: Praeger, 1999. Chapter entitled "Dealing with Stress" examines causes of stress. Other chapters deal with the stress related to obesity, a sedentary lifestyle, or such illnesses as AIDS, cancer, heart disease, or diabetes.

Ritchie, Sheila, and Peter Martin. *Motivational Management.* Brookfield, Vt.: Gower, 1999. One fourteen-page chapter deals specifically with stress and its implications in the workplace.

Schroeder, David A., ed. *Social Dilemmas: Perspectives on Individuals and Groups.* Westport, Conn.: Praeger, 1995. Most of the eleven essays in this book deal with the stress accompanying social dilemmas. Suggests ways of dealing with it.

SUBSTANCE ABUSE

Doweiko, Harold E. *Concepts of Chemical Dependency.* 5th ed. Pacific Grove, Calif.: Brooks/Cole-Thomson Learning, 2002. Consideration of the causes and manifestations of major addictions, including alcohol, tobacco, and both prescription and illegal drugs. Considers means of coping with substance abuse problems.

Horne, Arthur M., and Mark S. Kiselica, eds. *Handbook of Counseling Boys and Adolescent Males: A Practitioner's Guide.* Thousand Oaks, Calif.: Sage Publications, 1999. Of particular interest is Richard C. Page's "Counseling Substance-Abusing Young Males," the book's last chapter.

Schaler, Jeffrey A. *Addiction Is a Choice.* Chicago: Open Court, 2002. Solid presentation of compulsive behavior as related to substance abuse and addiction. Considers the psychological aspects of choice among substance abusers.

Solowij, Nadia. *Cannabis and Cognitive Functioning.* New York: Cambridge University Press, 1998. Considers how long-term use of cannabis affects people's ability to think. Concerned with how the effects of drugs can be reversed when use is discontinued.

Walters, Glenn O. *The Addiction Concept: Working Hypothesis or Self-Fulfilling Prophesy?* Boston: Allyn & Bacon, 1999. Walters deals with addiction in the light of its biological, psychological, sociological, and pragmatic constructs.

TESTING

Bormuth, John R. *On the Theory of Achievement Test Items.* Chicago: University of Chicago Press, 1970. Presents solid information fruitfully supplemented by Peter Menzel's excellent essay on the linguistic bases of the theory of writing test items.

Kaagan, Stephen S. *Leadership Lessons: From a Life of Character and Purpose in Public Affairs.* Lanham, Md.: University Press of America, 1997. The twenty-two page chapter entitled "Reestablishing the Educational Testing Service" is relevant to those interested in tests and measurements.

Lemann, Nicholas. *The Big Test: The Secret History of the American Meritocracy.* New York: Farrar, Straus, and Giroux, 1999. Presents an accurate history of intelligence testing, discussing elitism as it pertains to such testing. Emphasis on Henry Chauncey's contributions to standardized testing.

Lidz, Carol, and Julian G. Elliott, eds. *Dynamic Assessment: Prevailing Models and Applications*. New York: JAI, 2000. Useful suggestions for the psychological testing of handicapped children. Sensitive presentation of material on cognition in children.

Reynolds, Cecil R., and Randy W. Kamphaus, eds. *Handbook of Psychological and Educational Assessment of Children*. New York: Guilford Press, 1990. The contributions to this resource deal with psychological tests for children and with achievement tests in general.

R. Baird Shuman

WEB SITE DIRECTORY

AAASP Online: Association for the Advancement of Applied Sport Psychology

http://www.aaasponline.org/index2.html

Offers valuable background information that explains the nature of sport psychology, the growing variety and number of people who use it, the services provided by sport psychologists, and how to find a qualified sport psychology professional. The site also has a member services page which includes AAASP's code of ethics and explains how to become an AAASP certified consultant. Other features include a consultant finder, a list of AAASP publications, and links to other sport psychology sites.

abcnews.com: "All in Your Head" column

http://www.abcnews.go.com/sections/living/InYourHead/allinyourhead.html

This site provides the current installment and the archives of the ABC News occasional mental health column "All in Your Head." Most columns are accompanied by a summary, links to related stories, links to relevant Web sites, and responses from readers. The sixty columns in the archives treat widely varying topics, including "conversion therapy" to reverse the sexual orientation of gay men, the question of whether racists are "ill or evil," families coping with multiple tragedies, and the long-term effects of teachers' emotional abuse of children.

All About Depression

http://www.allaboutdepression.com

This small but attractive and well-designed site is maintained by Prentiss Price, who has a Ph.D. in counseling psychology and works for a college counseling center. The site's major sections are a general overview, causes, diagnosis, treatment, medication, and resources (contact information and/or links for organizations). Each topic's page has a table of contents along the left edge and a "professional recommendations" section highlighting the most important advice.

American Academy of Child and Adolescent Psychiatry (AACAP)

www.aacap.org

This organization hopes its site will aid the treatment and understanding of children and youth who have behavioral, mental, or developmental disorders. Particularly useful are the factsheets for family members and other caregivers. The Facts for Families series of more than fifty texts includes discussions of alcohol, bed-wetting, divorce, guns, lying, pregnancy, talking about sex, and violent behavior. The site also provides a downloadable glossary of symptoms and mental illnesses that might affect teenagers; AACAP policy statements on topics such as juvenile death sentences and psychoactive medications for children and youth; press releases about children on-line and the influence of music and music videos; and information for professionals.

American Association of Suicidology (AAS)

http://www.suicidology.org/index.html

This site's sections include a detailed background document featuring a focused outline for understanding and helping someone who is suicidal; an on-line bookstore, with resources grouped by topic and audience; recent suicide news; search forms for locating crisis centers or support groups by state and city; guidance on obtaining organizational or individual AAS certification; and a resource page, listing suicide statistics, school guidelines, specifics on suicide among youth and the elderly, and resources for the clinician who has lost a patient to suicide.

American Psychological Association (APA)

http://www.apa.org

This extensive site, from the world's largest professional association for psychologists, offers a wide range of information for a variety of audiences. Though content-rich and detailed, the site is clearly organized and easy to navigate. The main page has sections providing recent news; a featured article;

classified ads; portals for psychologists, students, and the public; membership information; APA books, videos, and databases; and quick links. Resources for the public include full text reports from APA's PsycPORT news site; links to information pages on twelve topics (including aging, children, depression, mind-body health, parenting and family, women, and violence); and links to help pages (including finding a psychologist, the help center, a series of on-line brochures, and psychology in daily life). Resources for psychologists include job search information, conferences, ethics statements, practice-related information (such as record-keeping guidelines), and patient brochures.

Association for the Study of Dreams
http://www.asdreams.org/index.htm

This international, nonprofit organization's site features information about the international conference; selected articles from the association's magazine, *Dream Time*, and its journal, *Dreaming*; educational pages, with answers to common questions about dreams and nightmares, and a science project file; the association's Dreamwork Ethics statement; and a classified list of dream-related and dream-sharing Web sites and e-mail lists.

Birth Psychology
http://www.birthpsychology.com

This site is provided by the Association for Pre- and Perinatal Psychology and Health (APPAH). Its sections include life before birth (fetal senses, sound, prebirth communication, and prenatal memory and learning); birth and the origins of violence; the birth scene (circumcision, obstetrics, and more); healing of prenatal and perinatal trauma; abstracts and index for APPAH's *Journal of Prenatal and Perinatal Psychology and Health*; a classified bibliography of one hundred books, videos, and journals; and a current list of practitioners and programs.

C. G. Jung Page
http://www.cgjungpage.org

This full-featured site aids novice readers with an introduction to Jungian psychology in the form of a Jung Lexicon. The site's Jungian Resources Page includes links to the Web sites of institutes and societies offering Jungian training. There are also links to the bibliography of the *Journal of Analytical Psychology*, covering 1991 to 2000; links to numerous full-text analytical psychology articles; and film commentaries, book reviews, and literary articles employing Jungian criticism.

catalyst. on computers and psychology
http://www.victoriapoint.com/catalyst.htm

This site's editor specializes in Internet addiction and other psychological issues related to the Internet. He provides topical pages (which link to Web-based articles) on hackers, on-line behavior, Internet addiction, on-line therapy, and Internet usability. Other sections of the site deal with human-computer interaction, psychology software, and "features" (a lengthy assortment of articles on a wide range of computers-and-psychology topics).

Center for the Study of Autism
http://www.autism.org

The Center, located in Salem, Oregon, conducts research on autism therapies and provides information for parents and professionals. The site's sections include a detailed overview of autism; texts on subgroups and related disorders; issues (seventeen topics, including auditory processing problems, self-injurious behavior, and how to determine whether a treatment has helped); interventions (more than twenty-five, including music therapy, the hug machine, and nutrition); the sibling center; interviews with autism experts; and a detailed, classified page of autism links.

Classics in the History of Psychology
http://psychclassics.yorku.ca

This site collects important public-domain scholarly texts from psychology and related fields. There are more than 150 articles and 25 books, with links to more than 200 related works on other sites. To aid undergraduates, some texts are accompanied by introductory essays written for the site. The texts can be accessed by author or by topic (including behaviorism, intelligence testing, psychoanalysis and psychotherapy, cognition, and women in psychology). Within topics, texts are arranged chronologically. Users can also search the entire site by keyword.

Community Psychology Net
http://www.communitypsychology.net

This site provides comprehensive information on community psychology for readers at all levels. The introductory page defines the topic, distinguishing it from sociology, social work, and public health. The site's organizing metaphor is the university campus. The library provides a classified grouping of links. The lecture hall has course syllabi and reading lists. The admissions office has links to forty universities offering graduate programs. The career planning center lists job ads.

Consumer Psychology

http://www.wansink.com/index.html

This small but effective site has two sections, both related to consumerism and food. The Food Psychology section covers nine topics (including "Do larger packages increase usage?" and "Measuring ad effects on brand usage"). For each topic, the site provides a one-paragraph overview, a more detailed Research Brief, and usually a link to a PDF file for a journal article on the topic written by the site editor. There are also lesson plans suitable for ages twelve to adult.

Criminal Profiling Research

http://www.criminalprofiling.ch

This Swiss site focuses on presenting the results of scientific research. Besides a detailed, referenced introduction to the topic, it offers brief accounts of how profiling is used in the United States and Europe, a case analysis page, bibliographies of books and journal articles, links to sites explaining how profiling is done, and a FAQ which includes information on profiling as a career.

depressedteens.com

http://www.depressedteens.com/indexnf.html

This educational site strives to help teenagers and their parents and teachers recognize and understand the symptoms of adolescent depression and ensure that depressed teenagers get help. An essential part of the site is information about, and a QuickTime preview of, the twenty-six-minute video *Day for Night: Recognizing Teenage Depression*. Other areas of the site are a factsheet on adolescent depression and a checklist and parent notification form for showing the video.

Dr. Ruth Westheimer

http://webcenter.drruth.aol.com/DrRuth

Dr. Ruth is a highly visible, long-time sex therapist who has written several books (including *Dr.*

Ruth's Encyclopedia of Sex) and worked as a professor at New York University, a lecturer, and a television and radio commentator. This content-rich site features a biographical sketch of Dr. Ruth, her answer to the question of the day, and a wide-ranging alphabetical archive of about 110 question-and-answer topics. The latter include affairs, children witnessing sex, fantasy, homosexuality and bisexuality, infidelity, sex aids, and sexual dysfunctions. In addition, the site provides a monthly archive of varied, practical, and fun-loving sex tips going back to January, 1998.

dotCOMSENSE

http://helping.apa.org/dotcomsense

This small site, based on a brochure produced by the American Psychological Association, guides Web users in protecting their privacy on bulletin boards, chat rooms, and Web sites (particularly on those dealing with mental health) that ask for personal information or use cookies. Also gives helpful guidelines for assessing the credibility and accuracy of sites providing mental health information. It lists other Web sites devoted to evaluation of on-line information.

Eating Disorder Referral and Information Center (EDRIC)

http://www.edreferral.com

EDRIC provides information for friends and family members as well as treatment referrals for individuals with all forms of eating disorders. The sections of the site include a referral form for searching for a therapist or treatment center, job openings at treatment centers, treatment scholarships, and recommended books and Web sites. Addresses such topics as how family members can deal with a loved one who has an eating disorder. Also examines movement therapy, causes, assessment, treatment, consequences, body image, introductory information on specific disorders, and eating disorders among males, athletes, and pregnant women.

ECT.org: Information About Electroconvulsive Therapy

http://ECT.org

This attractive site aims to be the Web's most comprehensive source of ECT information. Juli Lawrence, the site's creator, had ECT in 1994 and hopes her site, which discusses all sides of the topic, will help others considering ECT make an informed decision. The site provides attractive, clearly arranged links (with annotations) to information on these topics: effects (particularly memory loss and, possibly, brain damage); resources (studies, statistics, and official statements from organizations); news (breaking stories, personal stories, lawsuits, legislative battles); self-help (alternatives to ECT); community (message boards and event calendars); and the Hall of Shame ("the very worst ECT practitioners and researchers").

Encyclopedia of Psychology
http://www.psychology.org

This site, "intended to facilitate browsing in any area of psychology," provides access to more than two thousand Web sites. The main method of access is by category—including careers, environment behavior relationships (with forty-five subcategories and more than one thousand links), organizations, paradigms and theories, people and history, publications, and resources. All categories are further divided into subtopics. The Web page for each subtopic will include two types of links: those which go to texts and those which go to Web sites. An annotation for each site (usually detailed and often noting the level of user for whom it is appropriate) is generally provided.

Explorations in Learning and Instruction: The Theory into Practice Database
http://tip.psychology.org

This site provides brief but detailed summaries of fifty major theories of human learning and instruction. All the theories have extensive scientific support, and the summaries are drawn from published primary and secondary writings. The summaries include the name of the theory's originator, an overview of the theory, its principles and application, an example, references for further study, and sometimes a video clip or Web site links. The theories include adult learning, andragogy, cognitive dissonance, Criterion Referenced Instruction, experiential learning, lateral thinking, multiple intelligences, operant conditioning, and more.

Freud Net
http://www.nypsa.org

The site of the New York Psychoanalytic Institute's Abraham A. Brill Library. The library maintains what might be the world's largest collection of information on psychoanalysis. Provides a helpful page of selected links about Sigmund Freud: museum, exhibition, and library sites; links to texts of Freud's writings (with a warning that most of his works are still under copyright, so only the earlier, inferior translations are in the public domain); and writings about Freud.

Great Ideas in Personality
http://www.personalityresearch.org

This sites deals with scientific research in personality psychology. It provides detailed information on personality theories that are empirically testable, grouping them into twelve sections. The sections include behaviorism, evolutionary psychology, attachment theory, basic emotions, personality disorders, interpersonal theory, and more. The page describing each theory includes a brief description, the theory's beginning date, names of the theorists involved, references to published works, and links to additional Web sources. The site also features sections on personality in general, practical information for psychology students, links to personality journal sites, and links to personality courses sites for professors.

Health Emotions Research Institute
http://www.healthemotions.org

This clear, attractive site of the University of Wisconsin's Health Emotions Research Institute provides information on studies of positive emotions, their influence on the body, and the implications of this research for preventing disease, affecting definitions of health, and fostering resilience. The site explains the institute's mission and its current projects (both human and private)—including biological consequences of meditation, biological substrates of resilience, and biological bases of positive affective styles.

Holistic-online.com
http://holistic-online.com

This comprehensive site serves to provides accurate information on both conventional and alternative treatment options for a variety of conditions. It emphasizes treatment of the whole person, prevention of illness, and self care. Separate pages are devoted to conditions such as anxiety, back pain, depression, insomnia, migraine, panic attack, seasonal affective disorder, and stress. The alternative therapies featured include biofeedback, guided imagery, humor therapy, hydrotherapy, imagery, light therapy, massage, meditation, prayer healing, and yoga.

The Humor Project, Inc.

http://www.humorproject.com

The Humor Project, founded in 1977 by Joel Goodman, focuses on the positive power of humor by training individuals and organizations (through its lectures, workshops, conferences, and publications) to use humor and creativity. The site's playful spirit is immediately apparent in the visitor counter, with its constantly whirling numbers. The impressive list of clients who have used the project's services includes Xerox, Mobil Oil, NASA, Harvard University, and the American Hospital Association. The site provides descriptions of the speaker's bureau program offerings, the annual workshop, and the international humor conference (held annually for sixteen years); an on-line bookstore; a daily article, interview, and reader's "di-jest"; a spotlight column; and "today's laffirmation."

Internet Mental Health

http://www.mentalhealth.com

This award-winning site, established in 1995, is intended for both professionals and the general public. It functions as an encyclopedia for the fifty-four most common mental disorders. For each disorder, the site gives both the American and European description, treatment information (meant for therapists and written by the site's author), research information, booklets prepared by professional organizations and support groups, and magazine articles. The site has links to on-line diagnostic programs for personality, anxiety, mood, eating, and substance-abuse disorders, as well as for schizophrenia and attention-deficit hyperactivity disorder (ADHD). It also provides encyclopedic information on common psychiatric medications, a mental health magazine, and links to popular mental health sites.

Internet Psychology Lab

http://kahuna.psych.uiuc.edu/ipl

This award-winning site provides a multimedia, interactive system for psychology lab instruction at the University of Illinois, enabling the university's students—and visitors to the site—to work remotely on lessons, experiments, and demonstrations. The instruction modules include cognition, memory and learning, visual perception, and auditory perception. Experiments include the Stroop Effect, choice reaction time, visual cognition, basic reaction time, and chimeric faces.

Memory and Reality: Website of the False Memory Syndrome Foundation

http://fmsfonline.org

This foundation works to prevent False Memory Syndrome, investigate reasons for its spread, and help families affected by it. Includes a detailed FAQ; the current newsletter; a searchable archive of newsletter issues back to 1992; a document explaining hypnosis, hypnotic susceptibility, and their role in creating false memories; information about *USA v. Peterson, Seward, Mueck, Keraga, and Davis*, the first criminal trial to bring charges against therapists regarding false memories; a detailed page dealing with retractors; and discussions of scientific studies on whether people can actually repress memories and how false memories can be engendered.

MHN: Mental Help Net

http://mentalhelp.net

Developed in 1994, this award-winning site strives "to catalog, review, and make available to everyone all online mental health resources as they become available." Groups the sites into subject categories, which are divided into two lists: Issues and Disorders, and Information. For each topic, the page might include basic information (summarized from DSM-IV), links categorized by type, news, book reviews, self-help groups, and resources (such as treatment facilities, therapists, professional conferences, and clinical job openings). The site also contains a daily mental health news section and a professional area (where visitors can search for conferences or workshops, list their practice or clinic, or view licensure information).

NAMI: The Nation's Voice on Mental Illness

http://www.nami.org

This site represents the National Alliance for the Mentally Ill (NAMI), a support and advocacy organization for friends and family of people with severe mental illnesses—and for the individuals themselves. It contains a search form for locating NAMI affiliate organizations; information about the NAMI helpline; factsheets on specific illnesses, treatments, and medications; purchase information for NAMI's books, videos, brochures, and newsmagazines; public policy information and statements; and a research page with links to NAMI research reports.

National Association for Self-Esteem (NASE)
www.self-esteem-nase.org

This association works to integrate self-esteem into American society and thus enhance the personal worth and happiness of every individual. The site provides a review of research on self-esteem, relating it to problems such as substance abuse, violence, crime, teenage pregnancy, and suicide. There are also articles from NASE's newsletter, a categorized reading list, a list of published self-esteem educational programs, and a description of NASE's Parent Link Network for raising socially responsible children.

National Institute of Psychosocial Oncology (NIPO)
http://www.nipo.org

NIPO works with cancer patients, family members, and professionals to ensure that sufficient attention is given to patients' and family members' psychosocial needs. For patients, the site provides a clear, helpful article on how families can cope with cancer, as well as an archive of six others. Two of the topics included are denial and effective communication with doctors. In addition, there is information about the patient-communications presentations NIPO can offer and a "prepared patient's checklist" page.

Positive Psychology
http://psych.upenn.edu/seligman/pospsy.htm

This content-rich site is maintained by Martin Seligman, past president of the American Psychological Association and a researcher on positive psychology, optimism, and learned helplessness. The site offers several readable and well-documented articles, columns, and book chapters by Seligman that define and explore the parameters of positive psychology. There are also professional summaries, a concept paper for a network of positive psychology scholars, an e-mail directory of researchers, questionnaires (some downloadable) that researchers can use, and a grouping of essays, units, syllabi, and reading lists for teaching positive psychology.

Procrastination Research Group (PRG)
http://www.carleton.ca/~tpychyl

This clear, attractive site is provided by a university learning group at Carleton University's psychology department (Ottawa, Canada), but it collects research and information on procrastination worldwide. The Research Resources section includes a featured journal article, summaries of student papers (undergraduate through doctoral levels) written by the PRG, and a comprehensive procrastination bibliography. The site also has a useful self-help page. The latter includes a brief outline of signs of procrastination, suggested strategies for reducing it, a list of recommended readings, and a concise grouping of links to other sites.

Psybersquare: Strength and Healing Through Community and Self-Help
http://www.psybersquare.com/index.html

This award-winning site aims to provide compassionate advice and guidance to enable visitors to function well in their lives. Consists mainly of brief, warm, and helpful articles (many written by the site's author and most accompanied by recommended readings). Categories include "Me," "Us," "Family," "Work," "Women," "Men," "Anxiety," "Depression," and "Recovery." Each category covers a handful of topics. "Me" includes essays on "getting unstuck," resentment, expectations, learning new tools for strength and health, gratitude, motivation, self-esteem, holidays, self-assertion, and self-improvement. The site also provides support for coping with the terrorist attacks of September 11, 2001; telephone-based mental health information and support (for a fee); a bookstore; and step-by-step advice on selecting a therapist.

Psych Central: Dr. Grohol's Mental Health Page
http://psychcentral.com/grohol.htm

This award-winning site, in existence since 1992, provides links to more than 1,700 Web sites that have been personally reviewed by the author. Its main access point is the Resources section, which consists of thirty categories (some as specific as "Bipolar" and "Attack on America," others as broad as "Professional Psychology Resources"). Each category ("Sexuality and Gender," for example) is further subdivided into topics (such as men's issues, symptoms, and women's issues) and/or formats (such as books or support groups). The page for each of the 1,700 Web sites gives a brief but usually detailed description of the site, the date last updated, the number of hits it has received from *Psych Central*, the number of votes from *Psych Central* users, and its rating by those users. Besides the Web site links, *Psych Central* provides "What Is" texts (concise descriptions of symptoms and treatments for mental disorders), "Have I Got?" quizzes for several disorders, live chat, book reviews, several essays by Dr. Grohol, and psychology and mental health news.

Psychology

http://psychology.about.com/mbody.htm

This content-rich, attractively formatted site is one of thirty-two in About.com's Homework Help series. About.com focuses on using people (its guides) to carefully select and organize links, texts, Forums, and How-To's to answer questions. The site's main organization is its thirty "essentials" categories (including adult development, cognitive psychology, dreams, love, industrial and organizational psychology, sport psychology, and more). Each topic has additional sections. Leadership, for instance, has sections for background articles, book reviews, student development programs, pertinent journals, assessment tools, and background texts on leadership styles, theories, and researchers. Another access method, by subject, includes the essentials but adds about seventy additional categories. The site has numerous ads, but many are related to psychology.

Psychology Information Online

http://www.psychologyinfo.com

This site provides a wide range of information (aimed at consumers, college students, and psychologists) on the practice of psychology. The information falls into these categories: psychotherapy and counseling, diagnosis and disorders, psychological testing and evaluation, other forms of treatment, behavior therapy, forensic psychiatry, and psychological consultations for legal situations. There are separate access points for the three categories of users. In addition, users can consult the navigation guide, the list of links, or the alphabetical subject index for each category.

Psychology Virtual Library

http://www.clas.ufl.edu/users/gthursby/psi

This clear, attractive site is part of the World Wide Web Virtual Library, which evaluates each site it includes. The seventeen categories include academic psychology, books, journals, university psychology departments, clinical social work, directories of psychology sites, mental health, history of psychology, and more. Each category has its own subsections. The Stress Virtual Library includes, for example, links for books and publishers, e-mail lists and newsgroups, mental health resources, professional organizations, stress management, and commercial products. The links on each page are annotated.

RxList: The Internet drug index

http://www.rxlist.com

This site, founded in 1995, is maintained by Neil Sandow, a licensed, experienced California pharmacist. The site's primary content includes FAQs on more than 4,500 popular drugs, 1,000 professional monographs, and 1,500 patient-oriented monographs. Visitors can search for drugs by brand name, generic name, ID Imprint code, or NDC code. Each FAQ explains the purpose of the drug, who should not use it, how to take it, potential problems, and what to do if you miss a dose or overdose yourself. Other features include a search page for alternatives (such as homeopathies or herbal remedies) and a list of the top two hundred prescriptions filled in each of the last six years.

schizophrenia.com

http://www.schizophrenia.com

This site was established in 1996 by Brian Chiko in memory of his brother, a schizophrenia patient who committed suicide. Its purpose is to provide, free of charge, accurate information for those who have the disease or whose lives have been affected by it. The site's introduction to schizophrenia is clear and well organized. Other topics covered include causes, diagnosis, medication, managing depression, preventing suicide, getting financial assistance, and assisted or involuntary treatment. The site's only drawback is that it has not been updated recently.

Self Psychology Page

http://www.selfpsychology.org

This clear, attractive site is devoted to the study of psychoanalytic self psychology, a theoretical school founded by Heinz Kohut. Its "About" page provides a brief introduction to and definitions of self psychology. There are lengthy bibliographies on self psychology and on its approaches to topics such as children, the elderly, parenting, marital and family therapy, and addictions. The site also provides a news page, a page listing original self psychology papers, and a directory of self psychology training programs.

The Shyness Home Page

http://www.shyness.com

This small site is sponsored by the Shyness Institute in Palo Alto, California. It provides information on upcoming shyness workshops and an e-mail link enabling visitors to ask the institute questions. Finally, the site provides links to, or contact information for, a wide range of other shyness resources: newsgroups; shyness clinics; brochures and articles; organizations offering classes, workshops, and coaching; reading lists; and research papers.

Sleepnet.com

http://www.sleepnet.com

Provides information (not medical advice) to improve sleep and aims to link to all noncommercial sleep information sites. Sections include information on a wide range of sleep disorders and sleep-related conditions (sleep apnea, insomnia, narcolepsy, restless legs, shift work, and circadian rhythms); a detailed glossary; a categorized list of links to news articles; public sleep forums, grouped by topic; and an e-mail newsletter.

Social Phobia/Social Anxiety Association Home Page

http://www.socialphobia.org

The site explains that this frequently misdiagnosed condition is the world's third largest mental health problem. It provides definitions and background information, a weekly mailing list for individuals with social phobia, a link to the Social Anxiety Institute's page (offering a variety of therapy programs), and other social phobia links, including personal testimonies and reading lists.

Social Science Information Gateway: Psychology

http://sosig.esrc.bris.ac.uk/psychology

This well-organized, attractive site lists and describes high-quality Web sites and texts useful for all audiences. The sites are arranged into eighteen subcategories. Users can search by keyword or browse within the subcategories—including mental health,

general psychology, consumer psychology, animal psychology, psychological disorders, developmental psychology, sport psychology, and more. Each subcategory contains further groupings by subject and by type of site. The latter might include books, bibliographies, journals, educational materials, e-mail lists and discussion groups, organizations, research projects, and resource guides. The page describing each Web site gives a descriptive summary, keywords, the site administrator's name and e-mail address, and the site's language.

Society for Light Treatment and Biological Rhythms

http://www.sltbr.org

This society supports those with research or clinical interests in biological rhythm disorders—including seasonal affective disorder, sleep disorders, jet lag, shift work, and premenstrual syndrome—and therapies for those conditions. The information for the general public includes a detailed "Questions and Answers About Seasonal Affective Disorder and Light Therapy" page as well as links to other Web articles and sites about seasonal affective disorder, sleep disorders, melatonin, and circadian rhythm.

Stress Inc.—The Commerce of Coping

http://stress.jrn.columbia.edu

This creative, attractive site depicts ways in which society has moved from the 1950's, when stress was primarily an engineering term, to 1996, when Americans expended $9.6 billion to buy peace of mind. Sections of the site (representing the commerce of stress) include publishing, advertising, fitness (focusing on yoga), toys, consulting, ergonomics, and yoga. In addition, the site provides a brief history of stress, a stress quiz, information on fringe stress-relief techniques, and tension-breakers.

Traffic Psychology at the University of Hawaii

http://www.soc.hawaii.edu/leonj/leonj/leonpsy/traffic/tpintro.html

This site, maintained by Dr. Leon James, a psychology professor at the University of Hawaii, has extensive texts and references on the origins and theories of traffic psychology. In addition, James provides an inventory of driving behavior and the psychological aspects of traffic flow, a comprehensive bibliography on driving psychology, a self-test for individuals to determine how they would operate within the nine zones of the driving personality, an outline for presentations on aggressive driving and road rage, and a twenty-year overview of what James has learned from teaching his traffic psychology course.

The Whole Brain Atlas

http://www.med.harvard.edu/AANLIB

This site's sponsors include Harvard Medical School and the American Academy of Neurology. The images it provides were created using magnetic resonance, X-ray computed tomography, and nuclear medicine images. Sections of this award-winning site cover the normal brain (with images of normal aging), cerebrovascular disease, brain tumors, degenerative disorders (such as Alzheimer's and Huntington's diseases), and inflammatory or infectious diseases (such as multiple sclerosis, AIDS dementia, Lyme disease, and herpes).

WholeFamily

http://www.wholefamily.com/index.html

This site, enhanced by its comforting, inviting appearance, offers problem-solving texts (written by credentialed professionals) about situations encountered within family relationships. The site's main portals are its centers for marriage, parents, seniors, and teens. The Marriage Center, for instance, has segments on ten issues (including work, money, in-laws, communication, and parenting). "What's New" adds sections on additional topics. There are also Q and A's (such as "Am I asking too much?" and "Too much work, not enough intimacy"). The site also provides chat rooms, topical discussion-forums, "real life dramas," the editor's column, a family soap opera, and a site newsletter.

Glenn Ellen Starr Stilling

MEDIAGRAPHY

Psychology is a common theme in films, television programs, and literature. Therapists and patients represent many archetypes such as heroes, villains, and victims. Glen O. Gabbard and Krin Gabbard identified 450 films with mental health themes and characters, which they discussed in *Psychiatry and the Cinema* (2d ed. Washington, D.C.: American Psychiatric Press, 1999). Many of those films are adapted from books, plays, and short stories which portray psychology in such genres as drama, comedy, mystery, or horror.

Media depictions of mental health professionals and people with mental illnesses vary in accuracy. Psychiatrists and patients are often stereotyped, misrepresented, and either vilified or celebrated to extremes. Media sometimes distort realities of psychotherapy, cheer pathological behaviors, and show mental health professionals acting unethically, erratically, or irresponsibly. The following list describes selected representatives of psychological media.

FILMS

After Dark, My Sweet
DATE: 1990
DIRECTOR: James Foley

Based on Jim Thompson's 1990 novel of the same title. Mentally ill Collie (Jason Patric) tells Doc Goldman (George Dickerson) about being institutionalized and is advised to seek additional treatment. Instead, he joins a kidnapping plot and is killed. This film is presented from Collie's point of view, which causes audiences to wonder if his perceptions are accurate or blurred by his mental instability.

Analyze This
DATE: 1999
DIRECTOR: Harold Ramis

Dr. Ben Sobel (Billy Crystal) treats a gangster (Robert De Niro), who expects his therapist to focus only on him.

Antonia and Jane
DATE: 1991
DIRECTOR: Beeban Kidron

British. Lifelong friends Antonia McGill (Saskia Reeves) and Jane Hartman (Imelda Staunton) see the same therapist (Brenda Bruce). The women express their emotional feelings, including love, jealousy, and anger concerning their friendship.

Antz
DATE: 1998
DIRECTOR: Erich Darnell and Tim Johnson

Neurotic worker ant Z-4195 (Woody Allen) talks to a psychologist (Paul Mazursky) about his frustrations with work and romantic aspirations with Princess Bala (Sharon Stone).

As Good as It Gets
DATE: 1997
DIRECTOR: James L. Brooks

Melvin (Jack Nicholson) has obsessive-compulsive disorder. He begins taking his psychotropic medication when he falls in love with waitress Carol (Helen Hunt). Psychiatrists state that the character probably should have been described as having a personality disorder.

The Assault (Misshandlingen; Mistreatment, Assault and Battery)
DATE: 1969
DIRECTOR: Lasse Forsberg

Black-and-white Swedish film, based on a 1968 official Swedish sociopathy report. This fictional film resembles a documentary in its critical depiction of how the Swedish Social Democracy controlled radicals by manipulating the meaning of insanity in courts. Socialist Knut Nielsen (Knut Pettersen) is institutionalized in a psychiatric ward because of his protests. Characters denounce how mental institutions are used as weapons against dissenters. Psychologists assisted film production.

¡Átame! (*Tie Me Up! Tie Me Down!*)
DATE: 1990
DIRECTOR: Pedro Almodovar

Spanish. On his release from a mental hospital, Ricky (Antonio Banderas) tracks down a porn star, Marina (Victoria Abril), with whom he once had sex and holds her hostage in an attempt to make her love him. Oddly enough, it works.

A Beautiful Mind
DATE: 2001
DIRECTOR: Ron Howard

Based on Sylvia Nasar's 1998 book. Mathematician John Nash (Russell Crowe), a paranoid schizophrenic, is depicted as a genius who developed game theory and won a Nobel Prize despite his illness. His psychiatrist, Dr. Rosen (Christopher Plummer), treats Nash with insulin shock therapy and antipsychotic drugs. Psychiatrists served as film consultants. Film won the Academy Award for Best Picture. Nash was also the subject of *A Brilliant Madness*, a 2002 PBS *American Experience* documentary.

Beauty and the Beast
DATE: 1991
DIRECTOR: Gary Trousdale and Kirk Wise

Animated film in which an evil psychiatrist in control of an asylum accepts a bribe from the villain, Gaston, to commit the heroine's father so that Gaston can marry her.

The Bell Jar
DATE: 1979
DIRECTOR: Larry Peerce

Adapted from Sylvia Plath's 1963 autobiographical novel. Esther Greenwood (Marilyn Hassett) succumbs to depression.

Benny and Joon
DATE: 1993
DIRECTOR: Jeremiah Chechik

Benny (Aidan Quinn) protects his schizophrenic sister Joon (Mary Stuart Masterson) and is unwilling to institutionalize her as advised by Dr. Garvey (C. C. H. Pounder). Joon disrupts Benny's life and acts hostilely toward caretakers. She falls in love with eccentric Sam (Johnny Depp) but is briefly institutionalized after she has a public outburst. Sam and Benny cooperate to secure Joon's release.

Best in Show
DATE: 2000
DIRECTOR: Christopher Guest

A neurotic couple, Meg and Hamilton Swan (Parker Posey and Michael Hitchcock), take their dog to a therapist.

Betrayal
DATE: 1978
DIRECTOR: Paul Wendkos

Based on the case *Julie Roy v. Renatus Hartogs, M.D.*, Lesley Ann Warren stars in this drama about a woman who sues her psychiatrist after he seduced her.

Beyond Therapy
DATE: 1987
DIRECTOR: Robert Altman

Based on a 1982 Broadway play written by Christopher Durang. Couple Bruce (Jeff Goldblum) and Prudence (Julie Hagerty) consult their psychotherapists, Charlotte (Glenda Jackson) and Stuart (Tom Conti). Both therapists are portrayed as acting unethically and having personality disorders themselves.

Birdy
DATE: 1984
DIRECTOR: Alan Parker

An adaptation of William Wharton's 1979 novel of the same title. Vietnam veteran Birdy (Matthew Modine) is institutionalized in a Veterans Administration Hospital mental ward. Ineffectively treated by Dr. Weiss (John Harkins), Birdy lives in silence, obsessing about flying like the pigeons he raised as a teenager. Birdy's best friend, Al Columbato (Nicolas Cage), helps him regain his voice and retain mental stability despite the insanity of his surroundings.

Blue Sky
DATE: 1994
DIRECTOR: Tony Richardson

Manic-depressive Carly Marshall (Jessica Lange) disrupts her children's lives and the military career of her husband, Major Hank Marshall (Tommy Lee Jones), during the 1960's. Hank's credibility as a military scientist, recommending that underground nuclear testing should be conducted to avoid radiation contamination, is undermined by his wife's bizarre and adulterous behavior. Carly has a brief affair with base commander Vince Johnson (Powers Boothe), who forces her to have Hank hospitalized. There he is drugged to prevent him from revealing atomic hazards. Carly ultimately rescues her husband and attracts media attention to the dangers of atomic testing. Lange won a Academy Award for Best Actress for this role.

*The Cabinet of Dr. Caligari (Das Cabinet des
    Dr. Caligari)*
DATE: 1920
DIRECTOR: Robert Wiene

German expressionistic silent film. Francis (Friedrich Feher) is a delusional mental hospital patient. He conveys information about an evil hypnotist named Caligari and the somnambulist Cesare (Conrad Veidt) whom Caligari hypnotizes to kill people. When Caligari is accused of murder, he hides in the mental institution where Francis is committed. Viewers soon realize that Francis and many of the characters in his story, including Cesare, are mental patients and that Caligari is sane. Many film scholars consider this film the catalyst for quality German cinema. The film was remade in 1962.

Camille Claudel
DATE: 1988
DIRECTOR: Bruno Nuytten

French film based on Reine-Marie Paris's biography and the Claudel family archives. This film features the life of sculptor Camille Claudel (Isabelle Adjani) who became insane and was committed to a mental institution. Claudel was the lover of sculptor Auguste Rodin (Gérard Depardieu), who refused to marry her after using her artistic ideas. Her brother Paul Claudel's (Laurent Grevill) abandonment further agitated her precarious mental condition.

Captain Newman, M.D.
DATE: 1963
DIRECTOR: David Miller

Based on Leo Rosten's 1961 novel. Captain Josiah Newman (Gregory Peck) treats patients at a World War II neuropsychiatric ward. Neurotic Corporal Jackson Leibowitz (Tony Curtis) is an orderly.

Carefree
DATE: 1938
DIRECTOR: Mark Sandrich

Psychiatrist Dr. Tony Flagg (Fred Astaire) hypnotizes his best friend's fiancé Amanda Cooper (Ginger Rogers), to overcome her fear of commitment and reluctance to marry. The first hypnosis goes awry when she falls in love with Flagg instead; a second hypnosis to reverse the first causes her to hate him intensely. When Flagg realizes that he is in love with her himself, he must attempt a third hypnosis to erase the effects of his previous attempts.

Cat People
DATE: 1942
DIRECTOR: Jacques Tourneur

Psychiatrist Dr. Judd (Tom Conway) attempts to treat Irena Dubrovna (Simone Simon), who is obsessed by a family curse that she will become a panther and kill her husband if she is sexually aroused.

Catch-22
DATE: 1970
DIRECTOR: Mike Nichols

Based on Joseph Heller's 1961 novel. In this dark comedy, a World War II bombardier (Alan Arkin) pleads insanity in an attempt to avoid more missions. The "catch-22," however, is that knowing he is crazy is proof of mental competence.

Charly
DATE: 1968
DIRECTOR: Ralph Nelson

Adapted from Daniel Keyes's 1966 novel *Flowers for Algernon*. Surgery gives the mentally retarded adult Charly (Cliff Robertson) a genius intelligence quotient without emotional maturity. The effects are impermanent, causing tragedy when Charly begins to slip back into his preoperative state.

The Couch Trip
DATE: 1988
DIRECTOR: Michael Ritchie

Based on Ken Kolb's 1970 novel. John Burns (Dan Aykroyd) is a prisoner who switches places with his psychiatrist Dr. Baird (David Clennon). He travels to Los Angeles to substitute for radio psychiatrist, Dr. Maitlin (Charles Grodin), who is mentally disintegrating.

Das Testament des Dr. Mabuse (*The Last Will of
Dr. Mabuse, The Testament of Dr. Mabuse*)
DATE: 1933
DIRECTOR: Fritz Lang
German film in which Dr. Mabuse (Rudolf Klein-
Rogge), an insane criminal and mental patient in-
troduced in a 1922 film, seizes control of the lunatic
asylum from its administrator Dr. Baum (Oskar
Beregi), who cooperates with his criminal activities.
Chief Inspector Lohmann (Otto Wernicke) finds
the deceased Mabuse, whose spirit has possessed
Baum. Lang made *Die Tausend Augen des Dr. Mabuse*
(*The Thousand Eyes of Dr. Mabuse*) in 1950.

David and Lisa
DATE: 1962
DIRECTOR: Frank Perry
Adapted from a 1998 book based on a case study
by psychiatrist Dr. Theodore Isaac Rubin. This film
features interactions between two teenagers at a
school for mentally disturbed students. David Clemens (Keir Dullea), who is highly intelligent and obsessive, cringes at the suggestion of being touched.
Lisa (Janet Margolin) is schizophrenic and also displays a personality named Muriel. Dr. Alan Swinford
(Howard da Silva) observes the pair's friendship,
which aids the beginning of their recovery.

Diary of a Mad Housewife
DATE: 1970
DIRECTOR: Frank Perry
An unhappy housewife, Tina Balser (Carrie Snod-
gress), participates in group therapy to learn how to
resolve issues she has with her chauvinistic husband
Jonathan (Richard Benjamin), demanding daughters, and narcissistic lover George Prager (Frank Lan-
gella). Tina realizes she must become responsible
for her life to achieve happiness.

Dr. Dippy's Sanitarium
DATE: 1906
DIRECTOR: American Mutoscope and Biograph
Silent; the first film to depict a psychiatrist. Luna-
tics seize control of an asylum until the superinten-
dent restores order.

Eyes Wide Shut
DATE: 1999
DIRECTOR: Stanley Kubrick
Psychiatrist Dr. William Harford (Tom Cruise)
and his wife Alice Harford (Nicole Kidman) explore
their sexuality with patients, individually and in
groups.

Face to Face (*Ansikte mot Ansikte*)
DATE: 1976
DIRECTOR: Ingmar Bergman
Swedish. While in a coma after attempting suicide, psychiatrist Dr. Jenny Isaksson (Liv Ullmann)
recognizes the childhood sources of her repressed
anger. Her colleague, psychiatrist Dr. Helmuth Wan-
kel (Ulf Johansson), dismisses psychoanalysis as a
treatment. Isaksson heals by forgiving her grandparents who raised her. This film reveals the director's
personal interest in Jungian therapy and the sub-
conscious.

Family Life
DATE: 1971
DIRECTOR: Ken Loach
British. Adapted from the play *Two Minds*. Schizophrenic teenager Janice Baildon (Sandy Ratcliffe)
suffers a nervous breakdown aggravated by the domineering behavior of her parents (Grace Cave and
Bill Dean). Her condition is exacerbated by uncar-
ing medical and psychiatric treatment that appears
aimed at alleviating her parents' problems rather
than hers.

Frances
DATE: 1982
DIRECTOR: Graeme Clifford
Based on the life of 1930's actress Frances Farmer
(Jessica Lange), who has a nervous breakdown. She
is wrongly declared criminally insane and institutionalized by those who are threatened by her female independence and autonomy. Contains scenes
of Frances receiving a prefrontal lobotomy.

Freud: The Secret Passion
DATE: 1962
DIRECTOR: John Huston
Montgomery Clift portrays Sigmund Freud at the
beginning of his career. Public and professional rejection of his theories of the unconscious and infantile sexuality are depicted. The film portrays Freud's

interactions with patients, and the conscious and unconscious perceptions that molded his psychoanalytic theories.

Gaslight
DATE: 1944
DIRECTOR: George Cukor

The sadistic Gregory Anton (Charles Boyer) tries to make his wife, Paula Alquist (Ingrid Bergman), insane. Alquist, pondering her aunt's decade-old unsolved murder, suffers memory loss, delusions, and hysteria after she marries Anton. He constantly threatens to have her declared insane and institutionalized before he is exposed as her aunt's strangler.

Girl, Interrupted
DATE: 1999
DIRECTOR: James Mangold

Based the 1993 autobiography by Susanna Kaysen. A psychiatrist admits a teenager (Winona Ryder) to a psychiatric ward after she attempts suicide. Diagnosed as having borderline personality disorder, she is held forcibly and medicated. She interacts with other patients before being deemed fit for release.

Good Will Hunting
DATE: 1997
DIRECTOR: Gus Van Sant

Psychiatrist Sean McGuire (Robin Williams) counsels Will Hunting (Matt Damon) concerning his abusive childhood. In the process, McGuire unprofessionally reveals details of his life and is physically aggressive toward Hunting.

Grosse Pointe Blank
DATE: 1997
DIRECTOR: George Armitage

Professional hit man Martin Blank (John Cusack) forces his therapist Dr. Oatman (Alan Arkin) into continuing to treat him by threatening to kill his family. Nonetheless, he is hurt by Oatman's reluctance to listen to his problems.

Hannibal
DATE: 2001
DIRECTOR: Ridley Scott

Based on Thomas Harris's 1999 novel, the third one featuring former psychiatrist and cannibal Dr. Hannibal Lecter, now living free in Italy and still killing and eating victims.

Harvey
DATE: 1950
DIRECTOR: Henry Koster

Adapted from Mary C. Chase's Pulitzer Prize-winning play about fantasy versus reality. Veta (Josephine Hull) and her daughter, Myrtle Mae (Victoria Horne), attempt to have Veta's alcoholic brother, Elwood P. Dowd (James Stewart), committed to an asylum because he has an invisible human-size rabbit friend he calls Harvey. Veta admits to Dr. Sanderson (Charles Drake) that she, too, has seen Harvey and is admitted to the Chumley Rest Home. Psychiatrist Dr. Chumley (Cecil Kellaway) intends to help Elwood but instead sees Harvey. Veta decides to prevent Elwood from receiving an injection which would make him stop seeing Harvey because she realizes that Elwood would lose his amiable personality and that Harvey represents sanity.

Heavenly Creatures
DATE: 1994
DIRECTOR: Peter Jackson

New Zealand. Based on a true crime. Two teenage girls, Juliet (Kate Winslet) and Pauline (Melanie Lynskey), form an obsessive friendship based on their mutual creation of a fantasy kingdom. When Juliet's parents decide to move back to England, the two kill Pauline's mother, who they believe is standing in the way of Pauline accompanying her friend.

High Anxiety
DATE: 1977
DIRECTOR: Mel Brooks

Parody of psychiatrist films in general and *Vertigo* in particular, in which Brooks plays a psychiatrist who is the director of the Psycho-Neurotic Institute for the Very, Very Nervous.

L'Histoire d'Adèle H. (*The Story of Adèle H.*)
DATE: 1975
DIRECTOR: François Truffaut

French. Based on the life of the second daughter of French writer Victor Hugo. In 1843, Adèle (Isabelle Adjani) follows a man she believes to be her lover, the English Lieutenant Pinson (Bruce Robinson), to Halifax, Nova Scotia. Spurned by Pinson, she slowly descends into an obsessive madness.

Hombre Mirando al Sudeste (*Man Facing Southeast*)
DATE: 1986
DIRECTOR: Eliseo Subiela

Argentina. A man confined to a mental hospital claims to be an extraterrestrial, causing his psychiatrist to question his treatment.

Ikimono No Kiroku (*I Live in Fear*)
DATE: 1955
DIRECTOR: Akira Kurosawa

Japanese film created for the tenth anniversary of the Hiroshima and Nagasaki atomic bombings. Dentist Dr. Harada (Takashi Shimura) and businessman Kiichi Nakajima (Toshiro Mifune) represent the emotional impact of the atomic bombs on the Japanese. Dr. Harada responds with fear yet is optimistic. Nakajima becomes paranoid, then psychotic, and plans to move to Brazil, where he thinks he will be safe. His family tries to have him declared mentally incompetent. When Nakajima burns his foundry, he is placed in a psychiatric hospital. He believes his padded room is actually a fallout shelter and that Earth is burning from another atomic bomb. His psychiatrist (Nobuo Nakamura) questions whether it is more insane to be afraid of atomic weapons or to accept them.

I Never Promised You a Rose Garden
DATE: 1977
DIRECTOR: Anthony Page

Adapted from Hannah Green's 1964 book about schizophrenia. Psychiatrist Dr. Fried (Bibi Andersson) treats teenaged Deborah (Kathleen Quinlan) in an asylum. Deborah has constructed an elaborate fantasy world, which provided her comfort in her childhood years but which now threatens to overwhelm her and prevent her from facing adulthood.

Is This Goodbye, Charlie Brown?
DATE: 1983
DIRECTOR: Phil Roman

Short animated film in which Snoopy becomes responsible for Lucy's psychiatric booth when she moves out of town with her family.

Jacob's Ladder
DATE: 1990
DIRECTOR: Adrian Lyne

Jacob Singer (Tim Robbins) suffers from post-traumatic stress disorder as he has graphic nightmares and flashbacks about service in the Vietnam War and the death of his son (Macaulay Culkin). He becomes increasingly paranoid when his psychiatrist's car explodes. Aspects of the film suggest that Singer is actually the restless spirit of someone who is dead.

Kings Row
DATE: 1942
DIRECTOR: Sam Wood

Dr. Alexander Tower (Claude Rains) is a psychiatrist in a Midwestern town, where some characters are insane or suffer other mental disorders, including his own daughter Cassandra (Betty Field).

Klute
DATE: 1971
DIRECTOR: Alan J. Pakula

Prostitute Bree (Jane Fonda) sees a therapist, who learns about her weaknesses and strengths.

K-PAX
DATE: 2001
DIRECTOR: Iain Softley

Based on Charles Brewer's 1995 novel. Prot (Kevin Spacey) is a mugging victim who insists he is an alien from the planet K-PAX. Committed to a public mental hospital, Prot becomes the patient of Dr. Mark Powell (Jeff Bridges), who medicates Prot for delusions but then begins to question whether his claims might be true.

Lady in the Dark
DATE: 1944
DIRECTOR: Mitchell Leisen

Adapted from a play written by Moss Hart, influenced by his personal psychoanalysis experience. Magazine editor Liza Elliott (Ginger Rogers) undergoes psychiatric treatment to address her indecisiveness and fears. Psychiatrist Dr. Brooks (Barry Sullivan) helps Elliott understand childhood traumas and her need to dominate men. Dream sequences represent her unconscious.

Life Upside Down (*La Vie à l'envers*)
DATE: 1964
DIRECTOR: Alain Jessua

French. Depicts the alienated estate agent Jacques (Charles Denner), who prefers to live in a mental clinic rather than with his wife, model Viviane

(Anna Gaylor). She attempts suicide as a result of his odd behavior.

Lilith
DATE: 1964
DIRECTOR: Robert Rosen

Based on J. R. Salamanca's 1961 novel. Warren Beatty plays an occupational therapist at a mental hospital for wealthy schizophrenics.

Love Crazy
DATE: 1941
DIRECTOR: Jack Conway

William Powell plays a husband who pretends to be insane to prevent his wife (Myrna Loy) from divorcing him after she finds him with a former girlfriend.

The Madness of King George
DATE: 1994
DIRECTOR: Nicholas Hytner

British; adapted from Alan Bennett's play. This film portrays the period when King George III (Nigel Hawthorne) of England was temporarily insane in 1788. The film suggests that he had an organic psychosis such as intermittent porphyria. The king's supporters ask Dr. Willis (Ian Holm) to apply his expertise in psychological disorders to cure the king.

The Man Who Loved Women
DATE: 1983
DIRECTOR: Blake Edwards

Psychiatrist Marianna (Julie Andrews) relates incidents in the Lothario-esque life of former patient David Fowler (Burt Reynolds) at his funeral.

The Man with Two Brains
DATE: 1983
DIRECTOR: Carl Reiner

Neurosurgeon Dr. Michael Hfuhruhurr (Steve Martin), the inventor of Screw Top, Zip Lock Brain Surgery, marries a gold digger (Kathleen Turner) for her looks but falls in love with the brain—preserved in a jar by mad scientist Dr. Necessiter (David Warner)—of a chubby musician whose thoughts he can hear telepathically.

The Manchurian Candidate
DATE: 1962
DIRECTOR: John Frankenheimer

Based on Richard Condon's 1959 novel. American soldier Raymond Shaw (Laurence Harvey), son of a politically ruthless woman (Angela Lansbury) married to a McCarthyesque senator (John Gregory), is brainwashed by the Chinese during the Korean War to become a sleeper agent/assassin as part of a Communist plot.

Manhunter
DATE: 1986
DIRECTOR: Michael Mann

Adapted from Thomas Harris's 1981 novel *Red Dragon*. This film introduces the character Dr. Hannibal Lecter (Brian Cox), a psychiatrist gone insane who has become a cannibal.

M*A*S*H
DATE: 1970
DIRECTOR: Robert Altman

Based on Richard Hooker's 1968 novel. Korean War surgeons Hawkeye Pierce (Donald Sutherland) and Trapper John MacIntyre (Elliott Gould) cope with what they consider wartime insanity by tormenting unbearable colleagues. They provoke Major Frank Burns (Robert Duvall) to go berserk.

Me, Myself, and Irene
DATE: 2000
DIRECTOR: Bobby Farrelly and Peter Farrelly

An inaccurate portrayal of a mentally ill policeman (Jim Carrey) with two personalities (not schizophrenia, as the film states). Heavily criticized by psychiatric and mental health organizations for its negative images of psychology.

The Mirror Crack'd
DATE: 1981
DIRECTOR: Guy Hamilton

Based on a 1962 Agatha Christie mystery. Marina Rudd (Elizabeth Taylor) is an actress struggling to recover from a nervous breakdown.

Mr. Jones
DATE: 1993
DIRECTOR: Mike Figgis

Psychiatrist Dr. Libbie Bowen (Lena Olin), under the supervision of Dr. Catherine Holland (Anne Bancroft), treats Mr. Jones (Richard Gere), who suffers from bipolar affective disorder. Bowen falls in love with him. This film explores the psychiatrist-patient relationship, the use of the psychotropic drug Haldol, forced hospitalization, and Jones's resistance to accepting that he has a mental illness.

Mumford
DATE: 1999
DIRECTOR: Lawrence Kasdan

Dr. Mickey Mumford (Loren Dean) is a popular psychologist in the community where he has recently moved. His patients are unaware that he is recovering from drug addiction and has assumed a deceased friend's identity. Mumford's psychological methods to treat patients are unusual, and he gradually realizes why most psychologists are professionally educated and trained to practice competently.

Nell
DATE: 1994
DIRECTOR: Michael Apted

Adapted from Mark Handley's 1989 play *Idioglossia*. Nell (Jodie Foster) grew up in complete isolation because her mother was a recluse. When Nell's mother dies, physician Jerome Lovell (Liam Neeson) discovers Nell and is puzzled by her private language. He contacts psychologist Paula Olsen (Natasha Richardson), who assumes Nell is mentally disturbed. Psychiatrist Alexander Paley (Richard Libertini) decides to institutionalize Nell to protect her. Lovell removes Nell from the institution, and she speaks in court to demonstrate that she is mentally competent.

Now, Voyager
DATE: 1942
DIRECTOR: Irving Rapper

Based on Olive Higgins Prouty's 1941 novel. Psychiatrist Dr. Jaquith (Claude Rains) treats repressed Charlotte Vale (Bette Davis). Dr. Jaquith helps Charlotte function normally in the world and find love.

Nuts
DATE: 1987
DIRECTOR: Martin Ritt

Adapted from a play by Tom Topor. After prostitute Claudia Draper (Barbra Streisand) murders her client (Leslie Nielsen) in self-defense, her parents hire attorney Clarence Middleton (William

Prince) to convince the judge that Draper is mentally unfit to stand trial and should remain institutionalized. Middleton resigns when an angry Draper assaults him. Public defender (Richard Dreyfuss) is assigned her case and sides with Draper, arguing that she is competent. Psychiatrist Dr. Herbert A. Morrison (Eli Wallach) also evaluates Draper.

One Flew over the Cuckoo's Nest
DATE: 1975
DIRECTOR: Milos Forman

Adapted from Ken Kesey's 1962 novel. McMurphy (Jack Nicholson) and the inmates of a mental asylum rebel against the institutionalized system. Film graphically portrays shock therapy.

Ordinary People
DATE: 1980
DIRECTOR: Robert Redford

Based on Judith Guest's 1976 novel. Focuses on parents (Donald Sutherland and Mary Tyler Moore) coping with their suicidal son (Timothy Hutton), who feels guilty after he was unable to prevent his brother's drowning. The appealing Dr. Berger (Judd Hirsch) helps the family recover emotionally. Many psychiatrists identified his character as the type of therapist they aspire to be. Won the Academy Award for Best Picture.

Possessed
DATE: 1947
DIRECTOR: Curtis Bernhardt

Through narco-hypnosis, a schizophrenic (Joan Crawford) remembers events that led to her admission to a hospital psychiatric ward.

The Prince of Tides
DATE: 1991
DIRECTOR: Barbra Streisand

Adapted from Pat Conroy's 1986 novel. Dr. Susan Lowenstein (Barbra Streisand) helps Tom Wingo (Nick Nolte) deal with his sister's mental illness.

Prozac Nation
DATE: 2002
DIRECTOR: Erik Skjoldburg

Based on the 1994 memoir by Elizabeth Wurtzel. Dr. Sterling (Anne Heche) treats Wurtzel (Christina Ricci) for depression.

Psycho

DATE: 1960

DIRECTOR: Alfred Hitchcock

Based on a 1959 novel by Robert Bloch. Psychiatrist Dr. Richmond (Simon Oakland) declares Norman Bates (Anthony Perkins) insane after he kills guest Marion Crane (Janet Leigh) and a detective at the Bates Motel and his mother's mummified corpse is found. This film initiated a genre of films about psychotic killers.

Psycho II

DATE: 1983

DIRECTOR: Richard Franklin

In this sequel, psychiatrist Dr. Raymond (Robert Loggia) releases Norman Bates (Anthony Perkins) from the mental institution where he was committed after murdering motel guests. More murders soon occur, and Bates's sanity is uncertain.

Psycho III

DATE: 1983

DIRECTOR: Anthony Perkins

Another sequel which features murderous mayhem at the Bates Motel, where Norman Bates (Anthony Perkins) continues to be mentally unstable.

Psycho IV: The Beginning

DATE: 1990

DIRECTOR: Mick Garris

A made-for-cable film which attempts to explain why Norman Bates (Anthony Perkins) was mentally flawed.

Rain Man

DATE: 1988

DIRECTOR: Barry Levinson

Adapted from Barry Morrow's story. Autistic savant Raymond Babbitt (Dustin Hoffman), who is gifted mathematically, inherits $3 million from his deceased father. Younger brother Charlie Babbitt (Tom Cruise) abducts Raymond from his institution and challenges his guardian, Dr. Bruner (Jerry Molen), for Raymond's custody. Film won an Academy Award for Best Picture.

Random Harvest

DATE: 1942

DIRECTOR: Mervyn LeRoy

Based on a 1941 novel by James Hilton. World War I army officer Charles Rainier (Ronald Colman) has amnesia due to shell shock and is institutionalized. He escapes and marries Paula (Greer Garson). When Charles is in a car accident, he regains his memory but forgets his wife. She works as his secretary, and he eventually remembers that they are married.

Repulsion

DATE: 1965

DIRECTOR: Roman Polanski

Carol Ledoux (Catherine Deneuve) is a paranoid schizophrenic who kills men who try to befriend her.

Return to Oz

DATE: 1985

DIRECTOR: Walter Murch

Dorothy Gale (Fairuza Balk) is admitted to a mental hospital, where her Aunt Em (Piper Laurie) believes electric shock therapy administered by Dr. J. B. Worley (Nicol Williamson) will stop the girl's claims to have visited a fantasy land.

sex, lies, and videotape

DATE: 1989

DIRECTOR: Steven Soderbergh

Ann Millaney (Andie MacDowell) confides her feelings about sex and her unhappy marriage to her therapist (Ron Vawter).

The Shining

DATE: 1980

DIRECTOR: Stanley Kubrick

Based on Stephen King's 1977 novel. Jack Torrance (Jack Nicholson) becomes insane when his family is snowed in at the Overlook, a huge, isolated hotel where he works as the winter custodian. He had been told that a former caretaker had a nervous breakdown and murdered his family.

The Silence of the Lambs

DATE: 1991

DIRECTOR: Jonathan Demme

Based on Thomas Harris's 1988 novel. Held in a maximum security mental institution, cannibal and former psychiatrist Dr. Hannibal Lecter (Anthony Hopkins) antagonizes FBI agent Clarice Starling (Jodie Foster) as she pursues a serial killer.

The Sixth Sense
DATE: 1999
DIRECTOR: M. Night Shyamalan
Child psychologist Malcolm Crowe (Bruce Willis) helps Cole Sear (Haley Joel Osment) comprehend his visions of ghosts seeking his help.

Slingblade
DATE: 1996
DIRECTOR: Billy Bob Thornton
Karl Childers (Billy Bob Thornton) is released from a mental hospital for criminals and has difficulty adjusting when he returns home.

The Snake Pit
DATE: 1948
DIRECTOR: Anatole Litvak
Adapted from Mary Jane Ward's 1946 novel. Virginia Cunningham (Olivia de Havilland) plays a woman committed for insanity. Her psychiatrist Dr. Mark Kick (Leo Gunn) is resolved to cure her despite her recurrent breakdowns.

Spellbound
DATE: 1945
DIRECTOR: Alfred Hitchcock
Adapted from Hilary Aidan St. George Saunders's 1927 psychological mystery *The House of Dr. Edwardes*. When amnesiac J. B. (Gregory Peck) thinks he has committed a murder that he cannot remember, psychiatrist Dr. Constance (Ingrid Bergman) tries to exonerate him.

Sybil
DATE: 1976
DIRECTOR: Daniel Petrie
Made-for-television film in which a psychiatrist (Joanne Woodward) treats Sybil (Sally Field), who has seventeen personalities as a result of a childhood trauma.

Three Faces of Eve
DATE: 1957
DIRECTOR: Nunnally Johnson
Adapted from psychiatrists Corbett H. Thigpen and Hervey M. Cleckley's 1957 book based on a case study. Joanne Woodward won an Oscar for portraying a woman with three distinct personalities. The film depicts hypnosis during therapy sessions.

Through a Glass Darkly (*Sasom i en Spegel*)
DATE: 1961
DIRECTOR: Ingmar Bergman
Swedish film that begins a trilogy. Schizophrenic Karin (Harriet Andersson) breaks down mentally while on vacation. She realizes that she must be hospitalized but pleads not to be medicated with anything that might worsen her hallucinations.

The Vanishing
DATE: 1988
DIRECTOR: George Sluizer
Dutch. A sociopath (Bernard Pierre Donnadieu) taunts, then ensnares Rex (Gene Bervoets), who is obsessed by learning what happened to his girlfriend who disappeared.

Vertigo
DATE: 1958
DIRECTOR: Alfred Hitchcock
An acrophobic San Francisco detective (James Stewart) must cope with his phobia as he trails a woman (Kim Novak) in a very complicated plot.

The Virgin Suicides
DATE: 1999
DIRECTOR: Sofia Coppola
The five Lisbon sisters commit suicide, and psychiatrist Dr. Horniker (Danny DeVito) attempts to comprehend why. Their parents (James Woods and Kathleen Turner) are rigidly religious and did not allow the girls to interact in normal social situations as they matured.

What About Bob?
DATE: 1991
DIRECTOR: Frank Oz
Bob Wiley (Bill Murray) follows his narcissistic psychiatrist Dr. Leo Marvin (Richard Dreyfuss) on vacation, annoying him and befriending his family.

What's New, Pussycat?
DATE: 1965
DIRECTOR: Clive Donner
Written by Woody Allen. Incorrigible womanizer Michael James (Peter O'Toole) sees Viennese psy-

chiatrist Dr. Fritz Fassbender (Peter Sellers) to help him commit to one girlfriend.

When the Clouds Roll By
DATE: 1919
DIRECTOR: Victor Fleming

Silent. Dr. Ulrich Metz (Herbert Grimwood) is a psychiatrist—actually an escaped mental patient—who tries to cause Daniel Boone Brown (Douglas Fairbanks) to commit suicide.

Zelig
DATE: 1983
DIRECTOR: Woody Allen

In a film that is presented to resemble a 1920's documentary, psychiatrist Dr. Eudora Fletcher (Mia Farrow) helps hospital patient Leonard Zelig (Woody Allen) realize that he suffered identity crises throughout his childhood which resulted in him lacking a personality and mirroring the people whom he meets. Dr. Fletcher hypnotizes him in what are called the White Room Sessions, and his own personality emerges.

TELEVISION
Ally McBeal
DATE: 1997-2002

In this comedic drama, neurotic lawyer Ally Mc-Beal (Calista Flockhart) sees a therapist (Tracey Ullman) who is humorous but unprofessional, controlling, and mentally imbalanced.

The Bob Newhart Show
DATE: 1972-1978

In this situation comedy, Bob Hartley (Bob Newhart) is a Chicago psychologist who counsels patients individually and in group therapy. Patients seek help for phobias, depression, and neuroses. Elliot Carlin is a recurring character with a persecution complex. Hartley is more competent at handling his patients' problems than his own relationships.

Buffy the Vampire Slayer
DATE: 1997-

In one plotline of this tongue-in-cheek drama, Professor Maggie Walsh (Lindsey Crouse), Buffy's (Sarah Michelle Gellar) psychology teacher and an expert in operant conditioning, is revealed as the evil mastermind of a secret military force, the Initia-tive. The Initiative captures vampire Spike (James Marsters) and implants a chip in his brain, preventing him from harming any living creature. Subsequent seasons show Spike's behavior continually being modified by the implant. In the episode "Normal Again," Buffy is infected with a demon poison causing her to believe that her town is a hallucination and that she is a schizophrenic in a mental hospital.

Cheers
DATE: 1982-1993

This situation comedy includes characters Dr. Frasier Crane (Kelsey Grammer) and his wife Dr. Lilith Sternin Crane (Bebe Neuwirth). The uptight psychiatrists provide comic relief through their elitist and pretentious reactions to the problems of their acquaintances at a Boston bar.

Cracker
DATE: 1993-1996

In this British drama, Eddie "Fitz" Fitzgerald (Robbie Coltrane) is a criminal psychologist who works as a profiler. He is also a compulsive gambler and drinker. Psychologist Ian Stephen was a show consultant.

Days of Our Lives
DATE: 1965-

In this soap opera, leading character Dr. Marlena Evans (Deidre Hall) is pivotal to plots. Her office is often the scene of therapy sessions with other characters. Psychiatrist Dr. Laura Horton also is a recurring character.

Dr. Katz, Professional Therapist
DATE: 1995-1999

This animated comedy explores the world from the perspective of a psychiatrist.

ER
DATE: 1994-

This hospital drama often features psychiatric consultations by such characters as Dr. Kim Legaspi (Elizabeth Mitchell). Sally Field guest starred as Maggie Wycenski, the bipolar mother of nurse Abby Lockhart (Maura Tierney).

Felicity
DATE: 1998-2002

In this drama, college student Felicity (Keri Russell) undergoes counseling with Dr. Toni Pavone (Amy Aquino), who helps her cope with her parents' divorce. Other characters are in therapy and take antidepressants. Felicity's roommate, Meghan (Amanda Foreman), aspires to become a psychiatrist.

Frasier
DATE: 1993-

A spinoff of *Cheers.* Dr. Frasier Crane (Kelsey Grammer) is the host of a Seattle radio talk show which promotes "good mental health." His brother, Dr. Niles Crane (David Hyde Pierce), has a private psychiatric practice. The brothers' psychiatric interests, insecurities, and misunderstandings are the basis of most plots.

Friends
DATE: 1993-

In one episode of this ensemble comedy, actor Joey Tribbiani (Matt LeBlanc) plays Sigmund Freud in a musical titled *Freud!*

Futurama
DATE: 1999-2002

In one episode of this animated comedy, Bender and Fry are committed to a robot asylum after being falsely accused of robbing a bank and declared insane.

Good Advice
DATE: 1993

In this situation comedy, Susan DeRuzza (Shelley Long) good-naturedly attempts to help patients while experiencing chaos in her own life.

I'll Fly Away
DATE: 1991-1993

Set in a small Georgia town between 1958 to 1960, this drama features local district attorney Forrest Bedford (Sam Waterston), whose wife Gwen Bedford (Deborah Hedwall) is mentally ill and a resident of a private hospital outside of town.

King of the Hill
DATE: 1997-

In an episode of this animated comedy called "Naked Ambition," Boomhauer is mistakenly admitted to a Dallas state mental hospital. Friends Dale and Bill also are admitted when they attempt to have Boomhauer released. Hank Hill rescues everyone except Bill, a mentally troubled man who finds group therapy comforting.

Law and Order
DATE: 1990-

This dramatic series chronicles the efforts of the police and legal systems to bring criminals to justice. The characters often seek out the advice of police psychiatrists Dr. Elizabeth Olivet (Carolyn McCormick) or Dr. Emil Skoda (J. K. Simmons).

Mad About You
DATE: 1992-1999

The main characters in this situation comedy, Paul Buchman (Paul Reiser) and his wife Jamie (Helen Hunt), undergo therapy with Sheila (Mo Gaffney), who first appears in the episode "Therapy." Other episodes depict the Buchmans confronting Sheila about her steep therapy fees and searching for more affordable therapists.

Malcolm in the Middle
2000-

In this situation comedy, Andy Richter plays a psychiatrist who is asked to determine why the three brothers are so destructive. The brothers also see a school therapist in an attempt to avoid unappealing school activities.

M*A*S*H
DATE: 1972-1983

This wartime comedy based on the 1970 film features the supporting character of Corporal Klinger (Jamie Farr), who dresses in women's clothing in hopes of receiving a Section 8 discharge for insanity. The "Dear Sigmund" episode focuses on a visiting psychologist who comforts the characters and is amused by Klinger's efforts.

My Living Doll
DATE: 1964-1965

In this situation comedy, Bob Cummings plays Dr. Robert McDonald, a psychiatrist who finds himself in control of an attractive female robot.

Once and Again
DATE: 2000-2002

Edward Zwick plays a psychiatrist who helps teenaged Jessie (Evan Rachel Wood) with an eating disorder in this family drama.

Party of Five
DATE: 1994-2000

In this dramatic series, an education student, Kirsten Bennett (Paula Devicq) suffers depression and a nervous breakdown after her fiancé cancels their wedding and she is accused of plagiarizing her doctoral dissertation. She stabilizes with medication and later works as a children's counselor.

Profiler
DATE: 1996-2000

Dr. Sam Walters (Ally Walker) is a forensic psychologist for the Violent Crimes Task Force in this drama.

Seinfeld
DATE: 1990-1998

One plotline in this situation comedy has the psychiatrist of Elaine Benes (Julia-Louis Dreyfus), Dr. Reston (Stephen McHattie), fall in love with her.

Seventh Heaven
DATE: 1996-

Reverend Eric Camden (Stephen Collins) is a minister who counsels congregation and community members in this family drama. Episode themes often address mental health issues such as depression, suicide, abuse, and alcoholism.

The Simpsons
DATE: 1989-

In an episode of this animated comedy called "There's No Disgrace Like Home," the Simpson family participates in shock therapy with Dr. Marvin Monroe. In another episode, "Stark Raving Dad," Homer Simpson is placed in a mental institution with a man who claims he is singer Michael Jackson.

Sisters
DATE: 1991-1996

One of the sisters in this dramatic series, Georgie Reed (Patricia Kalember), is seduced by her therapist, Dr. Caspian (Daniel Gerroll), who takes her to a psychiatric conference and suggests that she was molested. She files ethics charges against him with the medical licensing board.

The Sopranos
DATE: 1999-

In this dramatic series, Mafia hitman Tony Soprano (James Gandolfini) is in therapy with Dr. Jennifer Melfi (Lorraine Bracco), who urges him to keep a journal.

thirtysomething
DATE: 1987-1991

Most of the characters undergo therapy at some point in this dramatic series. The episode "Therapy" features Elliott (Timothy Busfield) and his wife Nancy (Patricia Wettig) in marriage counseling.

Elizabeth D. Schafer

ORGANIZATIONS AND SUPPORT GROUPS

Organizations

- NORTH AMERICAN ORGANIZATIONS

American Psychiatric Association
1400 K Street, NW
Washington, DC 20005
Phone: (888) 357-7924
Fax: (202) 682-6850
E-mail: apa@psych.org
http://www.psych.org

American Psychoanalytic Association
309 East 49th Street
New York, NY 10017
Phone: (212) 752-0450
Fax: (212) 593-0571
E-mail: central.office@apsa.org
http://www.apsa.org

American Psychological Association
750 First Street, NE
Washington, DC 20002-4242
Phone: (202) 336-5500 or (800) 374-2721
TDD/TTY: (202) 336-6123
http://www.apa.org

American Psychological Society
1010 Vermont Avenue, NW
Suite 1100
Washington, DC 20005
Phone: (202) 783-2077
http://www.psychologicalscience.org

Canadian Mental Health Association
2160 Yonge Street, 3d Floor
Toronto, Ontario M4S 2Z3 Canada
Phone: (416) 484-7750
Fax: (416) 484-4617
http://www.cmha.ca

Canadian Psychiatric Association
237 Argyle Avenue
Suite 200
Ottawa, Ontario K2P1B8 Canada
Phone: (613) 234-2815

Canadian Psychological Association
151 Slater Street
Suite 205
Ottawa, Ontario K1P 5H3 Canada
Phone: 1 (888) 472-0657
E-mail: cpamemb@cpa.ca

National Mental Health Association
1021 Prince Street
Alexandria, VA 22314-2971
Mental Health Information Center: (800) 969-
  NMHA (6642)
Phone: (703) 684-7722
TTY Line: (800) 433-5959
Fax: (703) 684-5968
http://www.nmha.org

- SPECIALTIES

Academy for the Study of the Psychoanalytic Arts
31805 Middlebelt Road
Suite 305
Farmington Hills, MI 48334
Phone: (248) 626-6460
E-mail: AcademyAnalyticArts@yahoo.com
http://www.AcademyAnalyticArts.org

Academy of Organizational and Occupational Psychiatry
717 Princess Street
Alexandria, VA 22314
Phone: (877) 789-2667
Fax: (877) 789-6050

E-mail: staff@aoop.org
http://www.aoop.org

Academy of Psychosomatic Medicine
5824 North Magnolia
Chicago, IL 60660
Phone: (773) 784-2025
Fax: (773) 784-1304
E-mail: APsychMed@aol.com
http://www.apm.org

American Academy of Addiction Psychiatry
7301 Mission Road
Suite 252
Prairie Village, KS 66208
Phone: (913) 262-6161
Fax: (913) 262-4311
E-mail: info@aaap.org
http://www.aaap.org

American Academy of Child and Adolescent Psychiatry
3615 Wisconsin Avenue, NW
Washington, DC 20016-3007
Phone: (202) 966-7300
Fax: (202) 966-2891
http://www.aacap.org

American Academy of Clinical Psychiatrists
P.O. Box 458
Glastonbury, CT 06033
Phone: (860) 633-5045
Fax: (860) 633-6023
E-mail: info@aacp.com
http://www.aacp.com

American Academy of Neurology
1080 Montreal Avenue
St. Paul, MN 55116
Phone: (651) 695-1940
http://www.aan.com

American Academy of Psychiatry and the Law
One Regency Drive
P.O. Box 30
Bloomfield, CT 06002
Phone: (860) 242-5450
Phone: (800) 331-1389
Fax: (860) 286-0787

E-mail: office@aapl.org
http://www.emory.edu/APPL

American Academy of Psychoanalysis
One Regency Drive
P.O. Box 30
Bloomfield, CT 06002
Phone: (888) 691-8281
Fax: (860) 286-0787
E-mail: AAP@ssmgt.com
http://www.aapsa.org

American Academy of Psychotherapists
P.O. Box 1611
New Bern, NC 28563
Phone: (252) 634-3066
Fax: (252) 634-3067
E-mail: aapoffice@coastalnet.com
http://www.coe.iup.edu/aap/main.html

American Art Therapy Association
1202 Allanson Road
Mundelein, IL 60060-3808
Phone: (847) 949-6064 or (888) 290-0878
Fax: (847) 566-4580
E-mail: info@arttherapy.org
http://www.arttherapy.org

American Association for Emergency Psychiatry
15731 NE 105th Court
Redmond, WA 98052-2640
Phone: (425) 556-5430
    (888) 945-5430, membership inquiries
Fax: (425) 556-5420
E-mail: aaep@emergencypsychiatry.org
http://www.emergencypsychiatry.org

American Association for Geriatric Psychiatry
7910 Woodmont Avenue
Suite 1350
Bethesda, MD 20814-3004
Phone: (301) 654-7850
Fax: (301) 654-4137
E-mail: main@aagpgpa.org
http://www.aagpgpa.org

American Association for Marriage and Family Therapy
1133 15th Street, NW
Suite 300

Washington, DC 20005-2710
Phone: (202) 452-0109
Fax: (202) 223-2329
E-mail: Central@aamft.org
http://www.aamft.org

American Association of Children's Residential Centers
51 Monroe Place
Suite 1603
Rockville, MD 20850
Phone: (301) 738-6460
E-mail: info@aacrc-dc.org
http://www.aacrc-dc.org

American Association of Community Psychiatrists
c/o Frances M. Roton
P.O. Box 570218
Dallas, TX 75228-0218
Phone: (972) 686-5227
Fax: (972) 613-5532
E-mail: frdal@airmail.net
http://communitypsychiatry.org

American Association of Directors of Psychiatric Residency Training
Department of Psychiatry
University of Connecticut
10 Talcott Notch Road, East Wing
Farmington, CT 06030-6410
Phone: (860) 679-6766
Fax: (860) 679-6675
E-mail: aadprt@psychiatry.uchc.edu

American Association of General Hospital Psychiatrists
330 Mount Auburn Street
Cambridge, MA 02238
Phone: (617) 499-5008

American Association of Pastoral Counselors
9504A Lee Highway
Fairfax, VA 22031-2303
Phone: (703) 385-6967
Fax: (703) 352-7725
E-mail: info@aapc.org
http://www.aapc.org

American Association of Psychiatric Administrators
P.O. Box 570218
Dallas, TX 75357-0218
Phone: (800) 650-5888
Fax: (972) 613-5532
E-mail: frdal@airmail.net
http://www.psychiatricadministrators.org

American Association of Suicidology
4201 Connecticut Avenue, NW
Suite 408
Washington, DC 20008
Phone: (202) 237-2280
1-800-SUICIDE
Fax: (202) 237-2282
E-mail: ajkulp@suicidology.org
http://www.suicidology.org

American Board of Psychiatry and Neurology, Inc.
500 Lake Cook Road
Suite 335
Deerfield,IL 60015
Phone: (847) 945-7900
http://www.abpn.com

American College of Forensic Psychiatry
P.O. Box 5870
Balboa Island, CA 92662
Phone: (949) 673-7773
Fax: (949) 673-7710
http://www.forensicpsychonline.com

American College of Neuropsychopharmacology
320 Centre Bldg
2014 Broadway
Nashville, TN 37203
Phone: (615) 322-2075
Fax: (615) 343-0662
E-mail: acnp@acnp.org
http://www.acnp.org

American College of Psychiatrists
732 Addison Street
Suite B
Berkeley, CA 94710
Phone: (510) 704-8020
Fax: (510) 704-0113
http://www.acpsych.org

American Counseling Association
5999 Stevenson Ave
Alexandria, VA 22304
Phone: (703) 823-9800 or (703) 823-0252
http://www.counseling.org

American Group Psychotherapy Association
25 East 21st Street, 6th Floor
New York, NY 10010
Phone: (212) 477-2677 or (877) 668-2472
Fax: (212) 979-6627
E-mail: info@agpa.org
http://www.agpa.org

American Horticultural Therapy Association
909 York Street
Denver, CO 80206
Phone: (303) 370-8087
Fax: (303) 331-5776
E-mail: ahtaadmin@earthlink.net
http://www.ahta.org

American Mental Health Counselors Association
801 North Fairfax Street
Suite 304
Alexandria, VA 22314
Phone: (703) 548-6002 or (800) 326-2642
Fax: (703) 548-4775
http://www.amhca.org

American Neurological Association
5841 Cedar Lake Road
Suite 204
Minneapolis, MN 55416
Phone: (952) 545-6284
Fax: (952) 545-6073
http://www.aneuroa.org

American Orthopsychiatric Association
330 7th Avenue, 18th Floor
New York, NY 10001
Phone: (212) 564-5930
http://www.amerortho.org

American Psychiatric Nurses Association
Colonial Place Three
2107 Wilson Blvd
Suite 300-A
Arlington, VA 22201
Phone: (703) 243-2443

Fax: (703) 243-3390
http://www.apna.org

American Psychopathological Association
1051 Riverside Drive, Unit 14
New York, NY 10032
Phone: (212) 543-5880
http://www.appassn.org

American Psychosomatic Society
6728 Old McLean Village Drive
McLean, VA 22101-3906
Phone: (703) 556-9222
Fax: (703) 556-8729
E-mail: info@psychosomatic.org
http://www.psychosomatic.org

American Psychotherapy Association, Inc.
Association Headquarters
2750 East Sunshine
Springfield, MO 65804
Phone: 417-823-0173
Fax: 417-823-9959
E-Mail: member@americanpsychotherapy.com
http://www.americanpsychotherapy.com

American Society for Adolescent Psychiatry
P.O. Box 570218
Dallas, TX 75357-0218
Phone: (888) 877-4311

American Society of Addiction Medicine
4601 N Park Avenue, Arcade Suite 101
Chevy Chase, MD 20815
Phone: (301) 656-3920
Fax: (301) 656-3815
E-mail: email@asam.org
http://www.asam.org

American Society of Clinical Psychopharmacology, Inc.
P.O. Box 2257
New York, NY 10116
Phone: (212) 268-4260
Fax: (212) 268-4434
http://www.ascpp.org

American Society of Consultant Pharmacists
1321 Duke Street
Alexandria, VA 22314

Phone: (703) 739-1300 or (800) 355-2727
Fax: (703) 739-1321 or (800) 220-1321
E-mail: info@ascp.com
http://www.ascp.com

American Society of Group Psychotherapy and Psychodrama
301 N. Harrison Street
Suite 508
Princeton, NJ 08540
Phone: (609) 452-1339
Fax: (609) 936-1659
E-mail: asgpp@asgpp.org
http://www.asgpp.org

American Society of Psychoanalytic Physicians
Janice S. Wright, Executive Director
4804 Jasmine Drive
Rockville, MD 20853
Phone: (301) 929-1470
http://pubweb.acns.nwu.edu/~chessick/aspp.htm

American Society on Aging
833 Market Street
Suite 511
San Francisco, CA 94103-1824
Phone: (415) 974-9600
E-mail: info@asaging.org
http://www.asaging.org

Animal Behavior Society
Indiana University
2611 East 10th Street #170
Bloomington IN 47408-2603
Phone: 812-856-5541
Fax : 812-856-5542
E-mail: aboffice@indiana.edu
http://www.animalbehavior.org

Assisted Living Federation of America
11200 Waples Mill Road
Suite 150
Fairfax, VA 22030
Phone: (703) 691-8100
Fax: (703) 691-8106
E-mail: info@alfa.org
http://www.alfa.org

Association for Academic Psychiatry
Suite 4200

725 Concord Avenue
Cambridge, MA 02138
Phone: (617) 661-3544
Fax: (617) 661-4800
http://www.hsc.wvu.edu/aap/home.htm

Association for Advancement of Behavior Therapy
305 Seventh Avenue, 16th Floor
New York, NY 10001-60008
Phone: (212) 647-1890
Fax: (212) 647-1865
http://www.aabt.org

Association for Ambulatory Behavioral Healthcare
2301 Mount Vernon Avenue
Suite 100
Alexandria, VA 22301
Phone: (703) 836-2274
Fax: (703) 836-0083
E-mail: aabh@aabh.org
http://www.aabh.org

Association for Behavior Analysis
213 West Hall
Western Michigan University
1903 West Michigan Ave
Kalamazoo, MI 49008-5301
Phone: (616) 387-8341 or (616)387-8342
Fax: (616) 387-8354
E-mail: 76236.1312@compuserve.com
http://www.wmich.edu/aba

Association for Death Education and Counseling
342 North Main Street
West Hartford, CT 06117-2507
Phone: (860) 586-7503
Fax: (860) 586-7550
E-mail: info@adec.org

Association for Humanistic Psychology
1516 Oak St, #320A
Alameda, CA 94501-2947
Phone: (510) 769-6495
E-mail: ahpoffice@aol.com

Association of Behavioral Group Practices
325 Seventh Street, NW
Suite 625
Washington, DC 20004-2802

Phone: (202) 393-6700
Fax: (202) 783-6041
E-mail: naphs@naphs.org
http://www.naphs.org

Association of Black Psychologists
P.O. Box 55999
Washington, DC 20040-5999
Phone: (202) 722-0808
E-mail: Admin@ABPsi.org
http://www.abpsi.org

Association of Prenatal and Perinatal Psychology and Health
340 Colony Road
Geyserville, CA 95441
Phone: (707) 857-4041
Fax: 707-857-4042
E-mail: apppah@aol.com
http://www.birthpsychology.com

Association of Women Psychiatrists
P.O. Box 28218
Dallas, TX 75228
Phone: (972) 686-6522
E-mail: info@womenpsych.org
http://www.womenpsych.org

Child Neurology Society
1000 West County Road E
Suite 290
Saint Paul, MN 55126
Phone: (651) 486-9447
Fax: (651) 486-9436
E-mail: nationaloffice@childneurologysociety.org
http://www.childneurologysociety.org

Child Welfare League of America
440 First Street, NW, 3d Floor
Washington, DC 20001-2085
Phone: (202) 638-2952
Fax: (202) 638-4004
http://www.cwla.org

Children's Hospice International
901 North Pitt Street
Suite 230
Alexandria, VA 22314
Phone: (703) 684-0330 or (800) 2-4-CHILD
Fax: (703) 684-0226

E-mail: chiorg@aol.com
http://www.chionline.org

Coalition for Marriage, Family and Couples Education
5310 Belt Road NW
Washington, DC 20015-1961
Phone: (202) 362-3332
E-mail: Diane@smartmarriages.com
http://www.smartmarriages.com

Cognitive Neuroscience Society
Center for Cognitive Neuroscience
Box 90999
Duke University
Durham, NC 27708
Phone: (978) 749-0021
Fax: (978) 749-0025
http://www.cogneurosociety.org

Drug Information Association
501 Office Center Drive
Suite 450
Fort Washington, PA 19034-3211
Phone: (215) 628-2288
Fax: (215) 641-1229
E-mail: dia@diahome.org
http://www.diahome.org

EEG and Clinical Neuroscience Society (ECNS)
Brain Research Laboratories
New York University
550 First Avenue
New York, NY 10016
Phone: (212) 263-6288 or (888)-366-2203
Fax: (212) 263-6457

Federation of Families for Children's Mental Health
1101 King Street
Suite 420
Alexandria, VA 22314
Phone: (703) 684-7710
Fax: (703) 836-1040
E-mail: ffcmh@ffcmh.org
http://www.ffcmh.org

International Psychogeriatric Association
550 Frontage Road
Suite 2820

Northfield, IL 60093
Phone: (847) 784-1701
Fax: (847) 784-1705
E-mail: ipa@ipa-online.org
http://www.ipa-online.org/ipaonline/default.htm

International Society for Mental Health Online
E-mail: ismho@ismho.org
http://www.ismho.org

International Society for the Study of Dissociation
60 Revere Drive
Suite 500
Northbrook, IL 60062
Phone: (847) 480-0899
Fax: (847) 480-9282
E-mail: issd@issd.org
http://www.issd.org

International Society of Traumatic Stress Studies
60 Revere Drive
Suite 500
Northbrook, IL 60062
Phone: (847) 480-9028
Fax: (847) 480-9282
E-mail: istss@istss.org
http://www.istss.org

Jean Piaget Society (JPS)
Main Office: Kurt Fischer, Archivist, Jean Piaget Society
Department of Human Development
Graduate School of Education
Larsen Hall
Harvard University
Cambridge, MA 02138 (USA)
http://www.piaget.org

Justice in Mental Health Organization, Inc.
421 Seymour Street
Lansing, MI 48933
Phone: (517) 371-2266
http://members.aol.com/jimhofw/jimho.htm

National Association for Home Care
228 7th Street SE
Washington, DC 20003
Phone: (202) 547-7424
http://www.nahc.org

National Association for Human Development
1424 16th Street NW
Suite 101
Washington, DC 20036-2211
Phone: (202) 328-2191

National Association of Cognitive-Behavioral Therapists
P.O. Box 2195
Weirton, WV 26062
Phone: (800) 853-1135
Fax: (304) 723-3982
E-mail: nacbt@nacbt.org
http://www.nacbt.org

National Association of Psychiatric Health Systems
325 Seventh Street, NW
Suite 625
Washington, DC 20004-2802
Phone: (202) 393-6700
Fax: (202) 783-6041
E-mail: naphs@naphs.org
http://www.naphs.org

National Association of Psychiatric Treatment Centers for Children
1025 Connecticut Avenue, NW
Suite 1012
Washington, DC 20036
Phone: (202) 857-9735
Fax: (202) 362-5145
E-mail: naptcc@aol.com

National Association of School Psychologists
4340 East West Highway Suite #402
Bethesda, MD 20814
Phone: (301) 657-0270
Fax: (301) 657-0275
TDD: (301) 657-4155
http://www.nasponline.org

National Association of Social Workers
750 First Street NE
Suite 700
Washington, DC 20002-4241
Phone: (202) 408-8600 or (800) 638-8799
http://www.naswdc.org

**National Association of State Mental Health
    Program Directors**
66 Canal Center Plaza
Suite 302
Alexandria, VA 22314-1591
Phone: (703) 739-9333
Fax: (703) 548-9517
http://www.nasmhpd.org

**National Council for Community Behavioral
    Healthcare**
12300 Twinbrook Parkway
Suite 320
Rockville, MD 20852
Phone: (301) 984-6200
Fax: (301) 881-7159
http://www.nccbh.org

**National Federation of Societies for Clinical
    Social Work, Inc.**
P.O. Box 3740
Arlington, VA 22201
Phone: (703) 522-3866
Helpline: (800) 270-9739
E-mail: nfscswlo@aol.com
http://www.webcom.com/nfscsw

National Hospice and Palliative Care Organization
1700 Diagonal Road
Suite 625
Alexandria, VA 22314
Phone: (703) 837-1500
Fax: (703) 837-1233
E-mail: info@nhpco.org
http://www.nhpco.org

**National Psychological Association for
    Psychoanalysis, Inc.**
150 West 13th Street
New York, NY 10011-7891
Phone: (212) 924-7440
Fax: (212) 989-7543
E-mail: info@npap.org
http://www.npap.org

**Psi Beta National Honor Society in Psychology
    for Community and Junior Colleges**
1027 Westbridge Lane
Chattanooga, TN 37405
http://www.psibeta.org

**Psi Chi, The National Honor Society in
    Psychology**
825 Vine Street
P.O. Box 709
Chattanooga, TN 37401-0709
Phone: (423) 756-2044
Fax: (877) 774-2443
E-mail: psichi@psichi.org
http://www.psichi.org

Psychiatric Society for Informatics
5962 Whittaker Road
Ypsilanti, MI 48197
Phone: (734) 485-7513
E-mail: ann@psychinoformatics.org
http://psychinoformatics.org

**Psychologists for the Ethical Treatment of
    Animals**
P.O. Box 1297
Washington Grove, MD 20880-1297
Phone/Fax: 301-963-4751
http:// www.psyeta.org

Psychonomic Society
1710 Fortview Road
Austin, TX 78704
Phone: (512) 462-2442
Fax: (512) 462-1101

Reversal Theory Society
Midwest Research Institute
425 Volker Boulevard
Kansas City, MO 64110

**Society for Chaos Theory in Psychology and Life
    Sciences**
Kevin Dooley, President
Arizona State University
Department of Industrial Engineering
P.O. Box 875906
Tempe, AZ 85287-5906
http://www.societyforchaostheory.org

Society for Computers in Psychology
Western College Program
Miami University
Oxford, OH 45056
Phone: (513) 529-5670
Fax: (513) 529-5849

Society for Consumer Psychology
Dr. Larry D. Compeau, Executive Officer
Clarkson University School of Business
Box 5795
Potsdam, NY 13699
Fax: 315-268-3810
E-mail: scp@clarkson.edu

**Society for Development and Behavioral
  Pediatrics**
19 Station Lane
Philadelphia, PA 19118-2939
Phone: (215) 248-9168
http://www.dbpeds.org

Society for Disability Studies
Carol J. Gill, Ph.D., Executive Officer
Department of Disability and Human
  Development
University of Illinois at Chicago (MC 626)
1640 W. Roosevelt Road #236
Chicago, IL 60608-6904
Phone: 312-996-4664 (V/TTY)
Fax: 312-996-7743

**Society for Gestalt Theory and Its Applications
  (GTA)**
c/o Dipl.Psych. Michael Ruh
Klause 26, D-35066 Frankenberg, Germany
Phone: (+49) 6451-716700
Fax: (+49) 6451-718556
E-Mail: gestalttheorie.gta@t-online.de

Society for Judgment and Decision Making
membership information:
Sandra Schneider/JDM
Department of Psychology, BEH 339
University of South Florida
4202 E. Fowler Avenue
Tampa, FL 33620-8200
http://www.sjdm.org

Society for Mathematical Psychology
Dr. Thaddeus Cowan
Department of Psychology
Bluemont Hall
Kansas State University
Mannhattan, KS 66506
E-mail: tmcowan@ksu.edu
http://aris.ss.uci.edu/smp

Society for Neuroscience
11 Dupont Circle, NW
Suite 500
Washington, DC 20036
Phone: (202) 462-6688
Fax: (202) 462-9740
E-mail: info@sfn.org
http://www.sfn.org

**Society for Personality and Social Psychology
  (SPSP)**
Department of Psychology
University of Rochester
Rochester, NY 14627
http://www.spsp.org

Society for Psychophysiological Research
1010 Vermont Avenue, NW
Suite 1100
Washington, DC 20005-4907
Phone: (202) 393-4810
Fax: (202) 783-2083
E-mail: spr@aps.washington.dc.us
http://liberty.uc.wlu.edu/~spr

**Society for Research in Child Development
  (SRCD)**
University of Michigan
505 E. Huron
Suite 301
Ann Arbor, MI 48104-1567
Phone: (734) 998-6578
Fax: (734) 998-6569
E-mail: srcd@umich.edu
http://www.srcd.org

**Society for the Psychological Study of Social
  Issues (SPSSI)**
SPSSI Central Office
1901 Pennsylvania Avenue NW
Suite 901
Washington, DC 20006-3405
Phone: (202) 223-5100
Fax: (202) 223-5555
http://www.spssi.org

Society of Behavioral Medicine
7600 Terrace Avenue
Suite 203
Middleton, WI 53562

Phone: (608) 827-7267
Fax: (608) 831-5485
E-Mail: sbm@tmahq.com
http://www.sbm.org

Society of Biological Psychiatry
C/O May Clinic Jacksonville
4500 San Pablo Road
Research-Birdsall 310
Jacksonville, FL 32224
Phone: (904) 953-2842
http://www.sobp.org

Society of Psychologists in Management (SPIM)
Lorraine Rieff
Lorraine Rieff and Associates
SPIM Administrative Officer
318 South Halsted Street
Chicago, IL 60661
Phone: (312) 655-1150
Fax: (312) 655-1152
E-mail: Lrieff@naii.org
http://www.spim.org

Sufi Psychology Association
P.O. Box 2221
Davis, CA 95617-2221
http://sufi-psychology.org

• **International Organizations**

Australian Psychological Society, Ltd.
P.O. Box 38
Flinders Lane Post Office
Melbourne VIC 8009 Australia
http://www.psychsociety.com/au

British Psychological Society
St Andrews House
48 Princess Road East
Leicester
LE1 7DR UK
Phone: 0116 254 9568
Fax: 0116 247 0787
E-mail: enquiry@bps.org.uk
http://www.bps.org.uk

Canadian Psychological Association
151 rue Slater Street
Suite 205

Ottawa, Ontario K1P 5H3 Canada
Phone: 1-888-472-0657
E-mail: cpamemb@cpa.ca
http://www.cpa.ca

Canadian Society for Brain, Behaviour, and Cognitive Science
BBCS
Department of Psychology
McMaster University
1280 Main Street West
Hamilton, ON, L8S 4K1 Canada
http://www.csbbcs.org

Drug Information Association, Europe
Postfach 4012,
Basel, Switzerland
Phone: +41 61 386 93 93
Fax: +41 61 386 93 90
E-mail: dia@diaeurope.org

Drug Information Association, Japan
Level 32,
Shinjuku Nomura Building
1-26-2 Nishi-Shinjuku, Shinjuku-ku
Tokyo 163-0532, Japan
Phone: +81 3 5322 1336
Fax: +81 3 5322 2872
E-mail: diajapan@gol.com

European Federation of Professional Psychologists Associations
EFPA Head Office
Grasmarkt 105/18
B-1000 Brussels, Belgium
Phone: +32 2 503 49 53
Fax : +32 2 503 30 67
E-mail: headoffice@efpa.be
http://www.efpa.be

European Federation of Psychology Students' Associations
EFPSA p/a EFPA (European Federation of Professional Psychologists Associations)
Galery Agora, B 421
Grasmarkt 105/18
B-1000 Brussels, Belgium
E-mail: info@efpsa.intranets.com
http://www.efpsa.org

European Health Psychology Society
Dr. Britta Renner, EHPS Membership Officer
Institut für Psychologie
Ernst-Moritz-Arndt Universität Greifswald
17487 Greifswald, Germany
Phone: +49 3834 86 3755
Fax: +49 3834 86 3763
E-mail: renner@uni-greifswald.de
http://www.ehps.net

German Psychological Society
Geschäftsstelle der DGPs
Postfach 42 01 43
D-48068 Münster, Germany
Phone: (02533) 2811520
Fax: (02533) 281144
geschaeftsstelle@dgps.de
http://www.dgps.de

International Association for Cross-Cultural Psychology
Klaus Boehnke
Secretary-General
2000-2004
Department of Sociology
Chemnitz University of Technology
D-09107 Chemnitz, Germany
Phone: +49-(0)371-5313925/2483
Fax: +49-(0)371-5314450
E-mail: Klaus.Boehnke@phil.tu-chemnitz.de
http://www.tu-chemnitz.de/phil/soziologie/
   boehnke

International Association of Applied Psychology
Jose M. Prieto, IAAP Secretary General
Colegio Oficial de Psicologos
Cuesta de San Vicente 4, 5 Planta,
28008 Madrid, Spain
Fax: 34-91-5779172 and 5472284
http://www.iaapsy.org

International Association of Psychosocial Rehabilitation Services
601 North Hammonds Ferry Road
Suite A
Linthicum, Maryland 21090
Phone: (410) 789-7054
Fax: (410) 789-7675
TTY: (410) 789-7682
http://www.iapsrs.org

International Committee Against Mental Illness
P.O. Box 1921
Grand Central Station, NY 10163
Phone: (212) 263-6214

International Ergonomics Association
Prof. Perre Falzon
Laboratoire d'Ergonomie, CNAM
41 Rue Gay Lussac
75005 Paris, France
Phone: +33-1-44-107802
Fax: +33-1-43-253614
E-Mail: falzon@cnam.fr
http://iea.cc

International School Psychology Association
ISPA Central Office
Anders Poulsen, Executive Secretary
Hans Knudsens Plads 1A, 1st Floor
DK-2100 Copenhagen, Denmark
http://www.ispaweb.org

International Society for Traumatic Stress Studies
60 Revere Drive
Suite 500
Northbrook, IL 60062
Phone: (847) 480-9028
Fax: (847) 480-9282
E-mail: istss@istss.org
http://www.istss.org

International Society of Political Psychology
ISPP Central Office
Pitzer College
1050 N. Mills
Claremont, CA 91711
http://www.ispp.org

International Society of Sport Psychology (ISSP)
Prof. Dr. Dieter Hackfort, Treasurer
ISWS der Uni BwM
Werner-Heisenberg Weg 39
D-85577 Neubiberg, Germany

International Union of Psychological Science
http://aix1.uottawa.ca/~iupsys

Japanese Psychological Association
Hongo 5-23-13, Bunkyo, Tokyo, 113-0033 Japan

Organizations and Support Groups • 1775

Phone: +81-3-3814-3953
Fax: +81-3-3814-3954

Singapore Psychological Society
P.O. Box 192
Newton Post Office
Singapore 912207 Malaysia

Turkish Psychological Society
Mesrutiyet Cad. 22/12 Kizilay
06640 Ankara, Turkey
Phone: 0312-425 67 65
Fax: 0312-417 40 59
E-mail: bilgi@psikolog.org.tr
http://www.psikolog.org.tr/eng/index.htm

World Association of Social Psychiatry
645-375 Water Street
Vancouver, BC V6B 5C6 Canada

World Federation for Mental Health
1021 Prince Street
Alexandria, VA 22314-2971
Fax: (703) 519-7648
http://www.wfmh.org

• **SPECIFIC DISORDERS**

American Sleep Disorders Association
6301 Bandel Road NW
Suite 101
Rochester, MN 55901
Phone: (507) 287-6006
Fax: (507) 287-6008
http://www.asda.org

Anxiety Disorders Association of America
11900 Parklawn Drive
Suite 100
Rockville, MD 20852
Phone: (301) 231-9350
http://www.adaa.org

Association for Addiction Professionals
901 North Washington Street
Suite 600
Alexandria, VA 22314-1535
Phone: (800) 548-0497
Fax: (800) 377-1136
http://www.naadac.org

Association for Medical Education and Research in Substance Abuse
125 Whipple Street, 3d Floor
Suite 300
Providence, RI 02908
Phone: (401) 349-0000
Fax: (877) 418-8769
http://www.amersa.org

Brain Injury Association, Inc.
105 North Alfred Street
Alexandria, VA 22314
Phone: (703) 236-6000
Fax: (703) 236-6001
Family Helpline: 800-444-6443
http;//www.biausa.org

Child and Adolescent Bipolar Foundation
1187 Wilmette Avenue
P.M.B. #331
Wilmette, IL 60091
Phone: (847) 920-9498
http://bpkids.org

Children and Adults with Attention Deficit Disorders
8181 Professional Place
Suite 201
Landover, MD 20785
Phone: (800) 233-4050 or (301) 306-7070
Fax: (301) 306-7090
E-mail: national@chadd.org
http://www.chadd.org

Coma Recovery Association, Inc.
807 Carman Avenue
Westbury, NY 11590
Phone: (516) 997-1826
Fax: (516) 997-1613
http://comarecovery.org

Depression and Related Affective Disorders Association
Meyer 3-181
600 North Wolfe Street
Baltimore, MD 21287-7381
Phone: (202) 955-5800 or (410) 955-4647
E-mail: drada@jhmi.edu
http://www.med.jhu.edu/drada

False Memory Syndrome Foundation
1955 Locust Street
Philadelphia, PA 19103-5766
Phone: (215) 940-1040 or (800) 568-8882
Fax: 215-940-1042
E-mail: mail@fmsfonline.org
http://www.fmsfonline.org

Foundation for Depression and Manic Depression
952 5th Avenue
New York, NY 10021
Phone: (212) 772-3400

International Association of Eating Disorders Professionals
P.O. Box 35882
Phoenix, AZ 85069-8552
Phone: (602) 934-3024
Membership: (800) 800-8126
Fax: (775) 329-1597
E-mail: info@iaedp.com
http://www.iaedp.com

Learning Disabilities Association of America
4156 Library Road
Pittsburgh, PA 15234-1349
Phone: (412) 341-1515
Fax: (412) 344-0224
E-mail: info@ldaamerica.org
http://www.ldanatl.org

National Alliance for Research on Schizophrenia and Depression
60 Cutter Mill Road
Suite 404
Great Neck, NY 11021 USA
Main Line: (516) 829-0091
Research Grants Program: (516) 829-5576
Fax: (516) 487-6930
Infoline: (800) 829-8289
E-mail: info@narsad.org
http://www.mhsource.com/narsad

National Association for Children of Alcoholics
11426 Rockville Pike
Suite 100
Rockville, MD 20852
Phone: (301) 468-0985
http://www.nacoa.net

National Association for the Dually Diagnosed
132 Fair Street
Kingston, NY 12401
Phone: (845) 331-4336 or (800) 331-5362
Fax: (845) 331-4569
E-mail: thenadd@aol.com
http://www.thenadd.org

National Association of Anorexia Nervosa and Associated Disorders
P.O. Box 7
Highland Park IL 60035
Hotline: (847) 831-3438
Fax: (847) 433-4632
Information E-mail: anad20@aol.com
Advocacy and Media E-mail:
    AnadAdvocacy@aol.com
http://www.anad.org

National Attention Deficit Disorder Association
1788 Second Street
Suite 200
Highland Park, IL 60035
Phone: (847) 432-ADDA
Fax: (847) 432-5874
E-mail: mail@add.org
http://www.add.org

National Depressive and Manic-Depressive Association
730 North Franklin Street
Suite 501
Chicago, IL 60610-3526
Phone: (312) 642-0049 or (800) 826-3632
Fax: (312) 642-7243
http://www.ndmda.org

National Foundation for Depressive Illness
P.O. Box 2257
New York, NY 10116
Phone: (800) 239-1265
http://www.depression.org

Obsessive-Compulsive Foundation
337 Notch Hill Road
North Branford, CT 06471
Phone: (203) 315-2190
Fax: (203) 315-2196
E-mail: info@ocfoundation.org
http://www.ocfoundation.org

Organization for Bipolar Affective Disorders
1019 - 7 Ave SW
Calgary, Alberta T2P 1A8 Canada
Phone: (403) 263-7408
E-mail: obad@obad.ca
http://www.obad.ca

Schizophrenia Society of Canada
The Schizophrenia Society of Canada
75 The Donway West
Suite 814

Don Mills, ON M3C 2E9 Canada
Phone: (416) 445-8204
1 (888) SSC-HOPE (772-4673)
E-mail: info@schizophrenia.ca
http://www.schizophrenia.ca

Tourette's Syndrome Association
42-40 Bell Boulevard
Bayside, NY 11361
Phone: (718) 224-2999 or (888) 4TOURET
http://www.tsa-usa.org

Support Groups

AARP Grief and Loss Program
601 E Street, NW
Washington DC 20049
http://www.griefandloss.org

Aging Network Services
Topaz House 4400 East-West Highway
Suite 907
Bethesda, MD 20814
Phone: (301) 657-4329
http://www.agingnets.com

Agoraphobics in Motion
1719 Crooks Street
Royal Oak, MI 48067
Phone: (248) 547-0400
http://www.aim-hp.org

**AIDS Clinical Trials Information
    Service**
P.O. Box 6421
Rockville, MD 20849-6421
Phone: (888) 480-3739
http://www.actic.org

AIDS Health Project
1930 Market Street
San Francisco, CA 94102
Phone: (415) 476-3902
http://www.ucsf-ahp.org

Al-Anon/Alateen Family Group Headquarters, Inc.
1600 Corporate Landing Parkway
Virginia Beach, VA 23454-5617
Phone: (757) 563-1600 or (888) 4AL-ANON
http://www.al-anon.alateen.org

Alcoholics Anonymous
475 Riverside Drive
New York, NY 10115
http://www.aa.org

Alliance for Aging Research
2021 K Street NW
Suite 305
Washington, DC 20006
Phone: (202) 293-2856
http://www.agingresearch.org

Alzheimer's Association
919 N Michigan Avenue
Suite 1100
Chicago, IL 60611-1676
Phone: (800) 272-3900 or (312) 335-8700
http://www.alz.org

**Alzheimer's Disease Education and Referral
    Center**
P.O. Box 8250
Silver Spring, MD 20907-8250
Phone: (301) 495-3311 or (800) 438-4380
http://www.alzheimers.org

American Association of Homes and Services for the Aging
2519 Connecticut Avenue, NW
Washington, DC 20008-1520
Phone: (202) 783-2242
http://www.aahsa.org

American Council for Drug Education
164 West 74th Street
New York, NY 10023
Phone: (800) 488-3784
http://www.acde.org

American Federation for Aging Research
1414 Avenue of the Americas, 18th Floor
New York, NY 10019
Phone: (212) 752-2327
http://www.afar.org

American Foundation for Suicide Prevention
120 Wall Street, 22d Floor
New York, NY 10005
888-333-AFSP
Phone: (212) 363-3500
http://www.afsq.org

American Geriatrics Society
Empire State Building
350 5th Avenue
Suite 801
New York, NY 10118
Phone: (212) 308-1414
http://www.americangeriatrics.org

American Professional Society on the Abuse of Children
P.O. Box 26901
CHO 3B-3406
Oklahoma City, OK 73190
Phone: (405) 271-8202
Fax: (405) 271-2931

American Self-Help Clearinghouse
100 E. Hanover Avenue
Suite 202
Cedar Knolls, NJ 07927-2020
Phone: (973) 326-67893
Fax: (973) 326-9467
E-mail: ashc@cybernex.net
http://selfhelpgroups.org

Anti-Stigma Project
1521 South Edgewood Street
Suite C
Baltimore, MD 21227
Phone: (410) 646-0262 or (800) 704-0262
Fax: (410) 646-0264

Center for Mental Health Services Knowledge Exchange Network
The Substance Abuse and Mental Health Service
P.O. Box 42490
Washington, DC 20015
Phone: (301) 443-0383 or (800) 789-2647
http://www.samhsa.gov
E-mail: info@samhsa.gov

Children of Alcoholics Foundation, Inc.
C/O Drug Health
164 W. 74th Street
New York, NY 10023
Phone: (800) 359-COAF
http://www.coaf.org

Co-Dependents Anonymous, Inc.
P.O. Box 33577
Phoenix, AZ 85067-3577
http://www.codependents.org

Depression After Delivery
91 East Somerset Street
Raritan, NJ 08869
Phone: (800) 944-4773
http://www.Depression After Delivery.com

Disabled American Veterans
P.O. Box 14301
Cincinnati, OH 45250-0301
Phone: (859) 441-7300
http://www.dav.org

Dual Recovery Anonymous World Service Central Office
P.O. Box 218232
Nashville, TN 37221-8232
Phone: (877) 883-2332
http://draonline.org

Erasing the Stigma of Mental Illness Serving Hands International
4607 Mission Gorge Place

San Diego, CA 92120
Phone: (800) 219-4854

Freedom from Fear
308 Seaview Avenue
Staten Island, NY 10305
Phone: (718) 351-1717
http://www.freedomfromfear.org

Gamblers Anonymous—International Service Office
P. O. Box 17173
Los Angeles, CA 90017
Phone: (213) 386-8789
http://www.gamblersanonymous.org

Marijuana Anonymous
P. O. Box 2912
Van Nuys, CA 91404
Phone: (800) 766-6779
http://www.marijuana-anonymous.org

Moderation Management Network, Inc.
22 W 27th Street
New York, NY 10001
Phone: (212) 871-0974
http://www.moderation.org

Mood Disorders Support Group, Inc.
P.O. Box 30377
New York, NY 10111
Phone: (212) 533-6374
http://www.mdsg.com

Nar-Anon Family Groups
P.O. Box 2562
Palos Verdes Peninsula, CA 90274
Phone: (310) 547-5800

Narcotics Anonymous
P.O. Box 9999
Van Nuys, CA 91409
Phone: (818) 773-9999
http://na.org

National Alliance for the Mentally Ill
Colonial Place Three
2107 Wilson Boulevard
Suite 300
Arlington, VA 22201-3042

Phone: (703) 524-7600
NAMI HelpLine: 1-800-950-NAMI (6264)
http://www.nami.org

National Clearinghouse for Alcohol and Drug Information
P.O. Box 2345
Rockville, MD 20847-2345
Phone: (800) 729-6686
http://www.health.org

National Clearinghouse on Child Abuse and Neglect Information
330 C Street, SW
Washington, DC 20447
Phone: (800) 394-3366 or (703) 385-7565
http://www.calib.com

National Council on Alcoholism and Drug Dependence
20 Exchange Place
Suite 2902
New York, NY 10005
Phone: (212) 269-7797
http://ncadd.org

National Council on Child Abuse and Family Violence
1155 Connecticut Avenue, NW
Suite 400
Washington, DC 20036-4306
Phone: (202) 429-6695
http://www.nccafv.org

National Council on Patient Information and Education
4915 Saint Elmo Ave Suite 505
Bethesda MD, 20814-6053
Phone: (301) 656-8565
http://www.talkaboutrx.org

National Empowerment Center
20 Ballard Road
Lawrence, MA 01843
Phone: (800) POWER-2-U (769-3728)

National Families in Action
2957 Claremont Road
Suite 150
Atlanta, GA 30329

Phone: (404) 248-9676
http://www.nationalfamilies.org

**National Information Center for Children
and Youth with Disabilities**
P.O. Box 1492
Washington, DC 20013-1492
Phone: (800) 695-0285 or
(202) 884-8200 (V/TTY)
http://www.nichcy.org

**National Institute of Mental Health
(NIMH)**
6001 Executive Boulevard
Room 8184, MSC 9663
Bethesda, MD 20892-9663
Phone: (301) 443-4513
Fax: (301) 443-4279
E-mail: nimhinfo@nih.gov
http://www.nimh.nih.gov

**National Legal Support for Elderly People
with Mental Disabilities**
Bazelon Center for Mental Health Law
1101 15th Street
Suite 1212
Washington, DC 20005
Phone: (202) 467-5730
http://www.bazelon.org

**National Mental Health Association
Information Center**
1021 Prince Street
Alexandria, VA 22314-2971
Phone: (800) 969-NMHA
TTY Line 800/433-5959

**National Mental Health Consumers'
Self Help Clearinghouse**
1211 Chestnut Street
Suite 1000
Philadelphia, PA 19107
Phone: (800) 553-4539 or (215) 751-1810
http://www.mhselfhelp.org

**National Mental Health Services
Knowledge Exchange Network**
P.O. Box 42490
Washington, DC 20015
Phone: (800) 789-CMHS (2647)

E-mail: ken@mentalhealth.org
http://www.mentalhealth.org

**National Resource Center on Homelessness and
Mental Illness**
345 Delaware Avenue
Delmar, NY 12054
Phone: (800) 444-7415
http://www.prainc.com

National Self-Help Clearinghouse
c/o CUNY, Graduate School and University
Center
365 Fifth Avenue
Suite 3300
New York, NY 10016
Phone: (212) 817-1822
E-mail: ajgartner@gc.cuny.edu
http://www.selfhelpweb.org

Obsessive Compulsive Foundation
337 Notch Hill Road
North Branford, CT 06471
Phone: (203) 315-2190
http://www.ocfoundation.org

Phobics Anonymous
P.O. Box 1180
Palm Springs, CA 92263
Phone: (619) 322-2673

**Protection and Advocacy for Individuals with
Mental Illness**
401 State St
Schenectay, NY 12305
Phone: (518) 473-7378 or (800) 624-4143
http://www.cqc.state.ny.us

Save Our Sons And Daughters (SOSAD)
2441 W. Grand Blvd
Detroit, MI 48208-1210
Phone: (313) 361-5200
Fax: (313) 361-0055
E-mail: sosad@aol.com

• **HOTLINES**
1-800-488-DRUG
1-800-HEROIN
1-800-RELAPSE
1-800-SUICIDE (800) 784-2433

1-888-MARIJUANA (888) 627-4582

Action, Parent and Teen Support (800) 282-5660

AlAnon Family Groups (800) 344-2666

Al-Anon for Families of Alcoholics (800) 344-2666

AlAnon/Alateen (800) 356-9996

Alcohol and Drug Abuse Hotline (800) 729-6686

Alcohol and Drug Helpline (800) 821-4357

Alcohol Hotline (800) 331-2900

Alcoholics Anonymous (617) 426-9444

Alzheimer's Disease Education and Referral
    Center (800) 438-4380 or (301) 495-3311;
    fax: (301) 495-3334

American Association on Mental Retardation
    (800) 424-3688

American Council for Drug Education
    (800) DRUG-HELP

American Council on Alcoholism (800) 527-5344,
    (410) 889-0100 in Maryland

American Suicide Foundation (800) 531-4477

American Trauma Society (800) 556-7890, (301)
    420-4189 in Maryland, fax: (301) 420-0617

America's Crisis Pregnancy Helpline
    (800) 67-BABY-6

Anorexia and Bulimia Crisis (800) 227-4785

Ask a Nurse (800) 535-1111

Be Sober Hotline (800) 237-6237

Child Abuse Hotline (800) 540-4000

Child Abuse Hotline (800) 792-5200

Cocaine Anonymous (800) 347-8998

Cocaine Hotline (800) COCAINE (262-2463)

Crisis Helpline (800) 233-4357

Crisis Intervention Hotline (psychiatric)
    (800) 540-5806

Depression/Alcohol and Drug Addiction Trauma
    Hotline (800) 544-1177

Depression Awareness Recognition and Treatment
    Helpline (800) 421-4211

Family Support Network (800) TLC-0042

Grief Recovery Helpline (800) 445-4808

National Association for Children of Alcoholics
    (888) 554-2627

National Child Abuse Helpline (800) 262-2463

National Child Abuse Hotline (800) 422-4453

National Council on Alcohol and Drug
    Dependence HopeLine
    (800) 475-HOPE (4673)

National Council on Problem Gambling
    (800) 522-4700

National Domestic Violence Hotline
    (800) 799-7233 TDD: (800) 787-3224

National Drug Information Treatment and
    Referral Hotline (800) 662-HELP (4357)

National Help Line for Substance Abuse
    (800) 262-2463

National Institute on Drug Abuse Hotline
    (800) 662-4357

National Victim Center (800) FYI-CALL
    (394-2255)

Occupational Therapy Consumer Line
    (800) 668-8255

OCD Literature Request Line (800) 639-7462

Panic Disorder InfoLine (NIMH) 800-64-PANIC
    (647-2642)

Parental Stress Hotline (800) 632-8188

Prevent Child Abuse America - (800) CHILDREN
    (244-5373)

Prozac Survivors Support Group, Inc.
    (800) 392-0640

Rape and Abuse and Incest National Network
    (800) 656-HOPE

SAFE (Self-Abuse Finally Ends) Alternative
    Information Line (800) DONT-CUT
    (366-8288)

Shoplifters Anonymous (800) 848-9595

Therapist Referral Network (800) 843-7274, fax:
    (858) 481-5143

Youth Crisis Hotline (800) 448-4663

Elizabeth D. Schafer

PHARMACEUTICAL LIST

This appendix is divided into the following sections:

Psychopharmacologic Treatments for Clinical Depression

Antidepressant medications are grouped into four classes based on their effects on cerebral function:
- Tricyclic antidepressants (TCAs)
- Selective serotonin reuptake inhibitors (SSRIs or SRIs)
- Monoamine oxidase inhibitors (MAOIs)
- Miscellaneous (or atypical) antidepressants

Antidepressants work by enhancing the function of neurotransmitters. Depression seems to be caused by a highly complex and intricate change in sensitivity of receptors for these neurotransmitters, rather than the quantity of neurotransmitters present in the brain. Two neurotransmitters, norepinephrine and serotonin, are particularly associated with depression, and one or both are affected by almost all antidepressant drugs.

Tricyclic Antidepressants (TCAs). TCAs were introduced into clinical medicine in the late 1950's. Positive features include effectiveness in preventing relapse and recurrence and the ability sometimes to measure blood levels of TCAs to use as guidelines for adjusting dosage. Limitations include side effects (which often can be regulated by lowering dosage) and the fact that a prolonged period of dosage may be required to produce a therapeutic effect.

The most frequent side effects are sedation (due to antihistamine properties); orthostatic hypotension (sudden decrease in blood pressure leading to light-headedness or dizziness); and anticholinergic effects (due to a decrease in mucosal moisture production caused by acetylcholine), such as dry mouth, constipation, difficulty urinating, and blurred vision. For older men, the anticholinergic aspect may aggravate the symptoms of an enlarged prostate gland.

TCA Usage

Generic Name	Trade Name	Daily Dosage Range (approx.)	Side Effects
amitriptyline	Elavil	10-75 milligrams	drowsiness, possible blurred vision, urinary hesitation
amoxapine	Asendin	10-300 milligrams	drowsiness, possible blurred vision, dry mouth

(continued)

1782

Generic Name	Trade Name	Daily Dosage Range (approx.)	Side Effects
clomipramine	Anafranil	10-250 milligrams	drowsiness, headache, blurred vision, dry mouth, constipation
desipramine	Norpramin	10-75 milligrams	drowsiness, blurred vision, urinary hesitation
doxepin	Sinequan, Adapin	10-75 milligrams	drowsiness, blurred vision, urinary retention/hesitation
imipramine	Toframil, Aventil	10-75 milligrams	drowsiness, blurred vision, urinary retention/hesitation
nortriptyline	Pamelor	10-100 milligrams	drowsiness, blurred vision, urinary retention/hesitation
protriptyline	Vivactil	5-20 milligrams	drowsiness, blurred vision, urinary retention/hesitation
trimipramine	Surmontil	10-75 milligrams	drowsiness, blurred vision, urinary retention/hesitation

Selective Serotonin Reuptake Inhibitors (SSRIs or SRIs). SSRIs are the most widely used antidepressants in the United States and other parts of the world. They do not cause orthostatic hypotension or anticholinergic side effects and are preferred by some physicians for mild or moderately severe depression, reserving TCAs for the most severe depression. SSRIs are generally more expensive than TCAs. Prozac (fluoextine) was the first SSRI to become available in the United States, and it remains one of the most widely prescribed antidepressants in the world. It has a longer elimination half-life, which means that it can remain effective for a longer period of time, but the side effects also persist longer after discontinuance. Sarafem, another name for Prozac, is marketed as a treatment for symptoms of premenstrual dysphoric disorder (PMDD). Both Zoloft (sertraline) and Luvox (fluvoxamine) have broad therapeutic dosages and relatively few side effects, but upset stomach, bloating, and diarrhea can be common early in treatment. Paxil (paroxetine) tends to be sedating and may cause sporadic constipation, dry mouth, and trouble starting urination. Celexa (citalopram) has a longer half-life and is unique in that does not have significant interactions with other medications. An isomer of Celexa, Lexapro (escitalopram oxalate), was brought to market, with indications of faster action and reduced side effects in some patients.

SSRI Usage

Generic Name	Trade Name	Daily Dosage Range (approx.)	Side Effects
citalopram	Celexa	10-40 milligrams	restlessness, insomnia or drowsiness
escitalopram oxalate	Lexapro	10-20 milligrams	headache, nausea, insomnia
fluoextine	Prozac, Sarafem	5-40 milligrams, 10-20 milligrams	agitation, nausea, sexual dysfunction
fluvoxamine	Luvox	5-50 milligrams	somulence, nausea, headache, diarrhea
paroxetine	Paxil	5-20 milligrams	nervousness, nausea, sexual dysfunction
sertraline	Zoloft	12.5-150 milligrams	nausea, diarrhea, sexual dysfunction

Monoamine Oxidase Inhibitors (MAOIs). MAOIs were the first antidepressants prescribed. They were initially discovered (like many psychiatric drugs, by accident) in the 1950's and are now widely used throughout the world. MAOIs work by inhibiting the production of monoamine oxidase, which metabolizes norepinephrine and serotonin in the central nervous system. They can be effective when other drugs are not working, particularly when peo- ple are listless and apathetic. Side effects include changes in thyroid function and blood pressure. Sedation or stimulation is not uncommon in older patients. Some commonly prescribed vitamin and mineral supplements, herbal preparations, and pain medications tend to interact with MAOIs. In addition, there may be food interactions, with a synergistic effect on blood pressure that may lead to a potentially fatal stroke or heart attack.

MAOI Usage

Generic Name	Trade Name	Daily Dosage Range (approx.)	Side Effects
phenelzine	Nardil	7.5-30 milligrams	low blood pressure, weight gain, sexual dysfunction
tranylcypromine	Parnate	5-30 milligrams	weight gain, lowered blood pressure, sexual dysfunction

Miscellaneous (or Atypical) Antidepressants. Some of the newer antidepressants have diverse chemical properties and do not fit into standard medication categories. Wellbutrin (bupropion) has a broad dosing range and tends to increase physical energy. It may lead to agitation and insomnia and, in its original form, must be given more than once per day. Effexor (venlafaxine) has many of the pharmacological and therapeutic properties of TCAs but without the anticholinergic side effects. It has a very broad range of effective dosage. Its side effects are nausea, vomiting, and headache, and it may raise blood pressure. Serzone (nefazodone) has a broad dosing range and a moderate sedating effect, which may lead to daytime drowsiness over a prolonged course of therapy. It has the advantage of not causing hypotension or anticholinergic side effects. Like some SSRIs, it may interfere with enzymes that metabolize other medications, thus increasing their level in the bloodstream. Remon (mirtazapine) is one of the newest antidepressants. It does not cause orthostatic hypotension or have cardiac or anticholinergic side effects. It can function as a mild sedative and is potentially harmful for overweight patients.

Miscellaneous Antidepressant Usage

Generic Name	Trade Name	Daily Dosage Range (approx.)	Side Effects
bupropion	Wellbutrin	75-225 milligrams	possible increase in energy
mirtazapine	Remon	7.5-45 milligrams	very sedating, possible weight gain
nefazodone	Serzone	50-200 milligrams	very sedating, potential drug interactions
trazodone	Desyrel	25-200 milligrams	very sedating, useful as a sleep aid
venlafaxine	Effexor	12.5-225 milligrams	possible nausea, increase in blood pressure

Psychopharmacologic Treatments for Anxiety

Benzodiazepine Anxiolytics. A variety of medications, especially antidepressants, are used to treat anxiety, but benzodiazepines are still the most frequently prescribed drugs. Generally speaking, benzo- diazepines can be divided into two categories based on their elimination half-life, or the time that it takes for the medication to be cleared from the body. The long half-life medications remain in the system for sufficient time to become metabolized in the bloodstream, leading to some potentially serious side effects. The short half-life medications do not have this concern. Benzodiazepine drugs are sedative hypnotics, and their side effects may include a decrease in attention, unsteadiness when large doses are prescribed, and a tendency toward forgetfulness, particularly of recent events. A degree of physiological dependence often develops when a benzodiazepine is taken on a regular basis for more than a few weeks, and a mild withdrawal reaction may occur if the drug is abruptly discontinued. Prolonged usage may lead to a more intense dependency and more severe symptoms such as restlessness, agitation, and flulike discomfort if the medication is discontinued without a gradual reduction in dosage.

Benzodiazepine Anxiolytics Categorized by Half-Life

Long Half-Life	Short Half-Life
diazepam (Valium) 30-100 hours	alprazolam (Xanax) 12-15 hours
chlordizaepoxide (Librium) 50-100 hours	lorazepam (Ativan) 8-12 hours
clonazepam (Klonopin) 18-50 hours	oxazepam (Serax) 8-12 hours

---

Benzodiazepine Anxiolytics Usage

Generic Name	Trade Name	Daily Dosage Range (approx.)	Side Effects
alprazolam	Xanax	0.25-2 milligrams	drowsiness, dizziness, confusion, dependency
chlordizapoxide	Librium	10-40 milligrams	drowsiness, dependency, alcohol interaction
clorazepate	Tranxene	3.75-15 milligrams	drowsiness, dizziness, alcohol interaction
diazepam	Valium	2-20 milligrams	drowsiness, dizziness, blurred vision, alcohol interaction, dependency
lorazepam	Ativan	0.25-2 milligrams	drowsiness, alcohol interaction, dependency
oxazepam	Serax	10-45 milligrams	drowsiness, blurred vision, alcohol interaction

Atypical Antipsychotics. Newer drugs, such as buspirone (Buspar), are part of a different chemical subgroup, the azapirones, and are considered pure anxioselective agents. They do not result in sedation and are less likely to lead to physiological dependence. They do not interact with as many other compounds. Side effects may include dizziness or lightheadedness and nausea, and buspirone takes a longer time to become effective. Hydroxyzine (Atarax, Vistaril, Marax) is part of the piperazine chemical subgroup and is a sedating antihistamine sometimes used as a medication for anxiety. It is rapidly absorbed and has a half-life of three hours. Its powerful sedating qualities limit its usefulness.

Miscellaneous Anxiolytics Usage

Generic Name	Trade Name	Daily Dosage Range (approx.)	Side Effects
buspirone	Buspar	5-80 milligrams	dizziness, dry mouth, nausea
hydroxyzine	Atarax, Vistaril, Marax	25-100 milligrams	transient drowsiness

Psychopharmacologic Treatments for Mania

The alternation of mania and depression is known as bipolar disorder, a condition which tends to increase as a person ages such that the normal euthymic (nonsymptomatic) state between episodes may decrease to the point of nonexistence. Manic states are treated with lithium carbonate (anticonvulsant agents), which functions as a mood stabilizer. For more severe conditions, particularly among elderly patients, neuroleptic medications are utilized, so named for their tendency to cause neurological side effects or extrapyramidal symptoms (EPS). Typical neuroleptics, such as haloperidol (Haldol), have been used since the 1960's. They have a wide range of conventional side effects, such as oversedation and unsteadiness, as well as anticholinergic side effects including dry mouth, constipation, blurred vi-

sion, and prostate disorders. EPS include immobile facial features, slowed hand motion, and tremors similar to Parkinson's disease. Over a prolonged period of time, abnormal movements around the mouth and involuntary blinking may occur. Consequently, neuroleptics are usually prescribed in very small doses and carefully controlled. Atypical neuroleptics which do not produce EPS (or only infrequent and mild ones) have begun to replace neuroleptics, but each has individual side effects that affect usage. For bipolar disorders, a combination of a mood stabilizers and neuroleptic medications are often used, sometimes in conjunction with antidepressants, requiring a careful coordination of the various drugs.

Mood Stabilizers Usage

Generic Name	Trade Name	Daily Dosage Range (approx.)	Side Effects
carbamazepine	Tegretol	50-1,200 milligrams	possible decreased white blood cell count, possible interaction with other medications
gabapentin	Neurontin	150-2,000 milligrams	sedation
lamotrigine	Lamictal	12.5-50 milligrams	possible serious rash
lithium	Eskalith, Lithobid	75-1,200 milligrams	possible thirst, increased urination, forgetfulness, and mild tremors
valporic acid	Depakene, Depakote	125-1,800 milligrams	possible mild weight gain
verapamil	Calan, Isoptin, Verelan	120-480 milligrams	possible lower blood pressure

Typical Neuroleptics Usage

Generic Name	Trade Name	Daily Dosage Range (approx.)	Side Effects
chlorpromazine	Thorazine	10-200 milligrams	muscle stiffness, tremors, dry mouth, weight gain
fluphenazine	Prolixin	0.25-4 milligrams	muscle stiffness, dry mouth, hypotension
haloperidol	Haldol	0.25-4 milligrams	muscle stiffness, tremors, weight gain, tachycardia
loxapine	Loxitane	10-100 milligrams	mild sedation, dizziness, weight gain, dry mouth
mesoridazine	Serentil	10-200 milligrams	muscle stiffness, dry mouth, mild sedation

(continued)

Generic Name	Trade Name	Daily Dosage Range (approx.)	Side Effects
perphenazine	Trilafon	2-32 milligrams	mild sedation, dry mouth, muscle stiffness, jumpiness
pimozide	Orap	0.25-4 milligrams	muscle stiffness, tremors, weight gain
thioridazine	Mellaril	10-200 milligrams	sedation, low blood pressure, dry mouth
thiothixene	Navane	1-15 milligrams	muscle stiffness, tremors, weight gain
trifluoperazine	Stelazine	1-15 milligrams	muscle stiffness, tremors, weight gain

Atypical Neuroleptics Usage

Generic Name	Trade Name	Daily Dosage Range (approx.)	Side Effects
clozapine	Clozaril	10-100 milligrams	heavy sedation, anticholinergic effects
olanzapine	Zyprexa	2.5-10 milligrams	mild sedation, mild anticholinergic effects, possible weight gain
quetiapine	Seroquel	25-100 milligrams	possible unsteadiness and orthostatic hypotension
risperidone	Risperdal	0.25-2 milligrams	possible severe EPS in higher doses
ziprasidone	Geodon	10-20 mg	possible serious cardiac problems for patients with heart disease

Psychopharmacologic Treatments for Attention Disorders

It has been estimated that 3 to 5 percent of children have some degree of attention-deficient hyperactivity disorder (ADHD), a condition which may continue into adolescence and adulthood. There are three aspects of this disruptive behavior: inattention, hyperactivity, and impulsivity. Methylphenidate (Ritalin) was first used in 1950 to treat hyperactive children and has been joined by the stimulants dextroamphetamine (Dexedrine) and pemoline (Cylert) as effective agents. These drugs alter metabolic activity in the brain, lowering the neurotransmission of dopamine. Serious side effects may include growth

Stimulant Usage

Generic Name	Trade Name	Daily Dosage Range (approx.)	Side Effects
dextroamphetamine	Dexedrine, Dextrostat	5-40 milligrams	hyperactivity, insomnia, headache
dextroamphetamine saccharte/sulfate; amphetamine aspartate/sulfate	Adderal	40-50 milligrams	sleep disturbance, appetite suppression, irritability
methamphetamine hydrochloride	Desoxyn	20-115 milligrams	hyperactivity, insomnia, restlessness

(continued)

Stimulant Usage—continued

Generic Name	Trade Name	Daily Dosage Range (approx.)	Side Effects
methylphenidate	Ritalin, Metadate, Concerta, Methylin	10-60 milligrams	sleep disorders, appetite suppression, restlessness, irritability
modafinil	Provigil	100-400 milligrams	typical stimulant side effects, but less sympathomemitic
pemoline	Cylert	37.5-112.5 milligrams	hyperactivity, insomnia, hepatitis

retardation related to appetite supression leading to anorexia, impairment of cognitive performance, and (in the case of pemoline) liver toxicity, requiring monitoring every six months. Dextroamphetamine can be fatal if an overdose occurs, and all stimulants can result in insomnia. Because of the latter property, amphetamine-like stimulants can also be used to treat nacrolepsy. Ritalin-SR (extended release), Dexedrine-SR, Cylert, methamphetamine hydrochloride (Desoxyn), and modafinil (Provigil) have substantially helped but not cured narcolepsy.

Psychopharmacologic Treatments for Sleep Disorders

As people grow older, changes in normal sleep patterns occur frequently, due most fundamentally to age-related alteration in monoamine neurotransmission, as well as to a decrease in melatonin, the primary hormone that regulates sleep cycles. Antidepressants with sedating properties can be helpful in treating sleep disorders, since they affect benzodiazepine receptors in the brain and facilitate neurotransmissions. These drugs decrease the amount of time that it takes to fall asleep and increase the amount of total sleep time. However, steady use may make a patient totally dependent on the drugs and require them to fall asleep. In addition, abruptly discontinuing usage may lead to a rebound reaction resulting in severe insomnia. Benzodiazepine drugs are not physically addictive, and there is no sense of a physical craving, but they also tend toward a degree of mild memory loss and confusion on awakening. In addition, they can be very dangerous when used in conjunction with alcohol. The benzodiazepine drugs in this category are commonly called hypnotics. Zolpidem (Ambien) has fewer side effects, better long-term effectiveness, and less likelihood of dependency than the older hypnotics.

Hypnotics Usage

Generic Name	Trade Name	Daily Dosage Range (approx.)	Side Effects
donzepril	Aricept	5-10 milligrams	mild muscle cramping, nausea
tacrine	Cognex	20-80 milligrams	nausea, agitation

Psychopharmacologic Treatments for Dementia

A reduction in memory capability is likely to occur as people age, but there is a distinct difference between between age-associated memory impairment (AAMI) and dementia, a general diagnostic term to convey impairment in cognitive functions such as memory, concentration, orientation, and logical reasoning. Alzheimer's disease, a specific form of dementia, involves the production of abnormal proteins. While treatments for dementia are still being devel-

oped, two available medications, tacrine (Cognex) and donzepril (Aricept), can slow the progression of the disease and improve memory to some extent. Aricept has become the medication of choice due to its lesser side effects for most patients.

Cognitive Enhancer Usage

Generic Name	Trade Name	Daily Dosage Range (approx.)	Side Effects
estazolam	ProSom	0.5-2 milligrams	drowsiness the following day, anxiety and dizziness after effect passes
flurazepam	Dalmane	7.5-30 milligrams	prolonged drowsiness during the day, some withdrawal symptoms, unsteadiness, falls among the elderly
quazepam	Doral	7.5-15 milligrams	possible mild memory loss and confusion
temazepam	Restoril	7.5-30 milligrams	strong withdrawal symptoms, mild drowsiness
triazolam	Halcion	0.125-0.25 milligrams	very powerful drug leading to short-term memory loss, rebound insomnia, anxiety
zolpidem	Ambien	5-10 milligrams	fewer than with other hypnotics, some drowsiness possible

---

Interaction of Pharmaceutical Agents

One of the most important considerations in the use of psychiatric drugs is their interaction with medical drugs, an important element in many situations in which more than one pharmacologic agent

is required. In addition, psychiatric drugs also may interact to cause problems when treatment requires more than one prescription.

Medical Drugs Interacting with Psychiatric Drugs

Medical Drug	Psychiatric Drug	Interactive Effect
antiarrhythmics	TCAs	possible heart arrhythmias
antibiotics (doxycycline)	carbamazepine	decrease in the antibiotic effect
antibiotics (erythomycin)	nefazodone	increase in the blood level of nefazodone
antibiotics (tetracycline, spectinomycin)	lithium	increase in the effect and side effects of lithium
bromocriptine	neuroleptics	mutual interference with each other's therapeutic effect
caffeine	fluvoxamine	increased sleepiness, agitation

(continued)

Medical Drugs Interacting with Psychiatric Drugs—continued

Medical Drug	Psychiatric Drug	Interactive Effect
calcium channel blockers	TCAs	increased sedation, dizziness, dry mouth, urinary retention
cough medicine with dextromethorphan	SSRIs	flushing, sweating, elevated blood pressure
Coumadin (warfarin)	SSRIs, clozapine	increased risk of bleeding
Demerol (meperidine hydrochloride)	MAOIs	increased temperature, risk of death
diabetes medications	MAOIs	decrease in blood glucose levels
	neuroleptics	possible increase in blood glucose levels
digoxin	clozapine	serious cardiac effects
estrogen	imipramine	lethargy, headache, tremor, increase in blood pressure
	TCAs	increased sedation, dizziness, sweating, urinary retention
Hismanal (astemizole), Seldane (terfenadine)	Serzone (nefazodone)	cardiac arrhythmias
	SSRIs	potentially fatal heartbeat irregularity
Inderal (propranolol)	neuroleptics	increased blood level of Inderal, lowered blood pressure
labetalol	imipramine	increased imipramine level, more antidepressant side effects
nonsteroidal anti-inflammatory drugs (NSAIDs)	lithium	increased blood levels and side effects of lithium
prednisone, estrogen	nefazodone	increased steroid blood levels
Propulsid (cisapride)	SSRIs	potentially fatal heartbeat irregularity
quinidine	TCAs	dangerous cardiac arrhythmias, increased sedation
rifampin	neuroleptics	decreased neuroleptic effect
stimulants	MAOIs	increased blood pressure, risk of stroke and heart attack
Tagmet (cimetidine)	TCAs	increased sedation, dizziness, dry mouth, urinary retention
Tegretol (carbamazepine)	TCAs	decreased therapeutic effect
theophylline	Luvox (fluvoxamine)	increased blood pressure, rapid heart rate, shakiness, sweating
Tylenol (acetaminophen)	Luvox (fluvoxamine)	increased Luvox side effects
vasopressors	MAOIs	increased blood pressure, risk of stroke and heart attack

Psychopharmacologic Interaction

Psychiatric Drug	Interacting Drug	Clinical Effect
buproprion	carbamazepine	decreased buproprion effect
	haloperidol	increased haloperidol levels

(continued)

Psychiatric Drug	Interacting Drug	Clinical Effect
carbamazepine	benzodiazepine	decrease in clonazepam and alprazolam levels
	lithium	increased dizziness, ataxia
donepezil	carbamazepine	possible decrease in donepezil levels
	nefazodone, fluoxetine	possible increase in donepezil levels, side effects
MAOIs	buspirone	increased blood pressure
	lithium	tardive dyskinesia
	nefazodone	toxic reactions
	SSRIs	hyperserotonergic states
nefazodone	benzodiazepine	enhanced effects
	haloperidol	increased haloperidol levels
neuroleptics	anticholinergics	increased anticholinergic effect
	benzodiazepines	increased sedation, increased risk of respiratory depression
	buproprion	possible increase in haloperidol levels
	carbamazepine	decreased neuroleptic levels
	lithium	possible delirium, possible increased EPS
	MAOIs	hypotension, possible increase in effect of antipsychotics
	nefazadone	possible increase in haloperidol levels
	SSRIs	possible increase in fluoxetine levels
	TCAs	increased sedation, hypotension, possible ventricular arrhythmias, possible risk of seizures
	trazadone	possible increase of hypotension
SSRIs	lithium	fever, increased lithium levels
TCAs	anticholinergics	increased antiocholinergic effects
	antipsychotics	possible ventricular arrhythmias, increase in plasma levels, sedation, hypotension, risk of seizures
	benzodiazepines	increased sedation, confusion, impaired motor function
	carbamazepine	decreased TCA levels
	lithium	possible increase in lithium tremor
	MAOIs	increased incidence of mania, increase in TCA toxicity

Time Line of Psychotropic Drugs

- 1930's: Synthetic production of benzodiazepines
- 1948: Serotonin isolated from beef serum
- 1949: Discovery of therapeutic effects of lithium on mania; FDA bans lithium as a result of deaths of patients with cardiac disease

- 1951: Chlorpromazine used to reduce anxiety in surgical patients, suggesting therapeutic implications for neuroleptic agents
- 1952: Chlorpromazine (as Thorazine) used to treat mania; iproniazid identified as a MAOI

- 1955: Molecular structure of chlorpromazine altered, leading to development of antipsychotic agents haloperidol and fluphenazine
- 1957: Halodol developed from haloperidol
- 1958: Tricyclic antidepressants introduced in article in *American Journal of Psychiatry*
- 1960: Benzodiazepines (Valium) developed as effective medications; addictive considerations emerge later

- 1960's: TCAs introduced to treat depression; ban on lithium in the United States lifted
- 1980's: SSRIs (Prozac) developed as antidepressants; antiepileptic drugs Carbamazepine and Valproate discovered to have mood-stabilizing properties
- 1990's: Clozapine and risperidone introduced as new form of antipsychotic agents; cognex (Aricept) introduced as cognitive enhancer

SOURCES FOR FURTHER STUDY

Folks, David G., and Norman L. Keltner. *Psychotropic Drugs*. St. Louis: Mosby-Year Book, 1997. Divided into two parts, an overview of clinical psychopharmacology and a very detailed profile of more than one hundred psychotropic drugs. Designed for the serious student of psychopharmacology but organized so that the layperson can consult it about specific drugs and their properties. The individual profiles are very informative, and the numerous charts, diagrams, illustrations, and indexes complement the text well.

Gorman, Jack M. *The Essential Guide to Psychiatric Drugs*. New York: St. Martin's Press, 1997. Described by experts as "An outstanding book about these drugs for the nonphysican," Gorman's book offers an extensive overview of the discipline and its primary concerns. Presents specific data about the psychotropic drugs and their uses. Includes many tables, detailed discussions about issues and controversies, and sufficient scientific data to assist in an understanding about how psychotropic agents operate.

Hardman, Joel G., and Lee E. Limbird, eds. *Goodman and Gilman's The Pharmacological Basis of Therapeutics*. 10th ed. New York: McGraw-Hill, 2001. A standard reference work in which the contributors attempt to "be reliable in their efforts to provide information that is complete and generally in accord with the standards accepted at the time of publication." The book is directed toward medical students, and chapters 19 and 20 have extensive information about psychopharmacologic agents.

Salzman, Carl. *Psychiatric Medications for Older Adults: The Concise Guide*. New York: Guilford Press, 2001. A comprehensive, very clearly written, and well-organized presentation by the foremost expert in geriatric psychopharmacology. Provides an overview of the entire field of psychotropic drugs. Many charts and tables augment the text, which is accessible to the general reader as well as the health care practitioner.

Schatzberg, Alan F., and Charles B. Nemeroff, eds. *The American Psychiatric Press Textbook of Psychopharmacology*. Washington, D.C.: American Psychiatric Press, 1998. As the prefatory note indicates, the contributors to this volume "have worked to ensure that all information in this book concerning drug dosage, schedules, and routes of administration is accurate as of the time of publication," and the book is "intended to provide background information only." In spite of this cautionary note, this is as reliable a source as a searcher is likely to find. It is thorough, clearly presented, very comprehensive and unbiased. It includes historical data, numerous diagrams and illustrations, and extensive material about the scientific explorations leading to the development of psychotropic agents. While designed for the professional in the field, it is suitable for consideration by the layman as well.

Weiden, Peter J., Patricia L. Scheifler, Donald J. Diamond, and Ruth Ross. *Breakthroughs in Antipsychotic Medications: A Guide for Consumers, Families, and Clinicians*. New York: W. W. Norton, 1999. A thorough, informative discussion of the capabilities, advantages, and problems involved in the uses of psychototropic drugs, directed particularly to patients and their friends and families. Detailed information is combined with a directive narrative that introduces and examines the crucial issues of psychiatric approaches to psychotic disorders. An extensive glossary defines many important terms, and a section on resources provides information about support groups, Web sites, volumes on psychopharmacology, individual medications, and journals and newsletters.

WEB SITES

http://www.nami.org

The Web page for the National Alliance for the Mentally Ill, with up-to-date information about treatments for mental disorders.

http://www.cmhc.com/guide/pro22.htm

A Web page of pharmacology references, with basic information about various medications

http://uhs.bsd.uchicago.edu/dr-bob/tips/tips/html

This Web site is an indexed archive of the psychopharmacology discussion group, with information about the use of medications, including side effects. It is based on clinical experience, rather than research.

Leon Lewis

BIOGRAPHICAL LIST OF PSYCHOLOGISTS

Adler, Alfred (1870-1937). Originally a Freudian psychologist, Adler, by 1911, had broken from Sigmund Freud, resigning as president of the Vienna Psychoanalytic Society when the break became apparent. Adler was known for his work on individual personality and his theory of the creative self. He eschewed environment and heredity as the major governing factors in people's lives. He considered these factors raw materials that individuals can shape as they will.

Allport, Gordon (1897-1967). Allport was well known for his theory of functional autonomy, which disputes Sigmund Freud's notion that adult conduct stems from instincts, desires, and needs that all people share. He resisted classifying people according to such elemental motives. For him, each personality was unique and could not be categorized according to a preconceived set of motivations.

Bandura, Albert (1925-). The learning theory advanced by Bandura postulated that people learn largely through realizing what the consequences are of their behavior or of the behavior of others. He advocated observational learning. His social cognitive theory influenced learning theory in the last quarter of the twentieth century.

Beck, Aaron T. (1921-). Recognized for his work in cognitive therapy, Beck sought to alter the thinking of depressed patients by encouraging them to assess their problems in alternative ways capable of solution. He also moved his patients toward understanding how their problems might be the result of their own actions or inactions. The Beck Depression Inventory, a twenty-one-item instrument based on a four-point scale, is used as a quantitative tool for ascertaining the symptoms of depression in adolescents and adults.

Berkowitz, Leonard (1926-). A social psychologist, Berkowitz achieved worldwide reputation as an expert on human aggression, which he defined as an externally elicited drive to harm or injure others. He believed that aggression could be sparked involuntarily by stimuli from the surrounding environment.

Binet, Alfred (1857-1911). A French psychologist, Binet, collaborating with Theodore Simon, devised tests for measuring intelligence, later called intelligence quotient (IQ) tests. Although he originally contended that intelligence was too complex to be reduced to mere numbers, he ultimately accepted the simplified modes of measurement, devised by William Stern and refined by Lewis Terman, that considered IQ to be equal to mental age divided by chronological age and multiplied by one hundred. Terman added the last element so that IQ could be expressed in whole numbers rather than in numbers requiring decimal points.

Brentano, Franz Clemens (1838-1917). Brentano questioned the theories of the mind espoused by many contemporary psychologists and physicians who were mainly concerned with the brain as a physical entity. He denied the necessity of understanding the physiological mechanisms underlying mental events, contending that experimental psychology was more limited and limiting than many of his colleagues believed because it involves the systematic manipulation of variables, then noting their effect upon other variables. Brentano believed that any study of the mind should emphasize process over a material view of the mind's content.

Breuer, Josef (1842-1925). A noted physician and researcher, Breuer grew close to the young Sigmund Freud, fourteen years his junior. Freud said that while he was still a student preparing for his last examinations in medical school, Breuer applied the methods of psychoanalysis to one of his patients, Anna O., who suffered from hysteria and whom he treated systematically from 1880 to 1882, thereby, in Freud's eyes, inaugurating the field of psychoanalysis.

Cannon, Walter B. (1871-1945). A Harvard University professor of physiology, Cannon demonstrated the effects emotions have on the human body.

His work led to the mapping of the brain's hypothalamus and limbic systems. Cannon challenged the theory proposed by William James and C. G. Lange that situations caused by certain stimuli produce specific bodily reactions, such as increase heart beat or increases or decreases in blood pressure, pointing out that similar bodily reactions occur in a wide variety of emotional states. He noted that the viscera, with few sensory nerves, are unlikely to perceive changes, contending that autonomic reactions often have relatively long periods of latency.

Cattell, James McKeen (1860-1944). Convinced that applied psychology underlies every aspect of human activity, Cattell was a member of the functionalist school, which demanded that psychology be a practical science. Unlike the structuralists, the functionalists were concerned with the function of the mind rather than with its contents. The approach of Cattell and other functionalists was biological rather than physiological. He was elected president of the American Psychological Association at the age of thirty-five, succeeding William James in that post.

Dewey, John (1859-1952). Generally considered the most significant educational philosopher of the twentieth century, Dewey regarded the division of the elements of human reflexes into sensory, brain, and motor processes as inaccurate and misleading. He contended that there is a stream of behavior and that human reflexes are part of a coordinated system that cannot be viewed as anything but a unified whole. Dewey accepted the inevitability of social change but believed that it could be influenced favorably by proper planning. He is considered the father of progressive education.

Dollard, John (1900-1980). The frustration-aggression hypothesis of Dollard and his partner Neil Miller departs from the explanations of Sigmund Freud and Konrad Lorenz, which are essentially biological. Miller and Dollard place considerable emphasis on explanations that have to do with social learning and environmental factors. They collaborated on *Frustrations and Aggression* (1963).

Dix, Dorothea (1802-1887). While teaching inmates in a Boston prison, Dix concluded that many of the women confined as criminals were really mentally ill. She began a campaign to publicize and improve the treatment of the mentally ill in the United States and later in Europe. When she began her crusade in 1841, only 15 percent of people needing care received it. By 1890, that proportion had increased to 70 percent.

Ebbinghaus, Hermann (1850-1909). Ebbinghaus is best remembered for his systematic study of learning and memory, which flew in the face of Wilhelm Wundt's proclamation that the higher mental processes could not be studied experimentally. A rationalist, Ebbinghaus conducted experiments based on learning out-of-context groups of syllables from a pool of 2,300 that he had devised. His chief interests were in such topics as meaning, imagery, and individual differences in cognitive styles.

Egas Moniz, António (1874-1955). Egas Moniz was a Portuguese neurologist, who, aware of C. R. Jacobson's experiments in altering the behavior of chimpanzees by the removal of the frontal lobes of their brains, concluded that such procedures would produce similar results in humans. He was a pioneer in the now largely discredited area of psychosurgery. He was awarded the 1949 Nobel Prize in Physiology or Medicine for his discovery of the therapeutic value of leucotomy in certain psychoses.

Ellis, Albert (1913-   ). As a psychoanalyst and sex therapist, Ellis became disenchanted with the methods of psychoanalysis and sought new means of approaching his patients, which he outlined in *New Approaches to Psychotherapy* (1955). He devised a rational-emotive therapy (RET) which was initially scorned by most of his professional colleagues, many of whom eventually came to see the practical wisdom of this approach. His *Sex Without Guilt* (1958) was widely distributed and influenced much subsequent thinking about sex and sex therapy.

Erikson, Erik (1902-1994). In *Childhood and Society* (1950), one of the most influential books on learning theory in the last half of the twentieth century, Erikson defined eight developmental stages through which humans pass as they move from infancy to later adulthood. An understanding of these stages, particularly the first five that move from infancy to adolescence, substantially affected learning theory in the United States.

Eysenck, Hans (1916-1997). In his theory of personality, Eysenck related the dimensions of introversion/extroversion and neuroticism/stability to the way the nervous system is constituted. He enumerated the characteristics that distinguish behavior therapy from dynamic psychotherapy.

Freud, Anna (1895-1982). The youngest child of Sigmund Freud, Freud became, like her father, a psychoanalyst, dealing exclusively with children. She earned a worldwide reputation as a child psychoanalyst. Following her father's death, she was regarded as the worldwide leader of the Freudian movement in psychology.

Freud, Sigmund (1856-1939). Perhaps the most renowned figure in the field of psychoanalysis, Freud introduced the free-association technique into that field. From his patients' free associations, Freud realized that psychoanalysts have to determine the structure and nature of their patients' unconscious minds. He identified and named the Oedipus complex, which contends that on the unconscious level a male's mother is the object of his sexual desire, thereby setting up his father as a competitor. Freud also identified the id, the ego, and the superego as cornerstones of the human psyche.

Fromm, Erich (1900-1980). In his most renowned book, *Escape from Freedom* (1941), Fromm speculated that freedom is a frightening thing to many people and that when they recognize that they are free, they immediately attempt to affiliate themselves with people or organizations that will reduce or totally eliminate their choices. He concluded that being free places an enormous responsibility upon people, who are often willing to trade freedom for the security of having a structure and direction provided by an external force.

Gilligan, Carol (1936-   ). Gilligan served as chief investigator for a number of studies of the development of girls and women. Her major research interests were in adolescence, moral reasoning, and conflict resolution, with particular emphasis on the contributions women's thinking have made to psychological theory. She pursued her studies because of the lack of attention women and girls received in most psychological research. She uncovered a "deep sense of outrage and despair" over the disconnection women feel because they believe their feelings have been ignored. Her books *In a Different Voice: Psychological Theory and Women's Development* (1982) and *Meeting at the Crossroads: Women's Psychology And Girls' Development* (coauthored with Lyn M. Brown, 1992) have gained widespread recognition among psychologists concerned with matters of gender.

Hall, G. Stanley (1844-1924). A man of diverse talents, Hall was an antistructuralist who embraced the evolutionary theories of Charles Darwin and adapted them to psychology, particularly in his recapitulation theory, which hypothesized that every child from the embryonic stage to maturity recapitulates, first quite rapidly and later more slowly, every stage of development through which the human race has passed from its earliest, prehistoric beginnings. As president of Clark University in Worcester, Massachusetts, for thirty-one years (1888-1919), Hall made the university a major center for the study of psychology in the United States. He was the first person in the United States to call for sex education in public schools.

Horney, Karen (1885-1952). A physician, Horney denied that Sigmund Freud's theories on biological motivation were relevant for the people of her day. For her, social and cultural influences were preeminent. She contended that psychological problems grow out of disturbed human relationships, particularly those between children and their parents. Her essays about the psychology of women are cogent and were compiled in *Feminine Psychology* (1967).

Husserl, Edmund (1859-1938). Husserl contended that the methods employed by researchers in the natural sciences were not wholly appropriate in the study of areas related to psychology and to mental phenomena. He believed that it was incumbent on those studying human mental and emotional processes to understand their underlying mental essences. His phenomenological approach predated both Gestalt and existential psychology, both of which were indebted to Husserl's insights.

James, William (1842-1910). James's ideas sowed early seeds in psychological thought that eventually germinated into the school of functionalism. Wrestling with the implications of German materialism, Charles Darwin's theory of evolution—from which freedom of choice seemed to be absent—and predetermination, James finally, after reading an essay on free will by Charles Renouvier (1815-1903), moved in new directions that led inevitably to the pragmatism for which he is most remembered. His recognition of the importance of stream of consciousness led away from making generalizations about humans and their psychological constituents and led to a theory that emphasized the individuality and instinctuality of humans.

Johnson, Virginia E. (1925-   ). Johnson, along with her partner William H. Masters, was among the leading sexual therapists in the United States. They gathered scientific data relating to sex by means of electroencephalography, electrocardiography, and the use of color monitors. They worked with 694 volunteers photographed in various modes of sexual stimulation, carefully protecting their subjects' identities and privacy. They classified four stages of sexual arousal. Their work, especially *Human Sexual Response* (1966) and *Human Sexual Inadequacy* (1970), helped to spark the sexual revolution of the late 1960's and the 1970's.

Jung, Carl G. (1875-1961). Noted for his word-association research, Jung was essentially Freudian in his formative years as a psychologist, although the two began to part ways philosophically beginning in 1909. He employed Freud's notions of the preconscious and unconscious minds to arrive at the concept of the personal unconscious. This led him to his renowned theory of the collective unconscious that drew on common experience of people through the ages. Jung contended that predispositions of the human mind are inherited and that in the collective unconscious there exist archetypes, so that at birth the mind is not the blank slate postulated by John Locke (1632-1704), but rather that it contains structures inherited from previous spans of human existence.

Kelly, George A. (1905-1967). Notably iconoclastic, Kelly eschewed much of the theoretical psychology of his day, including a great deal of Sigmund Freud. In dealing with subjects, he concluded that whether a person has a psychological problem or not depends largely on how that person views life. While scientists create theories that help them to predict future events, the general public creates systems constructs to make similar predictions. His two-volume work *The Psychology of Personal Constructs* (1955) explains in great detail how nonscientists create their systems constructs.

Kinsey, Alfred (1894-1956). Kinsey had a distinguished career as a zoologist at Indiana University, where his early work dealt with the life cycle, evolution, geographic distribution, and speciation of the gall wasp. He gained his greatest renown, however, for his extensive studies of human sexual behavior, begun in the late 1930's. They culminated in the publication of his landmark study, *Sexual Behavior in the Human Male* (1948), which was followed by a similar study on the human female in 1953. At the time of his death, he was the founding director of the Institute for Sex Research of Bloomington, Indiana.

Kohlberg, Lawrence (1927-1987). Kohlberg's greatest contribution was his research on the moral development of children and adolescents. Kohlberg ran an extensive longitudinal study in which he recorded the responses of boys aged seven through adolescence to hypothetical moral dilemmas. He concluded that children and adults pass through six identifiable stages in their moral development, which stems from cognitive development. Older children shape their responses on increasingly broad and abstract ethical standards. He detected an evolution from self-interest to more principled, selfless behavior and developed a chronological hierarchy of moral development.

Kraepelin, Emil (1856-1926). Kraepelin's chief contribution to psychology was his formulation of a comprehensive list of mental disorders published in 1883. It was used worldwide for over a century until, in 1952, the *Diagnostic and Statistical Manual of Mental Disorders* (DSM) was published by the American Psychological Association. Kraepelin identified the mental condition of dementia praecox and demonstrated that it was treatable and manageable. He renamed the condition schizophrenia, which means "a splitting of the personality."

Lacan, Jacques (1901-1961). Lacan, a French psychoanalyst, was trained as a psychiatrist. In the 1930's and 1940's he worked with psychotic patients. In the 1950's, he began to develop his own version of psychoanalysis, based on the ideas he found in structuralist linguistics and anthropology. He questioned Sigmund Freud's notion of the unconscious. Whereas Freud believed that by bringing the contents of the unconscious into consciousness he could minimize repression and neurosis, Lacan contended that the ego can not replace the unconscious or control it. For Lacan, the ego or "I" self is only an illusion, a product of the unconscious itself, and the unconscious is the center of all being.

Lewin, Kurt (1890-1947). An early apostle of Gestalt psychology, Lewin applied Gestalt principles to such areas as motivation, personality, and particularly group dynamics. For Lewin, many psychologists clung too tenaciously to the notion that the inner determinants of behavior are foremost in shaping human events. This Aristotelian view was contrary to the Galilean view that how organisms behave depends upon the totality of forces acting upon them at any given time. For Lewin, human behavior can be understood only in the light of the many complex, dynamic forces acting upon a person. He viewed groups as physical systems comparable to the brain. He detected an interdependence within members of groups that dynamically affected their functioning.

Maslow, Abraham (1908-1970). Maslow made humanistic psychology a recognized branch of the field. His early experimental work with monkeys led him to conclude that physical strength had less to do with dominance than the inner confidence of animals, although as he matured, he saw little value in studying nonhuman animals. His emphasis was on studying individuals rather than groups and using subjective reality as the most effect key to understanding human behavior. Maslow's hierarchy of needs led to his concept of self-actualization, for which he is best known.

Masters, William H. (1915-2001). Masters, along with his partner Virginia E. Johnson, was among the leading sexual therapists in the United States. They gathered scientific data relating to sex by means of electroencephalography, electrocardiography, and the use of color monitors. They worked with 694 volunteers photographed in various modes of sexual stimulation, carefully protecting their subjects' identities and privacy. They classi-

fied four stages of sexual arousal. Their work, especially *Human Sexual Response* (1966) and *Human Sexual Inadequacy* (1970), helped to spark the sexual revolution of the late 1960's and the 1970's.

Meichenbaum, Donald (1940-). Meichenbaum, a founder of the "cognitive revolution" in psychotherapy, advocated the constructivist perspective. Professor of psychology at the University of Waterloo in Ontario, Canada, he has been a prolific writer, researcher, and lecturer. Meichenbaum wrote the influential book *Cognitive Behavior Modification: An Integrative Approach* (1977). His *Clinical Handbook/Treatment Manual for PTSD* (1994) is an impressive summary of information for clinicians and researchers working with persons suffering the effects of traumatic stress.

Menninger, Karl (1893-1990). Dealing psychoanalytically with patients, Menninger claimed that patients' guilt, which can make them seem unworthy in their own eyes, is attributable to the resistance of the superego. Menninger identified acting out as a manifestation of resistance and recognized that when patients go out of their way to please their analysts, they are engaging in what Menninger called "erotization resistance," which he related to the stages of psychosexual development.

Miller, Neal E. (1909-). The frustration-aggression hypothesis of Miller and his partner John Dollard departs from the explanations of Sigmund Freud and Konrad Lorenz, which are essentially biological. Miller and Dollard place considerable emphasis on explanations that have to do with social learning and environmental factors. They collaborated on *Frustrations and Aggression* (1963).

Mischel, Walter (1929-). Mischel refused to acknowledge that there exist stable characteristics of personality, contending that behavior depends upon specific situations. He questioned the validity of personality inventories and the data obtained from them. For Mischel, the assessment of personality based upon traits is specious because it overgeneralizes. Mischel's most notable works on personality are *Personality and Assessment* (1968) and *Introduction to Personality* (1971, revised 1981).

Murray, Henry A. (1893-1988) Murray had a background in a variety of disciplines, including psychology, chemistry, and biology. He taught at

Harvard from 1927 to 1968 and helped to establish the Boston Psychoanalytic Society. He drew his theory of personality from both Freudian and Jungian psychoanalysis, postulating an elaborate system of basic motivational forces. Murray developed the Thematic Apperception Test (TAT), widely used for assessing personality.

Pavlov, Ivan (1849-1936). Pavlov gained his reputation for his work on conditioned and unconditioned responses. Using dogs that were fed when a bell sounded, he accustomed the dogs to associating the sound of the bell with food. Once they were made this association, he found that sounding the bell caused them to salivate even though no food was forthcoming. Pavlov was a positivist whose life was centered on his laboratory work. He had a low opinion of psychology not because of its emphasis on consciousness but because of its use of introspection.

Perls, Fritz (1893-1970). Perls developed and popularized Gestalt therapy. In South Africa, where he emigrated from Europe, he establish a training institute for psychoanalysis before developing his unique theoretical method, which emphasized a phenomenological and subjective approach to therapy. He noted that people tend to split off experiences (emotions, thoughts, sensations) that are uncomfortable. One goal of his work is to encourage patients to own up to their experience and develop it into a healthy "Gestalt," or whole. Perls's book *Gestalt Therapy Verbatim* (1969) drawn from transcripts of his work, describes his approach.

Piaget, Jean (1896-1980). Piaget was a central figure in the study of human development. His theory of genetic epistemology links the development of intellectual ability to biological maturity and experience. He contended that when an experience fits a child's cognitive structure, assimilation takes place. When such an experience does not fit its cognitive structure, the cognitive structure is adjusted, by a process that Piaget called accommodation, so that it can be assimilated. His stages of intellectual development have been instrumental in teacher education.

Pinel, Philippe (1745-1826). Pinel's book *Philosophy of Madness* (1793) changed the way that many physicians viewed mental illness. Pinel was appalled at the treatment of mental patients, many of whom were chained and abused. He demonstrated that violent behavior among patients who were chained often disappeared when their chains were removed. Pinel also called for a cessation of the blood-letting that was a common means of treatment in his day.

Rogers, Carl (1902-1987). Renowned for his client-centered approach to psychotherapy, Rogers outlined his methods in his widely used book, *Client-Centered Therapy: Its Current Practice, Implications, and Theory* (1951). Rogers's nondirective approach was unique and was based on his belief that therapists function most productively when they seek to understand and accept their patients' subjective reality. His complex theory of personality is clearly articulated in *Client-Centered Therapy*.

Rorschach, Hermann (1884-1922). As a small child, Rorschach loved an activity called *Klecksography,* a way of making pictures by using ink blots. This enthusiasm led to his life's work. Undecided about whether to study medicine or art, he finally opted for medicine, but his continuing interest in inkblots caused him to devise a way to use them in exploring the human psyche. Rorschach began showing inkblots to school children, whose reactions he noted and analyzed. After receiving his medical degree in 1912, he tested three hundred patients and one hundred "normal" people, using inkblots to analyze their unconscious minds. In 1921, he published *Psychodiagnostics: A Diagnostic Test Based on Perception,* which fully described his unique diagnostic method.

Rush, Benjamin (1745-1813). Sometimes referred to as the first psychiatrist in the United States, Rush published *Diseases of the Mind* in 1812. He complained that mentally ill people were treated criminally and urged that their shackles be removed. Such patients should never be put on display for the amusement of others. Despite his revolutionary views, Rush nevertheless accepted bloodletting as a viable treatment for mental disorders, as well as rotating patients to relieve their confused minds and strapping them in tranquilizing chairs in order to calm those who were agitated.

Selye, Hans (1907-1982). Selye demonstrated how environmental stress and anxiety could lead to the release of hormones that, over time, could produce a number of the biochemical and physiological disorders common in industrial societies of the twentieth century. Selye's theory greatly affected popular views of stress. In *The Stress of Life* (1978), Selye reduced the research on stress to terms the general public could understand and appreciate.

Simon, Théodore (1873-1961). In 1904, Simon, an intern in a French institution for mentally retarded children, worked with Alfred Binet to create tests that would quantify intelligence, differentiating intellectually normal children from those who were intellectually deficient. Together, Simon and Binet in 1905 produced the Binet-Simon Scale of Intelligence, which led to the development of a broad range of tests to measure people's intelligence quotient (IQ).

Skinner, B. F. (1904-1990). Skinner's belief that behavior is controlled by environmental reinforcement mechanisms gave him reason to think that understanding such mechanisms can help to solve many of society's problems. In his view, it is more pressing to understand the environment rather than the mind or the inner self. His method was to manipulate environmental factors and note the effect that such alterations had on behavior. His approach has been designated "descriptive behaviorism."

Spencer, Herbert (1820-1903). Spencer applied the concept of evolution to the human mind and to human societies. For him, everything in the universe begins as an undifferentiated whole. Evolution leads to differentiation so that systems become increasingly complex. After Charles Darwin's *Origin of Species* (1859) appeared, Spencer shifted his emphasis from acquired characteristics to natural selection. He coined the term "survival of the fittest," which is widely associated with Darwinian thought.

Stern, William (1871-1938). A German psychologist who introduced the concept of mental age as opposed to chronological age, which led to the quantitative statement of people's intelligence quotients (IQs).

Stumpf, Carl (1848-1936). Stumpf, who studied with and was much influenced by Franz Brentano, stipulated that mental events should be studied holistically and not be broken down analytically. Stumpf considered mental phenomena rather than conscious elements the appropriate objects in the study of psychology. This view predated and led to the phenomenological approach that became a major underpinning of the Gestalt psychology that followed.

Sullivan, Harry Stack (1892-1949). An American psychiatrist, Sullivan, along with his teacher William Alanson White (1870-1937), extended Freudian psychoanalysis to the treatment of patients with severe mental disorders, particularly schizophrenia. Sullivan argued that schizophrenics were curable, blaming cultural forces for the condition of many such patients. His writing, especially *Schizophrenia as a Human Process* (1962), greatly altered the views of many psychiatrists.

Terman, Lewis M. (1877-1956). Working in the field of psychological testing and measurements, Terman abbreviated the term "intelligence quotient" to merely IQ. He modified William Stern's method of measuring IQ by adding one element to it. Once mental age had been divided by chronological age, he multiplied the result by one hundred so that it could be expressed as a whole number rather than as one with a decimal point.

Thorndike, Edward L. (1874-1949). A pioneer in the field of learning theory, Thorndike was also intrigued by and wrote in such fields as verbal behavior, transfer of training, the measurement of sociological events, educational methodology, and comparative psychology. Well known for his theories of the Law of Effect and the Law of Exercise, he subdivided the latter into the Law of Use and the Law of Disuse. The former stated that if an association led to a feeling of satisfaction, it would be strengthened, whereas if it led to an unsatisfying feeling, it would be weakened. He later repudiated these theories. In time the functionalism that he espoused was absorbed into mainstream psychology.

Tichener, Edward B. (1867-1927). British-born psychologist Tichener spent thirty-five years at Cornell University as director of its psychological laboratory, creating there the largest psychology doctoral program in the United States. Convinced that there was little value in applied psychology, Tichener dogmatically insisted that the field, in order to be truly scientific, must deal with pure knowledge. Despite his close relationship with John B. Watson, Tichener eschewed behaviorism and became the founder of the structuralist school of psychology, which opposed not only behaviorism but such other schools of psychology as functionalism and faculty psychology.

Watson, John B. (1878-1958). A major researcher in animal psychology, Watson was the founder of and the most significant figure in the behaviorist school of psychology. His academic career ended precipitously in 1920 when he was found to be having an adulterous affair with a research assistant. He began to write for the popular press and in 1921 joined the J. Walter Thompson Company, a leading advertising company, of which he became vice president in 1924, remaining with the company for the rest of his working life. Watson continued his interest and writing in psychology and had a significant effect upon the behaviorists who followed him.

Wundt, Wilhelm M. (1832-1920). One of the most prolific writers in the field of psychology, Wundt held that psychology was a scientific field and that it had become an experimental science. Whereas the other sciences were based on what Wundt termed "mediate experiences," psychology was based on "immediate experiences." He sought to use experimental psychology to discover the basic components of thought and to understand how mental elements combine into complex mental experiences. His method was based largely on introspection, or self-observation and analysis.

R. Baird Shuman

NOTABLE COURT CASES

1843

Rex v. M'Naghten

8 Eng. Rep. 718; 10 Clark & Fin 200, 210 Law Lords Council, England

This was the first appellate case involving a substantive insanity test. Nine experts deemed Daniel M'Naghten insane. The Scottish wood-turner had murdered Prime Minister Robert Peel's private secretary because he believed the man was plotting against him. Lord Chief Justice Tindal accepted expert testimony concerning M'Naghten's persecution complex. Judged not guilty by reason of insanity, M'Naghten was institutionalized in Bedlam, then in Broadmoor, where he died.

1927

Buck v. Bell

274 U.S. 200

The U.S. Supreme Court ruled that involuntary sterilization of the mentally ill for eugenic purposes was constitutional. Carrie Buck of the Virginia Colony for Epileptics and the Feeble-minded had undergone sterilization without her consent. Supreme Court Justice Oliver Wendell Holmes, Jr., justified his vote, saying that because Buck was mentally incompetent, she was unsuitable to produce offspring. As a result of this ruling, sterilization laws were enforced in many states and the number of involuntary sterilizations increased despite health risks and moral issues concerning privacy and reproductive freedom. Most people sterilized were either poor or institutionalized. These laws were later overturned.

1954

Monte Durham v. U.S.

214 Fed. Rptr. 2d 862 U.S. Circuit Court of Appeals for D.C.

Burglar Monte Durham pleaded not guilty by reason of insanity when tried for a 1951 arrest. A mentally ill repeat offender, Durham appeared at a bench trial without a jury. The judge insisted it was Durham's burden as defendant to prove he was mentally unsound when he committed the crime. Durham took right/wrong and irresistible impulse tests in an effort to measure his psychological state. He was found guilty. During appeals, Judge David L. Bazelon reversed the decision and shifted the burden to prove insanity to the prosecution. He said that the law would consider a defendant sane unless evidence to prove mental disease or defect was submitted.

1960

Dusky v. U.S.

362 U.S. 402; 80 S Ct 788 U.S. Supreme Court (Missouri)

The U.S. Supreme Court affirmed a lower court ruling that schizophrenic Milton Dusky was competent to stand trial for kidnapping a teenager and helping two other teenagers rape her. He was found guilty and sentenced to forty-five years in prison. In this case, the court defined competency to stand trial as meaning a defendant was capable of communicating with an attorney and could rationally comprehend the facts of the charges against him or her.

James Carter v. General Motors Corp. (Chev. Gear & Axle)

361 Michigan 575 Michigan Supreme Court

Schizophrenic James Carter received workers' compensation that he claimed was owed him because of work-related emotional pressures. The Michigan Supreme Court recognized that Carter did not have to cite a specific incident as provoking his inability to work. The court also declared that Carter's schizophrenia prior to employment did not render worker's compensation invalid. Such benefits would cease being applicable only if Carter's schizophrenia was no longer present. Carter's legal representation included expert psychological testimony. General Motors did not seek expert evaluation of Carter's psychological state. Michigan laws were subsequently rewritten to prevent employees who were mentally ill prior to their employment from securing worker's compensation from their employers.

1966

Charles C. Rouse v. Dale C. Cameron, Supt., St. Elizabeths

373 Fed. 2d. 451 U.S. Circuit Court of Appeals for D.C.

The plaintiff was committed for four years although the crime of which he was accused had a maximum sentence of one year. Judge David L. Bazelon declared that patients hospitalized based on the plea of not guilty by reason of insanity must be treated or released if they are not dangerous to society. Because of this case, plaintiffs were guaranteed the right to writ of *habeas corpus* and the precedent was set for mental patients to have the right for appropriate treatment.

Johnnie K. Baxstrom v. Herold

383 U.S. 107 U.S. Supreme Court (New York)

When prisoner Johnnie K. Baxstrom's sentence in a Department of Corrections psychiatric hospital concluded, he was supposed to be committed to a civil hospital. The state hospital refused to admit Baxstrom, and he remained in the prison hospital. All transfer requests and legal protests were not considered. The U.S. Supreme Court ruled that Baxstrom had been denied equal protection because civilly committed patients were guaranteed the right to a hearing. The court also denounced keeping Baxstrom in prison beyond his sentence.

1967

Thomas H. Washington v. U.S.

390 Fed. 2d 444 U.S. Circuit Court of Appeals for D.C.

Tried for rape, assault, and robbery, Thomas H. Washington pleaded not guilty by reason of insanity but was convicted. Because the defense's psychiatrist said Washington was mentally ill, Washington appealed his verdict. The two prosecution psychiatrists stated that Washington was mentally sound. Judge David L. Bazelon decided that juries determined if an insanity defense was credible and that an expert's testimony did not override jury decisions.

1970

In re Joseph E. Lifschutz, M.D., on Habeas Corpus

85 Cal. Rptr. 829 California Supreme Court

When a patient named Housek sued another person for emotional distress, the defendant subpoenaed records from Housek's psychiatrist, Dr. Joseph E. Lifschutz. Although Lifschutz appeared in court, he declined to testify, stating that doctor-patient interactions were privileged information. Housek had not requested such privacy, and Lifschutz was jailed for contempt of court. The California Supreme Court stated that patients have the right to exercise privilege, not their doctors. Because Housek revealed information about his treatment, the court had the legal right to Lifschutz's records.

1972

Alberta Lessard et al. v. Wilbur Schmidt et al.

349 F. Supp. 1078 U.S. District Court, Eastern Wisconsin

Two police officers detained schizophrenic Alberta Lessard, who was recommitted involuntarily to a mental hospital. The court declared that a law which permitted detaining mentally ill people in civil institutions for a maximum of 145 days with no civil rights was unconstitutional. The ruling said that people could be committed for protection and legal procedure for as much time as two weeks prior to a hearing only if their guilt was beyond a reasonable doubt and they posed risks to themselves or others. Specific procedures for committing people were outlined. Mental health professionals worried that many mentally ill people might not receive the care they needed because of this ruling. The court also stated that psychiatrists were required to inform patients of their Fifth Amendment rights when they questioned them for trials.

Theon Jackson v. State of Indiana

406 U.S. 715; 92 S. Ct. 1845 U.S. Supreme Court (Indiana)

Because burglar Theon Jackson was mentally retarded, deaf, and mute and could not communicate effectively, the court considered him incompetent to stand trial and committed him. Jackson's legal representative considered this a life sentence. The U.S. Supreme Court decided that the Indiana court's decision violated due process. The court stated that defendants considered incompetent to stand trial and who could not regain competency must either be released or be committed in a civil not a penal institution.

1973

Gilbert Seiling v. Frank Eyman, warden, Arizona state prison
478 Fed. 2d 211 U.S. Court of Appeals, 9th Circuit Arizona

When Gilbert Seiling was charged with assault with a deadly weapon and to commit murder, three psychiatrists who examined him said that Seiling was insane when he committed the crimes. Two of the psychiatrists determined that Seiling was competent to stand trial. Prior to the trial, Seiling pleaded guilty. Afterward, Seiling said he had not been competent to waive his rights. The appeal court decided that being considered competent to stand trial is not the same as being competent to plead guilty.

Kaimowitz v. Michigan Dept. of Mental Health
#73-19434-AW trial court Michigan

Gabe Kaimowitz was an attorney who represented Lewis Smith, who had raped and murdered a woman in 1965. Designated a criminal sexual psychopath, Smith was committed without a trial. By 1972, he consented to participate as a research subject in an experiment studying amygdaloidotomy versus cyproterone treatment at Lafayette Clinic. Kaimowitz argued that the clinic was illegally detaining Smith. The court said that Smith's consent to become a research participant was invalid because he had been denied due process and had not been found guilty in a trial. The court further stated that neither committed patients nor inmates could consent to participating in hazardous experiments.

Ricky Wyatt by his aunt Mrs. W. C. Rawlings v. Aderholt (Stickney)
503 Fed. 2d 1305 (1974) U.S. Court of Appeals, 5th Circuit Alabama

When the cigarette tax income designated for mental health services was revoked in 1970, Bryce State Hospital in Tuscaloosa fired ninety-nine employees. The hospital's five thousand patients suffered from deprivations caused by lack of sufficient funding. The state appealed a lower court injunction. Judge Frank M. Johnson, Jr., of the 5th Circuit Court was the first federal judge to rule that patients who were civilly committed patients had the constitutional right to receive individual treatment. The Wyatt Committee, the American Psychiatric Association, and the U.S. Department of Justice over-saw Alabama's mental health services, which were reformed and certified.

1974

Kenneth Donaldson v. J. B. O'Connor
493 Fed. 2d 507 U.S. Court of Appeals, 5th Circuit Florida

Kenneth Donaldson refused treatment at the Chattahoochee State Hospital because he was a Christian Scientist who did not believe in many medical practices. During his twenty years spent in the institution, Donaldson was forced to undergo milieu treatment, which involved interacting with other mental patients. A trial court awarded Donaldson compensatory and punitive damages from the hospital's superintendent, J. B. O'Connor, and the psychiatrist who treated Donaldson. An appeals court, basing its decision on the 1973 Wyatt case in Alabama, then stated that the treatment is commitment's sole purpose, and that patients have a constitutional right to receive treatment. This case was followed up in 1975.

1975

J. B. O'Connor v. Kenneth Donaldson
422 U.S. 563, 95 S. Ct. 2486 U.S. Supreme Court (Florida)

In a follow-up case to the 1974 case of *Kenneth Donaldson v. J. B. O'Connor*, the U.S. Supreme Court decided that hospital superintendent O'Connor was not liable unless he acted maliciously or was aware of a violation against patient. Damages were dropped. The court limited states' rights to commit and confine people, placing mental illness under direction of a federal civil rights statute. The justices did not rule on the right to treatment issue, only stating that they "can't commit without more" but not elaborating on meaning of "more."

1976

Julie Roy v. Renatus Hartogs, M.D.
381 NYS 2d 587 New York Appellate Court

Patient Julie Roy sued therapist Renatus Hartogs because she claimed she was emotionally damaged by his sexual treatments. Hartogs argued that seduction was not illegal. The court awarded Roy compensatory and punitive damages. An appeals court agreed that Hartogs was guilty of malpractice. That court dropped punitive damages because it declared Hartogs was incompetent, not malicious.

When Hartogs sued his insurance company for not covering his costs, the company successfully argued that Hartogs's treatment method for Roy was not considered professional treatment. A book and a film, both titled *Betrayal*, portrayed this case.

Vitaly Tarasoff v. Regents of University of California et al.
131 Cal. Rptr. 14, 551 p2d 334 California Supreme Court

After Prosenjit Poddar revealed to a university psychologist that he wanted to murder Tatiana Tarasoff, the therapist alerted authorities. The campus police questioned and released Poddar, who then killed Tarasoff. Her parents sued the university for failure to warn Tarasoff of Poddar's threat. A trial court said the university had "no duty" to alert Tarasoff. The California Supreme Court initially stated that "privilege ends where public peril begins" and emphasized the "duty to warn." Because this statement was vague, the state supreme court reheard the case, issuing the decision that a "therapist has an obligation to use reasonable care to protect a potential victim" and the "duty to protect." This was a landmark decision because it established a new cause for legal action. Many mental health professionals worried that this decision might interfere with therapist-patient confidentiality and cause liability issues because clinicians could not always detect dangerous patients before they acted violently.

1977

Ann Fasulo & Marie Barberi v. Mehadin K. Arafeh
173 Conn. 473 Connecticut Supreme Court

After being committed thirteen years and twenty-six years, respectively, at the state Connecticut Valley Hospital, two patients filed writs of *habeas corpus*. Laws at that time stated that either patients had to prove they were not mentally ill to be discharged or the hospital superintendent could approve their release. The Connecticut Supreme Court approved hearings, stating that commitment did not suggest patients were permanently mentally ill and could not recover. The court emphasized Fourteenth Amendment rights and designated any "scheme to set the mentally ill apart" as a possible civil rights violation.

Jane Doe v. Joan Roe, M.D. & Peter Poe, Ph.D.
400 NY Supp. 2d 668 Circuit New York Supreme Court

Psychiatrist Roe and her psychologist husband Poe treated Jane Doe. The couple published an autobiography which included information for which they said Doe gave oral consent for them to use. Because a New York statute states medical personnel cannot disclose patient information because of implied confidentiality and that oral consent is not sufficient, the court awarded damages to Doe and stopped the book's sale. The defendants could not convince the court of the book's scientific merit to resume sales.

1979

Beverly Ibn-Tamas v. U.S.
407 Atl. Rpt. 2d 626 U.S. Circuit Court of Appeals for D.C.

Beverly Ibn-Tamas murdered her husband when he beat her while she was pregnant. He had beaten her many times previously and was known to be violent against women. Ibn-Tamas claimed self-defense. Several witnesses testified that her husband had begged Ibn-Tamas to spare his life. The judge would not allow expert testimony concerning battered woman syndrome because the victim was not on trial. An appeals court disagreed.

Frank O'Neal Addington v. State of Texas
441 U.S. 418, 99 S. Ct. 1804 U.S. Supreme Court (Texas)

Frank O'Neal Addington was committed to an institution based on a "clear and convincing" standard which was unequivocal. When he appealed that commitment should require mental instability "beyond a reasonable doubt," the U.S. Supreme Court unanimously decided that "preponderance of evidence" was insufficient and "beyond a reasonable doubt" too strong. "Clear and convincing" was considered the most appropriate standard which recognized due process protection for civil commitments, although the word "unequivocal" was designated as being too strict. "Beyond a reasonable doubt" is valid in several states.

James Parham v. J. R. et al.
442 U.S. 584 U.S. Supreme Court (Georgia)

A trial court had said Georgia's lack of a law addressing the release of committed minors, particularly those who had recovered, was unconstitutional. The U.S. Supreme Court decided that parents or the state acting as a legal guardian can make mental health decisions based on a child's best interests regardless of the child's protests. The court ordered Georgia to establish posthospital evaluations.

Hawaii Psychiatric Society v. Geo Ariyoshi, Governor
481 F. Supp 1028 U.S. District Court for Hawaii

When Hawaiian legislators approved a law permitting Medicaid officials to search medical records to find incidence of fraud, the Hawaii Psychiatric Society stated that this violated patients' and physicians' privacy. The society's lawsuit protected patients from revealing their identities to protest the state's actions. The federal court decided that individuals' privacy was more important than Hawaii detecting fraud. The court allowed government representatives to cite reasons to secure warrants for suspect psychiatric records.

Paula Frendak v. U.S.
408 A.2d 364 U.S. Circuit Court of Appeals for D.C.

Paula Frendak murdered a coworker, fled the country, and was captured. Experts evaluated her during four competency hearings and determined that she was competent to stand trial even though she might be insane. Frendak did not want a defense of not guilty by reason of insanity but was ruled insane. The appeal court determined that a defendant considered mentally competent can decide not to pursue a not guilty by reason of insanity defense. They can choose prison incarceration over hospitalization. The court acknowledged that some crimes might be in protest of laws the defendants consider unfair, such as Martin Luther King, Jr., protesting segregationist laws, and that a not guilty by reason of insanity plea would weaken their objections.

Rogers v. Okin
478 F. Supp. 1342 (D. Mass. 1979)

A Massachusetts federal court interpreted that the privacy rights and freedom of speech for committed patients, both voluntarily and involuntarily, also allowed them to refuse to take medication if they were competent to make that choice. Incompetent patients could have guardians choose whether treatment should be administered. Prior to this ruling, mental health professionals had been allowed to make medication decisions and worried that such patient autonomy might interfere with treatment.

1980

Joseph Vitek v. Larry D. Jones
445 U.S. 480 U.S. Supreme Court (Nebraska)

The prisoner Larry D. Jones was transferred without a hearing from a prison mental hospital to a state mental hospital. Both the trial court and the U.S. Supreme Court ruled this action was unconstitutional. The Supreme Court emphasized that convicted felons had due process protection rights and that commitment to a mental hospital involves a "massive curtailment of liberty."

Ruth Ann Lipari and Bank of Elkhorn v. Sears, & Sears v. U.S.
497 F. Supp 185 U.S. District Court Nebraska

An involuntary patient at a Nebraska Veterans Administration Hospital outpatient clinic, Ulysses L. Cribbs, Jr., purchased a shotgun from Sears in September, 1977. The next month, he stopped going to therapy. He murdered Dennis Lipari at an Omaha nightclub in November, 1977. When Ruth Ann Lipari and her bank sued Sears for negligence, that corporation sued the Veterans Administration. A federal district court ruled that the Veterans Administration was not immune and its liability was equivalent to that of a private citizen. The court extended duty in *Vitaly Tarasoff v. Regents of University of California et al.* (1976) to warn "any foreseeable victim or to that class of victims."

1981

John Rennie v. Klein
635 Fed. 2d 836 U.S. Court of Appeals, 3d Circuit New Jersey

John Rennie, diagnosed as paranoid, was unwilling to take medication. The court ruled that an independent psychiatrist could treat Rennie and gradually introduce medications into his treatment. The court suggested that medical personnel should follow several steps. First, they should attempt to convince Rennie that medications were needed and encourage him to cooperate. The institution's medical director then should examine Rennie and monitor his treatment weekly. As needed, the medical director could consult an independent psychiatrist to evaluate Rennie.

State of New Jersey v. Paul Hurd
86 NJ 525 New Jersey Supreme Court

After Jane Sell was knifed by an intruder, she initially said her attacker had been a stranger. Later, when she was hypnotized, Sell identified her former husband, Paul Hurd, as the assailant. Her hypnotic identification was questioned because the police officer who had interrogated her suggested Hurd was guilty. The court ruled that hypnotized witnesses must be questioned by trained medical professionals who were independent of legal authorities. Prior to hypnosis, the examining experts must ask the witness to describe events and record all aspects of hypnosis sessions and expert-witness contacts in writing. Hypnotized witnesses can only testify in New Jersey if their hypnosis sessions are limited to the expert and witness participation.

W. J. Estelle, Jr., v. Ernest Benjamin Smith
451 U.S. 454 U.S. Supreme Court (Texas)

A psychiatrist declared Ernest Benjamin Smith competent to stand trial after his arrest for murder. After a guilty verdict, that psychiatrist testified during sentencing hearings that Smith posed a "danger to society." Smith had not been informed that the same psychiatrist who had examined him pretrial for the defense would later testify for the prosecution. The U.S. Supreme Court unanimously ruled that Smith's Fifth Amendment and his counsel's Sixth Amendment rights had been violated. Without warning that the psychiatrist's expertise would be used by the prosecution, Smith's lawyer had been unable to advise him sufficiently. The justices also thought Smith's due process rights guaranteed by the Fourteenth Amendment had been violated.

1982

Timothy Floyd Clities v. State of Iowa D.S.S.
322 NW 2d 917 Iowa Court of Appeals

When he was eleven years old, Timothy Floyd Clities was committed to a state institution because he was mentally retarded. Ten years later, the neuroleptics he received in treatment caused tardive dyskinesia. A court awarded him monetary damages for pain and suffering. The state of Iowa appealed, claiming that the amount was too high and that Clities had given informed consent. The appeals court disagreed, saying that the pharmacy had been poorly managed and citing Rogers v. Okin (1979), John Rennie v. Klein (1981), and Youngberg v. Romeo (1982), which addressed medicating and restraining committed patients and securing guardians' consent for mentally incompetent patients.

United States v. John Hinckley, Jr.
Cr. No. 81-3-306

John Hinckley, Jr., attempted to assassinate President Ronald W. Reagan in 1981. He was ruled not guilty by reason of insanity. This verdict outraged many Americans. Mental health professionals responded by saying that the insanity defense either should be abolished or require a stricter standard. Because the prosecution bore the burden of proving defendants' sanity beyond a reasonable doubt, psychiatrists suggested the defense should have this burden instead. Congress passed an act to shift burden of proof to defense attorneys and also prohibited defendants from claiming they could not control how they behaved because of impulses.

The American Psychiatric Association issued a statement on the insanity defense which outlined how states reacted to the Hinckley verdict. Some state laws were changed to limit insanity defense use. They also created review boards to evaluate people found not guilty by reason of insanity to monitor treatment and determine if individuals should be released from institutions. Each state and the District of Columbia has distinct insanity statutes. Some use an American Law Institute 1950's insanity defense test which determines the degree to which a person realized his or her behavior was wrong. Other states base their definition on modifications of the M'Naghten case. A few states do not have an insanity defense, and mentally ill defendants ruled guilty there are placed in prison.

Youngberg, Supt. Pennhurst State School v. Nicholas Romeo by his mother
457 U.S. 307 U.S. Supreme Court (Pennsylvania)

Because Nicholas Romeo was retarded and unable to communicate and take care of himself, he suffered injuries at the Pennhurst State School. Distressed about her son's condition, his mother sued the school's superintendent, claiming that Romeo's Eighth and Fourteenth Amendments rights had been violated. Her complaints included use of unsafe restraints. A trial judge ruled that Romeo's Eighth Amendment right had been violated. An appellate court reversed that decision. The U.S. Supreme Court supported the appeal decision, declaring that patients have the constitutional right to safe conditions according to medical professionals' decisions, which courts cannot overrule.

1983

Cynthia E. Petersen v. State of Washington
100 Wash. 2d 1016 Washington State Supreme Court

A schizophrenic burglar and drug addict named Knox caused an automobile accident with Cynthia E. Petersen within days of his being released from a mental hospital. He had stopped taking his medication, which no longer was active in his system at the time of the accident. When the injured Petersen sued the state, the trial court ruled in her favor. The Washington State Supreme Court disagreed with the state, which claimed in its appeal that it was not required to warn people when mental patients were released. Citing *Vitaly Tarasoff v. Regents of University of California et al.*, the supreme court stated that Knox was a danger to society and should be committed. The justices ruled that plaintiffs did not need expert testimony to prove defendants were hazardous and that state hospital mental professionals were equally accountable as private psychiatrists to protect the public from patients.

Michael Jones v. U.S.
463 U.S. 354, 103 S. Ct. 3043 U.S. Supreme Court (D.C.)

Charged with petty larceny in 1975, Michael Jones was committed to St. Elizabeths Hospital. He was considered competent to stand trial the next year and was found not guilty by reason of insanity. Jones was returned to St. Elizabeths and sued in 1980 because he was held beyond the one-year sentence for petty larceny. Courts refused to hear Jones's appeals. The U.S. Supreme Court split 5-4, determining that the ruling of not guilty by reason of insanity was sufficient to commit both nonviolent and violent criminals based on preponderance of evidence. These criminals are not considered responsible for their actions. The minority wanted clear and convincing proof that committed criminals posed a persistent threat.

People of California v. C. W. Stritzinger
688 P.2d 738 California Supreme Court

A psychologist reported to a law enforcement officer information divulged during sessions with C. W. Stritzinger and his teenaged stepdaughter, with whom the stepfather had been sexually involved. The psychologist testified about the sessions during the trial against Stritzinger. The stepdaughter became agitated and left the courtroom before

testifying. The California Supreme Court stated that psychological sessions involving Stritzinger were privileged information and that medical experts must verify that the stepdaughter could not testify.

Thomas A. Barefoot v. W. J. Estelle, Jr.
463 U.S. 880 U.S. Supreme Court (Texas)

When murderer Thomas A. Barefoot was convicted in 1978, the American Psychiatric Association filed an amicus brief which stated that psychiatrists are unable to predict if patients are dangerous. The U.S. Supreme Court declared that, even though such assessments are difficult to determine, they should be undertaken.

1984

State of Minnesota v. David Andring
342 NW 2d 128 Minnesota Supreme Court

David Andring voluntarily committed himself to a hospital because he sexually molested his stepdaughter and niece. He willingly divulged his crimes to medical personnel and people in his group therapy sessions. The state of Minnesota subpoenaed Andring's hospital records. The Minnesota Supreme Court declared that medical records and group sessions are confidential and privileged and that only limited information could be released for legal purposes.

U.S. v. John J. Torniero
735 Fed. 2d 725 U.S. Court of Appeals, 2d Circuit New York

When John J. Torniero was charged with transporting $750,000 of stolen jewelry across state lines, he said he was insane because of compulsive gambling. This plea was not permitted at his trial, and Torniero was declared guilty. He appealed because he said the jury had not heard his compulsive gambling defense. The court stated that compulsive gambling could not be legally used as a mental illness. The *American Journal of Psychiatry* said that compulsive gambling did not cause people to be unaccountable for their behavior.

1985

Commonwealth v. Kenneth Kobrin, M.D.
479 NE 2d 674 Massachusetts Supreme Court

The court ruled that patient records cannot be disclosed to grand juries because of psychiatrist-patient privilege but that records for fees paid, appointments scheduled, diagnosis and treatments plans, and somatic therapy could be introduced as evidence.

Glen Burton Ake v. Oklahoma
105 S. Ct. 1087 U.S. Supreme Court (Oklahoma)

When Glen Burton Ake was charged with two murder counts, he was initially declared incompetent to stand trial. Medicated with Thorazine, Ake was considered competent within six weeks, but a mental state opinion was not recorded. Ake pleaded not guilty by reason of insanity. Neither psychiatrists for the plaintiff nor state testified during the trial regarding Ake's mental state. Convicted, Ake received a death sentence plus one thousand years. His appeals were rejected by the state appeals court. The U.S. Supreme Court ruled that defendants must have access to a psychiatrist to insure due process.

1986

Alvin Bernard Ford v. Louie L. Wainwright
477 U.S. 399 U.S. Supreme Court (Florida)

When Alvin Bernard Ford was convicted and sentenced to death for murder in 1974, he did not plea he was insane. Eight years later, Ford began behaving erratically. A psychiatrist stated Ford was mentally ill and could not comprehend the reason for his execution. Three psychiatrists testified for the state that Ford was competent to undergo execution. The U.S. Supreme Court interpreted the Eighth Amendment to say that insane prisoners could not be executed.

Colorado v. Francis Barry Connelly
107 S.Ct. 515 - 147 U.S. 157 U.S. Supreme Court (Colorado)

Francis Barry Connelly willingly confessed to committing murder. He was read his Miranda rights, then talked about his crime without his attorney being present. Connelly later claimed that he heard voices which forced him to confess. His confession was not permitted into evidence during his trial because authorities said he had involuntarily accepted blame for murder. The Colorado Supreme Court agreed that the confession was involuntary. The U.S. Supreme Court disagreed and stated that involuntary confessions referred to being forced to accept criminal responsibility because of police action, not mental incompetency.

1987

Vickie Lorene Rock v. Arkansas
107 S. Ct. 2704 U.S. Supreme Court (Arkansas)

Vickie Lorene Rock was unable to recall shooting her husband. While hypnotized, she remembered the gun discharging without her finger pulling the trigger. An expert testified that the firearm she had held could fire without the trigger being activated. Arkansas courts refused to admit hypnotic testimony. The U.S. Supreme Court admitted hypnosis was not 100 percent accurate but stressed that excluding statements collected during professionally monitored hypnosis was unreasonable. The court said that such exclusion violated the Sixth and Fourteenth Amendments to rights to call witnesses and due process.

1989

Daley v. Koch
51 Fair Employment Practice Cases 1077, 1079 (2d Circuit 1989)

Both district and appeals court agreed that the New York City Police Department had not discriminated against Daley when it claimed he had undesirable behaviors based on the California Psychological Inventory and the Minnesota Multiphasic Personality Inventory. Daley claimed the police department treated him as if he were mentally ill.

Washington v. Harper
110 S. Ct. 1028 U.S. Supreme Court (Washington)

The U.S. Supreme Court ruled that states can forcibly treat mentally ill prisoners without a hearing, based on mental health professionals' recommendations, if the inmates are dangerous to the prison community or need treatment for urgent health reasons.

1992

Erik Menendez v. Superior Court of Los Angeles
834 P2d 786 California Supreme Court

Dr. L. J. Oziel was the therapist for Erik and Lyle Menendez. They told him that they had murdered their parents and then threatened to kill him, his wife, and his mistress if he revealed the brothers' guilt. Oziel told the intended victims. During the brothers' murder trial, session tapes were introduced as evidence despite the brothers' claims they were privileged information. Citing *People of California v. George Wharton*, the California Supreme Court ruled that privileged material is not confidential after the information has been disclosed. Related therapy sessions are also eligible for court. The court also approved the right of therapists to divulge any warnings made solely against a criminal's mental health professional.

State of Louisiana v. Michael Perry
610 So.2d 746 Louisiana Supreme Court

Michael Perry, a psychotic, killed his parents, two cousins, and a nephew. Against his attorney's advice, he pleaded not guilty. Perry was found guilty and received a death sentence. The U.S. Supreme Court returned Perry's appeal without issuing an opinion. The American Psychiatric Association had wanted the U.S. Supreme Court to rule that insane death row inmates would instead receive life sentences. The Louisiana Supreme Court stated that insane prisoners cannot be executed and that treatment cannot be required in an effort to achieve sufficient sanity for executions.

1993

Salvador Godinez, warden, v. Richard Moran
113 S. Ct. 2680 U.S. Supreme Court (Nevada)

After Richard Moran killed his wife and two men, two psychiatrists declared him competent to stand trial. He pleaded guilty knowing that the state of Nevada wanted the death penalty for him. Moran appealed after receiving a death sentence. He declared that he was mentally ill, which prevented him from defending himself legally. An appellate decision stated that competency to waive rights had priority over competency to stand trial. The U.S. Supreme Court disagreed, ruling that competency to plead guilty and to stand trial were equal.

1999

Olmstead v. L. C.
119 S. Ct. 2176

Institutionalized patients L. C. and E. W. were denied access to community services so they could be released. The state of Georgia said that insufficient funds, not discrimination, was the reason. The Supreme Court ruled in this landmark Americans with Disabilities Act case that states cannot unjustifiably segregate the mentally disabled.

2002

J. K. v. Eden
No. CIV-91-261-TUC-JMR (D. Ariz. March 20, 2001)

In 1991, a father sued the state of Arizona because its managed care system did not provide professionally recommended treatment for his son, who tried to kill himself before being committed. After ten years of discussions, litigants settled this federal class-action lawsuit out of court, initiating the first managed care state mental health reform in the United States.

State of Texas v. Andrea Pia Yates
230th District Court Harris County, Texas
Trial Court Case Nos. 880,205 and 883,590

Yates drowned her five children and was tried for the murder of two of them. She pleaded not guilty by reason of insanity. The jury watched forensic psychiatrist Phillip Resnick's interview with Yates, during which she revealed her delusional perceptions about her role of mother and that she thought she was saving her children from hell. Resnick stated that Yates was psychotic. The prosection agreed that Yates was mentally ill but that she knew her actions were legally wrong because she notified the police. Yates was convicted and sentenced to life in prison. The jury afterward said Yates was mentally ill but that Texas law required an insanity defense to prove the person could not differentiate between right and wrong and that Yates had admitted she knew what she did was wrong. Mental health advocates initiated attempts to change Texas insanity legislation.

Elizabeth D. Schafer

MAGILL'S ENCYCLOPEDIA OF SOCIAL SCIENCE

PSYCHOLOGY

COMPLETE LIST OF ENTRIES

CATEGORIZED LIST OF ENTRIES

ABILITY TESTING

Ability tests
Career and personnel testing
College entrance examinations
Confidentiality
Creativity: Assessment

General Aptitude Test Battery
    (GATB)
Giftedness
Intelligence tests
Kuder Occupational Interest
    Survey (KOIS)

Peabody Individual Achievement
    Test (PIAT)
Stanford-Binet test
Strong Interest Inventory (SII)
Testing: Historical perspectives

INDEX

Ainsworth, Mary, 176, 1001
Air rage, 73
Ajzen, Icek, 188
Akil, Huda, 1075
Al-Anon/Alateen Family Group Headquarters, 1777
Alarm reaction, 672, 714
Albers, Josef, 1669
Albert, Robert, 457
Alberta Lessard et. al v. Wilbur Schmidt et. al, 1803
Alcohol; aggression and, 73; domestic violence and, 531; reticular formation and, 1337
Alcohol dependence and abuse, 96-101; depression and, 494; suicide and, 1585
Alcoholic neuritis, 98
Alcoholics Anonymous (AA), 33, 98, 1590, 1777
Alcoholism, codependency and, 343
Aldosterone, 53
Aldwin, Carolyn, 1551
Alexander, Charles, 943
Alexander, Franz, 283, 712
Alexithymia, 1551
Algorithms, 1188
ALI rule, 17
Alicke, Mark, 1258
Alienation, 608, 928; denial and, 492; midlife crisis and, 979; parental alienation syndrome, 1084
Alienists, 928
Allele, 1705
Allen, Andrea, 990
Alliance for Aging Research, 1777
Allport, Floyd, 1510
Allport, Gordon, 101-102, 193, 292, 756, 758, 1017, 1130, 1233, 1289, 1322, 1794; prejudice and, 807, 1169, 1174; religion and, 1328; self-actualization and, 1394; self and, 1387; stereotyping and, 1435
Alpha press, 1138

Altered states of consciousness, 413; hallucinations and, 718; hypnosis, 767. *See also* Consciousness
Alternate personalities, 1013
Alternative assessment, 172
Alternative hypothesis of variables, 1534
Altman, Irwin, 596-597, 1395
Altruism, 64, 102-106, 734, 1705; ethology and, 603; paradox, 102
Altruistic suicide, 1583, 1614
Alvin Bernard Ford v. Louie L. Wainwright, 1809
Alzheimer, Alois, 106, 872
Alzheimer's Association, 106, 1777
Alzheimer's disease, 69, 81, 106-111, 368, 488, 1275, 1597, 1705; animal experimentation and, 953; Down syndrome and, 536; forgetting and, 659; neuropsychology and, 1036
Alzheimer's Disease Education and Referral Center, 1777
Alzheimer's Disease Prevention Initiative, 110
Amabile, Teresa, 461
Amato, Paul R., 1424
Amatrude, Catherine, 677
Ambiguity, helping and, 735
Ambivalence, racism and, 1287
Ambivalence-induced behavior amplification, 1287
American Academy of Addiction Psychiatry, 1765
American Academy of Child and Adolescent Psychiatry, 1765
American Academy of Clinical Psychiatrists, 1765
American Academy of Neurology, 1765
American Academy of Psychiatry and the Law, 1765
American Academy of Psychoanalysis, 1765
American Academy of Psychotherapists, 1765

American Art Therapy Association, 1765
American Association for Emergency Psychiatry, 1765
American Association for Geriatric Psychiatry, 1765
American Association for Marriage and Family Therapy, 1765
American Association of Children's Residential Centers, 1766
American Association of Community Psychiatrists, 1766
American Association of Directors of Psychiatric Residency Training Department of Psychiatry, 1766
American Association of General Hospital Psychiatrists, 1766
American Association of Homes and Services for the Aging, 1778
American Association of Pastoral Counselors, 1766
American Association of Psychiatric Administrators, 1766
American Association of Suicidology, 1766
American Association of University Women, 347
American Association on Mental Retardation, 507
American Board of Psychiatry and Neurology, 1766
American College of Forensic Psychiatry, 1766
American College of Neuropsychopharmacology, 1766
American College of Psychiatrists, 1766
American College Test (ACT), 380
American College Testing Assessment Program (ACTAP), 381